9/92

DATE DUE

MY 10 '05			

DEMCO 38-296

HANDBOOK OF RECONSTRUCTION IN EASTERN EUROPE
AND THE SOVIET UNION

Other recent current affairs and economics titles from Longman Group UK Limited include the following:

Political Scandals and Causes Célèbres since 1945: An International Reference Compendium (1990)

Political and Economic Encyclopaedia of Western Europe, edited by CIRCA Ltd (1990)

World Guide to Environmental Issues and Organizations, edited by Peter Brackley (1990)

Communist and Marxist Parties of the World (2nd edition), edited by Roger East (1990)

Youth Movements of the World, by William D. Angel (1990)

Political and Economic Encyclopaedia of the Soviet Union and Eastern Europe, edited by Stephen White (1990)

The European Parliament, by Francis Jacobs and Richard Corbett, with Michael Shackleton (1990)

Anti-Nuclear Movements: A World Survey of Opposition to Nuclear Energy, by Wolfgang Rudig (1990)

The Broken Mirror: China after Tiananmen, edited by George Hicks (1990)

The British Trade Union Directory, edited and compiled by Wolodymyr Maksymiw (1990)

Employers' Organizations of the World, edited by Martin Upham (1990)

World Development Directory, compiled and edited by Roger East, Miles Smith-Morris and Martin Wright for CIRCA Ltd (1990)

Political and Economic Encyclopaedia of the Pacific, edited by Gerald Segal (1990)

World Directory of Minorities, compiled by the Minority Rights Group (1990)

Religion in Politics, edited by Stuart Mews (1990)

Western European Political Parties: a Comprehensive Guide, edited by Francis Jacobs (1989)

Trade Unions of the World, 1989–90 (2nd edition, 1989)

CPA World Directory of Old Age, compiled by the Centre for Policy on Ageing (1989)

Elections since 1945: a Worldwide Reference Compendium, general editor Ian Gorvin (1989)

Reuters Glossary: International Economic and Financial Terms, edited by the Senior Staff of Reuters Limited (1989)

Political Parties of the World (3rd edition), edited by Alan J. Day (1988)

HANDBOOK OF RECONSTRUCTION IN EASTERN EUROPE AND THE SOVIET UNION

Edited by
STEPHEN WHITE

CONTRIBUTORS

**John B. Allcock, John D. Bell, Marko Milivojević,
Martin Myant, Daniel Nelson, Jonathan Osmond, Peter Rutland,
George Sanford, Vladimir Sobell, Nigel Swain, Gordon Wightman**

LONGMAN
CURRENT
AFFAIRS

HANDBOOK OF RECONSTRUCTION IN EASTERN EUROPE AND THE SOVIET UNION

Published by Longman Group UK Limited, Westgate House,
The High, Harlow, Essex, CM20 1YR, United Kingdom.
Telephone (0279) 442601
Telex 81491 Padlog
Facsimile (0279) 444501

Distributed exclusively in the United States and Canada
by Gale Research Company, Book Tower, Detroit,
Michigan 48226, USA

ISBN 0-582-08502-0

A catalogue record for this book is available from the British Library

Printed in Great Britain by Bookcraft (Bath) Ltd

CONTENTS

PREFACE

The two years that are the focus of this volume are two of the most momentous in modern history. At the start of 1989 communist governments were in power throughout Eastern Europe. They were allied, through the Warsaw Treaty Organization and Comecon, with the Soviet Union and communist-ruled states elsewhere. Nearly a third of the world's population was under communist rule. And after 40 years in power, it seemed that even in the more pluralistic societies of Eastern Europe a kind of *modus vivendi* had developed between communist governments and the populations over which they ruled based upon what some described as a "social contract". Under its terms, the populations concerned relinquished most of their democratic rights but in return received a range of social benefits including full employment, cheap housing and a wide range of welfare services.

By the start of 1991, when the detailed coverage of this volume comes to an end, communist governments had been replaced in Hungary, Poland and the German Democratic Republic (which had disappeared entirely as a separate state). In Romania, a National Salvation Front had overthrown the Ceauşescu regime and the communist party that sustained it. In Bulgaria, the communists — who renamed themselves the Socialist Party — won the largest share of the vote at free elections but had to concede a range of pluralising, marketising changes. Even in Albania, still under communist rule in January 1991, there were signs of change. And by the spring of 1991 the Warsaw Treaty Organization had shed its military function, and Comecon was to be replaced by a new form of association based upon world market prices.

Following up a successful *Political and Economic Encyclopaedia of the Soviet Union and Eastern Europe*, published by Longman/St James in 1990, the various contributors to this volume explore in detail the changes that have come about in Eastern Europe and the USSR over these recent years and months. All the chapters follow a similar format: there are chronologies to begin with, then overviews of recent political and economic developments, and then more detailed entries on economic sectors, foreign trade, key personalities, the media and foreign policy. We have incorporated a documentary section, which includes some of the most important treaty and constitutional texts of the period, and a detailed index. Once again, my thanks in preparing this volume are due both to the contributors and to John Harper and Nicola Greenwood of Longman, for the close and sympathetic attention they have devoted to it at all stages.

Stephen White
University of Glasgow

The Publishers wish to thank Ian Gorvin at CIRCA Research and Reference Information Ltd. for producing all the maps in this book, which are the copyright of CIRCA Ltd. Thanks are also due to the Novosti Information Agency (London) for supplying their transcript of the Constitution of the USSR.

NOTES ON CONTRIBUTORS

John B. Allcock is Lecturer in Sociology and head of the Research Unit in Yugoslav Studies at the University of Bradford, England. He is the author of numerous publications on Yugoslav affairs, including *Yugoslavia's Security Dilemmas* (with others, 1988), *Yugoslavia in Transition* (with others, 1991) and *Black Lambs and Grey Falcons* (with Antonia Young, 1991).

John D. Bell is Professor of History at the Baltimore campus of the University of Maryland, USA, and President of the Bulgarian Studies Association of North America. As well as numerous articles on modern Bulgarian history, Professor Bell is the author of two monographs: *Peasants in Power* (1977) and *The Bulgarian Communist Party: from Blagoev to Zhivkov* (1986).

Marko Milivojević is a freelance writer and consultant specializing in European affairs and also Honorary Visiting Fellow at the Research Unit in Yugoslav Studies, University of Bradford, England. His recent publications include *Swiss Neutrality and Security* (1990), *Yugoslavia's Military Industries* (1990) and *Yugoslavia in Transition* (with others, 1991).

Martin Myant is Senior Lecturer in Economics at Paisley College, Scotland. The author of several books and many articles on the economics, politics and history of Eastern Europe, his publications include *Socialism and Democracy in Czechoslovakia 1945–1948* (1981), *Poland: A Crisis for Socialism* (1982) and *The Czechoslovak Economy 1948–1988* (1989).

Daniel Nelson is Senior International Policy Co-ordinator at the Office of the Majority Leader, US House of Representatives, Washington DC, and was formerly at the Carnegie Endowment for International Peace and the University of Kentucky. A specialist on East European and communist politics, his recent books include *Elite-Mass Relations in Communist Systems* (1988) and *Romanian Politics in the Ceauşescu Era* (1988).

Jonathan Osmond is Lecturer in History at Leicester University, England. A specialist in GDR affairs (which he covered for the Economist Intelligence Unit) and German agricultural history, he has contributed widely to journals and symposia including Robert G. Moeller, ed., *Peasants and Lords in Modern Germany* (1986) and Martin Blinkhorn and Ralph Gibson, eds., *Land Ownership and Power in Modern Europe* (forthcoming).

Peter Rutland is a member of the Department of Government at Wesleyan University, Connecticut, in the USA. A specialist in Soviet political economy, his books include *The Myth of the Plan* (1985) and a forthcoming study on the politics of industrial stagnation in the USSR.

George Sanford is Senior Lecturer in the Department of Politics at Bristol University, England. A specialist in comparative communist and East European studies, he is the author of *Polish Communism in Crisis* (1983), *Military Rule in Poland* (1986) and *The Solidarity Congress, 1989* (1990); his *Democratization in Poland* will appear in 1991.

Vladimir Sobell is East European editor of the Economist Intelligence Unit, in London. A specialist on the East European economies and their foreign trade, his publications include *The Red Market* (1984) and more recently *The CMEA in Crisis* (1990).

Nigel Swain is joint Director of the Centre for Central and Eastern European Studies at the University of Liverpool, UK. His publications include *Hungary: A Decade of Economic Reform* (with others, 1981) and *Collective Farms which Work?* (1985). His new book, which analyses Hungary's economy and society during the 40 years of communist rule, will be published in 1991.

Stephen White is Professor of Politics and a Member of the Institute of Soviet and East European Studies at the University of Glasgow. His numerous publications include, most recently, *The Origins of Détente* (1986), *The Bolshevik Poster* (1988) and *Gorbachev in Power* (2nd ed., 1991). He has also edited the *Political and Economic Encyclopaedia of the Soviet Union and Eastern Europe* (1990).

Gordon Wightman is Lecturer in the School of Politics and Communication Studies and joint Director of the Centre for Central and Eastern European Studies at the University of Liverpool, UK. His most recent articles have appeared in *Electoral Studies, Representation* and *Parliamentary Affairs*, and he is presently working on the process of democratization in Czechoslovakia.

ALBANIA

Marko Milivojević

Government as at December 1990

Secretariat of the APL Central Committee
Ramiz Alia (First Secretary; also President of the Presidium of the People's Assembly and Commander-in-Chief of the Albanian Armed Forces)
Foto Çami (also APL ideology chief)
Xhelil Gjoni (also Tiranë First Secretary)
Abdyl Baçka

Politburo of the APL Central Committee
Above four persons, plus the following:
Adil Çarçani (also Chairman of the Council of Ministers, or Prime Minister)
Simon Stefani (also Chairman of the State Control Commission; Deputy Prime Minister)
Pali Miska (also Agriculture; Deputy Prime Minister)
Hekuran Isai (also Internal Affairs; Deputy Prime Minister)
Lenka Çuko (also Fier district First Secretary)
Vangjel Çereva
Muho Aslanni
Hajredin Çeliku (also Transport)

Gen. Kiço Mustaqi (also Defence)
Xhemal Dymylja (candidate member)
Niko Gjyzari (candidate member; also General Secretary of the Council of Ministers)

Other Members of the Council of Ministers
Foreign Affairs. *Reis Malile*
Justice. *Enver Halile*
State Planning Commission. *Bujar Kolaneçi*
Industry and Mining. *Besnik Bekteshi*
Light Industry. *Bashkim Sykaj*
Foodstuff Industry. *Ylli Bufi*
Domestic Trade. *Pajtim Ajazi*
Education. *Skenda Gjinushi*
Finance. *Andrea Nako*
Construction. *Ismail Ahmeti*
Foreign Trade. *Shane Korbeçi*
Public Services. *Xhemal Tafaj*
Minister to the Presidium of the Council of Ministers. *Farudin Hoxha*

Auxiliary Organizations
ADF (Chairwoman. *Nexhmije Hoxha*)
ULYA (Chairman. *Lisen Bashkurti*)

Abbreviations

ADF   Albanian Democratic Front
APL   Albanian Party of Labour
ULYA   Union of Labour Youth of Albania

ALBANIA

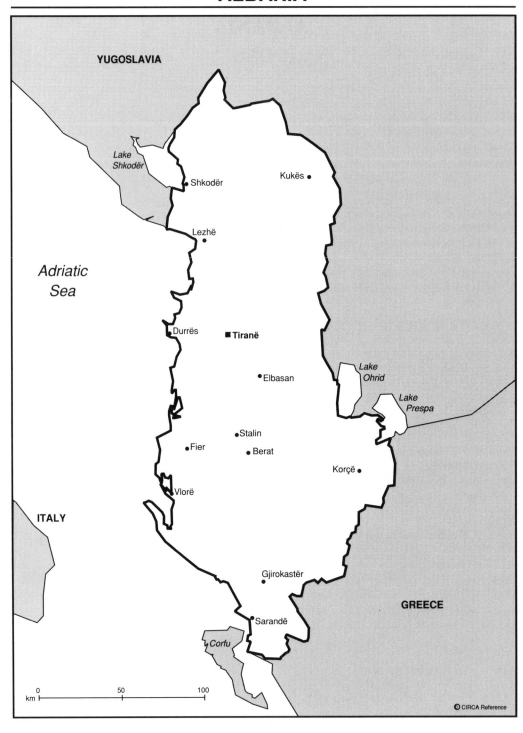

YUGOSLAVIA

*Lake
Shkodër*

• Shkodër

Kukës •

Lezhë
•

*Adriatic
Sea*

Durrës
•

■ **Tiranë**

•Elbasan

*Lake
Ohrid*

*Lake
Prespa*

•Stalin

• Fier

• Berat

Korçë •

Vlorë
•

ITALY

Gjirokastër
•

GREECE

• Sarandë

Corfu

0   50   100
km ├──────┼──────┤

© CIRCA Reference

Chronology

1989

February 1–2. Eighth Plenum of the Albanian Party of Labour (APL) Central Committee announces limited restructuring of party and government leadership.

March 28–30. Albanian Foreign Minister, Reis Malile, visits France, following visits to Turkey and Greece the previous month.

November 15. Presidium of the People's Assembly declares a limited amnesty (including some political prisoners) on the occasion of the 45th anniversary of Albania's liberation from Nazi occupation.

December 19. First Yugoslav report of anti-communist unrest and brutal police repression in Shkodër in northern Albania.

December 26. Central Committee Plenum of the APL's Union of Labour Youth of Albania (ULYA) replaces its First Secretary.

December 29. Niko Gjyzari, Chairman of the State Planning Commission (SPC), presents 1989 economic results and 1990 economic plan to the People's Assembly.

1990

January 1. President Ramiz Alia's New Year's message to the Albanian people claims all is well in the country, and that foreign reports of further unrest and repression in Shkodër, Durrës, Fier and Vlorë are untrue.

January 11. Large demonstrations in Athens to protest against the mistreatment of ethnic Greeks in southern Albania.

January 11–14. Demonstrations involving up to 7,000 people in Shkodër, according to Yugoslav reports later the same month.

January 25. Ninth Plenum of the APL Central Committee announces limited political and economic proposals.

January 26. First large demonstration in Tiranë, involving around 10,000 people, according to the later testimony of the dissident Xhu Lianol Çukol.

March 21. *Zëri i Rinisë*, newspaper of the ULYA, publishes an outspoken interview with the country's leading writer Ismail Kadare, who calls for the overthrow of the APL regime.

April 17. Speaking at the 10th Plenum of the APL Central Committee, President Alia declares an end to opposition to the restoration of diplomatic relations with both the Soviet Union and the United States.

April 15–16. First recorded political strike in Berat, following disturbances in Kavajë towards the end of the previous month, according to Western reports.

May 7–8. The People's Assembly approves a wide-ranging package of political and economic reforms.

May 11. UN Secretary-General Perez de Cuellar visits Albania.

July 1–7. Following anti-government demonstrations in Tiranë, around 5,000 Albanians seek refuge in a number of foreign embassies in the city.

July 7–9. Politburo personnel changes announced at the 11th Plenum of the APL Central Committee, followed by a reshuffle in the Council of Ministers.

July 9–13. All asylum-seekers in foreign embassies allowed to leave Albania in an operation co-ordinated by the UN.

July 30. Albania and the Soviet Union agree to restore diplomatic relations.

September 25–October 1. President Alia visits the United States, where he addresses the UN General Assembly in New York, and meets prominent Albanian émigrés in Boston.

October 24. Tiranë conference of six Balkan Foreign Ministers.

October 25. Ismail Kadare is granted political asylum in France, where he issues an open letter condemning the APL régime.

November 10. Promulgation of new electoral law to allow secret ballots and multi-candidate contests in elections of February 1991, following policy-making speech by President Alia to APL leadership earlier the same month.

November 19. Albania is granted observer status at the Paris Summit of the Conference on Security and Co-operation in Europe (CSCE).

December 9. Large demonstration of students in Tiranë broken up by riot police; further demonstrations in other towns followed.

December 11. Reshuffle of APL leadership. The big surprise was the removal of Foto Çami, but far more significant was the retention of Xhelil Gjoni, Tiranë First Secretary, a member of the Secretariat and a hardline conservative. Governmental changes were also made including the replacement of Andrea Nako by Qemal Disha as Finance Minister and of Nikos Gjyzari by Fatos Nano, a young and reformist economist, as General Secretary of the Council of Ministers.

December 25. Rally of over 10,000 organized by the Democratic Party of Albania in Kavajë; it demanded postponement of the elections due to be held on February 10, 1991 (conceded on January 16, 1991) and the release of all political prisoners.

December 26. A special one-day conference of the APL was held at which Alia's speech offered mild and qualified criticisms of Stalin but defended Hoxha.

End December 1990–January 1991. About 6,000 ethnic Greeks from southern Albania fled over the border to nearby Greece; further worsening of Greco-Albanian relations.

Political Overview

More than any other event during the Year of Revolutions in East-Central Europe, the violent overthrow of Ceauşescu in Romania in December 1989 sent a shock wave throughout Albania. For the country's alienated youth (half the population of 3,000,000 is under the age of 20), it was the impetus for both overt revolt in Shkodër and other cities, and the beginnings of covert political organization under the cover of the official Union of Labour Youth of Albania (ULYA). For Alia's atrophied Stalinist regime, which had done absolutely nothing to reform itself in 1989, it was a nightmare to be avoided by a confused mixture of limited reform and increased *Sigurimi* (secret police) repression during 1990.

Hoxha's legacy

In power continuously for 40 years prior to his death in 1985, Enver Hoxha remains as dominant in death as he was in life in Albania. The fearful and terroristic *Sigurimi-*

controlled Stalinist state he created remains largely intact. His widow, Nexhmije Hoxha, remains powerful and influential behind the scenes. Overtly, she retains full control of the Albanian Democratic Front (ADF) and the Institute of Marxist-Leninist Studies. Alia, a Hoxha protégé and Madame Hoxha's one-time student, has consistently avoided any real confrontation with the conservative Hoxharite-Stalinist diehards who continue to dominate the apparatus controlled by the APL-*Sigurimi* apparatus at all levels (APL — Albanian Party of Labour).

It was not until July 1990, for example, that Politburo personnel changes took place. Though this resulted in a nominal reformist majority in the Politburo, it is highly unlikely that Alia will carry out a long overdue purge of the lower echelons of the APL. And he dare not touch the *Sigurimi*, as the power and survival of the APL rests upon it. As was the case with Ceauşescu's *Securitate*, the *Sigurimi* is an essentially criminal organization. Its violent and terroristic operational methods, which have instilled a great fear among all Albanians, are absolutely central to the APL regime. Despite Alia's limited moves towards reform in 1990, this regime is basically unreformable. It can only operate through intimidation and fear. Once the latter begins to abate, as was the case during 1990, then it faces the prospect of being violently destroyed in a civil war. This will almost certainly happen if the APL regime attempts to cling indefinitely to absolute power in the future. This seems highly probable, if only because of a well grounded fear of a mass *gjakmarrje* (blood-feud or revenge killing) against the hated members of the APL-*Sigurimi* apparatus. Tens of thousands of people could die in such a bloodbath. Relinquishing power appeared as dangerous as hanging onto it in Albania in the early 1990s.

The need for change

Though the obstacles to meaningful political and economic change remain formidable in Albania, the need for such change is great. Hoxha's Stalinist communism has been an unmitigated disaster for the country. Politically, it has given Albania a deeply flawed system of government that can now only be removed by violence, up to and including actual civil war. It has also left Albania dangerously isolated internationally. Economically, it has pauperized the vast majority in a resource-rich country of immense economic potential. Only the most unreconstructed Stalinists could have managed to do this. Economic conditions were fast approaching the point of total collapse in 1990, with life becoming intolerable for the country's long-suffering population. Despite his many promises to improve matters, Alia appeared to have no idea how to begin to resolve this economic crisis.

Alia has failed completely as a reformer. For five years he did nothing. In 1990, under the pressure of external events and internal revolt, he finally recognized that something had to be done, but what he did was a clear case of too little, too late. Economically, the May 1990 reforms turned out to be less meaningful than they appeared to be at first sight. Politically, the November 1990 electoral law was equally meaningless, as it presupposed the very thing that the majority of Albanians did not want: continuing APL domination of the country's political and social life.

Against a background of large student demonstrations in Tiranë in December 1990, a Plenum of the APL Central Committee made a number of decisions that represented the most radical reform package announced to date by the Alia regime. Firstly, five senior members of the Politburo were sacked, including Foto Çami, Simon Stefani and Hajredin Çeliku. Secondly, and most importantly, a multi-party system of government was authorised, with the promise of an amended constitution to legalize opposition political parties before the February 1991 elections. Thirdly, an extraordinary APL congress was scheduled for June 1991.

Radical student leaders, who forced Alia into talks to discuss their grievances, immediately announced the formation of a political party called the Democratic League of Students and Young Albanian Intellectuals. If such groupings could have developed into a realistic political alternative in the future, and if Alia was serious in wanting to bring about meaningful and irreversible change, then there appeared to be a slight hope of a peaceful transition in Albania. However, historical traditions, present political realities, a collapsing economy, and time were all against the development of such a scenario. The option already mentioned, civil war, still seemed the most likely, although the probability of its breaking out in at least the foreseeable future was reduced by these momentous decisions.

Economic Overview

According to the World Bank and other Western sources, Albania's Gross National Product (GNP) was around US$2.5 billion in 1989, which gave a GNP *per capita* of around $800 in the same year. These are only estimates, as Albanian published economic statistics are extremely sparse, selective and often deliberately misleading. In addition, Albania's centrally planned economy uses the concept of Net Material Product (NMP) for its national accounts statistics. NMP is considerably smaller than the GNP or GDP concepts commonly used in the West. No official total NMP figure is publicly available, only annual NMP growth figures (total and by sector) expressed in percentages. These can be used to roughly measure economic performance.

Economic performance

As throughout the period of the eighth Five-Year Plan (1986–90), economic growth performance in 1989 was much lower than planned (see Table 1). Total NMP grew

Table 1:   Annual plan targets and performance (% growth)

	1989 Plan	Result	1990 Plan
NMP produced	5.0	2.0	—
Industrial output	6.8	5.6	8.6
Agricultural output	16.9	9.0	15.0
Fixed investment	2.2	1.5	1.4
Retail trade	5.7	2.0	—
Exports	19.6	4.5	33.4

Source: Albanian press reports.

by only 2%. With Europe's highest population growth rate (2.1% in 1989), Albania is effectively struggling to stay in one place. In the absence of genuine reform, real increases in living standards appeared unlikely. Performance in the crucial agricultural sector was particularly poor; a series of severe droughts in recent years have not helped matters in this part of the economy. Export performance was abysmal in 1989. All the signs pointed to even worse economic performance in the coming decade.

A rigid Stalinist political economy and the absence of external sources of economic aid are responsible for this state of affairs. The withdrawal of Soviet and Chinese economic aid in 1960 and 1978 resulted in sharp falls in the rate of economic growth in the periods 1961–65 and 1979–83 respectively. During the 1980s, NMP growth was regularly less than 50% of the target planned for in the seventh and eighth Five-Year Plans. The 1989 NMP growth rate was only 40% of that planned for that year.

The 1990 Economic Plan

This perhaps explains why no total NMP growth rate figure is to be found in the 1990 Economic Plan. Even more so than the 1989 plan, this document showed little sign of having been prepared by people with a knowledge of real economics. The plan's targets are totally unrealistic and, in the case of exports, pure nonsense. Only the target for fixed investment bears any relation to economic reality. Industry and agriculture, which are now reaching the point of total collapse, barely met 1989 output levels in 1990. Exports, which were meant to rise by a third in 1990, are reportedly down on 1989, as the Alia regime struggled to increase the supply of everything from electricity to food to the domestic market at a time of growing political instability in the country.

Economic policy changes

Like Alia's so-called political changes of late 1990, his economic policy changes of earlier the same year were more cosmetic than substantive. Only one economic policy change was meaningful to the average Albanian. This was the decree of May 1990 that allowed peasants to sell their private plot surplus produce at private markets. Though radical for Albania, this change did little to boost food supplies in 1990. This is because the surplus produced from tiny (currently 200 square metre) plots is limited, and there is little incentive to bring it to market given the dearth of consumer goods for peasants to purchase with their extra income.

Another decree (No. 228), apparently concerned with encouraging private enterprise in the consumer goods/services sector, was in fact nothing of the kind. Stalinist dogmas about private enterprise ensured a large number of restrictions that made it effectively impossible for anyone to start a private business in Albania. Yet the need for such enterprise was great, and the means available to create it at no cost to the state (Albania has a very high rate of private savings). Despite worsening economic conditions in 1990, no further economic policy changes have been forthcoming from the Alia regime.

Key Economic Sectors

Agriculture

Accounting for 31% of NMP and employing 51% of the working population of 1,500,000 in 1989, agriculture remains the most important sector of what is still very much an intermediate developing economy. At a time of rapid population growth, agricultural output growth has been falling in recent years. In 1990, by far the worst year to date, output totals are thought to be at the levels of 1989. This seems to be true for all the principal crops, which include wheat, maize, potatoes, vegetables, fruit and sugar beet. Consequently, severe food shortages are now the norm throughout Albania, which can no longer properly feed its people within its present economic system. A reduction in food exports does not appear to have improved this situation, which will almost certainly worsen in 1991, although not to the point of actual famine.

Industry

Accounting for 46% of NMP and employing 23% of the working population in 1989, Albanian industry is now in an even worse state than the country's agricultural sector. The largest industrial sector, food processing (25% of total industrial capacity in 1984 — see Table 2) is directly dependent upon agriculture. Despite considerable fixed investment in this sector during the 1980s, light industry has totally failed to keep up with the demand for consumer goods. The so-called engineering sector has long been mainly concerned with producing low-quality spare parts for the old and decrepit Soviet and Chinese machinery that largely makes up Albania's industrial base. Once it breaks down altogether, that

	1980	1984
Coal	1.3	1.5
Chrome	1.5	1.7
Copper	5.4	6.6
Ferro-nickel	2.9	3.7
Electricity	4.5	4.0
Chemicals	4.8	5.3
Engineering	13.8	15.4
Building materials	7.8	7.1
Timber & paper	5.9	5.6
Light industry	16.3	16.1
Food	24.9	25.0
Handicrafts & other	10.9	8.0
TOTAL	100.0	100.0

Table 2: Industrial production sectoral breakdown (% of total)

Source: 40 years of Socialist Albania (Tiranë 1985).

industrial base will be finished unless it is modernized with Western equipment and expertise.

Transport

With only 500 kilometres of railways and around 6,700 kilometres of motorable roads, Albania's transport infrastructure remains woefully inadequate, and thus a brake on future economic development. The railways, which carried around 50% of freight traffic in 1989, are mainly confined to the central coastal plains, linking Tiranë to Durrës and Fier, but not to Shkodër in the north and Vlorë in the south. Albania's sole international rail link, from Shkodër to Titograd in Yugoslavia, was opened as recently as 1986. The road network, though twice as large as it was in 1960, has yet to reach Albania's remote inland areas. There is also a serious shortage of vehicles (Albania is the only country in Europe where private cars do not exist).

Finance

Table 3 shows that the forecast annual state budget for 1990 was considerably larger than what it probably was: a little more than the actual figure for 1989. It may be even less, due to the 1990 economic crisis (virtually all revenues come from the economy; income tax does not exist). The average Albanian's social wage is thus now falling in such areas as health, social security and education. In the area of monetary policy, too much money is clearly chasing too few goods, which creates inflationary pressures in the economy. Much private money is thus saved at interest rates of 2–3%, but little can be productively invested for reasons already indicated.

Energy

Though largely self-sufficient in energy, Albania is now experiencing increasing problems extracting oil, gas and coal. Redundant machinery and lack of new fixed investment are

Table 3:   State budgets (million Lekës)

	1989 actual	1990 forecast
Revenue	8,558	9,650
Expenditure of which:	8,552	9,600
National economy	—	4,933
Social & cultural measures	—	3,042
Defence	—	1,030
Administration	—	175
SURPLUS	6	50

Source: Albanian press reports.

the two key problems. In the longer-term, and under a more rational economic system, prospects are very good, as Albania is rich in hydrocarbon resources and hydroelectric potential (80% of all electricity comes from this source), although recent droughts have led to regular power cuts throughout Albania. This has adversely affected industrial production. These short-term problems aside, the country has a good energy balance.

Mining

Though extremely rich in mineral resources (chromium, copper and nickel), Albania has consistently failed to realize its full potential in this area. The problems are the same as with oil, gas and coal. Output of the main mineral, chromium (Albania is the world's third largest producer) has slumped drastically in recent years. It is thought to have fallen to as low as 500,000 tonnes in 1989. The 1990 figure may be even lower. True to form, the unrealistic 1990 economic plan set a chromium output target 25% higher than the official and unattained figure of 900,000 tonnes for 1989.

Foreign Economic Relations

After having its foreign trade and payments generously subsidized to the tune of around $5 billion during the period 1945–78 (by Yugoslavia, 1945–48; the Soviet Union, 1948–60; and China, 1961–78), Albania was left to its own devices during the 1980s. During this decade, its foreign trade was largely with various Western countries, plus Yugoslavia and Romania in the East. Other than 1981 and 1986, this foreign trade was regularly in deficit (see Table 4). In 1989, after a dip in the previous year, imports increased sharply. Export performance remained poor, which meant large deficits now and into the foreseeable future. This in turn meant a larger hard currency foreign debt to finance these deficits.

As of 1989, Albania was trading with around 50 countries. Its most important trading partners in that year were, in decreasing order of importance, the following: Yugoslavia, Italy, Romania, Poland, Germany, Bulgaria and France. During 1989 and 1990, according to Western sources, trade with Italy and Germany increased considerably as regards both

Table 4:   Foreign trade with IMF members (US$ millions)

	1982	1983	1984	1985	1986	1987	1988	1989
Exports	255	219	193	173	243	194	—	—
Imports	–322	–242	–227	–228	–215	–228	–165	–245
Balance	–57	–23	–34	–55	28	–34	—	—

Source: IMF, *Direction of Trade Statistics* (Washington DC 1988), and press reports for 1988–89 data.

imports and exports. Albania also trades with both China and the United States, but not the Soviet Union, although this is now changing following the restoration of diplomatic relations between the two countries in July 1990.

Around 75% of the country's exports consist of oil, chromium ore, ferro-chrome, copper wire, ferro-nickel ore and electricity. The rest is made up of agricultural products, plus some consumer goods (handicrafts). Presently, food exports are being reduced so as to make more food available for the domestic market. Recent droughts have also reduced electricity exports. Production of oil and minerals for export is stagnant. As regards imports, the most important are raw materials (fuels, minerals and metals), capital goods (machinery, plus spare parts), chemicals, paper and rubber products, plus some consumer goods. Imports of all these items are now rising sharply.

Foreign investment in Albania

Until it was amended in May 1990, Albania's 1976 constitution forbade any type of foreign investment in the country, including the acceptance of foreign credits (or portfolio investments). Like much else in Albania, this strange rule was meaningless in practical terms. Albania has been borrowing in Western capital markets (mostly commercial banks and government export credits) for most of the 1980s, so as to finance its foreign trade deficits. The main source of credit seems to have been government export credit organizations, but there were also borrowings from commercial bank sources in 1986. In 1989, when a record $368 million was borrowed from BIS (Bank for International Settlements) banks, Albania's hard currency debt stood at around $85,000,000 at the beginning of the year. It was nearly five times greater at the end of it. Borrowing in 1990 is thought to have been as substantial as was the case in 1989. A total foreign debt of $1 billion by the end of 1991 was a real possibility.

With stagnating export earnings, the servicing of this growing foreign debt could become a problem in the short term. More generally, this type of high-interest rate and short-term debt is not the most suitable for a developing country. More government-to-government and multilateral agency credits would be far better, although to obtain these Albania would have to join the IMF and the World Bank.

Although political instability and uncertainty will deter many potential foreign investors in at least the short term, resource-rich Albania is now regarded as a good long-term investment opportunity in the West. Presently, it is having no trouble borrowing abroad, and prospective Western joint venture (direct investment) partners are now seeking business in Tiranë. Oil is the crucial area at the moment. *Agip* of Italy is looking for a major concession, and *Denimex* of Germany signed an offshore exploration agreement with Albania in late 1990. Other than oil, mineral extraction and processing and also tourism are of interest to foreign investors in the longer term.

Principal Personalities

Alia, Ramiz. Born in 1925 in Shkodër, joined the Albanian Party of Labour (APL) in 1943, its Central Committee in 1948, and the Politburo in 1961. After succeeding his mentor, Hoxha, in 1985, Alia did nothing to reform Albania until as recently as July 1990, when he made his first personnel changes in the Politburo. A very weak character, Alia both fears and avoids conflict with the APL-*Sigurimi* diehards, thereby making a mockery of his so-called reformist credentials. He would not survive long in the event of civil war in Albania.

Çami, Foto. A relative newcomer to the APL leadership, joining the Central Committee in 1971 and the Politburo as a candidate member in 1981. Alia's closest political associate, Çami served as Tiranë First Secretary before being elevated to his present position in 1985.

Çarçani, Adil. Born 1922 in Gjirokastër (Hoxha's birthplace), joined the Politburo with Alia in 1961. A shrewd administrator, Çarçani survived and profited from the fall of his old mentor, Mehmet Shehu (1913–81), becoming Prime Minister in 1982. Çarçani is a political opportunist with no great personal loyalty to Alia.

Hoxha, Nexhmije. Widow of Enver Hoxha (1908–85), remains a formidable figure behind the scenes in Albania, where she is the symbolic leader of the APL-*Sigurimi* diehards. Alia, who owes his job to her support in 1985, dare not touch her politically. One of her many ears in the present Politburo is Lenka Çuko.

Isai, Hekuran. Became Interior Minister in 1990 for the second time in as many years. He replaced the hardline Simon Stefani in this crucial job, although it is unclear as to how much operational power this outsider has over the *Sigurimi* security apparatus.

Kadare, Ismail. Born 1936 in Gjirokastër, became Hoxha's court poet in the early 1960s. With the publication of his first novel, *The General of the Dead Army* (Paris, 1970), he became his own man, although he was not a professional dissident: in 1989, for example, he became vice-chairman of the ADF. In 1990, however, he publicly split with Alia's regime, defecting to France in October of that year. Considered a future President of Albania.

Malile, Reis. Alia's Foreign Minister, is well regarded internationally for his activist diplomacy, which considerably lessened Albania's international isolation in 1989 and 1990. In terms of domestic politics, however, he counts for very little, as he is not a member of the Politburo. A typical Albanian politician, he would drop the APL without a second thought, but is not prepared to risk his own life to get rid of a regime he has had trouble defending internationally in recent years.

Mustaqi, General Kiço. Shadowy figure with extensive *Sigurimi* connections, became the *de facto* boss of the security and defence apparatus in 1982, following Hoxha's assassination of Shehu in 1981. It is he who has real operational power over the *Sigurimi*, which makes him a crucial figure in Albanian politics at the present time.

The Media

With around 300,000 television sets in the country in 1987, most Albanians are well aware of events beyond their borders through watching Yugoslav, Greek or Italian television broadcasts. Such foreign coverage of the Romanian revolution played a major role in bringing about a revolt in Skhodër in December 1989. Certain foreign radio and television stations also kept Albanians informed of events in their own country during 1990, which aided the spread of revolt nationwide. The APL-controlled audio-visual media, with its brazen lies and shrill propaganda, was totally discredited at this time.

The official printed media were less important, as around 40% of the population is illiterate (the highest level in Europe). The APL newspaper, *Zëri i Popullit* (Voice of the People), is also tedious in content and virtually unreadable. The ULYA newspaper, *Zëri i Rinisë* (Voice of the Youth), was more daring, publishing the now famous interview with Kadare in March 1990. It is, however, still unclear whether its editor did this on his own initiative or as part of some wider power struggle in the APL regime. The latter was far more likely than the former.

This interview was of great importance for the country's students and intellectuals, who also gave much attention to Kadare's glowing review of a 1989 book, *Knives*, which was highly critical of the *Sigurimi* secret police. This publishing sensation was almost certainly due to a power struggle in the APL regime. It certainly had no precedent in the post-war period in Albania.

Foreign Relations

Although Albania had diplomatic relations with over 100 countries in 1989, it remained relatively isolated internationally. In 1990, however, there was a marked and largely successful effort to begin to end this self-imposed state of international isolation.

The Balkan region

Following a brief *rapprochement* earlier in the decade, relations with Yugoslavia deteriorated in 1989 and 1990 due to developments in the neighbouring Yugoslav province of Kosovo, which is home to 2,000,000 ethnic Albanians and the birthplace of Albanian nationalism in the 19th century. Serbia's heavy-handed attempts to revoke Kosovo's autonomy is pushing the region towards civil war, and increasing the probability of its eventual secession from Yugoslavia in favour of union with Albania. To date, union with Stalinist Albania has not been an attractive option in Kosovo. A change of regime in Albania would alter everything in Kosovo overnight, thereby further complicating Yugoslav-Albanian relations.

After being relatively good in 1989, Greco-Albanian relations began to come under severe strain in 1990 on account of Tiranë's alleged mistreatment of the 400,000 ethnic Greeks resident in southern Albania. Like Kosovo, this issue has the potential to spiral out of control. By late 1990, however, the need for greater regional co-operation (as at the

Balkan Foreign Ministers' Summit in October) helped to keep these nationalist passions in check on both sides of the Greco-Albanian and Yugoslav-Albanian borders, but they could be rapidly reactivated for the worse in what promises to be an uncertain future in the Balkans.

Albanian relations with other powers

Having been granted observer status at the Paris Summit of the CSCE in November 1990, Albania has at last began to break out of its self-imposed isolation from mainstream European affairs. Actual membership of the CSCE, however, will not be possible until Albania improves its appalling human rights record. And democratic political change will have to come about before it can join the Council of Europe. As regards the EC, Albania has yet to establish diplomatic relations (this was expected to take place in 1991). Bilateral relations with Italy, Germany and France are good and improving, as Albania's pressing economic needs demands it. The United Kingdom, however, is still rebuffed, despite its periodic covert attempts to restore diplomatic relations in recent years.

Having restored diplomatic relations with Moscow in July 1990, President Alia met Soviet Foreign Minister Eduard Shevardnadze at the UN later the same year. Alia accepted an invitation to visit Moscow in the future, thereby finally ending one of the longest and bitterest conflicts in the communist world. Alia also met US President George Bush at the UN. The restoration of diplomatic relations with the US was expected to take place sometime in 1991. If that were to happen, then many other doors would be opened to Albania, including the IMF and the World Bank.

BULGARIA

John D. Bell

Council of Ministers as at January 1991

Chairman. *Dimitur Popov (Non-party)*
Deputy Chairmen. *Dimitur Ludzhev (UDF)*
    Alexander Tomov (BSP)
    Viktor Vulkov (BANU)
Finance. *Ivan Kostov (UDF)*
Industry, Trade and Services. *Ivan Pushkarov (UDF)*
Foreign Economic Relations. *Atanas Paparizov (BSP)*
Transport. *Veselin Pavlov (BSP)*
Justice. *Pencho Penev (BSP)*
Defence. *Yordan Mutafchiev (BSP)*

Foreign Affairs. *Viktor Vulkov (BANU)*
Internal Affairs. *Khristo Danev (Non-party)*
Agriculture. *Boris Spasov (BANU)*
Environment. *Dimitur Vodenicharov (Non-party)*
Labour and Social Welfare. *Emeliia Maslarova (BSP)*
Health. *Ivan Chernozemski (Non-party)*
Education. *Matei Mateev (BSP)*
Science and Higher Education. *Georgi Fotev (UDF)*
Culture. *Dimo Dimov (BSP)*

Party name abbreviations

BANU   Bulgarian Agrarian National Union
BSP   Bulgarian Socialist Party
UDF   Union of Democratic Forces

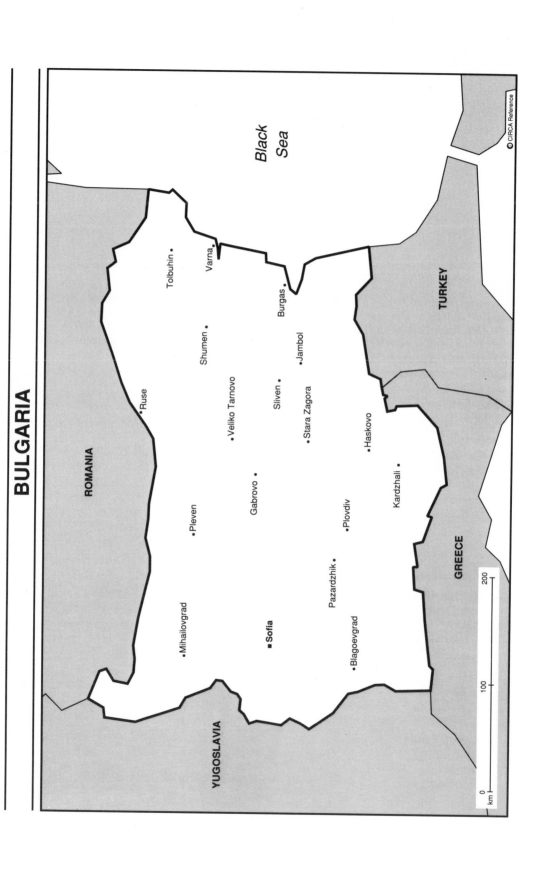

BULGARIA

ROMANIA

YUGOSLAVIA

GREECE

TURKEY

Black Sea

•Mihailovgrad

•Sofia

•Pleven

•Ruse

•Blagoevgrad

Pazardzhik•

Gabrovo•

•Veliko Tarnovo

•Plovdiv

•Tolbuhin

Shumen•

Sliven•

•Stara Zagora

•Jambol

Varna•

Burgas•

Kardzhali•

•Haskovo

© CIRCA Reference

km 0   100   200

Chronology

1989

January 11. Government launches crackdown on dissent with arrest of prominent human rights activists.

February 11. Independent trade union *Podkrepa* (Support) applies for official recognition.

February 20–21. Politburo of Bulgarian Communist Party meets with "representatives of the intelligentsia" to discuss reconstruction; Todor Zhivkov warns that attacks on socialism will not be tolerated.

March 17. Father Khristofor Sŭbev seeks recognition for his newly formed Committee for Religious Rights, Freedom of Conscience, and Spiritual Values.

May 5. Zheliu Zhelev and other dissidents are arrested for circulating an appeal for democratic reforms.

May 6. A group of ethnic Turks in Razgrad begins hunger strike to protest the government's forcing them to adopt Bulgarian names. Their example rapidly spreads to other areas inhabited by Turks and Bulgarian Muslims.

May 19–27. Thousands of ethnic Turks launch public protests; demonstration in Razgrad is attacked by security forces.

June 8–August 27. Turkish government opens border to refugees from Bulgaria; approximately 310,000 ethnic Turks flee Bulgaria or are expelled until border is again closed; Bulgaria widely condemned for human rights violations.

October 16–November 1. Conference on Security and Co-operation in Europe (CSCE) holds conference on environment in Sofia; Bulgarian dissidents launch public protests with many beaten and arrested in clashes with police.

November 10. The "resignation" of Todor Zhivkov is announced; Petŭr Mladenov becomes new state and party leader.

November 13. Government rehabilitates many dissidents and extends official recognition to opposition groups.

November 16. Central Committee plenum of Bulgarian Communist Party launches open attack on Zhivkov and begins purge of his closest associates.

December 7. Seven dissident organizations form Union of Democratic Forces with Zheliu Zhelev as chairman.

December 30. Government announces end to persecution of ethnic Turks and invites those who have fled to return; approximately 200,000 eventually do so.

1990

January 30–February 7. Bulgarian Communist Party holds "Congress of Renewal"; Aleksandŭr Lilov elected as new party leader.

February 1–2. Government of Prime Minister Georgi Atanasov resigns; Andrei Lukanov becomes new Prime Minister.

February 7. Government announces disbanding of secret police.

March 29. Bulgaria suspends payments on its US$10 billion foreign debt.

March 30. Round-table negotiations between Communists, Union of Democratic Forces, and Agrarian Union produce agreements on basic political reform.

April 3. National Assembly adopts round-table proposals on political parties, constitutional changes, and the electoral system; Petŭr Mladenov is elected to the new post of President of the Republic.

April 3. Communists change their party's name to "Bulgarian Socialist Party".

June 10 and 17. Elections are held for a Grand National Assembly to prepare a new constitution; Socialists win a plurality of popular vote and a small majority of seats in the Assembly.

July 6. Mladenov resigns as President.

August 1. Grand National Assembly elects opposition leader Zheliu Zhelev President; Petŭr Beron succeeds him as chairman of Union of Democratic Forces.

August 26. Rioters attack and partially burn the headquarters of the Socialist Party in Sofia.

September 22. Conservatives succeed in replacing pro-reformers at Socialist Party Congress, but Aleksandŭr Lilov is re-elected party leader.

October–November. Economic situation declines drastically; rationing introduced for most staples; a severe energy shortage develops in wake of Gulf crisis.

November 29. After failing to gain opposition support for his economic reform programme, and facing a growing strike movement, Andrei Lukanov resigns as Prime Minister.

December 3. Petŭr Beron, leader of the Union of Democratic Forces, resigns following charges that he had once worked for the State Security apparatus.

December 7. Dimitŭr Popov, a non-party jurist, is named to form a new government to hold power until new elections can be held the following year.

December 20. A cabinet is formed representing the three major parties.

Political Overview

On November 10, 1989, the day after the opening of the Berlin Wall, the resignation of Todor Zhivkov as general secretary of the Bulgarian Communist Party (BCP) and president of the State Council was announced to the country. Zhivkov had headed the BCP for 35 years and had combined state and party leadership for 27. He had been in power longer than any other living Soviet bloc leader, and an entire generation of Bulgarians had come to maturity under his regime.

In the long run, Zhivkov's downfall will probably be seen as the product of changes set in motion by Mikhail S. Gorbachev in the USSR, but a number of domestic factors were also significant. Among these were a declining economic situation (see below), the growth of internal dissent, and the effects of changes in Bulgarian society that proceeded through the communist era.

Zhivkov offered lip service to *perestroika*, but his Bulgarian version of it consisted of fiery rhetoric accompanied by repeated and confusing government reorganizations that made few real changes. Meanwhile, Bulgarian dissidents proved increasingly willing to mount open challenges to the regime. Members of the intelligentsia, particularly in the capital, joined Clubs for the Support of *Glasnost* and *Perestroika* (later renamed "Clubs for the Support of Democracy"). *Podkrepa*, an independent trade union, was organized in February, 1989, and quickly began to enroll thousands of members. In the city of Ruse, which was being slowly poisoned by chlorine gas emissions from a Romanian chemical combine across the Danube River, an organized ecological movement condemned the government's indifference to the destruction of the environment. Human rights organizations also appeared in various parts of the country.

Zhivkov's regime warned that it would not tolerate "national nihilism" or "negative attitudes towards socialism", and subjected its critics to police harassment, loss of employment, and abuse in the press. Dissident leaders, however, did not retreat into passivity. During the spring, protests among Bulgaria's ethnic Turks and Muslims against the suppression of Islamic names and the use of Turkish escalated rapidly and led to several violent clashes with the authorities. When the government of Turkey opened the border to refugees from Bulgaria, thousands fled or were driven from the country. By the time Turkey again closed the border, more than 310,000 refugees had abandoned Bulgaria, an exodus that focused worldwide attention on Bulgaria's human rights record.

Zhivkov's increasingly erratic leadership, compounded by his efforts to promote his wastrel son's career, caused an erosion of support among the party leadership. While the details surrounding his actual removal are still obscure, the key figures were Petŭr Mladenov, Minister of Foreign Affairs since 1971, and Dobri Dzhurov, the Minister of Defence. At a combined meeting of the BCP's Politburo and Secretariat on November 10, a small majority voted to accept the leader's "resignation". The fiction that he had resigned voluntarily lasted only days. Zhivkov soon came under attack for personal corruption and for establishing a "totalitarian" regime. His relatives and closest supporters were quickly purged or voluntarily went into retirement.

Mladenov, who filled Zhivkov's place as state and party leader, pledged to promote the development of pluralism in the country and to respect the rule of law along with the rest of the new leadership. To this end, they halted the persecution of the ethnic Turks and invited those who had fled to return to Bulgaria, allowed opposition groups to register as legal entities, and promised to eliminate the domestic role of the state security forces. Bowing to widespread demonstrations, the party also amended Article 1 of the constitution, which recognized the party as the guiding force in society.

By the end of February 1990, when the BCP held a "Congress of Renewal", a new distribution of power emerged. In a gesture toward the separation of powers, Mladenov left the party leadership while remaining head of state. Andrei Lukanov, widely regarded as the party's ablest statesman, became Prime Minister. And Aleksandŭr Lilov was elected chairman of a restructured BCP Supreme Council. Lilov had been purged from the leadership by Zhivkov in 1983, and was widely believed to favour liberalization. Auxiliaries of the old Communist Party, such as the Bulgarian Agrarian National Union, the Council of Trade Unions, and the *Komsomol* (the party's youth wing) declared their independence from the BCP.

The number of political parties and movements mushroomed — more than 50 sought official recognition — but by the end of 1989 the most important groups entered into a coalition, the Union of Democratic Forces (UDF) with dissident leader Zheliu Zhelev as president. The UDF quickly showed its ability to stage mass demonstrations in the capital, and its leaders gained the agreement of the communists to enter into round-table discussions on the future of the country. The round table, which functioned as a substitute parliament, reached decisions on three basic issues. The first provided for the election of a Grand National Assembly (GNA) to be composed of 400 deputies, half elected in single-member districts and half selected by proportional representation. Over a period of 18 months, the

GNA would function both as parliament and as constitutional assembly to design a new political structure for the country. A neutral commission whose membership was approved by both sides was set up to implement the election agreement. The round table banned the formation of political parties on an ethnic or religious basis, a measure aimed at preventing the organization of a separate, and perhaps separatist, party to represent Bulgaria's Turks and Muslims. Despite this provision, the Party of Rights and Freedoms, organized by Akhmed Dogan, quickly emerged as the *de facto* "Turkish Party".

The UDF entered the campaign with a high level of confidence. Assuming that if the populace were given the opportunity to vote freely it would automatically reject the BSP, the UDF sought to make the election a referendum on the past 45 years of Communist rule. UDF leaders pledged never to join a coalition with the BSP, and even turned down a Socialist proposal to sign an agreement on mutual nonviolence. The BSP, on the other hand, distanced itself as much as possible from the past and campaigned as the party of "responsible, conservative, change", stressing the experience of its leaders and minimizing its policy differences with the UDF. It denied seeking a monopoly of power and called for the formation of a coalition with its opposition either before or after the elections. While cultivating a new image designed to appeal to Bulgaria's middle-class urban voters, the BSP conducted a more traditional campaign in the countryside. Party and state officials put heavy pressure on the village population, whose habits of subordination, developed over the past 45 years, were not easily broken. This pressure was admitted by BSP leaders, who attributed it to over-zealousness on the part of local activists while denying that it was a tactic promoted by the national party leadership.

The election results, shown in Table 1, were a bitter disappointment to the UDF, but they were hardly the "overwhelming Socialist victory" that was reported in the Western press. The BSP failed to gain a majority of the popular vote, and some of its leading figures were forced into embarrassing run-offs or were actually defeated. The UDF dominated Bulgaria's cities, especially the capital, and enjoyed a commanding level of support from professionals and the young. And because decisions of the Grand National Assembly required a two-thirds majority, it could exercise a veto on any Socialist proposals.

The June elections in fact produced a prolonged political stalemate, as the BSP proved unwilling to enact painful reforms without the approval of the opposition, while the UDF steadfastly refused to be drawn into a coalition. As the economic situation deteriorated, popular feeling moved steadily toward the UDF. On July 6, President Mladenov resigned,

Table 1:   Bulgarian election results, 1990

Party	Votes	%	Seats
Bulgarian Socialist Party	2,886,363	47.15	211
Union of Democratic Forces	2,216,127	36.20	144
Bulgarian Agrarian National Union	491,500	8.03	16
Party of Rights and Freedoms	368,929	6.03	23
Others	158,279	2.59	6
TOTAL	6,121,198	100.0	400

Source: Bulgarian press reports.

after the broadcast of a videotape of him proposing that tanks be used against an opposition demonstration. When no candidate could garner enough votes in the Assembly to become his successor, the Socialists gave their support to UDF leader Zheliu Zhelev. Zhelev accepted the office, resigning from the UDF, and quickly acted with great vigour, making the office a focus of power. By the end of the year, polls showed him to be the most popular figure in the country.

The erosion of the BSP's position continued as the party itself threatened to break up, some of its parliamentary deputies declared their independence, and an open dispute broke out between Lukanov and Lilov. Unable to persuade the party leadership to remove Lilov, and faced with a deteriorating economy and growing strike movement, Lukanov resigned as Prime Minister at the end of November. The National Assembly turned the task of forming a new government over to Dimitŭr Popov, a non-party jurist who had won general approval for his work on the Central Election Commission that had administered the June elections. On December 20 a cabinet of 18 ministers was formed, consisting of eight Socialists, three members of the UDF, two Agrarians, and five independents. This government was expected to remain in power until new elections, projected for March 1991, could be held.

The resignations of Mladenov and Lukanov and the disarray in the Socialist camp contributed to a marked swing of public opinion in favour of the opposition shown in a number of polls. The UDF, however, experienced a sharp setback of its own when Petŭr Beron, Zhelev's successor as chairman, suddenly resigned following allegations that he had once worked for the state security service. He was replaced by Dimitŭr Filipov, a lawyer and vice-chairman of the Green Party.

Economic Overview

Up until the fall of Todor Zhivkov, the Bulgarian government issued optimistic reports on the country's economic progress. According to official statistics, during 1987 the economy grew at a rate of 6.2% with a 5.1% increase in the industrial sector. Even at the time, however, some Bulgarians expressed scepticism at this report, which contained glaring internal inconsistencies.

At the beginning of 1988 Zhivkov launched a new round of economic restructuring after admitting that earlier efforts had sown confusion among managers and alienated the workers. His new proposal was to make "the firm" the basic unit of production in the industrial and service sectors. According to the new regulations, firms could be established by state agencies, banks, co-operatives, or individual citizens, and would be permitted to issue their own stock or bonds. Firms operated by private citizens would be permitted to hire up to 10 workers on a permanent basis and an unlimited number on temporary contracts. Thousands of new firms appeared, at least on paper, apparently as the result of a simple reclassifying of existing enterprises.

Even Zhivkov admitted that the exodus of ethnic Turks during the summer created economic disruption, particularly in agriculture, but the government continued to issue confident reports on plan fulfilment through the third quarter of 1989. Zhivkov's fall, however, was followed by a turn toward economic realism and the frank admission that Bulgaria faced massive economic problems. Soon after Zhivkov's removal, Mladenov described the Bulgarian economy as "on the verge of a heart attack". The most critical problems he cited were that 40–45% of Bulgaria's production facilities were obsolete, that production of many critical goods had actually declined since 1980, that the growth of wages had outstripped the growth of consumer goods available to the population leading to shortages and inflation, and that the state budget had been operating at enormous deficits. Particularly alarming was the recent rapid growth in the country's hard currency debt, which had reached the level of $10 billion. Much of this debt had been run up by Zhivkov in order to forestall a sharp decline in living standards caused by the country's declining productivity. The old leadership was criticized for launching grandiose costly projects that were frequently left uncompleted; for allowing massive corruption to pervade the economic system; and for neglecting the needs of consumer industries. (See Table 2 for economic performance 1987–89.) For the first time, the new leadership also focused attention on the environmental damage that had been done to the country during the past decades of complete neglect.

In a general sense the governing Socialist Party and the opposition agreed on the nature of the reforms needed to promote economic recovery. These included the dismantling of the bureaucratic command structure and the closing down of unproductive state enterprises; the legalization of private property and the privatization of broad sectors of the economy; reliance on markets to set prices; and the reorientation of trade away from the countries of the CMEA, particularly the Soviet Union, and toward Western Europe. Real differences existed, however, over the scope and pace of change. In the months before the elections, the UDF endorsed a policy of economic "shock therapy", maintaining that a gradualist approach to change had not worked in the other countries of Eastern Europe. The Socialists, on the other hand, warned of the hardships that such a policy would bring to the majority of the population and promised a policy of "responsible change" that would lead to a painless transition to a market system. Lukanov's government also used the country's

Table 2:   Recent economic performance

	1987	1988	1989
Net Material Product at market prices (bn Lv)	28.21	30.08	30.01
NMP growth (%)	5.1	6.2	–0.4
Population (millions, end year)	8.97	8.99	8.99
Retail price inflation (%)	0.1	0.5	9.0
Hard currency exports ($bn)	2.8	2.7	2.2
Hard currency imports ($ bn)	3.2	3.9	3.7
Current account ($ bn)	–0.5	–1.2	–1.3
Gross external debt ($ bn)	6.2	7.6	10.8

Main foreign trading partners (1989):
Exports: USSR, GDR, Czechoslovakia, Poland, Romania.
Imports: USSR, GDR, Czechoslovakia, West Germany, Poland.

Source: Current press reports.

remaining hard currency reserves to prevent any sharp decline in living standards before the elections.

The Socialist economic programme was politically effective, but Lukanov was unable to deliver the painless transition his party had promised. The government suspended payments on the principal of its foreign debt at the end of March and stopped making interest payments in June. Almost immediately after the elections, basic commodities such as sugar, cooking oil, and detergent began to disappear from the shelves, forcing the government to introduce rationing. An energy crisis loomed as the USSR decreased its deliveries of oil and made it clear that after January 1, 1991 Bulgaria would have to pay for Soviet oil at world market prices and in hard currency. The expectation that energy needs would be met by Iraq, which had accumulated a $1.3 billion debt to Bulgaria during the Iran-Iraq war, was dashed by the crisis in the Gulf. Shortages of fuel and power combined with the inability to finance the importation of raw materials led to sharp declines in industrial and agricultural production. According to the government's office of statistics, during the first three-quarters of 1990 there was a decline of 11% in total domestic production which included a 13% decline in commodity production (see Table 3 for an overview of the economy at this time).

In October Lukanov proposed a comprehensive economic reform based on the recommendations of a team of American experts headed by Richard Rahn, vice-president of the US Chamber of Commerce. It called for the rapid denationalization of major state-owned holdings, the privatization of agriculture, and reliance on the market to set prices and wages. Lukanov warned that there was no alternative to this programme and that it was inevitable that it would be accompanied by sharp dislocations, increased unemployment, and a decline in living standards for the majority of the population. Because of the hardships involved, Lukanov refused to ask the National Assembly to approve the plan unless the political opposition would agree in advance to support it. The opposition, however, despite the fact that Lukanov's programme had come primarily from their proposals, refused to co-operate and seized on the moment to topple the government. The *Podkrepa* trade union took the lead, calling for a general strike that got widespread support. Lukanov resigned, leaving the formation of an economic programme to his successors. It appeared most likely that basic economic decisions would have to await the resolution of Bulgaria's political crisis, probably through new parliamentary elections projected for March 1991.

Table 3: The Bulgarian economy in 1990

	January	*November*	*% decline*
Total production (millions of lev)	6,834	6,116	10.5
Industrial production	5,441	4,783	12.1
Construction			4.9
Transportation			6.9
Housing (number of apartments)	37,575	22,545	40.0

The cost of living based on a shopping basket of 1,700 goods and services rose 36.5% between May and October.

Source: *Duma*, December 11 1990, pp. 1–2.

Key Economic Sectors

Agriculture

Bulgarian agriculture suffered from a host of long- and short-term problems. Years of neglect and mismanagement left this sector technologically backward. Moreover, for decades young Bulgarians have deserted the countryside for more rewarding occupations in the cities; the average age of villagers is 10 years higher than the urban average. More recently, agriculture has frequently suffered from drought, and this year the shortage of fuel for farm machinery led to serious delays in winter sowing. The exodus of ethnic Turks in 1989 created severe farm labour shortages, particularly in the south-east, disrupting the production of tobacco, a traditional staple of Bulgarian exports. During 1990 the state procurement system all but collapsed, as farmers resisted turning their crops over to state agencies, preferring to wait for market reforms to bring higher prices. While the government did raise the prices it was willing to pay, the increases were not large enough to bring significant supplies into the market.

The privatization of agriculture was delayed by the insistence of some parties in the Union of Democratic Forces that the land be restored to the same individuals it had been taken from during collectivization or to their legal descendants. While this demand rested on a degree of justice, the task of locating the "rightful owners" of the land promised to be enormously slow and complicated.

Manufacturing

Industrial manufacturing, the expansion of which was once the communist regime's proudest achievement, now constitutes an enormous problem. Many of the massive enterprises built in imitation of Soviet experience are now seen to be enormously wasteful of resources, environmentally damaging, and technologically obsolete. Particularly after the oil shock of the 1970s, the Bulgarian government began to subsidize unprofitable industries. In December 1989 the government announced that almost one quarter of national income was used for this purpose.

The metallurgical industry is the most striking example of Bulgaria's history of misdirected investments. It received 600 million Leva in subsidies during 1989. Although it generates only 1% of the national income, metallurgy accounts for 15–16% of Bulgaria's total energy consumption. The great Kremikovtsi iron works outside Sofia not only poisons the air of the capital, but is dependent on ore imported from the Soviet Union. On purely economic criteria, Kremikovtsi and other giant monuments to the Stalinist pursuit of heavy industrialization at any cost would be shut down immediately. The social and political problems created by the resulting unemployment, however, make this an unlikely possibility.

Energy

The problem of locating new sources of energy and finding the means to pay for it was the most pressing economic problem that developed during the year. Bulgaria had been accustomed to receiving oil from the Soviet Union at below-market prices. During the spring, however, Bulgaria was informed that not only would deliveries be reduced, but that after January 1, 1991, Bulgaria would have to pay in dollars. Moreover, Soviet oil deliveries during 1990 fell about 15% short of what had been expected. The crisis in the Gulf cut off another source of supply, and left the country with no alternative to strict gas rationing. Electric power for consumers was delivered in a two-hours-on-two-hours-off pattern and was also sharply reduced for industry.

Almost 40% of Bulgaria's electric power is generated by the nuclear power complex at Kozlodui on the Danube. The Soviet-designed reactors lack many of the safety features considered essential in the West; the German government closed down a similar plant in the former East Germany for safety reasons. Bulgaria's fledgling ecological movement has demanded the shutting down of Bulgarian nuclear plants, but the lack of alternative energy sources has made this impossible for the present.

Finance, transport and new technology

The political stalemate produced by the June elections delayed any governmental undertaking to deal with the country's financial problems, which became increasingly chaotic. Early in 1991 the government reported that the economic slowdown and administrative turmoil had created a situation in which almost no revenue was flowing into the state treasury. In the new government, formed on December 19, 1990, the key economic ministries (Finance along with Industry, Trade and Services) were turned over to experts from the Union of Democratic Forces who were charged with preparing new reform proposals.

The economic crisis hindered any improvements in transport and technological innovation. In late 1990 Bulgaria announced a joint agreement with *Club Med* of France to help develop the Black Sea tourist industry, but otherwise lagged behind comparable nations in developing partnerships with Western corporations. Several agreements were nonetheless concluded in the latter part of 1990, among them with *Citroën* of France (under which a company based in Varna will produce spare parts and sell 2,000–2,500 passenger cars annually in the local market); with *Festo Maschinenfabrik* of Austria (for the production and sale of pneumatic systems); with *Deltacam Systems* of the United Kingdom (a joint venture which will produce and market CAD/CAM systems); with the *European Investment and Development Company* (for a variety of forms of household and transport eqduipment); and with the Spanish companies *Miguel Bosser*, *Jaime Bertram* and *Comitexa* (for the modernization of the Bulgarian textile industry).

Foreign Economic Relations

During the communist era up to 80% of Bulgaria's foreign trade was with the countries of the Council for Mutual Economic Assistance (CMEA or Comecon); up to 60% with the Soviet Union alone. Over the years a series of agreements aimed at integrating the Bulgarian and Soviet economies. Consequently the collapse of the CMEA and the growing economic crisis in the USSR had a sharp impact on Bulgaria, which could no longer count on reliable sources of raw materials or secure markets for its manufactured goods. The Soviet decision to demand payment in hard currency for its exports beginning in 1991 was another severe blow to the Bulgarian economy. Bulgarian leaders hoped to reorient the economy toward Western Europe and the United States. After his election to the presidency, Zheliu Zhelev visited the USA, Western Europe, and Japan to plead for economic aid and co-operation, but results were slow to materialize. The government's suspension of debt payments made it all but impossible to secure credits from Western banks, and the prolonged political stalemate between the Socialists and opposition delayed the adoption of basic legislation that would provide a framework for foreign investment.

Bulgaria's economic difficulties, combined with its support for economic and military sanctions against Iraq, did create some sympathy in the West. By the end of the year, it was reported that the EC was preparing an aid package worth $500 million and that the USA would include Bulgaria in the emergency aid programme being developed for Eastern Europe and the USSR.

Principal Personalities

Dertliev, Dr Petŭr. Born 1916, active in politics before World War II, Dr Dertliev spent more than 10 years in prisons and labour camps after the communist takeover. During 1989 he reconstituted the long dormant Social Democratic Party, which became the largest component of the Union of Democratic Forces. He is, perhaps, the most respected of the senior leaders among the opposition.

Dogan, Akhmed. Born 1955. Trained in philosophy, one of the chief organizers of the ethnic Turkish resistance to the government's programme of Bulgarization. In 1989 he was sentenced to 10 years in prison, but released after Zhivkov's fall. He is the organizer and leader of the Party of Rights and Freedoms, the principal representative of Bulgaria's ethnic Turks and Muslims.

Karakachanov, Aleksandŭr. Born 1960, active in the formation of Bulgaria's ecological movement. During the CSCE environmental conference in Sofia he was among the demonstrators beaten by police. After Zhivkov's fall, he organized the Green Party and became its chairman. He was recently appointed mayor of Sofia.

Lilov, Aleksandúr. Born 1933 and educated in literature and philosophy, became one of the most powerful men in the Communist Party until purged by Zhivkov in 1983. He then headed the Institute for Modern Social Theories, a think-tank noted for harbouring "liberal" communists. After Zhivkov's fall, Lilov rejoined the party leadership and was elected head of the Party at its congress in February 1990. Lilov claims to want to make the BSP a "party of the modern European left", by separating it from the state and by democratizing it internally. During 1990 he was sharply criticized by both reformers and conservatives and barely survived a challenge to his leadership at the BSP congress in September.

Zhelev, Zheliu. Born 1935, Bulgaria's most prominent dissident, Zhelev was at odds with the regime since the early 1960s when he was not allowed to defend his dissertation in philosophy because of its disagreement with Lenin's views. His study of totalitarian government, *Fascism*, implicitly comparing communist and fascist regimes, was suppressed. Zhelev was the principal inspiration for the formation of "discussion clubs" among the intelligentsia that served as forums to criticize the Zhivkov regime, and when Zhivkov fell he was immediately chosen to lead the Union of Democratic Forces. On August 1, 1990, the Grand National Assembly elected him president of Bulgaria following the resignation of Petŭr Mladenov. As President, Zhelev acted with great force to seize the political initiative from the Socialists and to make the presidency a real focus of power.

Zhivkov, Todor. Born 1911, Bulgaria's former dictator spent 1990 under house arrest, facing the prospect of being brought to trial for embezzlement and abuse of power. Attempts to persuade him to appear before the National Assembly foundered on his demand to be granted immunity from prosecution. In an interview given on November 27, 1990, he stated that he had long had doubts about communism and that it had been a mistake for the West to turn Bulgaria over to Stalin after World War II. At the same time, he pointed out that life had been better under his leadership, and that the present government was bringing the country to ruin.

The Media

The Bulgarian media, particularly the press, were profoundly changed by the fall of Zhivkov's regime and the lifting of censorship. Although somewhat limited by shortages of newsprint and printing facilities, the Bulgarian press became free and a vigorous participant in the debates on the country's future. Most Bulgarian newspapers are published by the various political parties and movements. The UDF publishes *Democracy*, the Social Democrats *A Free People*, the Agrarians *Agrarian Banner*, and the Agrarian Union affiliated with the UDF *Popular Agrarian Banner*. The BSP changed its newspaper's name from *Workers Cause* to *Word*, and under the editorship of the reform-minded Stefan Prodev it became quite lively and informative. Some semi-official publications, such as the *Literary Front*, published by the Writers' Union, and *Review*, published by the Journalists' Union, have aggressively asserted their independence from the government and political parties.

Several publications have appeared aimed at satisfying the public's demand for satire, sex, and humour. The paper *168 Hours* is a weekly aimed at providing economic/business information to the country's aspiring capitalists.

Although radio and television remain state enterprises, their employees have fought hard and successfully to gain independence from strict government control. The elimination of Communist Party cells in the workplace has given greater freedom to the media professionals.

Foreign Relations

During his last year in power, Todor Zhivkov attempted to form an anti-*perestroika* bloc with the conservative communist governments of Czechoslovakia, the German Democratic Republic, and Romania. He defended the legitimacy of the 1968 Warsaw Pact occupation of Czechoslovakia and was rewarded by Prague's approval of his campaign against Bulgaria's ethnic Turks. Zhivkov also courted the orthodox regimes in Cuba and North Korea and expressed approval of the massacre in Beijing's Tiananmen Square as necessary to "protect the socialist gains of the working people". But Zhivkov's hope that conservatives in the USSR would oust Gorbachev was disappointed, and the collapse of communist regimes in Czechoslovakia and the GDR left Bulgaria entirely isolated. It is also widely believed that the Soviet Union encouraged Zhivkov's colleagues to move against him; at the very least the Soviet government publicly welcomed the change.

Both the governing Socialists and the opposition agreed that Bulgaria's foreign policy had to be reoriented toward the West. The crumbling of the Warsaw Pact and the absorption of the USSR with its own internal problems made it obvious that Bulgaria's security needs would have to be met in new ways. The government quickly moved to mend fences with Turkey by halting the persecution of the ethnic Turks and Muslims and by inviting those who had fled the country to return. Both as opposition leader and as president, Zheliu Zhelev was extremely firm on this point. The government also restored diplomatic relations with Israel and promised to co-operate fully in the removal of certain missiles whose presence on Bulgarian soil caused concern in the USA and Western Europe. President Zhelev also insisted on sending at least a token Bulgarian force (a medical team) to participate in the military build-up in Saudi Arabia.

Most Bulgarian leaders expressed the hope that regional and European-wide structures would supply the economic and military security that had been provided by the Warsaw Pact and CMEA. Their worst fear was that Bulgaria would remain isolated and forgotten in a region traditionally known for instability.

CZECHOSLOVAKIA

Gordon Wightman and Peter Rutland

Government as at January 1, 1991

Prime Minister. *Marián Čalfa (PAV)*
Deputy Prime Minister (economic reform). *Václav Valeš (Non-party)*
Deputy Prime Minister (legislation). *Pavel Rychetský (Non-party)*
Deputy Prime Minister (human rights and information policy). *Jozef Mikloško (CDM)*
Deputy Prime Minister and Minister of Foreign Affairs. *Jiří Dienstbier (CF)*
Defence. *Luboš Dobrovský(CF)*
Interior. *Ján Langoš (PAV)*
Finance. *Václav Klaus (CF)*

Economy. *Vladimír Dlouhý (CF)*
National Economic Strategy. *Pavel Hoffmann (Non-party)*
Labour and Social Affairs. *Petr Miller (CF)*
Transport. *Jiří Nezval (Non-party)*
Communications. *Theodor Petřík (Non-party)*
Federal Committee for the Environment (Minister and Chairman). *Josef Vavroušek (Non-party)*
State Control. *Květoslava Kořínková (Non-party)*

Abbreviations

CDM   Christian Democratic Movement
CF   Civic Forum
PAV   Public Against Violence

Note: It was reported on January 18, 1991, that Jozef Bakšay (PAV) was expected to be given the post of Minister of Foreign Trade which had been vacant since the death of Slavomír Stračár on August 21 1990. Imrith Klassik (CDM) was appointed to a new post as Minister in charge of the Federal Office for Economic Competition on January 19, 1991.

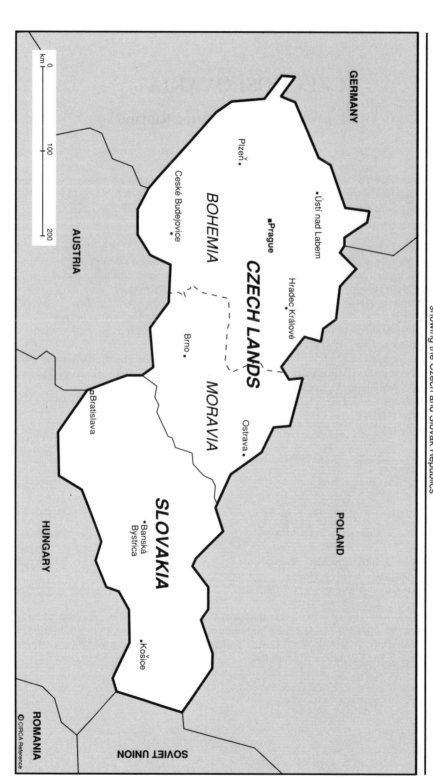

CZECHOSLOVAKIA
showing the Czech and Slovak Republics

GERMANY

POLAND

AUSTRIA

HUNGARY

ROMANIA

SOVIET UNION

BOHEMIA

MORAVIA

CZECH LANDS

SLOVAKIA

■Prague

Plzeň •

• Ústí nad Labem

České Budějovice •

Hradec Králové •

Brno •

Ostrava •

□Bratislava

• Banská Bystrica

• Košice

km
0   100   200

© CIRCA Reference

Chronology

1989

January 15–20. Week-long demonstrations take place in Prague on the anniversary of Jan Palach's suicide in 1969.

February 21. Václav Havel is sentenced to nine months' imprisonment on charges of incitement and obstructing a public official during the January demonstrations.

May 1. Official May Day celebrations in Prague's Wenceslas Square are followed by a pro-democracy counter-demonstration by 2,000 predominantly young people.

May 17. Havel is released from prison after serving four months of his sentence.

June 29. A petition calling for political reform is circulated under the title "A Few Sentences".

August 21. Several thousand take part in a demonstration in Prague on the anniversary of the Soviet invasion in 1968.

October 28. Almost 10,000 take part in an unofficial demonstration in Prague's Wenceslas Square on the 71st anniversary of the foundation of Czechoslovakia.

November 17. An officially sanctioned student demonstration in Prague to mark the 50th anniversary of the execution of Jan Opletal by the Nazis is attacked by security police.

November 19. As protests sparked off by the police brutality on November 17 spread, Havel and other opposition figures form Civic Forum to co-ordinate the pro-democracy campaign. In Bratislava the Public Against Violence is formed a few days later as a Slovak counterpart to Civic Forum.

November 20–26. Massive demonstrations in Prague's Wenceslas Square demanding the resignation of the country's communist leaders and an end to one-party rule spread throughout Czechoslovakia.

November 24. At an extraordinary session of the Communist Party Central Committee, the entire leadership resigns.

November 27. A two-hour general strike demonstrates workers' support for the opposition.

November 29. The Federal Assembly approves the deletion from the constitution of references to the Communist Party's leading role and to Marxism-Leninism as the basis of education.

December 3. The Communist Federal Prime Minister Ladislav Adamec forms a new 21-member Federal Government in which communists retain 16 seats.

December 7. Adamec, faced with the refusal of the opposition to accept his new government, resigns as Federal Prime Minister.

December 10. Gustáv Husák resigns as President of Czechoslovakia after swearing in a coalition Government of National Understanding led by Marián Čalfa, in which a majority of the 21 seats are given to candidates nominated by Civic Forum, the Public Against Violence and the non-communist political parties.

December 19. The Federal Government announces its intention to prepare for free elections and the transition to a market-based economy.

December 20–21. An extraordinary congress of the Communist Party elects Ladislav Adamec party chairman and former Youth Union leader Vasil Mohorita first secretary.

December 28. Alexander Dubček is elected Chairman of the Federal Assembly.

December 29. Václav Havel is elected President of Czechoslovakia by the Federal Assembly.

1990

January 18. Federal Prime Minister Čalfa resigns from the Communist Party.

February 6. Civic Forum's spokesman Petr Pithart replaces communist František Pitra as Czech Prime Minister.

February 26. An agreement on the complete withdrawal of Soviet troops from Czechoslovakia by July 1, 1991 is signed by the Soviet and Czechoslovak foreign ministers in Moscow.

March 10. Milan Čič, appointed Slovak Prime Minister on December 12, 1989, announces his resignation from the Communist Party.

April 18. Czechoslovakia joins the IMF and World Bank.

April 20. The Federal Assembly approves adoption of the name Czech and Slovak Federative Republic.

April 21–22. Pope John Paul II visits Czechoslovakia.

June 8–9. Elections to the Federal Assembly give Civic Forum and the Public Against Violence a clear parliamentary majority. Civic Forum wins two-thirds of the seats in the Czech National Council. The Public Against Violence becomes the largest party in the Slovak National Council with 48 of the 150 seats.

June 27. Čalfa forms a new Federal Government based on a coalition between Civic Forum, the Public Against Violence and the Slovak Christian Democratic Movement.

June 27. Vladimír Mečiar of the Public Against Violence replaces Čič as Slovak Prime Minister and forms a government comprising members of the Public Against Violence, the Christian Democratic Movement and the Democratic Party.

June 29. Pithart forms a new Czech government based on a coalition between Civic Forum, the Czechoslovak People's Party and the Movement for Self-Governing Democracy-Society for Moravia and Silesia.

July 5. Havel is re-elected Czechoslovak President by the Federal Assembly.

October 13. Finance Minister Václav Klaus is elected chairman of Civic Forum.

October 25. A bill on the privatization of small businesses (*zákon o malé privatizaci*) is approved by the Federal Assembly.

November 1. The Federal Government agrees a bill on the privatization of large-scale businesses (*zákon o velké privatizaci*) to be presented to parliament early in 1991.

November 8. The Slovak National Council approves a bill making Slovak the official language in Slovakia and according ethnic minorities limited language rights.

November 9. An agreement according Czechoslovakia Most Favoured Nation status is signed by President Bush.

November 16. The Federal Assembly approves a bill confiscating Communist Party property.

November 17. President Bush addresses crowds in Prague's Wenceslas Square on the anniversary of the 1989 revolution.

November 23–24. Local elections in the Slovak Republic put the Public Against Violence in second place to the Christian Democratic Movement.

November 24. Local elections in the Czech Republic confirm Civic Forum's dominance, though with a reduced share of the vote.

December 4. Miroslav Štěpán, former Communist Party chief in Prague, sentenced in July to four years' imprisonment for abuse of the powers of a public official against demonstrators in October 1988 and January 1989, begins his sentence, commuted on appeal to two-and-a-half years.

December 8–9. A meeting in Olomouc of delegates from local branches of Civic Forum recommends that its transformation from a broadly based political movement into a right-wing party with individual membership should be put to a Republican Assembly of the movement to be held in January 1991.

December 10. President Havel addresses the Federal Assembly on the crisis in Czech-Slovak relations which has arisen over a "competences" bill (*kompetenční zákon*) redefining the distribution of powers between the federal authorities and the republics. He introduces legislation providing for referenda and a Constitutional Court and promises to submit a bill extending presidential powers.

December 12. The Federal Assembly approves the "competences" bill.

December 13. A centrist Civic Forum Liberal Club is founded as a counterweight to the Civic Forum Interparliamentary Club of the Democratic Right formed in July.

Political Overview

The "velvet revolution" in Czechoslovakia at the end of 1989 came as a surprise to most observers. At the beginning of the year there was little to indicate that 41 years of communist rule would end less than 12 months later and that Czechoslovakia would become the first country in Eastern Europe in which a multi-party democracy was restored not by the ruling Communist Party but by its political opponents.

In the course of 1989 there were few changes of any significance in Communist Party policy and few signs that it might abandon its hardline course and fall wholeheartedly in line with reformist trends in the Soviet Union and elsewhere in the region. The 18th party congress which was planned for May 1990 and which was intended to be the occasion for the approval of a new party programme and a draft constitution provided the opportunity for a reassessment of policy but, as time passed, it looked increasingly unlikely that the party would undertake such a review and attempt to alter course.

Growing political dissent

In contrast with the immobility of the Communist Party leadership, there were increasing indications that the public was growing more restive and ready in ever larger numbers to express its dissatisfaction with the *status quo*. That change of mood, already evident in the latter half of 1988, made itself felt when demonstrations in Prague's Wenceslas Square took place to mark the suicide 20 years before of the student Jan Palach, who had set himself on fire in protest at the then Dubček leadership's concessions to Soviet demands for the reversal of the Prague Spring reforms.

The official response — police dispersal of the crowds (except on the third day, January 18, when no action was taken), the arrest of Václav Havel and other prominent dissidents, the nine-month prison sentence imposed on him on February 21 and new restrictions on demonstrations — failed to inhibit further protests. On May Day official celebrations in the Czechoslovak capital were followed by a counter-demonstration of 2,000 predominantly young people and the anniversaries on August 21 and October 28 were again marked, as they had been in 1988, by protesters prepared to ignore warnings of tough countermeasures.

At the same time, other forms of opposition were also finding increased support. Havel's arrest in January provoked not only a protest from the leader of the Catholic Church, Cardinal Tomášek, but also a call for his release signed by 700 members of the cultural community, by no means all from dissident circles. A petition demanding political reform, issued in late June by supporters of the Charter 77 movement under the title *Několik vět* (A Few Sentences), attracted around 11,500 signatories over the following month.

The "velvet revolution"

If the Communist Party leadership remained unshaken by these domestic events, the formation of a non-communist government in Poland in August 1989 and the fall of Honecker in East Germany in October dealt much more serious blows to its self-confidence. At the same time, those changes were a clear signal to the Czech and Slovak population that popular action could topple even the most entrenched regime.

There was, however, no reason to anticipate that the collapse of communist rule in Czechoslovakia would be triggered by the officially sanctioned demonstration on November 17, 1989, to commemorate the execution by the Nazis of the student Jan Opletal 50 years before. The spark that transformed what might have remained just another in a series of demonstrations into a prolonged popular protest against the regime was a brutal police attack on the student marchers — since alleged to have been instigated by the KGB in an attempt to discredit party leader Miloš Jakeš — and a rumour, subsequently disproved, that a student had been killed during that action. Within a matter of days protests spread from Prague to the Slovak capital Bratislava and other major cities as new political movements were established to co-ordinate the campaign for democracy — Civic Forum (*Občanské fórum*) in Prague on November 19 and the Public Against Violence (*Verejnosť proti násiliu*) in Bratislava a few days later.

Exactly a week after the initial demonstration, on November 24, Jakeš and the entire Communist Party leadership resigned and responsibility for resolving the crisis fell initially on the shoulders of the then Federal Prime Minister, Ladislav Adamec. Aware, thanks to a two-hour general strike on November 27 that they had the backing of a majority of the working-class, the opposition however rejected a new coalition government formed by Adamec on December 3, in which the Communist Party retained 16 of the 21 seats, and demanded a much more radical restructuring of the administration.

Adamec's resignation on December 7, in the face of opposition intransigence and continuing public protests, signalled the end of one-party rule. His successor as Prime Minister, Marián Čalfa, agreed to the formation of a Government of National Understanding (sworn in on December 10) in which the Communists retained only 10 of the 21 seats, including two ministers, the economists Valtr Komárek and Vladimír Dlouhý, who had been nominated by Civic Forum. The remaining places were allotted to members of other parties which had survived Communist rule, the Czechoslovak Socialist Party (*Československá strana socialistická*) and the Czechoslovak People's Party (*Československá strana lidová*), and seven other nominees of Civic Forum and the Public Against Violence.

The formation of similarly constituted coalition governments in the two constituent units of the Czechoslovak federation — in the Czech Republic on December 5, under the existing Prime Minister František Pitra, and in Slovakia on December 12, under a new leader, the communist Milan Čič — further reduced communist influence. The clearest indication however that power had effectively shifted from the Communist Party to the opposition, despite that party's retention of all three prime ministerial posts, was the election on December 28 of the former communist Alexander Dubček, the party's First Secretary during the Prague Spring, as Chairman of the Federal Assembly and the election the following day of the leading figure in Civic Forum, Václav Havel, as Czechoslovak President.

By February the Communist Party had agreed to the replacement of around half its deputies both in the Federal Assembly and the parliaments or National Councils in the two republics by representatives of the opposition. The severest blow to what remained of its influence however came with the resignation from the party of Čalfa, Komárek and Dlouhý in January and the replacement of Pitra as Czech Prime Minister on February 6 by Civic Forum's Petr Pithart (the Slovak Prime Minister Milan Čič also left the party, on March 10).

The restoration of a pluralist democracy

The first six months of 1990 were dominated by preparations for the election on June 8–9 of new federal and republic parliaments. New legislation provided for the return to the party list system of proportional representation which had been used in Czechoslovakia up to 1946, with the important provisos, designed to inhibit party fragmentation in the new assemblies, that only organizations (parties, political movements and coalitions of parties) with at least 10,000 members would be allowed to stand in the elections and that they would need to win at least 5% of the vote in one of the two republics to qualify for seats in the Federal Assembly and the Czech National Council (a lower 3% threshold was set for the Slovak parliament).

Table 1:   Parties, movements and coalitions standing in the June 1990 parliamentary elections

Czech Republic	*Slovak Republic*	*Both Republics*
Civic Forum	**Christian Democratic**	Alliance of Farmers and
Christian and Democratic	**Movement**	the Countryside
Union	Democratic Party	**Coexistence and Hungarian**
Electoral Grouping of	Freedom Party	**Christian Democratic Movement**
Interest Associations in	Gipsies	**Communist Party of**
the Czech Republic	**Public Against Violence**	**Czechoslovakia**
Friends of Beer Party	**Slovak National Party**	Czechoslovak Democratic Forum
Movement for Self-Governing		Czechoslovak Socialist Party
Democracy – Society for		Democratic-Republican Coalition
Moravia and Silesia		Free Bloc
		Green Party
		Movement for Civic Freedom
		Movement for Czechoslovak
		Understanding
		Social Democrats

Note: Parties in bold won seats in the Federal Assembly.

The months prior to the elections revealed that those precautions were wise as new political parties proliferated and, although only 22 contenders confronted the electorate, as many as 66 organizations had been registered as political parties with the authorities (see Table 1).

While electoral preparations went ahead reasonably smoothly, other more disruptive issues surfaced. Slovak nationalism made an early appearance in a month-long dispute over the country's official name which began in March after Havel suggested Czechoslovakia should no longer be referred to as a *socialist* republic. The issue was resolved only on April 20 when the Federal Assembly agreed on a formulation, "The Czech and Slovak Federative Republic" (*Česká a slovenská federativní republika*, abbreviated as *ČSFR*), which met Slovaks' demands that it reflect their status as a nation distinct from and equal with the Czechs.

The continuing strength of the Communist Party preoccupied press and politicians alike. Its size, though halved to around 900,000 by March, made it the most numerous party in the country. Its assets, partly acquired through state subsidy while it had been in power, were also an important resource and the occupation by its members of top posts within the state bureaucracy and in factory administrations were seen as potential obstacles to the transition to a pluralist democracy and a market economy. While the party itself surrendered many of its buildings to other organizations in the spring, the broader issue of its inordinate wealth was not resolved until November when the Federal Assembly approved legislation confiscating its property. A solution to its members' occupancy of top posts was found in some instances via the dismissal of incompetent staff and the obligatory refilling of some posts by competition but much less than more vociferous proponents of wholesale dismissals felt was necessary.

Much greater controversy was raised by fears that secret police agents and informers remained in key positions. Although the old security service (*Státní bezpečnost*) had been formally abolished and security matters entrusted to a new body, the Office for the Protection of the Constitution and Democracy (*Úřad pro ochranu ústavy a demokracie*), set up on February 1, concern was expressed that the Interior Minister Richard Sacher had acted too late to prevent the destruction of files on its network of agents and at the same time had allowed members of the old service to secrete information on its informers. Although available records were incomplete and, it was recognized, could lead to wrongful accusations against innocent people, the desire to ensure the new parliament contained no former collaborators, who might be susceptible to blackmail by their former "associates", led to the institution of vetting procedures which resulted in the resignation of a number of election candidates.

Although most of these took place discreetly, two cases achieved notoriety. On the eve of the poll, Josef Bartončík, the chairman of the Czechoslovak People's Party, was accused of having been an informer for 17 years — a charge he repeatedly denied, but which is thought to have lost support in the elections for the Christian and Democratic Union (*Křesťanská a demokratická unie*), the coalition within which the People's Party was standing. Where Bartončík nevertheless became a deputy in the new Federal Assembly and survived as party Chairman until September, the admission by Ján Budaj, a prominent figure in the Public Against Violence, that he had signed a collaboration agreement with the security police in 1978 had a more immediate effect. Although he denied having acted on that agreement, Budaj withdrew from the elections and political activity.

The June 1990 parliamentary elections

The elections on June 8–9 brought not only an astonishingly high 96% turnout but outright majorities for the combined forces of Civic Forum and the Public Against Violence in the bicameral Federal Assembly (87 of the 150 seats in the House of the People and 83 of the 150 in the House of the Nations) and for Civic Forum in the Czech National Council (127 out of 200). In the Slovak parliament, the Public Against Violence emerged as the largest party but with only 48 of the 150 seats (see Table 2).

Table 2:   Elections to the Federal Assembly of the Czech and Slovak Federative Republic, June 8–9, 1990

House of the People

	% votes	Seats
Czech Republic		
Civic Forum	53.1	68
Communist Party of Czechoslovakia	13.5	15
Christian and Democratic Union	8.7	9
Society for Moravia and Silesia	7.9	9
Others	16.8	—
TOTAL	100.0	101
Slovak Republic		
Public Against Violence	32.5	19
Christian Democratic Movement	19.0	11
Communist Party of Czechoslovakia	13.8	8
Slovak National Party	11.0	6
Coexistence	8.6	5
Others	15.1	—
TOTAL	100.0	49

House of the Nations

	% votes	Seats
Czech Republic		
Civic Forum	50.0	50
Communist Party of Czechoslovakia	13.8	12
Christian and Democratic Union	8.7	6
Society for Moravia and Silesia	9.1	7
Others	18.4	—
TOTAL	100.0	75
Slovak Republic		
Public Against Violence	37.3	33
Christian Democratic Movement	16.7	14
Communist Party of Czechoslovakia	13.4	12
Slovak National Party	11.4	9
Coexistence	8.5	7
Others	12.7	—
TOTAL	100.0	75

Sources: *Lidové noviny* and *Rudé právo*, June 11 and 14, 1990, and *Hospodářské noviny*, June 11, 1990.

For some Czech commentators, the massive overall support given by the electorate to Civic Forum and the Public Against Violence showed that they had regarded the elections as a plebiscite in which they had the opportunity to express their preference for democracy over totalitarianism. Nevertheless, the Communist Party had done moderately well, winning around 13.5% of the vote for both houses of the Federal Assembly and both republican parliaments.

The vote, however, revealed two areas of concern for the future of political democracy in Czechoslovakia. Firstly, there was much greater support than had been expected for separatism in Slovakia and regional autonomy in Moravia (a historically distinct province in the eastern half of the Czech Republic). The "success" of the Slovak National Party (*Slovenská národná strana*), which won 11% of the Slovak vote for the Federal Assembly and 14% for the Slovak National Council, suggested Slovak nationalism would be an even stronger factor in domestic politics than had been realized. Support for the Movement for Self-Governing Democracy-Society for Moravia and Silesia (*Hnutí za samosprávnou demokracii-Společnost pro Moravu a Slezsko*), whose 8–10% share of the Czech vote represented well over 20% of the electorate in Moravia, came as a shock for politicians in Prague who thought regional devolution was far from a live issue.

Secondly, the failure of all but eight of the 22 contenders to win seats in the federal parliament as a result of the 5% hurdle signalled a different problem: the absence of support for moderate left- and right-wing parties similar to those found in Western democracies. Only the Christian Democrats, separately organized in the two republics, made any headway, winning around 8.5% of the vote in the Czech Republic and between 16% and 19% in Slovakia. (The eighth party elected to the federal parliament, with 8.5% of the vote in Slovakia, Coexistence (*Együttélés*), drew most of its support from the Hungarian minority in southern Slovakia.)

The new governments

Despite the clear majority won by Civic Forum and the Public Against Violence in the Federal Assembly, and by Civic Forum in the Czech parliament, broader coalition governments remained in place after the elections. A key consideration in the decision to invite the Slovak Christian Democratic Movement (*Kresťanskodemokratické hnutie*) to join the new Federal Government, formed once more by Marián Čalfa on June 27, was the situation in Slovakia where, given its lack of a parliamentary majority, the Public Against Violence had little option but to form a coalition with the Christian Democrats (it also included the Democratic Party (*Demokratická strana*) which, along with the Greens (*Strana zelených*), had won seats in the Slovak parliament thanks to the lower 3% threshold in the elections). However the decision by Petr Pithart to invite members of the Society for Moravia and Silesia and the Czechoslovak People's Party to join Civic Forum in forming a new government in the Czech Republic suggests that a preference for a broader consensus within that and the federal administrations was no less significant a factor.

Although the Federal and Czech Prime Ministers remained unchanged, Čič was replaced as head of the Slovak Government by Vladimír Mečiar (from the Public Against Violence), who had served as Interior Minister in the outgoing Slovak administration. In all three governments there were important changes of portfolio. The most obvious break lay in the disappearance of the remaining Communist Party ministers and those from parties which had failed to win seats in the new parliaments. The departure of Valtr Komárek from the Federal Government on the other hand suggested that arguments over economic policy had been resolved in favour of the more radical strategy of the Finance Minister Václav Klaus.

The Slovak question

However much the new Federal Government expected the transition to a market economy to dominate its agenda for the remainder of 1990, in practice constitutional issues remained at the forefront of its concerns. If all three governments agreed on the need to move from the previous, highly centralized, sham federation to "an authentic federalism" in which there would be significant devolution to the two republics, there was less consensus on the optimal distribution of power between the two levels of government.

Much of the explanation for the crisis in Czech-Slovak relations, which peaked in December 1990 when constitutional amendments defining federal-republic arrangements reached the Federal Assembly in a "competences bill" (*kompetenční zákon*), derived from different perceptions in Bratislava and Prague of the issues at stake. For the Slovak Government, a desire to protect its flank against criticisms from extreme nationalists and to prevent what it believed to be centralist tendencies in Prague from restricting its power drove it to press for maximum control over Slovak affairs. For the Federal Government and the Czech population, on the other hand, some Slovak actions — the creation of a Slovak Ministry of International Affairs, the demand that Slovakia have its own currency-printing bank and the suggestion that oil and gas-pipelines should be split between the two republics — not only appeared to tread in areas that were seen as more properly federal responsibilities but raised doubts about Slovaks' commitment to a united Czechoslovak state. Fears on that point were only heightened when, in early November, the Christian Democratic Movement adopted a policy which favoured maintenance of a common state for the time being but argued that Slovakia should, when the opportunity arose, have its own representatives in the EC rather than join as part of Czechoslovakia.

Relations between Czechs and Slovaks were not made easier by a tendency among the former to regard extreme nationalist opinion in Slovakia as the norm. Attempts during the summer to rehabilitate the leader of the wartime puppet Slovak state, Jozef Tiso, though condemned by the Slovak authorities, were a case in point. Another was pressure from the Slovak National Party to promote legislation, prepared by the cultural organization *Matica slovenská*, making Slovak the sole official language in that republic. Although the Slovak parliament would not even debate that proposal and approved a government bill on November 8 which accorded the Hungarian and other minorities the right to use their own language in official contacts with their co-nationals in ethnically mixed areas, Czech perceptions of the Slovaks as nationally intolerant were only encouraged by the dispute.

The crisis which immediately preceded approval of the "competences bill" on December 12 arose when the Slovak Prime Minister was reported to have warned that, if the bill was rejected or substantially amended, as some deputies in the federal and Czech parliaments wished, his government would assert the priority of Slovak over federal legislation — a move seen as tantamount to separation by many Czechs. The bill, in slightly modified form, became law only as a result of direct intervention by President Havel, who appealed to the Federal Assembly on December 10 to approve the bill, submitted legislation providing for referenda on constitutional issues and for a Constitutional Court to settle intergovernmental disputes, and promised to bring in a bill which would extend the powers of the President to deal with similar crises.

Local elections

Elections in the autumn to newly established local councils showed some changes in political attachments as compared with voting patterns in June. The poll in Slovakia (held over two days on November 23 and 24) indicated a shift from the Public Against Violence to the Christian Democratic Movement, which became the most popular party, and a large decline

Table 3:   Local election results

Czech Republic, November 24, 1990

Party	% seats	% votes
Civic Forum	31.7	35.6
Independent candidates	27.7	10.6
Communist Party of Czechoslovakia	14.4	17.2
Czechoslovak People's Party	12.1	11.5
Movement for Self-Governing Democracy–Society for Moravia and Silesia	2.6	4.2
Czechoslovak Farmers' Party	2.5	1.5
Cooperative Farmers' Political Movement	2.1	n.a.
Czechoslovak Socialist Party	1.6	3.5
Czechoslovak Social Democracy	1.6	5.0
Greens	1.3	3.2
Christian Democratic Party	0.4	1.3
TOTAL	98.0	

Slovak Republic, November 23–24, 1990

	% seats
Christian Democratic Movement	27.4
Public Against Violence	20.4
Communist Party of Slovakia	13.6
Non-party	8.4
Coexistence	6.3
Independent candidates	4.4
Slovak National Party	3.2
Farmers' Movement	3.1
Hungarian Christian Democratic Movement	3.0
Democratic Party	2.3
Greens	1.2
Romany Civic Initiatives	0.6
TOTAL	93.9

In addition, one seat was won by the Independent Erotic Initiative.

Note: Different electoral systems applied in the two republics — proportional representation in the Czech Republic and a majority system in Slovakia.
Sources: *Lidové noviny* and *Rudé právo, November 26 and 28, 1990.*

in support for the Slovak National Party. In the Czech Republic (where the elections were held on November 24), Civic Forum lost some of its adherents to independent candidates, the Communist Party attracted a 3% higher share of the vote (albeit on a lower, 73.5% turnout) and the Society for Moravia and Silesia saw its support halved (see Table 3).

If the decline in support for extreme nationalism in Slovakia and for regionalism in Moravia was welcomed by Czechoslovak observers, the failure of parties like the Social Democrats or others on the right of the political spectrum to establish a following continued to cause concern. It was a factor which also contributed to a crisis within Civic Forum that seemed likely to reach its height early in 1991.

Whither Civic Forum?

Conceived in November 1989 as a loosely-organized movement which would unite all shades of democratic opinion, from reform communists in the *Obroda* (Reawakening) Club and the Trotskyist Left Alternative to the right-wing Civic Democratic Alliance, Civic Forum's demise has been repeatedly anticipated since its initial goal of ending one-party rule was achieved.

After the June 1990 elections, two views on its future surfaced within the movement itself. One, associated with Finance Minister Václav Klaus, envisaged its transformation into a right-of-centre political party based on individual membership. The second view, most clearly expressed by Foreign Minister Jiří Dienstbier, supported the maintenance until the next parliamentary elections in 1992 of the broad coalition which, he pointed out, the electorate voted into power in June 1990.

In practice, proponents of the first view appeared to be in a stronger position. Less than a month after the elections right-wing Civic Forum deputies in the federal and Czech parliaments set up an Interparliamentary Club of the Democratic Right (*Meziparlamentní klub demokratické pravice*). Three months later on October 13 they gained considerable influence within Civic Forum itself with the election of Klaus as its first chairman and on December 8–9 Klaus's proposals were endorsed by an overwhelming majority at a meeting in Olomouc of officials and delegates from Civic Forum branches throughout the Czech Republic.

Although support for the view that Civic Forum should remain a broad church was strong within the Federal and Czech governments as well as among deputies of those assemblies, it was slower to organize and it was not until December 13 that the formation of a Civic Forum Liberal Club (*Liberální klub Občanského fóra*), of which Dienstbier, Pavel Rychetský, his fellow Deputy Prime Minister, and Dagmar Burešová, the chair of the Czech National Council, were elected spokespersons, was announced.

Civic Forum thus entered 1991 with its future uncertain. Klaus's proposals were to be put to a Republican Assembly (*sněm*) of the movement on January 12 1991. Their approval would mean the exclusion of small parties and clubs, given his insistence on individual membership, and some individuals may also find its rightward shift unpalatable. Less certain was whether the two main currents — right-wing and centrist — would remain within Civic Forum or whether the movement would split into two or more political parties of a more conventional kind.

The consequences of a split could be very serious indeed in a year when the government faces the prospect not only of social unrest as the economic reform begins to bite but also of further Czech-Slovak conflict once new federal and republic constitutions are published.

Economic Overview

After 1968 Czechoslovakia was the most conservative of the central Eastern European states, both politically and economically. Under the leadership of Gustáv Husák, Czechoslovakia shunned any efforts at reform, while Hungary, for example, enjoyed 30 years of steady political liberalization and experimentation with economic reform. Poland also established extensive contacts with Western economies in the 1970s, and developed a small but thriving private sector after 1981.

The Czechoslovak GNP growth rate steadily declined, from 6% in 1975 to less than 2% in 1988 and 1989. As of 1985, Czechoslovakia had a GNP *per capita* of US$7,400 (47th place in the world), and *per capita* consumption of $3,390 (45th place). This meant a fall from 90% of Austria's GNP *per capita* in 1960 to 60% in 1985. The technological level of Czech industries was falling steadily behind that of their global competitors. North Bohemia, with a heavy concentration of brown coal power stations and steelworks, was on the brink of an ecological catastrophe. (For a summary of economic performance, see Table 4.)

Despite this poor record, it can be argued that Czechoslovakia has the best chance of creating a viable, internationally competitive market economy of all the Eastern European countries (leaving aside the special case of East Germany). She has three main advantages in comparison with neighbouring Poland and Hungary.

First, the failure of the earlier, partial reform experiments led to international debts of $1,000 *per capita* in Poland and $2,000 in Hungary. Czechoslovakia, in contrast, only has a $500 *per capita* debt (total amount $8 billion).

Second, by East European standards Czechoslovakia has a fairly developed and diverse economy, with a mixture of heavy and light industry and a lower dependence on agriculture than its neighbours (only 11% of the labour force are in farming). One in three families own a car and weekend cottage, and a refrigerator and colour television are the norm.

Table 4:   Economic performance

	1970	1980	1987
Population (000)	14,334	15,311	15,573
Active population (000)	8,158	8,709	8,812
Gross social product (Czech crowns, bn.)	732.3	1,233.8	1,614.7
Rate of growth of social output (1948 = 100)	442	702	803

Economic indicators, 1989
GDP growth: 1.7%
Trade balance: 3,978 mn crowns
Budget surplus: 2,846 mn crowns
Total external debt: US$7,900,000
Gross domestic product: 606,300 mn crowns (1988)
Gross national product: US$158,168 mn (1988)
Inflation rate: About 3%
Major trading partners: Soviet Union, Poland, West Germany, East Germany

Source: Statistická ročenka Československé socialistické republiky 1988 (Prague 1988) and current press reports.

Czechoslovak families spend 35% of their income on food — double the proportion found in West European family budgets, but half that of Poland or the USSR.

Third, the post-communist political situation has seen the emergence of a strong central leadership, and the resuscitation of a consensual political culture, both of which will be highly conducive to the sort of tough decisions needed to effect the transition to a market economy.

However, this is not to suggest that Czechoslovakia's path to pluralist democracy and a market economy is assured. All that could be said in the early 1990s was that it was moving, slowly, in the right direction, and seemed to have learned from some of the mistakes of its neighbours.

In 1990 the Czechoslovak economy basically marked time, as the old political institutions were dismantled and the new regime struggled to draw up a programme to transform Czechoslovakia into a market economy. In the course of 1990 industrial output fell 3.7% — although retail turnover rose 9.7%.

The emergence of the reform programme in 1990

The key developments in the economy in 1990 were political in nature: the emergence of a consensus for reform. The new government which emerged in the wake of the "velvet revolution" of November 1989 was deeply split over the wisdom of a rapid move towards a market economy. Deputy Prime Minister Valtr Komárek warned that "if a market economy were to start immediately, economic agony and chaos would result". However, Finance Minister Václav Klaus argued that the move towards the market was inevitable, and that it was delay in introducing reform which threatened catastrophe. Klaus persuaded the government that plans for economic reform had to be drawn up as soon as possible — even before the first free parliamentary elections, scheduled for June 1990. Komárek, having lost the argument, was removed from office, and an outline of the reform package was agreed on May 15 1990.

In the June elections (as noted above) Civic Forum won half the vote in the Czech lands and, together with its sister organization in Slovakia, Public Against Violence, won 170 of the 300 seats in the federal parliament. This gave the new government a firm mandate for change.

The situation was not quite so rosy in the provinces, however, where there were complaints that communists continued to occupy a majority of managerial positions, and were using their power to block economic reform or to turn it to their own personal advantage. President Havel had previously argued against the idea of a witch-hunt of communists, but in response to complaints from Civic Forum branches in Moravia he shifted his position, and in an August 19 speech he came down firmly in favour of a "second revolution" to bring about a market economy.

Amid fierce debate, parliament adopted a Scenario on Economic Reform on September 17. Key elements of the programme were the removal of price controls; the establishment of currency convertibility by January 1991; and the introduction within the next year of a programme of privatization of small and large-scale industry.

Commentaries on the programme were solicited from five academic institutes. Predictably enough, the five reports criticized the programme, and proposed five different solutions. The government did not want to get drawn into a protracted debate, and argued that every month's delay made it more difficult for the programme to succeed. A broad Transformation

Act laying out plans to change the ownership structure of large-scale state industry was introduced on November 1, but had not passed through parliament by early 1991.

Civic Forum itself continued to be deeply divided over the economic reform issue. While many socialist-inclined elements of Civic Forum's national leadership continued to adhere to the Komárek line, the majority of the provincial organizations were in favour of rapid reform. This provincial support enabled Václav Klaus to be elected chairman of Civic Forum on October 14, and he seemed a likely candidate for the post of Prime Minister. A pivotal Civic Forum conference in Olomouc on December 8–9 reaffirmed its commitment to rapid marketization, and declared that there was no "third way" between capitalism and Soviet-style socialism.

In local elections held in November 1990 (see above) Civic Forum held on with 35% of the vote, although the Communist Party polled a surprising 17%, testifying to their still strong local organization in many small towns and villages. A public opinion poll carried out in November 1990 showed 43% of the public supported the economic reform programme, 23% expressed no opinion, 10% expressed concern, and 23% voiced opposition. The opponents included the majority of agricultural workers, fearful of the loss of farm subsidies. However, 41% of Czechs and 61% of Slovaks expressed a willingness to use strike action if price increases were excessive.

These election results and polling data showed that the public was by no means united behind the reform programme. However, in several respects the situation was more promising than in Poland or Hungary. First, there was a solid core of public support for reform. Reform advocates had a firm grip on the national leadership, and their opponents had not yet come up with a plausible alternative programme. Second, the Czechoslovak leadership was proceeding carefully, and was anxious to avoid their neighbours' errors, such as Poland's over-zealous "shock therapy"; or the "spontaneous privatizations" in Hungary which saw the selling of valuable assets to foreigners and former communist officials at bargain prices.

Budgetary stabilization

At the beginning of 1990 Poland and Yugoslavia were facing inflation of 50% *per month*, and administered "shock therapy". By abruptly introducing currency convertibility and a tight monetary policy, they were more or less successful in bringing inflation under control. However, many East Europeans began to worry whether the cure might be more painful than the disease. Choking off credit for enterprises led to a 20–30% slump in economic activity, while the sinking currency meant prices continued to rise.

The Czechoslovaks were determined to learn both the positive and negative lessons from the experiments with "shock therapy". Czechoslovakia was better placed than its neighbours to avoid stagflation, since it did not face a heavy foreign debt, and the central authorities had not allowed monetary emissions to get out of control. In 1990, retail prices rose a modest 14%, while wages rose only by 3%. (The average wage at the end of 1990 was 3,250 crowns.)

However, as in all the socialist economies, they inherited the problem of a money overhang of 300 billion crowns in consumers' savings — 18,000 crowns *per capita*, equivalent to 17 months' average income. This meant that despite high prices, consumer durables such as washing machines disappeared from the stores as soon as they were put on sale.

The government revoked the original 1990 budget, which had been introduced on

November 30, 1989, in the dying days of the old regime. On March 28 Klaus persuaded parliament to adopt a new, tight budget, with a projected deficit for 1990 of only five billion crowns, (down from a seven billion crown deficit in 1989).

During 1990 Klaus kept a tight grip on government spending, and 1990 ended with a five billion crown budget surplus. The budget for 1991 stands at 117 billion crowns, broken down as follows: 28 billion for the armed forces; five billion transport subsidies; 27 billion compensation to consumers for food price rises; six billion compensation for energy price rises; and 1.5 billion compensation for former political prisoners. The biggest savings came in the slashing of subsidies to industry and agriculture. Farm subsidies, for example, were to be cut from 40 billion to 11 billion crowns. The annual 1.2 billion crowns payment to the Communist Party was eliminated (and the bulk of its assets seized). Ministry staff had already been cut by a third in 1988–89, so only another 5% were removed in 1990.

Price liberalization

The government's tight monetary and fiscal policy, and the maintenance of strict wage controls in industry, meant that retail prices only rose by 10% in 1990. However, the government recognized that in order to eliminate subsidies to industry and agriculture, prices would have to be freed, so as to allow supply and demand to determine which firms would survive and which would go under.

The general aim is to allow prices to float to world market levels, and to free 85% of retail prices by end of 1991. Price controls were relaxed initially on food and energy products. There is reluctance to free the prices of industrial goods before privatization gets under way, since many producers face weak competition, and would raise prices to exorbitant levels.

On 9 July 1990 subsidies on a wide range of food produce were eliminated, leading to an overall 26% price increase for food items. The government backed down in the face of a public outcry over the initial 75% rise in the price of top quality beef, and scaled back the increase to 40%. Over the whole year, meat of all sorts rose 40% in price, bread 53%, vegetables 48%, and dairy products 63%. On July 19 petrol prices were increased by 50%. A 50–60% increase in wholesale energy prices was introduced on December 1 1990, to be passed on to consumers in January 1991.

From January 1, 1991, price controls were relaxed for a broad range of products. New, higher maximum prices were set, and unfortunately most producers immediately raised their retail prices to the new ceilings. Bread, milk and egg prices doubled within a week, and meat rose 20% (on top of a 40% rise in July 1990).

Key Economic Sectors

Retailing and services

A series of laws approved in April 1990 abolished the previous legal prohibitions on private economic activity. The private sector expanded from 86,000 employees at the beginning of 1990 to about 300,000 employees by the year's end, although the bulk of these persons continued to hold full-time jobs in the state sector. Private entrepreneurs were given a three-year tax break (60% in the first year, falling to 20% in the third year), but still complained vigorously about cumbersome registration procedures; the shortage of premises; and administrative and financial problems when dealing with foreign suppliers.

Czechoslovakia is at a disadvantage in comparison with Poland and Hungary, both of whom relaxed controls on small entrepreneurs a decade ago. Czechoslovakia's "midget" entrepreneurs have a lot of catching up to do, in terms of locating suppliers, generating capital, learning consumer demand and so forth.

"Small privatization" legislation was unveiled by the government in September, and approved on October 25. A total of 70,000 small businesses and real estate properties which were nationalized between 1955 and 1961 would be returned to their former owners, or their heirs. Owners would not receive any compensation for damage to their property, and may indeed have to repay the state for any investments which have recently been completed. If the former owners could not be located, the properties would be put up for auction. Foreigners and non-residents would not be allowed to buy these properties. An additional measure passed on November 16 pledged to auction off 100,000 other small businesses, currently operated by state enterprises and local councils. In the face of strike threats by the shopworkers' union, the government agreed to provide loans equal to 50% of the purchase price for employees who wished to bid for the store in which they worked.

Auctions of small businesses began in January 1991, under the supervision of the newly created Ministry of Privatization, headed in the Czech Republic by Tomáš Ježek. The whole process should be completed by the end of 1991. Proceeds from the sales were to be split between the federal government and local authorities, in the proportion 70–30. The properties were to be sold by auction, with a minimum price of 50% set for the first round, and 20% for properties which had to be offered at a second round. Foreign citizens were to be allowed to participate in second-round auctions. The first auction was in Prague on January 26, at which 16 properties were sold for 22 million crowns. At the second auction, nine properties were sold for 2 million crowns. On February 23 the first auction outside Prague was held, in Bratislava. Many of the properties being sold are small, modest retail outlets, and in many cases the title to the property is not yet resolved, so it is two-year leases that are being auctioned.

Pressure to increase the pace of small privatization was reinforced when it was revealed that the IMF attached certain conditions to the $1.8 billion loan it granted Czechoslovakia on January 7, 1991 (which was primarily designed to compensate for the rise in the oil price). The full terms of the IMF loan have not yet been made known, but the IMF reportedly expects 13,000 small properties to be auctioned off by the end of June 1991 and 20,000 more by the end of the year. These goals seem excessively optimistic. Apart from doubts about the economic viability of the programme, several fundamental legal and political questions remain unresolved.

The small privatization programme is threatened mainly because of continuing disagreement over the restitution of properties seized between 1948 and 1955. Initially the Government hoped to exclude these properties from the programme altogether. Then, under parliamentary pressure, they proposed compensating former owners with government bonds, rather than returning their property, and also insisted on excluding all émigrés from the process. They argued that returning property to former owners among the 580,000 persons who emigrated since 1948 would be prohibitively expensive, possibly costing an additional 30 billion crowns. They fear that the whole restitution process is in danger of becoming a legal quagmire, and could derail the entire privatization programme. It can also be noted that, with the exception of East Germany, none of the other East European countries are seeking full restitution back to year one of communist rule. However, the Federal Assembly rejected the government's arguments, and on equity grounds are holding out for full restitution. This has triggered a major constitutional crisis between the government and parliament.

Agriculture

Czech and Slovak farming has been fairly successful, providing 95% of the country's food needs. However, farms were protected by heavy state subsidies, and it was not clear how many farms would be viable if they were forced to rely on retail sales alone to cover their costs. The country's 179 state farms were expected to be converted to joint stock companies as part of the large privatization programme (see below), while the 1,750 co-operative farms would remain more or less intact. The unified agricultural marketing organizations, in 1991 under criticism for the monopoly position they enjoy, would probably also be retained for the time being, in the absence of an immediate alternative.

By 1991 there were no plans to return farms seized under the first wave of expropriations, in 1948, to their former owners. It was argued that the process of identifying the current status of these assets would be too complicated, and could delay or derail the whole privatization programme.

However, it should be remembered that smallholders who were forced to join co-operative farms after 1948 retained the title to the land which they had "voluntarily" ceded to the collective. Those farmers were entitled to withdraw their land from the farm, under a procedure laid out in a law passed on May 3, 1990. To preserve the integrity of farms, smallholders were not entitled to receive their own land back, but may have to accept a plot of comparable worth on the periphery of the farm.

A mass exodus from co-operative farms was unlikely to occur, however. Agricultural workers remained dubious as to the economic viability of private farming, given the elimination of farm subsidies, and new worries about the availability of credit and equipment. A poll carried out by the Institute for Agricultural Economics in October 1990 showed 52% of farmers doubted whether private farming would be feasible in their village, and a further 41% thought it was definitely impossible. Only 10.4% thought that owning or renting a private farm could be economically viable.

Manufacturing industry

Among the initial tasks facing the government was the need to dismantle the inherited system of controls over all spheres of economic activity. Already, 10 years ago, Czechoslovakia had broken up the industrial planning ministries, and replaced them with collegial boards consisting of representatives of the major trusts in each sector.

A group of laws passed on April 18–20, 1990, empowered the government to break up the existing trusts, and laid the legal foundations for converting enterprises into joint-stock companies. In the first six months of 1990 the 100 large trusts which dominated the economy of the Czech Republic were broken up into 330 enterprises.

The system of central directive planning was dismantled. On July 18 the State Planning Commission and the Federal Price Office were abolished. Firms were no longer given output targets, nor did they have to report their production activities to any central office. However, a Price Control Commission was empowered to set maximum prices for a broad range of goods, and a law was passed on December 20, 1990, giving the government broad reserve powers for strategic economic planning. (The latter measure drew considerable criticism from pro-market radicals in Parliament.)

While these reorganizations were under way, the economy stagnated. Although a slump of Polish proportions was avoided, industrial output fell by 5–10%, as follows: coal 9.6%; metallurgy 2.8%; trucks 5%; chemicals 4.8%; cars 10%; and computers 25%.

There are three principal explanations for this fall in output. First, some Czechoslovak firms found that suppliers and purchasers in East Germany and the USSR broke their contracts or ceased trading altogether in the course of 1990. Second, many firms were monopoly producers, and sought to exploit their newly granted freedom by cutting output and raising prices. Third, in the absence of pressure from central planners, there was little incentive for managers to make an effort to increase production or profits, given that they were uncertain whether they would still be running their plant in a year's time.

The next phase in economic reform was to be the implementation of the "large-scale" privatization programme. State enterprises holding between 40–80% of the nation's total industrial assets of 3–5 trillion crowns ($110–180 billion), were to be converted into joint stock companies over the next five years. Only mines, railways and power generation enterprises will remain under state ownership.

About 20% of the stock will be made available to foreign buyers, 20% will be put up for public sale through a voucher system, and the remaining 60% will be retained by the newly created National Property Fund, to be sold off as and when the stock market gets into operation. The government rejected union proposals to sell 20% of the stock directly to employees, as is planned in Poland.

Each citizen will be allowed to buy 1,000 points of vouchers for 2,000 crowns ($70). In some firms vouchers will be exchanged directly for stock, in others stock will be sold at "Dutch auctions" (where the auctioneer works *down* from a starting price). The vouchers will be valid for one to two years, the expected duration of the large-scale privatization process.

That was the programme in outline. There are many practical problems as yet unresolved, which may generate political controversy and threaten the implementation of the reform. For example, there are problems of equity. Some enterprises had powerful political connections and received generous investment capital under the old regime. It was unfair to simply keep the old managers, turn the assets over to some sort of new owners, and expect other enterprises to compete with them. Such accusations have been levelled, for example, against the highly successful *Slušovice* agricultural co-operative, which diversified in the 1980s into a range of manufacturing activities, including computer assembly.

The old regime left behind an ambiguous ownership structure which is causing problems for the transformation process. Some workers' councils are powerful enough to try to block reorganization plans. (In many cases, they seem to be acting as a surrogate for the old communist management.) Local councils share dual ownership rights over many small industries with central trusts, and will fight plant closures planned for their district. Finally, there are now many disputes where subsidiary plants object to the privatization package put together by their controlling trust. Successful plants want to go it alone, while ailing plants resist closure plans.

For example, on December 11 workers in the *Budvar* brewery struck in favour in independence from the South Bohemia Brewery Trust, while workers in 13 North Bohemia coal mines threatened to strike *against* plans to give them economic independence from their former controlling trust. In both these cases, the government conceded the workers' demands.

Labour and the unions

In the initial period following the revolution the unions emerged as very powerful bodies. They exercised an effective veto power over decision-making in many plants, and exerted a powerful influence on the national government, being strong supporters of the Komárek line.

The old communist union organization, ROH, formally dissolved itself on March 3, 1990, creating a new Czechoslovak Confederation of Trade Unions. Unlike Hungary and Poland, no significant new independent unions have been created, apart from small organizations in Slovakia and for cultural unions. The new CCTU remains dominated by old regime appointees. The CCTU did, however, pledge not to align itself to any particular political party.

The original draft of the new enterprise law, introduced on March 23, included provisions expanding the role of workers' councils, and preserving the right of workers to elect plant managers. The government, led by Vladimír Dlouhý, insisted on removing these clauses, and the draft bill was withdrawn.

As the year progressed, Civic Forum's strong electoral performance increased the government's confidence, and the unions adopted a more conciliatory position. Their aim was to ensure their inclusion in the decision-making process, through the creation of a corporatist system of consultation between employers, unions and government.

One of the main concerns of the unions has been to try to limit the unemployment which market reform is expected to bring. Very few sackings have yet occurred, largely because the old labour legislation which was still in force mandated prior union approval before any workers could be fired. As of December 1990, there were 60,000 registered unemployed (less than 1% of the labour force), but the number is expected to reach 3–4% in Czech lands in 1991, and 8% in Slovakia. According to some estimates, 80,000 of the 350,000 steel workers and coal miners may face redundancy. The jobs of many of the 150,000–200,000 workers in the arms industry may also be at risk, although the government seems to have backed down from its initial statements.

Tripartite negotiations between unions, employers and the government in a "Council of Social Consent" produced a series of agreements in December 1990. Unions eventually called off threatened strike action through which they sought to stop a new law removing the right of workers to participate in the selection of managers.

New legislation agreed on December 3, 1990 will introduce a system of binding collective contracts, with pay-related strikes only allowed during the contract negotiation period. Sacked workers will receive from two to five months' severance pay, and unemployed workers who show a willingness to work will receive benefits for one year (60% of their former wage, falling to 50% after six months).

The three sides also agreed to limit wage increases to 5% for 1991, with punitive taxation of employers who violate the guidelines. They agreed on a minimum pension of 1,440 crowns a month, but in early 1991 were still in the process of negotiating a minimum wage. (The government proposed 1,850 crowns, the unions 2,350.)

Thus despite widespread worker agitation, and many short work stoppages or strike threats, a *modus vivendi* between organized labour and the pro-reform government seemed to be emerging.

The Slovak question

The Slovak question has mostly revolved around questions of national pride and political symbolism, but it also has a strong economic component. Radical Slovak politicians seem to have been manipulating the threat of secession in order to win more favourable economic terms. Polls and election results show little evidence of support for complete secession among Slovaks. Czech offers to hold a referendum on secession have been rebuffed by Slovak nationalists, probably because they fear defeat.

Under the old regime resources were to an extent diverted into Slovakia in order to promote its economic development. However, in mid-1990 Slovakia's share of the federal budget was cut from 42% to 38%, more in line with its 30% share of the country's population. In a series of meetings of Czech and Slovak leaders between August and November, the Slovaks pressed hard for economic concessions, such as the creation of a Slovak State Bank with an independent monetary policy. By December, 1990, after a firm intervention by President Havel, the two sides neared a compromise solution on the terms of the new confederation. It was agreed to split revenue from turnover tax between the federal, Czech and Slovak budgets in the proportion 35–40–25. Also, an independent stock company was created to manage the oil and gas pipelines which the Slovak government had been claiming as their exclusive property, on the grounds that all the refineries are located in Slovakia.

Foreign Economic Relations

All the successes of the post-war world have been cases of export-led growth (Taiwan, West Germany, etc.). Eastern Europe, unfortunately, is not likely to get an opportunity to replicate this pattern. Comecon had functioned as a trade-restricting union, which had prevented the international integration of the region's economies. As a proportion of GNP, Czechoslovakia's trade is at one sixth the level of comparable Western countries. Czechoslovakia's total external trade in 1988 was $30 billion, placing it 31st in the world. In 1988 this amounted to $3,031 of trade *per capita*, compared to $8,907 for neighbouring Austria. On top of these past distortions and missed opportunities, Czechoslovakia is now suffering severely from the double blow of the sudden collapse of markets in Comecon and the rise in the price of oil.

Around 60% of Czechoslovakia's trade in 1989 was with the Soviet bloc, half of that with the USSR, and only 18% with the European Communities. This amounts to some $5.5 billion of exports to the West, and nominally $20 billion to Comecon. Of these exports 57% are raw materials, and only 24% consumer goods. Czechoslovakia had run up a nominal 44 billion crown soft currency surplus with the USSR, although it traded at a deficit with the other Comecon members.

In 1990 this traditional trade pattern started to unravel. The bulk of Czechoslovakia's imports from the USSR consists of oil, gas and petrochemical products. In 1989 the USSR had been selling oil at $7.40 a barrel, when the world price was $19. In 1990 the Soviet oil and gas deliveries were cut by 15%, and will contract by another 20% in 1991. Czechoslovakia had to seek out Iranian supplies for 1991 in order to make up the Soviet shortfall, and the termination of supplies from Iraq.

Furthermore, the Soviets insisted on denominating Soviet-Czech trade in hard currency from January 1, 1991. The shift to dollar pricing for Soviet oil was expected to mean an effective price rise of 300%: in aggregate the equivalent of a $2 billion rise in imports for 1991. If oil stayed above $30 a barrel, the merchant bank Morgan Stanley estimated that 80% plus of Czechoslovakia's export earnings would have to be spent on energy imports (assuming exports stay at current levels).

In February 1990 Czechoslovakia withdrew from the Transferable Ruble system of handling intra-Comecon trade. Exports to Comecon fell by 20% in 1990, while imports fell by 8%. The largest falls were with Poland (40%) and Yugoslavia (34%).

Even in 1991, Czechoslovakia expected 25% of its trade to be with the USSR. Trade officials entered into protracted negotiations with their Soviet counterparts in the latter half of 1990 in an effort to construct a payments system to cover this trade in the wake of the demise of Comecon. Much of the trade with the USSR has been proceeding through barter deals. These are being negotiated at three levels: with national, republican and local authorities within the USSR. In December 1990 the first hard currency deal was signed, by *ČKD Locomotiva*, for the export of railway engines to the USSR. On December 18, 1990, an important agreement was signed by the Soviet and Czechoslovak ministers of foreign trade whereby the USSR promised to repay the old Soviet debt to Czechoslovakia at a ratio of one dollar to one ruble (i.e. terms quite favourable for the Czechs).

Trade with the West

Trade with the West rose 4.5% in 1990, mostly in the form of a surge of consumer durable imports. The Czechoslovak government moved to limit the flood of foreign imports, which could undermine domestic producers and fuel inflation. The former strict system of import licences was replaced by a 20% tariff on imports of consumer goods in January 1991. (Neoclassical economists are of course unanimous in the opinion that if protectionist measures are to be kept, tariffs are more efficient than quotas.)

Western nations have taken measures to lower barriers to trade with Czechoslovakia. On May 4 COCOM restrictions on the export of militarily sensitive technology to the Soviet bloc were relaxed for Czechoslovakia. The granting of Most Favoured Nation status to Czechoslovakia by the USA in December 1990 meant duty on exports to the USA fell (e.g. beer 13% to 1.6%, glass 60% to 20%, tyres 10% to 4%), and on imports from the US (e.g. wheat 30% to 7%, computers 15% to 5%).

On January 7, 1991, it was announced that Czechoslovakia was to receive the largest share — $1.8 billion — of the $5 billion in loans that the IMF would be giving to Eastern Europe in 1991. Czechoslovakia will also receive $1.5 billion of the $9 billion the World Bank will allocate to the region over the next three years. The USA itself will be giving $120 million to Czechoslovakia as emergency aid, and to provide capital for small businesses.

It was hard to predict which areas of trade would grow most rapidly. Apart from the public hunger for Western clothing and consumer durables, Czechoslovakia had acute needs for Western technology in re-equipping its machine tool industries and for rebuilding its telecommunications system, which is on the level of the USA of the 1950s.

The problem is finding sectors in which Czechoslovakia can generate the hard currency earnings to pay for these items. Tourism is likely to show rapid growth, since Czechoslovakia only earned $36 *per capita* in 1988, compared to $200–800 in Western countries. However, there is an extremely limited supply of hotel accommodation at present, and there is only 550 kilometres of highway in the country (and none connecting Prague with the West). In terms of classic trade theory, like the other Eastern European countries Czechoslovakia probably has a comparative advantage in agriculture, but this is likely to be of little relevance, given the protectionist policies of the EC.

Moves towards currency convertibility

The government accepted in principle the idea that Czechoslovak industry should expect to take world market prices as a measure of their performance, and moved the crown steadily towards full convertibility over the course of 1990. In January 1990 there was a 20% devaluation, bringing the rate to $1 = 16 crowns. On October 12 it was devalued again by 55%, from 16 to 24 crowns to the dollar. On December 28, 1990 there was a further 17% devaluation, and a fusion of the business and tourist rates, at 28 crowns to the dollar. (Previously the tourist rate had been 50% above the business rate.)

While businesses can now freely convert currency, there remain limits on the ability of private citizens to exchange crowns for hard currency. In the spring foreign buyers were attracted by food selling at 20% of the price in Austria, so on March 15, 1990, the government introduced a ban on export of food and alcohol. Presumably, now that food price increases have been put through, at some point in the future these restrictions will be lifted.

Joint ventures

Czechoslovakia has been slower, and more cautious than its Eastern European neighbours in developing joint ventures with Western partners. The government's philosophy is to liberalize domestic prices and de-monopolize the industrial structure *before* opening the door to Western partners. A law was passed in April 1990 creating the legal framework for joint ventures. Another law gave any Czechoslovak enterprise the right to engage in foreign trade (subject to a deposit of $50,000 bond — a significant disincentive for small companies). Foreigners were not allowed to buy land or property directly, but must operate through joint ventures.

Foreign firms have nevertheless been showing considerable interest in entering the Czech market and in acquiring Czech manufacturing capacity. As far as the car industry is concerned, for example, *Volkswagen* have acquired 25% of the *Škoda* works in Mladá Boleslav, over competing bids from *Renault* and *General Motors*. *VW*'s share will rise to

70% by 1995, as they contribute new investment funds. The plant will produce a modified version of the Škoda "Favorit" model, plus the VW Passat. *VW* are also negotiating with *BAZ* in Bratislava, while *Audi* are looking seriously at *Tatra* in Koprivnice.

As is true elsewhere in East Europe, co-operation with foreign firms has been hampered by the acute shortage of accommodation in Prague. The city council is maintaining tight control over the allocation of business premises, and office rents have already reached Western levels.

Principal Personalities

Adamec, Ladislav. Czechoslovak Prime Minister at the time of the November 1989 revolution. His failure to reach agreement with opposition representatives on the composition of a new government led to his resignation on December 7. Elected chairman of the Communist Party of Czechoslovakia on December 20, 1989, he resigned from that post in the autumn of 1990.

Benda, Václav. Chairman of the Czech-based Christian Democratic Party, founded in December 1989, and a deputy in the Federal Assembly. During the last two decades of communist rule, Benda was active in the Catholic opposition movement and a spokesman for the Charter 77 movement.

Burešová, Dagmar. Chair of the Czech National Council since June 26, 1990, Burešová was Minister of Justice in the Czech Government between December 1989 and the June 1990 elections. A lawyer by training, she represented reformists in legal actions contesting their dismissal from employment in the early 1970s and defended dissidents put on trial by the communist authorities. She became a spokesperson for the newly-formed Civic Forum Liberal Club formed on December 19, 1990.

Čalfa, Marián. Appointed Prime Minister of Czechoslovakia in December 1989, a post he retained after the June 1990 elections, Čalfa was the only member of the previous communist government still in office at the end of 1990. He resigned from the Communist Party in January 1990 and was elected to the Federal Assembly in June that year as a deputy for the Public Against Violence.

Čarnogurský, Ján. Chairman of the Christian Democratic Movement and First Deputy Prime Minister in Slovakia since June 1990. A defence lawyer who represented dissidents under the communist regime and who was himself under arrest at the time of the November 1989 revolution, Čarnogurský served as First Deputy Prime Minister in the Government of National Understanding formed in December 1989, but turned down offers of a post in the new Federal Government in June 1990 to take up his present post in Slovakia.

Dienstbier, Jiří. Czechoslovak Foreign Minister since December 1989 and a Deputy Prime Minister since April 1990. Dienstbier was Czechoslovak Radio's correspondent in the USA in the 1960s. Forced to take labouring jobs under the Husák regime, he was a spokesman for the Charter 77 movement. At the Olomouc meeting of Civic Forum in December

1990 he strongly advocated its continuation as a broadly-based movement as against its transformation into a more narrowly based right-of-centre party. On December 19 he was elected one of three spokespersons for the newly-formed Civic Forum Liberal Club.

Dlouhý, Vladimír. Federal Minister for the Economy since June 1990. A member of the Forecasting Institute of the Czechoslovak Academy of Sciences, Dlouhý was one of two members of the Communist Party nominated by Civic Forum for posts in the Government of National Understanding in December 1989 in which he was appointed Chairman of the State Planning Commission. He left the Communist Party in January 1990 and was elected to the Federal Assembly in June 1990 as a deputy for Civic Forum.

Dobrovský, Luboš. Appointed Minister of Defence in the Federal Government on October 18, 1990, Dobrovský became a reporter with Czechoslovak Radio in 1959 and was its Moscow correspondent in 1967 and 1968. He was forced to take a range of manual jobs between 1970 and the 1989 revolution. A founding signatory of Charter 77, he was active in *samizdat*, editing the journal *Kritický sborník* (Critical Album) and helping to produce the newspaper *Lidové Noviny* (People's News) during the last two years of communist rule.

Dubček, Alexander. Chairman of the Federal Assembly since December 28, 1989, Dubček was First Secretary of the Communist Party of Czechoslovakia during the 1968 Prague Spring. Expelled from that party in 1970, he re-emerged from the political wilderness during the November 1989 revolution and was elected to parliament as a candidate for the Public Against Violence in June 1990.

Gál, Fedor. Chairman of the Public Against Violence and Director of the Institute for Social Analysis at Comenius University in Bratislava, Gál was a leading figure in the ecological opposition movement in Slovakia in the 1980s.

Havel, Václav. Czechoslovak President since December 29, 1989, Havel first came to prominence in the 1960s as the author of a number of successful political satires including *The Garden Party* and *The Memorandum*. A founding signatory of Charter 77 and key figure in the Committee for the Defence of the Unjustly Persecuted (VONS) during the late 1970s and 1980s, he was imprisoned by the communist regime on a number of occasions for his activities. His prominence in pro-democracy demonstrations in 1988 and 1989 laid the basis for his emergence as the leading figure in Civic Forum at the time of the November revolution. He was re-elected President on July 5, 1990.

Husák, Gustáv. General Secretary of the Communist Party of Czechoslovakia between April 1969 and December 1987, Husák was also Czechoslovak President from 1975 until his resignation on December 10, 1989.

Jakeš, Miloš. General Secretary of the Communist Party of Czechoslovakia from December 1987 until November 24, 1989, Jakeš was responsible for the purge of reformists from the Communist Party after the Prague Spring.

Kanis, Pavol. Elected Chairman of the Communist Party of Czechoslovakia for a 12-month term at its 18th congress in November 1990, Kanis reached top levels of the Communist Party when he was elected to the Action Committee of the Slovak Party and to the Executive Committee of the Czechoslovak Party in December 1989.

Klaus, Václav. Appointed Finance Minister in the Government of National Understanding in December 1989, Klaus retained that portfolio in the administration formed after the June 1990 elections. A member of the Forecasting Institute of the Czechoslovak Academy of Sciences, he has described himself as a conservative who wishes to see tried and tested economic and political models applied in Czechoslovakia. He was elected Chairman of Civic Forum on October 13, 1990, and sees its future as a conventionally structured right-of-centre political party rather than as a broadly based movement.

Komárek, Valtr. Director of the Forecasting Institute of the Czechoslovak Academy of Sciences, Komárek, then a member of the Communist Party, was nominated by Civic Forum as First Deputy Prime Minister in the Government of National Understanding in December 1989. He was dropped from the government after the 1990 elections purportedly because of his inability to work as part of a team, but more probably because he did not share others' enthusiasm for a rapid implementation of radical economic reform.

Mečiar, Vladimír. Slovak Prime Minister since June 27, 1990, Mečiar was Interior Minister in the preceding government in Slovakia. A member of the Public Against Violence, his pursuit of Slovak interests and his aggressive political tactics have earned him wide popularity in Slovakia but have endeared him less among the Czech population and federal ministers who see some of his proposals as potentially detrimental to the interests of an integrated economy and the unity of Czechoslovakia.

Mikloško, František. Chairman of the Slovak National Council since June 26, 1990, and a member of the Public Against Violence, Mikloško is a mathematician by profession. Active in the Slovak Catholic opposition in the 1980s, he was one of the organizers of the demonstration by members of that faith in Bratislava in March 1988.

Moric, Vitazoslav. Elected a deputy to the Federal Assembly in June 1990, Moric was Chairman of the Slovak National Party until December that year when he resigned from that post purportedly to devote himself to his parliamentary duties.

Pithart, Petr. Appointed Prime Minister of the Czech Republic on February 6, 1990 after a short period as Civic Forum's chief spokesperson, Pithart retained that post after the June 1990 elections. A political scientist active in the reform wing of the Communist Party in the 1960s, he was a signatory of Charter 77 and author of *Osmašedesátý* (Nineteen Sixty-Eight), a critical study of the Prague Spring initially published in the West in 1980 under the pseudonym J. Sládeček.

Sládek, Miroslav. Chairman of the extreme right-wing Association for the Republic — the Republican Party of Czechoslovakia, which was unsuccessful in the 1990 parliamentary elections. Sládek achieved notoriety for his demands that foreign workers be deported from Czechoslovakia, attacks on Civic Forum politicians and accusations that that movement's political success represented a new form of totalitarianism. He attempted to disrupt proceedings on Wenceslas Square during President Bush's visit to Prague on November 17, 1990, at the head of a group of skinhead supporters.

Zeman, Miloš. A member of the Forecasting Institute of the Czechoslovak Academy of Sciences, Civic Forum deputy in the Federal Assembly and trenchant newspaper columnist. Though fully committed to a radical economic reform, he is one of the most effective critics of aspects of the privatization programme identified with Václav Klaus and a supporter of the Civic Forum Liberal Club formed in December 1990.

The Media

Both the restoration of political pluralism and the return to democratic elections benefited from the end of the Communist Party's control over the mass media following the November 1989 revolution. The first months of 1990 witnessed a rapid expansion of the press, despite a serious shortage of newsprint which was only partially resolved in April 1990 through cutbacks in supply to traditional newspapers — a move which hit the Communist Party's mass circulation daily *Rudé Právo* (Red Right) particularly hard.

Only a few of the new contenders in the June parliamentary elections, however, succeeded in establishing their own daily papers, notably Civic Forum, the Public Against Violence and the Christian Democratic Movement, with *Občanský Deník* (Civic Weekly), *Verejnosť* (The Public) and *Slovenský Denník* (Slovak Daily) respectively. However, before concluding this was a decisive factor in their electoral success, it should be noted that having its own well-established newspaper, *Svobodné Slovo* (Free Word), proved no advantage to the Czechoslovak Socialist Party which failed to win any parliamentary seats.

New titles were by no means all partisan in that sense and informed political debate benefited in particular from the emergence of a range of independent publications. The most important were the decidedly non-conformist Czech weekly *Respekt* and two new dailies — *Lidové Noviny* (People's News) in the Czech Republic, under an editorial team who had pointedly chosen the name of the most prestigious newspaper of the pre-war period when they began producing it as a *samizdat* monthly in 1988, and *Národná Obroda* (National Reawakening) in Slovakia.

Given insufficient print-runs to meet demand for most newspapers and the limited coverage of the political spectrum they provided, Czechoslovak television acquired a key role as a source of information. During the run-up to the elections a reasonable degree of neutrality was achieved in its news reports and the undoubted shortcomings in its overall coverage of the campaign may be attributed largely to the parties themselves. Their refusal to appear in televised debates until a week before polling day when two two-hour programmes were at last broadcast, involving representatives of all 22 contenders, seriously restricted coverage and abandoned the viewer to a repetitive series of very short party political broadcasts prepared by the parties themselves that resembled low quality, and largely uninformative, advertising spots.

Yet, if the press made a positive contribution overall to the restoration of a pluralist democracy, it suffered from the major defect that newspapers were divided along national lines. Only *Hospodářské Noviny* (Economic News), the former Communist Party economic weekly, now an official government daily, set out to be a paper with a state-wide remit and to provide balanced coverage of affairs throughout Czechoslovakia. That was little compensation, at a time when disputes were intensifying between Czechs and Slovaks, for the bias in other newspapers towards reporting events from the perspective of their own republic and thus doing little to reduce misunderstandings or defuse passions.

In that context, television's integrative role took on additional importance, and it was hardly surprising that demands from its Slovak staff in the autumn of 1990 that separate Czech and Slovak companies should be set up to run the two television channels in each republic were rejected by the authorities. While agreeing to the division of the second channel into separate Czech and Slovak services, they insisted on the retention of the first network as a "federal" station showing identical programmes throughout the country.

Domestic programmes were not the only television broadcasts available to Czechoslovak citizens. Most also had access to a third channel which had, during the last years of communist rule, relayed programmes from the Soviet Union that provided what had been, by contrast with domestic material, the refreshing wind of *glasnost'*. Its transformation in 1990 into a network transmitting programmes from a variety of foreign, mainly Western, sources was yet one more step — along with decisions to open up the radio airwaves to Western ideas and values by providing transmission facilities within Czechoslovakia to the French Europe 2 station, the US-backed Radio Free Europe and the BBC — towards ending the earlier isolation of Czechs and Slovaks from the outside world.

Foreign Relations

The collapse of communist rule and the formation of the Government of National Understanding in December 1989 brought a radical change in Czechoslovakia's foreign policy. Although the new rulers hoped a friendly relationship would be maintained with the Soviet Union, its previous subservience to Moscow in foreign affairs was abandoned and its top priorities under President Havel and his new Foreign Minister Jiří Dienstbier shifted towards the re-establishment of closer ties with the West and in particular Czechoslovakia's eventual integration into Western Europe.

Relations with the Soviet Union

No small part in establishing a more cordial relationship between the new government in Prague and the Soviet Union during the first months of 1990 than had been apparent during the last years of communist rule was played by Soviet promptness in responding positively to Prague's demands for the withdrawal of its troops from Czechoslovakia (an Agreement to that effect was signed in Moscow by Dienstbier and his Soviet counterpart, Eduard Shevardnadze, on February 26, 1990). At the same time Prague's willingness to accept, despite its initial insistence on their immediate departure, that for practical reasons the withdrawal of all Soviet troops would have to be phased over 17 months and could not be completed until June 1991 was evidence of its good will towards the Gorbachev leadership that must have been welcome in Moscow.

Prague's announcement that it would not abandon its existing commitments to the Warsaw Treaty Organization (Warsaw Pact) and the CMEA (Comecon) was yet another indication that the change of regime had not brought a government to power which was intent on breaking all its previous ties with the Soviet Union. Czechoslovakia made clear, however, that its continuing participation in those bodies depended on fundamental changes in their *modus operandi*, and in particular the transformation of the former from a military into a primarily political alliance in which all members would have an equal voice. At the same time Prague made no secret of its view that the Warsaw Pact's days were in any case numbered as a result of the changes in Eastern Europe and that Czechoslovakia planned to direct its efforts towards the eventual replacement of both the Warsaw Pact and NATO by a new pan-European security system based on the principles underlying the Conference on Security and Co-operation in Europe (CSCE).

Openings to the West

A major focus of Czechoslovakia's diplomatic activity throughout 1990 was its re-entry as an independent actor on the international stage. To that end, Havel alone was reported to have paid official visits to as many as 16 countries, predominantly in the West, in the 12 months to mid-December that year. A mark of his success, after four decades when Czechoslovakia had been virtually ignored by senior Western statesmen, was the succession of foreign leaders who visited the country, including Pope John Paul II on April 20–21 (following the restoration of diplomatic relations with the Vatican a few days earlier); Mrs. Thatcher in mid-September; and President Bush on the anniversary of the November 1989 revolution.

Czechoslovakia's early readmission to the IMF and World Bank (on April 18, 1990), its acquisition of Most Favoured Nation status from the USA (approved by President Bush on November 9) and the decision (in November) to site the CSCE Secretariat in Prague were major successes for its diplomacy. By contrast, its pursuit of admission to Western European institutions moved, as had been expected, at a somewhat slower pace. It was granted observer status in the Council of Europe relatively early in 1990 and at the end of the year the government was optimistic that it would acquire full membership of that body in the first months of 1991 once new legislation on human rights had completed its passage through the Federal Assembly.

That was, however, only the first step towards its ultimate goal of integration in Western Europe. Czechoslovakia recognized that its ambition to acquire full membership of the EC was at best a long-term aspiration but, as Dienstbier announced, in a foreign policy review delivered to the Federal Assembly on December 18, it had made intensive diplomatic efforts during the second half of 1990 to begin negotiations on the associate membership it hoped would be granted in the shorter term.

With its eventual adhesion to the European Communities in mind, Prague had, by the end of 1990, come to appreciate the value of closer co-operation with Poland and Hungary and the advantages of a joint approach from three states with comparable claims to membership. Nevertheless, that is a strategy which may not be easy to implement. Tension between Prague and Warsaw during the summer over entry restrictions on Polish tourists was one example of the kind of difficulty that may recur. Relations with Hungary remained good throughout 1990 and neither the treatment of the Hungarian minority in Slovakia nor the suspended Danube Dam project at Gabčíkovo-Nagymaros, to whose continuation the Hungarian government remained adamantly opposed and the Slovak government equally strongly committed, became an issue between Budapest and Prague. Both are nevertheless potential sources of conflict which could hamper co-operation between the two countries.

Nor were these the only areas of uncertainty in Czechoslovakia's foreign relations. By the end of 1990 the initial warm rapport between Prague and Moscow had begun to cool. Although three-quarters of Soviet troops had by then left Czechoslovak soil in line with the February Agreement, difficulties encountered in negotiations over Soviet oil and gas supplies and new terms of trade between the two countries occasioned some disenchantment within the Czechoslovak government. Moscow's postponement until 1991 of a crucial Warsaw Pact meeting to discuss changes in that organization and its increasingly hardline policy towards Lithuania and the other Baltic states at the end of 1990, however, brought much closer the possibility of a much more serious deterioration in Soviet-Czechoslovak relations.

GERMANY

Jonathan Osmond

The Kohl government, January 16, 1991

Chancellor. *Helmut Kohl (CDU)*
Foreign Affairs and Deputy Chancellor.
  Hans-Dietrich Genscher (FDP)
Interior. *Wolfgang Schäuble (CDU)*
Defence. *Gerhard Stoltenberg (CDU)*
Justice. *Klaus Kinkel (CDU)*
Economy. *Jürgen Möllemann (FDP)*
Finance. *Theo Waigel (CSU)*
Agriculture, Food and Forestry. *Ignaz
  Kiechle (CSU)*
Labour and Social Order. *Norbert Blüm
  (CDU)*
Family and Old People. *Hannelore Rönsch
  (CDU)*

Women and Youth. *Angela Merkel (CDU)* *
Health. *Gerda Hasselfeldt (CSU)*
Transport. *Günther Krause (CDU)* *
Environment. *Klaus Töpfer (CDU)*
Post and Telecommunications. *Christian
  Schwarz-Schilling (CDU)*
Construction. *Irmgard Adam-Schwaetzer
  (FDP)*
Research. *Heinz Riesenhuber (CDU)*
Education. *Rainer Ortleb (FDP)* *
Development. *Carl-Dieter Spranger (CSU)*

Note: * from the former GDR

Abbreviations

BFD	*Bund Freier Demokraten*: League of Free Democrats
CDU	*Christlich-Demokratische Union Deutschlands*: Christian Democratic Union
CSU	*Christlich Soziale Union*: Christian Social Union
DA	*Demokratischer Aufbruch*: Democratic Departure
DBD	*Demokratische Bauernpartei Deutschlands*: Democratic Farmers' Party of Germany
DSU	*Deutsche Soziale Union*: German Social Union
FDGB	*Freier Deutscher Gewerkschaftsbund*: Free German Trade Union League
FDP	*Freie Demokratische Partei*: Free Democratic Party
LDPD	*Liberal-Demokratische Partei Deutschlands*: Liberal Democratic Party of Germany
NDPD	*National-Demokratische Partei Deutschlands*: National Democratic Party of Germany
PDS	*Partei des Demokratischen Sozialismus*: Party of Democratic Socialism (formerly SED-PDS)
SDP	*Sozialdemokratische Partei*: Social Democratic Party (later SPD)
SED	*Sozialistische Einheitspartei Deutschlands*: Socialist Unity Party of Germany
SED-PDS	*Sozialistische Einheitspartei Deutschlands-Partei des Demokratischen Sozialismus*: Socialist Unity Party of Germany-Party of Democratic Socialism (formerly SED)
SPD	*Sozialdemokratische Partei Deutschlands*: Social Democratic Party of Germany (formerly SDP)

GERMANY

showing the *Länder* and the pre-unification boundary of the German Democratic Republic (East Germany)

DENMARK

Baltic Sea

North Sea

Rügen

Kiel •

Rostock •

SCHLESWIG - HOLSTEIN

MECKLENBURG - WESTERN POMERANIA

Bremerhaven

• Schwerin

• Hamburg

HAMBURG

BREMEN — • Bremen

LOWER SAXONY

BRANDENBURG

NETHERLANDS

Brandenburg •

Berlin

• Hannover

Potsdam •

Magdeburg •

NORTH RHINE - WESTPHALIA

SAXONY - ANHALT

Cottbus •

Essen •

• Dortmund

Halle •

• Duisburg

Leipzig •

• Düsseldorf

THURINGIA

SAXONY

Cologne •

Weimar •

Dresden •

Bonn ■

HESSEN

Erfurt • Jena • Gera • Chemnitz
(Karl Marx Stadt)

BELGIUM

RHINELAND - PALATINATE

Wiesbaden •

LUX.

• Mainz

• Frankfurt am Main

CZECHOSLOVAKIA

SAAR- LAND

Mannheim •

• Nuremberg

• Saarbrücken

BAVARIA

Stuttgart •

• Regensburg

FRANCE

BADEN - WÜRTTEMBERG

• Augsburg

• Munich

• Freiburg

AUSTRIA

0   100   200
km

SWITZERLAND

LIECHTENSTEIN

POLAND

© CIRCA Reference

Chronology

1989

January 1. New foreign travel regulations come into effect, but meet with little enthusiasm.

January 15. Eighty arrests follow Leipzig demonstration; official growth in 1988 net material product announced as 3% (target: 4.1%); real growth nearer 1.7%.

January 19. Erich Honecker declares Berlin Wall will last another 100 years.

January 23. Honecker announces cuts in armed forces and military spending.

February 5–6. Would-be escaper shot dead by GDR border police in Berlin; this and later incidents provoke West German protests.

March 3. People's Chamber approves electoral law giving local voting rights to certain categories of foreigners.

March 13. In West German television interview former GDR spy chief, Markus Wolf, speaks out for reform; demonstration in Leipzig for right to emigrate broken up by Stasi (GDR State Security Organization).

April 1. Revised travel regulations introduced in wake of criticism, but still very limited in scope.

May 2. Hungarians begin to dismantle border with Austria.

May 7. Local elections show slight increase in votes against single "National Front" list; unofficial observers accuse authorities of falsifying results to disguise real level of opposition.

May. Politbüro sends deputation to investigate alleged shortcomings in Dresden party organization of Hans Modrow.

June 5. Tiananmen Square massacre applauded by GDR authorities; popular demonstrations reject this.

June 11. Honecker attends reconsecration of renovated Greifswald cathedral.

June 22–23. SED Central Committee meets in East Berlin; Joachim Herrmann, party secretary for agitation and propaganda, delivers hardline report, singling out Hungarian reforms for criticism.

June 29. "Soviet Forces in Germany" renamed "West Group of Soviet Forces".

July 8. Honecker falls ill at Warsaw Pact summit in Bucharest and is forced to return home.

July 10. After hospital treatment for gall bladder complaint, Honecker goes on holiday.

July 31. West Germans announce that so far in 1989, 46,343 GDR citizens have legally migrated to West Germany.

August 8. West German mission in East Berlin forced to close under pressure of would-be emigrants.

August 13. West German embassy in Budapest similarly closed.

August 18. Honecker undergoes further surgery.

August 19. Several hundred GDR citizens break through Austro-Hungarian border.

August 22. West German embassy in Prague forced to close.

September 1. Honecker leaves hospital for convalescence.

September 11. Hungarians allow GDR citizens to cross to Austria; New Forum founded.

September 12. Democracy Now founded.

September 19. Meeting of Evangelical Synod in Eisenach calls for reform.

September 20. Manfred Gerlach, leader of LDPD, encourages questioning and new ideas.

September 21. New Forum denied official recognition.

September 25. Honecker takes up work again.

September 30. Genscher in West German embassy in Prague announces agreement on migration of refugees; that night trains begin to leave for West Germany via the GDR.

October 1. Democratic Departure (DA) founded.

October 6. President Gorbachev arrives for celebrations of 40th anniversary of the GDR.

October 7. Anniversary parade in East Berlin; Gorbachev warns "He who comes too late is punished by life"; Demonstrations throughout GDR meet with armed force; Social Democratic Party (SDP) founded.

October 9. Mass demonstration in Leipzig; Gewandhaus conductor Kurt Masur intervenes to help prevent bloodshed; in Dresden mayor Wolfgang Berghofer agrees to meet a delegation of protesters.

October 10–11. Politbüro meets to discuss crisis.

October 12. Politbüro issues appeal to solve problems with concerted strength.

October 14. Egon Krenz makes plans with Willi Stoph for removal of Honecker.

October 15. Krenz, Günter Schabowski and Harry Tisch meet at latter's home to finalize plans.

October 16. Over 100,000 people march through Leipzig demanding reform.

October 17. Politbüro votes to remove Honecker, Mittag and Herrmann.

October 18. Special meeting of Central Committee; Honecker, Mittag and Herrmann removed from all party offices; Krenz elected new General Secretary of SED; Krenz announces a "turning point" (*Wende*).

October 23. About 300,000 people demonstrate in Leipzig; other demonstrations take place elsewhere.

October 24. *Volkskammer* elects Krenz as Chairman of Council of State (26 votes against, 26 abstentions) and of National Defence Council (eight against, 17 abstentions).

October 26. In Dresden, Hans Modrow and Wolfgang Berghofer address meeting of 100,000 people; Helmut Kohl and Krenz discuss the situation by telephone.

October 27. Amnesty announced for those who had fled illegally; appeal that they return.

October 29. West Berlin mayor Walter Momper and (East) Berlin party secretary Schabowski meet in East Berlin.

October 30. Demonstration of over 200,000 in Leipzig.

November 1. Krenz holds talks with Gorbachev in Moscow.

November 2. Dismissal/resignation of Margot Honecker (Education Minister), Tisch (FDGB chairman), Gerald Götting (CDU chairman), Heinrich Homann (NDPD chairman) and of first two of SED district party secretaries; Krenz in Poland.

November 3. Krenz announces Politbüro action programme; departure from Politbüro of five members, including Erich Mielke (head of state security); resignation of mayor of Leipzig.

November 4. Largest protest demonstration yet: about 1,000,000 people take to the streets of East Berlin.

November 6. New travel law fails to meet demands of people; mass demonstrations continue.

November 7. *Volkskammer* committee rejects new travel law; Stoph government resigns, but continues in caretaker capacity.

November 8. Meeting of Central Committee (to 10th); Politbüro resigns and new election held;

votes for and against made public; Krenz re-elected General Secretary; Modrow joins Politbüro and is recommended as new Prime Minister.

November 9. At press conference Schabowski announces opening of borders to West Berlin and the FRG; throughout night thousands of people cross between two states in both directions; there is dancing on the Berlin Wall.

November 10. GDR citizens pour across the borders; Kohl interrupts visit to Poland to speak at rally in West Berlin, meeting hostile reception; Krenz addresses SED rally in East Berlin, with mixed reaction; Lothar de Maizière elected chairman of (East) CDU.

November 12. Central Committee calls for an extraordinary party congress.

November 13. Horst Sindermann (SED) resigns as *Volkskammer* chairman; Günter Maleuda of the Farmers' Party (DBD) elected in his stead, defeating Gerlach (LDPD); Modrow elected new Prime Minister on show of hands (one vote against).

November 16. Academy of Science rehabilitates disgraced members; change of editorship at *Neues Deutschland*.

November 18. Modrow government approved by *Volkskammer*: 28 ministers from SED (17), LDPD (four), CDU (three), DBD (two) and NDPD (two); commissions established to propose constitutional and electoral reforms; in East Berlin and other cities large demonstrations continue against the SED's leading role and for free elections; 15,000 attend New Forum rally in Leipzig.

November 20. Rudolf Seiters, head of Chancellor Kohl's office, meets Krenz in East Berlin.

November 22. Politbüro proposes "Round Table" discussions.

November 23. Mittag expelled from the SED.

November 24. New customs regulations come into force, to prevent goods in GDR being bought up by foreigners; Green Party founded.

November 26. Otto Graf Lambsdorff (FDP chairman) meets leaders of LDPD and DA in East Berlin.

November 27. 200,000 demonstrate in Leipzig.

November 28. Kohl announces his 10-point plan for German unity.

December 1. *Volkskammer* excises from the constitution the SED's leading role.

December 2. SED members demonstrate outside the Central Committee building, demanding resignation of leadership.

December 3. Krenz, Politbüro and Central Committee resign; 25-strong provisional committee replaces them; Honecker and others expelled from SED; Mittag and Tisch (FDGB) arrested; human chain of protest formed across GDR.

December 4. CDU leaves "Democratic Block" led by SED; calls for German unity begin to be heard at the continuing demonstrations.

December 5. Honecker and Mielke under house arrest at Wandlitz; Modrow and Seiters (on behalf of Kohl) agree on hard-currency fund to assist GDR citizens and on lifting of currency and visa requirements for FRG citizens.

December 6. Krenz resigns as Chairman of State Council and National Defence Council; provisionally replaced in former capacity by Gerlach (LDPD).

December 7. First meeting of Round Table, bringing together old parties, new groups and parties and church representatives.

December 8–9. SED party congress; Gregor Gysi elected party chairman, Hans Modrow and Wolfgang Berghofer as deputy chairmen.

December 11. US, British and French ambassadors to FRG and Soviet ambassador to GDR meet in Control Commission building in West Berlin.

December 13. Contacts established between SDP and West German SPD.

December 15–16. CDU holds special congress in East Berlin.

December 16–17. SED resumes party congress and renames itself SED-PDS (Party of Democratic Socialism); DA forms itself as a political party; Wolfgang Schnur elected chairman.

December 17. West German President Richard von Weizsäcker meets Gerlach in Potsdam.

December 18. Second session of Round Table.

December 19–20. Kohl visits Dresden and holds talks with Modrow; they decide to form "contractual community" between the two German states; Kohl receives rapturous welcome in Dresden.

December 20–22. President Mitterrand of France visits GDR.

December 22. Brandenburg Gate reopened by Kohl and Modrow.

December 31. 1989 total of GDR citizens leaving for FRG stands at nearly 350,000.

1990

January 2. President Havel of Czechoslovakia, visiting Berlin, envisages confederation of two German states.

January 3. Opposition groups threaten to leave Round Table if Modrow does not abandon plans for state security organization; six parties and groups, including SDP, DA and New Forum, form electoral pact; large demonstration in East Berlin, led by SED-PDS, against neo-Nazism and racism.

January 8. At Leipzig and other demonstrations the calls for German unity dominate.

January 11. Modrow presents government programme to *Volkskammer*, abandoning plan for state security organization; constitution altered to allow foreign participation in GDR enterprises; Krenz and Schabowski resign from *Volkskammer*.

January 12. SDP meets in Berlin and changes name to SPD.

January 13. Price rises announced for children's clothes and other items.

January 16. Modrow visits West Berlin.

January 20. DSU (German Social Union) founded in Leipzig.

January 21. Wolfgang Berghofer, mayor of Dresden, and 39 colleagues leave SED-PDS; Krenz and Schabowski expelled from SED-PDS.

January 22. Modrow offers opposition parties role in government.

January 23. First meeting in East Berlin of German-German Economic Commission; party symbol removed from SED-PDS headquarters in East Berlin.

January 27–28. New Forum agrees its constitution, but not as a political party.

January 28. *Volkskammer* elections brought forward from May 6 to March 18; proposal for Government of National Responsibility announced, to include opposition parties.

February 1. Modrow presents declaration on "path to German unity", proposing neutral confederation; new liberal travel law comes into force, also allowing GDR citizens to buy West German Marks.

February 4. SED-PDS changes its name to PDS in order to break clearly from the old ruling party; FDP founded in East Berlin.

February 5. Opposition parties furnish eight ministers without portfolio in Modrow government; CDU, DSU and DA form "Alliance for Germany" to fight March elections.

February 7. New Forum, Democracy Now and Peace and Human Rights Initiative form "Alliance 90" to fight elections.

February 10. In Moscow, Kohl meets Gorbachev, who agrees that Germans themselves should take decision on unity.

February 11. FDP, LDP and DFP form liberal electoral alliance, "League of Free Democrats"; first East German Green Party congress approves its programme.

February 13. In Bonn, Modrow and Kohl agree on commission to prepare monetary and economic union.

February 14. In Ottawa, two German foreign ministers and those of USA, USSR, UK and France agree to hold "Two-plus-Four" conference on German unity; Green Party and Independent Women's Association form electoral alliance.

February 15. Kohl rejects neutral Germany.

February 18. First congress of DSU in Leipzig.

February 20. New electoral law.

February 25. First SPD congress in Leipzig elects Ibrahim Böhme as chairman and Willy Brandt as honorary president; Modrow elected honorary president of PDS.

March 5. Round Table agrees "social charter" as basis for inter-German talks.

March 7. Modrow tries to enlist Gorbachev's help in preserving property relations in the GDR.

March 12. Last session of Round Table.

March 14. Preliminary Two-plus-Four talks begin in Bonn; Wolfgang Schnur resigns as chairman of DA, because of former Stasi links.

March 18. Elections to *Volkskammer*: CDU victory (163 seats) but even with allies no overall majority (192 seats out of 400); SPD 88 seats; PDS 66 seats.

March 19. DSU and CSU representatives meet near Hof in West Germany; Deutsche Kreditbank founded in East Berlin.

March 20. West German cabinet plans to abolish special measures for incoming GDR citizens; three liberal parties (LDP, FDP, DFP) propose merger.

March 21. Ibrahim Böhme elected chairman of SPD delegation in *Volkskammer*.

March 23. Mass grave of victims of Stalinism discovered at Fünfeichen, Neubrandenburg.

March 24. Honeckers prevented by popular protest from moving to government house in Lindow.

March 25. First *Lufthansa* flight from Frankfurt am Main to Dresden.

March 26. Ibrahim Böhme gives up SPD party posts and *Volkskammer* seat, pending investigations into alleged co-operation with Stasi; CDU leadership proposes Lothar de Maizière as Prime Minister; treason charges against Honecker and others dropped.

March 29. Demonstrations in several cities press for investigation of possible Stasi pasts of *Volkskammer* members; coalition negotiations begin between CDU and SPD.

March 30. Böhme, de Maizière and Gysi cleared of collaboration with Stasi.

April 1. *Bundesbank* proposal of 2:1 exchange rate meets with GDR protest.

April 2. CDU fraction proposes de Maizière for premiership; Böhme resigns from SPD leadership.

April 3. Coalition talks between Alliance for Germany parties, SPD and liberals; Honecker transferred to Soviet military hospital in Beelitz, Potsdam.

April 5. First meeting of newly-elected *Volkskammer*; Sabine Bergmann-Pohl (CDU) elected President; abolition of State Council approved; 100,000 demonstrate in Berlin against 2:1 exchange rate.

April 9. Coalition cabinet formed; de Maizière (CDU) Prime Minister; Meckel (SPD) Foreign

Affairs; Diestel (DSU) Interior; Romberg (SPD) Finance; Eppelmann (DA) Defence and Disarmament; 11 ministries for CDU, seven for SPD, three for liberals, two for DSU and one for DA.

April 12. New government approved by *Volkskammer*.

April 18. De Maizière delivers government declaration to *Volkskammer*, proposing German unity, democracy, and exchange rate for wages, pensions and savings of 1:1.

April 23. Bonn government proposes 1:1 exchange rate for wages and first tranche of savings and otherwise 2:1 rate.

April 24. Kohl and de Maizière agree on currency, economic and social union from July 1, 1990.

April 25. In Cologne, assassination attempt on Oskar Lafontaine, SPD chancellor candidate in West Germany.

April 27. Negotiations begin on state treaty between two Germanies.

April 29. De Maizière in Moscow talks with Gorbachev; GDR farmers protest against worsening agricultural situation.

May 2. Terms of state treaty on currency union published in Bonn; East Berlin government announces measures to alleviate agricultural crisis.

May 5. First Two-plus-Four meeting in Bonn.

May 6. In GDR local elections CDU, SPD, DSU and PDS all lose ground; advances by liberals, Farmers' Party and citizens' groups; CDU still well ahead.

May 13. SPD wins state elections in North-Rhine-Westphalia and Lower Saxony, depriving CDU of majority in West German *Bundesrat* (upper house).

May 18. State treaty on currency, economic and social union of the two Germanies signed in Bonn by respective finance ministers Romberg (SPD-GDR) and Waigel (CSU-FRG).

May 20. Lafontaine urges vote against state treaty, fearing economic collapse in GDR; in conflict with Hans-Jochen Vogel, party chairman.

May 21. Renewed mass farmer protests in GDR.

May 22. DSU fraction in *Volkskammer* votes for dismissal of Interior Minister Peter-Michael Diestel (DSU); Diestel and de Maizière resist.

May 31. *Volkskammer* decides that finances of all parties to come under government supervision and that GDR state symbol be removed from all public buildings.

June 1. Karl-Marx-Stadt renamed Chemnitz.

June 2. PDS demonstration in Berlin against *Volkskammer* vote, fearing eventual disbanding of party.

June 6. Susanne Albrecht, long-sought suspected terrorist, arrested in East Berlin; other arrests follow, showing how GDR had provided a haven.

June 9. Wolfgang Thierse elected new chairman of SPD in GDR.

June 11. De Maizière meets President Bush in Washington.

June 12. Gorbachev proposes initial German dual membership of NATO and Warsaw Pact; rejected by USA and FRG.

June 13. PDS discloses party funds of M 1.08 billion.

June 14. West German SPD leadership agrees to vote for state treaty.

June 15. Agreed between German governments that claims can be made for property in GDR confiscated since 1949, but not during occupation of 1945–49.

June 17. *Volkskammer* expunges socialist character of GDR constitution and approves Trust

Agency law, paving way for privatization; DSU attempt to push through immediate German unity fails.

June 18. De Maizière received by President Mitterrand in Paris.

June 21. Volkskammer approves state treaty.

June 22. Bundestag (federal parliament) approves state treaty; in *Bundesrat* only representatives of Lower Saxony (SPD) and Saarland (SPD and Lafontaine's state) vote against; "Checkpoint Charlie" dismantled; Two-plus-Four talks continue in Berlin.

June 23. Anti-fascist demonstration in East Berlin ends in violence against police.

June 25–26. Parliamentary chairwomen Bergmann-Pohl (GDR) and Süssmuth (FRG) visit Israel.

June 29. West German President Weizsäcker favours Berlin as new German capital; Detlev Rohwedder of Hoesch appointed chairman of Trust Agency.

June 30. Interior Minister Diestel leaves DSU, complaining of rightward drift; followed by other leading figures.

July 1. From midnight, currency, economic and social union of two Germanies; Deutsche Mark currency in GDR; inter-German border open.

July 2. GDR shops reopen with western goods and new prices.

July 6. Warning strike of 120,000 metalworkers in Berlin/Brandenburg.

July 8. (West) German victory in World Cup in Rome celebrated in GDR.

July 10. In Bonn and Berlin negotiations on second state treaty of unification.

July 14–16. Kohl with Gorbachev in Moscow and the Caucasus; talks result in Gorbachev's acceptance of all-German NATO membership.

July 16. Trust Agency begins work under chief executive Reiner Gohlke, formerly of *Bundesbahn*.

July 17. Polish foreign minister takes part in "Two-plus-Four" session in Paris; discussion of Oder-Neisse German-Polish border.

July 19. De Maizière insists on two separate territories for all-German elections; opposed by SPD and liberals.

July 23. Dispute continues in GDR government over timing of unification and mechanism of elections; SPD threatens to leave coalition.

July 24. Liberals announce withdrawal from coalition.

July 26. Parliamentary committees from GDR and FRG recommend joint electoral territory for all-German elections; no decision yet on 5% hurdle.

July 27. SPD decides to remain in coalition.

August 6. Under growing economic pressure in GDR, de Maizière announces that he and Kohl favour bringing all-German elections forward to October 14; protest from other parties and requirement for constitutional amendment force retreat.

August 12. FDP organizations in GDR and FRG join to form first united party (others will follow suit).

August 15. General Secretary of GDR CDU, Martin Kirchner, removed from office on suspicion of having collaborated with Stasi; mass demonstrations by GDR farmers; in East Berlin Agriculture Minister Peter Pollack pelted with eggs; de Maizière sacks Finance Minister Romberg (SPD) and Agriculture Minister Pollack (independent, nominated by SPD); Economics Minister Pohl (CDU), Justice Minister Wünsche (independent) and Foreign Minister Meckel (SPD) also resign; cabinet crisis leads to SPD withdrawing from coalition.

August 20. Reiner Gohlke resigns as chief executive of Trust Agency; to be replaced by chairman Detlev Rohwedder.

August 23. Volkskammer approves by necessary two-thirds majority the accession of the GDR to the Federal Republic of Germany at midnight on October 2–3.

August 24. Bundesrat approves unitary electoral law with 5% hurdle for parties to enter *Bundestag.*

August 31. GDR and FRG sign 900-page unification treaty in East Berlin.

September 12. Two-plus-Four talks concluded in Moscow; wartime allies abandon remaining responsibilities in Germany.

September 13. German-Soviet co-operation treaty signed; Soviet troops to withdraw from East German territory by 1994; Germany to contribute DM 15 billion to USSR.

September 28. GDR Housing Minister Axel Viehweger (FDP) resigns after admitting contact with Stasi.

September 30. Federal Constitutional Court in Karlsruhe rules electoral law unconstitutional on grounds of unfairness to GDR parties.

October 3. At midnight GDR joins the Federal Republic of Germany; Berlin capital of Germany (although government still in Bonn).

October 5. New *Bundestag* meets, with 144 delegated members from GDR; approves revised electoral law; de Maizière, Krause, Bergmann-Pohl, Ortleb and Walther join Kohl cabinet as ministers without portfolio.

October 12. Assassination attempt in Baden on Interior Minister Wolfgang Schäuble.

October 14. Elections to five reconstituted East German *Landtage* give CDU victory in four (53.8% of vote in Saxony); SPD ahead only in Brandenburg (38.3%); SPD loses ground in Bavarian election.

October 19. Police raid PDS headquarters in Berlin.

October 20. Colonel Joachim Krase (d. 1988), formerly deputy head of military intelligence service (MAD), revealed as Stasi spy.

October 25. Bundestag passes third supplementary budget, raising expenditure from DM 312 billion to DM 396 billion to pay for unification costs.

October 26. Gysi admits PDS illegally transferred DM 100 million to USSR; denies prior knowledge.

November 1. Last of five new *Land* governments formed in Brandenburg: Stolpe (SPD) leads coalition of SPD, FDP and Alliance 90; other governments: Gies in Saxony-Anhalt, Biedenkopf in Saxony, Gomolka in Mecklenburg-Western Pomerania, Duchac in Thuringia (all CDU, leading coalitions with FDP, except Saxony — CDU alone).

November 14. Germany and Poland sign border treaty, reaffirming Oder-Neisse line.

November 15. Alternative List (Greens) leaves coalition with SPD in West Berlin government over treatment of squatters in East Berlin.

December 2. Elections to all-German *Bundestag* won by Kohl coalition: CDU/CSU 319 seats (43.8% of vote); SPD 239 (33.5%); FDP 79 (11.0%); PDS 17 (2.4%); Alliance 90/Greens eight (1.2%); CDU tops poll in election to Berlin House of Representatives (CDU 40.3%; SPD 30.5%) and seeks to form grand coalition; in East Berlin SPD ahead (SPD 32.1%; CDU 25.0%; PDS 23.6%).

December 3. Coalition negotiations begin (lasting until mid-January); Economics Minister Helmut Haussmann resigns; Lafontaine declines leadership of SPD.

December 5. Vogel re-elected parliamentary chairman of SPD, but does not wish to continue as party chairman.

December 9. De Maizière denies renewed accusations of past Stasi activity.

December 11. Finance ministers of five new *Länder* and Berlin demand higher funding; renewed aspersions about Stasi past force Böhme to resign from SPD executive.

December 17. De Maizière resigns from government and deputy party leadership because of allegations of Stasi complicity; SPD executive proposes Björn Engholm, prime minister of Schleswig-Holstein, as next party chairman, succeeding Vogel.

December 20. Newly elected *Bundestag* meets in Berlin *Reichstag*, with 519 members from West Germany and 143 members from East Germany.

December 31. 642,200 unemployed in former GDR; 1,800,000 on short-time.

1991

January 16. Kohl cabinet announced; few major changes; FDP retains control of Economics Ministry (Jürgen Möllemann); posts for East Germans: Günther Krause (CDU) Transport, Angela Merkel (CDU) Women and Youth, Rainer Ortleb (FDP) Education.

Political Overview

The German Democratic Republic was defined by its politics, and when in 1989–90 the politics changed, the state disappeared. Although some other communist states face fragmentation in the wake of change, the GDR alone had no national justification once its German population could move freely to the Federal Republic of Germany. This is not to underestimate the geographical, linguistic, cultural and religious differences between Mecklenburg, Brandenburg, Thuringia and Saxony and the states of West Germany, but those latter states have amongst themselves distinct identities too. It is also evident that many people in the GDR feared and still fear the consequences of the rapid merger which took place in 1990, and there are those too in West Germany who are concerned about the change which has overtaken their state. Such reservations were, however, swept aside in the tumult of 1990, as the economy of the GDR collapsed and German unification seemed to provide the only option. That it happened so speedily astonished everybody.

The GDR had appeared the most loyal and the most stable of the Soviet satellites, but this stability had been bought at a high price. Restrictions on foreign travel and a massive system of state security placed the population of the country in a straitjacket, alleviated only by a relatively developed economy dependent on its West German links and by heavy subsidy of rents, transport and staple foods. There was opposition expressed, especially from an environmentalist and pacifist lobby within the churches, but this was lamed during the 1980s by the encouragement of emigration of the dissatisfied and by outright use of harassment and force.

The beginnings of the crisis

The crisis in the GDR was endemic, but it broke only when external circumstances changed. These were the appearance in Moscow of Mikhail Gorbachev as party leader and President and the growing political crises in Poland and Hungary. Erich Honecker and his closest comrades maintained to the last that the GDR had already undertaken the necessary economic reforms being essayed elsewhere, and they refused to admit the lack of democracy in the GDR. They knew, of course, that an opening up of the system would endanger the very existence of their state. Events were to prove them right.

There were signs early in 1989 that the rhetoric of *glasnost'* was beginning to have an impact in the GDR. Although the regime attempted to suppress discussion even in hitherto praised Soviet sources, the population was well informed by West German television of the changes which were taking place further east. In May local elections were held, and opposition groups dared to place observers at polling stations in order to monitor the staged ritual of approving the National Front. That they did so was partly the consequence of minor but much-publicized reforms in the system of selecting candidates announced by the chairman of the electoral commission, Egon Krenz. Their observations of voter refusal to return the official list unchallenged did not tally with the published results, and there were protests against ballot-rigging. As significant, however, was the fact that even the official results indicated an increased willingness on the part of the electorate to vote against the approved candidates.

The promptness of SED approval of the Tiananmen massacre in June (see section on Foreign Relations below) was a further indication of the tenseness of the regime in the face of change elsewhere. It looked as though in this one major instance a communist leadership had been able to reassert its authority, albeit at great cost. Less tractable was the problem emerging in Hungary (also see below). The major discontent of the GDR population, the lack of freedom to travel, was here being tapped by the Hungarians' opening of their border with Austria. Already in 1989 the number of legal emigrants from the GDR had been relatively high; now the possibility of unbureaucratic escape was offered. This was not, of course, what most East Germans wanted; their wish was for unrestricted access to West Germany, where many still had family and friends, and for the opportunity to travel in the wider world. Their frustration had been increased rather than diminished by hamfisted attempts by the GDR government to introduce new travel regulations in January and April 1989.

The crisis on the Hungarian border and the occupation of West German missions in Prague, Warsaw and East Berlin took place at a time when the SED leadership was weakened for other reasons. Up to this stage the only sign of any crack in the system had been the disciplining in May of Hans Modrow's Dresden party apparatus. Günter Mittag was particularly keen to scotch the attention being given to the allegedly reform-minded party secretary. Otherwise, there had been only hardline uncompromising speeches from, amongst others, Joachim Herrmann and Margot Honecker. In early July, however, Erich Honecker was flown back from a Warsaw Pact summit in Bucharest for an urgent operation on his gall bladder. He was absent from his normal duties for the best part of two months, and there were even rumours in the West German press that he was dying or had actually died. His chosen but not announced replacement during this time was Mittag, who did nothing to defuse the situation. Egon Krenz, who had emerged once more as Honecker's eventual successor, was meanwhile sent on holiday. It was during this time that he began to crystallize his thoughts on the urgent need for change.

The dismissal of Erich Honecker

If Krenz and others in the Politbüro were beginning to anticipate the end of Honecker, others outside the system were mobilizing too. New Forum and Democracy Now were founded in the second week of September, and Democratic Departure (DA) and the SDP at the beginning of October, all defying official proscription. From within the churches came appeals for change in order to avert tragedy in the GDR, and then one of the system's minor pillars, Manfred Gerlach of the LDPD, spoke out for new thought to be given to the nature of the GDR.

Honecker would have none of this, and thereby sealed his fate. His blind confidence at the 40th anniversary celebrations of the GDR bewildered Gorbachev, his guest of honour, and many of his Politbüro comrades. They recognized that the situation was far more dangerous than Honecker was prepared to admit. Aside from the official demonstrations in East Berlin, which themselves testified to an ominous enthusiasm for "Gorby", there were violent skirmishes between protesters and the security forces. On October 9 threatened the worst scenario, with what had become a regular Monday demonstration in Leipzig swelling to some 70,000 people. With slogans of "We are the people" and "We are staying here" (i.e. not emigrating), the crowds could well have been attacked by armed force. That they were not is an issue still shrouded in mystery. Günter Schabowski, otherwise sceptical of Krenz's assessments, does attribute to him a role in holding back the security forces.

Schabowski also maintains, however, that this matter was secondary at the time to the nascent plans for Honecker's removal. The Politbüro met on October 10–11 to discuss the crisis, but failed to come up with more than a jargon-ridden appeal for everybody to help solve the crisis. Meanwhile Krenz was beginning to canvas support for his putsch attempt. He and his co-conspirators, who came to include Willi Stoph, so long humiliated by Honecker, Harry Tisch of the trade unions, and Schabowski, had to be sure that they had sufficient backing not to fall victim to Honecker's revenge. By the time the Politbüro met on October 17, in advance of a Central Committee meeting the next day, Krenz and Schabowski had spoken to many of the Politbüro members and had gained the impression that Honecker's position was now weak. At the meeting Honecker had time only for some introductory words before Stoph interrupted him with the proposal that the removal of the General Secretary be discussed. Honecker permitted this, but tried to prompt those into speech whom he thought would support him. They did not. Even Mittag and Erich Mielke of the Stasi spoke in favour of Honecker's departure. The meeting voted unanimously for the dismissal of Honecker, Mittag and Herrmann. According to Schabowski, the latter did admit some responsibility for the failure of the official media to cope with the crisis.

Honecker had been dismissed, but he was allowed in public to resign. His opponents were afraid that there might be difficulties with the Central Committee if a respected leader were to be seen humiliated by his comrades. The speech which Honecker delivered to the Central Committee the next day was therefore a request that he be relieved of all his offices on health grounds. He proposed that Krenz replace him, an insertion which Schabowski regrets because it implied to the party, the population and the outside world that Honecker had engineered the succession and that policy would not change substantially. The official communiqué of the Central Committee thanked Honecker for his service, but merely reported the removal of Mittag and Herrmann.

Egon Krenz and the opening of the Berlin Wall

The initial impact of Krenz was of an insistence on the socialist purpose of the GDR, coupled with an admission that there were problems and that they could only be solved by opening up discussion within the country. Krenz made a point of visiting ordinary factory workers and of talking to church leaders. The change at the top did nothing, however, to dampen the weekly demonstrations taking place throughout the country, but particularly in Leipzig. In fact it encouraged the calls for democratic reform, and hundreds of thousands marched the streets. On November 4, East Berlin excelled even Leipzig in numbers, with up to 1,000,000 on the move.

No change would be possible without a substantial clear-out of the old personnel, and this began in early November. Politbüro members, ministers, regional party leaders, and the heads of the other political parties began to disappear from office, and then on November 7 the Stoph government resigned, followed the next day by the entire Politbüro. The Central Committee elections to replace the latter brought in a generally new line-up, with votes against being announced. Some of those chosen were unable to take office because they had meanwhile been spurned by their local party organizations, but the main figures held on. They were Krenz, Schabowski and — new to the Politbüro — Hans Modrow. He had not been party to the anti-Honecker conspiracy, but his reputation as a popular local figure and as a man in favour of change had already led to Schabowski suggesting to Krenz that he be brought into the central leadership. He was proposed as the new Prime Minister, replacing Stoph, and was approved by the *Volkskammer* (People's Chamber) on November 18.

That was only after the most extraordinary event in the whole history. On the evening of November 9 (by strange coincidence the anniversary of the Berlin revolution of 1918 and of Hitler's abortive putsch in 1923), Schabowski announced at his regular press conference that with immediate effect citizens of the GDR would be allowed to travel out of the country with a minimum of formalities. This was a recognition by Krenz that his previous attempt to amend the travel regulations had failed and that a radical step was the only way to defuse the situation. Krenz and Schabowski were aware of the nature of the announcement, but they still assumed that people would from the following morning avail themselves of the official procedures before taking advantage of the new freedom. Instead, the effect was immediate and electrifying. In Berlin in particular there was a rush to the border crossings along the Wall and some tension before the border guards yielded to the pressure and allowed people to cross to West Berlin. Visas were issued on the spot or in many cases forgotten altogether. West Berliners too joined in, with dancing on the Wall by the Brandenburg Gate and droves of people entering the eastern sector of the city without any controls whatever.

The events in Berlin and the storm of Trabant cars westwards along the other borders between the two Germanies were flashed across the world and were instrumental in encouraging what was to come soon afterwards in Prague and Bucharest. They did not, however, make the task of Krenz any easier. He was faced by demands, even from within his own party, for a more radical reconstruction of the GDR, he saw the first signs of the economic chaos consequent upon the erosion of the state frontier, and he heard now from Helmut Kohl the first proposals for German unification. Krenz and Schabowski, indeed all apart from Modrow, had little time left. The leading role of the party was abandoned on December 1, and two days later the whole party leadership resigned. Former leading members were expelled from the SED entirely and some, including Honecker, Mittag and Tisch, were arrested. Krenz ceased to be head of state on December 6, less than two months after his displacement of Honecker.

The government of Hans Modrow

The focus now shifted to Hans Modrow, whose government coalition of the "old parties" was from December 7 supplemented by meetings of an advisory "Round Table", representing a wide range of the new political groupings. All the problems of the GDR were now up for discussion: the lack of political freedoms, the failings of the economy, the catastrophe of the environment, and much besides. One issue was already threatening to replace these concerns, however. Just before Christmas Kohl visited Dresden and was accorded an ecstatic welcome. The slogan of "We are the people" was coming to be replaced by "We are one

---

Table 1: The Government of National Responsibility, February 5, 1990

Prime Minister	Hans Modrow (PDS)
Deputy Prime Minister for Economic Affairs	Christa Luft (PDS)
Deputy Prime Minister for Local State Bodies	Peter Moreth (LDPD)
Deputy Prime Minister for Church Affairs	Lothar de Maizière (CDU)
Defence	Theodor Hoffman (PDS)
Education	Hans–Heinz Emons (PDS)
Employment and Wages	Hannelore Mensch (PDS)
Environmental Protection	Peter Diederich (DBD)
Foreign Affairs	Oskar Fischer (PDS)
Foreign Trade	Gerhard Beil (PDS)
Health and Social Welfare	Klaus Thielmann (PDS)
Internal Affairs	Lothar Ahrendt (PDS)
Justice	Kurt Wünsche (LDPD)
Machinery Manufacturing	Hans-Joachim Lauck (PDS)
Science and Technology	Klaus-Peter Budig (LDPD)
Trade and Supply	Manfred Flegel (NDPD)
Transport	Heinrich Scholz (PDS)
Chairman of the Committee on the Economy	Karl Grünheid (PDS)
Government Spokesman and Head of Press Office	Wolfgang Meyer (PDS)
Without Portfolio	Tatjana Böhm (UFV)
	Rainer Eppelmann (DA)
	Sebastian Flugbeil (NF)
	Mathias Platzeck (GP)
	Gerd Poppe (IFM)
	Walter Romberg (SPD)
	Klaus Schlüter (GL)
	Wolfgang Ullmann (DJ)

Note: The party appellations refer to the political origins of the ministers; officially they were now non-party.

Abbreviations:

UFV	=	Independent Women's Association
NF	=	New Forum
GP	=	Green Party
IFM	=	Initiative for Peace and Human Rights
GL	=	Green League
DJ	=	Democracy Now

people", and Modrow found himself discussing with Kohl provisional arrangements for links between the two Germanies. At this stage, actual political unification was seen to be a long way off, even by Kohl. The kind of link being suggested was a so-called "contractual community", which would maintain the separate statehoods of the GDR and the Federal Republic, while forging ever-closer economic, cultural and political bonds.

Modrow was caught between his old party and the new forces in the GDR. The SED was itself changing, not only its leadership (to Gregor Gysi) and its name (to the SED-PDS and then to simply PDS — Party of Democratic Socialism), but also its function. It was no longer of right the ruling party, and its membership numbers were collapsing. Local leaders, such as Berghofer in Dresden, were abandoning the organization. Modrow tried to maintain something of the old apparatus, however, by proposing a continuation of a state security office. This attempt suggested that he was so tested by his circumstances as to fail in judgement. He was forced to retreat.

The new parties and the partially reformed old ones were gaining in confidence and were beginning to prepare for free elections. The sense of growing crisis in the GDR by early 1990, with continuing mass emigration and uncertainty about future exchange rates and the terms of eventual German unity, led Modrow at the end of January to invite the "opposition" parties into a "government of national responsibility" (see Table 1). At the same time he approved the bringing forward of the elections to a new democratic *Volkskammer* from the original May 6 to March 18. All the parties, except the SPD (the new name of the SDP), began to form electoral alliances. On the right was the Alliance for Germany, in the centre the liberal League of Free Democrats (BFD), and on the libertarian left the Alliance 90.

The Volkskammer *elections*

Early opinion polls gave the SPD a substantial lead, providing encouragement too to the West German party. It had seen support for Helmut Kohl's CDU in the Federal Republic falter during 1989, but it had not yet experienced any fillip for SPD fortunes. It looked now as though the GDR might provide it. In the event, the reverse occurred. The opinion polls began to register a swelling of support for the CDU, especially once it formed the Alliance for Germany with the small Democratic Departure (DA) and the Saxon-based DSU, and once Kohl came out openly with a promise of a 1:1 exchange rate for savings, wages and pensions. Kohl had the advantage over the opposition of being able to use his office to make such undertakings and to negotiate a favourable attitude on the part of the Four Powers. The SPD could not do this, and even appeared reluctant to envisage early German unity. By now this had become a priority on the part of a large section of the East German electorate, and the result of the elections exceeded Kohl's wildest hopes. The Alliance for Germany only narrowly failed to win an absolute majority of votes and of seats in the new chamber. It achieved this victory despite the long-term complicity of the East German CDU in the old regime and its scant involvement in the revolution of 1989. Even the admitted former involvement of the DA leader, Wolfgang Schnur, in the State Security organization (Stasi) dented only his party and not its allies. The new leader of the CDU and prospective Prime Minister, Lothar de Maizière, was also accused of past malpractice, but denied the allegations and survived.

The election result was a clear break from the previous communist system on the part of most of the electorate. The PDS (formerly the SED) did hold on to a respectable 16.4% of

Table 2:   Elections to the *Volkskammer* of the GDR, March 18, 1990 (turnout 93.4%)

	Valid votes	%		Seats	
CDU ⎱	4,710,598	40.8 ⎱		163 ⎱	
DSU ⎰ Alliance for Germany	727,730	6.3 ⎰ 48.0		25 ⎰ 192	
DA ⎰	106,146	0.9 ⎰		4 ⎰	
SPD	2,525,534	21.9		88	
PDS (= former SED)	1,892,381	16.4		66	
BFD (= liberal coalition)	608,935	5.3		21	
A90 (= New Forum and others)	336,074	2.9		12	
DBD (= Farmers' Party)	251,226	2.2		9	
Greens/Women's Association	226,932	2.0		8	
NDPD	44,292	0.4		2	
Others	111,307	1.0		2	
TOTAL	11,541,155	100.0		400	

the vote, helped by the recent performance of outgoing Prime Minister Modrow and new party chairman Gysi. It still had the backing of those whose lives had been wedded to the former ruling party and of those who saw it as the best defender of the positive socialist aspects of the GDR against encroaching capitalism and the spectre of unemployment. Most voters, though, used their first democratic opportunity to reject their former rulers.

The Social Democrats could take little comfort from the vote. There was clearly a communist core to their left which they could not yet hope to attract, but more seriously they had failed to make a convincing moderate socialist appeal to a broad swathe of public opinion. The very term "socialism" had become anathema to so many. Far from latching on to the pre-Nazi social democratic past of such states as Saxony and Thuringia, those were the areas which had swung most strongly toward the CDU and DSU. The SPD also suffered during the later stages of the election campaign from accusations of Stasi involvement by its leader, Ibrahim Böhme. Shortly after the poll he was forced to lay down his party offices temporarily, pending investigation. This resignation later became permanent.

The election saw the beginning of the end for the other block parties, the NDPD (later to merge with the LDPD) and the DBD, but the LDPD managed to survive by allying with other liberal groupings and eventually turning into an East German FDP. New Forum and other citizens' initiatives which had spearheaded the revolution of the previous autumn paid the price for not having party organizations to match those of the parties supported by West German counterparts. Their message of a humane democratic GDR sorting out its own problems before considering German unification also failed to satisfy by this juncture.

The government of Lothar de Maizière and the negotiation of currency union

De Maizière did not form a government immediately. Three weeks passed before he had constructed a cabinet. The main problem was that without an overall majority for the Alliance for Germany and with the exclusion of the PDS as a putative coalition partner, he had to win the support of the SPD. This was made difficult by the inclusion in the Alliance for Germany and thus of necessity in the new government of the DSU. This was a party which had made furious attacks on the SPD during the campaign and which was drifting markedly rightward. The SPD accused it of being too much like the far-right Republicans, who had made inroads into West German politics in the course of 1989. De Maizière managed the delicate balancing trick and in the end included both the DSU and the SPD in his new broad coalition government. The DSU was given the Ministry of the Interior and one other, the SPD Foreign Affairs, Finance and five others. The CDU dominated with 11 ministries (see Table 3).

The success of the East German CDU made Kohl's task much easier than it might otherwise have been. De Maizière and Kohl had agreed before the end of April that the two Germanies would enter currency, economic and social union on July 1, and negotiations began at once on the details. They were concluded with extraordinary rapidity, in awareness of the mounting economic crisis in the GDR but with perforce inadequate information. On May 18 in Bonn the "state treaty" was signed by the respective finance ministers of the two Germanies, Theo Waigel (CSU) of the Federal Republic and Walter Romberg (SPD) of the GDR.

De Maizière and, by proxy, Kohl had meanwhile faced another electoral test. In early May local elections were held in the GDR, and there were some changes (see Table 4). Turnout, though still high, was well down on the near unanimous participation in March. The elections confirmed the dominance of the CDU over its rivals, but it lost ground

---

Table 3:   The government of Lothar de Maizière, April 9, 1990

Prime Minister	Lothar de Maizière (CDU)
Chief of Prime Minister's Staff	Klaus Riechenbach (CDU)
Government Spokesman	Mathias Dehler (CDU)
Interior and Deputy Prime Minister	Peter-Michael Diestel (DSU)
Foreign Affairs	Markus Meckel (SPD)
Defence and Disarmament	Rainer Eppelmann (DA)
Economy	Gerhard Pohl (CDU)
Finance	Walter Romberg (SPD)
Environment and Energy	Karl-Hermann Steinberg (CDU)
Education and Science	Hans-Joachim Meyer (Ind)
Research and Technology	Frank Terpe (SPD)
Trade and Tourism	Sybille Reider (SPD)
Economic Co-operation	Hans-Wilhelm Ebeling (DSU)
Justice	Kurt Wünsche (BFD)
Labour and Social Affairs	Regine Hildebrandt (SPD)
Post and Telecommunications	Emil Schnell (SPD)
Transport	Horst Gibtner (CDU)
Construction	Axel Viehweger (BFD)
Regional and Local Affairs	Manfred Preiss (BFD)
Agriculture	Peter Pollack (Ind)*
Health	Jürgen Kleditzsch (CDU)
Media	Gottfried Müller (CDU)
Culture	Herbert Schirmer (CDU)
Women and Family Affairs	Christa Schmidt (CDU)
Youth and Sport	Cordula Schubert (CDU)

Note: *Nominated by SPD

Table 4:   Local elections in the GDR, May 6, 1990 (turnout 75%)

	%	Change from March election
CDU	34.4	−6.4
SPD	21.3	−0.6
PDS	14.6	−1.8
DSU	3.4	−2.9
BFD	6.7	+1.4
A90	2.4	−0.5
Farmers' Parties (including DBD)	5.7	+3.5
Others	11.5	+7.3
TOTAL	100.0	

considerably. Even more so did its partners in the Alliance for Germany. The DSU, which was by this stage visibly fragmenting into right and left wings, lost nearly half its support, and the DA ceased to be of any significance. The other two big parties also had to concede some ground, the PDS more than the SPD. Alliance 90, including New Forum, continued its decline. The gainers were — appropriately for these local elections — local citizens' groups and independents, and also the liberals of the BFD. There was also, at the expense of the CDU and DSU, an advance made by two farmers' parties. This emphasized the growing crisis in GDR agriculture, even before the strains of economic union.

As economic calamity began to bite, so the de Maizière coalition began to feel the strain. The DSU parliamentary fraction turned against its Interior Minister, Diestel, accusing him of soft-pedalling on the Stasi, and he and other colleagues resigned from the party at the end of June. The DSU also tried to pre-empt de Maizière and Kohl in mid-June by proposing in the *Volkskammer* immediate German political unity. The form of that unity was contested too between de Maizière, the SPD and the BFD. The former wanted two separate electoral territories for the all-German elections, whenever they might be. The effect of this would be to bolster the DSU, to face the SPD with difficult competition from the PDS, and perhaps to endanger the parliamentary survival of the liberals in the GDR. The SPD and BFD argued for one electoral territory with the same rules as in the present Federal Republic, namely a 5% hurdle before any *Bundestag* (federal parliament) seats could be claimed. The coalition was falling apart, until agreement was reached on one electoral territory, with perhaps a lower threshold than 5% to assist the parties in the GDR which did not exist in the Federal Republic.

From currency union to political unification

De Maizière's problems were not over. He and Kohl, faced by the evidence of mounting economic chaos in the wake of the currency union and fearful of losing all-German elections if they were held as late as December, tried to bring the date forward to October 14, shortly after the unification date of October 3 which was now becoming firmer. De Maizière announced the plan without apparently consulting Kohl, and the extent of their panic was revealed. To bring forward *Bundestag* elections was, however, a matter of constitutional significance and the West German SPD promised to block the manoeuvre.

As the elections approached, de Maizière began to flex his political muscles against his recalcitrant coalition partners. In mid-August he sacked all three of his economics ministers, Romberg at finance, Pohl at economy and Pollack at agriculture, the latter having been treated ignominiously by angry egg-throwing farmers. The impression given was that de Maizière was trying to push the blame for the economic mess onto his ministers. He was, however, also settling his scores with the SPD. The dismissal of Romberg led to the SPD quitting the coalition. With such a short time to go before unification, de Maizière compounded the indignity of his ex-ministers by not even bothering to replace them. State secretaries dealt with the remaining economic tasks, and in the run-up to the signing of the unification treaty de Maizière acted as his own foreign minister.

The voluminous unification treaty, signed on August 31, 1990, was in effect an extension of the laws of the Federal Republic into the territory of the GDR, but on a wide range of points there were clarifications to be made and temporary arrangements to be implemented. The West German Basic Law had to be altered in some respects, most notably in its provisional character. There was henceforth no implication that "other parts of Germany" might join the Federal Republic. This was a message that the unification of Germany was now regarded as complete and that there was no expectation of lost territories in the east being regained. After unification this was codified in the treaty with Poland of November 14, 1990.

The unification of Germany

At midnight on October 2–3, 1990, the German Democratic Republic ceased to exist. Its territory joined the Federal Republic of Germany and the united city of Berlin became once more capital of the country. On a new public holiday, replacing October 7 in East Germany and June 17 in West Germany, Germans in all parts of the country celebrated the conclusion of a tumultuous political year. The next day the *Bundestag* met symbolically in the *Reichstag* building in Berlin, enlarged by 144 members delegated from the parties of the former GDR. Five CDU and FDP delegates, including de Maizière, joined Kohl's cabinet as ministers without portfolio. This did not yet mean that Berlin was to become the seat of German government. The following day the *Bundestag* continued its business as usual in Bonn.

The question of the all-German elections, which had been vexing the political parties of both West and East Germany for months, was now resolved. The elections were to take place on December 2 and they were to be based on two electoral territories, with a separate 5% hurdle in each. This had been made necessary by a ruling of the constitutional court in Karlsruhe that the earlier plan would have been unfair to the new parties of the former GDR. The campaign now began in earnest, with Kohl hoping to ride high on his achievement of German unity within one year of Honecker's fall and without major diplomatic problems. His opponent, Oskar Lafontaine, continued to berate the chancellor for having botched the process of economic integration, with dire consequences to come.

The immediate political impact of "the five new federal states", as the former GDR came to be called, was to bolster the ruling coalition in Bonn. After elections to new state governments in October the CDU formed governments, either in coalition or on its own (in Saxony), in four of the five states. Only in Brandenburg could the SPD lead a coalition. Apart from this regional CDU dominance within the former GDR, this meant that the CDU and its partners now regained a majority in the Federal Council (*Bundesrat*),

Table 5: Elections to East German *Landtage*, October 14, 1990
(% of valid votes cast)

	Brandenburg	Mecklenburg–W. Pomerania	Saxony	Saxony–Anhalt	Thuringia
CDU	29.4	38.3	53.8	39.0	45.4
DSU	1.0	0.8	3.6	1.7	3.3
FDP-Liberals	6.6	5.5	5.3	13.5	9.3
SPD	38.3	27.0	19.1	26.0	22.8
Alliance 90	6.4	2.2	5.6	5.3	6.5
Greens	2.8	4.2			
New Forum	—	2.9	—	—	—
PDS	13.4	15.7	10.2	12.0	9.7
Others	2.1	3.4	2.4	2.6	3.0
Turnout	67.4	65.2	73.5	65.6	72.1

Germany's upper house. They had lost this in May 1990 when the SPD seized control in Lower Saxony (see Table 5).

In the *Bundestag* elections of December 2, 1990 the CDU and the FDP performed well in the former GDR, and the SPD very badly. The CDU polled 43.4%, which was marginally up on the elections in March 1990 to the now redundant East German *Volkskammer* and, together with the sharply diminished vote of the DSU, slightly above the combined result of the CDU and CSU in West Germany. The FDP put in a very strong showing in East Germany: 13.4%, compared to 10.6% in West Germany. The popularity of Genscher, Foreign Minister and himself born in East Germany, played a major part in this (see Table 6).

The SPD in East Germany did improve on its showing in March 1990 (from 21.9% to

Table 6: Elections to *Bundestag*, December 2, 1990 (% of valid votes cast)

	Germany	West Germany	(1987)	East Germany	(March)	Seats in new Bundestag
CDU	36.7	35.0	34.5	43.4	40.8	270
CSU	7.1	9.1	9.8	—	—	49
DSU	0.2	—	—	0.9	6.3	—
SPD	33.5	35.9	37.0	23.6	21.9	239
FDP	11.0	10.6	9.1	13.4	—	79
PDS	2.4	—	—	9.9	16.4	17
Greens	3.9	4.7	8.3	—	—	—
Greens/A90	1.2	—	—	5.9	—	8
Republicans	2.1	2.3	—	1.3	—	—
Others	1.9	2.4	1.3	1.6	14.6	—
TOTAL	100.0	100.0	100.0	100.0	100.0	662
Turnout	77.8	78.5	84.4	74.5	93.4	—

23.6%), but this was a dismal result for a party which had emerged so confidently in the course of the changes in the GDR. It is probable that Lafontaine did not recover in East Germany from the impression which he gave initially of being half-hearted about unification. In East Germany the SPD also had to its left a party taking votes. The PDS managed 9.9%. This was a substantial drop from 16.4% in March 1990, and once Germany elects on a unified national basis, not as this time in two separate parts, the PDS will find it hard to return to the *Bundestag*. The East German Greens, backed by the citizens' movements which spearheaded the revolution, just squeezed in with 5.9%, embarrassing their West German counterparts, who did not. The far-right Republicans failed to make any impact in East Germany; their 1.3% was less than the 2.3% in West Germany.

On the same day as the *Bundestag* elections, the process of restoring regional representation throughout Germany was completed, as the newly unified city of Berlin went to the polls. Berlin, which is for the moment at least a separate *Land* within the enlarged Federal Republic, now has once more a parliament of its own. Until just before the election West Berlin had been ruled by a coalition of SPD and the Alternative List. This had then fallen apart acrimoniously over the treatment of squatters in East Berlin. East Berlin had been ruled by a coalition also headed by the SPD. In these new elections, however, the SPD performed badly, and the CDU and FDP made strong advances. They did not quite have an overall majority between them, and the outcome of negotiations was a grand coalition between CDU and SPD, with Eberhard Diepgen (CDU) replacing Walter Momper (SPD) as governing mayor (see Table 7).

The SPD's losses were primarily in West Berlin, although it gave ground slightly even in East Berlin. They formed part of the general poor performance of the party in the national elections, but were also due to the controversial SPD-Alternative List government of the city in recent months. The CDU did well in both parts of the city, although there is still a large difference between the two. The CDU did, however, overtake the PDS in the former "capital of the GDR". The PDS still had over 20% of the vote in East Berlin, but

Table 7: Elections to the Berlin House of Representatives, December 2, 1990

	Berlin		*West Berlin*		*East Berlin*	
	%	*Seats*	%	*(Previous %)*	%	*(Previous %)*
CDU	40.3	100	48.9	(37.7)	25.0	(18.6)
SPD	30.5	76	29.5	(37.7)	32.1	(34.0)
PDS	9.2	23	1.1	(—)	23.6	(30.0)
FDP	7.1	18	7.9	(3.9)	5.6	(2.2)
GAL	5.0	12	6.9	(11.8)	1.7	(—)
A90/G	4.4	11	1.4	(—)	9.7	(9.9)
Reps	3.1	—	3.7	(7.5)	1.9	(—)

Abbreviations:

GAL   =   Greens/Alternative List
A90/G =   Alliance 90/Greens
Reps   =   Republicans

its position, as in the rest of East Germany, was being eroded. The FDP could be pleased with its showing; it had not been represented in the West Berlin parliament before this election, but then recovered in both parts of the city. The combined forces of the Green alliances in East and West amounted to nearly 10% of the vote. The final message from this election was that the appeal of the far-right Republicans has ebbed for the moment at least. Despite fears of extremism in both West and East, the Republicans could only muster 3.7% in West Berlin (previously 7.5%) and 1.9% in East Berlin (total for Berlin 3.1%).

This completed the initial political integration of East Germany into the enlarged Federal Republic of Germany. The former ruling party was rewarded for its 40-year custody of the country by being displaced by its former subordinate party, the CDU. Erich Honecker, it was announced rather blatantly on election day, was to be charged with multiple manslaughter, in connection with the shooting over the years of escapees. He immediately fell ill, however, and there is doubt whether it would be right to try a man in his condition. He and other prominent participants in the old system, including the men who opened the Wall, Egon Krenz and Günter Schabowski, have been publishing their accounts of the past. Honecker seems to have learned nothing from what has happened. Krenz tries unconvincingly to prove his good faith and desire for reform. Schabowski is most candid about the iniquities of the old regime. He and Krenz lay most of the blame with former secretary for the economy, Günter Mittag, whose fate is still to be decided. Harry Tisch, the former trade union boss, faced trial early in 1991 on charges of corruption and embezzlement.

In this, as in so many other respects, the past casts a long shadow over "the five new federal states". Both the PDS and the East German CDU have been beset by scandals of misappropriation of party funds. In the summer of 1990 began the rooting out of alleged West German terrorists who had been given refuge in the GDR. And again and again spy cases are revealed and accusations made about the past Stasi associations of public figures. The most prominent to fall was Lothar de Maizière himself in mid-December, just missing out on appointment to Helmut Kohl's new cabinet. The only political survivors were Günther Krause, formerly de Maizière's state secretary, and two other new ministers in Bonn. It will be a long while before political life in the east of Germany fully frees itself from its recent history.

Economic Overview

The political crisis of the German Democratic Republic derived in large measure from its economic crisis. The command economy had over many years failed to deliver the standard of living observable over the border in the Federal Republic, but by the end of 1988 the GDR economy was once more in a serious slowdown. That this should come at the very time when the example of political and economic reform was being held up elsewhere in central and Eastern Europe exacerbated the discontent of the population in the GDR and caused some of the country's leading politicians to consider a change at the top. The official line of Honecker, Mittag and others remained unmoved, however. They claimed that the GDR had already undertaken its economic reforms and had done so with great success.

The economy in the late 1980s

The economy of the GDR before the revolution of 1989 was primarily industrial — manufacturing, mining and electricity generating 72.3% of Net Material Product in 1988, the construction industry 7.4% — but with a surprisingly large agricultural sector (9.8% of NMP). The economy was almost entirely state-owned, with only about 3.5% of NMP deriving from private enterprises, and those operating under strict limitations. Energy for both industrial and private consumption came primarily from indigenous supplies of lignite in the southern part of the country. The mining and burning of lignite caused severe ecological and health damage. The GDR managed a full range of products, with an emphasis on engineering, vehicles, chemicals, optics and some consumer goods. The supply of the latter to the population was quite inadequate, however, in terms of both quantity and quality.

One major feature of the GDR economy which came to have deleterious effects both on the state budget and upon the responsiveness of industry and agriculture was the high level of subsidy on a wide range of goods and services. Most of these were staple food products and fares, but some items were included — such as cut flowers — which scarcely came into these categories. The result of these subsidies, which reached 18.5% of state expenditure in 1988, was to keep most staple prices at 1950s levels. The budget could not carry this; it was admitted after the *Wende* that the neatly balanced budgets of the GDR had in fact themselves been surreptitiously subsidized from hard currency borrowing which did not appear in the accounts. The effect on production of the artificially low prices was that there was no incentive to produce goods in response to demand; producers were guaranteed their income. Some curious anomalies resulted; bread, which was heavily subsidized, was cheaper than animal feedstuffs, so bread intended for human consumption was fed to pigs. The pigs were then bought by the state and sold at a loss.

The East German economy 1989–90

At the end of 1988 the GDR party and governmental apparatus once more went through the motions of approving the next year's plan and state budget. Both were presented with a greater clarity and detail than they had been in previous years, suggesting that changes in attitude were taking shape, but they showed no sign of a change in policy. Despite clear evidence from even the official figures (see Table 8) that the apparent economic upturn of

	1984	1985	1986	1987	1988	1989
NMP at 1985 prices (M billion)	229.9	241.9	252.2	260.6	268.1	273.7
Official NMP growth %	5.5	5.2	4.3	3.3	2.8	2.1

Table 8:   GDR Net Material Product 1984–89

Source: *Statistisches Jahrbuch der DDR 1990.*

the mid-1980s was a thing of the past and was being followed by a remorseless downward trend, the planners stuck to quantity growth with an emphasis on expensive new technology. In fact, this development programme of autarky in microtechnology, a project dear to the heart of Erich Honecker, had for years been drawing much needed investment away from dilapidated industries, without really being able to modernize production techniques on a significant scale.

The economy at this juncture was characterized by outdated plant, manned by disgruntled and underused workers on long shifts, producing goods according to plan rather than according to demand. If the plan looked in danger of not being fulfilled, short cuts were taken or statistics manipulated. Production was often delayed or halted because of supply bottlenecks, and the whole production process was marked by enormous damage to the environment.

For most of 1989 the official statistics maintained their usual fictions, with NMP growth from January to September reported at 4.0% in comparison with the same period of 1988, gross industrial output up 4.4%, net industrial output up 6.0% and labour productivity up 6.1%. Retail trade turnover was claimed to have risen by 4.0% and net money incomes by 3.1%. These figures were far from comforting, however, since they showed little improvement in the general position. In the autumn things did not only get worse, but it was now admitted that they were getting worse. Gross industrial output in November fell in comparison with November 1988 by 2.5%, and growth in NMP by the end of the year was only 2.1%. Over 40% of main plan targets were admitted to be behind schedule, and the state budget was M 5–6 billion in deficit.

The reasons for this dramatic decline were a greater honesty in the figures themselves, the political chaos of the last quarter of the year, and the drain on the labour force of emigration. Already in the summer the exodus via Hungary, Czechoslovakia and Poland had begun to deplete the workforce in key areas. It was precisely younger, skilled workers and professionals who were the first to leave, opening crucial gaps which were to become very serious indeed by the end of the year. At that point some 350,000 men, women and children had left the country altogether, reducing the workforce by at least 2%, and worse was to come. In the first 10 days of 1990 over 15,000 left the GDR to settle in the Federal Republic and this rate showed no signs of abating.

The first half of 1990 saw the downhill slide begin (see Table 9). In all sectors of the East German economy concerns faced shortages of supplies, critical gaps in the workforce, and competition from western producers. This was either because the latters' goods were being sold in the GDR or because East Germans in Berlin and near the border were doing their shopping in the Federal Republic. In the early summer western consumer goods, foodstuffs, alcohol and tobacco were being sold on the streets of the GDR, often from mobile stalls. Motor cars were being driven to the GDR for sale.

All these problems were exacerbated by the monetary union of July 1, 1990. From that date all wages and salaries had to be paid for in Deutschemarks and concerns' debts were converted at a rate of 2:1. The GDR's CMEA trade partners also now had to pay for goods in hard currency. All these aspects placed great strain on the viability of industry and agriculture, but of more immediate importance were the removal of price subsidies and the swamping of the East German market with western produce. The food and consumer goods industries almost overnight found that their produce was replaced by western alternatives more attractive to the population. West German suppliers saw the GDR as a huge untapped market and tried to relieve the East Germans of their now converted savings.

Table 9:   Economic indicators 1989–90 (% change on period previous year)

	1989 3rd qtr.	4th qtr.	1990 1st qtr.	2nd qtr.	3rd qtr.	4th qtr.	Year
Gross industrial output	3.8	–1.0	–4.5	–9.5	–48.1	–50.0*	–20.0*
Retail trade turnover	2.7	2.5	7.0	–0.6	–45.0	n.a.	n.a.

Note: * = estimate
Sources: *Statistisches Amt der DDR*, *Statistisches Bundesamt.*

By the last quarter of 1989 gross industrial output was down by 1.0%. The first half of 1990 had seen the position worsen. In the third and last quarters of 1990, output was half that in the equivalent periods of the previous year. The year-on-year outcome was of a fall in gross output of about 20.0% (see Table 9).

The fall in output was accompanied by an accelerating laying off of workers or placing them on short-time. Unemployment, which had officially been nil under the old regime, rose from 7,000 (0.1%) in January 1990, to 757,200 (8.6%) a year later (see Table 10). As significant was the level of short-time working, which in many cases amounted to unemployment, funded from the West German budget. In July 1990 there were 656,000 short-time workers; by January 1991 there were 2,617,000. Within the category of short-time there were changes too. At end December 1990, 41% of short-time workers had had their working hours cut by more than half. Only a month later this proportion had risen to 50%.

The support of short-time workers by the Federal Labour Institution (*Bundesanstalt für Arbeit*) became a matter of controversy. It was suggested by some entrepreneurs that it was discouraging people from looking for new opportunities. As the president of the Federal Association of German Industry (BDI), Heinrich Weiss, put it in February 1991,

Table 10:   Unemployment and short-time working in territory of GDR, 1990–91

	Unemployed '000s	%	Short-time '000s	Total '000s	%
Jan. 1990	7	0.1	—	7	0.1
Feb.	11	0.1	—	11	0.1
March	38	0.4	—	38	0.4
April	65	0.7	—	65	0.7
May	95	1.1	—	95	1.1
June	142	1.6	—	142	1.6
July	272	3.1	656	928	10.5
Aug.	361	4.1	1,500	1,861	21.0
Sept.	445	5.0	1,729	2,174	24.4
Oct.	538	6.0	1,767	2,305	25.9
Nov.	589	6.7	1,774	2,359	26.9
Dec.	642	7.3	1,800	2,442	27.8
Jan. 1991	757	8.6	1,860	2,617	29.8

Sources: *Zentrale Arbeitsverwaltung der DDR*; *Bundesanstalt für Arbeit.*

"I cannot expect from someone who is receiving 92% of his net wage for not working that he start looking for a new job with any great ambition". However, the political effect of withdrawing state support would be unacceptable to the government, so it has devised a scheme to extend the short-time provisions beyond the original deadline of June 1991, while insisting that workers in such a position participate in a retraining scheme.

Besides unemployment, there has been a significant reduction in the total labour force in East Germany. This may be as much as 15% (1,300,000). This is due to emigration, commuting to West Germany, early retirement, dismissal of working pensioners and foreign workers, and unemployment itself. This will ease the position in the longer term, as over-manned sectors of the economy trim down, but in the meantime unemployment, with its accompanying social tensions, remains high.

The costs of unification

At the forefront of the unification issue were and still are the questions of how much it will cost and who will pay for it. They are economic questions which allow no simple answer, but they are also political questions which have been exploited by all participants in the process. In the early stages of the debate it appeared that the East German economy, in crisis as it was, could nevertheless be integrated into the West German economy without major upheaval. The two Germanies were after all the economic leaders in their respective European camps. Well before economic and currency union, however, it became clear that the task was going to be much greater and much more costly than this. The massive depletion of the East German labour force and the reluctance of West German and other western business to invest in the GDR threatened to undermine the East German economy before the process of unification was even agreed. Currency union then itself posed problems, with politically determined exchange rates and sudden competition from West German produce. Industry and agriculture were collapsing, the state budget of the GDR was proving inadequate, and at the same time it was becoming clear how huge the task was going to be of modernizing the infrastructure of the GDR and repairing the environmental damage.

These problems were to be faced at the same time as the political parties geared up for first the *Volkskammer* elections in March 1990, and then the *Bundestag* elections in December. Chancellor Kohl, whose position in West Germany had been slipping, knew that he needed to win the GDR vote for the CDU. This would make the negotiation of unity easier and it would stand him in better stead in the eventual all-German elections. He and his colleagues in West and East Germany had to make economic promises before March and then deliver enough of them before December. Kohl also had to consider the impact on his West German constituency of a high bill for unification. As for the SPD opposition, its chancellor-candidate Oskar Lafontaine tried to exploit Kohl's earlier weakness, to seize the initiative in the GDR by emphasizing the social-welfare and democratic socialist credentials of his party, and to present what he claimed was a more honest costing of unification. He also took account of West German concern about the numbers of East Germans entering the Federal Republic by suggesting that the incentives for them to do so should be withdrawn and that the money be spent on rebuilding the GDR from within. As is now known, Kohl's strategy succeeded where Lafontaine's failed, but in the process the public costings of unification were manipulated and underestimated. Only after the elections of December 1990 did the Bonn government admit its mistakes.

Before the March *Volkskammer* election Kohl made a promise that the exchange rate between the two German currencies would be on a 1:1 basis, at least for personal savings. This was contrary to the advice given publicly to Kohl by the president of the *Bundesbank*, Karl Otto Pöhl, who argued for a lower, more realistic rate. Meanwhile, the East German CDU leader, Lothar de Maizière, promised that no-one in the GDR would lose by unification. The clear message of both was that a victorious CDU would use the resources of the booming West German economy to guarantee the savings, jobs and wages of the citizens of the GDR. It was a message which contributed to the CDU landslide win.

Negotiations then began on the terms of economic unification. The figure for the costs of unity agreed between the two Germanies was DM 115 billion over five years (DM 22 billion in 1990; DM 35 billion in 1991; DM 28 billion in 1992; DM 20 billion in 1993; and DM 10 billion in 1994). DM 20 billion was to derive from savings in the West German budget, particularly in the hitherto existing costs of the division of Germany. The remaining DM 95 billion, known as the German Unity Fund, was to be raised on the capital markets, half by the Federal government and half by the *Länder* of the Federal Republic. Thus unity was to be achieved at no direct cost to the West German tax-payer, with only a very modest increase in public borrowing, and without antagonizing the regional governments of West Germany.

Lafontaine cast doubt upon the figures, when he suggested that DM 100 billion p.a. was a more likely cost, five times as much as that agreed between finance ministers Waigel and Romberg. He was not the only one to do so. Most independent analyses came out with much higher estimates than those in the inter-German agreement. Already in June 1990, before currency union, a commentary in the *Süddeutsche Zeitung* suggested an extra borrowing requirement in the second half of 1990 of about DM 43 billion, in 1991 of DM 66 billion and in 1992 of DM 70 billion, thus well exceeding in three years the total amount allocated for five.

The crunch came with currency union on July 1, 1990. It was not so much the 1:1 exchange rate for the initial tranches of personal savings which caused the problem. There was something of a spending spree on western goods, but not to the degree feared. It was the 1:1 rate for wages and the 2:1 rate for industry's obligations which were too much to bear. The former, necessary perhaps to keep workers, nevertheless placed huge pressures on concerns now facing western competition, especially when unions began to press for wages nearer West German levels. The latter made the debts of East German industry soar in real terms. The effect of this was to land the *Treuhandanstalt* (Trustee Agency) and ultimately the West German government with the entire amount of approximately DM 120 billion.

This burden was from the past, exacerbated by the terms of the currency union, but it covered nothing of the costs of the future. East German agriculture alone in 1991 needs in the region of DM 19 billion to survive, over half the amount deriving from the German Unity Fund in that year. A study by the Institute for Ecological Economic Research adds then the costs of environmental improvement and restructuring in the fields of energy, transport, waste disposal and water. The estimate is of as much as DM 38–47 billion p.a. for 10 years. Since new investors in East German industry are not to be held responsible for existing environmental damage, these costs will have to be borne primarily by the public purse. As unemployment and short-time working in the former GDR rise they pose a burden on the Federal exchequer. Compensation is payable to those claiming back property confiscated by the communist regime, if that property cannot simply be returned.

And another possibly vast sum may have to be paid for the relocation of the capital in Berlin and in the reallocation of federal functions around the cities of the newly united Germany. The indications are that there is no hurry at the moment to take this expense on board.

To add to the political problem, in the run-up to the all-German elections in December 1990 Kohl and his ministers made firm undertakings that there would be no tax increases to fund unity. Like President Bush before them, they then had to eat their words. Very soon after the elections, Finance Minister Waigel was talking about forms of environmental taxation which might contribute, along perhaps with a privatization programme in West Germany.

It is impossible to put one clear figure on the eventual cost of unification, and other factors have to be taken into account. Germany's financial contribution to the war in the Gulf placed extra strain on state finances at exactly the wrong time. But on the credit side West German profits and employment benefit from the demand unleashed in the former GDR. This has already meant higher than expected tax revenue (an extra DM 4.2 billion in 1990). The overall impact, though is to increase the German public debt (DM 183 billion in June 1989), to reduce Germany's current account surplus (DM 104.1 billion in 1989, and DM 55.1 billion in January–August 1990), and to keep an upward pressure on interest rates to attract capital.

The privatization of the GDR economy

The mechanisms for transferring the almost completely state-owned economy of the GDR into private hands began under the premiership of the last communist leader of the country, Hans Modrow. One of the first major economic measures of his government was the Joint Venture decree of January 1990. Its purpose was to allow foreign capital into the GDR in order to stimulate the economy, without allowing a complete sell-out of domestic industry. It permitted foreign investment in a GDR concern of between 20% and 49%, but a higher proportion (effectively anything below 100%) could be allowed if this was seen to be in the interests of the national economy or was in small and medium-sized concerns. The de Maizière administration, with a stronger free-market orientation, placed less emphasis on the necessity for foreign investment to take place in co-operation with a GDR partner, and after economic and then political union these regulations became irrelevant. The privatization process became, however, no easier.

The Trust Agency (Treuhandanstalt). The body which was to effect the privatization was the Trustee Agency (*Treuhandanstalt*). This was established by the Modrow government in March 1990 as a public institution, subordinate to the government, and the new legal owner of all the businesses formerly classified as "people's concerns" (VEB) and "combines" (*Kombinate*). These and other categories within the state-owned economy were transformed either into limited liability companies (GmbH) or joint-stock companies (*Aktiengesellschaften* — AG). Excluded were the public enterprises of the *Deutsche Post* (postal and telephone service), the *Deutsche Reichsbahn* (railways), and the administration of roads and waterways. The Trustee Agency, initially under the chairmanship of the head of the West German *Bundesbahn*, Reiner Gohlke, sat in East Berlin, where it was subdivided into five trustee companies: for heavy industry, for the investment goods industry, for the consumer goods industry, for agriculture and forestry, and for trade and the service sector. The Trustee Agency had regional offices in each of the 15 districts (*Bezirke*) of the GDR.

The remit of the Trustee Agency was a large one. It could order enquiries into the operations and finances of the concerns and it could make funds available to restructure them. In the longer term its purpose was to sell them off. The process moved very slowly to begin with. By mid-July 1990 a quarter of the approximately 8,000 concerns involved had still not been transformed into capitalized companies, and of those now legally GmbH or AG, many did not yet have full complements of chairmen, boards and management. Another problem was that companies put in large claims for restructuring funds. The Trustee Agency had to make controversial choices about which businesses were viable in the longer term and should be supported for the time being. For the month of July 1990 alone claims totalled over DM 17 billion, of which 41% were approved.

The slow progress made by the Trustee Agency, the emphasis which it was forced to place on keeping ailing industries going rather than on selling them, and the accusations made that bureaucrats and managers still in place from the old system were hampering advance all took their toll, and only four weeks after his appointment Reiner Gohlke resigned. He said that the task of privatization was more difficult than he had originally assumed and that the GDR economy was in chaos. Gohlke was replaced by Detlev Rohwedder, chairman of Hoesch steel and already chairman of the Trustee Agency's supervisory board. Despite voicing many qualms himself about the efficacy of the Trustee Agency in the face of its enormous task, Rohwedder was persuaded by the West German government to carry on into 1991.

Even at the end of 1990 the progress made by the Trustee Agency was very limited. In addition to the "old" debts of East German industry, the Trustee Agency had paid out DM 28 billion in liquidity credits, unsure how much of this would ever be repaid by ailing companies. Its revenue so far from the proceeds of sales was only DM 2.5 billion, so the original aim of financing the whole operation through sales is a long way off. In October 1990 Detlev Rohwedder had estimated the assets of the Trustee Agency at DM 600 billion, but this now seems an over-estimate. By the end of the year the number of firms sold off was in hundreds rather than thousands.

Property claims. One of the main reasons why most East German concerns failed to excite immediate interest on the part of western investors was the question of property rights. Would-be purchasers were afraid that any property they might acquire would subsequently be claimed back by a former owner expropriated by the previous regime. The two German governments tried to regulate this matter in an agreement signed in June 1990. Under it no claims could be made for the restitution of property confiscated during the occupation period 1945–49. Property confiscated since without compensation would in principle be restored to the original owners or their heirs. If, however, land or premises had been converted into public amenities (for instance, a housing estate) or been absorbed into some larger economic enterprise, compensation would be given instead. Also, if GDR citizens had acquired property in an honest manner, the original owners would similarly receive compensation in lieu of the property itself. This was to avoid acrimony over East Germans being evicted from their homes, farms or businesses by returning former owners.

By the beginning of 1991 this agreement was seen as not having been enough to encourage investment, and new regulations were drafted by the Ministry of Justice and laid before the *Bundestag* in February. It was noted that the Trust Agency and the new *Land* governments had been faced with great difficulties over the property question. More than 1,000,000 restitution claims had been received for 1,500,000 properties. At least 9,000 claims related to small and medium-sized businesses which were now part of combines in the hands of the Trust Agency. Estimates of the extent of the claims ranged from 40% to nearly one half of all property in the former GDR. The purpose of the new draft law was to simplify procedures both for claimants and for those wishing to buy East German properties and businesses. The Trust Agency was to have greater scope in making suitable sale or rental arrangements for each individual case. Another change was the inclusion of the years of the Third Reich (1933–45) within the time for which claims could be made. The occupation years were still excluded.

Investment in the GDR. After the initial flurry of business interest in the GDR dating from the breaching of the Berlin Wall, most West German companies came to view the GDR primarily as an extended domestic market rather than as a focus for major investment. The president of the (West) German Chamber of Trade and Industry (DIHT), Hans-Peter Stihl, criticized the GDR's remaining legislative barriers for this, but in addition to any effect from this quarter there were the general uncertainties and the unwillingness to get involved before some of the mess was sorted out. As far as the added market of about 16,000,000 people was concerned, it could largely be supplied from existing capacity in West Germany.

This applied less to certain financial, service and infrastructural sectors. The large West German banks, particularly the *Deutsche* and the *Dresdner*, moved in smartly to develop a network of branches throughout the GDR, and *Allianz* insurance pre-empted its competitors by taking 49% (the maximum at that stage) of the state-run insurance system. The three electricity giants of the Federal Republic also stepped in to take over the GDR power network; *RWE* of Essen, *Bayernwerk* of Munich, and *PreussenElektra* of Hanover were on their way towards an agreement with the GDR, but they ran up against difficulties with the West German monopolies commission. Nearly half of the gas monopoly, *Verbundnetz AG*, was sold to *Ruhrgas AG* and *BEB Erdgas*, with the remainder being offered to seven other German and foreign interests, including *Wintershall AG* and *British Gas plc*. *Lufthansa* was to have taken over the East German airline, *Interflug*, but then withdrew from negotiations.

The West German *Telekom* section of the *Bundespost* and the East German *Deutsche Post* planned a crash programme to develop the woefully inadequate East German telephone system. The aim was to instal 100,000 instruments in 1990, and through glass-fibre cables to increase the inter-German capacity to 600,000 calls per day. They intend further to build modern telephone exchanges in nine cities, so that not all calls have to pass as at present through East Berlin or Magdeburg. Also to be developed are mobile telephones and David, Diva and Dasat satellite systems. In 1990 the *Deutsche Post* planned to spend DM 540 million (including DM 240 million borrowed from *Telekom*) and for *Telekom* to spend DM 110 million in the GDR. The total cost of the programme is estimated at DM 55 billion over seven years, to bring the GDR up to the standards of the Federal Republic. DM 30 billion of the total is to be raised on the capital markets from 1991. Further to ease the situation, the postal monopoly of telephone communications between the two states was lifted temporarily in order to permit satellite communications.

Although the emphasis in West German involvement in the East German economy has been on infrastructural problems, some major companies have set manufacturing projects in motion. Car-makers have been in the forefront. *Volkswagen*, spending DM 5 billion, plans an assembly plant producing 250,000 cars per year from 1994. This will be at Mosel, north of Zwickau, the town renowned for manufacturing the two-stroke Trabant. *Daimler-Benz* has been negotiating the takeover of the IFA works at Ludwigsfelde, south of Berlin. This would cost DM 1 billion, with a further DM 1–2 billion set aside for other investment. *Opel*, the German subsidiary of *General Motors*, plans to spend DM 1 billion on a 150,000 cars p.a. plant at Eisenach. This would replace the *Wartburg* production in the town, which has been axed by the Trustee Agency. Amongst other companies which have announced major investment in East Germany or are in the process of negotiating deals are *GKN*, *BP*, *Coca Cola*, *McDonalds*, *Gervais Danone*, *Elf Aquitaine*, *Villeroy & Boch*, *Solvay* and *RMC*.

Although these projects augur well for the future, there are problems involved. Even though the German government has made it clear that investors are not financially responsible for the environmental clean-up required, most have refused to take over the premises and plant of the East German companies; they are instead developing new greenfield factories. This leaves the problem of the old sites.

Other forms of new enterprise are also developing, particularly in the retailing and service sector. Here West German companies are establishing their presence in the towns and cities of East Germany, and some small East German entrepreneurs are establishing themselves. In 1990 an estimated 227,000 firms were founded. Most of these were very small, however, and will have difficulty in the face of experienced West German competition. The news is also not good for some established East German operations. *Pentacon* cameras of Dresden is closing, as are many breweries, displaced by demand for West German beer.

Key Economic Sectors

Agriculture

East German agriculture was overwhelmingly socialized, with nearly 95% of agricultural land organized in co-operatives (LPG) or state farms (VEG). Private production, including that on the individual plots of co-operative farmers, did, however, contribute significantly to the supply of eggs, livestock, fruit and vegetables. The mid-1980s had seen record cereal harvests (11,660,000 tonnes in 1986), but there had been a decline since then (10,800,000 tonnes in 1989). In any case, yields were only moderate in comparison with West Germany, some 15% lower in the case of wheat.

Revolution and unification threw the agricultural sector of the GDR into deep trouble. For a long time protected by subsidy from the rigours of the market, it faced an immediate slump in demand. Once the doors opened to West German foodstuffs on July 1, 1990, consumers avoided domestic produce. Rightly or wrongly, they considered it of inferior quality, and even price cuts failed to move it. In fact, in many shops GDR products were not available. West German milk went on sale, while GDR farmers poured theirs onto the fields. In the summer of 1990 it looked as though the total collapse of agriculture was imminent. Funds were lacking for all aspects of business, including paying wages, and the de Maizière government had to step in with emergency measures to hold the situation in check. These included a deal with the USSR to supply agricultural produce, particularly pork, from surplus production.

The agriculture of the GDR also suffered from structural problems which will take a long and painful time to solve. First, there were proportionately more people working in agriculture than in West Germany, 14 full-time workers per 100 hectares of land, compared to only seven in the West. Some of these were in ancillary functions in the co-operatives, but even so overmanning was high and unemployment soon bore down heavily on agriculture. Second, agricultural production was divided too rigidly into arable and livestock, which made for expensive and artificial flaws in the system and for over-specialized agricultural workers. Third, the environmental damage done by and to agriculture is bad for productivity and bad for marketing in an increasingly environmentally-conscious Europe. And fourth, as the entire economy is privatized, so the unclear property relations in the agricultural sphere become a problem. Strictly speaking, members of co-operatives did not surrender ownership of their land, but only the use of it. This means that larger co-operative farms could once more be divided up in ways which are not economically rational.

The Bonn government and the European Community have had to make transitional arrangements to prevent the collapse of East German agriculture. EC rules are to be introduced gradually in the region, and the government is to use intervention buying, production cutbacks, and the export of foodstuffs in an attempt to ease the transition.

Ironically, the performance of East German arable production was very good in 1990. The cereal harvest of 11,830,000 tonnes was a new record, exceeding even 1986. This, and the drop in domestic demand for fodder grain, has led to excess stocks. East German and West German grain production together make Germany the leading producer of barley in the EC and second only to France in wheat.

Manufacturing industry

Already before the revolution in the GDR certain important industrial sectors were showing signs of strain. These included chemicals, aspects of engineering, and light industry. These and other sectors suffered from the excessive attention being given in investment terms

Table 11:   Gross industrial output by sector, 1990 (index: 1989=100)

	May	June	July	August	September
Energy and fuels	92.3	87.9	59.9	52.3	61.6
Chemicals	85.2	79.9	59.8	48.5	49.8
Metallurgy	90.3	77.0	39.7	33.1	34.5
Building materials	97.4	97.3	63.0	40.6	34.3
Water industry	105.8	110.1	89.6	100.8	100.3
Machinery and vehicles	97.5	103.8	71.2	64.2	62.6
Electricals	98.9	93.4	67.3	53.3	53.3
Light industry	87.1	75.2	48.9	44.6	46.2
Textiles	81.2	72.2	48.7	44.9	45.7
Food	86.7	72.0	42.3	38.6	37.9
TOTAL	91.0	84.5	57.9	49.2	48.9

to microelectronics. After the changes, industrial production plummeted in almost every field. The worst hit sectors have been building materials, metallurgy, the food industry, textiles and light industry (see Table 11).

By the beginning of 1991 few major manufacturers had actually closed down, but all were being propped up by liquidity credits from the Trustee Agency and were keeping on staff on short-time. However, many closures are expected in 1991, with *Wartburg* following *Pentacon* cameras into obscurity. Some small private enterprises will emerge, but they will not primarily be in manufacturing. West German investment will produce new production lines in East Germany, particularly in the car industry, but the effect on unemployment will only be gradual.

Transport

The transport infrastructure of East Germany is quite woeful. Despite a programme of electrification in the 1980s, the railways of the *Deutsche Reichsbahn* move unbearably slowly. The new partnership with the *Bundesbahn* has a huge task ahead. The state of the urban and inter-urban roads of the region testifies to the reluctance of the old regime to let people travel anywhere. Since the opening of the inter-German border the pitted two- or even one-lane remnants of 1930s motorways have been overburdened by increased domestic traffic and by that of West German visitors. The accident rate has soared.

Hitherto faced by 15-year waiting lists for new Trabants and Wartburgs from domestic production, East Germans have now come to dominate the German used-car market. Many are also buying new western cars. This has meant a proliferation in the former GDR of motor dealers, petrol stations and accessory shops.

The East German airline *Interflug* was to have been taken over by *Lufthansa*. Other western airlines were also taking an interest. The Trustee Agency failed, however, to set attractive enough terms at the right time, and *Interflug* will now probably be liquidated.

Finance

In the course of the revolution in the GDR the previous state monopoly on banking was broken up, and from October 3, 1990 the finances of the "new *Länder*" fell under the general budget of the Federal Republic. Even before unification the major West German banks began to move into East Germany in order to set up premises and to capture personal and business accounts. They were very cautious at first, however, to fund investment.

The political change also unlocked huge demand on the part of the East German population, and people did have savings to spend. Under the old regime staple goods had been very cheap and all others difficult to find. Excess income therefore found its way into savings accounts (c. M 163 billion at end April 1990), which were in large measure converted into Deutschemark on July 1, 1990.

In the course of 1990 it became clear that even before the revolution the state budget of the GDR had been more frail than the official picture had led to believe. The surpluses announced had been based on a high degree of hard-currency borrowing. Gross debt at the end of 1989 was approximately $22.3 billion, and by March 1990 it had increased to about $32 billion. During 1990 the ability of the East German government to remain within the strictures of the economic union agreement broke down, and several supplementary budgets in Bonn were required. The crisis of the municipal and *Land* governments of East Germany by 1991 is even worse, and major help from Bonn is needed if they are not to break down entirely.

Energy

The GDR was heavily dependent on its sole large indigenous energy resource, lignite or brown coal. In 1988, 85% of electricity production was from this source, a proportion which had actually been rising during the 1980s. Nuclear energy provided nearly 10% of the total, a fall from 12% in 1980. Both these sources pose major problems. Lignite reserves, though still plentiful, are increasingly difficult to exploit, and the mining of them and the burning of the fuel have caused massive environmental destruction. This is evident in many parts of the country, where the air is thick with brown dust, and forests are denuded by acid rain. Nuclear power is not a satisfactory alternative because the safety levels at the power stations have been discovered to be quite inadequate. For these reasons, both a series of lignite power stations and the nuclear reactors at Greifswald and Rheinsberg are to be closed down.

The unification of Germany has forced East Germany to look westward rather than eastward for its energy future. The electricity and gas industries are currently being taken over by West German interests. *Vereinigte Energiewerke* (United Energy Works) has been founded to manage the distribution of electricity in East Germany, and West German electricity companies will gain a majority holding in the course of 1991. *Ruhrgas* and *Wintershall* (BASF) are competing to control the gas industry. Meanwhile Soviet oil exports to East Germany have been falling sharply. In the last quarter of 1990 supplies were set to reach only 1,850,000 tonnes, instead of the 4,500,000 tonnes originally envisaged.

New technology

The old Ministry of Electrical Engineering and Electronics was the darling of the old regime. It attracted the lion's share of investment and achieved remarkable official growth rates. On an index of 1980=100, net production rose by 1988 to 285. This was by far the most dynamic of the industrial ministries. Two main areas were of importance: industrial robots, which were in many cases no more than advanced machine tools by western standards, and chip production for indigenous computers. The problem was that the industry sucked investment from the rest of the economy in order to produce technology already outdated in the West and Far East. For instance, at the end of 1988 *NEC* (Japan) was producing 4,000,000 1 Megabyte chips per month. The first example of one from East German manufacture was with great pomp presented to Erich Honecker in September 1988.

Foreign Economic Relations

The communist regime of the German Democratic Republic made analysis of its foreign trade performance very difficult indeed, far more so than did its partners in the CMEA. The statistics issuing from East Berlin were incomplete and implausible.

In the first place, trade was not broken down by country into imports and exports.

This made it very difficult to assess the GDR's overall trade balance and the relationship between its CMEA and non-CMEA transactions. The problem was compounded by the fact that even the turnover figures country-by-country did not correspond to OECD mirror figures on a discernible pattern of exchange rates. This led to discrepancies between the relative trade volumes derived from western and from GDR statistics. According to the East Germans, for instance, Switzerland was their main capitalist trading partner after West Germany, whereas the OECD figures showed France taking that place. More seriously, the trade account with the Federal Republic of Germany assumed a rough parity between the two German currencies, an assumption which was far from reality. The result was that inter-German trade appeared lower down the list of trade turnover than other observations suggested.

There were other complications. Trade with the CMEA was largely on a barter basis and the money figures put on deals were sometimes in transferable rubles, sometimes in Valuta Marks (the GDR's foreign trade accounting unit, not entirely equivalent to the domestic Mark), and sometimes in the currency of the trading partner (Forints, Zloty etc.). In all instances it was not necessarily the case that actual money had changed hands; a notional value was being placed on complex deals. Furthermore, an undisclosed amount of trade with the USSR appears to have been in hard currency. This is still impossible to assess, as is hard currency trade with the Third World.

The trade pattern alleged by the old statistics was as presented in Table 12. Socialist countries (primarily CMEA) accounted for 69.1% of the GDR's foreign trade turnover in 1988, the industrialized countries of the capitalist world 27.6%, and the developing countries 3.3%. These proportions had been roughly stable for about two decades, although since 1983 the proportion of trade with the socialist world had risen once more after a decline before that. Within non-socialist trade that with developing countries had been in relative decline.

Table 13, again from the pre-1990 GDR statistics, shows the ostensible dominance of trade with the USSR (37.5% of total trade turnover in 1988), with Czechoslovakia (8.2%) and the Federal Republic of Germany (7.0%) a long way behind. Trade with other OECD states seemed of scarcely any significance.

These statistics, like those on the domestic economy, were bogus. They probably had as their main purpose a fudging of the crucial importance of inter-German trade to the GDR economy. With the ouster of Erich Honecker and the economic manipulator Günter

Table 12:   GDR foreign trade turnover 1985–88, according to old GDR statistics
(billions of Valuta Marks)

	1985	*1986*	*1987*	*1988*	%
Socialist countries	119.0	122.6	121.8	122.5	69.1
Industrial capitalist countries	52.9	51.4	48.0	48.9	27.6
Developing countries	8.2	7.9	6.7	5.9	3.3
TOTAL	180.2	182.0	176.5	177.3	100.0

Source: Statistisches Jahrbuch der Deutschen Demokratischen Republik 1986–89.

Table 13:   GDR foreign trade turnover by country 1985-88, according to old GDR statistics
(billions of Valuta Marks)

	1985	1986	1987	1988	%
USSR	69.9	70.6	68.5	66.5	37.5
Czechoslovakia	13.0	13.3	14.3	14.6	8.2
West Germany	15.0	13.1	12.5	12.4	7.0
Poland	9.8	11.0	11.4	12.3	6.9
Hungary	8.8	9.3	9.3	10.0	5.6
Bulgaria	5.2	5.7	5.7	5.7	3.2
Romania	5.0	5.2	5.1	5.1	2.9
Switzerland[1]	3.2	3.0	3.1	4.0	2.3
Austria	4.3	3.1	3.1	3.5	2.0
France	2.7	2.8	2.9	3.1	1.7
Yugoslavia	2.5	2.5	2.7	2.9	1.6
Netherlands	1.9	1.6	1.9	2.9	1.6
Cuba	2.1	2.3	2.6	2.5	1.4
United Kingdom	2.8	2.1	2.2	2.3	1.3
Belgium[2]	2.4	1.6	1.4	1.8	1.0
Sweden	1.7	1.4	2.0	1.8	1.0
Italy	1.0	1.3	1.3	1.5	0.8
China	0.8	1.1	1.1	1.3	0.7
Japan	1.6	1.2	1.5	1.3	0.7
Others	26.5	29.8	23.9	21.8	12.3
TOTAL	180.2	182.0	176.5	177.3	100.0

Notes: [1]Includes Liechtenstein.
[2]Includes Luxembourg.
Source: Statistisches Jahrbuch der Deutschen Demokratischen Republik 1986–89.

Mittag and then of SED rule entirely, the figures were entirely recast by the renamed Statistical Office of the GDR. Although, no doubt, future information will further enhance the picture, closer estimates can now be made of the structure and development of foreign trade in the last years of the GDR.

Table 14 shows the position in 1988–89, as now recalculated. The difference is remarkable. In 1988 turnover with West Germany at 19.7% of the total was much closer to that with the USSR (24.5%) than the 7.0% and 37.5% respectively published under the old regime. The position narrowed further in 1989 to bring trade with West Germany (20.6% of the total) very close indeed to that with the USSR (22.9%). Other hard currency trade also figured much more prominently than had ever been admitted in the past, with CMEA partners Bulgaria and Romania much lower down the list than they had been before. In fact in value terms "western industrial nations" (including West Germany) took 48.5% of GDR exports in 1989 and provided 53.1% of GDR imports. Nearly one third of GDR trade was conducted with the EC.

Naturally these new figures do not alter the fact that in volume terms the GDR traded vastly more goods within the CMEA than with other countries, but the old figures did not present the picture in volume terms either. The worth to the GDR of its western

Table 14:   GDR foreign trade 1988–89, according to new GDR statistics
(hard currency value in billions of Marks)

| | 1988 | | | | | 1989 | | | | |
	Exp.	Imp.	Bal.	Turnover	%	Exp.	Imp.	Bal.	Turnover	%
USSR	33.5	34.5	−1.0	68.0	24.5	33.5	31.9	1.6	65.4	22.9
West Germany	29.0	25.7	3.3	54.7	19.7	30.2	28.6	1.6	58.8	20.6
Czechoslovakia	8.0	6.9	1.1	14.8	5.4	7.7	6.7	1.1	14.4	5.0
Poland	6.2	6.1	0.1	12.4	4.5	6.4	6.4	0.0	12.8	4.5
France	4.0	3.5	0.5	7.4	2.7	4.4	6.1	−1.7	10.5	3.7
Hungary	5.6	4.7	0.9	10.4	3.7	5.6	4.9	0.7	10.5	3.7
Switzerland[1]	2.2	7.1	−4.8	9.3	3.4	3.5	6.8	−3.3	10.3	3.6
Austria	2.3	5.9	−3.5	8.2	2.9	2.4	6.6	−4.2	9.0	3.1
Netherlands	2.3	4.5	−2.2	6.8	2.5	2.7	3.6	−0.9	6.3	2.2
Romania	2.7	2.4	0.3	5.1	1.9	2.9	2.7	0.2	5.5	1.9
United Kingdom	2.6	2.8	−0.3	5.4	1.9	3.0	2.4	0.6	5.4	1.9
Bulgaria	3.1	2.7	0.4	5.8	2.1	2.8	2.7	0.1	5.4	1.9
Yugoslavia	2.2	3.1	−0.9	5.3	1.9	2.2	2.8	−0.6	5.0	1.7
Sweden	2.3	1.9	0.4	4.3	1.5	2.3	1.9	0.3	4.2	1.5
China	2.0	2.0	0.1	4.0	1.4	2.1	2.0	0.1	4.1	1.4
Italy	1.2	2.3	−1.1	3.5	1.3	1.4	2.7	−1.4	4.1	1.4
Belgium[2]	2.1	2.2	−0.1	4.3	1.6	1.9	2.0	−0.2	3.9	1.4
Cuba	1.4	1.2	0.2	2.5	0.9	1.4	1.3	0.1	2.8	1.0
Others	22.6	22.2	0.4	44.8	16.2	24.8	22.6	2.2	47.3	16.6
TOTAL	135.3	141.7	−6.4	277.0	100.0	141.1	144.7	−3.6	285.8	100.0

Notes: [1]Includes Liechtenstein.
[2]Includes Luxembourg.
Source: Statistisches Jahrbuch der Deutschen Demokratischen Republik 1990.

trade, particularly that with West Germany, was grossly underestimated in the statistics, for political reasons.

The structure of GDR exports and imports according to categories of goods has also been reclassified by the Statistical Office. In 1989, 36.5% of exports and 31.6% of imports were machinery, vehicles and transport equipment; 18.7% of exports and 18.6% of imports were finished goods; 12.1% of exports and 9.0% of imports were chemicals; and 8.3% of exports and 14.5% of imports were fuels and lubricants. The only changes of any consequence in the second half of the 1980s had been a rise in the importation of machinery and transport equipment, and a halving of exports and imports of fuels and lubricants. This last can be explained by the fact that the GDR used to depend for large hard currency earnings on the import, refining and re-export of mineral oil. This trade declined as price relationships became less favourable.

GDR engineering exports were most important for the other CMEA countries and the developing countries, much less so for developed countries, which provided a good deal of plant. Within the CMEA, particularly in relations with the USSR, the GDR had a role of providing relatively advanced quality equipment in exchange for raw materials and semi-finished goods. Exports to the developed countries (primarily West Germany) were — after oil re-exports declined from 1986 — largely finished goods, for example, furniture, toys, and clothing.

By 1989 GDR foreign trade was as sluggish as the rest of the economy, with exports as judged by the new statistics rising by 4.3% in value and imports by 2.1%. In dollar and volume terms these increases must have been even more marginal. The GDR's deficit with OECD countries (including West Germany) rose from $471 million in 1988 to $707 million in 1989, partly due to increased imports from France, Italy and Austria. Trade with West Germany saw exports up 6.1% in Deutschemark terms and imports up 12.0%, but in dollar terms exports were down 1.2% and imports up 4.3%. This was a continuation of the undynamic path of recent years. GDR trade with other CMEA countries saw exports down by 0.2% and imports by 3.2%.

If new openness on the part of the authorities makes analysis of the later 1980s somewhat easier, that of foreign trade of 1990 is further complicated by the political developments of the year. From July 1 currency and economic union and from October 3, 1990 full political unity meant that the contention over the decades by the West Germans that inter-German trade was not foreign trade became an undisputable reality. This and the transition to full Deutschemark accounting complicates assessment of performance in 1990 in relation to previous years. The GDR Statistical Office has published figures for foreign trade in the period January–July 1990 inclusive, expressed now in Deutschemarks. Exports in that period were worth DM 21.2 billion, imports DM 17.4 billion. This represented in comparison with the same period of 1989 a fall in exports of 8% and in imports of 24%. However, these assessments now exclude West Germany and leave the country-by-country

Table 15: GDR foreign trade January–July 1990 (excluding West Germany)
(billions of Deutschemarks)

	Exp.	Imp.	January–July 1990 Bal.	Turnover	%
USSR	9.29	6.96	2.33	16.25	42.1
Czechoslovakia	2.28	1.38	0.91	3.66	9.5
Poland	1.27	1.39	−0.12	2.66	6.9
France	0.44	0.44	−0.00	0.88	2.3
Hungary	1.56	0.98	0.58	2.54	6.6
Switzerland[1]	0.31	0.61	−0.31	0.92	2.4
Austria	0.18	0.57	−0.39	0.75	1.9
Netherlands	0.28	0.39	−0.11	0.66	1.7
Romania	0.85	0.35	0.49	1.20	3.1
United Kingdom	0.34	0.29	0.05	0.62	1.6
Bulgaria	0.91	0.51	0.40	1.42	3.7
Others	3.51	3.54	−0.03	7.05	18.3
TOTAL	21.20	17.40	3.80	38.60	100.0

Note: [1]Includes Liechtenstein.
Source: Statistisches Amt der Deutschen Demokratischen Republik.

breakdown looking like an exaggeration of the old communist statistics: 79% of exports were to CMEA countries, and 69% of imports were from them. The USSR accounted for 42.1% of turnover, and Czechoslovakia for 9.5%. Full details are in Table 15.

In the first half of 1990 (before economic union) GDR exports to West Germany were worth DM 3.93 billion, up 12.4% on the same period in 1989. Imports more than doubled (up 116.3%) to DM 7.85 billion. Combining these two sets of figures the West German share of total turnover in the first half of 1990 was an estimated 26.3%, the Soviet share 31.0%, both figures up markedly on the corresponding ones for 1989. The surge in West German supplies to the GDR was, of course, a result of the open border and the huge demand for consumer goods in the GDR. The figures for the first half of 1990 show massive increases in West German deliveries of foodstuffs, cars, clothes, tobacco and a whole range of other goods.

In non-German trade in the months January–July 1990 GDR exports only increased in food and livestock (by 20%), items which were being replaced in the GDR itself by West German produce. GDR exports of fuels and lubricants were down 53%. Imports of food were cut by 43%, and of engineering and electrical products and vehicles by 30%. The whole process represented the integration of the GDR into one German economy.

From July 1, 1990 inter-German trade was no longer foreign trade for the GDR and it is not yet possible to quantify developments. What is clear is that West German produce flooded the GDR market, while East German concerns strove to fulfil remaining export orders, especially to CMEA countries. The unleashing of demand in the GDR and the stimulation of demand in West Germany also meant a large increase in total German imports. In November 1990 the western part of Germany had a trade surplus of DM 762 million, compared to DM 10.6 billion in November 1989. Eastern Germany had a surplus of DM 2.5 billion, but this figure now excludes West German supplies and includes the final phases of filling previous CMEA orders.

Principal Personalities

Berghofer, Wolfgang. Born 1943, mayor of Dresden from January 1986, Berghofer was an associate of Hans Modrow. In October 1989 he was prepared to talk to opposition groups about the growing crisis. After Krenz's fall, Berghofer became a deputy chairman of the SED-PDS, but he resigned from the party on January 21, 1990. In April he faced charges of electoral fraud, in connection with the local elections of May 1989. On May 23, 1990 Dr Herbert Wagner of the CDU replaced Berghofer as mayor of Dresden.

Bergmann-Pohl, Sabine. Born 1946. A medical doctor who had been a member of the CDU since 1981, was propelled into prominence by being elected president of the *Volkskammer* on April 5, 1990. Acting head of state, she undertook a reconciliatory visit to Israel in June 1990 in the company of *Bundestag* president Rita Süssmuth (also CDU). Dr Bergmann-Pohl entered the *Bundestag* after German unity, and joined Chancellor Kohl's cabinet as minister without portfolio. She was elected on the CDU *Land* list for Berlin in December 1990, but did not receive a post in Kohl's reshuffled cabinet.

Bohley, Bärbel. Born 1945. An artist and peace campaigner, Frau Bohley came into conflict with the old GDR regime on several occasions. She was arrested in December 1983 and again in January 1988. Forced out of the country, she argued successfully to be allowed to return. In the autumn of 1989 she was a co-founder of New Forum, the initial impact of which subsided as calls for German unity increased in the GDR. Frau Bohley was critical of rapid union and the introduction of capitalism.

Böhme, Ibrahim. Born 1944 and brought up in an orphanage, Böhme followed a variety of jobs and professions. He joined the SED in 1967, but left in 1976 in protest at the expulsion of singer Wolf Biermann. In the autumn of 1989 he was a co-founder of the SDP (later SPD) and took part in the Round Table discussions. In February 1990 he was elected SPD chairman, and looked a prospective prime minister as the SPD initially rode high in the opinion polls. The CDU was nevertheless victorious, and Böhme's defeat was compounded a week after the elections by accusations that he had been a Stasi informer. He temporarily laid down his party posts and *Volkskammer* seat, pending investigations. Although these showed no proof of his complicity, Böhme's position was irretrievably weakened and his health suffered. He resigned from the party leadership in April and from the party executive in December.

De Maizière, Lothar. In the space of five months, Lothar de Maizière emerged from relative obscurity as a lawyer, musician and lay church leader to be Prime Minister of the GDR in early April 1990. His path to prominence depended on the autumn 1989 revolution and the election campaign and CDU victory in the spring of 1990. Born in 1940, the son of a lawyer, he joined the CDU as early as 1956. He studied first music (becoming a professional viola player), then law. From 1976 he was a member of the council of lawyers' associations, moving up to become a deputy chairman in 1987. He was involved in the defence of dissidents, and during this period came to know well Gregor Gysi, later chairman of the SED. De Maizière was also active within the evangelical church, becoming a vice president of the synod in 1986.

The autumn of 1989 brought crisis to all the political parties of the GDR, and when the longstanding chairman of the CDU, Gerald Götting, was forced to resign, de Maizière was elected in his stead in November. He was considered to be relatively untainted by the CDU's collaboration with the SED. Also in November de Maizière was appointed to the new Modrow cabinet as a Deputy Prime Minister with responsibility for Church Affairs. During the run-up to the March 18, 1990 elections, de Maizière resisted demands from Chancellor Kohl that the CDU withdraw from co-operation with the SED-PDS. He did, however, take his party into the conservative Alliance for Germany with the DSU and DA. The election result, more of a triumph for Kohl than for de Maizière, nevertheless propelled the latter into the limelight. For several weeks he appeared undecided as to whether to aspire to the premiership himself. However, negotiations began with the SPD and the Liberals on a grand coalition, and when the *Volkskammer* met on April 5, 1990 de Maizière was charged with forming a government. He announced his cabinet four days later.

Up to that point his relations with Chancellor Kohl had not been marked by cordiality, and he pledged his party to defending vigorously the interests of the GDR population. Once in power, his co-operation with Kohl increased as the two prepared the way for first economic then full political union. His government laid the ground for the abandonment of the socialist structures of the GDR, but was beset by mounting economic chaos. In the summer of 1990 this exacerbated conflict within the coalition and led to trouble with Kohl as well. In early August de Maizière embarrassed Kohl by announcing that the two of them planned to bring all-German elections forward. This was thwarted by West German constitutional requirements. Later in the same month de Maizière purged his cabinet of all three ministers in charge of the economy (Finance, Economy and Agriculture), prompting the departure from the coalition of the SPD. De Maizière did not reappoint ministers and took over the Foreign Ministry himself from Markus Meckel.

With German unity, de Maizière's post became redundant, and he joined Kohl's cabinet as Minister without Portfolio. On December 2, 1990 he was elected to the *Bundestag* on the *Land* list for Brandenburg and might have expected high office in the new government, had not the shadows of the past closed in once more. Even before he became GDR Prime Minister, de Maizière had been touched by the Stasi scandal which brought down two party leaders, Wolfgang Schnur (DA) and Ibrahim Böhme (SPD). He was accused of having been a collaborator with the Stasi under the code-name "Czerny". He denied this vigorously and survived. However, shortly after the all-German elections, renewed allegations were made in the press and although there was no concrete proof, de Maizière felt compelled to withdraw from public life. On December 17, 1990 he resigned from government and as CDU deputy chairman. Chancellor Kohl however continued to express trust in him.

Diestel, Peter-Michael. Born 1952. From his base as General Secretary of the DSU, Diestel, a lawyer, was appointed Minister of the Interior by Lothar de Maizière in April 1990. He very soon began to provoke public controversy and dissent from within his own party. He was accused of being too lenient with former members of the Stasi, even allegedly consulting them about how to dismantle the security apparatus. On May 22, 1990 the DSU *Volkskammer* fraction voted for the removal of Diestel from office, but he and de Maizière refused to comply. On June 30 Diestel resigned from the party, but continued his ministerial career until the day of German unity. He did not enter the *Bundestag* either in October or December.

Ebeling, Hans-Wilhelm. Born 1934. Founder chairman of the German Social Union (DSU). This was a party based in the south of the GDR, which for a time looked capable of developing a presence in Saxony comparable to that of the CSU in Bavaria. Ebeling, pastor of the Thomas Church in Leipzig, responded to the *Wende* in the GDR by founding in December 1989 a Christian Social Party of Germany. This he took into a merger with other groups, forming the DSU on January 20, 1990 with himself as chairman. The emphasis of the party was on "Christian values", German unity, the reestablishment of the old *Länder*, and the social market economy. On February 1, 1990, Ebeling, Lothar de Maizière (CDU) and Wolfgang Schnur (DA) met in West Berlin with Helmut Kohl to prepare a pact between their parties for the forthcoming *Volkskammer* elections. This "Alliance for Germany" was announced on February 5, 1990.

The DSU was not a full participant in the Round Table discussions, but it continued to gain ground in Saxony and Thuringia and performed creditably in the *Volkskammer* elections with 6.3% of the vote and 25 seats. Ebeling became Minister for Economic Co-operation in the de Maizière cabinet, alongside his fellow DSU member Peter-Michael Diestel at the Ministry of the Interior. Ebeling left the DSU chairmanship in April 1990, and the party itself began to fall apart over Diestel's handling of the Stasi issue and other matters. Ebeling, Diestel and others felt that the DSU was moving dangerously towards the right and by the beginning of July they had left the party. Ebeling did not enter the *Bundestag* either after October 3 or after the elections of December 2, 1990.

Eppelmann, Rainer. Born 1943. A Berlin pastor, Eppelmann had been active in the peace movement, and he was strangely appropriate as the last Minister of Defence of the GDR, a post which he expanded to include specific mention of disarmament. Eppelmann's party base was the new Democratic Departure (DA), which he helped to found in October 1989. On December 17 he was replaced as party chairman by Wolfgang Schnur, but he continued to play a prominent role as one of the DA representatives at the Round Table discussions and as a minister without portfolio in the Modrow "government of national responsibility" from February 1990. When Schnur resigned in disgrace on March 14 Eppelmann took over once more.

In de Maizière's cabinet Eppelmann was appointed Minister of Disarmament and Defence and had the task of supervising the dismantling of the National People's Army. The way he did this caused some surprise, as he continued to place large orders for weapons. Meanwhile, the DA was collapsing from within and Eppelmann resigned from it. By the *Bundestag* election of December 1990 he was a successful candidate for the CDU in Fürstenwalde, Brandenburg.

Gerlach, Manfred. Born 1928. From the final resignation of Egon Krenz in December 1989 to the first meeting of the democratically elected *Volkskammer* in April 1990, Manfred Gerlach was acting head of state (Chairman of the State Council) of the GDR. As such, he had largely ceremonial functions. He had been prominent in GDR politics for a long time. From 1967 to 1990 he was chairman of the LDPD, the "liberal" party in alliance with the ruling SED, and was a loyal deputy to Honecker. In the autumn of 1989, however, Gerlach began to speak of the need for new ideas in the GDR and was the first leader of one of the "Democratic Block" parties to do so. The LDPD left the Block on December 5, 1989. Gerlach had meanwhile failed to be elected chairman of the *Volkskammer* on November 13, but he was elected acting chairman of the State Council on December 6. He had, unlike most other politicians of the old regime, survived into the new, but he was criticized for opportunism and an unconvincing sudden change of heart.

On February 10, 1990 Gerlach gave up the LDPD leadership to Rainer Ortleb and on April 5 he was replaced as acting head of state by the new chairman of the *Volkskammer*, Sabine Bergmann-Pohl. From that point Gerlach retired from politics.

Gysi, Gregor. Born 1948 in Berlin to a partly Jewish family. His father, Klaus Gysi, had been a communist before the Nazi period and after the war rose within the SED to become party secretary for religious affairs. A souring of relations with the churches, however, forced his resignation in July 1988.

Gregor Gysi trained as a lawyer in the 1960s and joined the SED in 1967. From 1971 he practised as a lawyer and in 1988 became head of the council of lawyers' associations. He used his legal skills to defend dissidents in conflict with the authorities and this gave him a reputation for fair-mindedness and willingness to countenance reform. Gysi was a member of the group of party activists which engineered the downfall of Krenz, and he was a member of the temporary commission which succeeded him. On December 9, 1989 he was elected to the unenviable post of Chairman of the SED, and at the party congress waved a broom in the air to show his intentions. He led a party committee of 100 members, practically all of whom were new to the party leadership. Almost all of the old guard, including those who had instigated the *Wende* (turning point), were expelled from the party. Gysi tried to save the party by stressing its democratic potential (it changed its name to the PDS: Party of Democratic Socialism) and its break with the past. He fought a good election campaign in the circumstances, and the PDS emerged with 16.4% of the votes and 66 seats.

Gysi entered the *Bundestag* after German unity on October 3, 1990, as a delegate for the PDS. Later that month he was forced to admit that PDS funds of around DM 100 million had been syphoned off illegally to an account in the USSR. He denied any personal involvement and emerged relatively unscathed. On December 2, 1990, he was elected PDS member of the *Bundestag* for Berlin-Hellersdorf-Marzahn.

Honecker, Erich. Was the second leader of the GDR, succeeding Walter Ulbricht as First Secretary (later General Secretary) of the SED in May 1971, and becoming head of state (Chairman of the State Council) in 1976. Honecker supervised the entry of the GDR into the international community, while sparing little in the suppression of domestic political dissent. A Politbüro coup in October 1989 ousted Honecker and began the revolutionary process which culminated in the abolition of the GDR as a state and the assimilation of its territory into a united Germany.

Erich Honecker was born in 1912 in the Saar region of western Germany to a socialist then communist mining family. In his autobiography he claims to have been impressed by the Russian Revolution, although he was only five years old at the time. He was involved in political activities during his youth, joining the KPD in 1929. In 1930–31 he was sent to train in Moscow. The accession of Hitler to power did not immediately affect the now detached Saar territory, but Honecker was active in the Reich too, using several pseudonyms. He was arrested in 1935, and served 10 years' gaol in Brandenburg-Görden. After the war his career in the SED was rapid: he chaired the party youth section, the FDJ, from 1946 to 1955; he became a Politbüro member in 1958 and was responsible for security and defence; in 1961 he supervised the construction of the Berlin Wall; he was Ulbricht's chosen successor, but by 1971 he was also Moscow's choice to replace his awkward mentor.

Honecker's years in power were characterized by apparent economic success, a much enhanced international profile for the GDR, and fluctuating phases of domestic accommodation and repression. By the mid-1980s the official picture of the GDR economy presented by Honecker and his associates was of a major industrial state enjoying buoyant growth and moving rapidly into modern technologies. Much of this was a deception. Honecker enjoyed the role of international statesman, but his string of prominent visitors and his own visits abroad were intended to impress upon the domestic population the independence and international respectability of the GDR. This did increase as the GDR signed the Basic Treaty with the Federal Republic of Germany in 1972 and entered the United Nations in 1973. Honecker's rapprochement with the FRG culminated in his official visit in September 1987. He also visited Paris, Rome and Brussels, but was not allowed time to fulfil his ambition of being received in London and Washington.

At home Honecker appeared as a tough, ascetic, but not entirely cold character. He was prepared to be conciliatory on occasions, as with the churches from 1978, but individual or collective opposition was stamped on smartly. Honecker took a personal interest in censoring the press and in spying upon suspected dissidents. He claimed to allow collective leadership in the Politbüro, but in fact kept a tight rein on his comrades. He associated primarily with Günter Mittag and Erich Mielke, but deterred the formation of other cliques by at times disgracing even such favoured persons as Egon Krenz. Honecker enjoyed hunting, and revelation in 1989–90 of his numerous hunting lodges and other excessive perks of office caused resentment in the GDR.

There were many signs of crisis in the late 1980s, as Gorbachev sought change and the GDR economy faltered. Honecker's fall from power began when he had to return suddenly from Bucharest in July 1989 for a gall bladder operation. During his enforced absence from the scene, GDR policy drifted in the face of mass exodus of GDR citizens via Hungary and Austria. Growing street protests and police brutality then followed, marring Honecker's triumphant celebration of 40 years of the GDR. His adamant resistance to change was now seen as a liability by Politbüro colleagues and on October 17, 1989 a Politbüro meeting forced him to submit to the Central Committee the next day his resignation "on health grounds". He was replaced by Egon Krenz, the man groomed by him for the succession but by now convinced of the need for change.

At first Honecker's exit seemed fairly dignified, but then he was arrested and expelled from the party. He faced corruption charges, which were later dropped. Forced by his dismissal to leave the luxury party compound at Wandlitz, Honecker and his wife, Margot Honecker, underwent several changes of address, including spells in hospital and detention for Honecker. During early 1990 they were housed by Pastor Uwe Holmer in Lobetal near Bernau, and had to return there when local protest prevented their transfer in March to a government guesthouse at Lindow. On April 3, 1990, the couple were given a flat in Red Army barracks at Beelitz, south of Potsdam. Honecker still stood accused of ordering the shoot-to-kill policy on the GDR border, and an order for his arrest was given on the day of the first all-German elections on December 2, 1990. His Soviet hosts showed reluctance to hand him over.

Extended interviews with Honecker and his wife, published as a book entitled *Der Sturz* (The Fall) in December 1990, showed him unrepentant and bitter and highly critical of those who had ousted him. Honecker tried but failed to prevent publication of the book.

Krause, Günther. Born 1953. Krause studied construction engineering and information technology and was a lecturer at the technical high school in Wismar. He is reported to have had contacts with the CDU since 1975 but to have joined only early in 1990. He was elected to the *Volkskammer* for Rostock and, after a close poll, as *Land* chairman of the CDU in Mecklenburg-West Pomerania. His rapid advance continued as he became parliamentary chairman of the CDU and parliamentary state secretary to de Maizière, with special responsibility for economic affairs. Krause was closely involved in the negotiations toward the first state treaty on economic union and — alongside West German Minister of the Interior Wolfgang Schäuble — he was the main negotiator of the second treaty on German unity. He represented a line strongly in favour of rapid unification and the introduction of market structures into the GDR.

In August 1990 Krause decided against standing for the premiership of his *Land* and instead looked to a political career in Bonn. With German unity he entered the *Bundestag* and Kohl's cabinet as a minister without portfolio. He was elected for Mecklenburg-West Pomerania in December 1990 and in January 1991 was appointed Minister of Transport.

Krenz, Egon. Born 1937. Was briefly the third leader of the GDR, succeeding Erich Honecker in October 1989, first as General Secretary of the SED and then as head of state (Chairman of the State Council). Krenz had been, like Honecker, chairman of the FDJ party youth organization (from 1974). He became a full member of the Politbüro in 1983 and was made responsible for security and youth affairs. He was regarded as

Honecker's designated successor, although Honecker deliberately reduced his prominence in the mid-1980s for fear of him becoming a threat.

Krenz reappeared towards the end of the decade but made few friends when he supervised the fraudulent elections of May 1989 and visited Beijing to congratulate the Chinese leadership on its Tiananmen Square operation. During Honecker's illness in the summer of 1989, Krenz chafed at the lack of policy coming from stand-in Günter Mittag and began to plot with Günter Schabowski and others the removal of Honecker and Mittag. Although known as a hardliner, he initiated the *Wende* (turning point) in GDR politics and was responsible for the opening of the Berlin Wall on November 9, 1989. His concessions were never enough, however, and he failed to establish either his own trustworthiness or the legitimacy of the SED. He resigned in December 1989 and was expelled from the party in January 1990. Still living in Pankow, East Berlin, he began to make a living writing for the West German popular press. In the spring of 1990 he published his account of the revolution in the GDR, *Wenn Mauern fallen* (When Walls Fall). Its narrative and interpretations have been contested by his co-conspirator, Günter Schabowski.

Meckel, Markus. Born 1952. Was GDR Foreign Minister during the period of negotiations toward German unity. Son of a pastor, and a pastor himself, he was before the *Wende* active in the peace and human rights movement. He was a founder member of the SDP (later SPD), becoming a deputy chairman in February 1990. When Ibrahim Böhme was forced to lay down his party offices in March 1990, Meckel took over in a caretaker capacity, and in April was appointed Foreign Minister in the de Maizière government. He was a participant in the "Two-plus-Four" negotiations, but was eclipsed by his West German counterpart, Hans-Dietrich Genscher. Within the GDR he suffered from criticism for giving posts to friends and family members. In mid-August Meckel resigned from the cabinet in the wake of de Maizière's sacking of other SPD ministers.

Meckel was a member of the *Volkskammer* for Magdeburg. He did not join the *Bundestag* with Germany unity, but was elected for Prenzlau, Brandenburg on December 2, 1990.

Mittag, Günter. Born 1926, Günter Mittag rose through the party hierarchy from 1946, becoming a full Politbüro member in 1966. His specialism was management of the command economy, and he was party secretary for the economy for most of the period 1962–89, enjoying close contact with Erich Honecker. He was responsible for the gross inadequacies of the planning structure, which he tried to disguise by ordering the manipulation of statistics. From time to time he exposed flaws in the economy and demanded changes, but these interventions were largely cosmetic and designed to exert his political control over industry and the regional leaderships of the SED. Despite health problems (diabetes and a partly amputated leg), he was a vigorous representative of the GDR in West German economic circles. When Honecker fell ill in the summer of 1989, Mittag deputized for him, but in his resolution to avoid reform he failed to grasp the depth of the crisis. He was dismissed in October 1989 along with Honecker and party propaganda secretary Joachim Herrmann. Mittag and Herrmann did not even receive the thanks accorded to Honecker. Mittag was later expelled from the SED and charged with corruption and other offences.

Modrow, Hans. Born 1928. Appointed GDR Prime Minister in November 1989, Dr Hans Modrow was a key figure in the revolution which overtook the GDR regime in 1989–90, and he could be so because he had not been closely implicated in the abuses of the past. Although a loyal member of the SED from the beginning of the GDR, he was for a long time distrusted by the party leadership and deliberately kept at a distance and out of high office.

Modrow joined the FDJ, the FDGB and the SED in 1949. From 1952 to 1961 he was active in the Berlin section of the FDJ, thereafter in the party organization in Berlin. His progress was at times unusually slow, indicating that his career was deliberately being restrained. He only became a full member of the Central Committee in 1967, and during his 16 years from 1973 as party secretary for the Dresden district he was not admitted to even candidate Politbüro status. By mid-1989 Modrow had developed a reputation, particularly in the Dresden area itself, as an honest and reform-minded man who spurned the luxuries enjoyed by other party leaders. He was viewed with distrust, however, by the Politbüro and in mid-1989 a party commission was sent from Berlin to Dresden to deal with "political and economic shortcomings". In other words, Modrow was being investigated and disciplined. His main opponents were Günter Mittag and Joachim Herrmann.

When the crisis broke in the autumn of 1989 and Egon Krenz replaced Erich Honecker as party secretary, Modrow was increasingly mentioned as a necessary member of any reform government to give it credibility. Although not a close associate of Krenz, Modrow was elected to the Politbüro in November and proposed as the new Prime Minister (Chairman of the Council of Ministers). He took office on November 13, 1989, and appointed a coalition cabinet with many new faces. When Krenz was displaced as SED General Secretary and as head of state, Modrow effectively became the leader of the GDR (he was elected honorary president of the PDS on February 25, 1990).

From December 1989 Modrow entered into "round table" discussions with opposition groups and parties, but had difficulty holding them and his coalition together. He had, for instance, to backtrack on his decision to retain a state security service. By late January 1990 Modrow was announcing clearly that the GDR was in deep crisis and that he needed the help of the opposition. It was agreed by most opposition groups and parties that they were willing to participate in a grand coalition government, provided that all ministers, including Modrow himself, temporarily lay aside their party positions. Modrow had already done this in all but name when he said that he was acting on behalf of his country rather than his party. At the beginning of February Modrow took the step which no other SED politician had dared take before: he declared that the two German states should move towards one neutral federal fatherland with its capital in Berlin. The neutrality question remained the stumbling block with Bonn.

Modrow acquired a generally positive reputation at home and abroad, and this helped his party to more than survive the election of March 1990. The 66 seats and 16.4% of the vote were not enough, however, to allow Modrow to continue, and his was a caretaker administration until Lothar de Maizière was charged with forming a new coalition government in April. Despite pressure from the PDS, Modrow failed to be elected president of the *Volkskammer*. With German unity in October 1990, Modrow joined the *Bundestag* as a delegate for the PDS, but this was only until the election of December. Modrow was not thereafter publicly active.

Ortleb, Rainer. Born 1944. A mathematician by training and a professor in shipping technology, Ortleb steered the old LDPD into union with the West German FDP and into eventual coalition with Kohl's CDU. A member of the LDPD since 1968 and local chairman in Rostock, he was elected chairman of the party on February 10, 1990 to replace Manfred Gerlach. He took the party into an electoral alliance with the other liberal parties, as the

"League of Free Democrats" (BFD), and was elected to the *Volkskammer* for Dresden. The liberal parties of the GDR merged with the FDP of the Federal Republic on August 12, 1990. Ortleb joined the *Bundestag* in October and his seat was secured by election in December for Mecklenburg-West Pomerania. The strong performance of the FDP in the elections helped to win more ministries for the party in Kohl's new cabinet, and Ortleb was put in charge of education on January 16, 1991.

Romberg, Walter. Born 1928, a mathematician by profession. Was the man who signed the first state treaty between the GDR and the Federal Republic of Germany on May 18, 1990. As Finance Minister of the GDR, he and his West German counterpart Theo Waigel (CSU) were responsible for the terms of the economic, currency and social union which came into effect on July 1, 1990.

Romberg was an early member of the SDP (later SPD) in late 1989 and joined the Modrow government in February 1990 as a Minister without Portfolio. In April he became one of the six SPD ministers in de Maizière's new cabinet, and was faced immediately by the worsening economic and budgetary situation in the GDR. He had difficulty appraising the current state of affairs, and this led Waigel to criticize him for not having sufficient information to hand. Despite this, the negotiations toward the state treaty went ahead successfully.

After currency union Romberg had to reassess the GDR budget and make further claims on the Federal Republic, alleging that unity had been rushed. Romberg then in the summer of 1990 became a casualty of de Maizière's use of his three economics ministers (the others being Pollack at Agriculture and Pohl at Economics) as scapegoats. They were sacked on August 15 and replaced only by state secretaries. Romberg joined the *Bundestag* on October 3, but was not elected on December 2, 1990.

Schabowski, Günter. Born 1929. Was editor of the SED party newspaper *Neues Deutschland*, before becoming SED First Secretary for Berlin and a full Politbüro member in 1985. In 1989 he assisted Krenz in the ousting of Honecker and for a short time was the public spokesman of the new regime. It was Schabowski who gave the laconic announcement on November 9, 1989 that GDR citizens were to be allowed to travel freely. Like Krenz, he failed to master the rapidly changing situation and in the winter of 1989–90 was deprived of office and of his party membership.

In November 1990 a series of extended interviews with Schabowski was published as *Das Politbüro: Ende eines Mythos* (The Politbüro: End of a Myth). In it Schabowski describes in much greater detail than Krenz the workings of the Honecker regime and on many points contests Krenz's account. He is also much more open than Krenz or Honecker about the failings of the GDR which led to its demise.

Schnur, Wolfgang. Born 1944. Was the first chairman (elected December 17, 1989) of Democratic Departure (DA), one of the three parties in the conservative "Alliance for Germany". He participated in the Round Table political discussions in East Berlin, and also in the talks with Kohl, Ebeling and de Maizière in February 1990. On March 14, 1990, just before the *Volkskammer* elections, he resigned, after admitting he had been a collaborator with the Stasi. He was replaced by Rainer Eppelmann, but the scandal severely weakened the DA. It performed very badly in the *Volkskammer* election (four seats) and in all subsequent votes, losing leading members and eventually disappearing into the CDU.

Thierse, Wolfgang. Born 1943, son of a lawyer and brought up a Christian, Thierse studied German in East Berlin. His protest against the expulsion of Wolf Biermann in 1976 led to dismissal from his post in the Ministry of Culture. Thereafter he worked in the Academy of Science. In 1989 he was first with New Forum and then joined the new SDP (later SPD). In March 1990 he was elected for East Berlin to the *Volkskammer*, and in June was the surprise victor in the election of a new SPD chairman, replacing Ibrahim Böhme. He joined the *Bundestag* in October 1990, being elected for Berlin in December. With the union of the East and West SPD organizations, Thierse became a deputy chairman of the party.

The Media

The media in the old GDR were rigidly controlled by the political apparatus. Foreign material was strictly vetted and rarely allowed into the country. This even applied to some Soviet papers and films in 1988–89, which were thought too much in favour of reform. Alongside this paucity of critical information, however, was set the fact that most of the population of the GDR could and did watch West German television. This was of great significance when western reports showed the protests against the regime in the autumn of 1989, the fall of the Berlin Wall, and the demonstrations in favour of unification in 1989–90.

Günter Schabowski, himself a former editor of the SED party newspaper *Neues Deutschland*, is now highly critical of journalistic practice during the Honecker years. He admits that central control of the media before the *Wende* (turning point) was symptomatic of the rigidity of the old regime and of its unwillingness to face facts. He describes how Honecker used to exercise daily personal supervision of the main contents of *Neues Deutschland*, giving prominence to his own activities.

Neues Deutschland was supplemented by newspapers for the other political parties and mass organizations, whose line fluctuated little if at all from that of the SED. Examples were *Neue Zeit* from the CDU and *Der Morgen* from the LDPD. Local newspapers were published throughout the country, but they too had no scope for critical expression. The same could be said of the television and radio services.

The political changes in the GDR saw rapid transformation of the media. In mid-November the editorship of *Neues Deutschland* passed from Herbert Naumann to Wolfgang Spickermann, one of his former editorial team. There was no wholesale changeover in staff, but the tone of the paper began to alter. The emphasis was still on the SED's role in a socialist GDR, but there was more open reporting of developments and discussion of problems. From December 4, 1989, the paper appeared no longer as "Organ of the Central Committee of the SED" but as "Central Organ of the SED", reflecting the growing demands within the party for greater democracy. Two weeks later, at the time of the extraordinary party congress, this last reference to the party was dropped, and *Neues Deutschland* became simply a "Socialist Daily Newspaper". In practice, of course, it was still tied to and financed by the SED-PDS (later PDS). To complete the changes, a friendlier format was introduced on February 19, 1990, with a wider variety of articles and text broken down into smaller sections. While Modrow was still Prime Minister, *Neues Deutschland* had a continuing function as the principal newspaper of record, but on the changeover to de Maizière it became more and more the representative voice of the PDS in opposition. Because of this and because of the dramatic decline in party membership, circulation dropped sharply.

Similar changes overtook the other party newspapers, but the main alteration was the huge incursion of West German material. This did not just mean that West German (and other western) papers and periodicals became freely available in the GDR; they swamped the market. Western publishers began to buy out their East German counterparts (including the purchase of the SED publishing house by Robert Maxwell) and publish regional editions of their own papers. The Munich-based *Süddeutsche Zeitung*, for instance, began to issue a Saxon-oriented version. These developments endangered the survival of local initiatives which had sprung up in the aftermath of the *Wende*.

The television service also responded to the changes with many staff departures and a new, more open tone to programmes of current affairs. From mid-March 1990 the two channels were renamed from DDR1 and DDR2 to DFF1 and DFF2 and permitted to show commercials. They continued into the period of German unity, but they now have a primary function of reflecting local and regional interests and problems.

As in so many other respects, the political revolution in the GDR had in the media consequences not found elsewhere in central and eastern Europe. Although the press, television and radio all changed significantly and expressed the new freedoms, they almost immediately began to be replaced by West German products. The one aspect of German culture which probably means that distinctive newspapers and television channels will continue in eastern Germany is that already in West Germany the press and television were more decentralized than in, say, the United Kingdom.

Foreign Relations

The general trend

At the beginning of 1989 the German Democratic Republic was a loyal member of the Warsaw Pact and the Council for Mutual Economic Assistance (CMEA). It maintained friendly relations with numerous developing countries, particularly in Africa, providing them with economic and military assistance. Relations with the People's Republic of China had been improving for some years. The GDR had also shed some of its implacable hostility to the developed capitalist states, with Erich Honecker visiting Paris, Rome and Brussels during the 1980s. He had also in 1987 been the first East German head of state to visit the Federal Republic of Germany, and he had used the occasion to emphasize the separate statehood of the GDR. By the late 1980s, relations between the two German republics were far from cordial, but they did encompass a growing range of contacts in the economy, in environmental matters and between leading politicians. Great distrust remained, however, with each side, particularly the East Germans, maintaining a large espionage apparatus.

There was still a substantial legacy from World War II and the Cold War. Soviet Forces of about 380,000 were stationed in the GDR, facing NATO troops in the Federal Republic. The city of Berlin was still under the 1971 Four-Power Agreement and the "capital of the GDR", East Berlin, was not recognized as such by the western powers nor by the West Germans. The East Germans for their part did not recognize West Berlin as part of the Federal Republic.

By the end of 1990, the German Democratic Republic was no more, and the enlarged Federal Republic of Germany continued to be a staunch member of NATO and the European Community. The Warsaw Pact and the CMEA were themselves in a process of disintegration. That such a transformation had taken place so quickly and with so few diplomatic problems was remarkable. It testified not only to the pressure for change and for unity within the GDR, but also to the extent of Mikhail Gorbachev's withdrawal from eastern and central Europe. The western powers and the EC too had raised very few substantive problems with regard to German unification, and worries on the part of the Poles had been assuaged by German recognition of the Oder-Neisse line as the incontrovertible border between Germany and Poland.

The events of 1989–90

The process of change in the GDR was inextricably bound up with the international scene. The old regime was in 1989 distancing itself from the reform movements in the USSR, Poland and Hungary and was reaffirming its friendships with Czechoslovakia and Romania. When in June 1989 the Chinese leadership clamped down on the student reform movement in the bloodbath of Tiananmen Square, the Honecker regime was quick in its approval of the measure. Various Politbüro members, including Egon Krenz, visited China and expressed their support for the Beijing regime's approach to dissent. The message was intended as much for domestic consumption, implying an open threat to those contemplating mass protest. In this regard, however, it backfired, since many people in the GDR were appalled by the events and by their government's condoning them. They were if anything spurred on by the incident to greater criticism of the system. Also, it is likely that many within the SED hierarchy now shied back from confrontation with the dissidents; they had seen the bloody consequences of sending in the troops, and they realized the implications for the GDR's international position if such events were to be repeated in the centre of Europe. It is still not proven whether any individuals — Egon Krenz, for instance — actually intervened to prevent the use of force in October 1989, but the Chinese incident certainly informed developments in the GDR in the latter half of 1989.

Meanwhile, one of the GDR's Warsaw Pact allies was posing the problem which was to lead to the revolution in the GDR. From the beginning of May the Hungarian government had authorised the dismantling of the fortifications along the border with Austria. The significance of this was that thousands of East Germans each year holidayed in Hungary and might now be able to use that border to emigrate unofficially. This was not initially permitted by the Hungarians, because East German holders of West German passports issued at the embassy in Budapest did not have an appropriate visa. During the summer, however, the pressure built up and from September 11 the Hungarians allowed the East

Germans to leave. This provoked cries of outrage from East Berlin, with accusations that the Hungarians, in cahoots with the West Germans, were engaged in "trade in human beings".

The Czechs on the other hand were still regarded as trustworthy communist allies, but this did not prevent difficulties arising in Prague too. In August the West German embassy had to be closed because it was full of would-be East German emigrants. The reintroduction of visa requirements for East German travel to Czechoslovakia and promises of amnesty and favourable treatment of those returning home voluntarily failed to defuse the situation. West German Foreign Minister Hans-Dietrich Genscher then managed at the end of September to negotiate an agreement with the Czechs and the East Germans. On September 30, to tumultuous acclaim which was to stand him and his party, the FDP, in good stead in the coming year, he announced in the Prague embassy that those in refuge there would be allowed to leave by train for the Federal Republic. East Berlin's one stipulation was that the trains make a detour through the territory of the GDR.

A major actor in the unfolding disintegration of the GDR was Mikhail Gorbachev. His encouragement of reform in eastern and central Europe and his acquiescence in the separate paths followed by his various allies led inexorably to the possibility of German unity. His part was clear in October 1989, when he attended the 40th anniversary celebrations of the GDR. The crowds' enthusiasm was rather greater for Gorbachev than for his hosts. He also took the opportunity to press upon the latter the need to take action to avert major crisis. Honecker would not understand the message, but others in the Politbüro took encouragement.

Once the change had come in the GDR and the prospect of German unification increased, the USSR would not initially countenance the GDR becoming part of NATO. Gorbachev and the Modrow regime in East Berlin made proposals of German neutrality or dual membership of the Warsaw Pact and NATO. These were rejected by the West German government and its NATO allies, and it became clear to the Soviet government that the best that could be salvaged from the situation was a dignified abandonment of the GDR in return for West German goodwill and financial assistance. In July 1990, at the famous Caucasus meeting of the West German and Soviet leaders, Helmut Kohl received Gorbachev's assurance that the Germans should be able to take their own decisions on membership of alliances. In other words, a united Germany could remain in NATO without Soviet objection.

Even before this, the so-called Two-plus-Four negotiations had begun in order to reconcile German unity with the residual rights of the wartime victor powers in Germany. They involved several sessions, held in Bonn in May, in Berlin in June, in Paris in July, and in Moscow in September. The main issue of contention was German membership of NATO, but this was resolved when Gorbachev gave way. The resultant treaty of September 12, 1990 was remarkably brief and to the point. In it the four powers agreed that their "rights and responsibilities in relation to Berlin and Germany are hereby concluded"; that the eastern border of the new Germany would be the Oder-Neisse line, pending a treaty with Poland (which followed on November 14, 1990); and that Soviet forces would be gone from the territory of East Germany by 1994. In addition to the Two-plus-Four accord the Germans the next day signed a friendship treaty with the USSR, which included major German financial assistance for the upkeep and then withdrawal of the Soviet forces. This DM 15 billion was supplemented by other loans and aid.

It was also necessary to regularize the departure of the GDR from the CMEA and its entry into the EC, but this proceeded without difficulty. With German unity from October 3, 1990 the territory of the former GDR acceded automatically to the EC, although transitional arrangements were conceded by Brussels to take account of the precarious economic situation of industry and agriculture in the new *Länder* and of their trade links with the CMEA countries.

HUNGARY

Nigel Swain

Government as at December 1990

President. *Árpád Göncz (MP, AFD)*
Prime Minister. *József Antall (MP, HDF)*
Interior. *Péter Boross*
Foreign. *Géza Jeszenszky (HDF)*
Education. *Bertalan Andrásfalvy (MP, HDF)*
Justice. *István Balsai (MP, HDF)*
Industry and Commerce. *Péter Ákos Bod (MP, HDF)*
Defence. *Lajos Für (MP, HDF)*
Labour. *Sándor Győriványi (MP, ISP)*
International Economic Relations. *Béla Kádár*
Environment. *Sándor K. Keresztes (MP, HDF)*
Agriculture. *Ferenc József Nagy (MP, ISP)*
Finance. *Mihály Kupa*
Transport and Communication. *Csaba Siklós (MP, HDF)*
Public Welfare. *László Surján (CDPP)*
Without Portfolio (land reform). *Jenő Gerbovits (MP, ISP)*

Without Portfolio (prime minister's office: minorities, church affairs, youth problems etc.). *Gyula Kiss (ISP)*
Without Portfolio (relations with European organizations and EC). *Ferenc Mádl*
Without Portfolio (co-ordinating government relations with financial institutions and National Bank). *Katalin Botos (MP, HDF)*
Without Portfolio (supervision of Secretariat of Hungarians Living Beyond the Border and government-parliamentary relations). *Balázs Horváth (MP, HDF)*
Without Portfolio (National Technical Development Committee and National Atomic Energy Committee). *Ernő Pungor*
Without Portfolio (National Security Office and Information Office). *András Gálszécsy*

Party name abbreviations

AFD	Alliance of Free Democrats	HPP	Hungarian People's Party
AYD	Alliance of Young Democrats	HSDP	Hungarian Social Democratic Party
CDPP	Christian Democratic People's Party	HSP	Hungarian Socialist Party
		HSWP	Hungarian Socialist Workers' Party
HDF	Hungarian Democratic Forum	ISP	Independent Smallholders' Party

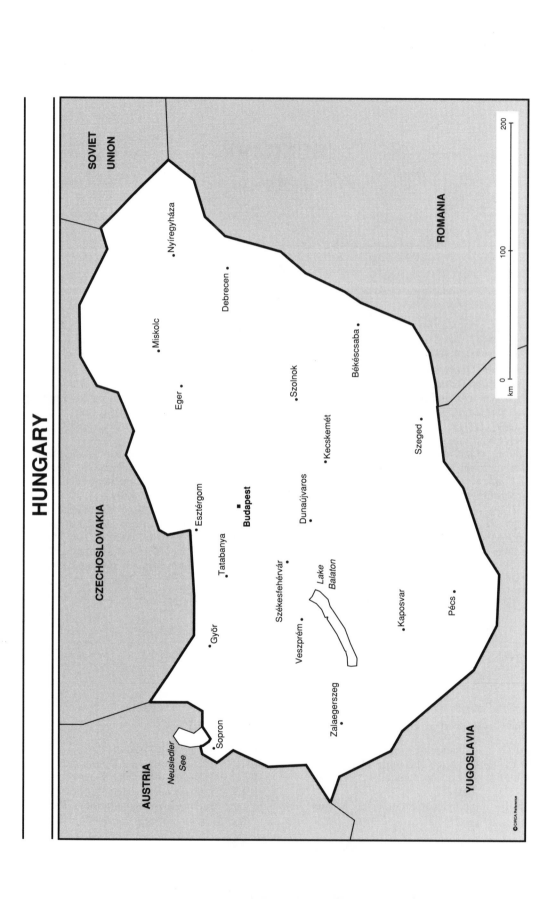

HUNGARY

SOVIET
UNION

CZECHOSLOVAKIA

AUSTRIA

ROMANIA

YUGOSLAVIA

Neusiedler
See

•Sopron

•Győr

Zalaegerszeg
•

Veszprém
•

Székesfehérvár
•

•Tatabanya

•Esztérgom

■
Budapest

Dunaújvaros
•

•Kecskemét

Lake
Balaton

•Kaposvar

•Pécs

Szeged
•

Eger
•

•Miskolc

Szolnok
•

Békéscsaba
•

Debrecen
•

•Nyíregyháza

km 0   100   200

© CIRCA Reference

Chronology

1988

May 20–22. Special Conference of the Hungarian Socialist Workers' Party appoints János Kádár to honorary post of party president and replaces him by Károly Grósz. A month earlier four prominent reformers had been expelled from the Party.

September–December. New parties formed and parties of the 1940s reconstituted.

1989

January 1. Company Act, authorising the creation of limited liability companies, and Foreign Investments Act come into force.

January 30. In a radio interview Imre Pozsgay refers to the events of 1956 as a "popular uprising".

February 7. First Reform Circle formed within the Hungarian Socialist Workers' (communist) Party in Csongrád county.

February 10–11. Central Committee of Hungarian Socialist Workers' Party accepts that Hungary will be a multi-party democracy.

March 11–13. First national assembly of the Hungarian Democratic Forum held in Budapest.

March 23. Eight opposition groups establish the Opposition Round Table as a vehicle for presenting a united opposition to the ruling party.

April–May. Successive attempts to establish negotiations between the Hungarian Socialist Workers' Party and the Opposition Round Table fail. The Reform Circle movement within the Party spreads and its congress is brought forward to October 1989.

May–June. IMF suspends an instalment of its credit agreement because its limits on external and internal debt are exceeded. An emergency budget revision is introduced.

May 1. Unofficial trade unions hold independent May Day celebrations.

May 2. Work begins dismantling the "iron curtain" with Austria.

May 8. János Kádár relieved of his post as Party president.

May 16. Work on the Gabčíkovo-Nagymaros dam is suspended.

June 13. National Round Table talks between the Party and the Opposition Round Table begin.

June 16. Huge crowds, including many famous dissidents from Hungary and abroad, attend the ceremonial reburial of Imre Nagy.

June 24. The leadership of the Hungarian Socialist Workers' Party is transferred to a four-man praesidium: Rezső Nyers, Miklós Németh, Imre Pozsgay (all reformers) and Károly Grósz.

July 6. Death of János Kádár.

August 19. "Pan-European picnic" at Sopron. A Hungarian delegation symbolically crosses the border to Austria.

September 11. Foreign Minister Horn announces that East German citizens will be allowed to emigrate legally via Austria.

September 18. The Round Table negotiations agree on cardinal constitutional reform necessary prior to elections, but the Free Democrats and Young Democrats refuse to sign the final document because they disagree with the proposal that a president should be elected prior to parliamentary elections and they object to the fact that the Party has made no commitment to withdraw from places of work, disband the Workers' Guard completely, or render an account of its property.

September 29. The Free Democrats and Young Democrats begin collecting signatures to force a referendum on the elements of the Round Table agreement they disagreed with.

October 7. The XIVth Congress of the Hungarian Socialist Workers' Party decides to transform itself into the Hungarian Socialist Party. The Congress then adopts a reformist programme and names Pozsgay as presidential candidate.

October 20–22. Second Congress of the Hungarian Democratic Forum.

October 23. On the anniversary of the Hungarian uprising, Hungary is declared a republic (rather than a people's republic).

November 26. Referendum on the four disputed aspects of the Round Table agreement. Both the government and the Hungarian Democratic Forum (which called for a boycott) are defeated on the issue of the President. Parliament had in the interim already decided the other issues in favour of the opposition. Henceforth the opposition is clearly divided.

December 21. Parliament passes the 1990 budget and Németh resigns from the Hungarian Socialist Party.

December 23. The chairman of parliament formally announces that parliament will dissolve on March 16, 1990 and elections will take place on March 25 and April 8.

1990

January 1. Constitutional Court begins work.

January 23. Interior Minister resigns over "Danube-gate" telephone-tapping scandal.

March 1. State Property Agency begins work.

March 15. IMF agrees the loan which was dependent on setting an acceptable 1990 budget.

March 25. First round of elections. The Hungarian Democratic Forum and the Alliance of Free Democrats are only 3% apart.

April 8. Second round of elections. The Hungarian Democratic Forum is the clear winner, but fails to achieve an overall majority.

April 29. Hungarian Democratic Forum and Free Democrats agree a pact concerning the passing of legislation requiring a 75% majority.

May 2. First session of new parliament.

May 14. Hungary receives a US$300,000 bridging loan from Bank for International Settlements.

May 23. Antall formally empowered by parliament to form a government. His government includes nine from the Democratic Forum, three Smallholders, one Christian Democrat and three independents.

June. Agreement with IMF to bring budget expenditure within approved limits.

June 5. Land sales suspended pending passage of a land law.

June 15. Agreement that religious education in schools would not be compulsory.

June 21. Budapest Stock Exchange reopens.

July 14. Final agreement on the pattern of religious education in schools.

July 16. Price increases to conform with IMF budget requirements.

July 19. The State Property Agency is placed under government rather than parliamentary supervision and a new head is appointed.

July 27. Parliament agrees the structure of local government reform.

July 29. Further referendum on method of electing the President is invalidated by a 13.91% turnout.

August 3. Parliament elects Árpád Göncz as President.

August 27. Justice Plan announced abolishing the privileges of the former regime.

September 14. First Privatization Plan announced.

September 23. Publication of the National Renewal Programme.

September 30. First round of local elections. Independents the most successful in villages and small towns.

October 2. Planned land law is ruled unconstitutional.

October 14. Second round of local elections. Liberal opposition are clear winners.

October 26–28. Taxi and lorry driver blockade brings country to a standstill. Petrol price increases are withdrawn.

November 6. Hungary joins Council of Europe and Antall announces his intention to reshuffle his government.

November 9. Pozsgay leaves Hungarian Socialist Party to form Citizens' Movement for the Republic.

December 15. Announcement of first stage of government reshuffle affecting independents and Hungarian Democratic Forum members.

December 21. Budapest Council further postpones a final decision on the Vienna-Budapest World Exhibition until April 1991.

December 30. Parliament accepts the government's 1991 budget proposals paving the way for a three-year agreement with the IMF.

The parliamentary electoral system

The parliamentary elections use a mixture of proportional representation and first-past-the-post, with a 4% of the total vote hurdle on the regional list to exclude minority parties. A total of 328 members of parliament is elected directly by the voters, and 58 enter parliament indirectly via a national list. Of the 328 directly elected members, 176 are elected in individual constituencies and 152 are elected on one of 20 regional lists (one for each county and one for Budapest). Voting takes place in one or two rounds. If the turnout is over 50% and a candidate receives more than 50% of the vote, that candidate is elected and no second round is necessary. If a second round is necessary, the candidate with the most votes wins. A second round of voting for the regional list is only necessary if turnout in the first round was under 50%.

Shares on the regional lists are converted into parliamentary seats for each party by means of a calculation, the essence of which is that the number of votes necessary to win a single seat is calculated and each party's vote is then divided by this figure to obtain a whole number of seats won and "remainder vote". The 58 seats available on the National List are distributed on the basis of the "remainder vote".

The local electoral system

The local electoral system is a mixture of proportional representation and first-past-the-post. In settlements of under 10,000, electors have two sets of votes, a single vote for a directly elected mayor, and a number of additional votes for each council seat, the precise number of which depends on the size of the settlement. In larger settlements, other than Budapest, the electorate has two votes: one for a district candidate, and one for a party list. Unlike parliamentary elections, there is no 4% of the total vote hurdle in these cases. Mayors of the larger settlements are elected indirectly by the newly formed council. Budapest constitutes a special case in that there is a second party list (making three votes in all) for the city-wide assembly, in this case including a 4% hurdle. The all-Budapest assembly of 88 is made up of 66 elected from this list and a delegate appointed from each Budapest district. Budapest's mayor is elected indirectly by the all-Budapest assembly.

Political Overview

In the two years between January 1989 and December 1990 Hungary peacefully transformed itself from a one-party communist state to a multi-party parliamentary democracy in which six parties, representing three broad ideological persuasions, vied for power. Popular participation in referenda and parliamentary and local government elections was rather low. Nevertheless, the newly formed political structures proved sufficiently mature to withstand and peacefully resolve the three-day taxi and lorry driver blockade which brought the country to a standstill in October 1990.

The birth of multi-party politics: January–June 1989

By January 1989 Hungary was already experiencing *de facto* multi-party politics. Four of the five new parties that eventually entered parliament had begun operations: the Hungarian Democratic Forum (HDF), the Alliance of Free Democrats (AFD), the Alliance of Young Democrats (AYD), and the Independent Smallholders' Party (ISP). The latter was a reconstitution of a pre-war party, as was the Christian Democratic People's Party (CDPP), formed on March 12, 1989.

In response to this upsurge in popular political activity, over the spring of 1989, the Party relinquished elements of its monopoly of political power, to the extent that by March it had announced its readiness to form a coalition government. Eight prominent opposition groups founded an Opposition Round Table that same month and, after initial obduracy and defeat by its own reformers on issues such as holding a congress in October and suspending work on the Gabčíkovo-Nagymaros dam, the Party leadership agreed that negotiations on how the political system might be transformed should begin on June 13.

Negotiations and the rise of reform communism: June–October 1989

The pace and pattern of the National Round Table talks were dictated by reformers within the Party, for whom it was imperative that the negotiations should have been successfully concluded before the Party Congress in October. Parallel with the negotiations, two significant political developments took place. First, the reformist wing of the Party strengthened its position by forcing Grósz (Kádár's successor) into a four-person praesidium including Nyers, Németh and Pozsgay (all prominent reformers). Second, the Hungarian

Democratic Forum finally took the decision to become a true political party, dropping its advocacy of the "third way" at the same time.

Negotiations concluded on September 18, 1989. For the opposition, their purpose had been to agree certain "cardinal laws" (the establishment of a new presidency, the creation of a Constitutional Court, an electoral law clarifying the status of political parties, and amendments to the criminal code) which the existing parliament should pass before elections could be held for a new, legitimate parliament which might carry democratic transformation further forward. When the successful conclusion of the negotiations was announced, the Free Democrats and the Young Democrats caused a furore by stating that they would not sign it for four reasons. They rejected the proposal that the election of a president by popular ballot should precede parliamentary elections, and they were unhappy that the Party had not committed itself to disband the workers' militia, withdraw from workplaces, and render a full account of its property. Their disagreement was such that they began collecting signatures to force a referendum on the four issues.

Attention now turned to the 6–9 October XIVth Party Congress. Following compromise between the Reform Alliance and the Popular Democratic Platform Party factions, the reformist proposal of creating a new party, rather than reforming the old one, won the day. A new Hungarian Socialist Party emerged carrying the bulk of the old Party with it, but leaving a rump Hungarian Socialist Workers' Party. The new party was committed to democratic socialism, a multi-party system, a market economy, and the withdrawal of Soviet troops. It later applied to join the Socialist International. By the conclusion of the Conference, the future political landscape seemed clear. Pozsgay would be elected President, and a Democratic Forum-led coalition (probably with Socialist Party support) would emerge from parliamentary elections.

Referendum and reform communism in decline: November 1989–February 1990

The Free and Young Democrats collected more than enough signatures to force a referendum, which was set for November 26. On a turnout of 58%, the crucial question of order of elections was won by the Free and Young Democrats (and their allies the Social Democrats and the Smallholders), 50.07% to 49.93%. (The other, by then uncontentious, issues were won by roughly 95% to 5% in each case.)

The November referendum marked a watershed in Hungarian multi-party politics. At a time when public opinion surveys revealed that political opinions were formed in an *ad hoc* fashion, and when the opposition groups elsewhere in Eastern Europe were only beginning to emerge as potent forces, the Hungarians were asked to break the simple Party versus Opposition dichotomy and decide between competing opposition parties. The referendum also marked the birth of the Free Democrats as a party with mass support. Surveys of hypothetical voting intentions reveal an upsurge in Free Democrat support in December and January following, first, its victory in the referendum and secondly its exposure of the "Danube-gate" telephone-tapping scandal. The Democratic Forum suffered a momentary loss of prestige after its failed call for a boycott of the referendum, but the biggest loser was the Socialist Party. The referendum proved that the Party could be defeated, and, when socialist regimes were collapsing in Hungary's neighbours, the Socialist Party's justifiable claim to be truly reformist cut little ice.

In January, as the election campaign began, the Constitutional Court came into being and parliament passed laws establishing religious freedom, permitting agricultural co-operatives to sell their land, and calling for the establishment of the State Property Agency, responsible to Parliament, to be created by the beginning of March. In its dying days parliament accepted an amendment, initiated by Zoltán Király, the independent member of parliament, that the President should be elected by popular ballot.

Parliamentary elections and their aftermath: March–April 1990

By the time of the parliamentary elections, some 84 parties had been formed, of which 64 were officially registered and 48 intended to run in the election. In the event, only 10 parties registered sufficient candidate nominations to be included on the National List and stand a realistic chance of power. They were joined by two essentially non-party organizations: the Agrarian Alliance and the Patriotic Election Coalition, a nominal party formed by the Patriotic People's Front to allow non-party candidates to stand.

The ideological stance of the six major political parties which gained parliamentary representation ranged from national-christian conservative (the Hungarian Democratic Forum, the Smallholders and the Christian Democratic People's Party), social-liberal (Alliance of Free Democrats and Alliance of Young Democrats) and left social democratic (the Hungarian Socialist Party). The larger opposition parties both contained significant minority groupings: a christian liberal orientation within the Democratic Forum, and a social democratic strand within the Free Democrats.

Turnout in round one of the elections on 25 March was approximately 65%, but it fell to around 40% for the second round on April 8. Whilst the battle between the Hungarian Democratic Forum and the Free Democrats was close in the first round (24.7% of the vote compared with 21.4%), in the second round the Forum was easily the largest party in parliament (42.5% of seats compared with 23.8% for the Free Democrats, its nearest rival), although it could not command an overall majority without support from elsewhere (see Tables 1 and 2).

The first session of the new parliament met on May 2 and on its eve the government

Table 1:   Parliamentary seats March–April 1990

	Regional List	Individual constituencies Round 1	Individual constituencies Round 2	National List	Number of seats
HDF	40	3	111	10	164
AFD	34	0	35	23	92
ISP	16	0	11	17	44
HSP	14	0	1	18	33
AYD	8	0	1	12	21
CDPP	8	0	3	10	21
Agrarian Alliance	—	0	1	—	1
Independent	—	2	4	—	6
Multi-party	—	0	4	—	4
TOTAL	120	5	171	90	386

Source: *Heti Világgazdaság*, 14 April 1990, p. 5 and *Parliamenti Almanach 1990*.

Table 2: Share of vote and seats[1] March–April 1990 (%)

	Regional List	Individual Seats
HDF	24.73	42.49
AFD	21.39	23.83
ISP	11.73	11.40
HSP	10.89	8.55
AYD	8.95	5.44
CDPP	6.46	5.44
HSWP	3.68	—
HSDP	3.55	—
Agrarian Alliance	3.13	0.26
Entrepreneurs' Party	1.89	—
Patriotic Electoral Coalition	1.87	—
HPP	0.75	—
Hungary's Green Party	0.36	—
National Smallholders' Party	0.20	—
Somogy Christian Coalition	0.12	—
Hungary's Co-operative and Agrarian Party	0.10	—
Independent Hungarian Democratic Party	0.06	—
Freedom Party	0.06	—
Hungarian Independence Party	0.04	—
Independent	—	1.55
Jointly sponsored	—	1.04

Note: [1]The first round was essentially for the lists and the second for the individual seats since the first round turnout generally exceeded 50% and was therefore valid; but only five deputies achieved over 50% of the vote and immediate election in the first round.
Source: *Heti Világgazdaság*, 14 April 1990, p. 5; *Magyar Nemzet*, 10 April 1990, p. 4, *Parlamenti Almanach* 1990; *Statisztikai Zsebkönyv 1989*, p. 250.

and opposition announced the choice of Árpád Göncz, a Free Democrat, as provisional President. The Democratic Forum and the Free Democrats also announced that they had entered into a pact whereby: (i) the Free Democrats would not use their parliamentary weight to block a range of other measures, which under the existing constitution formally required a 75% majority, in return for re-establishing the parliamentary election of the President as in the 1946 constitution; and (ii) agreements were made on, first, a number of fundamental issues (such as constitutional amendments, local government reform, electoral law, and the law on the press) for which a 75% majority would remain, and, second, a list of measures to be undertaken in the first 30 days of the parliament.

Antall's new government (announced on May 16 and formally passed on May 23) comprised eight members of the Democratic Forum, four Smallholders (agriculture, labour and two ministers without portfolio), one Christian Democrat (welfare), and three non-party experts (finance, international economic relations, and another minister without portfolio). Géza Jeszenszky, Foreign Minister, although a member of the Democratic Forum, was not a member of parliament. Only one of the three economics ministries was occupied by an elected party member (Péter Ákos Bod, the Minister for Industry and Commerce).

The first 100 days: May–September 1990

The four major non-economic issues of the government's first 100 days were the election of a President, local government reform, religious education in schools, and the land question (see section on agriculture below).

The pact between the Democratic Forum and the Free Democrats appeared to have resolved the first of these. Many in the Democratic Forum were committed to the direct election of the President however, not least Király Zoltán who had stood for the Forum in the elections but resigned over the issue. He began collecting signatures to force another referendum. The Democratic Forum was persuaded, after an uncertain Third Congress in June, to support Antall and the pact, so that the only institutional supporters of this new referendum call were representatives of the old regime: the Hungarian Socialist Party, the Hungarian Socialist Workers' Party, the communist youth organization DEMISZ, and latterly the old (but renamed) trade union movement. Turnout on July 29 was minimal, only 13.91% (although 85.91% of valid votes were in favour of the direct election of the President), and the referendum was declared invalid. On August 3 parliament elected Árpád Göncz President of the Republic.

All parties agreed on the need to restructure local government, but differed on details and especially on the role of the Lord Lieutenants, the representatives of central government at the local level. Since this was an area which, under the terms of the pact, required a 75% majority in parliament, the government was ultimately obliged to give up its centralist conception, and accept a compromise giving the Government Agents, as they were re-christened, much reduced powers.

A further issue during the first 100 days was religious education in schools. After earlier announcements indicating that it would be compulsory, the Minister of Education announced in June an agreement making it optional. This did not end the debate however, and, in a final agreement on July 13, he retreated further, indicating that the churches would pay the costs of religious education, and attendance and exam results would not be logged in the standard school record books. Other issues of the period were the national coat of arms, which was finally resolved in early July, and the Justice Plan, announced on August 27, which removed all privileges, such as supplementary pensions, awarded by the former regime.

The government's own assessment of its achievements during the first 100 days was understandably up-beat. It had restructured the ministries, transformed the Ministry of the Interior from a police ministry to one of public administration, begun the restructuring of the army, determined the principles of returning property to the church, introduced a new direction in foreign policy, restored foreign confidence in the economy, taken the first steps in privatization, and established a Compensation Office to help undo some of the damage caused by the former state. The opposition Free Democrat view was less forgiving: there still was no serious economic programme, price rises taken in isolation were inflationary, the government was excessively interventionist, and its nationalism frightened away foreign investment.

Local elections and their aftermath: September–October 1990

Turnout in the local elections was lower than in the parliamentary elections of the spring: 40.18% in the first round, 28.94% in the second. Forty-two of the 65 registered parties ran candidates, as did 647 social organizations and 12 national minorities; and there were also many more jointly sponsored candidates. The clear winners in the smaller villages were the independents, many of whom had previously held office in the local government, local

Table 3:   Local elections in 141 settlements of over 10,000,
September–October 1990 (%)

	Individual Candidates	List
AFD	17.2	20.7
AFD–AYD joint	16.9	5.0
Independent	14.9	—
HDF	12.0	18.3
AYD	8.4	15.3
ISP	6.0	7.8
CDPP	5.7	8.0
HSP	2.6	10.1
HDF–CDPP joint	2.5	2.5
HDF–ISP–CDPP joint	2.4	2.2
HDF–ISP joint	2.1	—
HSWP	—	1.3
Others	under 1.0	under 1.0

Source: *Magyar Hírlap*, 16 October 1990.

Table 4:   Election for Budapest Assembly
(first round invalid, second round turnout 35.4%),
September–October 1990 (%)

	Individual Candidates
AFD	34.7
HDF	27.3
AYD	18.2
HSP	7.3
CDPP	5.0
HSWP	3.6
ISP	2.3
Alliance[1]	0.72
Social Democrats	0.56
Budapest Alliance[2]	0.41

Notes: [1]Alliance of Budapest Town and Citizen
Organizations.
[2]Budapest Alliance of Industrial Bodies.
Source: *Magyar Hírlap*, 16 October 1990.

Table 5:   Local elections in 2,926 settlements
of less than 10,000, September–October 1990 (%)

	Mayors	"Small list"
Independent	82.9	71.2
ISP	3.7	6.2
HDF	2.3	4.3
AFD	1.9	4.0
CDPP	1.8	2.8
Agrarian Alliance	—	1.3
HSP	—	1.1
Other	—	under 1.0

Source: Magyar Hírlap, 16 October 1990.

party structure. The government was also roundly defeated in the larger communities. The coalition parties won a majority of seats in only one Budapest district and only five of Hungary's 19 counties, all, with one exception, in southern Hungary. They fared even worse in the county towns. Only in Kecskemét did the government parties win a clear victory (see Tables 3, 4 and 5).

The local election results indicate that the capital and the county towns were more opposition-inclined than the villages and small towns that surrounded them. In Budapest, the Free Democrats were favoured, but in the county towns, despite significant variations, a preference for the Young Democrats was apparent. The Young Democrats increased their vote amongst younger semi-skilled and white-collar workers, and generally attracted the dissatisfied from all camps with their as yet untainted no-compromise stance. The Free Democrats lost some support amongst their more elderly voters.

If local elections constituted a defeat for two of the three coalition parties (the Democratic Forum and the Smallholders), they represented a considerable victory for the Young Democrats who had, in Viktor Orbán, a leader of charisma and considerable personal popularity. The behaviour of the Young Democrats after the election led some to suspect that popularity and power, rather than the implementation of a political programme, were the party's overriding goals. Although they had entered the elections in many towns, including Budapest, in an apparent coalition with the Free Democrats, they shied away from responsibility and refused to participate in government after the elections in Budapest and some other towns.

The taxi blockade and after: October–December 1990

Out of the blue, Hungary's peaceful revolution was rocked by the direct action of a group of workers who, although neither numerous nor particularly underprivileged, manifestly enjoyed popular support. After months of postponing petrol price increases, the government announced an average 65% rise from midnight on Thursday October 25. Spontaneously, throughout the country, communicating by means of short-wave radio, lorry and taxi drivers blockaded towns, bridges, and border crossings during the course of the Thursday night.

The blockade lasted until the following Sunday evening. At first, the government stood firm, taking exception to a late-night television address by the President of the Republic in which he appeared to side with the demonstrators by asking the government to withdraw the increase until Monday when negotiations could take place. The situation then turned to stalemate as the Budapest police chief made it clear he would not use force against the crowds, and the barricades did not come down despite apparent agreement on the Saturday night. Negotiations on the Sunday, broadcast in their entirety live on television, were successful however: the government gave in, withdrawing the price rise until such time as petrol prices were fully liberalized and hence outside the political domain.

Public opinion surveys taken immediately after the negotiations revealed high levels of support for the drivers and criticism of the government, especially Horváth and Bod, who had taken the initial tough line. Following the blockade, Antall promised more consensus government and, on November 6, announced his intention to reshuffle his government. When the first stage of the reshuffle was announced, over a month later, Horváth was replaced as Interior Minister, although he retained a government post. The Minister of Finance resigned at his own request, and Antall sacked the Minister of State in the Prime Minister's Office in an attempt to bring to a close the debilitating argument over spheres of authority that had existed between the two bodies.

The taxi blockade impacted on party politics in two ways. Pozsgay resigned from the Socialist Party before the beginning of its Congress on November 9 to form a new Citizens' Movement for the Republic. A Hungarian Centre Alliance was similarly formed by other political groupings which had performed badly in the elections. Both looked for support to the mass of non-voters who had expressed their dissatisfaction with the current political choice by supporting the taxi-blockade. Within the coalition parties, factional divisions became more apparent, although the Party Congresses of the Democratic Forum and the Smallholders held in mid-December papered over most of the cracks.

Economic Overview

Despite being the most radically reformed of the Eastern European economies at the end of 1988, Hungary also had the highest level of *per capita* external debt. It enjoyed a head start over its neighbours in terms of institutional reform, trade and price liberalization, and internal equilibrium and, hence, was not an immediate candidate for "shock therapy". The democratically elected government's reluctance to take painful decisions in its first 200 days of office whittled much of that lead away however, and radical measures, if not "shock therapy", were being proposed by the end of 1990.

See Tables 6–9 outlining the main economic trends 1988–90.

Hungary's head start

During the long decade of economic stagnation from 1978 to 1989 the Hungarian economy underwent successive minor reforms which, cumulatively, provided the basis for stabilization and privatization before the radical political changes of 1989 and 1990 were in train. The New Economic Mechanism of 1968 swept away the traditional compulsory plan

Table 6:   External relations (percentage of equivalent period in previous year)

	1988	1989	1990[1]
Total foreign debt	20.21	20.96	20.29
Foreign convertible currency debt	19.63	20.61	20.01
Foreign assets	6.34	6.73	6.10
Balance of trade	+0.47	+0.54	+0.50
Current account balance of payments	−0.81	−1.44	+0.19
Tourism	+0.04	−0.35	+0.13

Note: [1]first three quarters of 1990
Source: Hungarian National Bank.

Table 7:   Domestic production and economic activity
(percentage of equivalent period in previous year)

	1989	1990[1]
GDP	99.8	95.0[2]
Domestic absorption	99.6	NA
of which domestic consumption	99.7	NA
gross accumulation	99.4	NA
Investments[3]	116.2	101.8
Total industrial production[4]	97–99	90–93
Industrial employment	98.3	91.5
Production per employee	100.7	98.3
Retail trade turnover	98.9	87.8
Construction activity	101.6	87.4

Notes: [1]first three quarters of 1990
[2]Minister for International Foreign Relations' estimate for full year.
[3]In current prices. Other indices based on comparable prices.
[4]Depends on precise method of calculation.
Source: Hungarian Central Statistical Office.

targets. Ministerial and small business reforms in the early 1980s increased competition. An embryonic capital market began following the introduction of enterprise bonds in 1983. Total economic autonomy from the administrative apparatus was achieved in 1985. The banking system was reformed in 1987, and the tax system in 1988. In 1988, the Party accepted a radical economic reform plan which reduced subsidies and abandoned controls on 67–68% of consumer prices and 35–40% of imports. It also passed the Company Act, which made possible the formation of limited liability companies and the ownership by individuals (corporate and natural) of shares as well as bonds, while a new law on foreign investment provided generous conditions for inward investment, offering tax concessions for low levels of investment, and permitting the repatriation of profits. Both came into force on January 1, 1989.

Table 8:   Wages, incomes and prices
(percentage of the equivalent period in the previous year)

	1989	1990[1]
Real incomes	102.5	NA
Real wages of workers and employees	100.4	NA
Real earnings of agric. co-op workers	96.8	NA
Gross average earnings	—	124.2
Industrial price index	114.6	118.6
Agricultural producer price index	119.1	127.4
Consumer price index	117.0	127.2
for food products	117.7	134.4
for other industrial goods	122.4	126.1

Note: [1]first three quarters of 1990. The gross average earnings figure is given as a proxy because real wage and income figures are not available for the first three quarters of 1990.
Source: Hungarian Central Statistical Office.

Table 9:   Unemployment, vacancies and new company formation

	1988	1989	1990[1]
Registered unemployment	15,000	23,000	60,000
Unfilled vacancies	71,000	36,000	23,000
No. of limited liability companies	567	4,792	16,155

Note: [1]first three quarters of 1990. The expected figure for the full year is between 80–100,000 which is equivalent to 3–4% of the working population.
Sources: *Figyelő* (Hungarian economics weekly, various issues) and Hungarian Central Statistical Office.

Key economic measures necessary for removing disequilibria and initiating privatization thus preceded the birth of political democracy in Hungary.

The Németh government: November 1988–April 1989

Németh's reform communist government continued the policies of liberalization and reform. By 1990 some 65–70% of convertible currency imports could be acquired without special authorisation, controls had been lifted on the majority of food prices, and a series of reform commissions, official and unofficial, had produced ever more radical reform proposals.

Németh's government twice had to take radical measures to bring budget expenditure in line with IMF prescriptions. In May 1989 the IMF suspended an instalment of its credit agreement because of increasing government expenditure. An emergency plan had to be introduced in June, resulting in price increases in July and September, mainly for food products. One key factor in Hungary's deteriorating external balance was spending by Hungarian tourists on consumer durables abroad (US$77,000,000 in two days in April

1989). In the autumn, the government acted to stop this by introducing, on November 20, an annual entitlement to foreign currency of only $50.

It proved equally difficult to bring the 1990 budget within IMF recommendations. The IMF insisted on reform to the housing finance system, which granted loans at hugely subsidized interest rates. Parliament finally passed the necessary legislation, but only after Németh had resigned from the Party. The price rises which followed in January and February included increases of 32% for meat, 42% for milk, 35% for rent and 45% for transport. On March 14, 1990, the Constitutional Court ruled the government's housing finance changes unconstitutional (although they were repealed only by the Antall government on June 25), but the IMF nevertheless authorised the credits it had made conditional on passing an acceptable budget, encouraged, perhaps, by the government's radicalism in suspending ruble-denominated trade.

Despite the inauspicious start, the Németh government, judged by 1989 figures, was not unsuccessful. Hungary's current account balance of payments registered a record deficit of $1.44 billion, but much of this was accounted for by the record deficit in tourism, and measures had been taken to reverse this trend. Price and trade liberalization had resulted in higher inflation, but it was a long way from hyper-inflation. The economy was in recession. GDP was 99.8% of the previous year, and domestic absorption registered 99.6%. Industrial production, industrial employment, investment, retail turnover, and construction activity all declined and unemployment increased. But this was an inevitable concomitant of stabilization, and the creation of 4,225 new limited liability companies indicated some initial success in economic restructuring.

The Németh government more or less coincided with the era of "spontaneous privatization" as astute managers made use of the possibilities of the Company Act to transform themselves into owners. "Spontaneous" privatizers were invariably accused of undervaluing state assets, although this criticism was equally true of state-sponsored privatization. After a series of scandals (Tungsram, HungarHotels, Ganz-Hunslet, ÁPISZ, and the Budapest Ship Factory, for example) the government decided in September 1989 that state control of the privatization process was necessary. Legislation was passed in January, and the State Property Agency began work at the beginning of March. The State Audit Office later revealed that under "spontaneous privatization" 98–99% of property worth 47 billion forints had remained in state hands; only 3.2 billion forints-worth of foreign capital had been attracted; and it had been common for foreign investors to take out of the country more than they put in.

The Antall government: May–December 1990

The Antall government continued the reform policies of its predecessor with regard to price and import liberalization, the encouragement of small businesses, taxation, and (more rigorously than its predecessor) forcing insolvent enterprises into bankruptcy. Despite declarations by individual politicians to the contrary, it also remained firmly committed to not defaulting on, or even rescheduling, foreign debt. It differed from its predecessor in its attitude to the State Property Agency, however, which, after highly publicized and unjustified criticisms of its performance, was transferred to government rather than parliamentary supervision.

After winning the election, the Democratic Forum promised speedy tax reform, a reduction of inflation to 10% over three years, and a reduction of the state sector to 35% of the economy in three to five years. It also promised to take note of the recommendations of the international Blue Ribband and domestic Bridge Group proposals for economic reform. Despite this overabundance of expert advice, the government's major economic statements (the 100-day short-term action programme, the emergency stabilization plan for 1990, and the Programme for National Renewal) have done little more than list desirable, sometimes mutually contradictory, goals.

The government weathered three short-term crises in addition to pursuing its stabilization and restructuring policies. First, in May, there was a credit crisis, the result of uncertainty in the financial community occasioned by Bulgaria freezing debt repayments and Antall's delay in forming a government, and the government was obliged to obtain a loan of $300,000 from the Bank for International Settlements. Second, the IMF made it clear that future loans would be dependent on bringing the budget deficit and foreign debt in line with the targets already agreed with the Németh government, and this required a new austerity package, including price increases, which was finally passed in July as part of the emergency stabilization plan, after acrimonious debates in parliament about the constitutionality of the proposals. Third, there was the 1991 budget. The IMF agreed to the government's hastily reduced budget proposal in mid-December of a deficit of 78 billion forints (it had been over 100 billion in early November) and external debt of $1.2 billion; and at 11 p.m. on December 30 parliament accepted the budget, putting the government on course for a three-year agreement with the IMF, an ambition the Németh government had sought but failed to achieve.

In terms of overall performance, the trends of 1989 continued in 1990, but even more markedly: the drop in output, retailing, investment, and construction activity was greater; unemployment was higher, but so was the number of new company formations, by a factor of well over three. Official estimates put the contribution of new small business to industry at 9% and construction at 40% in the first half of 1990. Tourism returned to surplus, and the trade surplus with the West was set to increase, although in November it declined considerably because of the need to buy oil on the open market. The burden of inflation fell increasingly on the consumer as subsidies were removed, and particularly on food and rents.

In December, measures were taken to permit Hungarian companies to pay directly for their imports in local currencies. This, it was argued, virtually completed *de facto* convertibility of the forint for companies, since most imports were liberalized and foreign investors' profits could be repatriated. Full convertibility of the forint has been predicted for 1991, but, given Hungary's shortage of foreign currency reserves, 1993 is more likely.

Privatization

Antall's government committed itself to privatization (the sale of previously socialized assets to new owners) rather than reprivatization (their return to previous owners), despite pressure to the contrary from certain sections of the Smallholders' Party, and despite the creation of a Compensation Office on the grounds that it could not afford the financial cost or the time required for reprivatization. The first element in the privatization programme to go through parliament was the "pre-privatization" of state retail, catering and consumer services activities. Central to this programme were the National Small Enterprise Development Office, which began operations on November 1, and the *Egszisztencia* Fund, to be administered partly by the former with the task of providing loans for prospective purchases. The implementation of the *Egszisztencia* Fund was delayed because of uncertainties about who would underwrite bad debts, and was expected to be introduced in January 1991.

The government prescribed three paths to privatization proper: state-initiated, privately initiated by the enterprise concerned, and privately initiated by an external party. Twenty enterprises listed in the government statement on September 14 constituted the first step in the state-initiated path. The government expected an income of 25–40 billion forints from the first sales, and hoped that up to 150 enterprises would be sold in the first 18 months, valued at 80–120 billion forints. Once in full swing in 1991, state-initiated privatization is planned to take place on three or four occasions a year, each offering some 40–60 enterprises to the private sector, so permitting 500–600 enterprises, roughly a third of state property, to be privatized over the course of the first three years. The programme envisaged privatization via the sale of shares on the Stock Exchange or through sale by tender for either the whole or reorganized parts of state enterprises. It further envisaged the mechanism for each round of state-initiated privatizations itself being put to tender (privatization of privatization) to consultancy companies. A second state-initiated round was planned for 1990 but, in the event, the first round was only partially completed. Some 250 tenders were received, but only 12 of the 20 privatization proposals had been announced by the end of 1990, with western consultancy companies being awarded the bulk of the contracts. Only one privatization was to be handled entirely by a Hungarian company (*Co-Nexus*), and an Anglo-Hungarian consortium (involving the Inter-Europa Bank) won a second.

The second and third paths for privatization essentially continued "spontaneous privatization", but under stricter control by the State Property Agency. No timetable was prescribed for enterprise-initiated privatizations, by which 300–400 enterprises were expected to be sold. By mid-October, the State Property Agency had published a guide on how to purchase a state company in order to facilitate privatizations of this type, and 60 privatizations outside the state programme had been authorised, fixing an average sale price of 148% of book value.

Key Economic Sectors

Agriculture

Agricultural production fell in both 1989 and 1990, and this was compounded in 1990 by the effects of a drought. Livestock figures indicate a fall in the volume of sales of live animals and animal products in both 1989 and in the first nine months of 1990. (Live animal sales were 96.2% in 1989 and 94.5% after the first nine months of 1990 of the equivalent period in the previous year; sales of animal products fell to 98.5% and 92.1% respectively.) Crop sales by volume in 1989 were mainly down on 1988. (Wheat sales were 90.2%, rye 103.4%, maize 96.1%, sugar beet 113.4%, sunflowers 97.1%, tomatoes 96%, green peppers 52% and wine 52% of their 1988 value.) This trend continued in the first nine months of 1990. (Cereals generally registered 81.0%, wheat 73.1%, maize 177.6%, sugar beet 119%, tomatoes 129.1%, green peppers 76.5%, and wine 74.8% of the preceding year's production in the equivalent period.) Output of food products was up by 1% on 1988 in 1989, but in the first nine months of 1990 had fallen to 97.8% of the equivalent period in 1989.

In the first half of 1990, it looked as if the previous year's $1.7 billion-worth of agricultural exports would be exceeded by $200–300 million. Estimates in October, however, suggested that the effect of the drought on convertible currency trade would be $150 million; $90,000,000 for importing seed maize and wheat for fodder, and $60,000,000 in lost wheat and canned goods exports. At home, there were reports of breeding pigs being slaughtered and of meat costing almost £4 per kilo because of the combined effects of drought, shortage of fodder, and increases in energy prices.

The major issue in agriculture during 1989 and 1990 was the question of land ownership. For much of 1989, the agrarian policies of the newly forming parties generally agreed that the collective farms should be transformed into service centres for new authentic co-operatives, and that the key issue was to increase the efficiency of both large-scale and small-scale agriculture by creating a market in land. In this spirit, the Németh government regularized the sale of agricultural land in January 1990.

By the time of the elections, however, the Smallholders' Party had developed its distinctive policy of returning land to its (pre-collectivization, post-land reform) 1947 owners; and, because Smallholders' Party support was necessary for the formation of Antall's coalition, the government was obliged to adopt the Party's agricultural policy. A prohibition on all further sales of land was promulgated at the beginning of June; but then the government prevaricated. The Smallholders issued a deadline of August 20 for presenting a bill to parliament, but this passed with no breakup of the coalition. The government then submitted its proposed land bill to the Constitutional Court which, to the relief of the opposition and many in the government, ruled, on October 3, that the policy was unconstitutional: by introducing reprivatization and full compensation into agriculture but not other sectors of the economy, it would be acting in a discriminatory manner. Despite subsequent agreement on the need rapidly to reformulate and pass a law on land ownership, no such bill came before parliament before the end of 1990, and all reports that a compromise solution in terms of compensation bonds had been reached were followed by denials from various Smallholders' spokespersons. Figures released by the Ministry of Agriculture in October indicated that, despite the uncertainty occasioned by this prolonged and undecisive debate, harvesting had progressed normally.

Manufacturing industry

The recession induced by economic restructuring was felt throughout industry. Industrial output fell in almost every branch of industry in 1989 and 1990. In 1989, mining fell to 94.8% of the previous year, and in the first nine months of 1990 fell to 88.6% of the equivalent period in 1989. Metallurgy and engineering marginally increased in 1989 (104.4% and 100.2%), before falling in the first three quarters of 1990 (79.3% and 84.4%). Light industry and the chemical industry registered a decline in output in both years (95.2% and 96.1% respectively in 1989, and 88.7% and 92.6% respectively in the first nine months of 1990). Industrial employment fell by orders of magnitude equivalent to the drop in output, except for mining and metallurgy where the earlier implementation of a redundancy policy resulted in a much larger drop in employment (92.0% and 91.9%

respectively in 1989, and 83.2% and 81.7% respectively in the first nine months of 1990). This resulted in significant productivity gains in mining in both 1989 (103%) and the first nine months of 1990 (106.5%), and, in the case of metallurgy, in a larger productivity gain in 1989 only (113.6%).

This fall in output was associated with an increase in bankruptcies. In the case of enterprises heavily dependent on Soviet trade such as *Ikarus*, the bus producer, this was a consequence of restrictions on ruble-based trade introduced in January 1990. On August 2 the government published a list of seven enterprises against which state-initiated bankruptcy proceedings would begin. New company formations, although more significant in the commercial sector, reached over 1,000 in both engineering and light industry.

Transport

Transport statistics also reflect the effects of the recession. The 1989 figure for the total weight of goods transported was 90% of that of 1988, and that for kilometre-commodity-tonnes 97.5%. Decline in the first nine months of 1990 was greater: 71.5% for the total weight of goods transported and 88.8% for kilometre-commodity-tonnes compared with the equivalent period in 1990. Passenger transport figures in passenger-kilometres reveal that, in 1989, long distance travel increased marginally (100.9% of 1988), but local transport declined to 95.1%. Figures for the number of passengers in the first nine months of 1990 registered a decline in both long distance (90%) and local (91.3%) passenger transport.

Although the total length of motorways and metros did not increase in 1989, in 1990 15 kilometres of the MO Budapest ring road and four kilometres of the Budapest's north-south metro line were opened. Following the abolition of the Post Office's postal monopoly at the beginning of 1990, the Australian-based TNT established an express parcel delivery service. It had already entered into a joint air freight venture with *MALÉV*, the Hungarian airline, in 1988. There was also discussion of the desirability of completing the Vienna-Budapest motorway and constructing a rapid rail link with Vienna in time for the proposed Vienna-Budapest World Exhibition. A final decision about this exhibition which was proposed before the change of system passed numerous deadlines. The government ultimately deferred a decision until the newly elected Budapest Council had taken a view; and, in December, the Budapest Council prevaricated further, announcing it would support an Exhibition in 1996 rather than 1995 if seven conditions were met by April 1991.

Finance

The most visible development in the financial sector in Hungary in 1989 and 1990 was the opening on June 21, 1990 of the Budapest Stock Market. With the development of a bond market since 1983, and the introduction of treasury bills and other forms of financial instrument in the course of 1988, rumours of the stock market reopening persisted throughout 1987 and 1988, and for a long time March 1990 was the expected date. By the end of the year, not only had the stock market been opened, it had also chalked up its first case of insider dealing when the State Securities Supervisory Board announced that the brokerage company *Attitüd Ltd* had been guilty of insider dealing following the launch of *Dunaholding plc* onto the market on November 19.

Attracted by the relatively well developed financial system that made the launch of the stock market possible, nearly all of the world accountancy and management consultant firms (*Price Waterhouse*, *Ernst and Young*, *Touche Ross* and so on) established themselves in Budapest over the course of 1989 and 1990, as did numerous other world financial institutions such as *Crédit Suisse*, *First Boston* and *Nomura Securities*. Governments proved wary about permitting the takeover of Hungarian banks by foreigners however. Under the Németh government, the State Property Agency stopped attempts by *Westdeutsche Landesbank* and the Dresdner Bank in conjunction with the *Banque Nationale de Paris* from taking 25% each in the Hungarian Credit Bank and the National Commercial and Credit Bank. A moratorium was placed on all sales of banks to foreigners until September 30, since when no takeovers or direct investment in Hungarian banks has taken place. Nevertheless, new ventures abound. In December, the formation was announced of four banks with varying degrees of foreign participation from Germany, France, Austria, the USA, Italy and Japan, and the press noted a boom in banking while production in the real economy fell. By the end of 1990, seven insurance sector public limited liability companies operated in Hungary, of which five have foreign participation.

Energy

The most significant development in the field of energy in 1989 and 1990 was the shortfall in Soviet oil supplies in 1990. This shortfall impacted on the trade balance (in that it necessitated unplanned imports from the West) and on the political situation (in that it was a contributory factor in the build-up to the taxi blockade). Press reports in the spring of 1990 predicted shortfalls because of planned Soviet reductions in deliveries, and in July the flow of oil along the Friendship pipeline stopped for a day and a half, with the result that third quarter deliveries were 30% below planned levels and Hungary had to spend $60,000,000, when oil prices were at their Gulf crisis peak, buying 280 million tonnes of oil on the open market. The flow of Soviet oil stopped for six days in September, obliging further open market purchases, and only 4.5 million of the contracted 6.5 million tonnes is expected for the year as a whole.

The link between energy supplies and political stability was recognized by Western European governments at the time of the taxi blockade. Promises of help were immediately forthcoming, and within days it was reported that Germany would send 500,000 tonnes of coal and 150,000 tonnes of coal briquettes to Hungary from its strategic reserves, and that Austria and Italy had already offered emergency fuel supplies.

The decision in principle to stop work on the Gabčíkovo-Nagymaros dam across the Danube was made as early as May 1989. The issue remained unresolved by the end of 1990 however. Negotiations between the Hungarians and Slovak authorities were still in train concerning how the landscape was to be restored; but in mid-November the Austrian and Hungarian contractors (*Donaukraftwerke* and *Oviber*) agreed on damages for the Austrian party of 2.6 billion schillings.

Mines in the Pécs and Borsod regions have been closed and special funds created to ease employment problems, but the interest expressed in August by the Irish company *Glencar* in the region's uranium mines, together with drastic staff reductions, led the government to suspend its decree to close the mine at the end of 1990.

New technology

At the beginning of 1989 the Hungarian computer industry was at its peak. Although the state sector stagnated, numerous Small Co-operatives (a particular form of loosely regulated co-operative) had made the most of the personal computer boom and were becoming very wealthy assembling the latest generation of *IBM* PC compatible computers. Hungary was the only Eastern European country where domestically-produced 32-bit personal computers were available as early as 1987.

The virtual abolition of COCOM restrictions following democratic parliamentary elections destroyed the market for technically obsolescent CMEA-produced mainframe and mini-computers; and trade liberalization cut into the highly protected market which the Small Co-operatives had created for themselves. State enterprises and Small Co-operatives alike either diversified into other products, set up legitimate dealerships, or entered into joint ventures with the major European and American computer producers. *Groupe Bull*, *DEC* and *Siemens* all set up joint ventures in Hungary in 1990. *IBM* had maintained a presence in Hungary during the 40 years of socialism, but radically increased its profile in 1990, donating computers to the three Budapest universities.

In telecommunications, despite the interest of North American corporations and *Northern Telecom*'s joint venture with the major telephone equipment supplier *BHG* in early 1990, the major tender for the improvement of Hungary's telephone system went to two European companies: *Siemens* and *Ericsson*. The Hungarian partner in the *Ericsson* bid, *Műszertechnika*, was the most successful of the Small Co-operatives, whose entrepreneurial chief is a member of the leadership of the ruling Hungarian Democratic Forum.

Foreign Economic Relations

Over the course of 1989 and 1990 a dramatic restructuring of Hungary's economic relations took place. Trade was reoriented away from the Soviet Union and former CMEA partners towards the West, especially Germany. In addition, the domestic economy was reopened to western private corporations, especially from the German-speaking nations of Europe, at the expense of inter-governmental co-operation within the context of the CMEA.

The changing pattern of trade

Two abiding problems of the Hungarian economy in the 1980s were its mounting trade surplus with the Soviet Union and its declining share of western markets. These worked together to reinforce Hungarian technological backwardness. The problems had proved intractable because, on the one hand, it was in the interests of the managers of the large state companies which dominated the economy to supply on long contracts to the relatively undemanding CMEA market and, on the other, the Party apparatus was politically committed to the CMEA. By the end of 1989, however, the Németh government was sufficiently convinced of the need for reform to take on these two natural allies and replace years of exhortation by administrative restriction. On January 18, 1990 the government unilaterally suspended all licences for exports denominated in rubles, and in the subsequent months turned a (relatively) deaf ear to cries of anguish from management and workers in enterprises with significant Soviet trade.

The results of these measures were striking. By the third quarter of 1990, although the

Soviet Union continued to be Hungary's major trading partner, with a total value of imports into Hungary of 72 billion forints and exports of 82 billion forints, the Federal Republic of Germany (pre-unification) already provided Hungary with 61 billion forints-worth of imports and received 66 billion forints-worth of exports. If the 21 billion forints-worth of imports and the 14 billion forints-worth of exports with the former GDR are added to these figures, the territory of the united Germany was already Hungary's major trading partner in 1990.

Comparing figures for the first three quarters of 1990 with the same period in 1989, imports from West Germany increased 12% and exports 56%, resulting in a five billion forint trade surplus. Imports from the Soviet Union, on the other hand, fell to 85.6% of the previous year, and exports to 77.6%, so reducing the trade surplus with the Soviet Union from 21.4 to 9.9 billion forints. Similar swings are visible in trade with the rest of the CMEA (exports to Bulgaria 41%, to Poland 47%, to Czechoslovakia 77.6% of the equivalent period in the previous year) and the rest of the European Community (exports to Belgium up by 41%, to the UK by 19%, to Italy 29%, and to the Netherlands by 32%). Trade with Japan and South Korea also increased, although on the import rather than the export side. Imports from Japan increased by 31.4% and from South Korea by 79.8%. Exports to South Korea increased by 26%, but exports to Japan fell to only 97.2% of the previous period. Trade with the German-speaking nations (Germany, Austria and Switzerland) is even more significant than with Germany alone. Even in 1989, 40.8% of Hungary's imports came from these countries, not so very much less than the 44.1% of 51 years earlier in 1938.

These trends can only increase in the 1990s as trade within the CMEA is converted to world prices denominated in dollars. The immediate effect of this change is expected to be a $1.5–2 billion increase in Hungary's balance-of-payments deficit, and a 50–70 billion forint increase in the budget deficit. This large increase in the budget deficit is in part due to the fact that the difference between CMEA prices and world prices constituted a source of revenue for the national budget.

Inward investment

The Company Act and Foreign Investment Acts which came into effect on January 1, 1989 were successful in convincing a large number of western corporations, large and small, to invest directly in Hungary. Many of the large joint ventures with major multinationals were established under the Németh administration before the State Property Agency had been created. These include the creation of *Ganz-Hunslet* in June 1989 (51% British, 49% Hungarian); the sale of *Tungsram* to *General Electric* in November 1989 (at $150 million the biggest investment to date); the purchase in December by the German insurer *Allianz* of 49% of *Hungária Biztosító*; the announcements, both in January, that *General Motors* and *Suzuki* would set up assembly operations in Hungary; and the sale, in February, of part of the Ózd Iron and Steel Works to a West German, Austrian, and private Hungarian consortium. The latter was signed on the last day before the creation of the State Property Agency because it did not conform to the new regulations.

In April, after the State Property Agency had begun operations, Hungary's other major insurer, the State Insurance Company (the only state insurer before a token competitor was created in the 1980s) took a 60% share in a Hungarian, Italian and Austrian consortium, and *Guardian Industries* of the USA embarked on a float glass venture. In May, the German

AEG returned to Hungary after a 40-year absence in a deal with *Transelektro*. Not all attempts at attracting foreign capital were successful. Protracted negotiations from autumn 1989 to spring 1990 between the Péti Nitrogen Works and a Swiss partner finally ended in failure. The works was bought by a Hungarian consortium.

Foreign direct investment under the Antall government has attracted less publicity, partly because the deals were smaller, partly because it had become an everyday occurrence. *Ford* announced a venture using a site provided by the soon-to-be-bankrupt *Videoton* factory on June 16, 1990. German interest continued, for example, with a deal between *Compack* and Hamburg-based *Tchibo-Rost Kaffee GmbH* to create *Compack-Tchibo RT*; state-owned Italian companies took interests in the Salgotarjan Iron and Steel Works and another element of the former *Ganz* conglomerate; the Indian hotel group *Oberoi* entered into a venture with *HungarHotels*; and in November the ultimately state-controlled French pharmaceutical company *Safofi* took a 40% state in *Chinoin*, Hungary's second largest pharmaceutical company. The fate of *Ikarus* and *Csepel Auto* had not been determined by the end of 1990, but foreign participation in the solution was almost certain, and the favoured candidate appeared to be a joint venture between enterprises from some Soviet republics in conjunction with the Toronto-based *Central European Investment Company* rather than famous names such as *Daimler Benz*.

The interest of Japanese and South Korean investors, although quite small, should be noted. In addition to the *Suzuki* deal, *Nomura Securities*, Japan's largest stockbroker, announced plans at the end of November to establish a 51% stake in a joint venture investment bank in Hungary. *Samsung* and Hungary's *Orion* television set producers established a joint venture in late 1988, and the company was supplying colour TVs to Austria, Hungary and the Soviet Union by April 1990, and *Daewoo Securities* set up a joint venture with the Hungarian Credit Bank.

Despite a dearth of reliable statistics, the following patterns in inward investment can be discerned. First, while most interest has been directed towards tourism and the services, there has been interest in industrial sectors such metallurgy, engineering, and chemicals. But this interest was largely expressed either in the early days, when assets could be picked up cheap, or by state-owned western companies, relatively sheltered from market forces. Second, although there is a numerical superiority of joint ventures from surrounding countries such as Germany and Austria, much of this investment is small-scale. German predominance is not all-pervasive as far as major international companies are concerned. It should also be noted that, by 1990, the stake of foreign companies amounted only to some 2% of Hungarian industry, compared with 20–40% in smaller Western European countries such as Austria, Ireland and Portugal (see Table 10).

An entirely new development in 1990, when it became clear that the political changes in Eastern Europe were irreversible, was the formation in the West of investment funds and corporations geared to attracting investment to Eastern Europe. By late 1990, the view was circulating with regard to these funds (such as the First Hungary Fund, established in conjunction with the Hungarian National Bank, John Govett's Hungarian Investment Company, Salomon Brothers' Fund for Eastern Europe, the Merrill Lynch-organized Austro-Hungarian Fund, the Hungarian-American Enterprise Fund) that the euphoria had faded, the pool of opportunities was so small that all institutions were chasing the same ones, and the majority of the funds collected were still on deposit in the West. Such views overstated the case. Although slow to start, and despite threats from certain quarters in mid-1990 to take their money elsewhere, by the end of the year funds such

Table 10:   Inward investment by country of origin:
November 1990 (approximate figures only)

	Number of joint ventures
Germany	1,000
Austria	1,000
USA	260
Switzerland	250
UK	150
Italy	130
Sweden	130
The Netherlands	85
France	65
Japan	12
South Korea	3

Source: *Heti Világgazdaság* (Hungarian current affairs weekly), 8 December 1990, p. 84.

as the Hungarian Investment Company claimed significant investments in listed securities and companies such as *Graboplast* (a producer of synthetic materials), *Terimpex* (a meat trader), and *Nikex* (an industrial trading and holding company). Nevertheless, when a politician on the populist wing of the Democratic Forum, Dénes Csengey, heard that money raised for First Hungarian Investment Fund was still on deposit (in fact in London), he caused a minor scandal by accusing one of the fund's administrators, the Canadian businessman of Hungarian origin, Andrew Sarlos, of investing it in New York to further his personal ends.

Despite the opening of the Budapest Stock Exchange in June 1990, opportunities for portfolio investment have been restricted as Lajos Bokros, president of the Budapest Stock Exchange, warned they would following the opening of the exchange. The Austro-Hungary Fund, launched in June 1990, was the first to concentrate on investment in listed equities.

Principal Personalities

Antall, József. President of the Hungarian Democratic Forum since October 1989. Formally appointed Prime Minister in Hungary's coalition government on May 23, 1990. His father was a member of the Smallholders' Party and held ministerial rank in the post-war coalition. Took part in the brief resurrection of the Smallholders' Party in 1956 and, following the uprising, under a publication and teaching ban, worked as a librarian and archivist, finally becoming Director General of the *Semmelweis* Medical Museum, Library and Archive. He was offered posts in both the Smallholder and Christian Democrat Parties before committing himself to the Democratic Forum. He entered parliament via the National List.

Bíró, Zoltán. A leading figure in the early days of the Hungarian Democratic Forum and one of the four members of the Hungarian Socialist Workers' (communist) Party, expelled April 1988 immediately prior to the May Party Conference which effectively removed Kádár from power. He faded from the political limelight after the rise of Antall, and in November 1990 indicated that he might be willing to join Pozsgay's new political movement.

Bod, Péter Ákos. Minister for Industry and Commerce in the Antall government. After completing university he worked as an economist in the National Planning Office's Planned Economy Institute. He was one of the many contributors to *Turnabout and Reform*, an influential reform economist publication in 1987 which turned the intellectual climate in favour of property reform. His performance during the taxi blockade negotiations was rated poorly, but he was not replaced in Antall's December reshuffle.

Csurka, István. Writer, sometime editor of *Magyar Forum*, member of the leadership of the Hungarian Democratic Forum. Together with Sándor Csoóri and Dénes Csengey is one of the best known figures on the nationalist-populist wing of the party. It is in his writings and speeches that those critical of the Forum find examples of chauvinism, anti-semitism and only a weak commitment to democracy.

Demszky, Gábor. Major figure in the dissident movement in the 1980s, organizer of the AB Independent Publishers which produced *samizdat* on an illegal printing press hidden on an isolated farm, and editor of *Hírmondó*, a *samizdat* journal. Was elected Free Democrat member of parliament for Budapest's VIIth district in spring, but resigned in the autumn to run, successfully, as Mayor of Budapest. His first act on taking office was to address the problems of the Budapest homeless and illegal parking in Budapest.

Göncz, Árpád. Formally elected President of the Republic on August 3, 1990 after two referenda and endless parliamentary manoeuvring had resolved the question of how the president should be elected. Born in 1922, he was politically active for a time in the Smallholders' Party. He worked as a labourer following the communist takeover in 1948, attended the Gödöllö Agricultural University, and spent six years (of a life sentence) in prison because of his activities in 1956. He then worked as a translator and writer, becoming a member of the Writers' Association. Was a founder member of the Alliance of Free Democrats, and entered parliament on their regional list.

Grósz, Károly. Joint First Secretary of the Hungarian Socialist Workers' Party and Prime Minister following the May 1988 Party Conference which removed Kádár, he relinquished the premiership to Miklós Németh on November 24, 1988. His position was fatally weakened on June 24, 1989 when a collective leadership including three prominent reformers was announced. When the Party reconstituted itself as the Hungarian Socialist Party he stayed with the rump Hungarian Socialist Workers' Party, although Gyula Thürmer took over as first secretary. He resigned from its Central Committee on October 6, 1990.

Hankiss, Elemér. Prominent literary theorist turned sociologist and political scientist who came into prominence in the 1980s when he published numerous articles on Hungary's "second society" and dual value system. Was appointed head of Hungary's state television service in July 1990.

Haraszti, Miklós. After flirting with Maoism in his university days, he worked in the Red Star Tractor Factory, wrote *Worker in a Workers' State* (for which he received an eight months' suspended sentence) and became an editor of *Beszélő*, the *samizdat* journal of the "democratic opposition". He is a member of the leadership of the Free Democrats and represents the XIth district of Budapest in parliament.

Horn, Gyula. Foreign Minister under the Németh government who began the westward reorientation of Hungarian foreign policy and took the decision to allow East German holiday-makers to emigrate across the Austrian-Hungarian border. He took over from Rezső Nyers as president of the Hungarian Socialist Party in May 1990. He entered the new parliament on the regional list and chairs its foreign policy committee.

Horváth, Balázs. A lawyer and Democratic Forum member from the provincial town of Veszprém who was Minister of the Interior from May to December 1990. Following what was regarded as a poor performance during the taxi blockade, he was one of the victims of Antall's government reshuffle and became a minister without portfolio but with responsibility for the Secretariat for Hungarians Living Beyond the Border. Antall made it clear that he retained full confidence in him and announced that he would recommend to the Democratic Forum that he be appointed executive deputy secretary of the party.

Jeszensky, Géza. Minister for Foreign Affairs and a founding member of the Hungarian Democratic Forum (also related to Antall by marriage). He is a historian, won a Fullbright scholarship to the United States in the 1980s, and has taught at the University of Los Angeles. He is not a member of parliament.

Kádár, Béla. Former director of the Planned Economy Institute, deputy secretary of the Economic Science Association and co-ordinator of Bridge Group which published a report on prospects for the Hungarian economy immediately before the elections. He is Minister for International Economic Relations and a believer in supply-side intervention. He is neither a party member nor a member of parliament.

Király, Zoltán. Stood for election to parliament in 1985 as alternative candidate and won. He was one of the four expelled from the Hungarian Socialist Workers' Party in April 1988. In October 1989 he was proposed as presidential candidate by the Szeged Social Democratic party, but stood for the Democratic Forum in the parliamentary elections. Joined the independent seats almost immediately because of disagreement over the pact with the Free Democrats.

Kis, János. One of the leading dissidents in the 1970s and 1980s, former member of the Lukács-School and Lukács-Kindergarten, joint author of the *samizdat* classic *Is a Critical Political Economy Possible?* and (under the pseudonym Rakovski) *Towards an East European Marxism*, he was instrumental in the decisions, taken in 1976/77, to begin the production of *samizdat* on a more or less regular basis and to form the "democratic opposition". He is president of the Alliance of Free Democrats, but declined to stand for parliament, preferring to keep party and parliamentary roles distinct.

Kupa, Mihály. Appointed Minister of Finance in Antall's December government reshuffle. Did not complete his secondary school studies and worked as a manual worker in the *Chinoin* pharmaceuticals company between 1959 and 1969 while studying for an economics degree in evening classes. He then worked in the Central Statistical Office, the Finance Research Institute, and finally the Ministry of Finance. From July 1990 was managing director of *DRT Hungary*, the Hungarian arm of the international accountancy and management consultancy company *DRT International*.

Matolcsy, György. A former employee of *Finance Research Ltd*, Matolcsy made names for himself in the early property reform debates as an advocate of "enterprise cross ownership" and during the early "spontaneous privatizations" as a wealthy businessman. When approached by Antall, he accepted the challenge of applying his theories in practice and, despite his youth, was made Minister of State in the prime minister's office and chair of the committee in charge of privatization. Was a leading force in the decision to submit the land ownership proposals to the Constitutional Court. He clashed publicly with the Minister of Finance and lost his post in the December government reshuffle.

Németh, Miklós. Made Prime Minister on November 24, 1988, he had the thankless task of overseeing the demise of the old regime. Although a reformer and in favour of the creation of the new party in October 1989, he resigned from the Socialist Party in December, partly because of difficulties in getting the party to accept necessary budget measures, partly because he wanted to be sure of re-election in March. He was one of only five members of parliament elected on the first round and combines parliamentary duties as an independent with a new business career.

Nyers, Rezső. One-time Social Democrat and Hungary's most prominent advocate of economic reform (the father of the 1968 New Economic Mechanism), was somewhat by-passed by the even more radical reforms of 1989–90. Elevated to joint party leader on June 24, 1989, he was president of the Hungarian Socialist Party between the October Conference and its second conference in May 1990 when he was replaced by Gyula Horn.

Orbán, Viktor. The faction leader of the Alliance of Young Democrats in parliament and by far its most prominent leader. Came to national prominence for virulently anti-establishment and anti-Soviet comments at the June 1989 reburial of Imre Nagy, and has been a consistent critic of nationalist and authoritarian demagogy, especially from the Smallholders, in the new parliament. He is seen in some quarters as leader of a potential strong government of the centre-left.

Petrasovits, Anna. Leader of Hungary's Social Democratic Party, and the only woman who was a major political figure in 1989–90. She had no political pedigree before the rebirth of the party in the spring of 1989, and came almost from nowhere as a candidate to unite the party in the summer of 1989. She retained her post despite the poor performance of her party in both parliamentary and local elections.

Pozsgay, Imre. The most prominent of reform communists, the Party man who dubbed the events of 1956 a "popular uprising", who first talked openly about multi-party politics, attended the founding meeting of the Hungarian Democratic Forum in 1987, and helped transform the Hungarian Socialist Workers' Party in the Hungarian Socialist Party, Pozsgay was by-passed by the events of late 1989 and 1990. He became faction leader of the Socialists in the new Parliament, but before the Congress of November 1990 left the party to form the Citizens' Movement for the Republic.

Rabár, Ferenc. Minister of Finance between May and December 1990. After working his way up through commercial and communications companies, the Communications Ministry, and the Industrial Economics Institute, he took a post in the Budapest Economics University. He has visited universities in the US and the UK, and intermitted for three years in the National Planning Office. He asked to resign following disagreements over his sphere of authority and personal differences of opinion with Matolcsy. He is neither a member of parliament nor a member of the Hungarian Democratic Forum.

Tölgyessy, Péter. Researcher at the State and Law Institute who came from nowhere in the opposition movement in the spring of 1989 to give constitutional and legal advice to the Free Democrats at the time of the beginning of the Opposition Round Table. Played a central role in these negotiations and in determining the democratic institutions that emerged from them. He entered parliament on the Komáron regional list and until October 15 was faction leader for the Free Democrats in parliament.

The Media

During the course of 1989 and 1990 fundamental changes took place in the ownership, control, and preoccupations of the media. The previously unpublishable became publishable, irrespective of whether its suppression had been because it was politically subversive or pornographic; state-subsidized newspapers gained new private-sector owners, many of them foreign; but the nature of the relationship between government and both the printed and the broadcast media remained unresolved.

Samizdat *to pornography*

In the first half of 1989 Budapest was awash with *samizdat*. All the materials of the "democratic opposition" and other opposition groups which previously had only been available at the "boutique" in László Rajk's appartment were on sale on nearly every street corner. A series of books on 1956, the prison camp at Recsk, the lives of Stalinist politicians were published by a myriad of new publishing houses, as were Orwell's *1984*, Koestler's *Darkness at Noon*, and other dissident classics. *Beszélő* the *samizdat* journal of the "democratic opposition" which had helped change the intellectual climate with its special issue on the social contract in the summer of 1987, became legitimate in October 1989. But by this time the climate was changing. The backload of previously unpublishable material had dried up, and demand switched radically to depoliticized subjects such as astrology, romance, and pornography.

Foreign ownership of the press

The first Hungarian publication in which there was partial foreign interest in the guise of the German *Springer* organization was the news magazine *Reform*, in which the Hungarian Socialist Workers' (Communist) Party was also financially interested. Capitalizing on its experience of the Hungarian market and the political uncertainty of the period between the two rounds of the parliamentary elections, *Springer* acquired, in the spring of 1990, at minimal cost, seven regional papers previously run by the Party. The incident caused a scandal, but was eventually ruled to have been legally correct. By the end of 1990, 25 national and regional newspapers had foreign ownership ranging from the 9% Austrian participation in the strongly anti-government *Kurír*, to the 100% Swedish in the business daily *Üzlet*. Of the major dailies, the former Party organ *Népszabadság* was 41.2% owned by the German *Bertelsmann* company, *Magyar Hírlap* 40% by Robert Maxwell's Mirror Group, the relatively new *Mai Nap* and *Mai Reggel* both 50% by Rupert Murdoch's News International, and, after much discussion, 40% of *Magyar Nemzet*, once the paper of the Patriotic People's Front, was sold to the French *Hersant* group in December.

Given the depth of the economic recession, it is not surprising that nearly all circulations were falling towards the end of 1990. The only dailies with an increasing circulation between January and August 1990 were some of the *Springer*-purchased local papers and *Világgazdaság* (world economy) which is aiming to become the *Financial Times* of Hungary. The fall in circulation hit old and new publications alike. Newspapers in (or rumoured to be in) financial trouble towards the end of 1990 were the relatively new *Világ*, *Ring* and *Magyar Napló*, and the longer standing *Film Színház Muzsika*.

The government and the media

Whilst the Free Democrat opposition manoeuvred for the creation of supra-government bodies that might ensure the freedom of the media from government control, the government appeared intent on extending its influence over the media. In the case of the press, this meant resolving a situation in which no major daily supported it. In May, István Csurka, leading figure in the populist wing of the Forum, advocated party control of the press and the distribution of titles in proportion to the votes gained in each election, and throughout the second half of 1990 the government appeared to be using its influence to prevent *Magyar Nemzet* from establishing a venture with the Swedish group which owned *Dagens Nyheter* as the latter had published an article critical of the Forum to which the Forum took great exception. In December 1990, Csurka renewed demands that the government should have its own press paid for out of central funds. He also announced that his mouthpiece, *Magyar Fórum*, which had ceased publication at the end of the summer 1990, would restart in January 1991.

With regard to the broadcast media, the Free Democrats waged what they saw as an unceasing battle against first socialist then nationalist government intervention. The two focal points of this opposition were, first, changes inspired by Pozsgay to the management of Hungarian TV and especially its news and current affairs programmes in January 1990; and, second, following the election of the Antall government, the long-running argument about who should appoint the new heads of the radio and the television service. At the end of July it was decided they should be appointed by the President, but on the recommendation of the Prime Minister.

If the government enjoys little press support, it is generally agreed that the first, and most widely received, television channel is pro-government. Channel Two is less pro-government, and the radio programme "168 hours", which broadcast Pozsgay's interview in January 1989 describing 1956 as a "popular uprising", tends towards the opposition.

Foreign Relations

Hungary has had no tradition of an independent foreign policy since the end of World War II. In the 1950s it was a loyal satellite of Moscow, and from the 1960s the essence of the "Kádár compromise" was that Hungary should follow the Moscow line to the letter in foreign policy in return for licence in domestic policy. Responding to pressures from the newly forming political parties, an independent foreign policy began to emerge in the spring of 1989, which became increasingly pro-West (and pro-West German) and decreasingly pro-Soviet as, first, the reform communists began to dominate the Party, and, then, a non-communist government was formed by a democratically elected parliament. By the end of 1990 the government was trying to rebuild bridges with the Soviet Union; but it remained adamant on one central aspect of its independent foreign policy — its right to defend the interests of Hungarian minorities abroad.

Openings to the West

In the spring of 1989, the still-communist Hungarian government, responding to pressures for greater democracy, announced that work should begin on May 2, 1989 dismantling the "iron curtain" on the border with Austria. At this stage it was essentially a domestic issue, extending the logic of the "world passports" for Hungarian citizens introduced in 1988. But for citizens of other countries in Eastern Europe it was a chink in the "iron curtain" which could be used to advantage, and by the late summer of 1989 thousands of would-be East German holiday-maker émigrés were in camps in Hungary. The government had to choose between loyalty to its Warsaw Pact (Warsaw Treaty Organization) ally or improved relations with its major Western trading partner. Since East Germans could cross the border illegally in any case (as publicly demonstrated by the participants in the "pan-European picnic", organized in part by the Debrecen Hungarian Democratic Forum, on August 19) and hence effective allegiance to East Germany would require the reimposition of the barbed wire, Foreign Minister Horn's decision to permit the Germans to leave legally was not surprising. It was nevertheless momentous. It increased the pressure on East Germany to ease its own foreign travel restrictions, so triggering the fall of the Berlin Wall.

The Antall government extended this foreign policy reorientation towards the West. On coming to power, it announced that the Minister of International Economic Relations would have regular meetings with counterparts in West Germany, Austria, Switzerland and Czechoslovakia. It also stated its intention to join the European Communities, although it has yet to submit a formal application. Despite optimistic statements by Otto Habsburg, member of the European Parliament and heir to the Hungarian throne, that Hungary could be a member by 1995/96, Chancellor Kohl's assessment of membership by the end of the decade seems more realistic. Meanwhile, Hungary signed a co-operation agreement with EFTA in June, voted for membership of the European Bank for Reconstruction and Development in October, and formally became a member of the Council of Europe on November 6.

The new government has made a number of additional gestures to the West. On a visit to Brussels on July 18 Antall announced the establishment of official relations with NATO. By sending military-medical volunteers to the Gulf in October, Hungary aimed to prove itself the most responsive Eastern European nation to US requests for support; and in the same month the government announced an agreement to allow Hong Kong Chinese to settle in Hungary provided they had $100,000 *per capita* to invest.

An additional aspect of the new foreign policy has been in the context of the *Pentagonale* group of countries. This began in November 1989 under the communist government when a meeting was held between the heads of the Italian, Hungarian, Austrian and Yugoslav governments. Czechoslovakia joined the group in the spring of 1990, so making it a group of five. Although Antall expresses commitment to the group, its significance is restricted to such issues as the environment, motorways, and minorities policy. It is not intended as an economic trading association to counter EFTA or the EC, nor as a political alliance to rival NATO.

By the end of 1990 reciprocal visa requirements with most Western European nations had been abolished; but voices were being heard advocating improving border controls, and even introducing visa requirements, to limit the expected influx of economic migrants from the East.

Withdrawal from the East

The twin issues of the return of Soviet troops and withdrawal from the Warsaw Pact spiced domestic politics throughout 1989 and 1990. Although, in considered contexts such as party manifestos, there was not a great deal of difference in policy (all parties, including the former communists, wanted Soviet troops to leave; all, except the former communists, had a long-term goal of neutrality), anti-Soviet demagogy became a virility test of commitment to reform at which the Smallholders and the Young Democrats were most successful. Even the Socialist Party (the former communists) participated, floating the idea of joining NATO in February 1990, and delaying the signing of the 1990 trade agreement with the Soviet Union until March 22; and the Free Democrats attempted to steal the Democratic Forum's thunder by calling, in the first session of the new parliament, for the immediate implementation of the Nagy government's 1956 resolution to leave the Warsaw Pact.

By the time the Antall government was in power, neither Soviet troops nor the Warsaw Pact were live issues. The Németh government had come to an agreement with the Soviet Union on March 10 concerning the departure of Soviet troops by June 30, 1991, and the Warsaw Pact was scarcely a political reality. By November and the agreement on the allocation of conventional forces signed in Budapest, it was being predicted that the military wing of the alliance would disappear before the end of 1991. The Antall government nevertheless pursued an anti-Soviet policy to the extent that ignored the Soviet Union diplomatically and fostered independent diplomatic relations with the Soviet republics. In late September the Hungarian President visited the Ukraine as head of state without even paying a courtesy call to Moscow, and in October a permanent commercial representation was opened in Estonia. This neglect backfired somewhat at the end of the year when the prospect of the new dollar-based trading system within the CMEA forced the Hungarian Minister for Industry and Commerce to go to Moscow to discuss trade. On December 9 it was announced that Antall, who had visited Washington, most European countries, and even the British Conservative Party Conference, had been invited to Moscow in February 1991 to sign a political agreement regulating the new principles of the relations between the two countries.

Hungarian minorities in neighbouring countries

A consistent feature of Hungary's new independent foreign policy was its commitment to defend the interests of Hungarians everywhere, most problematically those living in two of Hungary's immediate neighbours: Romania and Slovakia. (Relations with Yugoslavia are relatively good.)

The spectre of nationalism was rekindled under the Németh government when, in November 1989, the Hungarian Socialist Party refused to attend the congress of its fraternal party in Romania because of the Romanian treatment of its Hungarian minority. In his New Year message, the provisional President of the Republic stated that the new republic was responsible for the fate of 15–16,000,000 Hungarians, of which only 10,000,000 lived in Hungary. In March, before the elections, Foreign Minister Horn sent a stern warning to the Romanians concerning anti-Hungarian atrocities in Transylvania. The new government entrusted one of its ministers without portfolio to deal with the affairs of Hungarians abroad, and in June, on the anniversary of the Trianon Treaty of 1920 under which Hungary lost 67% of its territory and 58% of its population, although all parties issued a joint statement recognizing existing borders however unjustly they might have been determined, parliament held a minute's silence for the loss, and Antall's speech included reference to feeling himself to be Prime Minister of 15,000,000 Hungarians. The Christmas message from the Foreign Ministry repeated the theme: as a committed believer in human rights, Hungary was vitally interested in the evolution of the situation of Hungarians abroad.

Although Hungary's concern for the treatment of the Hungarian minorities in Romania and Slovakia are not ungrounded, its own minority policy, as minority groups in Hungary have observed, is not faultless; and the government's failure to condemn its own members for participating in irredentist demonstrations appears at best ambiguous in an atmosphere of heightened tension. Relations with Romania and Slovakia deteriorated to such an extent that parliament's foreign affairs committee discussed a secret document in October considering how they might be improved. In November 1990 proposals emerged for a summit meeting between Hungarian and Romanian leaders, but the two sides had not succeeded in agreeing mutually convenient dates by the end of the year.

POLAND

George Sanford and Martin Myant

Governments of September 1989 and December 1990

Mazowiecki's government, September 12, 1989 to December 14, 1990

Prime Minister. *Tadeusz Mazowiecki (OKP)*
Deputy-Premier and Finance. *Leszek Balcerowicz (OKP)*
Deputy-Premier and Agriculture, Fisheries and Food. *Czesław Janicki (ZSL), replaced by Janusz Byliński (Solidarity RI/PSL)*, September 1990
Deputy-Premier and Technological Progress. *Jan Stanisław Janowski (SD)*
Internal Affairs. *Czesław Kiszczak (PZPR), replaced by Krzysztof Kozłowski (OKP)*, July 1990
Head of the Office of the Council of Ministers. *Jacek Ambroziak (OKP)*
Justice. *Aleksander Bentkowski (ZSL)*
Culture and Arts. *Izabella Cywińska (OK)*
Environmental Protection and Natural Resources. *Bronisław Kamiński (ZSL)*
Health and Social Welfare. *Andrzej Kosiniak-Kamysz (ZSL)*
Labour and Social Policy. *Jacek Kuroń (OKP)*
Domestic Trade. *Aleksander Mackiewicz (SD)*
Housing and Construction. *Aleksander Paszyński (OKP)*

Education. *Henryk Samsonowicz (OKP)*
Defence. *Florian Siwicki (PZPR), replaced by Vice-Admiral Piotr Kołodziejczyk (non-party)*, July 1990
Foreign Affairs. *Krzysztof Skubiszewski (non-party)*
Foreign Trade and Co-operation. *Marcin Święcicki (PZPR)*
Industry. *Tadeusz Syryjczyk (PZPR)*
Transport, Shipping and Commerce. *Franciszek Wielądek (PZPR), replaced by Ewaryst Waligórski (OKP)*, July 1990
Central Planning Office. *Jerzy Osiatyński (OKP)*
Communications. *Marek Kucharski (SD), replaced by Jerzy Slezak (SD)*, September 1990
Without Portfolio (Rural Development). *Artur Balazs (Solidarity RI)*
Without Portfolio (relations with political associations). *Aleksander Hall (OKP), resigned in October 1990 and not replaced*
Without Portfolio (Economic Council). *Witold Trzeciakowski (OKP)*

cont'd overleaf

Bielecki's government, January 14, 1991*

Prime Minister. *Jan Krzysztof Bielecki (KLD)*

Deputy-Prime Minister and Finance. *Leszek Balcerowicz (Non-affiliated)*

Labour and Social Policy. *Michał Boni (Non-affiliated)*

Justice. *Wiesław Chrzanowski (Christian-National Union)*

Central Planning Office. *Jerzy Eysmont (Centre Alliance)*

Local Economy and Housing. *Adam Glapiński (KLD)*

National Education. *Robert Głębocki (Non-affiliated)*

Defence. *Vice-Admiral Piotr Kołodziejczyk (Non-party)*

Economic Collaboration with Abroad. *Dariusz Ledworowski (Non-affiliated)*

Ownership Transformation. *Janusz Lewandowski (KLD)*

Interior. *Henryk Majewski (Non-affiliated)*

Environmental Defence, Natural Resources and Forestry. *Maciej Nowicki (ROAD)*

Culture and Arts. *Marek Rostworowski (Non-affiliated)*

Foreign Affairs. *Krzysztof Skubiszewski (Non-party)*

Health and Social Welfare. *Władysław Sidorowicz (Non-affiliated)*

Communications. *Jerzy Slezak (SD)*

Agriculture and Food. *Adam Tański (Non-party)*

Transport and Maritime Economy. *Ewaryst Waligórski (OKP)*

Industry. *Adam Zawiślak (KLD)*

Head of the Office of the Council of Ministers. *Krzyztof Żabiński (OKP)*

*The Bielecki government was formed at a moment of exceptional fluidity of political labels and currents in Poland. Only a few of its members were elected representatives belonging directly to parliamentary clubs such as the original OKP which itself split into rival currents at this time. Non-affiliated therefore denotes general Solidarity background and support, while non-party is used in the accepted way.

Abbreviations

KLD *Kongres Liberalno-Demokratyczny:* Liberal-Democratic Congress

KOR *Komitet Obrony Robotników:* Workers' Defence Committee

NZS *Niezależny Związek Studentów:* Independent Students' Union

OKP *Obywatelski Komitet Parlamentarny:* Civic Parliamentary Committee

OPZZ *Ogólnopolskie Porozumienie Związków Zawodowych:* All-Poland Alliance of Trade Unions

PSL *Polskie Stronnictwo Ludowe:* Polish Peasant Party

PZPR *Polska Zjednoczona Partia Robotnicza:* Polish United Workers' Party

ROAD *Ruch Obywatelski Akcja Demokratyczna:* Civic Movement "Democratic Action"

SD *Stronnictwo Demokratyczne:* Democratic Party

SdRP *Socjal-Demokracja Rzeczpospolitej Polskiej:* Social-Democracy of the Polish Republic

TKN *Towarzystwo Kursów Naukowych:* Association for Academic Courses

ZSL *Zjednoczone Stronnictwo Ludowe:* United Peasant Party

Chronology

1989

January 16–18. Second half of PZPR 10th plenum.

January 27. Kiszczak-Wałęsa talks at Magdalenka.

February 6–April 5. Round Table negotiations continue at various levels.

February 5–9. Strike at the Bełchatów lignite mine. Suspended as result of Solidarity mediation and Wałęsa's call for a six-week strike moratorium.

March 7. Government press spokesman Jerzy Urban for the first time officially accuses the Soviet Union of responsibility for the Katyń massacre.

March 31. PZPR 11th plenum approves Kiszczak's report on Round Table and empowers the signing of the final agreement.

April 7. Sejm enacts the Round Table decisions.

April 14. Electoral Commission lays down that 425 *Sejm* Deputies will be elected in 108 constituencies and the remaining 35 on a National List.

April 15. PZPR 12th plenum discusses electoral preparations and its forthcoming National Delegates' Conference.

April 17. Warsaw provincial court formally re-legalizes Solidarity.

April 17. Bush announces US economic aid package of $1 billion for Poland.

April 18. SD congress; 780 delegates representing 140,000 members, elect Jerzy Jóźwiak as chairman.

April 19–22. Wałęsa meets Italian President and Prime Minister and the Pope in Rome.

April 20. The Warsaw Provincial Court registers Rural Solidarity (RI) led by Józef Ślisz.

April 27–28. Jaruzelski visits Moscow. He discusses the "radical transformations" in Polish-Soviet relations and historical blank spots, notably Katyń.

May 3. Visit of Italian President Francesco Cossiga and Prime Minister Giulio Andreotti.

May 4–5. PZPR Second National Delegates' Conference ratifies the party's electoral declaration and the resolution on "Removing the Remnants of Stalinism in Poland".

May 8. Appearance of first number of Solidarity's daily, *Gazeta Wyborcza*, with an initial print-run of 150,000 copies.

May 16–18. Violent anti-Soviet demonstrations in Kraków and attempts to storm Soviet Consulate elicit protest by Soviet ambassador.

May 17. Sejm passes three laws regulating Church-State relations.

May 22. Signature of Polish-East German treaty regulating their dispute (running since 1985) over their maritime boundary at the mouth of the river Oder.

May 23. Warsaw Court's refusal to register NZS, because of the right to strike in its statutes, provokes demonstrations in Warsaw, Łódź, Wrocław, Gdańsk and Kraków.

June 2. Solidarity's weekly, *Tygodnik Solidarność* (No. 38) reappears with Tadeusz Mazowiecki as editor.

June 3. Mitterrand's visit brings promises of French credits for tourist and rural development.

June 4. First round of *Sejm* and Senate elections.

June 6. Jaruzelski invites Solidarity to join a Grand Coalition.

POLAND

Baltic Sea

Gdynia
Gdańsk
● Koszalin
● Elblag
●Olsztyn

Szczecin

Bydgoszcz ●   ●Torun   Bialystok ●

● Gorzów Wielkopolski   ●Wloclawek

Poznan ●

Warsaw ■

Łódz ●

Radom ●
Lublin ●

Wrocław ●
Czestochowa ●   Kielce ●
● Walbrzych
●Opole

● Katowice
Rzeszów ●
● Kraków
Tarnów

GERMANY

SOVIET UNION

CZECHOSLOVAKIA

km 0   100   200

© CIRCA Reference

June 18. Second round of *Sejm* and Senate elections.

Mid-June onwards. The Auschwitz Carmelite Convent controversy breaks out.

July 4. The *Sejm* elects Mikołaj Kozakiewicz (ZSL) as its Marshal (presiding officer) and appoints the State Tribunal chaired by a communist, Adam Łopatka. The Senate chooses Andrzej Stelmachowski as its Marshal.

July 9–11. During his visit, Bush addresses a joint-session of *Sejm* and Senate and meets Jaruzelski and Wałęsa. His economic aid package disappoints Solidarity who had asked for $10 billion. So does his observation that "a new prosperous Poland" would develop "not overnight, not in a year but in your lifetime".

July 16. Restoration of diplomatic relations between Poland and the Vatican.

July 19. Jaruzelski elected to the newly established office of President.

July 24. Wałęsa-Jaruzelski meeting. An invitation for Solidarity to participate in government is refused.

July 28–29. PZPR 13th plenum elects Mieczysław F. Rakowski as First Secretary in Jaruzelski's place.

August 1. The Rakowski government's abolition of food price controls and meat rationing leads to huge price increases and panic buying.

August 2–3. Kiszczak is confirmed as Premier-designate. The *Sejm* also establishes Extraordinary Commissions to examine the Rakowski government's performance and Deputy Tadeusz Kowalik's (OKP) charge that the security services had committed up to 100 political murders since December 1981.

August 7. Wałęsa declares that Solidarity should form and lead the new government.

August 11. Senate condemns the 1968 invasion of Czechoslovakia. *Sejm* does likewise on 17th.

August 14–16. Kiszczak withdraws. Alternative proposals fail to take off. Intensive Solidarity-ZSL-SD negotiations.

August 19. The Solidarity National Executive Committee in Gdańsk backs Wałęsa's proposal after much controversy.

August 19. Stormy PZPR 14th plenum accepts participation in a Solidarity-led Grand Coalition.

August 20. Jaruzelski charges Mazowiecki to form a government "based on broad agreement among Poland's political and social forces".

August 24. Change of alliances by the ZSL and SD ensures the *Sejm*'s confirmation of Tadeusz Mazowiecki as Premier-designate. He promises "fundamental reform of the state" and a market economy.

September 11. ZSL chairman Roman Malinowski is replaced by Dominik Ludwiczak. The divided party quarrels with Rural Solidarity over the allocation of the Agriculture portfolio.

September 12. Mazowiecki cabinet is confirmed by the *Sejm*.

September 22. Jaruzelski appoints Gen. Michał Janiszewski as Head of his Presidential Office. His prominent PZPR lieutenant of the 1980s, Józef Czyrek, becomes Minister of State to represent him in the government office.

September 22. Supreme Court upholds the NZS's appeal for official registration.

September 19 onwards. Rejection of Romanian protest against the political changes in Poland.

September 29. After sharp debate the *Sejm* accepts an emergency budget for October and amendments to the one for 1989 which increase the deficit by 1,500 billion Zl to 4,500 billion Zl. It revises the Law on Income-Indexation on October 14.

October 3. PZPR 15th plenum sets January 27, 1990 as date for its 11th Congress.

October 19–21. Mazowiecki's first foreign visit to Italy and Vatican.

November 2 and 9–14. Visits of Egon Krenz (Chairman of GDR Council of State and SED First Secretary) and West German Chancellor, Helmut Kohl.

November 18. Sejm passes amnesty, appoints Professor Mieczysław Tyszka (SD) as President of the Constitutional Tribunal, revises the Criminal Code and abolishes Department for Religious Affairs.

November 23–25. Mazowiecki visits USSR.

November 25. Jaruzelski-Glemp meeting calls for support for the Mazowiecki government's economic austerity measures.

November 27. ZSL congress renews itself as PSL-Odrodzenie (Polish Peasant Party-Rebirth) with Józef Zych and Kazimierz Olesiak as the chairmen of its directing committees.

December 17–19 and 29–30. In a series of prolonged debates the *Sejm* passes the Balcerowicz budget and the IMF-backed economic reform and austerity programme and promulgates a major constitutional amendment.

1990

January 2. Sharp price increases come into force (coal six-fold, electricity, gas and petrol four-fold).

January 16–19. Silesian coal-mine strikes.

January 27. The PZPR dissolves itself at its 11th and final congress.

January 28–29. SdRP Founding Congress and formation of US (Social-Democratic Union).

February 5–6. Confirmation of the IMF's standby credit of $723 million and the World Bank's loan of $360 million for economic restructuring.

February 15. Mazowiecki meets with Solidarity and OPZZ delegations led by Wałęsa and Miodowicz to discuss growing worker discontent.

February 18. Dorota Simonides (OKP) elected as Senator for Opole, although her German minority opponent gains 32% of the vote.

February 28. SD elects Aleksander Mackiewicz (Minister of Domestic Trade) as new chairman.

March 9. Mazowiecki receives support on the confirmation of the Polish-German border during his visit to France.

March onwards. Growing policy and personal disputes develop between Wałęsa and Mazowiecki supporters.

March 20–28. Mazowiecki visits the USA and Canada.

March 22. Sejm votes to liquidate the RSW-Ruch press co-operative. Law passed on verification of the Procuracy.

April 9. Bratislava Summit of Polish, Czechoslovak and Hungarian leaders.

April 11–14. Jaruzelski's visit to Moscow is marked by the first official Soviet acceptance of NKVD responsibility for Katyń.

April 19–25. Second Solidarity Congress in Gdańsk re-elects Wałęsa as chairman. He subsequently declares his intention to run for the presidency.

May 21–25. Strikes by Słupsk and Koszalin railway workers.

May 27. Local elections.

June 1. OPZZ second congress re-elects Miodowicz as chairman.

June 7. Warsaw Pact Political Consultative Committee meeting in Moscow agrees to the fundamental transformation of the alliance from a military to a political one.

June 22. Sejm passes laws abolishing the ANS, Academy of Social Studies (PZPR party-school) and on limiting profits of so-called *"nomenklatura* co-operatives". Appoints Solidarity lawyer and Senator, Adam Strzembosz, President of the Supreme Court.

June 22. Centre Alliance, set up in late May to support Wałęsa's presidential candidacy, calls for Jaruzelski's resignation. Bujak and Frasyniuk establish ROAD while Jerzy Turowicz organizes the Democratic Alliance to support Mazowiecki.

June 29. Force is used to end the occupation of the Ministry of Agriculture by peasants. Rural discontent continues, especially in traditional areas of south-eastern Poland. Growing public disillusion is demonstrated by a 13% turnout in a Senate by-election in Lublin won by the Civic Committee candidate with 51% of the vote.

July 1. Conference of Civic Committees continues a long-running debate about their role and policy with Wałęsa and Mazowiecki.

July 6. Resignations of prominent communist ministers.

July 13. Sejm passes Privatization Law.

September 10–13. Skubiszewski's official visit to USSR.

September 18. Jaruzelski lets it be known that he agrees to resign.

September 27. The *Sejm* sets November 25 as the date of the presidential election by universal suffrage. It had already decided, in principle, also to cut short the term of both parliamentary chambers. Although it passes a new electoral law after much controversy there is no agreement on when elections should take place, on whether the new or the old *Sejm* should pass the constitution and on the need for a referendum on these issues.

October 4. Mazowiecki announces his presidential candidacy, but the Solidarity National Executive Committee backs Wałęsa.

October 25. The State Electoral Commission officially registers six (out of the 14 candidates) who had successfully collected the required 100,000 signatures for nomination. The Spokesman for Citizen's Rights (Ombudsman), Professor Ewa Łętowska, is definitely not running.

November 14. Signing of Polish-German Treaty.

November 25. The first ballot of the presidential election fails to produce a winner with an outright majority.

Early December. Mazowiecki offers his resignation as Premier after his elimination by Tymiński. He rallies half-heartedly behind Wałęsa and forms the Democratic Union.

December 9. Wałęsa wins the presidency by defeating Tymiński.

December 22. Wałęsa is sworn in before a joint session of *Sejm* and Senate.

Late December. Bielecki takes over the formation of the government from Jan Olszewski and announces his cabinet in early January 1991.

Political Overview

Polish politics during the 1980s are usually described in terms of political and social deadlock and economic deterioration. Martial law failed, in the long run, to reassert communist power. So did the Jaruzelski regime's subsequent policies of selective incorporation and reform from above. The turn towards more radical reform in autumn 1987 was motivated by Gorbachev's *perestroika* and the need to gain social support for the second stage of the economic reform. The November referendum failed, however, to gain sufficient support to prevent the industrial strikes of spring and summer 1988 in protest at growing price increases.

Under such pressures the Polish United Workers' Party (PZPR) plenum of August 27–28, 1988 took the fateful decision to work for an Anti-Crisis Pact. General Czesław Kiszczak, the Minister of the Interior, was to lead a general negotiation with what was described as the "constructive opposition", designed to incorporate it in the system. The aim was a broadened PZPR-led coalition platform for the next *Sejm* (parliament) election to gain national support for socio-economic reform and its consequential sacrifices. The autumn negotiations, however, bogged down over the issues of the conditions and extent of political and trade union pluralism involved in the re-legalization of Solidarity. The official All-Poland Alliance ("Understanding") of Trade Unions (OPZZ) led by Alfred Miodowicz obstructed the process although they were given the credit for the replacement of Zbigniew Messner as Prime Minister (Chairman of the Council of Ministers) in late September by the reformist Mieczysław F. Rakowski.

The political logjam was broken by two crucial developments. Firstly, Lech Wałęsa, after a successful television debate with Miodowicz, formed a Civic Committee on December 18, 1988. This set the limits to the constructive opposition which he came to lead. Solidarity opponents of Round Table talks and of transitional and incomplete agreements with the communist system, led by such "historic" (1980–81) chieftains as Andrzej Gwiazda, Marian Jurczyk and Jan Rulewski, consequently split away to form a "working-group". Wałęsa marginalized them as well as the "Fighting Solidarity" and "Solidarity 1980" opposition to his main Civic Committee strand during the spring.

Secondly, the second half of the PZPR 10th plenum replaced conservatives with reformists. It was overawed by the threatened resignation of Wojciech Jaruzelski (PZPR First Secretary and Chairman of the Council of State), Kiszczak, Rakowski and Florian Siwicki (Minister of Defence) into accepting political and trade union pluralism, the relegalization of Solidarity and the forthcoming Round Table talks by 143 votes to 32 with 14 abstentions. It also agreed to the PZPR's democratization. Bitter debate by newly emergent factional currents over its future character ensued during the whole of 1989.

The two camps entering the Round Table negotiations, dubbed the government-coalition and the Solidarity-opposition sides, had divergent aims from the outset. The former wished to maintain PZPR domination within a framework of relative pluralism and subordinate opposition. The latter viewed their participation in such a broad-based plebiscitary *Sejm* election as only the first step towards the full democratization of competitive elections. Both sides wanted the process to be controlled and limited by the two wings of the pro-reform élite. This aspect came to be symbolized by the secret meetings between Kiszczak and Wałęsa and their closest advisers, held at the Ministry of the Interior (MSW) villa in the township of Magdalenka outside Warsaw. These prepared the Round Table talks and struck the deals required to unblock the negotiations during its course.

The Round Table opened and closed with formal plenary sessions of all 57 participants on February 6 and April 5. Substantive negotiations were carried on by three major Groups on Trade Union Pluralism (10 sessions), Economic and Social Reform (13 sessions) and Questions of Political Reform (nine sessions). More detailed discussions were carried on by their working parties and by specialist sub-groups on ecology, education, housing, agriculture, health, youth, mass media, judicial reform, associations and local government.

The relegalization of Solidarity and its rural equivalent (RI) raised few difficulties. Deadlock ensued over the registration of the Independent Students' Union (NZS) which organized violent demonstrations, which turned anti-Soviet, in Kraków on February 24. The principles of a revised electoral law permitting Solidarity participation and representation but safeguarding the PZPR coalition's majority and the establishment of a new Senate and presidency were agreed early on. The exact details of the proposed deal, especially the precise powers and composition of the latter institutions, however, caused weeks of acrimonious negotiation. Agreement was only reached through recourse to Magdalenka "summits". Other contentious issues, eventually resolved by the sub-groups, concerned wage-indexation, housing, legal reform and access to the mass media. The most important political agreement laid down that the forthcoming elections were to be wholly free to the Senate but curial for the *Sejm*. The Solidarity-opposition side would be permitted to contest 35% of the *Sejm* seats; it was understood that the PZPR's coalition partners, the United Peasant Party (ZSL) and the Democratic Party (SD), would hold the balance in the new *Sejm*. There was also, at the very least, an informal agreement that Jaruzelski would occupy the new presidency in order to maintain communist control over the military and security forces and to reassure communist allies. The economic, social and sectoral agreements were extremely detailed. The general expectation was that they could now be fulfilled within the favourable framework of developing political and economic pluralism and flexible PZPR coalition hegemony.

The *Sejm* hastened to enact the Round Table decisions in the form of a constitutional amendment, new *Sejm* and Senate electoral laws and laws on associations and trade unions which legalized Solidarity and its rural branch (Solidarity RI). It also established the National Council for the Judiciary (KRS) to guarantee its independence.

The government-coalition side ran a confused and badly organized election campaign. It dissipated its weak resources by fielding numerous candidates in its allocated constituencies. The Civic Committee, on the other hand, achieved almost total discipline in endorsing a limited, mainly single number of candidates, per seat and in excluding opposition elements outside its control. The first round of voting on June 4 produced a 62.1% turnout and an almost complete Civic Committee victory. Wałęsa's team won 92 out of the 100 Senate seats and 160 out of the 161 *Sejm* seats available to it. The defeat for the government-coalition was overwhelming. Only two out of its 35 candidates on the National List were elected by receiving the required 50% of the votes cast. The defeated candidates, including major figures like Rakowski, Kiszczak, Siwicki and Miodowicz, had to withdraw. The Council of State decreed the election of their replacements in special *ad hoc* constituencies in order to maintain the Round Table contract. In the second round on June 18 the Civic Committee won its last *Sejm* seat and seven out of the eight remaining Senate seats. The government-coalition candidates won with low votes on a low turnout. Very significantly, about 55 were elected against other official candidates because of either open or informal Civic Committee recommendation. The *Sejm*'s final composition therefore conformed to the Round Table deal (PZPR 173, Civic Committee 161 who formed the Civic Parliamentary Club — OKP, ZSL 76, SD 27, PAX 10 and Christian Social Union — PZKS, five). The overall consequence was, however, a great psychological-political defeat for the communist camp which accelerated its growing decomposition. Solidarity, which had gained something like 65% of the votes cast and 40% of the total electorate (as measured by the best indicator of the free national Senate vote), was very quickly during the summer to become the dominant political force in Poland (see Table 1).

The first part of the PZPR 13th plenum on June 30 supported Jaruzelski's candidacy for the presidency despite his recommendation of Kiszczak. Jaruzelski was barely elected

Table 1:   Elections to the National Assembly, June 1989

	Seats allocated to govt. opposition	Seats: unallocated
Sejm (lower house)	299	161
Polish United Workers'Party (PZPR)	173	—
United Peasant Party (ZSL)	76	—
Democratic Party (SD)	27	—
Catholic/other	23	—
Solidarity Civic Committee	161	—
Senate (upper house)		100
Solidarity Citizens' Committee		99
Independent		1

Source: Polish press Reports.

President for a six-year term by a joint session of *Sejm* and Senate on July 19 due to the abstention of some Solidarity leaders who wished to maintain the Round Table contract.

Jaruzelski's nomination of Kiszczak as Premier-designate was accepted by the *Sejm* by 237 votes to 173, but the latter's long-drawn-out efforts to form a government failed. So did attempts to float alternative nominations such as those of Roman Malinowski (ZSL chairman and ex-*Sejm* Marshal) and Władysław Baka (PZPR politburo member and secretary for economic reform). Kiszczak withdrew after Wałęsa's declaration on August 7 that Solidarity should lead a coalition government. The idea had first been floated by Adam Michnik, the editor of Solidarity's daily *Gazeta Wyborcza*, as early as July 4, in his celebrated article "Your President — Our Premier". After much controversy the idea was accepted by Solidarity's National Executive Committee (KK) in Gdańsk and by the OKP. Exploratory talks between Solidarity and the ZSL and the SD led to the latter's change of alliances. This made a Solidarity-led government possible but the minor parties insisted that it should be a Grand Coalition with communist participation.

Jaruzelski then nominated Tadeusz Mazowiecki as Premier-designate (on the basis of three names proposed by the OKP, the other two being OKP chairman, Bronisław Geremek, and Jacek Kuroń). The *Sejm* confirmed his appointment by 378 votes to four with 41 abstentions on August 24; but complicated and long-drawn-out negotiations were necessary before it could endorse his cabinet list (402 to zero, 13 abstentions) on September 12 (see Mazowiecki's government above). The government's main features were that the PZPR received only four portfolios, but crucially Kiszczak remained at the Interior and Siwicki at Defence. The economic posts fell into the hands of Solidarity neo-liberals led by Leszek Balcerowicz (Deputy-Premier and Finance Minister), determined to take the advice of Harvard economics professor, Jeffrey Sachs, to go for rapid "big-bang" marketization. The PZPR also lost control of Foreign Affairs at the outset. This went to Krzysztof Skubiszewski, an independent professor of international law from Poznań and member of Cardinal Józef Glemp's (Primate of Poland) Social Council. The ZSL was too divided to profit from its control of agriculture and incapable of allaying peasant discontent, but Bentkowski proved a great success at Justice.

In outlining his government's programme to the *Sejm* on September 12 Mazowiecki promised to turn Poland into "a sovereign, democratic state subject to the rule of law". It would be "open to Europe and the world" and would contribute to the dissolution of the two military blocs. The economy would be transformed in the long run through the privatization of state industry, the creation of a stock exchange and capital markets, a convertible currency and a shift away from heavy industry towards consumer goods while inflation and tax evasion would be tackled in the short term. The rapid and easy dismantling of the communist system was then facilitated by communism's rapid collapse in the rest of Eastern Europe in late 1989 and the challenges posed by the Soviet Republics.

Among the main highlights in the establishment of a law-based state were the depoliticization of the army, the transformation of the Citizen's Militia (MO) into an ordinary police force (with criminal, traffic and preventive branches) and the abolition of its Volunteer Reserve (ORMO). The much hated ZOMO riot police was replaced by 22 provincial public order groups and the secret police (SB) had its functions taken over by the Bureau for State Protection (UOP). All members of the judiciary and procuracy were verified and considerable numbers were not reappointed, a process which likewise applied in the preceding cases. The informal "no-victimization" aspects of the Round Table deal were maintained although the question of the wider responsibility for Father Popiełuszko's murder was reopened in mid-1990. A gradual personnel turnover was set in train at all administrative and political levels (deputy ministers, department heads, provincial governors, municipal presidents and ambassadors) and public sectors which included university rectors, school inspectors and directors and the like. Local government was decentralized. A fundamental reorganization was attempted following the local elections of May 1990. This produced a 42.27% turnout with the Civic Committee winning about 43%, independents 38%, PSL 6.5%, and Solidarity RI 5% of the seats.

The above process was symbolized by the constitutional amendment of December 1989 and its associated changes. Article 3 enshrining the PZPR's leading role was abolished, the socialist Polish People's Republic (PRL) became the democratic Polish Republic (PR). Sovereignty was transferred from "the working people of town and countryside" to the "nation". Article I defined Poland as "a law-based state implementing the principle of social justice". The crown was now restored to the head of the white eagle national coat of arms, while somewhat later the communist National Day (July 22) was replaced by the traditional May 3.

At the same time the political forces of the communist order either collapsed or were transformed. The Patriotic Movement for National Rebirth (PRON) dissolved itself in November 1989. The PZPR spent the second half of 1989 debating whether it should choose the July 8 movement's social democratic or a reformed Marxist-Leninist option. In the end it chose the former very decisively. It wound itself up at its 11th congress before reconstituting itself as the Social Democracy of the Polish Republic (SdRP). It elected Aleksander Kwaśniewski, a 36-year-old ex-Sport and Youth Minister as chairman and the darling of the progressive communist intelligentsia, 44-year-old Leszek Miller as Secretary-General. Although a complete break with the PZPR's Leninist, let alone Stalinist, past was promised about 100 delegates led by *Sejm* Vice-Marshal Tadeusz Fiszbach (the Gdańsk province First Secretary who had collaborated with Solidarity in 1980–81) found this insufficient and hived off to form the Social Democratic Union (US, later PUS). In the new *Sejm* Club of the Parliamentary Left (PKLD), 22 initially belonged to the SdRP, 30 to the US, while 116 chose independence.

With democratization a proliferation of new political organizations and clubs occurred while existing bodies changed their leaderships and policies and attempted to revise their images. This ferment produced a fluid kaleidoscope of rapidly changing labels and leaders on the Polish political scene. All this was, however, largely marginal to developments within the Solidarity Civic Committee camp. Here Wałęsa remained as chairman of the Solidarity trade union. He was re-elected triumphantly with 77.5% of the vote by its second congress in April 1990. Through Zdzisław Najder he generally controlled the civic committees which now replaced the communist *aktyws* at every local and social level. A new Solidarity élite emerged at the levels of government headed by Mazowiecki and parliament led by OKP chairman Geremek.

Wałęsa had presided over the process of agreement between Solidarity and communist élites which had so quickly moved on from the negotiation of power-sharing to power-takeover. Although he did not stand for parliament or take governmental office he initially counselled patience on Polish society during the early euphoric period of democratization and marketization which culminated in Balcerowicz's dramatic taming of the hyper-inflation of early 1990 (described below). The rapid growth of industrial and social unrest at mounting unemployment, drastic cuts in living standards and burgeoning inequality, presented what was now called the Second Solidarity, with pressing identity and legitimacy problems. The First Solidarity of 1980–81 had wanted to correct communist deformations as it was in many respects a really socialist and egalitarian movement. The introduction of capitalism by the Mazowiecki-Balcerowicz government naturally presented Solidarity with acute dilemmas. Wałęsa's answer was to distance himself from Mazowiecki from spring 1990 onwards in order to raise his falling popularity and to protect the political capital of his historic myth as a great labour tribune. He called for a more social welfare approach and an "acceleration" of the removal of the communist *nomenklatura*, many of whose members had used their connections to turn smoothly into capitalist businessmen. The main political issue was the call for the resignation of Jaruzelski and for the election of the president through universal suffrage in order to strengthen his democratic legitimacy.

Solidarity consequently split into two political camps in summer 1990. Two "historic" regional chieftains, Zbigniew Bujak (Mazowsze) and Władysław Frasyniuk (Lower Silesia), who had opposed Wałęsa's authoritarian running of the union, formed ROAD (Civic Movement "Democratic Action"); it was designed to underpin Mazowiecki's presidential candidacy although he took a long time to declare himself. Wałęsa had no such inhibitions. He made an early start with his camp organizing the Centre Alliance. His close ally, Jarosław Kaczyński, had been imposed much earlier on *Tygodnik Solidarność*. The weekly organ became his mouthpiece against Michnik's pro-Mazowiecki daily *Gazeta Wyborcza* which was deprived of the use of the Solidarity logo. Wałęsa eventually gained the support of most civic committees and Solidarity regions while the very badly divided OKP replaced Geremek with his supporter Mieczysław Gil. The presidential campaign revealed differences of style and timing rather than programme between Wałęsa and Mazowiecki. The former was desperate to use his popular charisma and symbolism to get into power before volcanic socio-economic discontent shattered the Polish political scene yet again. The latter proved a poor campaigner, much too wedded to the élitist and intelligentsia conceptions of the Round Table period.

Kiszczak and Siwicki had already been replaced in summer 1990 as they had fulfilled their functions of preventing a communist backlash. The same also now applied to Jaruzelski who, exhausted by a turbulent decade of office, willingly agreed to resign. The election of a

President by universal suffrage with two ballots if no candidate got an absolute majority on the first round, on the French Fifth Republic model, preceded the definition of his powers in the new constitution. It was, however, envisaged that the *Sejm* would be dissolved in spring 1991. Its fully democratically elected successor would then promulgate the constitution in time, symbolically, for the 200th anniversary of the constitution of May 3, 1791.

Six presidential candidates met the requirement that their nominations be supported by 100,000 signatures; another eight hopefuls failed to do so and were therefore not registered. Surprisingly, Wałęsa failed to gain outright election on the first ballot of the presidential election on November 25 as he only got 39.96% of the 60% turnout. Even more dramatically a late surge favoured a completely unknown Polish-born émigré millionaire from Canada and Peru, Stanisław Tymiński, who with 23.1% eliminated Mazowiecki who got only 18.8%. Tymiński benefited from a backlash against the idea of two Solidarity candidates monopolizing the second ballot, from the partly Poujadist socio-economic discontent with the hardship caused by Mazowiecki's measures and from the rallying of ex-communist sectors to the strongest anti-Wałęsa candidate. The other candidates also got more support than originally predicted. Włodzimierz Cimoszewicz (SdRP), the personable young PKLD chairman, got 9.21% for the broad left, Roman Bartoszcze (PSL chairman) received 7.15% while Leszek Moczulski the chairman of the extremist Confederation for an Independent Poland (KPN) ended up with 2.5%. Having slapped Wałęsa's wrist the electorate, faced by an almost unelectable alternative, had no option but to favour him, somewhat less than triumphantly, by 74.75% to 24.25% on a 53.4% turnout.

Wałęsa was sworn in as President before a joint session of the *Sejm* and Senate on December 22. The same day, Ryszard Kaczorowski, "President" of the London Polish Government-in-Exile, transferred his insignia and powers to him. Wałęsa appointed his close collaborators Jacek Merkel as Head of his Presidential Office and Jarosław Kaczyński as Minister of State for Security Questions. After Jan Olszewski, a lawyer who had defended dissidents during the 1980s, abandoned his soundings to form a government, Wałęsa entrusted the task to a largely unknown economist and Gdańsk *Sejm* Deputy, 39-year-old Jan Krzysztof Bielecki. His heavily Liberal-Democratic Congress (formed just before Wałęsa's election) and Gdańsk-based cabinet, confirmed by the *Sejm* in early January 1991 (see Bielecki's government above), was largely new, although Balcerowicz, Skubiszewski and Admiral Kołodziejczyk remained in their posts. It was envisaged as seeing Poland through to the free elections of the spring and the promulgation of the new constitution.

The imponderable at that time was whether Wałęsa would attempt to emulate the Gaullist Fifth Republic experience by writing his own constitution and by moulding a strong executive presidency which would mobilize a presidential majority around his new Liberal Democratic Congress in the parliament. Would he retire at the end of the constituent phase of anchoring democracy? If he continued how would he cope with social impatience with insufficient economic development which threatened to overload the emerging democratic system in the "Argentinian" form of a nationalist-authoritarian-corporatist backlash? Or, more hopefully, would democratic mechanisms and legitimacy form sufficiently strong enough new élites, social interests and values to support the system through the painful transition to a market system and incorporation in the world economy?

Economic Overview

Background

As with other countries of Eastern Europe, the system based on central planning and autarkic development showed some potential for growth and structural change in the 1950s and even into the 1960s. The Polish economy, devastated during World War II, was rebuilt and large-scale industries developed around the basic sectors of energy, steel, petrochemicals, ships and also consumer goods. By the end of the 1960s, however, the potential for growth seemed to be largely exhausted. Real wages were almost stagnant in the years up to 1970 while even other Eastern European countries were still expanding. This contributed to the discontent that culminated in the strikes in the Baltic shipbuilding ports of December 1970 and to the replacement of Gomułka by Gierek.

The economic strategy of the 1970s was essentially to overcome stagnation by high levels of investment financed from foreign borrowing. In the freer international atmosphere, hard currency debts could rise from US$0.8 billion in 1971 to $25 billion in 1980, but much of the resources were actually spent on consumption for the population. Even those funds that were used for investment were often misdirected into prestige projects or into new factories which could never be used owing to the lack of wide enough technical expertise, the shortage of key materials or even the absence of demand for the finished products. The naivety of the Gierek strategy was exposed towards the end of the 1970s when debts had to be repaid. Nothing like enough new and modern industry was operating to win export markets. Total hard currency exports were not even enough to cover the costs of servicing existing debts. Poland therefore entered a phase of catastrophic crisis in which balance of payments difficulties forced drastic cuts in imports while all possible goods were sent for export. Domestic industry, starved of vital inputs, experienced a 23% decline in output between 1978 and 1982. Net Material Product per head fell by 27%. Personal consumption showed a fall of 11% while accumulation, which contributes to investment for the future, fell by over 60%. This made possible a small hard currency trade, and even balance of payments surplus from 1982, but it was still insufficient to enable a reduction in the debt burden.

With the rise of Solidarity in 1980, the government adopted a policy of economic reform, proposing a new mechanism that would use market relations to create a new form of socialism that would actually work. Even after the imposition of martial law, a considerable body of economists continued to hope that the government was serious in its talk of reform and looked forward to some sort of recovery. Ultimately, however, the key issue was the willingness of the population to accept a considerable fall in living standards so that the debt burden could be reduced. Reform of the system could never be enough on its own. Moreover, in the post-martial law situation, the authorities were always willing to water down proposals in the interests of compromise with diehard opponents of change.

In fact, the 1980s were a dismal decade with only a very partial recovery which was petering out by 1986. A recovery in personal consumption, to 12% above the 1978 level in the peak year of 1988, was bought largely at the expense of a reduction in the hard currency trade surplus which had practically disappeared by 1989. This meant, in view of the need to service existing debts, a balance of payments deficit from 1985 allowing debts to escalate to $36 billion by the end of 1989. By 1989 Net Material Product per head, still 9% below the 1978 level, was falling again. Throughout the decade there were absolutely no signs of the economy overcoming its more fundamental weaknesses. Cutting imports meant that the degree of economic autarky actually increased and there were minimal resources for importing modern equipment. Incentives to innovate were reduced still further by the lack of international contacts. The industrial structure, biased previously towards extractive and raw material processing industries, swung still further in that direction and away from light, consumer goods industries as well as high technology sectors. Depression meant, quite literally, stagnation with the Polish economy totally incapable of adapting to the modern world.

A further attempt was made to start on economic reform in January 1988 with sharp price rises, including 140% for food and even higher increases for fuel and energy. It was met with the re-emergence of a strike movement on a scale unprecedented since the banning of Solidarity. Management in many large enterprises capitulated, thereby fuelling an inflationary spiral. The centre's control over economic processes seemed to be collapsing again, as in 1980, as strikes continued and industrial production went into decline. For some time before the Round Table discussions, there were practically no economists left who held out any hope for recovery under the existing system. There had already for some years been voices arguing that reform was meaningless without a transformation of ownership relations. By the end of the 1980s expert opinion had clearly shifted towards acceptance of the necessity to abandon socialism in total and seek the quickest possible means for a transition to a capitalist system which, it was hoped, would resemble the advanced economies of Western Europe.

The change in direction was already started under the Rakowski government, formed in October 1988. A subsequent parliamentary investigation of that government's activities revealed two conflicting views. According to one account, Rakowski opened the way for reforms that were later implemented. According to the alternative view, which won majority backing in parliament on July 26, 1990, his government should rather be seen as making the last desperate effort to hold back genuine reform. Two of the crucial issues were his privatization policy and his attempt to close the Gdańsk shipyard. Superficially these could appear as the most obvious moves towards a market system. On the latter, the government argued that the shipyard was unprofitable and had no prospects for recovery and therefore declared it bankrupt in November 1988: work continued on projects already under way, but the workforce began to drift away over the following months. Solidarity, however, claimed that the decision was essentially politically motivated and it did appear that arguments in business terms were confusing and possibly unclear. Nevertheless, it has proved impossible to find a foreign buyer interested in running the shipyard. An offer from US millionairess Barbara Piasecka-Johnson finally fell through when the conditions, in terms of redundancies, wages and labour discipline, were judged unacceptable by the local Solidarity organization. Instead, as of April 1990, the shipyard has been reinstated as a state-owned joint stock company in which the employees will be offered 20% of the shares at half the market price.

On privatization generally, Rakowski's policy centred on the creation of joint stock companies which typically involved joint ownership by state-owned enterprises and by individuals. This created scope for the emergence of so-called "*nomenklatura*" companies. The point was that, with the collapse of effective centralized control over state assets, directors of state enterprises had the power effectively to transfer resources into new firms in which they had a shareholding as individuals. The arrangements were often very complicated and required contacts between a number of individuals, believed to be

Table 2   The first effects of the marketization of food in 1989

	August	September	October	November	December
Prices	40	34	55	22	18
Food prices	80	45	65	17	12
Animals for slaughter	−17	18	9	4	−9
Wages	81	13	33	25	48
Consumer spending (employees)	31	39	37	16	39

Note: All figures are percentage change on previous month.
Source: *Statistical Information on Economic Situation of Poland*, October 1990.

linked through the old *nomenklatura* system. Several thousand of these joint stock companies emerged in 1989 and 1990. Many were believed to be taking advantage of ambiguities in or conflicts between aspects of Poland's very rudimentary company laws, but they generally breached no existing legal codes. There were complaints in sections of the press which exposed some of the machinations involved, but the Ministry of the Interior finally announced on November 6, 1990 that it was not interested in investigating the cases any further as no laws were being transgressed.

The last important act of the Rakowski government was the "marketization" of food, meaning the freeing of practically all food prices and the elimination of state subsidies. The immediate consequences, as indicated in Table 2, were very rapid inflation (rising from an average monthly figure of 8.5% in the January to July period to an average of 34% for the rest of the year) and considerable chaos in food supplies as a stable market emerged only gradually. Confusion was exacerbated by some farmers holding back deliveries in the expectation of higher prices later, contributing to the fall in animals for slaughter in August. Under the new Solidarity-dominated government, people were prepared to tolerate the obvious inconvenience. They were protected by an indexation system, agreed to at the Round Table, which guaranteed wage increases equal to 80% of the increase in the cost of living. Comparisons of increases in wages, prices and consumer spending suggest that firms allowed still higher pay rises so that there was no fall in living standards in the latter part of 1989 and there is no reason to suppose that higher prices absorbed much of the personal savings in the hands of the population. The "inflationary overhang", a body of forced savings built up over the years when consumer goods supply could never satisfy demand, was still believed to exist.

The Balcerowicz programme

While the market for food was gradually stabilizing, the new government had to work out its economic programme. Work began immediately in August 1989 under the supervision of Finance Minister and Deputy Prime Minister Leszek Balcerowicz. An important stimulus was a visit from Jeffrey Sachs of Harvard University who had worked with the IMF in advising various Third World countries. He won an enthusiastic hearing from Solidarity MPs when he proposed a transition to a market economy "in one leap". A rapid transition, he believed, was necessary in political terms because Latin American experience showed political instability to be a fertile soil for demagogues who could block painful but necessary measures. The clear implication was that concern about the social effects of the transition to a market system had to take second place. He also argued that speed would make possible a link between macroeconomic "shock therapy", meaning sharp deflation to eliminate inflationary pressures, and systemic change creating a competitive environment and privatizing state enterprises. He assumed that this creation of a functioning market economy would lead to the appearance of automatic mechanisms for controlling inflation. Although his rhetoric referred to a rapid process, he actually accepted that privatization would have to be slow and gradual. That implied the need for strong, government-directed deflationary measures for some time to come. A final point in his proposal was that considerable outside assistance, starting with IMF backing, should be sought to overcome the burden of the massive hard currency debts: a programme of dramatic internal change would, he argued, make international assistance more likely.

His ideas were welcomed by the free-market oriented Solidarity advisers who started with the belief that systemic change, involving substantial privatization, could come simultaneously with macroeconomic stabilization. They even considered speeding up the process with the free distribution of shares. Balcerowicz, however, working closely with the IMF, was more cautious. The government programme, published in October 1989, carried forward the assumption that the aim was "to construct a market system, similar to that prevailing in economically advanced countries", but effectively ignored ideas for rapid privatization. Instead, it was to proceed purely by the sale of shares which, in view of the low level of savings in the hands of the population in relation to the total value of state assets, meant that it could advance at a snail's pace only. Balcerowicz claimed that macroeconomic stabilization had to come first, but that it could then be combined with the preparation for or start to systemic change. In fact, early 1990 saw a shift in emphasis with deflation ever more clearly taking first place while systemic change was continually put off into the future. Whenever there was conflict between the two objectives, anti-inflationary policies took priority.

The actual programme, as introduced on January 1, 1990, included the freeing of practically all prices, the freeing of imports and the introduction of limited currency convertibility, a savagely restrictive monetary policy and strict wage controls. The sudden unleashing of market forces and the elimination of state subsidies led to phenomenal price rises at the start of January, but official figures, given in Table 3, suggest that inflation was

Table 3:   Macroeconomic indicators for 1990

	Jan	Feb	March	April	May	June	July	Aug	Sep
Retail prices	79.6	23.8	4.3	7.5	4.6	3.4	3.6	1.8	4.6
Food prices	82.8	17.2	−0.2	10.8	5.1	1.8	0.8	0.2	3.5
Wages	2.5	15.4	40.1	−8.8	−3.8	1.4	10.8	4.8	7.4
Consumption (employees)	4.3	15.7	26.3	7.7	0.8	10.7	—	—	—
Employment	−1.1	−1.1	−1.3	−1.3	−1.9	−1.1	−1.6	−1.6	−1.2
Industrial output (real)	−31.6	−2.1	0.9	−1.5	0.3	4.9	−12.2	7.6	7.2

Note: All figures are percentage changes on the previous month.
Source: Statistical Information on Economic Situation of Poland, October 1990.

then brought down fairly quickly to significant but not catastrophic proportions. To some extent this conceals a continuing instability of the market as prices of individual goods fluctuated and varied enormously between different parts of the country. There were also significant changes in price relativities with those for food generally rising more rapidly.

There is controversy over which factors were the most important in bringing inflation under control. The major factor affecting individual enterprises was, without question, the restriction of consumer demand as money incomes failed to keep up with prices, but this could have been the result either of the wages policy or of monetary policy. The latter involved interest rates set at 38% to 46% in January and a sharp cut in state subsidies from 41% of profits of all state enterprises in the January to August period of 1989 to only 13% in the equivalent period of 1990. This contributed to a budget surplus discussed below in the section on Finance. A number of monetarist economists believed that these measures alone were enough to restrict enterprises' ability to grant wage increases and hence to control inflation.

The alternative view places the emphasis on the wage control policy. The system of 80% indexation, argued for at the Round Table by Solidarity, was considered sacrosanct until the end of the year. In January it was replaced by a system which fined enterprises with a 200% tax for increasing the wage bill by more than 30% of the previous month's increase in the cost of living. For February and March the policy was tightened still further with allowance for only 20% compensation. In later months it was relaxed to 60%. In practice, wage increases were generally below the allowed level, but that does not prove the monetarist case. Wage control could still have been the main factor holding back wage increases and hence demand while some firms would have been unable to afford even the allowed level of wage rises thereby pulling down the overall average. In any event, the IMF was convinced of the necessity of wage controls.

As Table 3 indicates, inflation slipped back up after its rapid fall towards a monthly figure of 5%. It was even slightly higher for the last three months of the year while a 7% monthly figure could still imply an annual rate of roughly 70%, which is clearly above the 1988 level. Inflation for the whole year was almost 200% instead of the 70% mentioned in the letter of intent for the IMF. Moreover, as figures in the Table show, the fall in inflation was accompanied by a drop in industrial output of over 30% in January (at least 23% for the full 12 months), while the government had forecast a fall of 5% for the year as a whole. Net Material Product has fallen by around 18% against a forecast of 3%. Unemployment rose more slowly, but also more steadily over the year as a whole, and is well above the 2% of the employed labour force predicted at the start of the year. Output and living standards seem to have stabilized quickly, and certainly within the first three months, but claims of a later general recovery need to be treated with caution. Industrial output in December was still 24% below the 1989 level.

The government nevertheless claimed a great success in bringing hyper-inflation under control and in achieving, for the first time in over 40 years, the transformation of a situation of chronic shortage into a buyers' market. Moreover, there were arguments that the official statistics might be exaggerating the extent of the fall in production and living standards. The fall in output could be partly accounted for by an end to enterprises fiddling their figures so as to achieve plan targets. It could also include the ending of some production of no social value which again had just helped attain plan figures. These factors, however, are unlikely to have been very important.

Figures on unemployment, which appeared in January 1990 with a new legal framework allowing enterprises to set their own employment levels, were also challenged with journalistic investigations in June suggesting that up to 40% of those registering had not been working before: many had been housewives. Moreover, even many who had worked could well be occupied in the rapidly expanding street trade sector which would not have prevented receipt of benefits of up to 90% of previous earnings. There were very few cases of mass redundancies, while "collective dismissals" still accounted for only 13% of the unemployed in September. It is therefore not surprising that Jeffrey Sachs was unmoved by rising unemployment, reaching 5% of the economically active population in September, which he saw as still way below any conceivable "natural" rate. There is, however, no doubt that job opportunities have been disappearing. Employment in the state sector fell by 967,000 (or 14%) from December 1989 to September 1990 while unemployment rose to 926,000 and notified vacancies fell to a mere 61,000.

Even more discussion has surrounded the extent of the fall in living standards. The drop in real wages must be a deceptive measure when shortages meant that goods were often not available except at inflated black market prices. Moreover, merely the fact that goods were visibly available, even if at high prices, could give the impression that things were improving. During 1990 the "unofficial" trading sector, based on enormous street markets, grew rapidly, first selling food and imported goods but then, as the demand constraint began to bite, even selling the products of the domestic consumer goods industry. The number of people involved is unknown, but prices tend to be 20–25% lower than in state-run shops. The implication is that official inflation figures may be exaggerated and that figures on retail sales may give too low an impression of living standards. There is, fortunately, some further sketchy data on consumption in real terms. Table 4 does suggest that the drop in food consumption, possibly 30% of which is accounted for by street traders, may be very small. It is certainly likely to be less than the extent suggested by the figures in Table 5 which show the drop in sales from state shops. Official estimates suggest a 16% fall in sales for the whole year, made up of a 35% fall in state and co-operative shops alongside a 4.5 times increase in private trade. There is, however, no doubting the sharp decline for many manufactured consumer goods with output figures showing almost as large a drop as the falls in sales.

Privatization and acceleration

By the end of March it was fairly clear to the government that the first stage of its programme, overcoming inflation, had been achieved. The question arose of how to proceed

Table 4:   Percentage change in consumption per head
of some foods, 1989–90

Bread	1.5
Meat	–2.6
Milk	–4.4

Note: All figures compare the January–September periods.
Source: *Statistical Information on Economic Situation of Poland*, October 1990.

Table 5   Percentage change in supplies to market
of consumer goods, 1989–90

Butchers' meat	–12.2
Milk	–19.8
Washing machines	–26.6
Cars	7.0
Clothing	–28.2
Footwear	–37.6

Note: All figures compare the January–September periods.
Source: *Statistical Information on Economic Situation of Poland*,
October 1990.

with broadly three possibilities. One was to continue with an unchanged deflationary policy. Another was to switch to an anti-recession policy, while the third was to maintain the existing restrictive policy while switching attention to "systemic" change. This last option was given verbal support, but the practice was for an eclectic mixture. Anti-inflation elements persisted in restraints on some prices, such as coal, which conflicted with the logic of the transition to the market, and in the continuation of the wage control policy. The significance of this was that, as it operated through a tax on the wage bill, it effectively prevented the growth of any sectors or significantly sized enterprises, both state and privately owned, that might want to expand in response to market signals. Wage control was therefore blocking structural change and adaptation. Anti-recession elements were also visible in a slight relaxation of policy in June including a cut in interest rates (although they were still at the level of 34%) and a decision to increase public spending after the unexpected budget surplus in the first half of the year. Some additional subsidies were given to some sectors facing possible bankruptcies.

The progress of systemic change was extremely slow. The key measure was to be privatization. The Round Table bequeathed the objective of a "pluralist ownership structure" with the insistence that privatization should be under parliamentary control and dependent on "the consent of the employees' council preceded by a referendum among all employees". The new government had a clearer commitment to a predominance of private ownership, but reaction against the *"nomenklatura"* companies encouraged a strong emphasis on a public process with shares sold at auctions. It was to prove impossible to combine this with speed.

A series of schemes (amounting to 13 draft laws from September 1989 to March 1990) were worked out in the newly created Office for Ownership Transformation. They all concentrated on "big" privatization, meaning large enterprises. The creation of a private sector based on small firms was largely ignored although it could have produced speedier results. Proposals started with firm opposition to "giving away" shares either to the public or to employees, but successive drafts represented a gradual process of compromise in which more possible means of privatization were accepted although ultimate control was always left with the single state agency.

In mid-March the government finally approved a draft law which was then put to parliament. It allowed for the creation of a new, powerful controlling body, the Agency for Transformation, with the status of a government ministry. Practically all shares were to be sold for their full value while, as a concession to the self-management lobby, 20% were to be made available to employees on preferential terms. More significantly, employees would hold one third of the seats on enterprise supervisory boards. Prior to privatization, state enterprises would be converted into state-owned joint stock companies but would then have to be fully privatized within another two years. The assumption was that the process would be started with the sale of a few, very good enterprises. The parliamentary debate ended in the passing of two laws on July 17. Very little had been changed although there was a clearer recognition of the possibility of "non-equivalent" privatization by the issuing of vouchers to the public exchangeable for shares. The law as passed effectively ruled out some options. It restricted the extent of employee preferences and created legal barriers to the old *nomenklatura* gaining control of property. At the same time, it left the government with important options for the future. Its first step, in October 1990, was to draw up a list of seven excellent companies ready for sale. These flotations proved to be oversubscribed, but evidence from several surveys suggests that even those who support privatization will not be spending much money on shares. Those with significant savings are more likely to want to invest in buying or setting up their own business.

The slow pace of privatization helped reinforce the growing impression that the Balcerowicz programme was simply a recipe for permanent depression. The depth of discontent should not be exaggerated. Some strikes occurred in May, notably on the railways, and in November, mostly in coal mining and urban public transport, but they were not protests against the logic of the Balcerowicz programme as a whole. The issue was rather declining relative wages in sectors that were not allowed to raise prices as they would like (about 5% were still controlled) or, as in the case of coal mining, that could not export their product without restriction because of continuing domestic shortages. In other words, allowing an extension of the free market into these sectors would have relieved the discontent. This, however, the government was not prepared to do, owing to the threat to the stability of the rest of the economy.

Nevertheless, the Solidarity leadership began voicing concern in public and in meetings with the government as early as March. The first targets were rising unemployment, the "*nomenklatura*" companies and the continued presence of officials of the former regime in high positions. The view was expressed increasingly strongly that "the workers have gained nothing" and privatization was presented as the key step for aiding economic recovery. Speeding this up was seen to require non-equivalent exchange while the Solidarity leadership was also pressing for more vigorous measures to sell off smaller enterprises. The problem there was that an enormous number of laws needed to be changed and that took time as the government was insisting on doing everything by the proper parliamentary procedures. Wałęsa's suggestion of December 1989 that powers should be taken to change obstructing laws by decree was firmly rejected.

Other political groupings were also formulating their economic policies. A "left" within Solidarity was generally doubtful of the benefits of privatization while also concerned that the government's non-interventionist approach was exacting too heavy a social cost without any promise of recovery to come: it advocated a more active approach centring on interventionist economic policies rather than systemic change, but never produced a real alternative to the government's policies. The ROAD group, later to emerge as Mazowiecki's supporters in the presidential election, was at first cautiously critical of

Balcerowicz, advocating "capitalism with a human face" and, in very vague terms, a more active policy on industry and to help agriculture.

The initiative, however, was with Wałęsa's supporters. His notion of "acceleration" was given some meaning in relation to privatization by some of his advisers and especially Janusz Lewandowski who was later to be appointed the minister in charge of privatization. He advocated placing the emphasis first of all on selling off smaller enterprises to individual owners, while bigger firms could be privatized in a series of blocks in exchange for vouchers issued to the public. Offering these firms for sale would, it was argued, simply limit the funds available for investment in smaller businesses. His main economic adviser, however, long-standing supporter of market systems Stefan Kurowski, concentrated on more direct criticisms of the Balcerowicz programme and advocated an anti-recession policy based on the classical Keynesian instrument of higher public spending on social services and the infrastructure alongside a relaxation of wage controls. The logic of his position was that inflation at the start of the year was largely just a one-off adjustment to the freeing of prices. It was now firmly under control.

Mazowiecki's supporters rejected this last assertion and uninspiringly argued that restraint had to be maintained for the foreseeable future while recovery would be a long, hard and very slow process. Wałęsa himself was very careful not to attack Balcerowicz whose removal from the government could jeopardize IMF support. He has preferred to suggest some "corrections" which are likely to involve at least verbal commitment to efforts at a more active employment policy, a change in relation to agriculture, a faster pace for "small" privatization and an attempt to formulate a clearer industrial policy. The implication of Wałęsa's campaign and subsequent statements is that a rigorous application of market principles will be tempered by an awareness of public concern at the social consequences. In practice, this could amount to a continuation of post-March eclecticism.

Key Economic Sectors

The results for different sectors of the economy in 1990 depended primarily on their ability to cope under the new conditions created by the collapse in consumer demand. Table 6 shows changes compared with 1989 although, as will be argued, a fall in output is often a deceptive measure of the prosperity of the sector.

Generally speaking, as the figures show, the small private sector did better, but it too suffered from the low level of demand and even where output increased it was rarely associated with investment for the future. Elsewhere, those large state enterprises that enjoyed a monopoly position fared well. The government did not link freeing prices with changes to the organizational structure of the economy and estimates suggested that 70% of production is in the hands of a monopolist, meaning that most firms could raise prices at the start of the year. Profitability in the state sector, measured as a proportion of sales, actually rose to 36% in the first quarter, falling only slightly to 32% for the whole January to August period, compared with 26% for the same period in 1989. These high profits are one of the main sources of tax revenue and this has contributed to the high budget surplus.

Table 6: Percentage changes in net output for individual sectors, 1989–90

	All	State & co-operative	Private
All	−17.5		
Industry	−23	−25	+8
Construction	−9	−17.6	−2
Transport	−15	−15.7	−4
Agriculture	−1.2		

Source: *Zycie Gospodarcze*, 1991, 1 and 4.

It was even suggested that some firms could be deliberately restricting output, thereby contributing to the overall fall in industrial production, so as to push up prices and reap monopoly profits.

Financial results were further helped by delaying the implementation of the Balcerowicz programme until January 1990 which gave enterprises several months in which to stock up raw materials at the lower, pre-free market prices. It also seems even that many enterprises which have faced financial difficulties have been able to build up debts with each other, thereby by-passing the restrictive monetary policy which itself has not been applied absolutely rigorously by the banks. The result overall has been very few bankruptcies. Unemployment has risen generally through the failure to replace those who leave, while the drop in employment has been most marked in internal trade with a 20.8% drop from December 1989 to September 1990 as turnover collapsed due to low consumer demand and competition from street traders. Employment also fell rapidly in construction where it was down 14.1%, but in all sectors the decline was less than the fall in output and took place more gradually.

Agriculture

Some sectors were better placed than others to exploit their market power, but the worst placed was probably agriculture. It inherited an outdated structure with 2,700,000 private smallholdings, most of which were under five hectares in 1987 while only 7% were over 15 hectares. These occupy 76% of the cultivated land with the rest in the hands of large state or co-operative farms which generally achieve a lower output per hectare. The level of mechanization is low, with 1,000,000 horses and only slightly more tractors, of which two-thirds are in the private sector. Despite incomes of around 85% of the level in industry, agriculture did relatively well in the 1980s with production in 1989 16% above the 1982 level. The sector actually benefited in some respects from the decline in domestic industry as depopulation of the countryside was held up by the lack of employment opportunities elsewhere. The proportion of the active labour force employed in agriculture in 1989 was still 26%, against 29% in 1976.

The government's philosophy in 1990 was essentially to avoid any specific agricultural policy. Instead, the free market was allowed to take its toll, meaning that farmers had to face escalating input prices, including imports and the products of domestic industry, while they lacked the power to control their own output or prices. Many farmers, obviously unable to raise output before the next harvest, responded by selling off equipment to keep up interest payments on debts. Throughout the year their only strategy for maintaining living standards was to maximize production, which contributed to the excellent results in physical terms with a much smaller drop in output than in industry. Good harvests, however, were accompanied by a relative decline in state purchase prices and hence in farmers' incomes. The position for animal products was slightly different as farmers were confronted by monopsonistic processing firms which both cut purchases and forced down the prices paid to individual farmers in the face of falling domestic demand for the final product.

The figures in Table 7 show that in some cases state purchase prices actually fell and the overall rise was nowhere near the 297.7% rise in consumer prices that farmers had to pay for the goods they bought, or even the 265% increase in food prices that consumers had to pay. There evidently was scope for some high profits in some sectors of the food processing industry, although even there there were cases of firms with high capital costs that could not raise prices enough and were faced with bankruptcy. The clearest example was the creameries which made repeated demands for support to maintain a minimum price for milk products.

Overall, farmers' real living standards may have fallen by 50% from the 1989 level with a drop to possibly 70% of the average in industry. There is, however, no immediate danger of a collapse of the sector as unemployment elsewhere in the economy means that farmers cannot abandon their businesses and leave. It is, however, likely that the government will make concessions to their demands for some form of subsidy (the food industry still accounts for 7% of total subsidies, although that represents a massive reduction on the 1989 level) and for special credit terms that recognize the seasonal nature of agricultural output.

Manufacturing

Manufacturing enterprises typically could respond to falling demand by raising prices. Although productivity is estimated to be around a third of the Western European level, imports represented no serious threat in view of the extremely low exchange rate as well as the tariff protection. The first price rises were followed by attempts to increase sales of the existing product range, sometimes by exporting and typically with little success. Enterprises

Table 7:   State purchase prices and state purchases from agriculture

	Prices September 1990 (December 1989=100)	Purchases January–September 1990 (January–September 1989=100)
Wheat	209.5	102.0
Potatoes	108.5	101.5
Sugar beet	138.5	105.8
Pigs	272.2	75.8
Milk	131.9	87.1

Source: Statistical Information on Economic Situation of Poland, October 1990.

typically also reacted by cutting production, but there were very few cases of a vigorous attempt to adapt to the new market environment. The low incidence of redundancies, the gradualness of the rise in unemployment (employment in September 1989 was still only 9.2% down on December 1989, although output was almost 30% down) and the lack of interest in retraining possibilities are indicative of how few cases there were of a major reorganization of production.

Typically, management lacked the ability or resources to undertake a major change of approach, or even to seek new markets abroad. They were left able only to wait and hope that good times would one day return. That often meant holding down individual wages to maintain employment and relative earnings in industry fell while those in construction, transport and internal trade rose substantially, thanks partly to slightly faster adaptation to the lower demand. Directors were also widely believed to lack the moral authority as they were faced with powerful trade unions and employees' councils. Survey evidence, however, suggests that this was not the decisive factor. Directors who took decisive steps generally won support from the workforce as there were widespread fears that inactivity could lead to bankruptcy and closure.

The most successful enterprises were those already exporting a significant proportion of output to the West. There were few of them, but they often reacted immediately by entering into discussions with Western firms. In some cases they had already made preparations over the preceding years so that they had the right contacts and market knowledge.

The worst placed were in light industry and especially textiles and garments where the large number of relatively small enterprises means that monopoly power is low. By the end of April the textile town of Łódź was reporting a 30–50% fall in sales, a 30% drop in output and a 50% fall in real wages. Many factories were already on a three- or four-day week. The quality of products and low level of technology made an export orientation impossible, especially as high interest rates and tariff restrictions ruled out the import of modern equipment. In fact, demand was hit further by a cut in exports to the USSR and by imports allowed in from the Middle and Far East. A report in late November showed that out of 68 firms in a state of liquidation, 20 were in light industry and 10 in Łódź.

In this situation current profitability is a very unreliable guide to the true potential of an enterprise. It depends on price and cost changes which may be beyond its control. It also may depend on the costs of past investment decisions, decided on by the central authorities in previous years. Particularly difficult were cases related to agriculture where the purchasing power of farmers had collapsed. The government was faced with a major crisis in the Ursus tractor factory, expanded enormously in the flawed investment drive of the 1970s, which was confronted with a halving of sales. It now has to pay tax measured on the value of useless capital equipment. There was some success with increasing exports, but that still left a 40% drop in production. The management, backed by employees' representatives, believed that its product was well adapted to the needs of Polish agriculture and therefore called for government assistance. Balcerowicz and his closest advisers have remained at least verbally opposed to such deviations from their philosophy, but in such cases solutions are generally being found that still hold up outright bankruptcy.

Transport

The transport sector has been hit by a sharp drop in goods transported while passenger levels have remained more stable. The country was already suffering from an outdated network in which there had been minimal investment for many years. Railways had suffered the worst. They accounted for roughly the same number of passenger-kilometres as road transport, but their share of goods transport, by value, had been declining. Thus from a level of 27% of all net transport revenues in 1985, the figure in 1989 had fallen to 24%. Road transport was steady at 33% while air transport was up from 3% to 4%. There had been a slight shift towards the private sector which accounted for 3.4% of the value of all transport output in 1985, rising to 6.3% in 1989. 1990 saw a decline in all recorded branches. Total loads carried were down by 41% by weight for the year as a whole. The state railways saw a drop of 37.6% while public road transport was down 54.5%, suggesting some relative shift back towards the traditional railway system, which is the main carrier of heavy loads.

The fall in employment had reached 10% by the end of September, which is significant when set against the 12.8% fall in output over the same period. Price controls have been maintained on much of public transport so as to prevent exploitation of monopoly positions. To avoid financial catastrophe, state subsidies have continued at roughly the 1989 level. Relative wages actually rose from 85.2% of the average for all employees in December 1989 to 97.3% in September 1990. Some sectors, such as urban public transport, did somewhat worse and sporadic strikes in November pushed the government towards further subsidies.

Energy

Poland is heavily dependent on its own domestic coal production which provides 76% of its energy needs. Oil accounts for another 13.5%, while gas, all from the USSR, provides 8%. In view of uncertainties over the future of trade with the Soviet Union (see below), coal is becoming even more crucial. At its peak in 1979, output reached 200 million tonnes, but then fell to 163 million tonnes in 1981 after miners had been granted a five-day week. With the banning of Solidarity, working hours were increased by 15% again and annual output rose to slightly over 190 million tonnes. The Round Table, however, led to a new agreement on miners' working conditions and output in 1989 was back down to 178 million tonnes. 1990 saw a further 17% fall. This has not led to a breakdown in energy supplies, thanks to a mild winter in 1989–1990 and to lower demand from the rest of the economy.

Nevertheless, to maintain domestic supplies, the government has limited coal exports, which would be highly profitable at the current exchange rate, to a level 8% below that achieved in 1989. It has also kept controls on the domestic price, after allowing a sharp rise in January, so that coal mines cannot exploit their monopoly position to fuel further inflation. The result has been a squeeze on profits and a unique escalation of state subsidies. From a negligible level in 1989, coal mining now accounts for 37% of total state help.

Even the enormous increase in subsidies for coal mining was, however, not enough to prevent relative wages from falling from 61% above the average level in the first nine months of 1989 to only 50% above in the same period in 1990. The result has been continual strike threats and even warnings that relative earnings, for an occupation in which geographical isolation and a tradition of employing no women often means that there is only one breadwinner, could be falling so low as to threaten recruitment and hence the stability of production.

New technology

There was little chance throughout the depressed 1980s of developing new technology. The greater degree of autarky and hence isolation of the economy meant that equipment and know-how was imported on a lower level than ever before. It also meant that there was no pressure on domestic firms to innovate or to seek to keep up with foreign rivals or partners. This stagnation has continued into 1990 with all the emphasis on restrictive macroeconomic policy and state non-involvement. Even where Poland once had some sort of start, it has generally slipped further behind over the past decade. For example, the country was reasonably well placed producing its ODRA computers in the 1970s. They were, however, never used as a basis for CMEA-wide development for which the Soviet-made RIAD was favoured. By 1980 development of the Polish product had effectively stopped and almost all the output was going for export so that the use of computers remained minimal within the domestic economy. Imports were restricted by the high prices and by COCOM regulations. The shortage of software was so serious that the government chose not to introduce software copyright laws. Now, with COCOM restrictions eased, more computers can be imported, albeit still at a very high price, but a new legal framework will be required before the software problem can be fully resolved. Some steps are already being taken, largely by private firms sometimes collaborating with Western partners. There is even a small firm assembling personal computers from imported components with the final product going to the domestic market and finding export success in the Soviet Union and some Western countries.

Finance

Although financial policy has been absolutely central to the government's thinking, and has been a major element causing the drop in both inflation and output during 1990, information on this sector is still very patchy. Official statistics continue to centre on production and the results of state enterprises. Precise details on both the state budget and on the banking sector are lagging behind. There is, however, no doubt that the state budget moved from a deficit general throughout the 1980s, with a high point in 1989, to a strong surplus in early 1990. Some relaxation of Balcerowicz's restrictive policy in later months led to a sharp reduction in the overall surplus and probably contributed to higher inflation and to a rise in consumer goods imports. If the trend of the first eight months of the year had been maintained, the total surplus would have been around 8.5% of state expenditure against a deficit of 10% of spending in the latter half of 1989.

This turnaround has been achieved by a 31% growth in revenues relative to personal incomes while expenditure has remained in line with incomes. This, of course, means that spending in real terms has been cut. There was a small 13% real growth in social security spending, which is remarkably low considering the new demands imposed by unemployment, but practically every other major expenditure item has been cut. The most important reduction was in subsidies which had accounted for around 40% of spending in the 1980s. Food subsidies, previously 15% of the state budget and 6% of Net Material Product, fell in 1990 to under 8% of the 1989 level.

This restrictive policy succeeded in sucking demand out of the economy. Consumer spending is discussed under the Balcerowicz programme. The stock of money fell by 24% in real terms from December 1989 to August 1990. The official measure includes cash, bank deposits and hard currency holdings. The last of these fell relative to price increases by 68%, made up of an 88% fall in the enterprise sector and a 43% drop in the personal sector: the reason is explained in the section below. Nominal money holdings rose more slowly in the enterprise sector leading to a fall in real terms of 30% against only 21% for the personal sector. This is consistent with the squeeze hitting enterprises first so that they could not pay out wages in line with inflation. How far they were able to compensate by running into debt with each other or by taking out bank loans is still unclear. Banks, however, appear not to have been excessively soft and probably made healthy profits in 1990. Figures to prove this are not yet available.

Foreign Economic Relations

International trade looks like the main success story for the Polish economy in 1990. The initial prediction was for a hard currency deficit of $0.8 billion and for a surplus of 0.5 billion Transferable Rubles (TR) with the non-convertible currency area. Instead there were surpluses of, respectively, $4.7 billion and TR 4.8 billion. The changes in exports and imports in 1990 compared with 1989 are shown in value terms in Table 8. Fixed prices would show a still sharper drop in hard currency imports. Hard currency exports grew with the fall in demand on the domestic and non-convertible currency markets. Judging from figures for the first nine months only, the biggest increase was in construction which also showed the biggest decline in any category in exports to CMEA (Comecon) countries. The cut in imports was most marked for agricultural produce, down to 12% of the 1989 level and accounting for only 1.7% of imports. There were increases for machinery (up 16.5%) and, especially, for fuel (up 94.2% as supplies from the USSR declined). The decline in imports from the non-convertible currency area was spread across all categories of goods, with fuel and power declining to 58.6% of the 1989 level which is little different from the average figure.

Trade relations within the CMEA have been hit by the reunification of Germany and falling demand for imports throughout the area. The most important development, however, has been the cut in raw material deliveries from the USSR. Poland needs 15,000,000 tonnes of oil annually and 85% of this came from the USSR in 1989. A

Table 8:   Foreign trade in 1990 as a percentage of 1989 figures

	Total	Convertible currency	Non-convertible currency	Soviet Union
Exports	110.1	134.0	88.8	89.3
Imports	71.5	86.5	60.0	58.4

Note: Figures for the Soviet Union are for the first nine months only.
Source: *Statistical Information on Economic Situation of Poland*, October 1990; *Zycie Gospodarcze* 1991, 4.

similar amount, 12,800,000 tonnes, was contracted for 1990, but deliveries have fallen short by possibly 30%. Efforts were made to replace this and it was announced in July that an agreement had been reached with Iraq for 1,000,000 tonnes. That quickly fell through with UN sanctions after Iraq's invasion of Kuwait. An agreement was then signed for 500,000 tonnes from Iran. Poland is now actively searching for additional supplies to see it through 1991. It has the capacity at Gdynia to pump 8,000,000 tonnes annually from tankers, although it would be easier to import along the pipeline from the Soviet Union.

Trade with the USSR from January 1, 1991 is to be based on dealings in hard currency at world prices. It is still unclear what this will mean but preliminary agreements suggest that about half Poland's oil needs will be supplied. A key Polish export in exchange, it is hoped, will continue to be machinery. Around 30 large engineering enterprises are geared exclusively to the Soviet market and would otherwise face closure while the engineering industry as a whole provided over 60% of exports to the USSR in 1989. The justification for optimism is that the USSR may still face a hard currency shortage while Polish made equipment, even if of too low a quality to be saleable elsewhere in the world, is appropriate to the technological level of Soviet industry. It remains very unclear what mechanism will be devised for setting the prices of Polish exports, but the expectation is that 1991 will see a deficit with the USSR of around $2 billion. That, however, is treated as only a very rough guess.

The improvement in the trade balance in hard currency is largely the result of depressed domestic demand. Imports are down by roughly the same proportion as industrial production as the demand for inputs has fallen. Moreover, the exchange rate and a 20% tariff on practically all imports has created special problems for import-dependent sectors, such as much of light industry, contributing to the decline in domestic production. The growth in exports is, as has been seen, largely a desperate response to falling demand and does not represent any fundamental reorientation of production or overall improvement in competitiveness.

The exchange rate was set in January 1990 at the existing free market level of 9,500 Zl to $1. This was way below any conceivable purchasing power parity level and implied average monthly earnings of around $66. The justification for the chosen level was that Poland had at the time minimal hard currency reserves and the request had not even been granted for a stand-by loan from the IMF. In Sachs' view, it was better to set the exchange rate at a level that could be held firm, so that it could be used as a definite target and as a means of checking whether the stabilization policy was being adhered to rigorously. In practice it did remain stable throughout the inflation of the following months. It even helped to reverse the "dollarization" of the economy. The point was that, over the previous months of rapid inflation, savings had been converted into dollars and even many domestic transactions were being conducted in hard currency. In 1990, with a stable exchange rate, high interest on domestic savings deposits and rapid inflation, it became disadvantageous to hold savings in hard currency with its declining real value.

Total hard currency debt now stands at $45 billion (with net debt at around $41 billion). The Polish government throughout 1990 tried to persuade creditors to give some relief, but one of the strong criticisms from Wałęsa's election campaign was that their approach was too cautious. It was claimed that the IMF terms for Poland's stabilization programme had been accepted with the implicit understanding that it would lead to the writing off of past debts. Wałęsa made the firm promise that he would appeal for a 50 year moratorium and his supporters suggested that he had the international standing to achieve it.

Principal Personalities

Bielecki, Jan Kryzsztof. Born May 3, 1951. An economist by training. MA in maritime transport at the Higher Economic School in Sopot 1973. Went on to doctoral studies at same School but did not submit thesis. Assistant at Gdańsk University. Worked in Ministry of Machine Engineering and Mining. Full time Solidarity functionary in Gdańsk Regional Committee 1980–81. After 1982 he ran a private handycrafts business, the *Doradca* co-operative. Elected as *Sejm* Civic Committee Deputy for Gdańsk in June 1989. Nominated by Wałęsa as Prime Minister-designate on New Year's Eve 1990. Formally appointed by the *Sejm* in early January 1991 to head a government of so-called technicians (but one that was in fact dominated by the Liberal Democratic Congress) until the *Sejm* elections envisaged for the spring.

Bugaj, Ryszard. Born in 1944, educated as an economist at Warsaw University. Worked in Planning Commission (1973–82) and then PAN. KOR and Solidarity adviser. Main spokesman for the "Realist" economic strand at the 1981 Solidarity congress. Interned 1982. Elected *Sejm* Deputy, he became the influential chairman of its Economic Committee.

Bujak, Zbigniew. Born 1954. Ursus technical worker and leader of the summer 1980 strikes there. From 1980–89 chairman of Solidarity's Mazowsze region and KK member. Organizer of underground resistance 1982 until his arrest in May 1986. Civic Committee member. Did not stand for election to parliament in 1989. With Frasyniuk, co-founder of ROAD in 1990 and sharp critic of Wałęsa.

Geremek, Bronisław. Born 1932, became historian of medieval France and Europe in PAN's Institute of History from 1955–85 and again after March 1989. Co-founder of "Flying University" (TKN) in 1978. Prominent Solidarity adviser and activist (chairman of Programme Commission at 1981 congress). Interned during 1982 and rearrested. Co-chairman of the Group on Questions of Political Reform at the Round Table. Candidate for Prime Minister in August 1989. OKP chairman September 1989–November 1990.

Jaruzelski, Wojciech. Born 1923, promoted Poland's youngest General 1956. Head of Main Political Department (GZP) 1960–65, Chief of Staff 1965–68, Minister of Defence 1968–83. PZPR Politburo candidate 1970, full member 1971–90. Chairman of Council of Ministers February 1981–85. PZPR First Secretary October 1981–July 1989. Chairman of the Council of State December 1985–July 1989. President July 1989–December 1990.

Kaczyński, Jarosław. Born 1949. Lawyer. Warsaw University lecturer at its Białystok campus. KOR-Solidarity activist, director of Mazowsze's Centre for Social Studies. Senator for Elbląg. Imposed by Wałęsa as Editor of *Tygodnik Solidarność* from October 1989 to December 1990. Appointed Minister of State for Security Questions by President Wałęsa.

Kaczyński, Lech. Born 1949, identical twin brother of Jarosław. Lawyer and adjunct-lecturer in labour law at Gdańsk University. KOR and Free Trade Unions of the Coast activist 1976–80. Solidarity adviser and functionary in Gdańsk 1980–81, interned till October 1982. Along with his brother, one of Wałęsa's closest collaborators. KK Secretary (rumoured as Wałęsa's eventual replacement as chairman) and Civic Committee member. Senator for Gdańsk.

Kiszczak, Czesław. Born 1925. Head of military intelligence in 1970s. Minister of Interior 1981–90. PZPR politburo candidate 1982, full member 1986. His proposal of talks with the opposition in August 1988 initiated the process which led to the Round Table, during which he headed the government-coalition side. Considered as a possible candidate successively for the posts of President and Prime Minister in summer 1989.

Kuroń, Jacek. Born in 1934, long-time opposition activist and theorist; imprisoned by the communist authorities on and off since the mid-1960s. KOR co-founder and its most prominent spokesman, 1976–80. A Solidarity adviser, he was interned and re-imprisoned after martial law. A Civic Committee member, he was elected as a *Sejm* Deputy in Warsaw in June 1989. Considered as a possible Prime Minister he became Minister for Labour and Social Policy in the Mazowiecki government. Probably the most influential opposition-Solidarity political writer and strategist up till the formation of the Civic Committee he was universally regarded as the least elegantly dressed man on the Polish political scene!

Mazowiecki, Tadeusz. Lawyer, born 1927. An organizer of Warsaw Catholic Intellectuals Club (KIK). Editor of Kraków Social-Catholic quarterly Więż 1958–81. Znak *Sejm* Deputy 1961–71. TKN organizer. Chairman of Committee of Experts in Gdańsk shipyard August 1980. Interned for whole of 1982. Subsequently a close adviser of Wałęsa's and the KK as well as a link to the episcopal hierarchy. Civic Committee member. Co-chairman of the Group on Trade Union Pluralism at the Round Table. Chairman of the Council of Ministers from September 1989 to December 1990. Came third in the Presidential election November 1990. Chairman of the Democratic Union.

Merkel, Jacek. Born 1954. Shipbuilding engineer in Gdańsk shipyard. Solidarity activist there and in the Gdańsk regional executive 1980–81. Interned in 1982 and dismissed from his job. Chairman of the Gdańsk strike-committee (MKS) in August 1988. Member of Civic Committee. Appointed by Wałęsa to be Director of his Presidential Office in December 1990 after strong rumours that he was considered as a prime ministerial candidate.

Michnik, Adam. Born 1946. Warsaw University opposition activist 1966–68 (sentenced to three years' imprisonment). Worked as a welder and completed his interrupted history degree externally at Poznań University. Co-founder of KOR with Kuroń and TKN organizer. Adviser to Solidarity's Mazowsze region and the Lenin Works in Nowa Huta. Interned 1982 and reimprisoned till the 1984 amnesty and again in 1985–86. Member of Civic Committee. Round Table participant. Elected *Sejm* Deputy in 1989. Editor of *Gazeta Wyborcza* from June 1989 onwards. Fell into renewed conflict with Wałęsa in 1990 and started to move back towards his socialist roots. Author of notable books such as *The Church, the Left, Dialogue* (1977) and works in Polish on opposition strategy and values.

Olszewski, Jan. Born 1930, lawyer specializing in defending dissidents from 1976 onwards with Władysław Siła-Nowicki. KOR and Solidarity adviser 1980–81. A link-man between Solidarity and the authorities during the various consultations of the late 1980s. Informally designated by Wałęsa to sound out his chances of forming a government in December 1990 but withdrew.

Rakowski, Mieczysław F. Reformist persona created as the Editor of *Polityka* 1958–81. Deputy-Chairman of Council of Ministers from February 1981–85 (responsible for trade union questions and for negotiations with Solidarity in 1981). *Sejm* Vice-Marshal and chairman of the Socio-Economic Council 1985–88. PZPR CC Secretary summer 1988. Chairman of the Council of Ministers from September 1988 to August 1989. PZPR First Secretary from July 1989 to January 1990.

Wałęsa, Lech. Born 1943, electrician in Gdańsk shipyard. Strike leader and Solidarity chairman 1981–90 (re-elected by 1981 and 1990 congresses). Interned 1982. Reconstituted Solidarity's Temporary Council in September 1986 which became the KK in 1987. Formed his Civic Committee in December 1988. Cleared way for the Round Table negotiations and agreement through his meetings with Kiszczak at Magdalenka. Did not stand for parliamentary election but was instrumental in bringing about the victory of his "team". He kept to the Round Table deal and ensured Jaruzelski's election as President, but again intervened crucially from August 7, 1989 to bring about a Solidarity-led government headed by Mazowiecki. Growing disputes with the latter led him to call for early presidential elections by universal suffrage which he won on the second ballot against Tymiński in December 1990. He then constituted the Bielecki government.

The Media

The organizational framework for running the mass media in communist Poland was very similar to that of other Marxist-Leninist states. The main differences lay in more flexible cultural and ideological policies and more critical and less controlled mass organizations, journalists, writers and film makers who presented recurrent challenges, especially in crisis periods, to all post-1955 regimes.

The Round Table sub-group on the mass media, chaired by Bogdan Jachacz and Krzysztof Kozłowski, in its extremely detailed final report, agreed on the need to abolish censorship and to build "a new system of information" rejecting all monopolies and responsive to social pluralism (*Porozumienia Okrągłego Stołu*, Warsaw, 1989). The Solidarity press was to be relicensed, its paper supply would be assured and *Gazeta Wyborcza* was to appear in time for the electoral campaign. Communist control over the press was to be replaced by judicial registration. It would be regulated by the new laws on associations and economic activity. Solidarity called for the break-up of the PZPR-controlled RSW *Prasa-Książka-Ruch* monopoly conglomerate. The form and extent of pluralist access to radio and TV were agreed in general terms after much controversy. It was unclear what Solidarity understood by the "shift from a monopolistic to a social model of pluralist radio and TV" and whether their demand to control a new third channel would be conceded. The ZSL and SD called in a separate declaration for the establishment of a Council, reflecting the parliamentary balance of forces, to supervise the Radio-Committee.

The government press spokesman, Jerzy Urban, resigned in early April 1989 to become chairman of the above-mentioned Committee for Polish Radio and Television (PRiTV). He did not last long, being replaced by Mazowiecki's nominee, Andrzej Drawicz, in September 1989. The distinctively bald-headed Drawicz was a philologist and literary critic associated with the Kraków catholic weekly, *Tygodnik Powszechny*. A prominent KOR, Flying University and Solidarity activist he was interned for most of 1982. He exercised a dominant, although controversial, influence in this sphere, resuming the broadcasting of religious programmes and masses in October and opening up the media to a wide range of individuals and opinions. Although he sacked his two PZPR deputy-chairmen, J. Królikowski and J. Słabicki in December he was criticized by the Wałęsa camp for not instituting sufficient organizational and personnel change and for his tardiness in commercializing the second TV channel. He was also charged with not satisfying old scores left by the martial law dismissals and verifications and of being too partial towards his boss, Mazowiecki, in the presidential campaign. The Solidarity PRiTV branch voted no confidence in him in October 1990, ostensibly over issues of wages and conditions, but also over the balance of access to the channels. Hardly surprisingly Wałęsa's victory meant his replacement by Marian Terlecki.

The most important formal change of the period was the abolition of censorship in April 1990 which was replaced by the judicial registration of publications. The Main Bureau for the Control of Publications and Spectacles (GUKPiW) which had exercised a more irritating than effective control during the 1980s also went. The second main aspect of the breaking of communist control was the partial privatization of the press. Here a Liquidation Committee was established under Docent Jerzy Drygalski to dispose of the titles of the huge *RSW-Ruch* press conglomerate. Immediate editorial changes were effected amidst charges of the misuse of political influence. It went on to attempt to auction off the more popular titles. Foreign investment became possible. The French *Hersant* group, for example, bought an interest in the official government daily *Rzeczpospolita*. It was envisaged that others like the weekly *Polityka* would be bought out and run by an employees' co-operative. The exercise involved great and bitter controversy from all sides. The SdRP, as the PZPR's successor, offered to cede over 90% of the RSW titles but argued that the total expropriation, finally imposed by the *Sejm*, was excessively vindictive.

1990 saw the massive and confusing proliferation of new titles. PZPR publications like *Nowe Drogi*, *Życie Partii*, *Ideologia i Polityka* vanished with the party although *Trybuna Ludu* transformed itself into a fairly high quality daily, *Trybuna*. The new left journals like Rakowski's *Dzis* or Urban's *Nie* predictably failed to establish a mass appeal. The reappearance of traditional interwar titles like the Kraków conservative daily *Czas* or the reformist *Po Prostu* with its exciting connotations of the Polish "Spring" of 1956 met with greater success. Other journals like *Wokanda* filled gaps left by the disappearance of long-established titles like *Tygodnik Kulturalny*. The list of publications which died, such as PAX's *Kierunki* or *Argumenty*, and their replacements as well as the editorial and ownership transformations of those who survived is far too long to be chronicled here.

Both film production and book-publishing had been subsidized very heavily by the communists, although a partial price was paid in terms of censorship. Fears were now expressed about the very survival, let alone shrinkage of the former. The latter had to introduce huge price rises which increased book costs relative to that of other goods two- or even three-fold. Western book prices were still prohibitive as a £4 Penguin would need to sell at about 40,000 Zl in Poland compared to the average price of a Polish paperback of about 12–15,000 Zl in late 1990.

Communist Poland always had lively and contestatory associations in the cultural and mass media spheres. The writers' (SSP/ZLP), journalists' (SDP), theatrical workers' (ZASP), film-makers' (SFP) and other ancilliary or successor organizations all responded to freedom, democratization and new pluralist conditions from summer 1989 onwards by changing their executive committees and statutes and by having predictably heated debates about past responsibilities and future tasks.

Foreign Relations

Poland's foreign relations during 1989–90 were dominated by the domestic shift from a communist system tied to the Soviet bloc to a budding democracy striving to reincorporate itself within the western and capitalist world order. The main problems were therefore four-fold. Firstly, the relationship with the USSR and with the Warsaw Pact and Comecon, which had been the organizational frameworks for its hegemony in Eastern Europe, had to be reshaped. Secondly, there was the need to confirm its western frontier on the Oder-Neisse definitively and to readjust to the other consequences, present and potential of German reunification. Thirdly, "the return to Europe" meant that Poland had to define new relationships with the EC, within the Conference on Co-operation and Security in Europe (CSCE) and to the wider disarmament negotiations ultimately designed to dissolve the two military blocs in Europe. Lastly, the vacuum caused by the withdrawal of Soviet power was not filled immediately by German influence. This provided the possibility for regional collaboration in what had been the "Northern Tier" of what is now generally described as the East-Central sub-region of Europe.

All aspects, especially the first two, were remarkably closely inter-linked. The anti-Soviet resentments of Polish public opinion against the post-war decades of Soviet control and alleged economic exploitation had very quickly to be balanced against the realities of the resurgent German threat. Mazowiecki's government therefore wanted to transform the Warsaw Pact from a military bloc into a largely defensive political alliance confirming the *status quo* of frontiers and providing protection against aggression. This process was well in train by the time of the Pact's Advisory Political Council meeting in June 1990. Jaruzelski called there for "more partner-like internal relations" and restructuring to match its new role as an instrument of East-West rapprochement. The Poles were therefore less decided and slower than the Hungarians and Czechoslovaks in asking for the withdrawal of the 50,000-strong Soviet garrison (after about 7,000 left during 1990), whose presence had been regulated by Gomułka's December 1956 agreement. The Soviet government offered negotiations on their withdrawal in February 1990 but met with a divided Polish response. Wałęsa wanted them out by the end of 1990. Jaruzelski agreed in principle, but preferred them to stay until a new European security order covering the united Germany had been achieved. His position was generally supported for tactical reasons by the Mazowiecki government. The tone hardened by September, when under pressure of Wałęsa's presidential campaign, Skubiszewski handed ambassador Kazlov an official demand for immediate negotiations on Soviet troop withdrawals and for compensation for the damage caused by their stay. The USSR then also hardened its line on the issue and over the terms and costs of Soviet transit across Poland for the evacuation of its huge garrison in what had been East Germany in late 1990. Another example of rapid change in the international situation was Defence Minister Kołodziejczyk's Madrid declaration in late September 1990 that Poland regarded the presence of American troops in Europe (i.e. Germany) as a stabilizing force; any withdrawal would have to be managed very carefully.

Balcerowicz's rapid marketization also meant that Poland was foremost in pressing for Comecon's demise and for foreign trade to be put on a purely hard currency basis which occurred by early 1991. Official Poland, very sensibly, did not raise a whisper about its Eastern frontier and the Eastern Territories annexed by Stalin in 1939. The whole nation, however, was now free to express its resentment against the repressions carried out there.

Painful World War II episodes such as the NKVD's massacre at Katyń of Polish officers, prisoners of war from the Kozielsk camp in 1940, were only slowly regulated by the official Soviet admission of responsibility gained during Jaruzelski's April 1990 visit; this made inquiries possible about the precise fate of the remainder from the Starobielsk and Ostaszkow camps whose bodies had never been found.

There was also strong public sympathy for the cause of Baltic independence especially of Lithuania, great concern over the fate of the over one million-strong Polish minority within the USSR and ambivalent attitudes regarding its break-up, especially the possibility of an independent Ukraine. The Polish-Soviet declaration at the end of Jaruzelski's April 1990 visit made it clear that their mutual relations were now based on equality, non-interference in domestic affairs and a free choice of socio-political system, that the Warsaw Pact would remain as a stabilizing force until military blocs were dissolved and that German unification would have to be accompanied by the recognition of all existing borders. The hardline Soviet ambassador in Poland, W. Brovikov, was replaced by Yuri Kazlov soon afterwards. Skubiszewski reciprocated during his first official visit to the USSR (taking in Moscow, Kiev and Minsk) in October 1990 by calling for "change in stability". He declared that Poland would not interfere in Soviet affairs even though she had "a multi-track policy" towards the nationalities. Even such issues as Lithuanian independence, which Poland supported, would first have to be settled directly between Moscow and Vilnius. This doctrine was bitterly attacked by the Wałęsa and nationalist camps.

Chancellor Kohl's interrupted visit of reconciliation to Poland between November 9–14, 1989 was preceded by an official Bonn statement on the inviolability of the German-Polish border. He met Mazowiecki, Foreign Minister Skubiszeski, Jaruzelski and Wałęsa to discuss German economic aid for Poland and Polish concessions to the German minority in Silesia, but the issue of compensation for Polish war victims of Nazism remained unresolved. The final declaration committed West Germany categorically on the central issue of the border. Kohl's office raised a storm on March 2, 1990 however, by declaring that German minority rights in Poland and war reparations would have to be regulated by treaty, implying that the border question was also still dependent on this. Angry French and EC reactions and pressure by Free Democratic Foreign Minister Hans-Dietrich Genscher ultimately forced Kohl to accept that the governments and parliaments of both Germanies would confirm the border quite separately from the resolution of the contentious issues. This was done, the *Bundestag* affirming that the Poles' "right to live in secure borders will not now or in the future be questioned by us Germans". Federal German President, Richard von Weizsacker, also confirmed the renunciation of all German territorial claims and the inviolability of the Polish-German frontier during his official visit to Poland in May 1990. This chapter was closed by the Kohl-Mazowiecki meeting in Frankfurt on Oder in mid-November 1990, which went some way towards allaying Polish fears of a new Rapallo, just before the Kohl-Gorbachev agreement in Bonn. Skubiszewski and Genscher then signed the long awaited treaty confirming the inviolability of their sovereignty, borders and territory on November 14.

Skubiszewski, at a meeting of Warsaw Pact Foreign Ministers in Prague on March 17, 1990 had supported the Hungarian and Czechoslovak view, against the USSR, that a neutral united Germany could prove dangerous and that it was better for it to be controlled within NATO. Poland also gained by being invited by the four victorious World War II powers to join in the "two plus four" talks of summer 1990 which regulated the international aspects of German unification.

The main aims of Polish foreign policy, as defined by Skubiszewski's *Sejm* exposé of May 1990, were: (i) disarmament and the creation of a European security system based on the CSCE; (ii) relations with the USSR were now based on mutual equality and partnership, but Poland would begin negotiating the eventual withdrawal of Soviet troops; and (iii) Poland was prepared to regard German unification as a stabilizing factor if both Germanies would sign a treaty on their borders and if this document were then signed and ratified by the united Germany.

Significantly, Skubiszewski placed little emphasis on East-Central European regional collaboration despite the cordiality of Havel's February 1990 visit to Poland. Gnawing problems over their trade and border crossings which Prague closed at times in order to prevent the notorious Polish "tourist trading" (the Poles did likewise to their Soviet frontier) did not augur well for the future. The absence of basic disputes with neighbours did not compensate for Polish public opinion's dislike of Czechs and Ukrainians, contempt for Bulgars and Romanians, growing disillusion with Magyars and Serbs and patronization of Slovaks, Lithuanians and White Russians, although the élites naturally expressed more subtle views.

A summit of Czechoslovak, Hungarian and Polish presidents, prime ministers and foreign ministers meeting in Bratislava on April 9, 1990 made only minor progress on regional collaboration except on some economic and ecological issues, the proposed establishment of a Central European University and that they should produce a joint viewpoint for the next Helsinki Conference in 1991. Similar attitudes were shared towards their mutual problems but symptomatically discussion of their future integration into the EC was vague and optimistic. The only specific proposal for their "return to Europe" was the Czechoslovak idea, backed strongly by the Poles, of a European Security Commission to be composed of the 35 CSCE states as a step towards Pan-European Confederation. Predictably the Poles were most concerned to break out of their regional backyard and to reassert their place in Europe. Not too much attention should, however, be paid to the renewal by extremist elements like the KPN of frothy inter-war concepts of a Polish dominated *międzymorze* ("between-the-seas bloc") in Eastern Europe. The Polish élites are only too aware that their foreign debt and perilous economic situation make them dependent on Western and IMF support. While they are favoured by the absence of direct disputes with their regional neighbours, historical prejudices work just as strongly against Poland's assumption of what it might consider to be the natural role which it is entitled to in terms of population, cultural level and dynamic socio-economic potential.

ROMANIA

Daniel Nelson

Council of Ministers as at January 1, 1991

Prime Minister. *Petre Roman*
Minister of State responsible for industry and commerce. *Anton Vatasescu*
Minister of State responsible for quality of life and social security. *Ion Aurel Stoica*
Minister of State responsible for economic orientation. *Eugen Dijmarescu*
Deputy Premier; Minister for Reform and Relations with Parliament. *Adrian Severin*
Foreign Affairs. *Adrian Nastase*
Defence. *Col.-Gen. Victor Atanasie Stanculescu*
Finance. *Theodor Stolojan*
Interior. *Doru Viorel Ursu*
Justice. *Victor Babiuc*
Resources and Industry. *Mihail Zisu*

Trade and Tourism. *Constantin Fota*
Agriculture and Food Industry. *Ioan Tip*
Communications. *Andrei Chirica*
Public Works, Transport and Territorial Planning. *Doru Pana*
Education and Science. *Stefan Gheorghe*
Environment. *Valeriu Eugen Pop*
Culture. *Andrei Gabriel Plesu*
Health. *Bogdan Marinescu*
Labour and Social Security. *Ctalin Zamfir*
Youth and Sports. *Bogdan Nicolae Niculescu Duvaz*
Secretary of State at the Ministry of Foreign Affairs. *Romulus Neagu*
Secretary of State at the Ministry of Education and Science. *Andrei Tugulea*

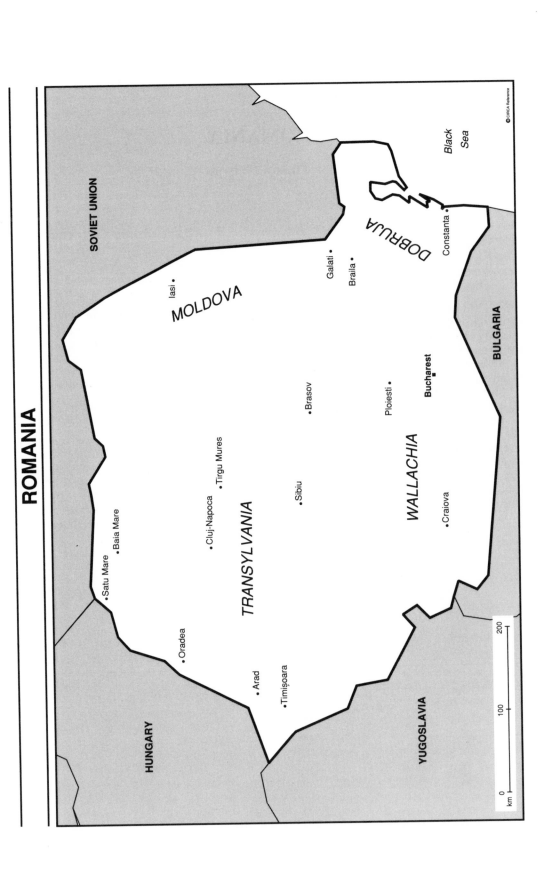

ROMANIA

Chronology

1989

January 7. Week-long celebrations of Elena Ceauşescu's birthday.

January 11. Romania agrees not to block final draft of concluding document of Helsinki review conference in Vienna but insists on January 15 that it will not feel obliged to honour all the provisions on human rights and will make a selective interpretation in accordance with its own law and traditions.

January 19. Radio Budapest says all cultural relations between Hungary and Romania are to cease after failure of bilateral talks on cultural, educational and scientific co-operation.

March 1. Six former party and government officials issue open letter highly critical of Ceauşescu for systematic violation of constitution, cult of self and family, ideological dogmatism and mismanagement of public affairs; all six detained by *Securitate* (secret police).

April 12. Romanian authorities announce all foreign debt has been repaid and endorse proposal to ban any future borrowing; trade emphasis to be on barter and co-operative deals.

April 19–20. Two days of speeches in National Assembly and mass rallies on daily basis to praise Ceauşescu for liquidation of the debt.

May. Ceauşescu visits Czechoslovakia. Subsequent joint communiqué reiterates criticism of Hungarian reforms.

June 17. Romania registers "vigorous protest" to Hungary over the "fascist hostile manifestations" in Budapest on occasion of reburial of Imre Nagy, interpreted as a direct threat to Romania.

June 26. Announcement that 1,000 European communities had "adopted" 1,000 Romanian villages in order to discourage their demolition.

Reports that Romania had reinforced its border with Hungary by wire fence to deter refugees followed within weeks by its being dismantled.

June 7–8. Warsaw Pact summit in Bucharest; relations with Hungary reach a new low in heated debate between Romanian and Hungarian delegates.

June 10. Harsh criticism in Romanian press of President Bush's discriminatory policies towards Eastern Europe on eve of his visits to Hungary and Poland.

June 11. In speech to Arab Inter-Parliamentary Union Ceauşescu castigates West for manipulation of Third World debt to plunder and impoverish debtor nations and to finance subversion. The EC suspends negotiations for trade and co-operation agreement, in progress since 1987.

August 1. Hungarian TV interview with King Michael in which the King accuses Romania of being an absolute monarchy in which people are treated like cattle and sold for hard currency if they wish to emigrate. Romania recalls its ambassador to Hungary in protest.

August 8. Hungarian TV broadcasts part of interview by Canadian TV with László Tőkes, Hungarian priest in Timişoara, who is then briefly detained by police. Later reported that 21,000 had crossed the border from Romania to Hungary since mid-1987, 2,600 alone in September 1989, of whom a third were ethnic Romanians.

October 17. László Tőkes reported to have been ousted as head of his Reformed Church congregation in Timişoara.

November 20–24. 14th Congress of Romanian Communist Party. Ceauşescu unanimously elected to further five-year term.

December 15. Deportation order served on László Tőkes in Timişoara.

December 16. Several hundred blockade his home to obstruct the order.

December 17. Street protests continue and are fired on by *Securitate* police and troops; 71 killed (earlier reports gave greatly inflated totals).

December 18–20. Demonstrations reported from other parts of the country as protests grow in Timişoara.

December 20. Troops withdraw from streets after workers occupy and threaten to blow up petrochemical plant in Timişoara. 50,000 demonstrate and Communist Party offices ransacked. Timişoara committee formed to demand free elections and an end to repression meets Prime Minister Dascalescu.

Ceauşescu returns from state visit to Iran and declares state of emergency in Timişoara.

December 21. Ceauşescu calls staged rally in Bucharest; his authority collapses and troops fail to intervene. *Securitate* police fire on demonstrators on clashes in Bucharest and elsewhere.

December 22. Ceauşescu calls national state of emergency and tries to address crowds who break into Communist Party Central Committee buildings as he and Elena flee by helicopter from roof.

Army joins people and battles with *Securitate* after shooting of Defence Minister for non-compliance with orders to shoot crowds. Crowds capture TV and radio stations and National Salvation Front is organized with headquarters in TV station. Heavy fighting with *Securitate*.

Ceauşescus detained and held in armoured car until tried and shot on December 25.

Council of the Front set up including well-known dissidents and religious leaders.

December 26. National Salvation Front (NSF) named interim government pending elections in April 1990; Ion Iliescu named NSF Chairman and Petre Roman Prime Minister.

December 27. Final small-scale *Securitate* assault on TV station. Many *Securitate* shot on capture.

NSF government announces programme of comprehensive political and economic reforms. Abolition of death penalty. Prominent dissident Doina Cornea voices suspicion of composition and intentions of new government.

December 29. Army withdraws from streets of Bucharest.

1990

January 1. *Securitate* formally abolished.

Iliescu announces partial redistribution of state agricultural and land assets to farm workers and returning city migrants, retaining co-operatives in a free market.

January 3. Ceauşescu's ban on foreign borrowing lifted; emphasis on urgent need of new technology imports.

January 8. Passports to be freely issued for foreign travel. Growing criticism of NSF and charges that it is too closely identified with Ceauşescu regime, and calls for postponement of April elections.

January 12. 10,000 demonstrate outside NSF headquarters in Bucharest. Iliescu tells crowd that Romanian Communist Party outlawed, but this decision reversed the following day. Signs of power struggle in NSF.

January 18. Seizure of all assets and property of Communist Party including 60 industrial enterprises, 50,000 hectares of land and 21 palaces used by Ceauşescu.

January 23. Elections rescheduled for May.

January 26. Village systematization plan cancelled; grandiose construction and prestige project halted. Food exports stopped by serious shortages necessitate emergency EC food aid.

February 1. Round table talks of 29 opposition parties agree to power-sharing arrangement with NSF in Council for National Unity.

February 2. Four senior Ceauşescu officials sentenced at start of series of show trials.

Economic reforms proposed involving cautious move towards market and extension of farmworkers' rights to land, assets and sales. Major currency devaluation.

February 9. Council for National Unity expanded to a total of 37 parties.

February 12. Air Force officers from Timişoara begin three-day occupation of NSF headquarters in protest at continuity of Ceauşescu and *Securitate* elements in the military.

February 14. Demonstration in support includes officers, cadets and conscripts. Iliescu pledges investigation of Defence and Interior Ministers.

February 16. Defence Minister replaced.

February 18. Demonstration of 5,000 in Victory Square denounces NSF and invades its headquarters.

February 19. Several thousand miners arrive in Bucharest to rally in support of Iliescu and NSF.

March 1. Suicide of judge who condemned Ceauşescus to death on December 25.

March 2. Trials of police and *Securitate* officials begin in Timişoara.

March 17. Electoral law sets out detailed rules for procedure and financing of general election to be held on May 20.

Conflicts between Romanian nationalists and Hungarians in Transylvania; three die in clash on March 20.

March 20. 70,000 Hungarians demonstrate in Bucharest; government denounces attacks upon them and sets up commission of inquiry.

April 11. NSF debars King Michael from entry.

April 24. Government legalizes Eastern Rite Orthodox Church.

April 25. New security service, the Romanian Intelligence Service, inaugurated in place of *Securitate*.

May 15. Vatican re-establishes diplomatic relations.

May 20. Parliamentary and presidential elections.

June 9. New parliament convenes for first session.

June 13. University Square in central Bucharest, occupied by anti-communist demonstrators since April 22, cleared by police in a dawn raid; followed by three days of violent clashes in which demonstrators were attacked by miners brought to the capital on June 14. Health Ministry announces six deaths and 502 hospitalized.

June 20. Inauguration of President Iliescu.

June 21. Lt.-Gen. Nicolae Andruta Ceauşescu, younger brother of late President, sentenced by a military tribunal of the Supreme Court to 15 years' imprisonment.

July 25. Bill on reorganization of state economic enterprises adopted.

August 22. Further demonstrations in University Square, Bucharest.

Workers' protests in Brasov.

August 27–30. Strike in Brasov Tractor Enterprise.

August 28. Mayor of Bucharest declares indefinite ban on all meetings and demonstrations in central Bucharest's main squares.

August 31. National Privatization Agency established.

September 21. Nicu Ceauşescu, younger son of late President, sentenced to 20 years' imprisonment for "instigating aggravated murder".

November 15. Protests against price rises.

Political Overview

The Ceauşescu regime

Nicolae Ceauşescu was Secretary-General of the Romanian Communist Party (RCP) from 1965 to December 1989 and state president from 1974 to 1989 (in 1989 this was extended for a further five-year term, cut short by his execution on December 25, 1989). He was also chairman of the Council of State and of the Supreme Council of Socio-Economic Development. The head of an increasingly authoritarian and nepotistic regime, Ceauşescu appeared firmly in power at the start of the year in which he met his death. Rejecting all concepts of reform or *glasnost'*, despite some pressure to modify his position by the Soviet Union and its allies, his report delivered to the Party Congress in November 1989 was triumphalist in tone and his re-election to the party leadership was with the customary unanimity. There were persistent rumours of ill health, possibly cancer; nonetheless if any replacement was likely the consensus was that it was likely to be his wife Elena, a first deputy prime minister and full member of the party's Political Executive Committee and of its Permanent Bureau. Ceauşescu's son Nicu, a prominent party official despite his dissolute life-style, was a longer-term bet.

In early 1989 there were some signs of disaffection in an open letter written by six senior members of the Romanian Communist Party, three of them former members of the leadership. The letter, released in the West in March, charged the President with violating Romania's constitution and failing to observe the country's international treaty commitments, thereby isolating Romania from the rest of the world. Ceauşescu responded by ordering the harassment or house arrest of the letter's signatories. The fate of the six protestors was a clear warning to would-be critics within the party. Perhaps for that reason an appeal, issued in September 1989 to the RCP congress and calling for the removal of Ceauşescu from the General Secretaryship, was circulated anonymously. Its signatories chose to call themselves the National Salvation Front — a name that was to be adopted in December by the post-Ceauşescu administration.

Notwithstanding the appeal, the RCP's 14th Congress, held on November 20–24, 1989, amounted to little more than a display of adulation for the Romanian leader, his wife Elena and their supposed achievements. Ceauşescu's keynote speech was interrupted for no fewer than 125 standing ovations. As expected, the congress reaffirmed Romania's resistance to the kinds of reforms that were already sweeping across the rest of Eastern Europe. The resolutions unanimously approved by the delegates denounced the restoration of multi-party politics and insisted on the RCP's continuing right to the monopoly of power. Economic policies remained wedded similarly to Marxist-Leninist orthodoxy; even the expansion of small-scale private enterprise was denounced on the grounds that it would lead to the restoration of capitalism.

The austerity measures which had already brought an unparalleled reduction in living standards in the 1980s continued unabated during the year. Most Romanians had to endure severe hardship in the form of shortages of food, energy and other basic commodities. The gap between official pronouncements and the realities of living grew wider than ever before. In October 1989 the President announced that the cereal harvest for the year amounted to 60,000,000 tonnes — nearly twice the yield claimed by officials for 1988. The post-Ceauşescu government in December 1989 eventually revealed that the real size of the harvest was in fact less than a third of the figure Ceauşescu had claimed.

Not even the repayment of Romania's foreign debt, announced by the President with great fanfare in April 1989, led to any relaxation in the policy of austerity. Although some doubt remained as to the veracity of the claim, it appeared that Romania had indeed repaid all its debts to Western commercial banks by the end of March and that any outstanding debts to foreign governments were negligible.

In any case, Ceauşescu's policy of wiping out his country's foreign debt ahead of schedule was not motivated by financial considerations but by a desire to free himself of reliance on the West. In that he succeeded, but at the cost of making Romania more isolated from the international community than any other European state apart from Albania. Having delayed the conclusion of the Vienna Conference on Security and Co-operation in Europe (CSCE) by its objections to a range of human rights provisions, Romania finally signed the document on January 18. Foreign Minister Ioan Totu, however, immediately declared that Romania would implement only those provisions of the accord that did not clash with its constitution. Romania's harsh treatment of its few open dissidents, and occasionally of Western journalists and diplomats, led to the suspension in April of negotiations on a planned trade and co-operation agreement with the European Community, and in the same month the United Nations Commission on Human Rights (in Geneva) voted to appoint a special rapporteur to investigate the situation.

The overthrow of Ceauşescu

It was, in fact, the courage of an outspoken Lutheran priest, László Tőkés, an ethnic Hungarian who had received considerable moral support from Hungary, that precipitated the Romanian revolution. Pastor Tőkés had refused to tone down his defence of religious and ethnic rights and disobeyed instructions to move from his parish in Timişoara to another part of the country. Attempts to remove him forcibly on December 16 met with resistance by members of his largely Hungarian-speaking congregation. The following day security forces fired on demonstrators, who by now included both Romanians and Hungarians.

It was the carnage in Timişoara that led to the revolution and the overthrow of the Ceauşescu dynasty. The protest against repression and poverty was inspired, in part, by the success of pro-democracy demonstrations in East Germany, Czechoslovakia and Bulgaria. Yet Ceauşescu, it appeared, still believed his position was impregnable. He even left on a three-day visit to Iran, from where he returned on December 20. The following day he sought to demonstrate that he was firmly in control by staging a demonstration in Bucharest, but his attempt backfired when the crowds turned against him. As anti-Ceauşescu demonstrations broke out in the capital, the fate of the revolution hung in the balance on the night of December 21–22; with support from the army, Ceauşescu might have survived. However, the army command was in no mood to repeat the violence of Timişoara. The Minister of Defence, General Vasile Milea, died in mysterious circumstances after he refused to support the President's last-ditch attempt to retain power. Ceauşescu's fate was sealed when the army changed sides and joined the crowds that surged towards the Romanian Communist Party headquarters on the morning of December 22. Meanwhile, a newly-formed National Salvation Front (NSF), consisting mainly of anti-Ceauşescu communist officials, dissident intellectuals and army officers, announced it had taken over power.

The now-deposed President and his wife escaped from Bucharest in a helicopter but were later captured. On December 25, at a summary trial held in secret, they were found guilty on charges ranging from genocide to corruption and immediately shot. The Ceauşescus' execution weakened the resistance of the hated secret police, the *Securitate*, who had been mounting indiscriminate attacks on army units and civilians in an unsuccessful attempt to crush the revolution. There were no official figures by the end of the year for the number of casualties. Some estimates, however, put them at hundreds of dead, making the Romanian revolution the bloodiest event in Europe since the Hungarian uprising of 1956.

Violence on this scale, combined with the legacy of the Ceauşescu years, presented the NSF with a difficult task of reconstruction. Most of the senior figures in the 11-man leadership of the 150-strong Front were former high-ranking communist officials. They included the NSF chairman, Ion Iliescu, who also became Romania's interim President; his deputy, Dumitru Mazilu; and the foreign policy strategist, Professor Silviu Brucan. In comparison with these seasoned officials the new Prime Minister, Petre Roman (a hydraulics engineer by profession), lacked political experience. The new Minister of Defence, General Nicolae Militaru, had considerably more power than his post would normally have commanded because of the importance of the army both during the revolution and in the period of consolidation that followed it.

In the chaotic conditions of the revolution the NSF acted quickly to reverse the Ceauşescu regime's most unpopular policies. It abolished food rationing, halted the village destruction programme, brought the secret police under military control, promised freer travel and legalized abortion. It also pledged to hold free, multi-party elections in April 1990. Although public discontent with the dominant role of Communists in the NSF soon emerged, the revolution was widely regarded as having brought the Romanian people relief from many years of oppressive and increasingly irrational rule.

The elections of 1990

Plans for free elections were endangered by an imposing list of difficulties. The lack of experience of anything like a competitive democracy was, from the moment Ceauşescu was deposed, a serious handicap. Neither the guiding principles nor the specific procedures of such a system were widely understood in Romania, and there was no time to engage in a massive re-education effort. Far more than (for instance) Poles or Hungarians, Romanians had lived in a truly totalitarian state for decades.

A related complication was the nature of the opposition parties that declared themselves as participants in the electoral campaign. Several "historical" parties with direct lineage from pre-war parties were reborn, and a number of elderly émigrés returned to Bucharest to play leading roles in these organizations. Most prominent among them were the two largest parties of the 1918-to-early-1930s period (which had also played roles in the 1944–47 coalition government), the National Liberals and the National Peasants.

The National Liberals, evoking pre-war nationalist sentiments mixed with vehement commitment to the "free market", were led in the election by Sorin Botez and Radu Campeanu. Botez, now elderly, was a post-World War II Liberal who was sentenced at that time to 20 years of hard labour for his anti-communist politics. Campeanu was one of three candidates for President. In the inter-war period, the Liberals were the political expression of Romania's business elite — a tiny, but very powerful stratum.

Seventy-four-year-old Cornel Coposu reactivated the National Peasants' Party. Coposu had been the party's leader immediately after the war, and resumed that role more than 40 years later. Ion Ratiu, who had departed from Romania more than four decades earlier and amassed a fortune in Britain, returned to run for President under the National Peasants' banner. Although harbouring some monarchical sentiments, the National Peasants were the party of landowners and they retained their advocacy of less government, and local autonomy.

A Social Democratic Party led by Sergiu Cunescu (as executive president) and Adrian Dimitriu (as honorary chairman, representing the older post-war generation) also re-emerged. Between the wars, socialists, not communists, held the loyalty of Romania's small industrial working class, and an effort to recreate such an appeal within the huge labour stratum of the 1990s may be a key test for Romania's political future. In the elections, however, the party fared very badly.

Among the dozens of other political associations, only four groupings had a chance of electoral viability. Although these proclaimed themselves as parties, each formed around a distinct issue or segment of the population — respectively, intellectuals, environmentalists, students, and ethnic Hungarians. The Front, competing as a party, commanded the loyalty of most urban workers; miners and employees of the huge "23 August" enterprise in Bucharest were, for example, prominent among pro-Front demonstrators in early 1990 — a loyalty not lost on Ion Iliescu and those around him.

There was never any doubt that few of the many competitors had any chance whatsoever of playing a visible role in Romanian politics. The Front was certain to gain a sizeable proportion of the vote due to its immediate linkage to events in December, Iliescu's well-known name, and the organizational head-start it had as compared with the opposition. But the Liberals and Peasants were thought to have a chance as well, with a coalition government not improbable. Divided as they were, however, the opposition parties were unable to expand their base of support very broadly.

Romania's electorate was thus presented with a huge array of parties, only a few of which had any broad appeal. Almost 16,000,000 voters were eligible for the franchise, and the May 20 1990 election required the selection of 396 members of the Lower House and 119 members of a new Upper House or Senate. Constituencies for the Assembly were drawn on the basis of population distribution, while the Senate was meant to guarantee the representation of all countries and minority groups. The presidential election, held simultaneously, was a direct, popular vote. Voting for the Upper and Lower Houses was complicated by the extraordinarily large number of candidates for many seats, by the need to fill places in both an Upper and a Lower House for the first time, and by other circumstances that made the ballot paper very long and the interpretation of results very difficult. Computers helped in tallying results and the outcome was clear by the evening. As in most of the other East European elections, international observers helped to ensure the fairness of the whole exercise.

In the event (see Table 1), the National Salvation Front and interim President Ion Iliescu won convincing victories on May 20. Charges of electoral fraud and countercharges became increasingly heated in the last days of May and the early days of June, as electoral observers' judgements were employed to support both the Front's contention that the vote was, by and large, fair and that incidents of intimidation or fraud were too infrequent and minor to have affected much of the outcome — and to reinforce the opposition's contention that there was "moral fraud" in the election. Most observers accepted that the campaign was an imperfect one, including many incidents that endangered the opposition's capacity to mount a nationwide electoral effort. At the same time international observers generally concluded that the result on May 20 was a genuine expression of the wishes of the electorate.

Table 1: Election results, May 1990

	% of total	Vote total	Seats
Presidential election			
Ion Iliescu (National Salvation Front)	85.1	12,232,498	—
Radu Campeanu (Liberal)	10.2	1,529,188	—
Ion Ratiu (Peasants)	4.3	617.007	—
Lower House of Parliament (Assembly of Deputies)			
National Salvation Front	66.3	9,089.659	263
Hungarian Democratic Union of Romania	7.2	991,601	29
National Liberal Party	6.4	879,290	29
Romanian Ecological Movement	2.6	358,864	12
National Peasants' Party	2.6	351,357	12
Romanian Unity Alliance—RUA	2.1	290,875	9
Agrarian Democratic Party	1.8	250,403	9
Romanian Ecological Party	1.7	232,212	8
Socialist Democratic Party	1.1	143,393	5
Other votes split among more than 50 parties			(20)
Upper House (Senate) of Parliament			
National Salvation Front	67.0	9,353,006	92
Hungarian Democratic Union of Romania	7.2	1,004,353	12
National Liberal Party	7.1	985,094	9
National Peasants' Party	2.5	348,687	1
Romanian Ecological Movement	2.45	341,478	1
Romanian Unity Alliance—RUA	2.15	300,473	2
Romanian Ecological Party	1.4	192,574	1
Other votes split among more than 50 parties			(1)

Source: Rompres wire service, May 25 1990.

There appeared, moreover, to be a strong aversion among Front leaders to dictatorial or Leninist roles in the Romanian politics of the future. Even if Iliescu or Roman wished to exercise such power, they lacked the institutional control necessary to effect such a goal. More important, they and their advisers lacked an inclination of this kind. Many of those who headed the National Salvation Front were engineers, economists or political scientists — generally pragmatic, and new to the game of mass politics. Their fault, if any, was to see as threatening events that (for example) a Greek or Spanish leader would simply have regarded as disruptive. There was additionally a tendency to be troubled by attacks on their ethics or qualifications; intolerance, however, was not enough to identify them with the practices of the regime they had displaced.

Iliescu and most of those around him were members of the Communist Party, and Iliescu had served as head of the Young Communist League in the late 1960s to 1971, and as first party secretary in Iasi county in the early 1970s. But his break with Ceauşescu had been no less than 18 years before the revolution and, although he retained a post in the party hierarchy until the early 1980s, he had become an increasingly outspoken critic over the decade. Iliescu's opponents also had pasts that were somewhat chequered; and he repudiated the Ceauşescu period without reservation, many of those around him having taken a direct part in the fighting.

The demonstrations of June 1990

University Square in central Bucharest, which had been occupied by anti-communist demonstrators since April 22, was cleared by police in a dawn raid on June 13, provoking three days of the most violent clashes seen in the country since the December revolution. Several attempts were made to open a dialogue between the government and the protestors, who were demanding the resignation of all high-ranking former communists from Iliescu's provisional National Salvation Front government. Adopting as a mark of defiance the name *golani* (tramps), as Iliescu had disparagingly described them, they claimed that the NSF had "stolen" the May 20 general election by deceit and intimidation. Government spokesmen had indicated on June 11 a willingness to consider one of the protestors' later demands, the opening up of an independent television station. On June 12, however, it acceded to a request made by the Prosecutor's Office to restore order in the square on the grounds that it had become a "temporary haven for drug trafficking, prostitution and black marketeering". In the early hours of the morning of June 13 riot police armed with truncheons and electric prods moved in, burning down the tents and arresting 263 people.

The police action brought thousands of demonstrators back to the centre of Bucharest. Unidentified groups of rioters attacked and set on fire the city police headquarters, where it was believed that some of those arrested earlier in University Square were being held. Others attacked the Ministry of the Interior, formerly the headquarters of the *Securitate* (secret police), the Romanian Information Service and the Romanian Television building. For a while the television channel went off the air as protestors swarmed into the building, before troops and government supporters pushed them out. Amid mounting chaos, Iliescu issued a radio appeal to factory workers and others to come on to the streets to defend the revolution and eliminate this "fascist rebellion".

Miners (who had come to Bucharest once before, in February, to demonstrate their support for the NSF) were brought into Bucharest by truck, train and bus in the early hours of June 14. They set about attacking anyone suspected of being an anti-government protestor, using clubs and iron bars. According to Health Ministry figures, four people had been killed and 93 injured up to the time of the miners' arrival on the scene. By the end of the three days of what one eyewitness described as a "vigilante rampage" the Health Ministry announced that six people were dead and 502 hospitalized, seven in a serious condition. The figures gave the overwhelming impression that the miners (estimated at around 10,000) were responsible for most of the injuries. One of the first to be beaten up and hospitalized was Marian Munteanu, the President of the League of Students and one of the leaders of the University Square protest. He was later arrested and, with others, charged with inciting violence.

The miners were supposed to have come to Bucharest "spontaneously", but had been fed and lodged in government-owned sports halls. They attacked not only students but also gipsies, the homes of prominent opposition politicians and the offices of the leading opposition newspaper, *Romania Libera*, demanding that it be closed. Iliescu congratulated the miners on their action; the Prime Minister, Petre Roman, admitted that at times they had been out of control and had committed violence against innocent people, although he supported their mobilization to aid the government. Given the ineffectiveness of the police and indecisive action by the army, Iliescu called for the establishment of a specially trained national guard; he also replaced the Interior Minister with Doru Viorel Ursu, a lawyer and president of the Bucharest military tribunal. Western governments, concerned by the brutality with which the demonstration had been suppressed, threatened to withhold economic assistance, and the United States and other representatives boycotted the inauguration of President Iliescu on June 20. Iliescu, in his address, referred to the "excesses" committed by the miners, but remained unapologetic about his decision to call them in.

The new Romanian government was presented to parliament on June 28. Headed by Petre Roman, it announced a radical economic programme involving a rapid transition to market relations and the "liquidation of inertia and conservatism" in the state bureaucracy. The development of these policies over the latter part of the year is considered below.

Economic Overview

The economic inheritance

Romania's economic development, like her constitutional history, has been handicapped by a late start, except in oil extraction and refining. Up to 1945 Romania was thought of primarily as an agrarian country and a food exporter. Both Nazi Germany and the Soviet Union (under Khrushchev) saw the Romanian economy in that light. At least since Gheorghiu-Dej (party leader from 1944 to his death in 1965) nationalism has been to the fore in official economic priorities, and this has been expressed in strivings towards self-sufficiency as it was understood at that time, that is in the direction of emphasizing ferrous metallurgy, machine-building and other industry. Furthermore, the hardline Ceauşescu regime showed a preference for extremist policies, emphasizing growth in statistical terms and self-reliance at the expense of present satisfactions and to some extent even despite the absence or shortage of basic necessities.

Under Ceauşescu the economy was planned, in the Stalinist way: there were one- and five-year plans and a comprehensive system of ministries, including even a ministry of tourism. The intermediate body was called a *Central*. Similarly, the banking system was centralized. On the other hand, during the previous decade self-reliance had been promoted. Regions in effect traded what they had in surplus for what they were lacking. For instance, Transylvania exchanged natural gas for petrol.

Draft, revised and approved versions of five-year plan targets were published. The plan for 1986–90, for instance, approved the following percentage growth rates on average per annum: national income 9.9–10.6, net industrial production 13.3–14.2, gross agricultural production 6.1–6.7. Despite the impressive results that were reported (see Table 2) these targets were over-optimistic and planning irrationalities were obvious. These included severe shortages of food and electricity, or the completion outside Suceava in 1986 of a

Table 2:   Recent economic performance

	1987	1988	1989
Net Material Product at market prices (bn Lei)	693	695	640
NMP growth (percentage)	—	3.2	–9.9
Retail price inflation (percentage)	0.4	—	1.1
Population (millions, mid-year)	23.01	23.11	23.15
Exports to OECD fob $bn	4.1	4.0	3.9
Imports from OECD fob $bn	1.3	1.3	1.2

Main foreign trading partners:

Exports (1987): USSR, Italy, West Germany, USA
Imports (1987): USSR, Egypt, Iran, GDR

Note: It should be noted that official statistics produced during the Ceauşescu era are of doubtful accuracy.

Source: Current press reports.

huge ultra-modern ball-bearings factory which by June 1989, if not later, had still yielded no output.

The main factor in Romania's economic difficulties of the late 1980s, however, was not inefficient planning in itself but the priorities chosen by the Ceauşescu regime: to undertake grandiose projects, demolish and replace dwellings and other structures, and to repay foreign debts as quickly as possible, despite the impact on living standards and in particular on food supplies. The fact that in the late Ceauşescu years economic statistics became increasingly unreliable may have contributed towards this mistaken undertaking, if sycophants failed to present an honest assessment of the real state of the economy to the leadership. In April 1989 the policy appeared to have yielded at least one tangible result: Ceauşescu was able to announce that all foreign debts had been repaid.

The policies of the NSF government

In presenting his new government, largely composed of young technocrats without previous government experience, to the Romanian parliament in June 1990, Prime Minister Roman called for a rapid transition to a market economy. The publication in July 1990 of the half-yearly figures for industrial production indicated a lack of improvement in the overall state of the economy — one of the most highly industrialized in Eastern Europe under Ceauşescu. During the first six months of 1990 industrial production fell by more than 18% and output was worth 532,000 billion Lei as compared with 656,000 billion Lei in the same period of 1989. Imports, mostly of crude oil and food, rose by 46% while exports fell by 43% in the first six months of 1990, dramatically affecting the country's balance of payments. While the price of materials had risen, labour productivity had declined appreciably due to work stoppages and a failure of management, according to the government, which sought ways of relating wages more closely to output.

On July 10, 1990 the government announced that as a result of its decision to withdraw subsidies "for commodities in ever-growing demand that cannot be met by domestic production" it would (i) almost double the price of fuel; (ii) increase the price of luxury goods, newspapers and books; and (iii) double the price of mineral water. It blamed the rise in fuel prices on the three-fold increase in fuel consumption in the first half of the year. However, an assurance was given that, in order not to affect the living standards of those on low incomes, a list of 100 key products would be drawn up whose prices would remain unchanged. Earlier, in June, the Finance Minister, Theodore Stolojan, had said it was not possible suddenly to remove controls on prices without creating an inflationary spiral in the ensuing price-wage explosion, although he agreed that the current pricing mechanism distorted prices and adversely affected supply and demand. The danger of inflation was underlined by figures which showed that there were 15.4 billion Lei more in circulation on May 21, 1990 than at the same time in 1989. Although there had been an appreciable rise in incomes, supplies in the state shops continued to be poor, encouraging a growing black market (efforts were made in August to clamp down on their activities). Farmers' incomes had also increased as a result of rises in the state purchasing price for produce, but retail prices had not risen.

The Prime Minister's undertaking to move swiftly towards a market economy was given tangible form on July 20, 1990, in the presentation to parliament of bills to create the legal framework for such an economy and to turn the great majority of state-owned businesses into autonomous enterprises and companies with share capital. In the first instance the government was aiming to foster a private sector in small and medium-sized enterprises. At the same time, the administrative structures overseeing some of the country's bigger concerns would be dismantled. Economic decision-making and private ownership would then be transferred to production units. In an interview with the newspaper *Adevarul* on July 11, Adrian Severin, a deputy prime minister and the Minister for Reform and Relations with Parliament, singled out a shortage of competent people, the bureaucratic resistance to change and the tendency to "over-rate the social cost of reform" as being among the major obstacles to the implementation of the transitional economic programme. The fear of future unemployment, he believed, was exaggerated and existed at the moment "as a heavy legacy of dictatorship". He supported the measures recently announced to protect those who would be affected by the transition, which included unemployment benefits and retraining opportunities.

As the National Salvation Front government implemented its radical economic programme in the months that followed, sharply reducing subsidies and allowing some prices to find their market level, protest demonstrations took place in November in response to the consequent steep price rises. The November 15 protests in Bucharest were the largest since the crushing of demonstrations in the capital by miners in June. In view of Romania's rapidly worsening economic situation, Prime Minister Roman argued that the government could no longer continue to pay subsidies to keep prices artificially low. According to Eugen Dijmarescu, Minister of State for Economic Orientation, the state was paying out some 30 billion Lei every month in subsidies, while the population's total monthly income amounted to no more than 26 billion Lei. The government itself was running a monthly deficit amounting to US$1 billion every three months. Imports had risen dramatically, by more than 28% over their 1989 levels, and imported goods now accounted for 56% of all goods on sale. The Gulf crisis had worsened Romania's fuel problem, with Iraq refusing to honour its trade debt and the Soviet Union stopping sales of subsidized oil and demanding payment in hard currency. Industrial output in 1990 was expected to be down by 60% as compared with 1989.

Against this background the government decided to bring forward its economic programme as a matter of urgency, adjusting prices as the first concrete step towards the development of a free market economy. Goods and services were classified in three groups: prices for electricity, gas, home heating fuels and rents would be raised on January 1, 1991, and remain fixed for a year; prices of 99 basic products, including bread, milk, meat and children's clothes, would be adjusted every three months, with equivalent wage adjustments; and prices of all other goods would be freed from all controls. On November 1, 1990, the Leu was devalued by a further 60% and fixed at US$1 = 35 Lei, a move designed to pave the way for partial convertibility of the Romanian currency which the government planned to introduce in January 1991. The devaluation and cuts in subsidies resulted in price increases of between 100% and 120%. To cushion the blow, wages and pensions were increased. The government set a new minimum wage at 2,300 Lei (US$65) a month, but factory managers were given the power to determine wage policy for their own enterprises and could set pay levels above the minimum. Meanwhile, parliament voted on November 12 to give the government special powers over the following six months to implement the economic reform programme, including the authority to change prices and taxes and to negotiate foreign credits.

The so-called "price liberalization" precipitated protests across the country which continued intermittently throughout November 1990. The largest anti-government demonstrations were staged on November 15 to coincide with the anniversary of demonstrations which had taken place in Brasov in 1987 against the Ceauşescu regime. More than 100,000 demonstrators marched through Bucharest in a demonstration co-ordinated by the recently formed Civic Alliance, comprising dissident intellectuals and workers, and were addressed by student leader Marian Munteanu. Union leaders criticized the government for introducing the price rises before implementing privatization measures and before passing laws on unemployment benefit and other social protection measures. A rally of 20,000 NSF supporters gathered on November 20 to hear Roman defend his government's record, but the NSF postponed its national conference from December to January 1991 amid reports of a growing split. In these tense circumstances the Romanian Communist Party re-emerged, in late November, under the name of the Socialist Labour Party; there were widespread protests from other parties and organizations.

Key Economic Sectors

Agriculture

Romania is generally favoured for agricultural production, although the climate is continental with hot summers and cold winters. Rainfall is adequate, and Romania has much bigger water resources than Bulgaria, though drought can have adverse effects and the most fertile soils have low and unreliable rainfall. Arable comprises 42% of Romania's territory. A good balance of plains, hills and mountains provides a range of microclimates.

As elsewhere in Eastern Europe, land is farmed partly by co-operatives, partly by state farms and partly by individual peasants. The shares farmed in these ways, in late 1989, were respectively about 61%, 30% and 9%. Private ownership (especially of hills, mountain tops, irregularly shaped plots and in general broken ground) remained substantial even before the establishment of an avowedly marketizing regime after the overthrow of Ceauşescu. In more open ground there are large massifs of land belonging to state or co-operative farms and privately owned animals had (at least until 1990) to graze along the edges.

The range of crops grown is very wide, comprising grains (wheat especially in Wallachia, maize almost everywhere, oats, rice between northwards-flowing parallel channels of the Danube), industrial crops (hemp and sugar beet in the south-west, sunflower), vines (on southward-facing slopes of the Carpathians and in the Dobrogea), hops (mainly in Transylvania, where most breweries are located), potatoes and vegetables, fruit, flowers (in hothouses), and reeds (in the Danube delta). Home-made wine is made from elderflower. Since 1961–65 the potato yield has risen about three-fold. Livestock (cattle, sheep, pigs) are numerous. Meat comes especially from private peasant production (possibly over 45% of the total) whereas eggs and chickens, up to 1990, came mainly from henhouses within the state sector. Fish comes mainly from the Danube delta. Since 1981, the harvests of maize and potatoes have shown a tendency to increase, but harvests of wheat have remained static. Outputs of meat and milk have shown little tendency to rise, but hens' eggs and wool have fared better.

Irrigation is on quite a big scale and is supported by appropriate equipment such as large-dimension sprinklers. Since 1974–76 the area of irrigated land has doubled. More surprisingly, given the favourable land-to-people ratio, the Ceauşescu government showed some concern to reduce the areas taken up by villages. Major land reclamation schemes were put into effect: for instance Sculeni-Gorban, completed in 1987, created over 200,000 hectares of ameliorated fields. The level of mechanization is uneven.

Over the past 40 years the labour force employed in agriculture has fallen from 75% to under 30%, a trend which is obviously related to the policy of village systematization. Still more relevant is the fact that the proportion living in the countryside has not declined proportionately, which appears to indicate that country-dwellers commute to work in towns; yet this is not visibly taking place and indeed seems to be precluded by transport limitations. A partial explanation may be that mainly younger and more able-bodied people commute while older people, especially women (grandparents and others) remain behind to work on the co-operative farm or on a private plot. This, however, implies a fall in the quality of agricultural labour, and labour insufficiency in agriculture has been officially cited. On the other hand, those left behind may retain links with urban migrants and provide something to supplement their skimpy rations. Those lacking such support have had a much harder time.

Energy

Romania's mineral resources include oil, coal and natural gas. Oil production (centred around Ploiesti and Pitesti) was in the past sufficient to allow Romania to export oil but the country is now a net importer. Natural gas output has been declining due to exhaustion of reserves which may be entirely gone by 1995 unless extraction is restricted (as the 1990–95 plan originally envisaged). Hard coal is mined, but is less than a fifth of total output; the rest is lignite and brown coal of much lower calorie content. Other minerals include small quantities of iron ore, bauxite, copper, lead and zinc as well as gold, silver and uranium.

Manufacturing industry

Romania under Ceauşescu pursued a policy of rapid industrialization and the structure of its economy reflects these priorities. The employed population in 1986 was 10.7 million, of whom three million worked in agriculture but 4.8 million in industry and construction. The output of main products in 1987 was as follows: (in tonnes) pig-iron, 8,673; steel, 13,885; steel tubes, 1,394; coke, 5,826; rolled steel, 9,765; chemical fertilizers, 2,897; washing soda, 894; caustic soda, 817; paper, 712; cement, 13,583; sugar, 646; edible oils, 392: (in units) radio sets, 618,000; television sets, 484,000; and washing machines, 242. Fabrics included 710 million square metres of cotton cloth and 139 million square metres of woollen cloth. In 1985, 39% of the total workforce, and 43% of the industrial workforce, were women. Up to 1990, about 72% of the economically active population worked in the state sector.

Finance

The National Bank of Romania (founded in 1880, nationalized in 1946) is the state bank under the direction of the Ministry of Finance. Half of its profits, up to 1990, were allocated to the state budget. There are also a Bank of Investments, a Foreign Trade Bank, an Agriculture and Food Industry Bank and a Savings Bank. In 1974 the American bank Manufactures Hanover Trust Co. opened a branch in Bucharest, the first Western bank to do so in a (then) communist-government country. In 1988 budgetary revenue and expenditure were planned to balance at a level of 433,094 million Lei.

New technology

Despite substantial efforts, inspired in part by nationalistic considerations, new technology is not a significant feature of the Romanian economy.

Foreign Economic Relations

Romania is a full member of the (now moribund) Council for Mutual Economic Assistance (CMEA or Comecon). In addition, since 1972 Romania has been a member of the International Monetary Fund, and also of the World Bank and GATT. This gives her an unusually broad basis for relations with both Eastern and Western economic institutions. Romania's foreign trade is accordingly more diversified geographically than that of most of her Balkan neighbours. In 1985, 39% of her exports went to "socialist" countries, while 48% of her imports came from them. Trade with the USSR comprised less than 20% of her total trade, whereas the Bulgarian proportion in the late 1980s (for instance) exceeded 55%. After the USSR, Poland and East Germany were Romania's main trading partners in the East, while Italy, the United States, West Germany and France were the most important Western ones. Among developing countries, both Iraq and Iran were important. Unlike other Soviet bloc countries, Romania co-operates both economically and technically with Israel.

Among commodity groups, Romania exports especially machinery and equipment, secondly fuels, minerals and metals, and thirdly industrial consumer goods, while she imports primarily fuels, minerals and metals, and secondly machinery and equipment.

Joint ventures with Western firms have been allowed since 1971; the Western share, however, was not (until 1990) allowed to exceed 49%. The legislation, as originally conceived, was rather restrictive and not many new ventures were started, although some collaborative agreements, for instance with *Citroën* to produce the Oltcit car, were important. After 1981 Romania followed a unique trade policy of seeking to repay her foreign debt as quickly as possible. At the end of 1981 this was at a peak level of $10.2 billion. By the end of 1986 this had been reduced to $6.4 billion, and on April 12, 1989, Ceauşescu was able to announce that the debt had been entirely repaid. This was achieved through a positive balance approaching, and occasionally exceeding, an annual figure of $2 billion. This extremely high rate of repayment was the central fact in the Romanian economy throughout the 1980s; it was achieved by reducing imports while increasing exports, and running down gold and foreign exchange reserves.

The policies followed by the National Salvation Front from 1990 onwards assumed a much closer relationship to the international economy, with more liberal policies in relation to foreign investment and currency movements. Particular importance was attached to negotiations with the EC, which were suspended in June 1990 after the suppression of the demonstrations in Bucharest. The EC was proposing an economic co-operation agreement which would have given Romania trade benefits and access to Community markets. However, on July 3 Community officials met government and opposition leaders in Bucharest to reassess the situation. The EC team also spoke to representatives of the Students' League and the Group for Social Dialogue, whose members included many leading intellectuals. Despite Ceauşescu's repayment of foreign debt it was expected that Romania would need to borrow abroad once again before the end of the year. It was reported in June 1990 that credit needs were expected to expand dramatically even though Romania was owed some $3,000 billion from abroad and had very substantial hard currency reserves.

Principal Personalities

Iliescu, Ion. President of Romania. Elected by an overwhelming majority in May 1990, President Iliescu is the most prominent of the former communist officials who have come to play a leading role in the National Salvation Front. Iliescu was born on March 3, 1930, and educated at Bucharest Polytechnic Institute. He joined the Romanian Communist Party in 1953 and rose through its ranks to become a candidate Central Committee member in 1965 and then a full member from 1968 to 1984. He was an alternate member of the Executive Political Committee of the Central Committee from 1969 to 1979, and was party first secretary in Jassy county from 1974 to 1979. In 1979 he became chairman of the National Council for Water Resources, moving in 1984 to a technical publishing house. Iliescu was a member of the Bureau of the National Council of the Socialist Unity Front (a regime-sponsored umbrella organization) from 1968 to 1972, and became a member of the Academy of Social and Political Sciences in 1970. He was President of the National Salvation Front from December 1989 to February 1990, and was then President of the

Provisional Council for National Unity from February 1990. On May 20 he secured 85% of the vote in the presidential ballot and became formally as well as *de facto* the leading figure in post-Ceauşescu Romanian politics.

Roman, Petro. Prime Minister. Born 1946, Roman was educated at Bucharest Polytechnical Institute and the National Polytechnical Institute of Toulouse in France. He later became professor and head of department at the Faculty of Hydraulics, Bucharest Polytechnical Institute, before assuming the premiership in December 1989. His nomination to the post was confirmed by the newly elected Romanian parliament in June 1990.

Stanculescu, Lt.-Col. Victor. Minister of National Defence. Born 1928, Stanculescu was educated at the Military Artillery Officers' School and Military Academy. He was deputy minister of national defence from 1981 to 1986, first deputy minister 1986 to 1989, Minister of National Economy from 1989 to 1990, and then transferred to his present post in March 1990.

The Media

In the late 1980s Romania published 36 daily and 24 weekly newspapers and 435 periodicals, including 11 dailies and three weeklies in minority languages. Some 3,063 book titles were published in 1985 in 66.3 million copies; 376 of the book titles were in minority languages (particularly Hungarian). The Romanian press, under Ceauşescu, was devoted almost obsessively to the actions of the President and his family, and open criticism was all but totally eliminated. The establishment of the Iliescu government led to a more diverse picture, but opposition publications encountered some difficulties and the press as a whole was adversely affected by shortages of newsprint and equipment, industrial disruption by printing and transport workers, and inflationary pressures.

Foreign Relations

Bordering entirely on what were (until 1989) communist countries and on the Black Sea, decisively weaker than one of these (the USSR) and unable for economic reasons to spend much on defence, Romania might have appeared at first sight to have little capacity to conduct an independent foreign policy. Romania, however, is too large for her subjugation to be viewed as a minor adventure. Any incursion from outside would evoke a strong nationalism, while the weakness of her armed forces is in some degree compensated by physical barriers — the Carpathians and the Danube — which also restrict the usefulness of occupying Romania with a view to further military advance. Having no borders with NATO countries, Romania (unlike Czechoslovakia) offers no corridor of access from the West. This combination of strength, weakness and strategic unimportance allowed Romania, before 1990, to pursue a more independent policy in foreign relations than any other country in what was then the Soviet bloc. Romania did not take part in the invasion of Czechoslovakia in 1968 (indeed she appeared to be threatened for some time by invasion herself). Romania maintained relations with China while these were broken off by the Soviet Union, kept up relations with Israel, and took part — the only communist-ruled country to do so — in the 1984 Olympic games. Only in Romania, similarly, were there large-scale demonstrations in favour of nuclear disarmament, although these were of course officially sanctioned.

During the Brezhnev administration the Romanians made it clear that they did not agree that Warsaw Treaty Organization (Warsaw Pact) defence expenditure needed to be further increased. So far as international economic relations were concerned, Romania rejected Soviet suggestions that she should not build up heavy industry and ensured that no planning organ covering the whole Eastern bloc was set up. On the other hand, certain limits were not transgressed. Within Romania itself, party control and censorship remained in force. Romania did not withdraw from the Warsaw Pact; although objecting, Romanian representatives eventually agreed to its extension in 1985 for a further 20 years (although the President's brother stated in 1989 that he did not believe the USSR would defend any other Pact member against capitalist attack). Much the same propagandist shibboleths continued to be proclaimed in Romania as was the case in other Soviet bloc countries until not long before. No irredentist claim was made concerning Bessarabia though most Romanians considered it to be unjustly within the USSR. The inviolability of frontiers within the Soviet bloc conversely allowed Romania, rather than Hungary, to retain control of Transylvania.

Foreign relations under the National Salvation Front

The transition to non-communist rule in both Romania and Hungary in 1989 led to a more open expression of differences on frontiers and the treatment of their respective nationals. The ethnic tensions in Transylvania arose out of heightened Hungarian expectations and increasing demands for the restitution of their national rights. Matters of this kind reached a crisis point in February and March 1990, culminating in serious disturbances in several Romanian towns. The most serious rioting took place in Tirgu Mures on March 19-20, following celebrations by Hungarians on March 15 of the anniversary of their revolution of 1848. In expressing his regret at the violence, Prime Minister Roman reinforced the Romanian government's commitment to minority rights, at the same time pleading for an understanding of the views of Transylvanian Romanians, who had suffered greatly between 1940 and 1944 when northern Transylvania had been under Hungarian rule.

An attempt by the Romanian authorities to place controls on the import of Hungarian books provoked a strong protest from Bucharest. The action reflected the fears in Bucharest of Hungarian interpretations of Transylvanian history and geography which would contradict those of Romania. Although the authorities insisted that the customs ban applied only to large consignments of books, which had to be sent via the Ministry of Culture in Bucharest, the Hungarians continued to complain that the Romanian post office was failing to deliver Hungarian-language publications to subscribers, who were forced to form their own distribution networks. The dispute also coincided with demands by ethnic Hungarians in Transylvania for the immediate reopening of their own schools and the re-establishment of the Hungarian-teaching Babes-Bolyai University, which had been closed by Ceauşescu in his campaign to assimilate the Hungarian minority. Despite an attempt by the Romanian government to defuse the language problem in Transylvanian schools by the appointment of an ethnic Hungarian, Attila Palfalvi, to the post of deputy education minister, local communities began to assert direct control over the schools in their areas.

The 70th anniversary on June 1, 1990 of the Treaty of Trianon, under which Hungary had ceded Transylvania to Romania, was marked by nationalist speeches in both countries. Speaking at a rally in Budapest, the Hungarian Prime Minister József Antall said that he condemned the treaty "historically speaking", but noted that Hungary had signed the 1975 Helsinki Final Act renouncing the violent changing of frontiers. However, he concluded by insisting on the upholding of rights for Hungarian national minorities. In Transylvania such sentiments were attacked by the right-wing Romanian national organization, *Vatra Romaneasca* (Romanian Hearth), which set itself in opposition to the rising tide of expectation on the part of Hungary. The unspoken Hungarian aim, in *Vatra*'s view, was the incorporation of Transylvania into Hungary. An attempt by the Hungarian émigré organization, Transylvanian Magyar World Federation, to organize a cross-border demonstration was widely condemned in both countries and did not materialize. Despite the seriousness of such incidents, agreements were reached in 1990 between the two governments on cultural co-operation (in February) and on the opening of a passport office (in June) in the former Hungarian consulate building in the Transylvanian capital of Cluj.

Relations with other countries were seriously affected by the crushing of the demonstration in Bucharest in June. This caused an outcry among EC countries, and especially in the United States. In August, France began moves towards healing the breach, indicating the traditional importance of that country's dealings with the West. Roman, a fluent French speaker, had trained in France and established cordial links with French ministers during his visit to Paris in February 1990. The Romanian government maintained cordial relations with the Soviet Union, taking a cautious approach to the situation in the neighbouring republic of Moldavia, most of the territory of which had formed the Romanian region of Bessarabia before its annexation in 1940. With the Soviet Union accounting for 33% of Romania's foreign trade, the visit to Moscow in May 1990 of Alexandru Margarietescu, then Minister of Foreign Trade, was seen to be of special significance. An expansion of cultural contacts between Soviet Moldavia and Romania was the object of the visit to Moldavia in May 1990 of Razvan Teodorescu, director of Free Romanian Radio and Television.

THE SOVIET UNION

Stephen White and Peter Rutland

Government as at January 1991

President. *Mikhail Gorbachev* (since March 1990)

Vice-President. *Gennadii Yanaev* (since December 1990)

Prime Minister. *Valentin Pavlov* (since January 1991)

First Deputy Prime Ministers.
    V. Kh. Doguzhiev (since January 1991)
    V. M. Velichenko (since January 1991)

Deputy Prime Ministers.
    N. P. Laverov (since January 1991)
    Yu. D. Maslyukov (since January 1991; and chairman, State Planning Committee — Gosplan, since February 1988)

Minister of Culture. *Nikolai Gubenko* (since 1989)

Minister of Defence. *Marshal Dmitri Yazov* (since 1988)

Minister of Foreign Affairs. *Alexander Bessmertnykh* (since January 1991)

Minister of the Interior. *Boris Pugo* (since December 1990)

(Other members of the Cabinet of Ministers had still to be nominated and approved by the Supreme Soviet.)

SOVIET UNION

showing the 15 Union Republics

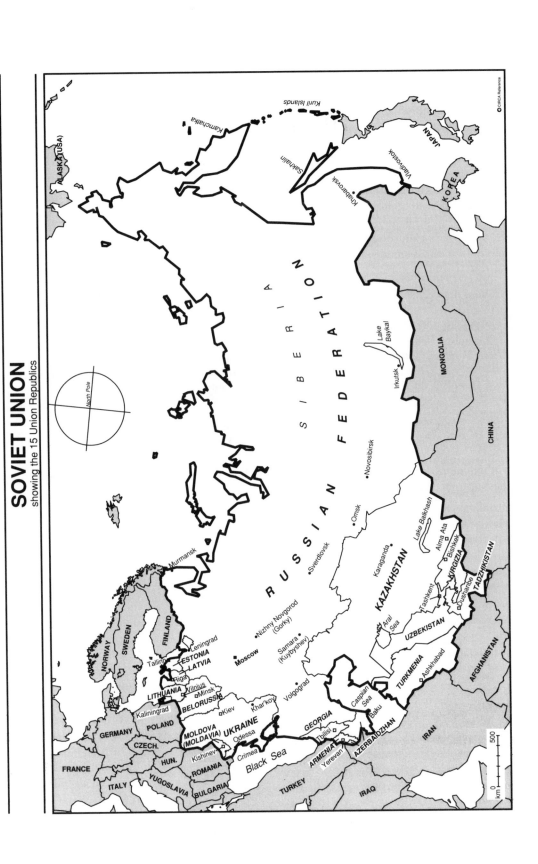

Chronology

1989

January 6. Announcement of mass rehabilitation of thousands of citizens who were victims of Stalin purges between 1930 and 1950.

January 12. Nagorno-Karabakh region placed under direct Moscow administration.

January 23. Earthquake in Tadzhikistan; 274 dead.

February 4. Talks in Beijing between Eduard Shevardnadze and Chinese Foreign Minister.

February 15. Soviet troops complete their withdrawal after nine years' occupation of Afghanistan.

February 21. USSR sends its first permanent ambassador to the EC.

March 26. Elections to Congress of People's Deputies; first since the revolution to take place on a largely competitive basis.

April 2. President Gorbachev begins three-day state visit to Cuba; talks with Irish Prime Minister Charles Haughey during a brief stop-over at Shannon airport.

April 5. President Gorbachev begins three-day state visit to Britain.

April 9. Pro-independence demonstrations in Tbilisi, Georgia, dispersed by Soviet troops; at least 21 dead; resignation (14 April) of Georgian party first secretary.

April 25. Central Committee plenum; "retirement" of 74 members (including former Foreign Minister Andrei Gromyko) and 24 candidate members.

May 15. President Gorbachev begins three-day official visit to China; first Sino-Soviet summit for 30 years; his schedule in Beijing and Shanghai severely disrupted by pro-democracy demonstrators.

May 25. Convening of first session of newly elected Congress of People's Deputies; Gorbachev elected Chairman of Supreme Soviet as sole nominee; election of 542-member working Supreme Soviet (May 26).

June 4. Gas pipeline explosion on Trans-Siberian railway; 400 dead.

June 11. At least 100 reported dead in week of ethnic violence in Uzbekistan between Uzbeks and Meskhetian Turks.

June 12. President Gorbachev begins four-day state visit to West Germany; on June 15, he pledged that the Berlin Wall "will come down".

July 4. President Gorbachev makes three-day official visit to France; addresses Parliamentary Assembly of Council of Europe (July 6).

July 18. State of emergency declared in towns of Abkhaz ASSR, Georgia, where 16 had died in three days of unrest.

July 19. Striking miners return to work after President Gorbachev had warned that their action was a threat to *perestroika* and the national economy; more than 1,000,000 tonnes of coal production reported lost.

July 29. Latvia declares itself "sovereign".

August 23. More than 2,000,000 people in the Baltic republics form a human chain in nationalist demonstration marking 50th anniversary of non-aggression pact between Soviet Union and Nazi Germany.

August 27. 250,000 take part in nationalist demonstrations in Kishinev, Moldavia.

September 2. Thousands of Azerbaidzhanis demonstrate in Baku in support of nationalist demands.

September 8. Formation of Ukrainian Popular Front.

September 19–20. CPSU plenum on the nationality question.

September 20. Central Committee plenum: many conservatives "retired" in favour of reformists.

October 6. President Gorbachev makes two-day visit to GDR on occasion of its 40th anniversary.

October 8. At annual conference in Riga, Latvian Popular Front announces intention of seeking independence from the USSR.

October 9. New labour law includes right to strike, but Soviet parliament votes to ban strikes in key industries.

October 19. Viktor Afanas'ev replaced by I. T. Frolov as editor of *Pravda*.

October 22. Formation of Russian Popular Front in Yaroslavl'.

October 24. Constitutional amendments approved by Supreme Soviet; later ratified by Congress of People's Deputies.

October 25. President Gorbachev begins three-day official visit to Finland.

November 12. Estonian Supreme Soviet votes to effectively annul 1940 unification with the USSR.

November 17–19. Meeting of Georgian Supreme Soviet declares the republic sovereign.

November 28. End of Moscow administration in Nagorno-Karabakh; control reverts to Azerbaidzhan.

November 29. President Gorbachev begins three-day official visit to Italy; on December 1 meets the Pope, the first Soviet leader ever to do so.

December 2. Two-day informal summit between President Gorbachev and President Bush aboard ships anchored at Malta; at end of talks Cold War declared over.

December 7. Lithuanian Supreme Soviet votes to remove guaranteed CPSU monopoly from Article 6 of republican constitution, preparing the way for multi-party system; first republic to vote to this effect.

December 9. Central Committee plenum; formation of Russian Bureau of CPSU.

December 12–24. Second session of Congress of People's Deputies; approves (December 19) Ryzhkov report on economy in 13th Five-Year Plan and transition to "socialist market economy".

December 14. Death of Andrei Sakharov, aged 68.

December 18. Foreign Minister Shevardnadze, in Brussels, signs 10-year agreement on trade and co-operation between EC and USSR.

December 20. Lithuanian Communists vote overwhelmingly for independent political status outside CPSU.

December 23. Commission headed by Alexander Yakovlev finds 1939 Nazi-Soviet Pact "legally invalid".

December 25–26. Central Committee plenum on Lithuanian party issue.

December 31. Riots along border between Soviet Azerbaidzhan and Iran; 80 injured and one killed when police dispersed demonstration by Azerbaidzhan People's Front on December 29–30.

1990

January 4–6. Gorbachev meets leadership of Lithuanian Communist Party and Sajudis in Moscow.

January 11–13. Gorbachev visits Lithuania; announces draft law on secession in preparation and envisages restructuring of USSR as a federation of sovereign states.

January 11. Latvian Supreme Soviet abolishes Article 6 of republican constitution, opening way for establishment of a multi-party system.

January 13–15. Continuing large-scale demonstrations in Baku lead to anti-Armenian pogrom in Baku; 60 killed.

January 19. Troop assault on Baku leads to restoration of central control.

January 22. Azerbaidzhani Supreme Soviet issues secession ultimatum and general strike starts.

February 4. 150,000 strong demonstration in Moscow in favour of reform.

February 5–7. Central Committee plenum to consider new party platform; Gorbachev announces intention to seek an end to the constitutionally guaranteed monopoly of power, and proposes establishment of Presidency.

February. Continuing intercommunal violence in Central Asia and Moldavia.

February–March. Local and republican elections in most Soviet republics; elections in RSFSR, Ukraine and Belorussia on March 4.

February 24. Lithuanian Supreme Soviet passes into hands of Sajudis in multi-party elections.

March 11. Lithuania declares unilateral independence; Vytautas Landbergis elected President.

March 13. Third Congress of People's Deputies convenes and approves establishment of Presidency and reformulation of Article 6 of the constitution establishing CPSU as sole "leading and guiding force".

March 15. Gorbachev elected President as sole candidate. Lithuanian independence declaration declared invalid.

March 17. Lithuania forms non-communist coalition government.

March 25. Estonian Communist Party votes for independence of CPSU after six-month transitional period.

March 30. Estonian Supreme Soviet declares start of transition to independence.

April 3. Law on secession approved by Supreme Soviet.

April 6–7. Split in Latvian Communist Party; minority opts for independent status.

April 18. Economic blockade of Lithuania begins.

April 20. Gavriil Popov elected head of non-communist Moscow Soviet following local elections.

April 26. Adoption of fundamentals of economic relations between the USSR and the union and autonomous republics.

May 1. Unprecedented protests at May Day procession in Moscow.

May 3. Death of Patriarch Pimen; election of Metropolitan Aleksei of Leningrad and Novgorod in his place (June 7).

May 4. Latvian Supreme Soviet votes in favour of transition towards independence; 1922 constitution reinstated; formation of nationalist government.

May 8. Estonian Supreme Soviet restores five key articles of 1938 constitution.

May 12. Baltic Council of 1934–40 re-established.

May 14. Presidential decree holds Latvian and Estonian independence votes legally invalid.

May 16. Estonian Supreme Soviet passes law establishing provisional system of government for the republic during the transition to independence.

May 17. USSR assumes observer status in GATT.

May 23. Anatolii Sobchak elected head of non-communist Leningrad Soviet following local elections.

May 24. Economic reform proposals presented to Supreme Soviet by Ryzhkov; plans approved in outline but call for more developed proposals to be submitted by September 1. Increase in price of bread rejected (June 14) but announcement of proposals to this effect leads to panic buying and introduction of restrictions on purchases by non-residents in Moscow and other cities.

May 29. Election of Boris Yel'tsin as chairman of Supreme Soviet of the RSFSR.

May 29–30. Gorbachev makes official visit to Canada.

May 31–June 6. US-Soviet summit in Washington; agreements signed on June 1; joint news conference (June 3).

June 12. Sovereignty declaration by Russian Republic. USSR Law on press freedom adopted.

June 19. Foundation of Communist Party of Russian Republic; election of Ivan Polozkov as its first secretary (June 21).

June 20. Sovereignty declaration by Uzbekistan.

June 23. Sovereignty declaration by Moldavia.

June 29. Lithuanian declaration of independence suspended in order to allow negotiations to take place.

June–July. Ethnic violence in Kirgizia; at least 212 dead.

July 2–13. 28th Congress of CPSU. Gorbachev re-elected General Secretary on July 10 by 3,411 votes to 1,116. Vladimir Ivashko elected Deputy General Secretary on July 11.

July 16. Sovereignty declaration by the Ukraine.

July 25. Presidential decree rules that trade within Comecon to be conducted in convertible currency from January 1, 1991.

July 27. Sovereignty declaration by Belorussia.

August 4. Election of nationalist President of Armenia, Levon Ter-Petrosyan, and nationalist Prime Minister (August 13) following republican elections.

August 9. USSR Council of Ministers resolution allows individuals to establish, buy and sell businesses and to hire labour.

August 22. Sovereignty declaration by Turkmenia.

August 23. Armenia votes in favour of "independent statehood".

August 25. Sovereignty declaration by Tadzhikistan.

September 14. RSFSR Supreme Soviet adopts radical Shatalin "500 days" reform programme.

September 24. Emergency powers granted to Gorbachev to "stabilize the country's sociopolitical life" for 18 months.

October 1. Law on freedom of conscience and religious organizations.

October 9. Law on public associations formally establishes the basis for a multi-party system.

October 19. USSR Supreme Soviet approves outline programme to create a market economic system.

October 23–27. All-Union Central Council of Trade Union reformed as General Confederation of USSR Trade Unions.

October 25. Sovereignty declaration by Kazakhstan.

October 26. Gorbachev arrives in Spain for official visit.

October 28. Elections to Georgian Supreme Soviet won by nationalist Round Table/Free Georgia bloc.

October 28. Gorbachev arrives in France for official visit.

October 30. Sovereignty declaration by Kirgizia; last of the 15 republics to adopt a declaration of this kind.

October–December. Continuing intercommunal tensions in Moldavia; Russian and Gagauz Turks establish their own forms of government; presidential decree on "normalization of the situation" in the Moldavia Soviet Socialist Republic, December 22.

November 7. Revolution parade in Red Square; man arrested after shots fired at Gorbachev.

November 9. Gorbachev begins official visit to Germany.

November 17. Gorbachev "programme of action" presented to the Supreme Soviet foreshadows constitutional change.

November 18. Gorbachev arrives for "short working visit" to Italy.

November 20. Treaty on limitation of conventional forces in Europe signed in Paris; Gorbachev report to Supreme Soviet on the treaty negotiations, November 26.

November 24. Publication of draft "union treaty" in the central press.

December 10. Law on trade unions adopted.

December 10–11. Central Committee plenum.

December 17. Opening of Fourth Congress of People's Deputies. Surprise resignation (December 20) of Eduard Shevardnadze as Foreign Minister. Votes (December 24) to retain the Soviet Union as a "renewed federation" and not to change the name of the state. Approves (December 25) outline of new union treaty. Approves (December 26) constitutional amendments establishing executive Presidency. Elects (December 27) Gennadi Yanaev as first ever Vice-President. Adopts (December 27) law on referenda.

Political Overview

On its leadership's own admission, the late 1980s were the most difficult years that had yet been encountered in implementing the policy of *perestroika* (restructuring) launched in 1985. Internationally, there were considerable advances, including the first Sino-Soviet summit for 30 years and a continuation of the series of Soviet-American summits with the new US President, George Bush. Politically, there was a steady extension of the programme of "democratization", launched in 1987, as the first ever elections on a largely competitive basis were held to a new "super-parliament", the USSR Congress of People's Deputies, and then to republican assemblies. Mikhail Gorbachev, General Secretary of the Communist Party since 1985, strengthened his own position by a series of promotions and resignations, and more particularly by securing his re-election to the General Secretaryship and, in 1990, to a new executive state Presidency.

In other respects, however, there was less to applaud. Economic performance (discussed in detail in the following section) failed to respond as had been hoped to the attempts that were made to move towards a "socialist market", and nationality differences, already acute in several parts of the country, extended still more widely. Social tensions, including crime and differences between rich and poor, became greater, and the President began to assume increasingly draconian powers to deal with public disorder and challenges by the republics to Moscow rule. By the early 1990s the combination of these difficulties was such as to place the continuation of *perestroika* in some doubt and the Soviet President himself in some public disfavour.

Reforming the state system

For all the importance of individual changes of personnel and policy, it was the establishment of a qualitatively different representative system that was perhaps the single most important political development of the late 1980s. Under the previous electoral system, which was governed by the 1936 and then the 1977 constitutions, there was no choice of candidate and very little opportunity, in practice, to reject the single candidate. Only one party, the Communist Party (CPSU), had a legal standing, and it either nominated candidates directly or arranged for its preferred nominations to be made by the other bodies that enjoyed this right, such as the trade unions and the *Komsomol* (Young Communist League). No candidate at the national level, since the introduction of this system in 1937, had ever been defeated, and the reported turnout had never fallen below 99% (at the last national elections under this system, in 1984, it achieved the record level of 99.99%).

Under constitutional amendments approved in December 1988 these arrangements were changed considerably. A choice of candidate was to become normal (although not obligatory). Candidates were to live in the areas they represented, they were required to put forward election manifestos, and had the right to appoint campaign staff to assist them. The voters themselves were to pass through screened-off booths before casting their vote, ending the earlier practice by which they had been discouraged from voting against the single candidate by the need to make use of the booth to do so. The forthcoming elections, set for March 1989, would be "unlike all those that had preceded them", the Central Committee promised at its meeting in November 1988; probably few inside or outside the USSR realized quite how different they would be.

Under the new arrangements, candidates were to be nominated and then approved by a selection conference; in the second stage they would compete with each other for the support of their respective electorates, who would then cast their decisive ballots. There had been some resistance, in the discussion of the constitutional amendments, to these somewhat elaborate provisions. Selection conferences came in for particular criticism, with some letters to the press asking who needed these "elections before elections". There was also some hostility to the most novel feature of the revised arrangements by which a wide range of public bodies, from the CPSU and the trade unions to stamp collectors and film fans, had the right to elect specified numbers of deputies to the new Congress. Was not this a violation of the principle "one person one vote", it was asked, and what, in any case, had stamp collecting to do with affairs of state? The new arrangements, notwithstanding these criticisms, were approved almost unanimously by the outgoing Supreme Soviet and they served as the basis of the first ever elections to the Congress of People's Deputies on March 26, 1989.

Electing the Congress of People's Deputies

In both the public bodies and ordinary constituencies the electoral process took a variety of forms. A number of public bodies, in the end, approved no more candidates than the seats available: the CPSU itself was one of these, agreeing to nominate just 100 candidates for the 100 seats it had been accorded under the constitutional amendments. In the vote, at a special plenary meeting of the Central Committee on March 15, 52 candidates were elected unanimously; 12 votes were cast against Gorbachev but 78, the largest number, against the prominent "conservative", Yegor Ligachev. The elections in the Academy of

Sciences were much more vigorously contested. A number of leading reformers, among them the physicist Andrei Sakharov and the space scientist Roald Sagdeev, were not originally selected as nominees for the Academy's 20 seats. In the elections that followed only eight of the 23 nominees secured the necessary majority, and further elections had to be held at which Sakharov, Sagdeev and other reformers were successful (Sakharov, who went on to become an outspoken and controversial parliamentarian, died the following December). Practices in the constituencies varied still more widely, some constituencies dispensing with selection conferences and approving up to 12 nominations for a single seat, while others, particularly in the southern republics, much more frequently approved a single candidate in the traditional manner.

In the end, 2,884 candidates were selected to contest the 1,500 constituency seats; in 384 of them, despite the intentions of the new law, there was just a single nomination. The first and in some ways most significant result was the turnout. The election legislation and official commentaries had made it plain that the abuses of earlier years would not be tolerated, and voting took place over a slightly shorter period than usual. In the circumstances a reported turnout of 89.8%, although well down on previous recorded levels, suggested that the new arrangements had succeeded in their primary task, to engage the interest and involvement of the Soviet mass public. More remarkable, however, were the results themselves. In three constituencies there was no result at all because the turnout had fallen below 50%; and in a further 271 constituencies there was no decision because none of the candidates had secured a majority of votes cast (these seats were later filled by by-elections).

Most unexpected of all, however, were the defeats that were suffered by Party and government officials at all levels of the system, even when they were standing unopposed. The list of unsuccessful candidates included the Prime Minister of Latvia, the Prime Minister and President of Lithuania, the mayors of Moscow and Kiev, and a total of 38 regional or district party secretaries throughout the country. The former Moscow party leader, Boris Yel'tsin, enjoyed a spectacular success in the capital's no. 1 national-territorial seat, where he secured 89.4% of the vote despite attempts by the central party apparatus to hinder his campaign. The most striking series of defeats occurred in Leningrad, where the list of casualties included the regional party first secretary (a candidate member of the Politburo), the regional second secretary, the chairman of the city soviet and his deputy, the chairman of the regional soviet and the city party secretary. Gorbachev, addressing the Central Committee a month later, professed to see the elections as a victory for *perestroika* on the grounds that the victims had been predominantly conservative officials who were less than fully committed to its success. The results were nonetheless difficult to interpret as other than a humiliating snub to the Communist Party, and in some respects, such as the sweeping victories achieved by nationalist candidates in the Baltic republics, they appeared to prejudice the unity of the Soviet state itself.

Establishing a presidential system

There were further changes in the Soviet constitution in 1990, particularly in March, when the CPSU's guaranteed "leading role" was abolished and a new executive Presidency was approved. The creation of the new Presidency had been among the radical proposals announced by Gorbachev at the February 1990 Central Committee plenum at which the constitutionally guaranteed "leading role" was formally relinquished. The introduction of the new system, for which there was no precedent in Russian or Soviet political practice, was justified by Gorbachev as a means of ensuring that swift executive action could take place in circumstances that required it. Despite claims from some deputies that powers of this kind were a step towards dictatorship, Gorbachev insisted that there was an urgent need to "enhance the mechanism of executive authority in order to ensure the laws work", and he secured the necessary majority at the Third Congress of People's Deputies on March 13. He was elected to the Presidency himself two days later, although by only 59% of the vote in an uncontested ballot.

Any citizen aged between 35 and 65 could be elected to the Presidency for a maximum of two five-year terms. The President was normally to be elected by universal, equal and direct suffrage, although in the difficult circumstances that then obtained it was agreed that the election — exceptionally — would be made by the Congress itself. The President was to report annually to the Congress of People's Deputies and would brief the Supreme Soviet on the "most important questions of the USSR's domestic and foreign policy". He would propose candidates for the premiership and other leading state positions; he had a suspensory veto over legislation; and he could dissolve the government and suspend its directives. He could also declare a state of emergency, and introduce direct presidential rule. The President headed a new Council of the Federation, consisting of the presidents of the 15 republics, with responsibility for inter-ethnic and inter-republican issues; he also headed a new Presidential Council, which was responsible for the "main directions of the USSR's foreign and domestic policy".

In September 1990 these already impressive powers were extended by parliamentary vote, giving Gorbachev the right to institute emergency measures to "stabilize the country's sociopolitical life" for a period of 18 months. Several further changes were made by the Fourth Congress of People's Deputies in December 1990, which completed the move to a fully presidential administration. The Council of Ministers was replaced by a more limited "Cabinet", headed by a Prime Minister who (together with his colleagues) would be nominated by the President and accountable to him as well as to parliament. The President became head of a new Security Council with overall responsibility for defence and public order (he himself appointed its other members). He also appointed a new Vice-President, responsible for carrying out the functions that were entrusted to him (Gennadi Yanaev, a member of the CPSU Secretariat who had formerly worked in the trade union movement and *Komsomol*, was elected to this position on December 27, 1990). The Presidential Council, formed the previous March, disappeared completely, and a reconstituted Council of the Federation headed by the President became, in effect, the supreme state decision-making body.

The Communist Party in transition

The 28th Congress of the Communist Party of the Soviet Union (CPSU) took place in July 1990. By the time it convened the party had already lost a substantial part of the authority it once commanded. The most important single development in this connection was the decision taken by the Central Committee in February 1990 to relinquish the guarantee of its "leading role" contained in Article 6 of the 1977 constitution. Gorbachev, who had resisted a challenge to Article 6 at the Congress of People's Deputies the previous December, argued that the leading role had already been overtaken by events, in particular the establishment of a wide range of independent political groupings. The party, however, should seek to retain a position of "political leadership" through the electoral process.

The constitution was amended accordingly by the Third Congress of People's Deputies in March; henceforth, the new Article 6 suggested, the Communist Party would share the task of forming and administering public policy with other parties and social movements.

The formal loss of its leading position was only one of the ways in which the CPSU saw its formerly unchallengeable position erode over the late 1980s and early 1990s. (For its composition at the start of 1990, see Table 1.) The party, for instance, began

---

Table 1: The Communist Party of the Soviet Union, January 1, 1990

Membership

Members	18,856,113
Candidates	372,104
TOTAL	19,228,217

Of which women 5,813,610, or 30.2%

Occupational composition

Workers	5,313,524
Collective farmers	1,466,361
White-collar staff	7,793,048
Students	101,415
Pensioners, housewives etc.	3,344,981

National composition

Russians	11,183,749
Ukrainians	3,113,560
Belorussians	747,261
Uzbeks	499,250
Kazakhs	416,829
Tatars	399,921
Georgians	338,502
Armenians	304,558
Azerbaidzhanis	375,925
Jews	204,767
Lithuanians	148,377
Moldavians	120,598
Chuvash	108,074

and other nationalities with fewer than 100,000 members

Educational composition

Higher	6,808,715	(35.4%)
Incomplete higher	358,350	(1.9%)
Secondary	8,605,207	(44.7%)
Incomplete secondary	2,246,495	(11.7%)
Primary	1,154,880	(6.0%)
Without primary education	54,570	(0.3%)

Source: *Izvestiya TsK KPSS*, 1990, no.4, pp. 113–14.

to lose members: nearly 1.5 million of them between January and September 1990, of whom 800,000 had simply resigned. The existing membership became increasingly divided, despite the formal prohibition of "factions" within its ranks. The two groupings that secured the widest attention in the run-up to the Congress were the "Democratic Platform", whose members called for the CPSU to abandon its Leninism in favour of a purely parliamentary role, and the "Marxist Platform", whose members called for a party based more closely on the interests and participation of the industrial working class. The party press lost circulation: *Pravda*, for instance, had only 30% of its 1990 subscribers in 1991. Members and whole branches began to withhold their dues, and party income as a whole fell by about half. The party's public standing, as measured by opinion polls, declined sharply. Perhaps (for its leaders) most alarming of all, the party began to fragment as a national organization. In December 1989 the Lithuanian party organization seceded; in March and April 1990 the Latvian and Estonian party organizations split into pro-Moscow and independent factions; and in December 1990 the Georgian party organization followed the Lithuanians by opting for full independence.

The 28th Congress of the CPSU

The 28th Party Congress, which met in Moscow from July 2–13, 1990, was accordingly a very different gathering from the party congresses that had preceded it. It was the first to meet against a background of demonstrators shouting "Down with the red fascists!" It was the first congress, for many years at least, at which members of the leadership rendered individual account. It was the first congress at any time at which there was a direct contest for the party leadership: Gorbachev originally faced nine challengers and had to be content with three-quarters of the vote in the final choice between himself and a district party secretary. It was the first congress since the late 1920s that adopted no "Guidelines" for the forthcoming Five-Year Plan, reflecting the view that this was the responsibility of government alone. An entirely new set of Party Rules was adopted, and a new "Programmatic Declaration" which was meant to guide the party's activities until a new Party Programme could be adopted. There were calls for the party to drop the word "Communist" from its title, and the "Internationale" as its anthem. The Congress concluded by electing its first ever deputy leader and a newly constituted Politburo, including the party first secretaries of the 15 republics. (Table 2 lists the leadership of the Politburo and Secretariat at the start of 1991.)

Gorbachev, in his opening address, described the process of *perestroika* as one by which a "Stalinist model of socialism" had been replaced by a "civil society of free men and women". The political system, more particularly, had been "radically transformed" with the establishment of "genuine democracy" based upon free elections, a multi-party system, human rights and popular self-government. An atmosphere of "ideological domineering" had been replaced by one of freedom of thought. The crimes of the past had been "resolutely condemned". There had been a "real revolution in people's thinking"; life had become fuller and richer, the "absurd bans" of the Stalinist years had been removed, and scientists and intellectuals had been given a much more prominent place in the party's decision-making processes. And new opportunities had opened up for the development of culture, literature and the arts, or what Gorbachev rather grandly called the "ecology of the soul".

The Congress adopted a formal position on these and other matters with its approval of

---

Table 2:   The CPSU leadership, January 1991

The Politburo
M. S. Gorbachev, General Secretary
V. A. Ivashko, Deputy General Secretary

Members:
M. M. Burokiavicus, 1st Secretary, Lithuanian CP
A. S. Dzasokhov, CC Secretary
I. T. Frolov, CC Secretary
G. G. Gumbaridze (former) 1st Secretary, Georgian CP
S. I. Gurenko, 1st Secretary, Ukraine CP
I. A. Karimov, 1st Secretary, Uzbek CP
P. K. Luchinsky, 1st Secretary, Moldavian CP
A. A. Malofeev, 1st Secretary, Belorussian CP
A. M. Masaliev, 1st Secretary, Kirgiz CP
K. Makhkamov, 1st Secretary, Tadzhik CP
A. N. Mutalibov, 1st Secretary, Azerbaidzhani CP
N. A. Nazarbaev, 1st Secretary, Kazakh CP
S. A. Niyazov, 1st Secretary, Turkmenian CP
N. K. Pogosyan, 1st Secretary, Armenian CP
I. K. Polozkov, 1st Secretary, Russian Republican CP
Yu. A. Prokof'ev, 1st Secretary, Moscow CP
A. P. Rubiks, 1st Secretary, Latvian CP
G. V. Semenova, CC Secretary
E.-A. A. Sillari, 1st Secretary, Estonian CP
E. E. Sokolov, 1st Secretary, Belorussian CP
O. S. Shenin, CC Secretary
E. S. Stroev, CC Secretary
G. I. Yanaev, CC Secretary

The Secretariat
M. S. Gorbachev (General Secretary)
V. A. Ivashko (Deputy General Secretary)

CC Secretaries:
O. D. Baklanov, A. S. Dzasokhov, V. M. Falin, B. V. Gidaspov,
A. N. Girenko, V. A. Kuptsov, Yu. A. Manaenkov, G. V.
Semenova, O. S. Shenin, E. S. Stroev, G. I. Yanaev

Members of the Secretariat
V. V. Aniskin, V. A. Gaivoronsky, I. I. Mel'nikov, A. I.
Teplenichev, G. Turgunova

---

a declaration entitled "Towards a humane, democratic socialism". The declaration made it clear that, for the party at least, the origins of Soviet difficulties lay in deformations of socialism rather than the socialist project itself. Party dictatorship had led to popular alienation and lawlessness; nature had been plundered without restraint; and dogmatism had reigned supreme in the world of culture. *Perestroika* meant a "radical turn towards a policy aimed at the country's renovation"; the CPSU itself was presented as a party of the "socialist choice and communist perspective", seen as a natural stage in the advance of civilization. The declaration incorporated a set of "urgent anti-crisis measures", including a new union treaty and normalization of the consumer market. Longer-term measures included strengthened civil liberties, a "stage-by-stage transition to a market system", international co-operation and democratization of the party itself. The declaration was to serve, in effect, as the party's Programme until a new Programme could be adopted at a conference or congress in the first half of 1992.

Gorbachev discussed democratization of the party in his opening address, noting that the party's own organization and role required constant reappraisal. For many years, he suggested, the party had served as an extension of the command-administrative system, leading to serious mistakes in its choice of personnel and policies. Millions of party members had been removed from direct control over its affairs, and the result had been a "climate of indifference, apathy and passivity" in party branches. What would an "updated CPSU", freed of these defects, look like? It would, Gorbachev suggested, be a party of the "socialist choice and communist perspective", committed at the same time to the common ideals of humanity. It would be a party "freed of its ideological blinkers", promoting its policies through dialogue and co-operation with other progressive social and political forces. It would be a tolerant party, based on a recognition of the rights of minorities and "total freedom of debate". It would be a "vanguard" as well as a parliamentary party, organizing in the workplace and armed forces as well as in residential areas. And it would be a self-managing party, based upon the freedom of action of branches and the independence of republican party organizations within a common programme and statute.

The Congress formalized its decisions on these matters with the adoption of an entirely new set of Party Rules, which introduced some quite significant changes as compared with drafts published earlier in the year and still more so the Rules that had been adopted at the previous congress in 1986. The important principle of democratic centralism was retained, after some discussion, in the final version. There was much more emphasis, however, upon the rights of ordinary members, who were given greater access to information about party committees at all levels and the right to "evaluate" their work. Branches were to be allowed to express their views on particularly contentious issues before they were considered by the Central Committee, and had the right to retain up to half of their membership income. The changes as compared with the Rules of 1986 were still more dramatic, including the explicit right to form "platforms" if not organized factions, greater respect for the rights of the minority, and official endorsement of "horizontal" structures such as political clubs and seminars of a kind that had hitherto been regarded as incompatible with democratic centralism. It was nonetheless unclear, after the Congress, if these and other changes would be sufficient to encourage the degree of commitment from party members that would be necessary if it was to retain the dominant position it had enjoyed for more than 70 years.

Nationalities and the republics

If the late 1980s saw the exacerbation of longstanding economic difficulties, they also saw the Soviet Union's nationality differences acquire a still more open and sometimes violent form. Nationality differences involving the Kazakhs had erupted in December 1986; similar tensions among Crimean Tatars and the Baltic peoples emerged publicly in 1987. In 1988 a complicated dispute between Armenia and Azerbaidzhan over the mountainous enclave of

Nagorno-Karabakh led to demonstrations and substantial loss of life. All of these disputes continued into 1989 and 1990, and they were joined by others hardly less serious in their implications. The party itself convened a much-postponed plenum on the national question in September 1989, but the "platform" it approved attracted little support and it was unclear which of the republics would be willing to negotiate a "new union treaty" as a fresh basis for their association. By the early 1990s the continuation of the USSR in any form had been placed on the agenda by the agreement to conduct a referendum on this question in early 1991.

The Baltic republics, in what soon became the most serious challenge to central authority, introduced legislation establishing a favoured position for their native languages, and adopted legislation on sovereignty which permitted all-union laws to have effect on their territories only after they had been approved by the republican parliaments. A set of constitutional amendments adopted by the Estonian Supreme Soviet in May 1989 proved particularly controversial in that they restricted the right to vote to those who had lived for a certain period in the republic. After an extended strike by the republic's Russian-speaking population and a ruling by the Supreme Soviet Presidium the legislation was modified, dropping the residence requirement for voting but retaining it for the candidates themselves.

Developments in the Baltic provoked the central party leadership to issue a formal statement in late August 1989, warning against the activities of "extremist" and "anti-socialist forces" that were pursuing a separatist path with "growing persistence and aggressiveness". Pressures of this kind, however, had relatively little effect, not least because party and state leaders in the republics were also influenced by the strength of local nationalist sentiment. On August 23, the 50th anniversary of the Nazi-Soviet Pact, an estimated two million citizens formed a human chain across the Baltic republics in the biggest demonstration that had yet been seen; and the popular fronts, which articulated nationalist feelings in all three republics, became more openly committed to outright independence rather than a greater degree of self-government within the USSR. Perhaps most alarmingly of all from the point of view of the central leadership, the Communist Party organizations in the three republics began to press for a greater degree of autonomy, establishing direct links with other ruling parties and adopting their own programmes and statutes. In December 1989, as we have noted, the Lithuanian party formally opted for an independent status; and then on March 11, 1990, following elections in which Sajudis had secured a clear majority, Lithuania itself formally declared its independence, followed (in more guarded terms) by Estonia on March 30 and Latvia on May 4.

Gorbachev, addressing the Congress of People's Deputies, described the Lithuanian action as "illegitimate and illegal" and refused to open negotiations with what remained, in his view, an integral part of the USSR. The central authorities issued an ultimatum demanding the withdrawal of the declaration of independence; when the Lithuanians refused to comply with this an economic blockade was imposed on April 18. The Lithuanian declaration of independence was suspended by parliamentary vote on June 29, the blockade was ended, and discussions began to attempt to resolve the dispute; they had not reached an agreed conclusion by the end of the year. Matters, indeed, reached a still more critical pass in the first weeks of 1991 as Soviet paratroopers moved into the three Baltic republics in an ostensible bid to enforce conscription into the armed forces. In Lithuania itself an attack on the main television station left 14 demonstrators dead and 144 wounded; Soviet troops also seized a police academy in Latvia leaving five dead. Although it was unclear that these hard line moves had been directly authorised by President Gorbachev, they did appear to reflect the view he had expressed in his New Year message that preserving the integrity of the USSR was a "sacred duty".

The nationalist tensions that emerged elsewhere in the USSR were more "communal" in character, involving disputes between different Soviet ethnic groups rather than a clear and widely supported movement towards independence. The dispute over Nagorno-Karabakh proved particularly intractable; the establishment of a "special form of administration" in January 1989 produced no lasting improvement in the situation and was brought to an end in November, when the area reverted to Azerbaidzhani rule. The Kremlin's special representative in the area, Arkady Vol'sky, told the press that the conflict was in danger of becoming the Soviet Union's "home-grown Lebanon". In January 1990 the long-running dispute flared into open violence once more, provoked by an Armenian decision to extend the provisions of their republican budget and electoral law to Nagorno-Karabakh. Tens of thousands took to the streets in Baku alone, up to 60 people (mostly Armenians) lost their lives in pogroms, and there were further fatalities when a state of emergency was declared by the USSR Supreme Soviet and troops were used to restore order. The death toll from the conflict was officially put at more than 200; the Azerbaidzhani first secretary, Vezirov, whose party organization had been powerless to influence events, lost his position as a result.

There was further loss of life in a savage flare-up in the summer of 1989 between Meskhetian Turks and the native Uzbek population in the Ferghana valley in the east of that republic. The violence, which erupted suddenly, left nearly 100 dead and over 1,000 injured in the space of a fortnight. Longstanding tensions also emerged during 1989 in Georgia, inspired both by Georgian nationalism and by the separate and conflicting claims of the minority Abkhazian population within Georgia itself. Nationalist pressures became stronger when a seven-party Round Table/Free Georgia coalition secured 54% of the vote at republican elections in October 1990, as compared with 23% for the Communists. The veteran dissident Zviad Gamsakhurdia became president and a parliamentary resolution was adopted which, like those in the Baltic and in Armenia the month before, committed the republic to a gradual transition to full independence. There were intercommunal clashes in Kirgizia in June and July 1990, which left at least 212 dead; in Moldavia there were tensions between the indigenous majority and substantial Russian and Gagauz Turkic minorities, which attempted to establish their own forms of government in late 1990. All told, the Procuracy reported in August 1990, inter-ethnic conflict since early 1988 had cost 949 lives; 8,652 had been wounded and about 600,000 had become refugees in their own country.

National assertiveness reached by far the largest of the Soviet Union's republics, the Russian, in May 1990, following elections to the republican Congress of People's Deputies at which radical candidates affiliated to "Democratic Russia" won about a third of the votes (and majorities in Moscow and Leningrad). After several ballots the former Moscow party secretary, Boris Yel'tsin, was elected chairman of the Russian Supreme Soviet, or *de facto* president, on May 29. Yel'tsin's political programme had combined calls for radical political reform with a strong appeal for Russia's sovereign rights, including separate citizenship, ownership of all the republic's natural resources, an independent foreign policy, and the primacy of republican legislation over that of the USSR as a whole ("reversing the pyramid", as Yel'tsin put it to a news conference shortly after his election). The Russian Congress of People's Deputies resolved to this effect on June 12; in a separate development a Russian Federation Communist Party was established on June 21 and Ivan Polozkov, a relatively conservative first secretary from Krasnodar, was elected its first secretary. Other Russian republican institutions, including an Academy of Sciences and a trade union organization, began to be established during the year.

Declarations of sovereignty were adopted by all 15 republics during 1990, and by many lower-level bodies as well. In some cases the affirmation to this effect was still more categoric than in the Russian Republic. The Ukrainian and Turkmenian declarations, for instance, proclaimed their republics nuclear-free zones. The Armenian declaration, which followed elections at which nationalists had won a majority of seats, included an assertion of the republic's "independent statehood", including the right to form its own military units and to control its own natural resources. A Central Committee plenary meeting in September 1989 agreed to deplore these and other manifestations of national hostility, but failed to advance a set of policies which would provide a framework for their peaceful resolution. By early 1990 the terms of the debate had moved still further, to a "new union treaty" based upon a free association of sovereign republics, and it appeared to have been accepted that this would allow a variety of forms of association ranging from home rule (in the Baltic republics) to a slightly more evenly balanced relationship between the centre and the republics (in Central Asia, which tended to gain rather than lose from its status as a part of the USSR). The Fourth Congress of People's Deputies, meeting in December 1990, approved the basic principles of a "new union treaty" of this kind, but a number of republics refused to take part in the discussions (and the Moldavians withdrew while they were taking place). The difficulties that arose in concluding a national budget for 1991 showed one of the ways in which these continuing national tensions could be apparent.

Economic Overview

Five years after Gorbachev took office, his programme of economic reform was overtaken by political and economic disintegration. On December 18, one week before the heart attack which prompted his resignation, Prime Minister Nikolai Ryzhkov bluntly stated that "in the form originally conceived, *perestroika* has failed to be realized". Soviet economic performance under Gorbachev has been no better than it was under Chernenko, Andropov or Brezhnev, whether one chooses to measure economic performance in terms of GNP growth, industrial output, factory productivity, the availability of consumer goods, or whatever.

This leaves two important questions to be answered. First, why did the economic reform efforts come to naught, and what are the chances of a breakthrough to radical reform in the forthcoming year? Second, how bad has been the economic slump, and how much worse can it get?

The stalemate over reform

The initial package of economic reform measures, introduced in 1987–88, failed to have the desired effect. They weakened the authority of the central planning authorities, without stimulating more output from enterprises. The central supply system, for example, cut the number of products it allocated from 10,000 in 1988 to 610 in 1990, with the remainder supposedly procured on the basis of direct contracts with suppliers.

In 1989, the breakdown in the industrial supply system, and mounting shortages in consumer markets, triggered a wave of social unrest and a flurry of strikes in coal mining regions. The Gorbachev leadership concluded that more radical reform measures were needed. Since that time, however, there has been a progressive paralysis of the central leadership. On one hand, Gorbachev has been unable to reach agreement with the USSR Supreme Soviet on a reform programme. Simultaneously, the political authority of all the central political institutions has eroded, with all of the republican parliaments declaring their sovereignty. By the end of 1990, the problem was not simply devising a national reform programme, but getting it implemented throughout the country.

The roots of reform. It is worth summarizing the key stages in the reform debate, to underline the erratic and frustrating nature of the process. The latest cycle began in July 1989, when Leonid Abalkin, a reform-minded economist, was brought in as Deputy Prime Minister to head a State Commission on Economic Reform. Abalkin reportedly clashed with Prime Minister Nikolai Ryzhkov and the conservative planners in Gosplan. On November 19, 1989, the USSR Supreme Soviet rejected the initial reform plan put forward by Ryzhkov, on the grounds that it was not radical enough. The plan stressed the virtues of horizontal market relations over central plan directives, but was firmly opposed to private ownership of the means of production, and ruled out any major change in the system of property relations.

In spring 1990 Gorbachev was under extreme political pressure from the "left", with communist functionaries having lost control of the local soviets in two-thirds of Russia's cities in the March 1990 elections. It began to look as if Gorbachev decided that radical economic reform was unavoidable. He appointed pro-reform economists to his inner circle: in January Nikolai Petrakov became a personal aide, and in March Stanislav Shatalin joined the new Presidential Council. In his inaugural address as President on March 15, Gorbachev tried to regain the initiative by renewing his commitment to radical economic reform. Meanwhile, the Abalkin team had prepared a new, more ambitious plan, entitled "Basic propositions for turning the economy into one based on market relations". The plan argued that only radical economic reform could stave off the "growing centrifugal forces" which threatened the economy, and proposed a package of 20 new laws which would dismantle the system of central planning and quickly abolish price controls (with compensation for consumers). Many of the key elements of the Abalkin programme were to resurface six months later in the Shatalin plan.

Ryzhkov was unwilling to accept the full Abalkin programme. On May 24 he advanced an alternative plan for a gradual transition to a "regulated market economy", the most striking feature of which was a proposal for an immediate wave of price increases, aimed at cutting food subsidies from R 130 billion to R 45 billion. On July 1, 1990, the price of bread, which had cost 25 kopecks for 30 years, was to be tripled, and on January 1, 1991, other retail prices would be increased by 30%, and food by 100–200%. A compensation package would be prepared: consumers would be given a 15% salary increase or a grant of R 40 per month (whichever was the higher). This macro-stabilization programme would not however be accompanied by the liberalization of the planning system. The existing system of state orders was to be maintained until 1992. In a humiliating defeat, the USSR Supreme Soviet rejected the Ryzhkov plan on June 14, and gave the government until September 1 to come up with an alternative. This rejection of the programme made it abundantly clear that the Ryzhkov government had lost its ability to steer economic policy.

The failure of the Ryzhkov plan can be largely attributed to political considerations. (Many would argue that there were also good economic reasons for rejecting the measure.) The idea of starting the programme with a tripling of bread prices was a symbolic mistake, particularly given popular fears that the government was about to introduce "shock therapy" of the sort which had been administered in Poland in January 1990. Also, there was a feeling that the Ryzhkov government was not really committed to the idea of reform, but was simply manoeuvring to keep itself in power. As one Baltic deputy put it, "the government has lost its trust, and this programme is too good for this government".

Soviet and Western economists then set to work to devise a programme capable of meeting the various conflicting demands being made on Gorbachev. In the course of the summer, six different teams of economists were closeted in various dachas working on draft programmes, under the auspices of different government agencies. At one point the Council of Ministers set up a Commission to Evaluate Alternative Variants of the Transition to a Market Economy, to sort through the 80 or more alternative programmes which were in circulation.

Shatalin headed a group working for Boris Yel'tsin. Shatalin returned to some of the radical drafts from the previous autumn, and presented a "500 days" plan to the RSFSR parliament in June. Meanwhile, Gorbachev's rhetoric seemed to shift in favour of radical reform. He announced to the 28th Party Congress on July 10 that "all the world's experience has shown the advantages of the market", and that "the old approach brought the country to the brink of bankruptcy". In a speech to military leaders on August 17 he used the word "privatization" for the first time.

In late July Gorbachev and Yel'tsin entered into talks to seek a compromise programme, and on August 2 the teams of advisers serving Gorbachev and Yel'tsin created a joint working group under Stanislav Shatalin. Leonid Abalkin, Ryzhkov's deputy, subsequently withdrew from the group, and Ryzhkov was to present his own plan.

The Shatalin plan. The famous "500 days" plan of Shatalin won the backing of Yel'tsin and the Russian parliament, and gave renewed hope to Western observers that the USSR was finally on the market reform path. Key elements of the Shatalin plan were as follows:

Days 1–100   abolish ministries and plan targets
abolish all subsidies to loss-making enterprises
encourage private farming
create an independent central bank along the lines of the federal reserve system
move towards a unified ruble exchange rate
cut spending on defence (10%), KGB (20%) and foreign aid (75%)
preserve a unified, open market across the USSR.

Days 102–250   create joint stock companies
privatize half the shops and cafés
phased removal of price controls, while indexing wages
give republics taxation power and the right to sell their natural resources.

Days 250–500   move towards 70% of industry in joint stock companies (JCS)
in these JCSs approximately R 100–150 billion of state assets (about 10%
of the total, estimate at R 2.6 trillion) would be sold off to private owners
introduce a convertible ruble.

The Shatalin plan was not very specific in explaining how subsidies could be reduced, while retail price controls would be maintained until the second phase. It argued, unpersuasively, that rapid sales of assets such as apartments and shops could close the gap in the state budget. Shatalin suggested that a sale of 1% of the housing stock would produce R 5 billion, and even proposed selling half of the 700,000 cars operated by state agencies, at 10,000 rubles each. It is not clear that this approach would be sufficient, even in the short run. For example, early in 1990 the Leningrad soviet tried to sell off apartments to tenants, but found no takers. People were unwilling to sink their savings into property when they could continue paying subsidized rents (estimated at one sixth of the cost of the housing). Also, there was massive uncertainty as to the political and economic conditions affecting the buying and selling of property in the future.

In addition to the Ryzhkov and Shatalin plans, Abel Aganbegyan produced a third plan, on Gorbachev's instructions, which tried to compromise between the other two. In mid-September the USSR Supreme Soviet asked Gorbachev to merge the three plans, and granted him extraordinary presidential powers to run the economy in the interim. (By September the outline production plan for the next year is usually approved.)

On October 1 the RSFSR parliament decided to press ahead on its own with the Shatalin plan, in order to create what Prime Minister Ivan Silaev called a new "economic alliance of sovereign states". Meanwhile, most of the other republics were unhappy with the Gorbachev *and* Shatalin plans, since both seemed to them to leave too much central control in Moscow. In the case of the Shatalin plan, for example, they objected to reliance on a single currency issued by a federal reserve bank in Moscow.

On October 16 Gorbachev countered with his own programme, "For the stabilization of the economy and the transition to a market economy", which emphasized the urgency of stabilization and offered no specific timetable for the dismantling of central planning. Gorbachev's own former economic advisers, S. Shatalin and N. Petrakov, denounced his plan on November 4, as did most of the republics. Shatalin, exasperated with the seemingly endless debate over the merits of the alternative plans, commented that "this is not a choice between London and Paris, but between survival and the grave".

Throughout the autumn, Yel'tsin played a complicated game of bluff and counter-bluff with Gorbachev. Many of Yel'tsin's economic advisers resigned, exasperated with the political manoeuvring, and unsure whether Yel'tsin was really prepared to break with Gorbachev. Deputy RSFSR Prime Minister Grigory Yavlinski, the author of the "400 days" plan which preceded the Shatalin programme, resigned on October 16, and RSFSR Finance Minister Boris Fyodorov resigned on December 28.

Gorbachev reasserts his control. Amid a growing sense of panic and open talk of a "Jaruzelski variant" among party officials, Gorbachev pressed ahead with his own stabilization/reform programme. The USSR Supreme Soviet approved his request for authorisation to issue presidential decrees to stabilize the economy. On November 2 he announced that 40% of all dollar earnings of enterprises would be directly confiscated by the state budget. On November 15 prices of "luxury items" like jewellery and furniture were increased, followed by across-the-board increases in retail prices in January. In January 1991 all 50- and 100-ruble notes were abruptly withdrawn from circulation, in a bid to cut back on the excess cash in circulation. There has also been a crackdown on "economic crime", with a new network of workers' control organs and an enhanced role for the KGB in the struggle with economic "speculation".

As for industrial planning, the centre is still trying to operate according to the old rules. On December 14 Gorbachev issued a decree obliging all enterprises to guarantee the same level of contract deliveries for 1991 as for 1990 (although the 1991 plan reportedly includes compulsory state orders at considerably lower levels than in previous years). The problem lies not so much with the state orders, as with the system of "direct links" through which firms are supposed to negotiate for supplies and sell the remainder of their output. Firms have been reluctant to sign such agreements, and are insisting on barter deals rather than cash payments.

The government seems to be pursuing a policy of increasing wholesale prices first, while postponing the more politically sensitive retail prices to a later date. Wholesale prices for energy, wood and metals prices were raised by 50% in January 1991. This policy is beneficial to primary producers, but is squeezing manufacturing and retail enterprises, who are forbidden from passing on their cost increases to consumers.

The consensus among Soviet economists as of December 1990 was that Gorbachev himself had become an obstacle to reform. They argue that Gorbachev simply does not understand the economics of reform, nor is he inclined to listen to those who do, preferring to follow his political instincts and patch together compromise measures. Above all, Gorbachev's reluctance to follow through on the path of economic reform can be attributed to his commitment to the preservation of the union. Gorbachev balked when it became clear that reform would involve ceding substantive economic power to the republics.

Gorbachev finally had his new draft union treaty approved by the all-union Supreme Soviet on December 3, 1990. However, five republics indicated that they would refuse to accept the treaty, and continue to insist on the legitimacy of their sovereignty decrees. Rather than accepting Gorbachev's formula of "a strong centre and strong republics", the republics seem to want a horizontal union of equals. Similarly, the Council of the Federation approved the 1991 plan in January, but Lithuania and Moldavia immediately announced that they would refuse to accept it (and others may follow).

In sum, one can conclude that economics took a back seat to politics in the late 1980s and early 1990s. No more progress with reform plans is likely until the political situation stabilizes. Most of the reform models being offered by Western specialists are flawed because they are built around the assumptions of a unified market, the common interests of the republics, and a strong central government with effective instruments for the implementation of the programme. These assumptions do not describe the current reality of the USSR, and one can argue that they have never really been characteristic of the Soviet economic system.

The situation in the republics

In view of the stalemate in Moscow's reform efforts, and given the breakdown in the system of supplies, the republics began looking for ways to insulate themselves from the mounting economic chaos as 1990 progressed. In what appears to be the creeping "Balkanization" of the Soviet economy, firms and regional administrations have been ignoring state orders and reneging on negotiated contracts. Teams of representatives from republics and city soviets have fanned out into other regions, and even into Eastern Europe, arranging barter deals: oil for textiles, coal for food, etc.

From June 1 the *Moscow* city soviet, under the control of radicals since March 1990, restricted sales of food and key consumer goods to residents. In retaliation, neighbouring provinces cut back on food deliveries, triggering the winter food crisis in the capital. The Baltic republics nominally introduced "regional self-management" on January 1, 1990, but have faced a hard struggle to turn this into a reality. *Lithuania* found itself under an economic blockade after its declaration of independence in March 1990, and its GNP fell by over 10% as a result. Ryzhkov threatened all three Baltic states with a blockade in November 1990, when they refused to accept his draft of the 1991 plan. *Estonia* has been the most active in trying to carve out its economic independence. It is taking steps to introduce its own currency, the kroon, and approved foreign currency as legal tender in December 1990. Estonia raised food prices by 225% in July, and then in August imposed border controls and a ban on all grain exports, to prevent store shelves from being stripped by buyers from Leningrad and Belorussia. Similar bans on the export of food and consumer goods were introduced in Lithuania in September, and in *Kazakhstan* in October. *Ukraine* froze all above-plan grain deliveries outside the republic, and took a step towards issuing a parallel currency on November 4. Coupons were issued to residents alongside their regular pay cheques, which had to be used when buying food or consumer goods. The republics of *Central Asia* had few exports to ban: 90% of their manufactured goods are imported. These regions were already the poorest in the USSR, and have slipped still further behind during the current economic slowdown. *Turkmenistan* is now officially posting an unemployment rate of 19% (compared to a national rate of 1.5%).

All the republics in varying decrees have tried to block or delay many of the emergency stabilization measures introduced by Gorbachev: Uzbekistan refused to raise food prices, for example. Of course, the strikes and civil violence which have plagued many regions of Central Asia and the Caucasus have played havoc with economic life, and has created the additional burden of 600,000 refugees who must be housed and fed.

There are limits to the autonomy which the republics can exercise in the present situation. The vast bulk of Soviet industrial plants remain subordinate to ministries or all-union associations based in Moscow. For example, 60% of the plants in the Ukraine are outside the jurisdiction of republican ministries. Secondly, although the locus of executive political power may have shifted to the republics, after 60 years of central planning their economies remain heavily interdependent. In most republics, 40–60% of GNP is traded with other regions. Russia and the Ukraine are nearest to self-sufficiency, trading 18% and 35% of GNP respectively (although the Ukraine, for example, has to import 42% of its energy needs). Only Russia, the Ukraine, Belorussia, Georgia and Azerbaidzhan have a surplus in current ruble prices. Using dollar prices, it is possible that only Russia would have a surplus (because of its energy exports).

Macroeconomic stabilization

The question of the macroeconomic balance of the economy has been surprisingly downplayed by Soviet reform economists, while it has come to dominate the thinking of the central leadership. This oversight is unfortunate, as one of the most striking features

---

Table 3: Macroeconomic data

	value in 1989, billion rubles
Official national income	950
Shadow economy	50–150
Government budget:	
expenditures	483
deficit	81
Money supply	
M1 (cash)	110
M2 (cash plus savings deposits)	357
M3 (M2 plus enterprise funds)	704

	%
Estimates of growth in 1990:	
average monthly wage	10.0
average household income	14.5
M1	21.4
M2	15.3
national income (official estimate)	–2.0
(unofficial estimate)	–4.0

Source: W. Nordhaus, "Growth in national output in the Soviet Union", unpublished paper, Yale University, January 1991 (used with the author's permission).

---

of *perestroika* was the breakdown of the tight control over monetary variables which Soviet governments had successfully exercised for decades. Money supply (M1) was allowed to rise by 55% between June 1987 and June 1990 (see Table 3).

The government alerted the public to the problem of the yawning budget deficit in October 1988. Even so, monetary emissions continued to accelerate. The financial plan allowed for the printing of R 10 billion in 1990: in the end, R 25 billion were issued. It can be argued that by mid-1990 the government's main concern was to regain budgetary balance, and it was this, and not a desire to introduce a market economy, which dominated their approach to the formulation of a recovery programme.

Between 1985 and 1988 government spending rose by a fairly modest 5.5%. The main problem was that revenues were declining, because of falling oil prices, a slump in alcohol taxes of R 7 billion a year, and a collapse in profits in many industrial and agricultural enterprises. (See Table 4 for a summary of the budget deficit 1985–90.)

However, balancing the budget necessitates spending cuts, since the taxation system is not capable of generating additional revenue in its present form, and is in need of complete overhaul. The turnover tax is a crude revenue vehicle being calculated in ruble amounts, rather than *ad valorem*, and varying from sector to sector. Turnover tax is being reduced, while a basic profits tax of 45% has been introduced, and payroll taxes are likely to increase from 10% to 30%. A new retail sales tax of 5% was introduced from January 1, 1991, on all goods except food.

Table 4:   Soviet federal government budget deficit as % of
GDP

1985	2.5
1986	6.0
1987	7.5
1988	11.0
1989	13.0
1990	9.0

Source: IMF/World Bank Report, *The Economy of the USSR*, Washington D.C., 1990, p. 5.

The process of balancing the budget for 1991 was complicated by the breakdown of relations between the centre and the republics. After much political bluster and bickering, the Federation Council finally agreed to the budget for 1991 on January 3, 1991. In December, the RSFSR parliament had initially offered a mere R 23 billion to the federal budget, plus R 56 billion in royalties from resource extraction. This proposed contribution of R 79 billion fell far short of the R 142 billion which Russia had handed over in 1990.

The new federal budget for 1991 will see a considerable devolution of activity to the republics. The federal budget aims to spend R 250 billion, and run a R 27 billion deficit. R 4.9 billion will go the KGB, and R 97 billion will be spent on defence, of which R 46 billion will be devoted to weapons expenditure (a 15% reduction). The largest cut has been in capital investment — 20%, down to R 45 billion. Subsidies to industrial and agricultural enterprises have crept up by 5% a year for the past five years, and stand at roughly R 115 billion. (Some estimates run as high as R 150 billion.) For 1991 they will be split between the federal and republican budgets, in a manner which is not yet clear.

Economists spent much of 1989–90 discussing ways of tackling the ruble overhang of R 400 billion or so in circulation, in cash and in savings accounts, which is the equivalent of 12 months of retail turnover. The overhang was caused by enterprises granting excessive wage increases, while being kept afloat by government subsidies. Much of the overhang is circulating in the "black economy", which Soviet economist A. Shults estimated is equal to one quarter of legal consumer spending, or R 90–110 billion a year. (Of this he attributed R 30 billion to black market sales, and R 20 billion to the resale of illegal imports.)

Proposed solutions to the overhang ranged from the introduction of a new currency, possibly tied to gold or the dollar, to administrative measures to freeze savings deposits and enterprise funds. Most economists argued against a confiscatory money reform. Data showed that the 2,300,000 savings accounts with more than R 10,000 only contain 10% of total deposits. In order to make serious inroads into the ruble overhang, the accounts of small savers would also have to be frozen. This would be clearly unjust, and would enrage the public.

In the end, Gorbachev abruptly took action in January 1991, removing 50-and 100-ruble notes from circulation and allowing people to exchange the notes they hold only up to the equivalent of one month's salary. Withdrawals from savings accounts were also limited to R 500 a month. The withdrawal of notes was supposed to be aimed at black marketeers, but in fact they had long ago moved their cash into small bills or hard currency. Initial estimates are that this measure removed a mere R 8 billion from circulation.

Key Economic Sectors

Overall Soviet performance since 1985 has been disappointing, but neither the official Soviet data nor CIA reconstructions of that data show evidence of a complete economic collapse. The USSR has not yet experienced the sort of slump which hit Poland in 1980–81 and 1988–89, where real incomes fell by more than 25% in a single year. However, Soviet data is so unreliable that the situation may turn out to be worse than the data suggest. In particular, factories have been artificially maintaining their output figures through disguised price inflation, for example by withdrawing underpriced items from production. (Table 5 gives a summary of economic performance in 1990.)

Overall estimates are that Net Material Product was 4% down in 1990. Industry was down by 1.5%, agriculture was roughly constant, and transport and construction were 5% down. Some consumer industries expanded considerably: colour TV production, for example, rose 14%. The overall decline in NMP was partially offset by a rise in services, such that GDP is around 2% down. Oil production peaked at 4.6 billion barrels in 1988, and fell by 5% in 1989 and 1990.

The real loser has been *capital investment*. Net fixed investment was slashed by about 5% per year in 1988 and 1989, and by 20% in 1990. Soviet industry could not afford such cuts, since the average age of their industrial machinery is around 20 years — more than double the average age of equipment in Western factories. One official reported that the defence industries which took over the plants of the Ministry of Light Industry in 1988 found that 60% of the machinery was simply unusable. The abrupt cutback in capital investment has exacerbated the chronic Soviet problem of uncompleted projects, and has left many major sites hanging in the air. For example, R 1 billion has been sunk into the *Yelabuga*

Table 5:   Soviet economic performance in 1990

	1990 as % of 1989
Gross national product	98.0
National income produced	96.0
Labour productivity	97.0
Industrial production	98.8
Agricultural production	97.7
Salaries of workers and office staff	111.0
Foreign trade turnover	93.1

Source: *Ekonomika i zhizn'*, no. 5, 1991, p. 9.

car manufacturer, but it is still years from completion. The construction completion rate fell from 59% in 1988 to 40% in 1989.

These cutbacks in central spending have severely affected the performance of Soviet science and technology. The vast network of research institutes were funded on the state budget, and were ill-prepared to adjust to the new requirement that they be "cost accounting", i.e. generate their own revenues to cover their costs. There has been an exodus of research professionals: either literally, to Israel and the USA, or to jobs in the co-operative sector, where salaries are two to five times higher than in state institutes.

The environment

The USSR faces huge environmental problems: Chernobyl, the devastation of the Aral sea, and hundreds of chemical and industrial plants pouring unfiltered pollutants into the atmosphere and water supply. An Academy of Sciences report classified 16% of the territory as being "ecological disaster" zones. The country is 30 years behind the West when it comes to developing the technical, legal and economic measures necessary to cope with these problems. In the short run this shows up in the waste of energy and materials and the despoilation of land; and in human terms greater morbidity and mortality and a lower quality of life overall.

Only slow progress is being made in developing the tools to cope with the ecological problems. However, political forces have mobilized over the environmental issue, and have demanded immediate action. Most often, this has taken the form of terminating new projects or closing down existing polluting plants.

Many new and existing forestry, chemical and energy projects have run into stiff opposition from the new environmentalist groups. Many of the local soviets newly elected in March 1990 have supported these campaigns, and it is estimated that over 1,000 polluting plants have been closed, usually over the objections of the central ministries. For example, opposition from the Kuibyshev soviet prevented the commissioning of the new facility in Chapaevsk which was supposed to destroy chemical weapons in accordance with the new US-Soviet agreement on the subject. The construction of 40 to 50 nuclear power stations has been halted by popular opposition. In fact, no new nuclear plant has been commissioned since Chernobyl in 1986.

Manufacturing industry

The monopoly problem. The problem of monopoly is severe, and has barely been broached by reform economists. In a vain attempt to make their job easier, planners preferred to concentrate the production of a given product in a single factory. Reliable figures are hard to come by, but there seems general agreement that some 30–40% of output comes from single producers. A total of 180 engineering plants produce 80% of the country's machine tools, for example. According to one set of semi-official estimates, 90% of output of the following goods was concentrated as follows:

in a single plant: sewing machines, automatic washing machines, trolleys, forklift trucks, diesel locomotives, tram rails, concrete mixers, cooking equipment.
in two plants: hydraulic turbines, steam turbines, tin plate, stainless steel pipe, freezers.

One negative consequence of the monopoly structure is already being felt. The extreme concentration of production makes the economy extremely vulnerable to supply breakdowns in a single plant, which are in turn exacerbated by the overloaded transport system and the emergence of inter-regional trade barriers. Against the background of the general goods shortage and consumer hoarding behaviour, this has triggered repeated crises in the distribution system. The soap shortage of mid-1989, and the cigarette panic of mid-1990, were respectively triggered by technical breakdowns and strike activity at chemical plants and a cigarette wrapping factory in the Caucasus.

However, the main worry arising from this monopoly structure is that firms will respond to the liberalization of central controls by raising prices and cutting output. Much of the 4% plus decline in industrial output in 1990 can probably be attributed to this sort of behaviour by managers.

Reformers respond to this point in one of two ways. Some suggest opening the Soviet economy to foreign competition, so as to force domestic producers to sell at competitive prices. The danger with this, of course, is that the vast majority of Soviet producers would prove unable to compete. Output would slump, imports would mushroom, the ruble would plummet, and hyper-inflation would take hold.

The second response of reform economists is to argue that price liberalization cannot be delayed, and that there is simply no time to try to devise a programme to demonopolize the economy. Even to try to maintain price controls to prevent profiteering is unwise, since it would merely give the bureaucrats an excuse to continue their stifling controls. In any case, ministry planners are so inefficient that they would probably be unable to distinguish between efficient enterprises and those charging excessive prices. Monopoly distortions are likely to be no worse than ministry distortions, and will hopefully be reduced as competition picks up.

In January 1991 the government created an Anti-monopoly Committee, and promises to set about "demonopolizing" Soviet industry. They seem to be taking US anti-trust structures as a model, which could be a mistake. In the USA, the focus of anti-trust is on excessive prices. In the USSR, prices are only a reflection of far deeper structural problems: enormous barriers to entry for new firms, the lack of a market and transport infrastructure, and so forth. Simply regulating prices will do nothing to tackle these problems, and may even make it more difficult for new competitors to enter the market.

New ownership structures. Reformers concur on the need to remove enterprises from the *diktat* of the central ministries, but are uncertain as to what ownership structure to put in the place of the centralized system.

In 1988 enterprises began to sign "leases" (*arendy*) with their ministry, instead of being directly employed by them. A work collective which converts itself into a "leaseholder" benefits from lower taxation and more lax wage controls. Leased firms almost always see an increase in wages: in some cases productivity rises and employment falls. Their big advantage over co-operatives is that they remain under the legal protection of their ministry, and are allocated supplies under the central plan, although the latter is an advantage of diminishing value. (See Table 6.)

Even among the more radical advocates of changing the ownership structure, the talk is of "destatization" (*razgosudarstvlenie*), rather than privatization. Both ministries and enterprises are looking for ways to give themselves more autonomy. Ministries are trying to convert themselves into "consortia", along the lines of holding companies, although there is

---

Table 6   Leasing of state enterprises to work collectives

	No. of enterprises	% of turnover
Industry	2,100	4.6
Construction	800	3.6
Trade and catering	24,000	10.6
Services	1,700	7.3

Source: *Ekonomika i zhizn'*, no. 49, December 1990, p. 3.

---

little expectation at this stage that private share ownership will become an important feature of the reform.

Since October 1988 enterprises have been allowed to issue shares (*aktsii*), their goals being to raise revenue and, in certain cases, to circumvent wage controls. The creation of joint stock companies is proceeding slowly, as their precise legal status is obscure, and was only partially clarified by a Council of Ministers' decree of June 19, 1990. A State Property Agency is to be created to supervise the conversion of enterprises into joint stock companies (JSCs). Enterprises primarily seek the status of a JSC as a way of escaping ministerial control. It does not usually involve a change in management, or the generation of significant additional capital. Shares are usually sold to the workers, and amount to a form of pay incentive.

However, the motives for creating a JSC can vary. For example, 70 firms in Latvia turned themselves into JSCs because their predominantly Russian workforces wanted to escape from the jurisdiction of the Latvian government. Similarly, Russian-dominated enterprises in Estonia were united in the "Integral" association in July 1990.

Finance

The banking system, and accounting practices in general, are among the most poorly developed components of the Soviet economic system. A massive amount of training and restructuring will have to be done before the financial infrastructure can sustain profit-seeking enterprises, and there is little sign that this is happening.

In the meantime, the state banking system consists of the following institutions: Gosbank, the Savings Bank, the Foreign Trade Bank, the Housing and Social Construction Bank, the Industry and Construction Bank, and the Agriculture Bank. Since the Law on Co-operatives of 1988, some 600 single-branch commercial banks have sprung up. There has been considerable chaos and licence in the supervision of these banks, which (it has been estimated) poured an additional R 25 billion into the economy in 1989. In the course of 1990 Gosbank began tightening its control, intervening and closing some banks (e.g. the Russian Commercial Bank, in July). In an attempt to stem credit creation the reserve ratio was increased from 5% to 10% on August 1, and interest rates were raised from 3–4% to 9–10% on November 1, 1990 (still way below the rate of inflation). Gosbank has redoubled its efforts to keep control of monetary flows out of the hands of republican authorities. For example, the Kiev city council set up special shops to sell consumer goods at free prices (five to six times higher than those in state shops). The scheme was considered a resounding success — until Gosbank stepped in and seized all the profits.

From 1988 on the central financial authorities began to lose control over enterprise accounts. The last two years have seen a boom in inter-enterprise credits (18% in 1988), and the seepage of funds from non-cash (*beznalichnye*) accounts into wage funds. The proportion of wages paid out in bonuses and special payments rose from 25% in 1980 to 42% in 1990; and the ratio of rise in wages to the rise in productivity fell from 0.68 in 1987 to 1.6 in 1988 and 5.8 in 1990.

October 1989 saw the introduction of a confiscatory tax on enterprises which grant wage increases above 3%. This had an immediate impact in curtailing wage increases, and helps explain why wages only rose 10% in 1990, considerably below the rate of inflation. This tax is a very blunt instrument, however, which will undermine the viability of state enterprises and accelerate the exodus of workers into the co-operative sector and the black economy.

In theory, the long run economic reform programme envisions the transformation of state enterprises into joint-stock companies (see above). In practice, the stock issued thus far is held by employees and is not tradeable. Some very halting steps have thus been taken with a view to the creation of a capital market. In December 1990 a stock exchange was due to open in Moscow (although the opening was then postponed for a year), and small stock and commodity exchanges already exist in Leningrad, Ryazan, Novosibirsk and Chelyabinsk.

The military sector

In a dramatic speech to the United Nations in December 1988, Gorbachev announced that the USSR would cut defence spending by 14.2%, and military procurement by 19.5%. Since then, much attention has been given to the campaign to convert military plants to civilian production. The idea of conversion was not in principle a new one. For many years, a majority of many types of consumer durables (cameras, motorcycles, sewing machines, etc.) were produced in plants run by one of the five defence ministries. Defence plants have their own, integrated, priority supply system, and for some time central planners had pondered how to utilize the superior management performance of the defence sector to aid the hard-pressed Soviet consumer.

During *perestroika*, concrete steps towards transferring this expertise began to occur. For example, in January 1987 the defence sector's system of outside quality controllers was extended to all industries. In March 1988 the Ministry of Light Industry and Household Appliances was closed down, and its 220 enterprises transferred to defence ministries.

This process accelerated after Gorbachev's December 1988 speech. Civilian goods produced by defence plants totalled R 27 billion in 1989, accounting for 40% of the sector's total output, and rose by 9% p.a. in 1988–90. In the 1991 plan they are scheduled to rise by 18%. However, contrary to initial hopes, conversion has not proceeded according to an orderly central plan. Defence plants were abruptly transferred to a cost-accounting basis in January 1989. Major plants suddenly found their contracts for helicopters, missiles or tanks cut by 50%, and scrambled to find alternative sources of income. In the short run, many plants have tried to survive by trading the machinery and semi-finished products they have at their disposal. A national conversion plan was not issued until September 28, 1990, and efforts to steer defence industries in certain directions have been crude and ineffective, almost farcical. The press is replete with examples such as an Uzbek missile plant being converted to ice-cream production, or the Ministry of Medium Machine-Building (which produces nuclear weapons) being given responsibility for cheesemaking equipment.

Defence plants have little knowledge of the needs of civilian customers, and are used to functioning as part of an integrated hierarchy rather than acting independently. It is estimated that these plants would need R 10–50 billion in new investments if they were really to be converted to the mass production of consumer goods. Needless to say, such funds are not forthcoming, and in the interim conversion has not had a significant impact on the production of consumer goods.

Co-operatives

The euphoria about the scope for the growth of a vibrant private sector from below has subsided since the adoption of the Law on Individual Labour Activity in 1986, and the Law on Co-operatives in 1988. Even while they show great willingness to use the services of co-operatives, a large proportion of the Soviet public, and the majority of Soviet officials, have been hostile to the co-operative sector, for several reasons.

First, private economic activity, particularly buying and selling, is considered to be intrinsically unjust, although necessity may dictate its acceptance within certain limits. Of course, officials may be objecting because the co-operatives undermine their own powers and privileges. The second objection one encounters is that co-operatives serve as a cover for laundering wealth illegally acquired through black market operations. Finally, a more recent complaint is that privileged officials are using the new co-operative and leasing arrangements to "convert" their old bureaucratic power into market-based wealth. Bureaucrats arrange joint ventures in which their children obtain lucrative positions, or a factory transforms itself into a co-operative, thereby cutting its tax burden and evading wage limits. 1990 saw the exposure of the *ANT* scandal, in which a co-operative exported an assortment of valuable raw materials and army tanks outside of the official foreign trade channels.

Thus, despite the formal legalization of co-operative and private entrepreneurs, local authorities have been given considerable leeway in regulating co-operative and private-sector activity. More than 3,000 different sets of rules are now applied to co-operatives in different cities, including price controls. In December 1988 rules were tightened to bar co-operatives from such politically sensitive and/or lucrative areas of activity as publishing, medical care, jewellery and precious metals.

Nevertheless, by October 1990 there were 215,000 co-operatives, and including individual workers accounted for 5,200,000 workers (4% of the total labour force). Many of their employees, perhaps more than half, also keep a job in the state sector. The state job serves as insurance against possible closure, and may provide access to food and housing. Co-operatives generated R 40.3 billion in 1989 and R 27.3 billion in the first six months of 1990 (5.7% of national income). Only R 4.8 billion of their income stemmed from the manufacture of consumer goods, and the bulk of the remainder comes partly from consumer services but mainly from buying and selling of industrial inputs.

Outright sales of state or local council enterprises to co-operatives have been proceeding rather slowly. As of June 1990 3.5% of shops (21,000), 3.2% of cafes (9,000) and 7.1% of service outlets (13,000) had been sold to co-operatives or private owners.

Personal consumption

Soviet consumers are suffering, but it is hard to calibrate just how badly their situation has deteriorated. *Per capita* GDP in 1990 stood at R 3,200 ($1,750, at the official commercial exchange rate). The average wage earner earns 280 rubles a month, and finds it difficult to make ends meet. More than 30% of income is spent on food, and ownership of more advanced consumer items remains at low levels (only 5% of families have a car, and there are only 10 phone lines per 1,000 inhabitants). Thus the USSR has the sort of consumption pattern usually associated with a middle-level third world country, such as Mexico.

During the first three years of *perestroika*, Western economists criticized Gorbachev for continuing to pour massive investments into the machine tool sector in the vain hope that this would "accelerate" the Soviet economy. 1989 finally saw a shift of emphasis in the central plan towards satisfying consumer demand. The 1990 plan called for a R 66 billion increase in consumer goods production, compared to R 17 billion in previous years. The avowed aim is to increase consumption from 40% to 65% of GNP by 1995. In parallel to these trends, in the early years of *perestroika* imports of consumer goods fell from 15% of total sales in 1985 to 12% in 1987, but in 1989 and 1990 the USSR began making extensive purchases abroad.

In the short run, retail turnover has shown a substantial increase, from R 340 billion in 1987 to R 430 billion in 1990, but it is hard to know what has really been happening to living standards. A CIA estimate is that while 50% of food items were routinely available in state stores in 1984, the proportion had fallen to below 25% by 1989. Of 220 food items monitored by central authorities, only 24 were regularly available in 1988, and 10 in 1989. In 1990 the decline continued, and spread, finally, to Moscow and Leningrad. In 1989, of 1,000 consumer goods monitored by central authorities, only 57 were described as regularly available in state stores. By 1990 the number had fallen to four. Meat and butter began to be distributed through ration coupons in some provincial cities 10 years ago, and sugar has been universally rationed since 1988. By the end of 1990 rationing had spread to nearly all cities. Leningrad introduced rationing of meat and dairy products in December 1990. However, in many cases rationing does not alter the situation, since city authorities often cannot even obtain the supplies to cover the ration requirements.

However, it may be misleading to judge food consumption solely on the basis of availability in stores. A large proportion of food and consumer goods is sold to employees at their place of work through the system of special orders (*zakazy*). Reliance on the *zakaz* system seems to have increased in the last two years, but little reliable data on this system is available. The official trade union now collects its own cost-of-living data. It estimates that 40% of food is distributed through the *zakaz* system, and that food prices inflated by 7% in 1990 (against a government estimate of 2%). Thus, despite the empty store shelves, large-scale malnutrition does not seem to be a realistic proposition at the present time (although Soviet diets have been poor for years, which undoubtedly contributes to the high morbidity and mortality rates).

It is very difficult to estimate the level of retail inflation in the Soviet economy, since goods are rationed by availability, not price, and are often resold illicitly at higher prices. The official retail price index rose 7% in 1990, but other estimates range as high as 80%. Prices in the farm markets for food did not rise rapidly between 1985 and 1989, but seem to have risen from 200% of the state price up to 300% during 1990. Another worrying sign is the apparently increasing "dollarization" of the economy. According to William Nordhaus of Yale, the estimated value of dollars in circulation as a proportion of rubles (M1) rose from 8% in July 1990 to 40% in November 1990.

Apart from the question of the availability of goods in stores, the infrastructure of stores and warehouses themselves leaves a great deal to be desired. Only 7% of the workforce is engaged in retailing (less than half that of Western societies), and packaging, handling and advertising operations are primitive and starved of investment.

Labour and social issues

Strikes. July 1989 saw half-a-million coal miners strike for higher pay and benefits, improved consumer supplies, and more economic independence. The strikes of Kuzbass and Donbass were the most dramatic development in working-class politics in the USSR since the 1920s, and the government scurried to limit the damage by promising to address the miners' demands. The short-term, immediate demands were met (the hasty dispatch of meat and medical supplies, bonus increases, etc.). However, a commission set up to bring the mines full economic autonomy ran foul of bureaucratic confusion and mounting economic chaos. In the course of the year the miners became increasingly radicalized. They developed strong local organizations which seized control of regional soviets (particularly in the Kuzbass), but have been less successful in creating a national organization. Not until November 1990 did they finally agree to break with the official union and form a new, independent miners' union.

Also, the unrest of the miners did not trigger extensive labour unrest in other sectors. The exception is ethnically-related unrest in the Baltic and Caucasus, which led to the loss of 7,000,000 workdays in 1989.

However, there were some work stoppages or strike threats in the steel and oil industries. In January 1990 wholesale energy prices were raised, which ate into the profits of heavy energy users, like steel mills. Iron and steel workers around the country threatened strike action to protect their bonuses. The government caved in, agreeing to pay additional subsidies to affected industries. Then in March 1990 oil workers in the Tyumen region, which produces 60% of the USSR's oil and gas, threatened to cut production by 15% if consumer supplies were not improved and the price of oil raised. Like the miners, they noted the discrepancy between the internal price of oil (R 30 a tonne) and the international price ($100–150).

Unemployment. The mass lay-offs which had been predicted after the introduction of enterprise "cost accounting" in 1988 did not apparently materialize. Unemployment currently stands at some 2,000,000 (1.5% of the workforce), and is heavily concentrated in Central Asia. In 1987 the government had begun preparing for the appearance of large scale unemployment, by creating a national network of employment offices. In June 1990 Ryzhkov predicted that unemployment would rapidly rise to 6–8,000,000 if his "regulated market" reform was implemented. The preservation of the archaic wage tariff system is also seen as a way of protecting lower-paid workers and enforcing equity. There is little evidence that it works that way in practice, but it most definitely constrains managers trying to improve worker incentives.

1990 saw something of a reactivation of the official trade union organization, which adopted a new federal structure in March, and became a vociferous advocate of the interests of workers and the poor. One setback for them was the amended Law on

State Enterprise of June 1990, which removed the right of work collectives to elect their managers. In December 1990 a new trade union law guaranteed three months' notice in the event of a plant closure, but declined to give the trade unions any veto power over such decisions. Redundant workers were to receive one month's severance pay, then unemployment benefits from their local council for 18 months (at 70% of pay, declining to 50% after three months).

Poverty and welfare. Under *glasnost'* the Soviet public have become newly aware of the degree of poverty within their society. For example, economists have shown that the current price subsidy system does not in fact work to the benefit of the poor, as had been widely assumed. Most of the food subsidies go on meat, but poor families do not eat meat. This concern over poverty has been redoubled by fears that market reform may lead to mass unemployment and inflation which would hit those on fixed incomes. The official poverty line as of 1990 was R 75 a month — and has been widely criticized as being too low. Meat, for example, costs R 20 a kilo in peasant markets in Moscow. The newspaper *Sotsialisticheskaya industriya* suggested a poverty line of R 125 in 1988. Data indicate that at least 30,000,000 people are living below the official poverty line. Much of the poverty is concentrated in the country's pensioners. In 1989, 20,000,000 of the nation's 58,000,000 pensioners were living in families where at least one adult was receiving the minimum pension of R 50 (see Table 7).

Table 7:   Average *per capita* income distribution
(rubles per month, 1988)

Rubles/month	Individuals (millions)
0–75	38
76–100	45
101–125	51
126–150	45
151–175	35
176–200	26
201–250	28
251 plus	21

As part of the preparations for market reform, August 1990 saw a generous but expensive overhaul of the pension and welfare systems, which had been created in 1956 and were clearly outdated. Benefits were improved (for example, the minimum pension was raised from R 50 a month to R 70), and eligibility conditions relaxed. Unfortunately, of course, the market reform programme was not adopted — but the welfare reform went through anyway, at considerable burden to the state budget.

All the variants of market reform discussed in 1990 included plans for near-full compensation for consumers for any retail price increases. The December 1990 Gorbachev programme envisions 100% indexation for those on fixed incomes and 50–70% for wage-earners. The government rejects compensating consumers for price increases in alcohol, tobacco and luxury goods.

Agriculture

Agriculture remains a weak link in the Soviet economy. Farming still occupies 19% of the labour force, something like 30% of investment over the past decade was poured into agriculture and related industries, and yet 40% of farms run at a loss, draining R 95 billion from the state budget each year. Moreover, the output of these farms is unable to satisfy consumers' needs. Private plots continue to account for about one quarter of Soviet food production (with a value of R 50 billion in 1988), including two-thirds of all animal production.

The recent problems cannot be attributed to bad luck with the weather. In fact, the USSR has seen several years of reasonable harvests, with production in the last five years being 15% up over the first half of the decade. The grain crop has fluctuated as follows:

1987	211 mn tonnes
1988	195 mn tonnes
1989	211 mn tonnes
1990	215 mn tonnes

Deficiencies in the transport and storage systems, however, mean that 20–40% of the crop is lost en route to market. The giant administrative agency *Gosagroprom* was abolished in March 1989, and republican and regional authorities took on responsibility for food procurement. The new system meant more food was kept in the localities. In 1989, grain deliveries to state purchasers stood at only 59,000,000 tonnes, against a plan target of 86,000,000.

Throughout the past three years, the USSR has continued to spend heavily on grain imports, bringing in some 35,000,000 tonnes a year. Although the grain harvest was good in 1990, meat and milk deliveries did fall, as did vegetable production (by 15%).

For the most part, central and provincial authorities have obstinately clung to their traditional administrative methods for running the agricultural sector. In July 1990, party committees were ordered to mobilize resources for the harvest, and many regions declared themselves harvest emergency zones. A Council of Ministers' decree ordered all enterprises to send 15% of their trucks and drivers to help with the harvest. These measures belie the statements of Gorbachev and others that the central leadership wants to step back from detailed management of the economy.

In marked contrast to the Chinese pattern, where the first reform measures adopted were aimed at improving the food supply, Gorbachev avoided a serious look at the agricultural question until 1988. 1986 saw some liberalization of the restrictions on the sale of produce in the "free markets", and collective farms were encouraged to contract out work to family "links". In March 1988 Gorbachev launched a drive to expand the contract system, arguing that families should be granted leases of up to 50 years. Only a few tens of thousands of peasants opted to take advantage of these lease arrangements, although they would seem to hold great promise for improving livestock rearing. Peasants are uncertain as to the future availability of credit and supplies, and fear possible future reversals in state policy. Also, in most areas, farm chairmen and regional officials actively obstructed the reforms.

Much to the disappointment of reform advocates, the March 1989 Central Committee plenum on agriculture backed away from radical reform, and opted basically to preserve the collective farm system. When the new land law was finally introduced in the USSR

Supreme Soviet in February 1990, it stopped short of legalizing the buying and selling of land. Instead it merely allowed lifetime leasing of land, with rights of inheritance for heirs. Similarly, the land laws passed in the Russian, Ukrainian and Belorussian republics in December 1990, also failed to legalize the buying and selling of land between individuals. Under the RSFSR law, farmers who "buy" land can sell it after 10 years — but only to the state! In Estonia, farm privatization is proceeding more rapidly.

A central problem is the weakness of economic incentives to farmers, since the procurement prices paid by the state do not cover the costs of production. In August 1989 a new programme was introduced, involving hard currency payments to farmers for above-plan deliveries. It was ineffectively administered and had a minimal impact. In December 1989, R 74 billion of farm debts were written off, easing the burden on the inefficient producers but of little help to the productive farms. In May 1990, the grain procurement price paid to farmers was increased by 50% (from R 196 per tonne to R 300) — although the Supreme Soviet subsequently refused to triple the retail price of bread. Unfortunately, even the new price of R 300 was still substantially below the cost of production, and less than the price grain was fetching on the free market (R 1,000). The central government declined to raise the procurement price for meat, since without retail price increases this would merely increase the need for subsidies and worsen the budget deficit. In October 1990 the RSFSR parliament tried to increase the meat procurement price of its own accord. The Ukraine has also tried to raise its procurement prices, complaining that they are arbitrarily fixed by Moscow at around 75% of the standard prices paid in the RSFSR.

Foreign Economic Relations

Trade flows and foreign debt

The Soviet economy has developed in a highly autarkic manner. Only around 15% of Soviet GNP is traded, and Soviet external trade accounts for just 4% of total world trade (below the level of Russia in 1913). This relative under-development of the USSR's trade potential, and the overall weakness of the Soviet economy, suggests that there is great room for trade expansion — and yet this has not yet been happening. As shall be shown in subsequent sections, this is because there are still severe organizational impediments to freer trade.

The USSR remains locked in a trade pattern characteristic of a developing country, exporting raw materials and importing finished goods. Although the USSR produces a wide range of manufactured goods at low cost, for the most part they are of sub-standard quality and technologically outmoded. Total Soviet exports in 1990 were roughly $110 billion, of which $16–18 billion were weapons, $4 billion gold, and $70 billion oil and gas. (This involves attaching rough dollar estimates to CMEA trade.) At 11 million barrels a day, the USSR accounts for 20% of world oil production. More than 75% of Soviet imports are industrial machinery, the remainder being food and consumer goods. Traditionally, 50–60% of its trade was with fellow members of the Council for Mutual Economic Assistance (CMEA or Comecon), and 12–15% with developing countries. US-

Table 8: Foreign trade turnover (billion rubles)

Total turnover		Exports	Imports
1984	140	74	65
1985	142	73	69
1986	131	68	63
1987	129	68	61
1988	132	67	65
1989	141	69	72

Source: Vneshnyaya torgovlya, various years.

Soviet trade, for example, amounted to $3.6 billion in 1989, about the same as trade between the USA and Haiti.

As Table 8 indicates, the external trade balance stood at around plus $5 billion in 1986–88, but plunged to minus $5 billion in 1990 due to a 12% fall in exports (in value terms) and inability or unwillingness to rein in imports. In 1989 R 37 billion was set aside for emergency purchases of consumer goods in the West (soap, razors, cassettes, shoes, etc.) — a sum equal to 10% of consumer spending.

Exports fell due to a decline in domestic oil output, and because the oil price charged to members of CMEA, based on a five-year moving average, was still falling. (The world oil price went from $27 a barrel in 1985 to $10 in 1986 and $17 in 1989.) Estimates of the impact of the slump in oil prices in the late 1980s are in the range of R 40 billion, or $20–25 billion. Despite the rally in oil prices in 1990, the trade balance will probably continue to be negative, because specialists are predicting a 17–25% fall in Soviet oil production in 1991.

External debt climbed from $29 billion in 1985 to $54 billion in 1989, with debt service accounting for 25% of hard currency export earnings. It is predicted to rise to $60 billion in 1991. In March 1990 there was a flurry of reports of missed payments to foreign suppliers, and Western bankers estimated that the USSR was up to $400 million behind in debt repayments. This was probably due to administrative confusion rather than inability to meet their obligations: a debt service ratio of 25% is worrying but not critical. A further complication in foreign trade was that as part of the economic blockade of the Baltic between March and July the Foreign Trade Bank suspended all repayments for enterprises based in the Baltic republics.

The USSR has been courting entry to international economic organizations. In May 1990 they were granted observer status to GATT, but full participation is still a long way off, since this would require price liberalization and the dismantling of the domestic producer subsidy system. In November 1990 the USSR announced it would not be joining the IMF and World Bank, largely because the USSR would have had to lodge $3.5 billion with the IMF as a condition of entry. The USSR is a member of the newly created European Bank for Reconstruction and Development, but the USA is insisting that it not be allowed to be a net borrower from the organization.

Western economic assistance to the USSR in all forms (credits, food shipments, etc.) totalled some $35 billion by the end of 1990. Half of this is tied to the agreement reached with Chancellor Kohl in June 1990 for the removal of Soviet troops from East Germany. In

December 1990 the USA announced its own modest contribution ($1 billion in emergency food aid) and promised to lift the Jackson-Vanik ban on Most Favoured Nation status for the USSR in recognition of the acceleration of Jewish emigration. Imports of consumer goods had been trimmed by 10% in 1989, but throughout 1990 the USSR dipped into its hard currency reserves to buy consumer goods on the world market (such as cigarettes in August). In November 1990 $18 billion in loans were arranged to cover such imports.

A major feature of *perestroika* has, of course, been the slashing back of the USSR's expensive foreign commitments. For example, the USSR buys one third of its sugar from Cuba, at eight times the world price, which is equivalent to a subsidy of $3 billion a year. According to the Rand Corporation, the annual cost of subsidizing client states around the world mushroomed from $6.4 billion in 1971 to $43 billion in 1981, easing back to $29 billion in 1983. This is roughly equivalent to 8.5% of Soviet GNP (far above the average level of aid spending by Western states). Rand estimates that over 10 years the Afghan war cost some $100 billion, and that outstanding debts owed the USSR in 1990 were as follows:

Cuba	$27 bn
Mongolia	$15 bn
Syria	$11 bn
Iraq	$6 bn
Algeria	$4 bn
Vietnam	$15 bn
India	$14 bn
Poland	$8 bn
Afghanistan	$4 bn

The ruble weakens as a currency

In practice, the ruble simply does not function as an international medium of exchange. Trade deals are conducted through an elaborate system of Differentiated Currency Coefficients, which means that the ruble has more than 3,000 shadow exchange rates. In 1990 the ruble lost its value at an accelerating rate. Between the beginning of 1989 and the end of 1990 the black market ruble/dollar exchange rate collapsed from R 5–8 per dollar to R 18–21 per dollar. The tourist rate was devalued in November 1989 from 0.55 to 5.5 rubles/dollar, and a commercial rate of 1.8 was introduced for business transactions. Since November 1989 there have been a dozen auctions where enterprises were authorised to bid for hard currency. In the course of 1990 the price of a dollar at these auctions rose from 15 to 30 rubles.

Currency convertibility became something of a buzzword for radical reformers in 1990. A succession of Western economic teams passed through Moscow, and repeated the neoclassical orthodoxy that protectionism is bad and free trade is good, and that rapid exposure to world market prices will provide the price information which the Soviet economy desperately lacks. There also seemed to be a widespread (and quite erroneous) view that a convertible currency is a necessary symbol of one's membership in the international community of nations. By the end of the year, however, it was clear that the ruble was too weak to be opened up to convertibility. The availability of hard currency would simply drive the ruble out of circulation, and unleash hyper-inflation.

The organization of foreign trade

Plans to liberalize foreign trade have made slow progress. The traditional system involved a monopoly of foreign trade by a small number of Foreign Trade Organizations, all closely controlled by the Ministry of Foreign Trade (MFT). After 1977, certain enterprises had the right to trade directly with firms within the member countries of the Council for Mutual Economic Assistance (CMEA).

A new State Foreign Economic Commission was created in 1987 to oversee the decentralization of the foreign trade system. In that year 100 ministry departments and major enterprises were given the legal right to engage directly in foreign trade, although the MFT kept a legal monopoly over the export of raw materials. By 1989 the number of firms allowed to engage in direct trade had increased to over 11,000, and they were responsible for around a third of Soviet foreign trade. In April 1989 co-operatives were also given the right to conduct foreign trade, and 2,500 had registered by 1990. There was a flurry of scandals arising from dubious import/export deals carried out by co-operatives. For example, the "BIT" co-operative swapped 550 tonnes of titanium for 880 VCRs and 480 PCs. An export licensing system was reintroduced in March 1989, under which only producers, not middlemen, were allowed to export products.

Thus foreign trade remains subject to a complex and frustrating system of export licensing, and controls over foreign currency accounts are still in place. Gorbachev's November 2, 1990 decree seizing 40% of all enterprise hard currency accounts typifies the uncertainty facing companies engaged in foreign trade.

The situation has been still further complicated by the collapse of the Soviet bloc in East Europe. Under the old system, trade deals between CMEA countries were written into national plans, and were notionally paid for in "transferable rubles". Through complicated barter negotiations the assumption was that trade could be balanced: no money actually changed hands within the CMEA system. In January 1990 the transferable ruble accounting system broke down, partly because of the confusion in East Europe (particularly East Germany), and partly because Soviet firms started revoking their contracts with East European suppliers and purchasers. In particular, oil and gas deliveries abruptly dropped by 15–20% of their 1989 levels.

On January 5, 1991, the Council for Mutual Economic Assistance was dissolved, and is to be replaced with a new Organization for International Economic Co-operation. In future, all trade with the former CMEA countries will be conducted in hard currency, or by means of barter deals. In December 1990 the first hard currency deals were signed with Hungarian and Czech firms. In autumn 1990 Hungary and Czechoslovakia negotiated the conversion of their transferable ruble debt into dollars, at a rate of R 0.92 to the dollar.

Joint ventures

The philosophy behind joint ventures (JVs) is simple. The Soviets want access to Western technology, and more importantly Western management skills which can put that technology to effective use. The Western partners' goals are varied. Some operators see a chance to parlay their specialized knowledge and contacts into a quick profit. Others dream of gaining access over the long haul to 300 million Soviet consumers, desperate for Western goods. The most pragmatic entrepreneurs focus their efforts on gaining a slice of the USSR's lucrative raw materials exports.

JVs were legalized in a series of decrees in 1986–87, and are granted a two-year exemption from taxes. Until a new regulation was issued in December 1988, however, foreign partners were limited to a 49% share. JVs still face formidable bureaucratic hurdles, great uncertainty in the regulatory environment in which they operate, and an acute shortage of accommodation and business premises.

A major barrier to the spread of JVs is their inability to convert their ruble profits (which are quite easy to come by) into hard currency. Repatriation of profits remains virtually impossible, despite repeated announcements that a policy change allowing repatriation is imminent. On January 1, 1991, it was announced that foreign firms will be allowed to participate in the ruble/dollar auctions which have been periodically held for the past year (and which were formerly limited to certain Soviet firms). It remains to be seen whether this will actually take place. In the meantime, JVs have to find hard currency revenues of their own, through barter deals or by tapping foreigners inside the USSR. Understandably, Soviet foreign trade organizations have been jealously keeping control over the overseas sale of raw materials. With a handful of exceptions, they have managed to keep them out of the hands of both foreigners and independence-minded republics.

Some 2,000 JVs are now formally registered, but less than 400 are actually conducting business operations. They have capital of $5 billion, and around $1 billion of turnover in 1990, of which exports account for only 10%. More than half of all the JVs are based in Moscow. Only a few dozen JVs are actually involved in manufacturing activity, such as a Finnish-Estonian shoe plant, or the 35 *Pepsi Co.* bottling plants. About 14% are German, 13% Finnish, 8% Italian, 7% Austrian, and only 6% American.

January 1990 saw the first Macdonalds opening in Moscow, and its four-hour queues became a fixed feature of Pushkin Square. Macdonalds sank $50 million into creating their own supply network, with their own farms and a food processing plant. Later in the year they were joined by the TrenMos restaurant, Baskin Robbins and Pizza Hut. These vanguard units of US consumerism are of symbolic importance, but the only way they can generate hard currency profits is through direct sales to tourists.

The biggest trade deals of the year were *Pepsi*'s renewal of its barter based operations (swapping Pepsi for vodka), with a $3 billion contract signed. *General Motors* signed sold $1 billion-worth of car emissions control technology to the *VAZ* car manufacturer. *General Electric* sold $150 billion-worth of airbus engines, and *Anglo-Suisse* signed a $100 million oil exploration deal. An innovative Connecticut real estate company set up a project to build a $150 million, 500-unit condominium complex just outside Moscow, for foreign residents.

Some attention has been attracted to the regions which have been allowed to declare themselves "free economic zones" in an attempt to emulate the success of the Chinese coastal regions. As yet seven Russian provinces, from Karelia on the Finnish border to Sakhalin in the far east, have declared their intention to establish such zones, but these remain largely paper entities.

Principal Personalities

Bessmertnykh, Aleksandr Aleksandrovich. Minister of Foreign Affairs. Formerly the Soviet Ambassador to the USA, Bessmertnykh became Foreign Minister in January 1991 following the unexpected resignation of Eduard Shevardnadze. A Russian, born on November 10, 1933, he graduated in 1957 from the Foreign Ministry's academy, the Moscow State Institute of International Relations, and holds the degree of candidate of juridical sciences. A member of the CPSU since 1963 and of the Central Committee since July 1990, Bessmertnykh has been a career diplomat with postings in the United Nations and the Foreign Ministry itself as well as in the US Embassy.

Gorbachev, Mikhail Sergeevich. General Secretary of the Central Committee of the CPSU (from March 1985, re-elected in July 1990) and President of the USSR (from March 1990). Gorbachev was born on March 2, 1931 to peasant parents in a village in the Stavropol territory. In 1955 he graduated from the Law Faculty of Moscow State University, and in 1967 took an external degree at the Stavropol Agricultural Institute. He has been a party member since 1952. According to his official biography Gorbachev began work at the age of 13 in a Stavropol collective farm, moving to *Komsomol* and party work after his university graduation. In April 1970 he became first secretary of the Stavropol territorial committee of the CPSU, and the following year he joined the Central Committee. His rapid ascent to power began in the late 1980s, apparently with the support of influential mentors such as Fedor Kulakov, responsible at this time for party work in agriculture. In November 1978, following Kulakov's death, Gorbachev became a Central Committee Secretary, in November 1979 he became a candidate member of the Politburo, and then in October 1980 he was promoted to full voting membership.

In March 1985, after the death of Konstantin Chernenko, he became the party's General Secretary. He was re-elected to the position, this time in a competitive ballot, at the 28th Party Congress in July 1990. He also headed the CPSU's Russian Bureau from its formation in December 1989 to its dissolution the following June. Gorbachev's state responsibilities began when he succeeded Andrei Gromyko in October 1988 as chairman of the Presidium of the USSR Supreme Soviet. In May 1989 he was elected by the Congress of People's Deputies to the newly established post of Chairman of the USSR Supreme Soviet, and then in March 1990 he became the USSR's first ever President. His wife Raisa, whom he met at university, lectured for more than 20 years and then became active in public life after his election, partly in her own right and partly as a Soviet "first lady" accompanying the General Secretary on his trips abroad. The architect of *perestroika*, his domestic standing, initially very high, began to decline as *perestroika* itself ran into increasing difficulties.

Ivashko, Vladimir Antonovich. Deputy General Secretary of the Central Committee of the CPSU. A Ukrainian, Ivashko was born on October 28, 1932 in a worker's family in Poltava. In 1956 he graduated from Khar'kov Mining Institute, and he holds the degree of candidate of economic sciences. At first a college lecturer, Ivashko moved subsequently into party work. He became Khar'kov first secretary in 1978, and then first secretary in Dnepropetrovsk in 1987. In 1988 he became second secretary of the Ukrainian party, and then in September 1989 he was promoted to the first secretaryship. In June 1990 he became chairman of the Supreme Soviet of the Ukraine, or republican president. On July 11, 1990, defeating Yegor Ligachev, he became the CPSU's first ever Deputy General Secretary. In 1986–89 he was a candidate, and then from April 1989 a full member of the CPSU Central

Committee. He moved into the Politburo itself in December 1989. As Deputy General Secretary, Ivashko is automatically a member of the Politburo and presides over meetings of the Secretariat. Widely regarded as a moderate conservative.

Landsbergis, Vytautas. Chairman of the Supreme Council (in effect President) of Lithuania. Born in Kaunas in 1932, Landsbergis was educated at Vilnius Conservatoire. A musicologist specializing in 19th and early 20th century Lithuanian music, he became Lithuanian President on March 11, 1990, when he defeated the outgoing President and first secretary of the republican Communist Party, Algeziras Brazauskas, who declined nomination as Deputy President. A somewhat unworldly figure, Landsbergis was widely regarded as a genuine patriot with perhaps unrealistic assumptions about the rapidity with which his republic could move to a fully independent status.

Maslyukov, Yuri Dmitrievich. Deputy Prime Minister of the USSR and chairman of the State Planning Committee (Gosplan). Maslyukov, a Russian, was born on September 30, 1937, in Leninabad. In 1962 he graduated from Leningrad Mechanical Institute, and subsequently worked at an Izhevsk engineering works before moving in 1974 to the ministry of defence industry. In 1982 he became first deputy chairman of Gosplan, and then from February 1988 chairman. Maslyukov, a party member from 1966, became a member of the CPSU Central Committee in 1986; he was a candidate Politburo member from 1988 to September 1989, when he was promoted to full membership. He left the Politburo in connection with its reorganization in July 1990 but remained a member of the Central Committee, and in January 1991 was re-elected to the Soviet government. Maslyukov is widely regarded as a moderate conservative and has been openly critical of proposals for greater regional economic autonomy.

Pavlov, Valentin Sergeevich. Prime Minister of the USSR. Pavlov, a Russian born on September 26, 1937, graduated in 1958 from the Moscow Finance Institute and holds a higher doctorate in economics. A career financial official, he became chairman of the State Prices Committee in 1986, Minister of Finance in 1989, and Prime Minister in January 1991 in succession to Nikolai Ryzhkov. A party member since 1962, Pavlov became a member of the Central Committee in July 1990. He is widely regarded as capable but conservative in matters of economic management.

Polozkov, Ivan Kuz'mich. First Secretary of the Communist Party of the RSFSR, and a member of the CPSU Politburo. Born on February 16, 1935, Polozkov was brought up in a village in Kursk region to collective farmer parents. In 1965 he graduated as an external student in finance and economics; in 1977 he acquired further qualifications from the Higher Party School, and in 1980 from the Academy of Social Sciences attached to the CPSU Central Committee. He has been a party member since 1958. After an early career in the army and agriculture, Polozkov took up full-time *Komsomol* and party work. From 1975 he worked in party headquarters in Moscow, and then in 1983 became a secretary (from 1985, first secretary) of the Krasnodar territorial committee of the CPSU. In April 1990 he became additionally the chairman of the territorial Soviet, and then in June 1990 at its foundation congress he was elected first secretary of the Communist Party of the Russian Federation. A Central Committee member from 1986, Polozkov became a member of the Politburo itself following the 28th Party Congress in July 1990. Widely regarded as a conservative, Polozkov's proposals for reform have generally emphasized discipline and strict controls on the newer forms of economic activity, such as co-operatives.

Pugo, Boris Karlovich. Minister of the Interior. Pugo, a Latvian born on February 19, 1937, graduated in 1960 from the Riga Polytechnic Institute and began his working life as an engineer, but almost immediately became involved in *Komsomol*, party and (from 1976 to 1984) KGB work. He has been a CPSU member since 1963, was a Central Committee member from 1986 to 1990, and a candidate Politburo member from September 1989 to July 1990. First Secretary of the Latvian party organization from 1984, Pugo became chairman of the Committee of Party Control in July 1990 before moving to his present position in January 1991.

Ryzhkov, Nikolai Ivanovich. Chairman of the USSR Council of Ministers (Prime Minister) from 1985 to 1990. Ryzhkov, a Russian by nationality, was born in a village in the Donets region on September 28, 1929. In 1950 he graduated from the Kramatorsk engineering college, and in 1959 he completed his education at the Urals Polytechnical Institute. He joined the CPSU in 1956. Ryzhkov began his working life at the massive "Uralmash" engineering works in Sverdlovsk, where he rose steadily through the ranks until he became (in 1965) chief engineer and then (in 1975) general director. After 1975 he held a succession of party and (more often) government positions, becoming a first deputy minister of heavy and transport engineering in 1975, and then in 1979 first deputy chairman of the State Planning Committee (Gosplan). In 1982 Ryzhkov became a member of the Central Committee Secretariat, where (until 1985) he headed its economic department. In September 1985 he became chairman of the Council of Ministers, securing nomination to that position again in 1989 and holding it until it was abolished in December 1990 (a serious heart attack at this time in any case made it unlikely he would remain active in the Kremlin leadership).

Ryzhkov was elected to the CPSU Central Committee in 1981, 1986 and again in 1990, and became a full member of the ruling Politburo in April 1985 without passing through the customary candidate or non-voting stage. He lost his Politburo position when that body was reconstituted in July 1990, but was elected to the Congress of People's Deputies in 1989 and became an *ex officio* member of the Presidential Council on its establishment in March 1990. Ryzhkov became an increasingly prominent member of the Gorbachev administration during the late 1980s, consistent with the efforts that were being made to shift executive authority from party to state institutions. He enjoyed a position of particular importance during the Armenian earthquake of December 1988, when he took responsibility for relief operations on behalf of the Politburo, and he headed party or state missions on other occasions, for instance in Uzbekistan during the inter-ethnic disturbances in the summer of 1989. A mild-mannered, efficient and popular man, it was perhaps his heavily managerial background that made it difficult for Ryzhkov to adapt successfully to the more politicized atmosphere that developed in Soviet politics at the end of that decade.

Silaev, Ivan Stepanovich. Chairman of the Council of Ministers (Prime Minister) of the Russian Republic. Silaev, a Russian, was born on October 21, 1930 and graduated from Kazan Aviation Institute in 1954. He has been a member of the CPSU since 1959. Silaev spent the earlier part of his working life at the Gorky aviation factory, where in 1971 he became director. In 1974 he moved into the Soviet government, becoming a minister in 1980 and heading the ministry of the aviation industry from 1981. He became the Russian premier in June 1990; widely regarded as a conservative, he has nonetheless proved an effective representative of Russian interests both at home and abroad.

Yanaev, Gennadii Ivanovich. Vice-President of the USSR. Yanaev, a Russian born on August 26, 1937, graduated in 1959 from the Gorky Agricultural Institute and in 1967 took a law degree on a part-time basis. His career has been largely in the *Komsomol* and trade union movements, heading the All-Union Council of Trade Unions from April until July 1990. The same month, following the 28th Congress of the CPSU, he became a member of the Politburo and a full-time member of the Secretariat, specializing in foreign affairs. A party member since 1962, Yanaev became a member of the Central Committee in July 1990. In December 1990, after an inconclusive first ballot, he was elected the first ever Vice-President of the USSR.

Yazov, Dmitrii Timofeevich. Minister of Defence. A Russian, Yazov was born on November 8, 1923. He has been a member of the CPSU since 1944. After a military education, service during World War II and a series of postings he became (in 1980) commander of the Central Asian military district, and then (from 1984) of the Far Eastern military district. Since 1987 he has served as Deputy and then as Minister of Defence, serving from 1981 to 1987 as a candidate and then from 1987 as a full member of the CPSU Central Committee. Yazov was also a candidate member of the Politburo from June 1987 until its reconstitution in July 1990.

Yel'tsin, Boris Nikolaevich. Chairman of the Supreme Soviet of the RSFSR (in effect, President of Russia). Yel'tsin was born on February 1, 1931 in the village of Butko in the Talitsky district of Sverdlovsk region. According to his autobiography, published abroad in 1990, Yel'tsin had a hard upbringing. Local harvests were bad, there were always shortages of food, and the family would not have survived the war but for the milk and sometimes warmth of the family nanny-goat. Yel'tsin lost two fingers in an accident during his schooldays, and contracted typhoid fever; his father was a harsh disciplinarian. He did well at school, however, and went on to study as an engineer at the Urals Polytechnical Institute, where he met his future wife and perfected his volleyball technique.

After some years in the building trade, Yel'tsin began to make his way up the political ladder. He joined the CPSU in 1961 and from 1968 onwards became first a department head, then a secretary, and from 1976 first secretary of the Sverdlovsk regional party committee. In 1985, according to his autobiography with some reluctance, he was persuaded to move to Moscow to take up a position as head of the construction department of the central party apparatus. From 1985 to 1986 he was a member of the CPSU Secretariat, becoming Moscow party secretary in December 1985. His outspoken criticism of the central leadership, particularly at a meeting of the Central Committee called to celebrate the 70th anniversary of the revolution in November 1987, led to his removal from the Moscow party secretaryship shortly afterwards, and from the Politburo (where he had become a candidate member in 1986) in February 1988.

Yel'tsin became first deputy chairman of the State Construction Committee at the end of 1987 and his political career appeared to be in eclipse. In March 1989, unprecedentedly in recent years, the Central Committee decided to investigate his increasingly outspoken views and determine if they were compatible with party membership. Yel'tsin, however, began to enjoy an increasingly large public following (in opinion polls in 1989 he was placed second, after Gorbachev, in order of esteem), and at the much more open elections to the Congress of People's Deputies in March 1989 he won over 89% of the vote in the Moscow national-territorial seat in a contest with the officially favoured candidate. Yel'tsin in turn became a member of the newly elected Supreme Soviet (after one of the deputies originally chosen had stepped down), and in further elections in March 1990 he was overwhelmingly elected in Sverdlovsk to the Russian Congress of People's Deputies. In May 1990, following several rounds of voting, he became republican president.

Yel'tsin had by this time become joint chairman of the radical Inter-Regional Group of Soviet deputies and an increasingly outspoken critic of official privilege and inequality. As Russian president he became an equally strong exponent of the rights of the Russian Republic in relation to the all-union government. Yel'tsin's programme, as he set it out in his autobiography and to the Central Committee in February 1990, involved the private ownership of land, independence for the republics, financial autonomy for factories and farms, freedom of political association and freedom of conscience. Part of this programme, particularly its attack on privilege, enjoyed widespread support; logically, however, it entailed substantially higher prices and probably unemployment. This left Yel'tsin with a substantially larger following as an anti-establishment figure than as a political alternative to Gorbachev in his own right.

The Media

Newspapers and periodicals

The Soviet leadership has consistently attached great importance to the development of the mass media — particularly so, perhaps, to newspapers, which played an important part in the Bolsheviks' conquest of power and were for some time the only effective means of mass communication within the country. The output of newspapers, and of magazines and periodicals, has accordingly grown rapidly over the years of Soviet rule. Although newspaper titles declined somewhat during the 1960s and 1970s, the number increased rapidly thereafter, and by 1989 there were 8,811 separate publications. The total circulation rose similarly from 40,012 million copies a year in 1980 to 50,505 million in 1989, with an average daily print of 230 million copies. Periodical publications showed no comparable increase in titles in the 1980s (5,236 in 1980, 5,228 in 1989), but their circulation expanded just as rapidly from 3,226 million copies a year in 1980 to 5,085 million in 1989.

"A newspaper", Lenin observed, "is not only a collective propagandist and collective agitator; it is also a collective organizer". Soviet newspapers and periodicals, accordingly, have different tasks to perform and are rather different in their coverage and layout from their Western counterparts. The Communist Party daily, *Pravda* (Truth), for instance, founded in 1912, normally contains an agitational message with a special emphasis on production achievements upon its front page; its other five pages are devoted to party affairs, correspondence, foreign news (mostly supplied by TASS, the official Soviet news agency), sport, TV programmes and the weather (on the back page). *Pravda* had 6.5 million subscribers in 1990, rather fewer than the 10–11 million of the 1970s and early 1980s; its loss of readership was not untypical of party publications in general, some of which disappeared altogether at this time. *Pravda* had lost further ground by 1991, retaining only 30% of its subscribers of the previous year (an increase in cover price, as with other Soviet publications, explained at least some of this fall).

Other important daily papers, which differ from *Pravda* in their coverage and (increasingly) in their editorial orientation, are *Izvestiya* (News), the government daily; *Komsomol'skaya pravda*, the *Komsomol* daily; *Sel'skaya zhizn'* (Rural Life), a party newspaper intended for a rural readership; *Trud* (Labour), the trade union paper, which enjoyed a spectacular rise in circulation during the 1980s (by 1990 it had 20 million subscribers); and *Krasnaya zvezda* (Red Star), the daily organ of the Ministry of Defence. Weekly magazines and periodicals of note include the best-selling *Argumenty i fakty* (Arguments and Facts), which specializes in brief but informative reports on sensitive matters and which in 1990 attained a circulation of over 30 million; the party theoretical journal *Kommunist*; the literary monthly *Novy mir* (New World); the illustrated weekly *Ogonek*; the weekly *Literaturnaya gazeta* (Literary Gazette); and the humorous weekly *Krokodil*. *Ogonek* and the weekly paper *Moscow News* (published in Russian and foreign languages) were the most outspoken supporters of Gorbachev's policy of *perestroika* after 1985; the Russian newspaper *Sovetskaya Rossiya* (Soviet Russia) and the *Komsomol* journal *Molodaya gvardiya* (Young Guard) were among the publications identified with more conservative positions.

Media consumption and glasnost'

Sociological studies conducted within the USSR suggest that the majority of adults make considerable use of this substantial diet of newsprint. A study conducted in Leningrad, for instance, found that 75% of those polled read the newspapers every day (a further 19% did so three or four times a week), and even in relatively remote areas at least half the local population normally reported reading a newspaper daily, with the younger and better educated more likely to so than the local population as a whole. Soviet newspaper readers also discuss articles in the press relatively frequently with their family and friends, cut out and keep articles of interest to them, and place some value upon the paper's ability to deal with local difficulties and shortcomings. More than 670,000 Soviet citizens wrote to *Pravda* alone in 1988, for instance, and the total mailbag of the national press is estimated at 60 to 70 million. No more than a small proportion of the letters can be published, but all are supposed to be answered and followed up and in some cases inquiries of this kind have led to the dismissal of officials who have acted improperly.

The role of Soviet newspapers and the electronic media expanded still further after 1985 as a result of Gorbachev's policy of *glasnost'* or openness in all areas of public life. "The better people are informed", the new leader told the Central Committee plenum that elected him, "the more consciously they act, the more actively they support the Party, its plans and programmatic objectives". The Gorbachev leadership was accordingly associated with a determined attempt to expand the boundaries of legitimate debate within the columns of the official media. A whole range of issues that had hitherto been taboo began to receive extended and sometimes sensational treatment. The crimes of the Stalinist years were explored in unprecedented detail, and so too were contemporary issues like prostitution, drug abuse and violent crime. For a small minority, *glasnost'* meant that the achievements of the Soviet past were being improperly neglected; for the great majority, however, *glasnost'* was the single most welcome development of the Gorbachev years, and most newspapers and journals rapidly increased their circulations.

The 1990 Press Law

Glasnost' did not, however, mean a free press in the Western sense. Gorbachev declared himself in favour of *glasnost'* "within and for the sake of socialism", and the law on the press and mass media that was approved in June 1990 required all legal publications to "register" with the authorities and to refrain from appeals for the forcible change of the government or social system. The law, which came into force on August 1, stated that citizens of the USSR were guaranteed the "right to express opinions and beliefs and to seek, select, receive and disseminate information and ideas in any form". It further stated that "censorship of mass information is not permitted" but listed a number of publishing or broadcasting activities that were illegal, including the disclosure of state secrets, calls for the violent overthrow of the state and social system, expression of racial or religious intolerance, pornography and incitement to commit criminal acts.

The law also featured legal guarantees of privacy for individuals, and defined the procedures for redress in cases of slander or libel of an individual or organization. A key clause defined freedom of information: journalists had the right to demand information (including access to documents) from state bodies, social organizations and officials, and to appeal to higher bodies or officials and ultimately to the courts if their demands were refused. The right to "found a mass information medium" was granted (subject to official registration) to state bodies, political parties, social organizations, mass movements, creative unions, associations "formed in accordance with the law", work collectives and individual citizens. A monopoly on any medium was forbidden, and editorial offices had the right of complete economic and financial autonomy.

The law was widely welcomed by leading Soviet journalists, but it was pointed out at the same time that true press freedom would only be achieved when state control of paper production and of distribution and ownership of print works had been ended. Moreover, prospects for new publishing ventures seemed bleak at a time when the print-runs of even state-owned newspapers were being crippled by an acute paper shortage caused by inefficiency and technological obsolescence in the timber and pulp-and-paper industry. Further difficulties arose in the early 1990s from increases in the cost of paper and of distribution, which had hitherto been subsidized. These circumstances were reflected in substantially higher cover prices and a fall in the number of subscribers. *Izvestiya*, for instance, retained only 38% of its 1990 subscribers into 1991; *Novyi mir* kept 33%, *Kommunist* 32%. As the official press discussed contraction, staff dismissals and even closures, a lively unofficial press developed in its place and by the early 1990s was clearly catering more successfully for the demand for commercial, life-style and (in some cases) erotic coverage.

Radio and television

The first experimental radio broadcasts in the USSR were made in Nizhny Novgorod (later Gorky) in 1919. The construction of a central radio station was undertaken in Moscow the following year, and it began broadcasting in 1922. Further stations were opened in 1924 in Leningrad, Kiev and Nizhny Novgorod, and regular broadcasts throughout the USSR began in the same year. By 1937 some 90 radio transmitters were in operation; by 1988 there were 176 radio broadcasting centres and over 5,000 local radio stations throughout the USSR, broadcasting a total of 1,372 hours of programmes daily in 72 Soviet languages. All of these facilities come under the control of the State Committee for Radio and Television of the USSR, whose chairman is a member of the Soviet government, and under its counterparts at republican and lower levels of government.

The central radio network broadcasts 14 main programmes with a total output which in 1989 exceeded 484 hours daily. The first programme, as with television, is the main national network for informational, socio-political and cultural broadcasts (about 20 hours a day); the second programme, "*Mayak*" (Beacon), broadcasts news and music on a 24-hour basis. The third programme concentrates upon educational, literary and musical programmes for about 16 hours daily; and the fourth broadcasts music for about nine hours daily. The fifth programme provides informational, socio-political and cultural broadcasts for Soviet citizens resident abroad; and the other programmes relay these broadcasts to more remote parts of the country. In 1990 practically the whole country could receive direct radio reception from wired-up speakers, a degree of coverage to which television could not yet aspire; about 60 million citizens, a particularly substantial proportion of them in the main urban areas, could also receive foreign radio broadcasts.

There were 92.4 million televisions in service in 1989, as compared with 84.8 million radios and 117.2 million wired-up speakers. In 1980 13.5% of the population were still unable to receive television transmissions, but by 1989 this had been reduced to a mere 2.9%. Of the 97.1% of the total population who could receive regular programmes, 45.9% could receive three channels, 46.1% two channels and 5.1% a single channel. A total of 494.7 hours of television programmes were produced daily in 1989; of this 169.9 hours were produced by Central TV, 130.6 hours by stations in the Russian Republic, and 194.2 hours by stations in other republics. Programmes were broadcast in 50 languages, of which 46 were languages spoken in the USSR itself.

Central TV, based in Moscow, produced four main programmes in 1989. The first is the basic national network for informational, socio-political, cultural, educational, artistic and sporting programmes; it is broadcast for about 14 hours daily. The second programme, which is also intended for the USSR as a whole and which concentrates upon cultural, educational and artistic matters, is also broadcast for about 14 hours daily. These are the two main national "all-union" programmes, and both are re-broadcast in five different reception areas for viewers in other time zones. The third programme is intended for Moscow city, Moscow region and the Ryazan region, and is broadcast for about five hours daily. The fourth programme, broadcast for about four hours a day in Moscow, Moscow region and Kiev, is educational in character. Of the total daily output of 169.9 hours in 1989, 15.2 hours were accounted for by informational programmes, 44.8 by socio-political programmes, 11.4 hours by sporting programmes, 10.3 hours by educational programmes and most of all, 76.2 hours, by "artistic" programmes (including much that would be regarded elsewhere as light entertainment).

Most urban residents watch television fairly regularly, and for many it is clearly an important source of news and information. According to surveys, of the events in the outside world that are covered by the Soviet media 86% are known to the public through television, 77% through the newspapers, and 62% from the radio. The most important of all television programmes is the news, "Vremya", which is carried on all channels at 9 p.m. and is watched by an estimated 150 million of the population (including all members of the Soviet armed forces). In other respects, however, the Soviet public appear to favour less directly political programmes, much as they prefer to read different kinds of articles in the newspapers. A study in Leningrad, for instance, found that feature films, documentaries and variety programmes were the most popular of all the programmes shown (91.5%, 85% and 84% of those who were asked preferred such programmes). Social and political themes were less popular; and only 4% of respondents opted for more programmes on economic matters, the least popular of all the 27 categories that were included in the survey. More than 70% of those polled said they regarded television as a "means of entertainment"; more than 41% said that too few entertainment programmes were shown, and 48% thought their quality should be improved.

These preferences have had some effect upon TV output, leading to improvements not only in entertainment programmes but in the nature of the coverage that has been given to news and current affairs. Since about the time of Gorbachev's accession, for instance, there has been more emphasis upon live audience response. An enterprising show called "12th Floor" has been one of the most notable newer-style programmes; viewers can phone in during the show and responsible officials are often asked to reply to criticisms on the spot. There have also been several "spacebridges" linking up ordinary people (on the first occasion, in Leningrad and Seattle) for discussion of whatever most concerns them. Television news has been improved by greater use of portable video equipment to allow quicker responses to events, and much more emphasis has been placed upon live interviews including those with visiting Western politicians. Television, more than the printed media, however, remained subject to direct political influence, and the appointment of a more conservative figure to head the State Radio and Television Committee in late 1990 was followed by the cancellation of the popular weekly programme "*Vzglyad*" (Glance), which had been intending to carry an interview with the former foreign minister Eduard Shevardnadze.

Foreign Relations

"New thinking" in foreign relations

Soviet foreign relations were affected by the accession of Gorbachev perhaps more profoundly than any other sphere of policy. The new General Secretary's early pronouncements in fact gave little indication that one of the main features of his new administration would be "new thinking" in its relationship with the outside world. Gorbachev's address to an ideology conference in December 1984, shortly before he took office, stressed the "necessity of a fundamental change through accelerated economic development" and pointed to *glasnost'* as a means of promoting this process. The section on foreign policy, however, was much more orthodox, accusing capitalism of resorting to "wars and terror" in order to further its objectives; it was constantly seeking "social revenge" on a global scale, and its leading representative, US capitalism, was accused of having joined together with the multinational corporations to declare a "crusade" against communism. In relations between the two "opposing systems", conflict clearly took precedence over competition.

A somewhat different tone began to emerge relatively quickly, particularly in an address that Gorbachev gave to British members of parliament later the same month. In the speech the General Secretary expressed a wish for renewed dialogue and co-operation, above all in relation to the threat of a nuclear war in which there could be "no winners". This, however, was only one example of the kind of issue that required the concerted action of states with different social systems. Another was the need to resolve regional issues peacefully; others were the fight against famine and disease, protection of the environment and the global supply of energy. The atomic age, Gorbachev suggested, required a "new kind of political thinking", above all the recognition that the peoples of the world lived in a "vulnerable, rather fragile but interconnected world". Whatever divided them, they had to share the same planet; and this dictated a "constructive dialogue, a search for solutions to key international problems, for areas of agreement". Gorbachev also made clear the reason why he advocated a position of this kind: it was to be found in the interconnection between foreign and domestic policy. The Soviet Union, for itself, required peace so as to be able to achieve its "truly breathtaking creative plans".

Several aspects of this new approach became apparent during the early months of his administration. His election address of February 1985, just before his accession, stressed the importance of better relations within the European "common home". The speech he delivered on his election laid most emphasis upon domestic priorities, but called also for better relations with the "great socialist community", particularly China, and for a relationship with the capitalist world that included the complete abolition of nuclear weapons. A speech to French parliamentarians in October 1985 pointed to the need for closer co-operation in ecological and cultural matters, and for inter-state relations to be kept free of ideological differences. In January 1986 Gorbachev was able to announce a unilateral moratorium on nuclear testing, and his speech to the 27th Party Congress the following month broadened the call for East-West co-operation to social democratic parties and religious movements. The "Delhi declaration" of November 1986 committed the Soviet leader to a "non-violent" as well as nuclear-free world; and in the military sphere, there was a shift to "reasonable sufficiency" in place of the earlier emphasis upon substantial numerical preponderance.

The early Gorbachev years saw many of these declarations of principle translated into reality. There were substantial cuts in Soviet military spending and troop numbers from 1989 onwards; much more information was made available on the structure and size of the military budget, and on troop and weapons deployments; and those deployments became more defensive in character. A superpower dialogue with the United States, initiated at Geneva in 1985, led in December 1987 to an historic agreement on short- and intermediate-range land-based missiles which for the first time provided for the elimination of an entire category of weaponry. A series of agreements, concluded in Geneva in April 1988, provided for the withdrawal of the "limited contingent" of Soviet troops from Afghanistan; the last Soviet troops left, as scheduled, in February 1989. At the same time a determined effort was made to develop relations with the widest possible range of states, including South Africa, Israel and the Arab monarchies. The General Secretary made a considerable personal contribution to the success of these new policies, travelling tirelessly abroad and persuading a wide section of Western public opinion to drop the "enemy image" of the USSR and its foreign policy.

Soviet foreign policy in the late 1980s

In the late 1980s, indeed, Gorbachev began to enjoy rather more success in his dealings with the outside world than in his efforts to promote *perestroika* within his own country. In 1989 the Soviet leader visited Cuba in early April, taking the opportunity to sign a friendship treaty between the two states. The same month saw the first ever Soviet-Irish summit, a brief stopover at Shannon airport, and a more extended visit to the United Kingdom. The centrepiece of the UK visit was an address delivered in London's Guildhall; later the same day the Soviet leader and his wife were received by the Queen and Prince Philip at Windsor Castle, in the course of which an invitation was extended to them to make an official visit to the USSR. In June 1989 the Soviet leader visited West Germany, where he met with a particularly enthusiastic reception. A series of agreements on economic and cultural matters was concluded, and further arrangements were made for West German involvement in the modernization of the Soviet Union's light and food industries. In July 1989 Gorbachev visited France, in the course of which he delivered an address to the Parliamentary Assembly of the Council of Europe; and in December he visited Italy and the Vatican and then shared an informal summit off the coast of Malta with the new US President, George Bush. A more formal meeting between the two leaders took place in the summer of 1990.

Perhaps the most significant development of the late 1980s, however, was the resumption of friendly relations with the People's Republic of China after a period of estrangement that had lasted 30 years. The way was prepared by a visit by the Chinese Foreign Minister to Moscow in December 1988, and then by Shevardnadze's visit to Beijing early the following year. Both sides agreed on the need for "Chinese-Soviet relations of a new type". Gorbachev, who had for some time sought such a meeting, was finally able himself to visit the People's Republic in May 1989. The talks, inevitably, were overshadowed by public demonstrations of support for the Soviet leader, which in turn contributed to a wave of public resistance to the policies of the Chinese government itself. Gorbachev was nonetheless able to claim that relations between the two countries had reached a "qualitatively new stage", and in the concluding communiqué both sides welcomed the normalization of relations between the two countries and between their two ruling parties. Although differences remained on the future of Kampuchea, the intended Vietnamese withdrawal was applauded, and it was agreed that any remaining territorial or other differences should be resolved on the basis of international law. The Chinese leaders were themselves invited to the USSR so that the discussions could be continued.

As the year concluded, it was the dramatic pattern of events in Eastern Europe that most directly engaged the attention of Soviet (and Western) foreign policy-makers. Speaking to the Central Committee in December, Gorbachev argued that the processes of change occurring in Eastern Europe were a version of the *perestroika* on which the Soviet Union had itself embarked, although it had led to outcomes for which there was little precedent. In Hungary and Poland the local Communist parties had lost their role in government; and Communists in East Germany and Czechoslovakia had also lost ground politically. New political forces had appeared, some of which supported socialism and others of which opposed it. Communists in these countries, Gorbachev suggested, would have to develop a new strategy and tactics to win back their popular support; the USSR, meanwhile, welcomed the "positive changes" taking place in the countries concerned. It was equally clear, the Soviet leader went on, that the post-war frontiers of Europe must be unaffected, and that there must continue to be two German states, any modification of which would threaten to destabilize Europe. There would clearly be no Soviet attempt, on the basis of these statements, to resist the process of change in Eastern Europe; but every effort would be made at the same time to ensure that the security of the USSR was not adversely affected.

Soviet opposition to German unity and even NATO membership had to be dropped in 1990; but this led to a greater emphasis upon Europe-wide security and the importance of continuing the "Helsinki process" begun in 1975. At the same time the dialogue between the superpowers continued, particularly at a summit meeting in the United States in May–June 1990. The summit was the second between Gorbachev and the recently elected US President, following their informal meeting off the coast of Malta. The summit was hailed as a new beginning in US-Soviet relations, despite acknowledged and continuing differences on a number of key bilateral and international issues. Formally speaking, the summit resulted in several agreements, including a convention banning the production of chemical weapons and a series of bilateral agreements on arms control, trade, and co-operation in the transport, energy, educational and cultural fields. The Soviet Union, in particular, secured "most favoured nation" access to the US market for the first time for 50 years. A more far-reaching agreement on reductions in strategic nuclear arms, which at the time of the Malta summit had been thought imminent, was deferred for further discussion. The two leaders nonetheless signed a framework agreement on the major elements of a START treaty; issues that remained in contention were to be taken further by negotiating teams based in Geneva. Gorbachev, at the two leaders' concluding press conference, described the summit as an "event of enormous importance for our bilateral relations and in the context of world politics", and added that one could now speak of a "new phase of co-operation" between the USA and the Soviet Union.

The US visit followed a two-day visit to Canada; the Soviet leader also visited Germany, Italy, France and Spain in the autumn, and attended the Paris summit in November for the conclusion of a far-reaching agreement on the reduction of conventional arms within the CSCE framework. The Soviet leader's visit to Spain in October led to the conclusion of political and economic agreements; his visit to France resulted in a joint agreement on co-operation (and a doubling of French aid to the USSR). The Soviet leader's visit to Germany in November (where a 20-year friendship and co-operation treaty was signed) followed a meeting between himself and Chancellor Kohl at Stavropol in July at which it was agreed that a newly unified Germany would be "sovereign in every way", including its liberty to join the military alliance of its choice (in practice NATO). NATO structures, however, would not be extended to the former GDR so long as Soviet soldiers were stationed there. Soviet troops still in East Germany would be withdrawn over three or four years, in the course of which the West Germans would underwrite their costs; the number of German troops would also be reduced to 370,000 within a comparable period.

The solidity of East-West understanding was tested in late 1990 by the outbreak of the Gulf crisis. The Soviet Union had traditionally maintained friendly relations with Iraq (and had, in fact, concluded a friendship treaty with its government). Foreign Minister Shevardnadze, however, in a speech at the UN General Assembly on September 25, characterized Saddam Hussein's invasion as an "act of terrorism against the nascent new world order" and added that the Soviet Union would be prepared to support the use of force against Iraq within a United Nations framework. Shevardnadze's resignation on December 20, 1990, delivered without warning to the Fourth Congress of People's Deputies, occasioned some concern that his policies on these and other matters might be modified. The Congress, however, supported the position that had been taken by Soviet representatives on the matter and insisted in its resolution upon the withdrawal of Iraqi forces and the full restoration of Kuwaiti sovereignty.

The USSR continued to widen its international relations as the decade concluded. In

May 1990 it became an observer in GATT (the General Agreement on Tariffs and Trade), and in September 1990 a member of Interpol. These moves were part of a much broader reintegration into the world political community, a development paralleled by the establishment of closer relations with the world economy and moves to establish a convertible ruble. The Warsaw Treaty Organization signalled a shift from military to political purposes as several of its member-states acquired non-communist governments. In July 1990 a presidential decree announced that the economic association of the communist states, Comecon or CMEA (the Council for Mutual Economic Assistance), would move towards a hard currency basis for its trade as from January 1991. The steady expansion of the network of Soviet foreign relations continued as Shevardnadze met Albanian representatives in September 1990 (the first such meeting for 30 years), and as relations were established with South Korea, whose President made an official visit to the USSR in December 1990. Nonetheless, as events in the Baltic in early 1991 made clear, Soviet foreign and domestic policies remained closely linked, and in both directions. If Soviet foreign policy successes made it easier to tackle the challenges of *perestroika* domestically, a harder line towards nationalist movements within the USSR itself was likely to harm East-West relations and to prejudice the willingness of outside powers to help to restore the Soviet economy.

YUGOSLAVIA

John Allcock

Government 1989–90

Federal Presidency

President. *Borisav Jović (Serbia)*
Vice-President. *Stjepan Mesić (Croatia)*
Members. *Nenad Bućin* (Montenegro)
    Dragutin Zelenović (Vojvodina)
    Riza Sapundžiu (Kosovo)
    Vasil Tupurkovski (Macedonia)
    Bogić Bogičević (Bosnia & Hercegovina)
    Janez Drnovšek (Slovenia)

Federal Executive Council (Cabinet)

President (Prime Minister). *Ante Marković*
Vice-Presidents. *Aleksandar Mitrović*
    Živko Pregl

Federal Secretaries (Ministers)
    Foreign Affairs. *Budimir Lončar*
    National Defence. *Veljko Kadijević*

Internal Affairs. *Petar Garačanin*
Finance. *Branko Zekan*
Foreign Trade. *Franc Horvat*
Trade and General Economic Affairs.
    Nazmi Mustafa
Justice & Organization of Federal
    Administration. *Vlado Kambovski*

Presidents of Federal Executive Committees
    Agriculture. *Stevo Mirjanić*
    Transport & Communications. *Jože Slokar*
    Labour, Health, Social Security &
        Veterans' affairs. *Radiša Gacić*
    Development. *Božidar Marendić*

Other members. *Nikola Gašoski, Dževad
    Mujezinović, Branimir Pajković, Veselin
    Vukotić.*

League of Communists of Yugoslavia (LCY)
The Presidency of the LCY has been replaced by a temporary Committee for the preparation of its XVth congress, intended to reconstitute the League on a new basis. In the interim the Committee is chaired by Miroslav Ivanović.

YUGOSLAVIA

showing the republics and provinces, and the distribution of nationalities, by percentages

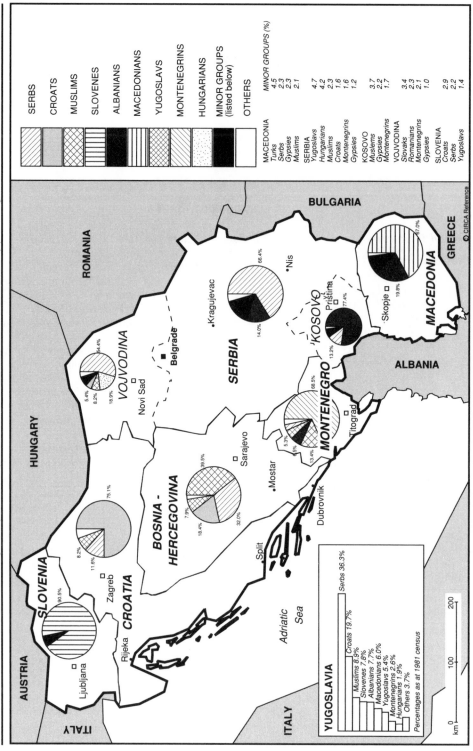

Legend:

- SERBS
- CROATS
- MUSLIMS
- SLOVENES
- ALBANIANS
- MACEDONIANS
- YUGOSLAVS
- MONTENEGRINS
- HUNGARIANS
- MINOR GROUPS (listed below)
- OTHERS

MINOR GROUPS (%)

MACEDONIA
Turks 4.5
Serbs 2.3
Gypsies 2.3
Muslims 2.1

SERBIA
Yugoslavs 4.7
Hungarians 4.2
Muslims 2.3
Croats 1.6
Montenegrins 1.6
Gypsies 1.2

KOSOVO
Muslims 3.7
Gypsies 2.2
Montenegrins 1.7

VOJVODINA
Slovaks 3.4
Romanians 2.3
Montenegrins 2.1
Gypsies 1.0

SLOVENIA
Croats 2.9
Serbs 2.2
Yugoslavs 1.4

YUGOSLAVIA
Serbs 36.3%
Croats 19.7%
Muslims 8.9%
Slovenes 7.8%
Albanians 7.7%
Macedonians 6.0%
Yugoslavs 5.4%
Montenegrins 2.6%
Hungarians 1.9%
Others 3.7%
Percentages as at 1981 census

© CIRCA Reference

Chronology

1988

December 30. Resignation of the Yugoslav government (Federal Executive Council — FEC), led by Branko Mikulić, because of the obstruction of its programme of economic and political reforms. This is the first government resignation in post-war Yugoslavia on the basis of the loss of a vote of confidence in the Federal Assembly.

1989

January 11. The New Year opens with the first moves towards political pluralism, as the Democratic Alliance is launched in Ljubljana, led by writer Dimitrij Rupel. This is the first political organization in post-war Yugoslavia openly to declare itself to be a "party" in opposition to the ruling League of Communists of Yugoslavia (LCY). On *January 16* the Praesidium of the Socialist Alliance (SA — an umbrella "popular front") declares it to be "unconstitutional". (This claim is never contested in the courts.)

January 11. Echoes of the earlier attempt by supporters of Serbia's Slobodan Milošević to affect political development in other republics continue, as the Republican Presidency and leading officials of the LC in Montenegro resign over their handling of popular demonstrations the previous October. On *January 20*, a new leadership of the LC in Vojvodina is elected following the collective resignation of its Praesidium, after similar demonstrations in Novi Sad, also in October. The Serbs fail, however, on *January 30*, in the Plenum of the CC (Central Committee) of the LCY in Belgrade, to force the resignation of Stipe Šuvar (a Croatian, and its President) because of his intervention in the Kosovo crisis.

Although losing the fight against Šuvar, two days later Milošević supporters secure the dismissal of the popular Albanian representative Azem Vllasi (and others) from the CC of the LCY.

January 19. Mikulić is replaced by Ante Marković as President of the FEC.

February 2. Movement for a Yugoslav Democratic Initiative is launched in Zagreb. Supported by Serb and Slovene as well as Croatian intellectuals, it is the first federation-wide opposition group to emerge. This is the first of several groups which initially agree to operate under the umbrella of the SA.

February 14. Major strike begins in the lead and zinc mines at Trepča near Kosovska Mitrovica, as a protest against the fate of Vllasi, and soon spreads to other enterprises. Work resumes temporarily after a personal appeal by Rahman Morina, the newly elected head of the LC in Kosovo; but on *February 20* more than 1,000 miners begin a hunger strike in the pit, demanding the dismissal of Morina, whom they accuse of being too pliant under Serbian pressure, and rejecting proposed changes to the republican constitution. The next day students from the University at Priština begin a sit-in in support.

February 23. Changes to the Serbian constitution, abrogating the distinctive status of the Autonomous Provinces, are adopted by the republican Assembly. The situation deteriorates over the next few days, and on *February 25* troops begin armed patrols in Kosovo.

Two days later, Morina offers his resignation, as do Husamedin Azemi (party leader in Priština) and Ali Šukrija (Kosovo member of the CC of the LCY). The strike in Kosovo has become virtually general. "Special measures" are announced to deal with the unrest in the province.

February 28. An estimated 700,000 demonstrators mass in front of the Belgrade Federal Assembly to demand the reinstatement of Morina and enforcement of the new constitution in Kosovo, and to protest against support given by senior Slovene communists to Albanian demands. There are token counter-strikes by Serb and Montenegrin workers.

March. Throughout the month some of the most serious disturbances in the post-war years develop in Kosovo. At an emergency meeting of the Federal Assembly on *March 1*, Lazar Mojsov (Macedonian representative in the Federal State Presidency — FSP) announces the discovery of a plan for armed insurrection in the province. A ban is imposed on public assembly in Kosovo, and restrictions placed on news reporting there.

Further massive demonstrations are held in Belgrade, demanding the reinstatement of Morina, Azemi and Šukrija, and the arrest of Vllasi. Demonstrators disperse after Slobodan Milošević (leader of the Serbian Party) comes to the steps of the Assembly to promise this. Within 24 hours, Vllasi is arrested, along with two directors of the Trepča mine and others, and on *March 5* they are charged with "counter-revolutionary activities".

A wave of further strikes ensues in Kosovo: and by *March 19* an estimated 25,000 miners and roughly the same number of other industrial workers in Kosovo are staying away from work. A school boycott begins.

Resistance in the LCY to Albanian demands stiffens, however, and the Kosovo Provincial Committee refuses to accept the resignations of Morina and others, on the grounds that they have been submitted "under pressure".

March 10. The provincial Assembly of Vojvodina, in Novi Sad, ratifies the draft changes to the constitutional position of the province within the Serbian republic and on *March 23* the Assembly of the Autonomous Province of Kosovo finally ratifies them, effectively signalling the end of its own autonomy. The republican Assembly of Serbia ratifies the changes to the constitutional position of the provinces on *March 28*.

Civil disturbances continue to be widely reported throughout Kosovo, especially in Priština and Uroševac. At special courts, several hundred miners are given prison sentences of up to 60 days for their participation in the strikes, or are suspended from their jobs.

The deaths of two policemen and a demonstrator in the province on *March 27* lead to the imposition of a curfew, and other restrictions on public assembly. By the end of the month there have been 29 deaths (official figures), many injuries and a total of 254 arrests.

March 15. The Federal Assembly finally approves the budget for 1989 — the issue over which the Mikulić government was compelled to resign the previous December. The following day the Assembly approves the composition of the new FEC proposed by Ante Marković, with only 19 members. The personnel changes reflect major organizational changes to the running of the federal government. Marković delivers an outline of his reform programme to the Assembly.

At the end of the month a new Republican Executive Council finally takes over in Montenegro, replacing the one ousted in January.

April. Although order is largely restored in Kosovo by the beginning of the month, recrimination about the problems of the province continues. At an emergency meeting of the Kosovo Party Committee on *April 1*, three members of its Praesidium resign, and Vllasi is expelled from the LCY for his alleged support of the disturbances in November 1988, and the February strikes. A purge of all Party officials associated with the disturbances is initiated.

April 2. Election of Janez Drnovšek in Slovenia as the republic's candidate for the Federal State Presidency in the country's first direct popular ballot. The following week, however, the Croatian Secretariat for Internal Affairs refuses to register the Movement for a Yugoslav Democratic Initiative, in Zagreb, on the grounds that it has political objectives. On *April 11* elections to the Federal Presidency are spoiled in Bosnia-Hercegovina by accusations that one of the candidates (known as a critic of the political establishment) has been the victim of a smear campaign run by the LC.

April. Internal divisions in the ruling LCY become more obvious. At an acrimonious meeting of its Central Committee, on *April 19*, it is determined that its XIVth Congress (previously brought forward, and due to be held in June 1990) will have the status of an extraordinary congress. The Slovene LC votes unanimously against the holding of the congress. Stipe Šuvar is nominated as the Croatian representative on the collective FSP. This is interpreted as a directly anti-Serbian move, and exacerbates ill feeling between the two republics.

May. It becomes clear that inter-ethnic conflicts in Yugoslavia are by no means confined to Serbia. Tension mounts in Macedonia when on *May 3* the republican Assembly passes a constitutional amendment declaring the republic to be the "national state of the Macedonian nation" — implicitly questioning the citizenship of Albanian, Turkish and other minorities.

On *May 8* an estimated 30,000 people assemble in Ljubljana in a demonstration of support for the military non-commissioned officer and three journalists associated with the paper *Mladina*, who had been sentenced in July 1988 for offences against state security. Following the hearing of their appeals, the "Slovene Four" were ordered to begin their prison sentences on *May 5*.

The "special measures" introduced to control public order in Kosovo in the spring are partially lifted on *May 21*. (There had been limited relaxation of these earlier in the month.) It is reported that since the April 1 emergency meeting of the Kosovo Party Committee more than 300 officials have either resigned or been dismissed.

The new Federal State Presidency takes office for a five-year term on *May 15*. Janez Drnovšek (Slovenia) is named as President, and Borisav Jović (Serbia) as Vice-President. Its reforming intentions are soon announced in a draft law presented to the Federal Assembly which facilitates the holding of multi-party elections. This is in response to the growing number of "political associations" which have already emerged throughout the federation. These continue to multiply rapidly throughout the summer.

June. The month sees a significant manifestation of the particular cultural content of Serbian nationalism. On *June 25* the new Cathedral of St Sava is consecrated in Belgrade, attended by some 150,000 people. It is said to be the largest church in the Balkans. More importantly, on *June 28* celebrations take place in Kosovo Polje to mark the 600th Anniversary of the Battle of Kosovo, which is regarded as a major symbolic declaration of Serbian rights to hold the province. An estimated one million Serbs take part. The occasion passes without significant public disorder among the majority Albanian population of the province, although there are serious outbreaks of violence in Knin, (Croatia) when on *June 8 and 9* Serbs returning from the Kosovo Polje celebrations clash with local Croat residents.

The province is sufficiently quiet to permit the lifting of all special measures to control public disorder in Kosovo on *July 11*.

September 4–7. Although domestic politics is dominated by constant ethnic bickering throughout the summer, the Yugoslav government presents a confident front to the world when the Ninth Summit of the Non-Aligned Movement (NAM) opens in Belgrade, attended by delegations from the 102 member-states. For the first time observers are present from all six Warsaw Pact (Warsaw Treaty Organization) countries. Drnovšek is elected to succeed Robert Mugabe as President of the NAM.

September 11. While one pillar of the Yugoslav political credo is affirmed, however, another crumbles. A further session of the CC of the LCY on *June 11* wrestles with the question of the arrangements for its extraordinary congress. Still no clear plan for the event emerges. General Kadijević, Federal Secretary for Defence, warns of the dangers facing Yugoslavia from an impending split in the LCY. On *September 11* yet another meeting of the CC of the LCY is devoted to the arrangements for the congress. Consideration is given to important constitutional changes within the League's ruling bodies, in the attempt to reduce the damage done to Party unity by regionalism.

September. While a great deal of political energy is devoted by Yugoslavia's leadership to the question of regional struggles, during the month the deteriorating economic position begins to have obvious political consequences. On *September 13* a demonstration of 10,000 people in Belgrade demands government action to curb inflation, and threatens a general strike. On *September 20*, in Nikšić (Montenegro) a "Rally against Hunger" draws a crowd of 30,000. These are followed by other organized protests and strikes.

September 26. Over the summer concern grows in the other republics as Slovenia moves steadily towards the adoption of important revisions to the republican constitution. The CC of the LCY, in emergency session, adopts a resolution urging their postponement. The meeting of the Federal Assembly is boycotted by the Slovene delegates; and on *September 27* Slovenia adopts the amendments to the constitution of the republic, which include the affirmation of the right to secession from the Yugoslav federation, the narrowing of the powers of the Federal State Presidency with respect to the control of the armed forces within the republic, and the provision for political pluralism.

More than 50,000 people demonstrate in Titograd on *September 27* against the Slovene constitutional changes, and on *September 28* further demonstrations along these lines are reported in several Serbian towns. In *October* the Constitutional Court is empowered by the Federal Assembly to begin an examination of the proposed revised republican constitutions which (especially the Slovenian) are alleged to conflict with the federal constitution.

October 1. With great ceremony, the remains of former King Nikola Petrović of Montenegro return from Italy for ceremonial reburial in Cetinje.

October 8. In Solin (Croatia), around 7,000 people attend a mass celebrated by Archbishop Ante Jurić, to mark the 900th Anniversary of the death of King Zvonimir of Croatia. The event, widely regarded as a Croatian response to the Kosovo Polje ceremonies, causes great offence particularly among the Serbian population, as the Archbishop denies that Croats engaged in genocide during the 1941–45 war.

October 10. The Central Committee of the LCY finally agrees to postpone the extraordinary congress until January 20–22, 1990 — "for procedural reasons". A sensation is caused on *October 20* by the discussion materials for the forthcoming congress, which include a policy paper calling for political pluralism, free elections, and the protection of human and civil rights.

October 30. Start of the trial in Kosovska Mitrovica of Vllasi and others accused of "counter-revolutionary actions endangering the social order", associated with another upsurge of public disorder. Five people are shot dead in Priština during demonstrations on *November 1–2*, and more than 500 people are reported injured. The Federal State Presidency rejects an official plea by Slovene representatives to annul the charges against Vllasi. By the end of the week 138 Albanians are imprisoned for their part in the disturbances.

November. Throughout the month the suppression of dissent in Kosovo becomes an increasingly serious occasion for friction between Serbs and Slovenes, as the latter tend to side with the Albanians. On *November 29* the Slovene authorities announce the banning of a rally planned by Serbs, to take place in the Slovene capital on *December 1*, as a "Meeting of Truth" to present the Serbian case in Slovenia. On the day, the Slovene police turn back prospective demonstrators at the republic's borders. Only about 70 manage to assemble in Ljubljana. There are five arrests. Demonstrations against the Slovene action take place in several Serbian towns.

In retaliation, the following day, the Belgrade Chamber of Commerce responds to a demand of the Serbian SA, and orders about 160 large enterprises in the republic to cut off ties with Slovenia. (It later transpires that fewer than a third do so.) Slovenia in turn responds on *November 3* by closing its border temporarily to traffic from Serbia.

December 19. The Federal Assembly votes additional powers to the government to deal with the rising wave of economic disorder in the country. 1989 is declared a record year for strikes in Yugoslavia, of which there have been around 1,900, involving more than 470,000 workers.

December. The year ends with several indications of the increasing openness of Yugoslav politics. Also on *December 19*, the articles of the legal code permitting prosecution for "verbal delicts" are repealed. The celebration of Christmas is given public acknowledgement for the first time since the war (although on grounds of the secular nature of the state, requests to make it a public holiday are refused). On *December 26* Yugoslavia's first post-war stock exchange is opened in Ljubljana.

1990

January 2. The year opens with the introduction of Yugoslavia's new currency, which is fully convertible, and valued in relation to the Deutschmark at 7:1 — a central plank of the Marković platform. Wage increases are pegged to the exchange rate. Over the next three months inflation (which reached an annual rate of more than 2,500% in 1989) temporarily disappears.

January 13. The tide of pluralism reaches Serbia, and the Serbian authorities ban the Movement for Serbian Renewal — the ultra-nationalist party led by Vuk Drašković. In the same week, however, the Radical Party (originally founded 1881) is relaunched in Belgrade.

A new trade union for journalists is launched, based on an initiative from Vojvodina, on *January 17*, largely in response to growing pressure from nationalist political groups on the press. Branches are set up in all major cities.

January 20. The LC finally begins its XIVth (extraordinary) Congress in Belgrade. The main item on the agenda is the commitment of the Party to political pluralism. The Slovene LC presents proposals for the reform of the Party into eight independent parties. This is fiercely attacked by Serbian delegates. On *January 22* the renunciation of the constitutional guarantee of the "leading role of the League of Communists" is adopted with only 28 votes against. The Slovene proposals are resoundingly defeated, as are proposals on a clear commitment to civil rights. The Slovene delegation withdraws from the Congress.

After bitter debate over the conditions under which the congress could continue, it is adjourned on *January 23* with no date set for its reconvention. The press announces "*SKJ više ne postoji*" — the LCY no longer exists. Marković declares that "Yugoslavia continues to function with or without the LCY",

January 24. After a period of relative calm in Kosovo, a demonstration of up to 40,000 people in Priština gathers at the provincial headquarters of the LC to demand extensive political reforms. The police break up the meeting with water cannon and tear gas. There are more than 100 arrests. This begins a week of rioting in the province, which spreads to other towns. Special militia units are drafted into the province on *January 26* in an attempt to restore order. Over the next four days at least 26 people are killed (including a police officer) in various locations. The riots are the worst seen in the province in the post-war period.

A vigil is begun in Belgrade outside the Federal Assembly by tens of thousands of Serbs, on *January 30*, demanding that the army be sent into Kosovo. A similar demonstration is mounted in Titograd. On *January 31* the FSP announces "special measures" in Kosovo. There are clear signs of acute disagreement between the members of the Presidency over the appropriate response to the situation.

February 1. For the first time units of the Yugoslav National Army are used to control public order in Kosovo. There are more deaths among rioters. Slovene militia units are withdrawn from Kosovo. On *February 5*, Milošević calls for a "mobilization for Kosovo", which would include the resettlement of thousands of Serbs in the province. On *February 20*, a curfew is imposed in Priština.

February. Throughout the month more prospective political parties declare their hand in all parts of the federation. The vast majority of these serve an explicitly ethnic constituency. Particularly noteworthy is the formation of an All-Macedonian Action Movement in Skopje on *February 25*. The Green parties and the Social Democrats appear to present some kind of cross-regional solidarity. It is estimated that by now more than 60 parties have declared themselves throughout the federation.

February 4. The Slovene LC holds a congress at which it formally renounces links with the LCY and commits itself to multi-party elections in the republic. The party is renamed the "Party of Democratic Renewal".

February 22. Slovene independence is expressed in another form when the Slovene government retaliates against Serbian economic sanction by withholding 15% of its contribution to federal funds — a proportion which represents economic aid to Serbia. On *March 8* the Slovene

Assembly finally adopts the controversial amendments to the republic's constitution, dropping the word "socialist" from the name of the republic and all its institutions. At the end of March the mutual economic boycott between Serbia and Slovenia (which began in December) is relaxed.

March 19. On the economic front the news is generally good; and external recognition of this is indicated by the agreement reached with the IMF for an 18-month standby credit of up to US$600 million.

March 30. LCY fails to assemble a quorum for its plenum, which has been called to address the collapse of the XIVth Congress in January. Members from Croatia and Macedonia, as well as Slovenia, absent themselves, and after the start of the meeting the CC members from Bosnia also withdraw.

March 22. After a brief respite, violence flares again in Kosovo following allegations and rumours of the mass poisoning of Albanian students and children. More than 100 people are injured in Podujevo alone. Troops are deployed in order to quell the resulting unrest and a curfew is imposed. Following an official enquiry, on *March 28* the claims about poisoning are officially dismissed, but Jusuf Karakusi (Provincial Minister of the Interior) resigns. The incident illustrates the permanently unstable condition of the province.

April 3. Jusuf Zejnulahu, the provincial premier, and other provincial ministers in Kosovo, resign in protest against the excessive brutality of the security forces towards Albanians in the province. The Provincial Assembly later refuses to accept the resignations which would leave government in the hands of the ethnic Serb members. Croatia announces the withdrawal of its militia units from Kosovo.

April. The long-awaited round of multi-party elections begins, with the first round of balloting for the Slovene Assembly. The election on *April 8* is contested by DEMOS, a powerful alliance of six opposition groups. The second round (on *April 22*) results in a victory for DEMOS. With nearly 55% of the vote it takes 47 of the 80 seats in the Socio-Political Chamber. The Party of Democratic Renewal (former LC) is still the largest single party, with 14 seats, and its candidate, Milan Kučan, is elected as President of the Slovene Presidency.

On the same day, the first round of the Croatian Assembly elections also take place on a multi-party basis. On *April 11*, the Federal Assembly passes temporary legislation, extending its own mandate until the end of the year, in order to allow multi-party elections of its members to be organized.

April 13. Fadilj Hodža, a prominent former state and LC official, is charged with incitement to racial intolerance and religious hatred in connection with the disturbances in Kosovo. Civil order is restored, even so, enabling the "special measures" to be suspended on *April 18*. The Serbian Ministry of Internal Affairs takes direct control of security arrangements in the province from federal authorities. 108 persons arrested during the disturbances are released from custody. More significantly, on *April 24* Azem Vllasi is released from custody, acquitted, together with the others formerly charged with him, of counter-revolutionary activity.

May 4. The changing political climate of Yugoslavia is symbolized as much as anything else when, on the 10th anniversary of the death of former President Tito, a demonstration in Belgrade of about 2,000 Serbs, organized by three of the new parties, calls for the removal of his remains to his native Croatia, and an end to the "cult of personality".

May 6–7. In the second round of the Croatian Assembly elections the Croatian Democratic Union, led by Franjo Tudjman, wins a sweeping victory, on a right-wing and highly nationalistic platform. The party takes 197 of the 353 seats in the three Chambers.

May 15. In the regular rotation of the presidency of the FSP Borisav Jović, a supporter of the Milošević line, takes over from Drnovšek. His vice-president is Croatia's Stipe Šuvar. The presidency is thereby seriously hampered as an agency for effective and united government. The likelihood of stalemate at the top is suggested when, on *May 28*, President Jović introduces to the Federal Assembly a package of measures designed to promote a more centralized and less liberal constitution, and which sets aside those constitutional changes already adopted unilaterally by individual republics. The session ended the following day without adopting the Jović plan.

May. During the month there are further indications of the future political importance of non-communists. On *May 16*, a member of the Christian Democratic Party, Lojze Peterle, is elected as President of the Slovene Republican Executive Council (REC), and its "Prime Minister". On *May 30* Franjo Tudjman is elected as president of the Croatian presidency, and another member of his party, Stjepan Mesić, president of the Croatian EC.

May 16. The Federal Assembly approves an amnesty for all political prisoners charged under Article 133 of the Penal Code (hostile propaganda), and those accused of "slandering the state" (Article 157).

May 25. Ante Marković announces plans to set up an all-Yugoslav party, which will contest elections to the Federal Assembly on the basis of support for his reform programme. The following day, the suspended XIVth Congress of the LCY is finally resumed, in spite of a boycott by Croatian, Macedonian and Slovene delegates. It votes for a relaunch of the Party at a XVth Congress, planned for September 1990.

June 13. The distinctive pattern of Serbian politics is underlined when a crowd of about 30,000 demonstrators assembles in Belgrade to demand the holding of early elections in Serbia. Opposition parties are still technically illegal, and their representatives denied access to the media.

June 26. The trial of Fadilj Hodža is abandoned after allegations of judicial irregularity.

June 30. The Marković government presents the second stage of its programme of economic reforms to the Federal Assembly. This includes proposals to privatize socially owned enterprises. He emphasizes that the future of the entire stabilization and restructuring process depends upon the co-operation of the republics.

July 2. Referendum in Serbia on the proposed changes to the republic's constitution. These include the abolition of the special status of the "Autonomous Provinces" and deletion of the description "socialist" from the name of the republic. It is claimed that 96.8% of the vote is in favour, but the event is largely boycotted in Kosovo, where some 400 polling stations fail to open. Nevertheless, on *July 5* Kosovo Assembly is declared abolished by the Serbian Assembly. Immediately, a group of 114 Albanian delegates to the provincial Assembly issue a statement that Kosovo is now independent of Serbia, and a full republic within the SFRY.

Senior staff of the Albanian language daily *Rilindja* and the Kosovo radio and TV services are replaced by staff loyal to Serbia. The following day token one-hour strikes begin each day in Kosovo in protest against constitutional change and Serbian control of the mass media.

These developments are condemned on *July 11*, by LC and other political bodies in Serbia, Montenegro and Vojvodina. The Federal State Presidency also issues a condemnation.

July 17. The Serbian LC votes to combine with the Socialist Alliance in the republic to form a new party, to be known as the Serbian Socialist Party. No change of policy attends this move. Slobodan Milošević is elected as its president by 1,299 votes to 66.

July 25. Amid the excitement in Serbia, it attracts little attention when on *July 2* the Slovenian Assembly formally declares the full sovereignty of the republic. On *July 25*, the Croatian Assembly approves 12 constitutional changes, including the removal of the word "socialist" from the constitution.

July 25. Legislation passed in the Federal Assembly permits the formation of parties "of a general Yugoslav character". One of the first to take advantage of this is Ante Marković himself. At a rally in Kozara, Bosnia on *July 29*, attended by some 100,000 people, he launches his own Yugoslav-wide party, the Alliance of Reform Forces. The move is a reflection of Marković's frustration at the lack of co-operation he is receiving from politicians in ethnically and locally based parties.

July 29. At a rally in the village of Srb, a gathering of 100,000 Croatian Serbs declare their own autonomy from Croatia. Two days later, leaders of Serb communities in Croatia form a Serbian National Council, which rejects recent amendments to the Croatian constitution and determines to conduct a referendum on questions of cultural autonomy.

Almost immediately the Croatian Ministry of Justice bans the proposed referendum. In the Croatian towns of Knin and Benkovac — areas with ethnic Serb majorities — disorder breaks out on *August 17* in connection with the referendum. Serb settlements are blockaded to exclude the republican police force. The Croatian government declares there to be an armed insurrection against the Croatian state.

On *August 19* the referendum among ethnic Serbs in Croatia begins in 11 communes. Several days later polling booths are opened in Belgrade for residents born in Croatia. The Croatian Assembly votes on *August 24* to recall Stipe Šuvar as the republic's representative on the FSP, following accusations that he had not been sufficiently vigorous in pursuit of Croatian interests during the affair. He is replaced by Stjepan Mesić.

August 23. Hajrullah Gorani, leader of the newly founded independent trade union movement in Kosovo, is jailed for 60 days for his advocacy of a general strike. The union calls a general strike in the province on *September 3*, and claim participation by 200,000 people, to protest against the dismissal of thousands of ethnic Albanian officials, and their replacement by Serbs, and the institution of compulsory loyalty oaths.

Earlier in the week (*August 29*) US Senator Robert Dole and a delegation of American congressional representatives make a fact-finding visit to Priština. They are greeted by strikes and violent demonstrations, which are dispersed by the use of batons, tear gas and water cannon. Officials from the International Helsinki Federation human rights group, visiting Kosovo on *September 4*, are detained by the police in Prizren, and ordered to leave the country within 48 hours.

The Albanian delegates to the dissolved Kosovo provincial assembly convene on *September 7* in the village of Kačanik, and proclaim a constitution for the "Republic of Kosovo" within the SFRJ. Over the next week the authorities begin arrests, and the majority (including the prime minister, Zejnulahu) flee the country or to other republics. It is estimated that 10–15,000 officials and others have been dismissed in the province, and replaced often by Serbs and Montenegrins drafted in from their own republics.

September 7. Attention now turns to Bosnia where, following several public disturbances in the town of Foča, the republican government dissolves the town council and prohibits public gatherings. There are further disturbances of public order over the following week involving clashes between Serb and Muslim residents. On *September 9*, police in Novi Pazar (Bosnia) clash with Muslim supporters of the republic's Democratic Action Party, who try to disrupt a rally of the extreme Serbian National Renewal.

September 17. Following talks over the previous month, Italy and Yugoslavia sign the "Adriatic Initiative" on environmental protection, transport, tourism and infrastructure.

September. By now the federal government is experiencing acute frustration in relation to its reform programme. Republican assemblies will not pass essential measures until after the forthcoming round of elections. Proposals for federal constitutional reform emanating from Slovenia and Croatia secure no support, and indeed experience consistent discouragement from the Jović presidency.

The new Serbian constitution finally comes into force at the end of the month, opening the way for elections in the republic. The controversial new Slovene constitution also comes into force.

October 2. The region of southern Croatia which witnessed civil disorder in 1989 after the Kosovo anniversary celebrations again erupts, when in Knin and five neighbouring settlements with large Serb majorities an independent Serb enclave is declared within the Croatian republic. Road blocks are erected and rail lines cut. Two policemen are shot and weapons seized from local arsenals. President Jović cuts short his visit to the USA, but the FEC is unable to agree on a course of action. The republican authorities seal off the area, but refrain from intervention on the insistence of the federal government. The violence continues sporadically into November.

November 10–12. The first round of direct elections in Macedonia gives the lead to a coalition of nationalist parties. In Bosnia and Hercegovina, on *November 18,* elections yield results roughly in keeping with the republic's ethnic mixture. Even in their reformed mode, the former communists typically do poorly.

A new twist is given to the story of political pluralism at the end of November by the formation of a new Movement for Yugoslavia — a fraction of the former LCY, headed by about 80 senior military officers including two members of Marković's own cabinet. Military figures are regularly (and disturbingly) outspokenly critical of the direction which Yugoslav politics is taking.

December 9. The first round of the Serbian elections confirmed the dominance of Milošević, with an absolute majority for his Serbian Socialist Party, which is emphatically underlined in the second round on *December 23.* Elections are also completed in Montenegro.

By the end of the year, therefore, popularly elected governments are installed after free elections in all areas of Yugoslavia — except in Kosovo, where the entire electoral process is boycotted by the Albanian parties. Although these may be said to have a mandate for the negotiation of any future form for a Yugoslav state, the year ends with a large question-mark over the future of federation, as a referendum in Slovenia on *December 23* returns a substantial majority in favour of the republic's withdrawal from Yugoslavia.

The results of the 1990 elections are shown in detail in Tables 1–6 below.

Table 1:   The 1990 elections — Slovenia

Presidential Election	First Round: April 8 (%)	Second Round: April 22 (%)
Candidate		
Milan Kucan (LCS-PDR)	44.5	58.4
Jože Pučnik (DEMOS)	26.2	41.7
Ivan Kramberger (Indep.)	18.9	
Marko Demsar (USYS)	10.5	
Socio-Political Chamber: Assembly	Vote (%)	Seats
DEMOS	55	47
CD	13	11
PU	13	11
LCS-PDR	17	14
USYS-Liberal	14	12
Others	14	7

Note: The elections to the Chamber of Associated Labour were not competed for on a party basis.

Abbreviations

CD   Christian Democrats

DEMOS   the Democratic Opposition of Slovenia — consists of an alliance of six parties, namely: Christian Democratic Party; the Peasants' Union; Democratic Alliance; League of Social Democrats; Liberal Democratic Party and Green Party

LCS-PDR   League of Communists of Slovenia-Party of Democratic Reform — the reformed LCY in Slovenia

PU   Peasants' Union — the first independent post-war political organization to be founded in Slovenia

USYS   Union of Socialist Youth of Slovenia — the former official communist youth organization, long known for its independent and radical stance, working in alliance with the Liberals

Table 2:   The 1990 elections — Serbia

Presidential Election	*Concluded in First Round:* *December 9 (%)*
Candidate	
Slobodan Milošević (SPS)	65
Vuk Drašković (MSR)	17

Note: Altogether 32 candidates stood in the first round.

Socio-Political Chamber: Assembly	*Concluded in Second Round:* *December 23*	
	Vote	Seats
SPS	77.6	194
MSR	7.6	19
Independents	3.2	8
Democratic Party	2.8	7
DUMV	2.0	5
Others	6.8	17

Note: The election was boycotted by the major Albanian party in Kosovo, The Democratic Alliance.

Abbreviations

DUMV   Democratic Union of Magyars of Vojvodina

MSR   Movement for Serbian Renewal

SPS   Socialist Party of Serbia — the reformed LCY in Serbia

Table 3:   The 1990 elections — Bosnia and Hercegovina

Presidential Election	First Round: November 18	Second Round: December 2

The Republic is headed by a collective Presidency, which must reflect its ethnic diversity. Of the seven members, two must be Muslims, two Serbs and two Croats. A seventh member represents other minority groups. In an extremely complex process, in which 28 candidates stood, the following were confirmed in the Second Round.

Candidate
Fikret Abdić (44%) and Alija Izetbegović (37%) (Muslim: PDA)
Nikola Koljević (25%) and Biljana Plavšić (24%) (Serb: LC–SDP)
Stjepan Kljujić (21%) and Franjo Boras (19%) (Croat: CDU)
Ejup Ganić (PDA)

A third Serb (Nenad Kecmanović) stood for the ARF, but secured only 21%.

Joint Result:
Socio–Political Chamber and
Chamber of Municipalities

	Seats
PDA	86
SDP	70
CDU	45
LC–SDP	19
ARF	12
Independents	5
Others	12

Abbreviations

ARF	Alliance of Reform Forces
CDU	Croatian Democratic Union
LC–SDP	League of Communists–Social Democratic Party — the renamed LC in Bosnia and Hercegovina
PDA	Party of Democratic Action — the principal Muslim party in the Republic
SDP	Serbian Democratic Party

Table 4: The 1990 elections — Croatia

Presidential Election	*Concluded in First Round:* *April 22*
Candidate	
Franjo Tudjman (CDU)	"overwhelming"
Ivica Racan (LCC-PDC)	
Ivo Družić (CNA)	

Assembly: *Chamber of* *Municipalities*	*Concluded in Second Round:* *May 6–7* *Seats*
CDU	67
LC–PDC	21
Socialists	9
Others	19
Socio–Political Chamber	
CDU	52
LCC-PDC	10
Others	18
Chamber of Associated Labour	
CDU	78
LCC–PDC	35
Democratic Party	7
CNA	5
Independents	12
Others	20

Abbreviations

CDU Croatian Democratic Union

CNA Coalition of National Agreement — a coalition of nine minor parties principally seeking a non-ethnic basis for politics and the defence of the Yugoslav federation.

LCC–PDC League of Communists of Croatia–Party of Democratic Change — the reformed LCY in Croatia

---

Table 5:   The 1990 elections — Macedonia

| *Presidential Election* | *First Round: November 9*
Because of "irregularities" in 176 voting districts, this was rerun on November 25.
Second Round: December 9 |

Because no candidate has secured the requisite support of 50% of the electorate, the Presidency is still undecided.

Assembly	*Resolved in the Second Round* *December 9* *Seats*
IMRO–DPMNU	37
LC–PDT	31
PDP	25
ARF	18
Socialists	5
Others	4

Abbreviations

ARF	Alliance of Reform Forces
IMRO–DPMNU	Internal Macedonian Revolutionary Organization–Democratic Party for Macedonian National Unity. (IMRO was an influential nationalist revolutionary organization before World War I. There is no direct continuity between this and the present party.)
PDP	Party of Democratic Prosperity (based in Tetovo, it has principally Albanian support).

Table 6:   The 1990 elections — Montenegro

Presidential Election	First Round: December 9	Second Round: December 23 (%)
Momir Bulatović (LCM)		76
Ljubiša Stanković (ARF)		
Novak Kilibarda (NP)		

Note: A second round was necessary as the President needs to secure the votes of more than 50% of the electorate.

Collective Presidency	28 candidates stood in the First Round
Svetozar Marović (LCM)	
Milica Pejanović–Djurišić (LCM) }	elected in First Round
Hazbo Nuhanović (LCM) }	
Slobodan Vujačić (LCM) }	elected in Second Round

Assembly	Seats
LCM	83
ARF	17
Democratic Coalition	13
National Party	12

Abbreviations

ARF	Alliance of Reformed Forces
LCM	League of Communists of Montenegro
Democratic Coalition	An alliance of Muslim parties: the Party of Democratic Action (based in Bosnia), the Party of Equality and the Democratic Alliance (an Albanian party based in Kosovo)
National Party	Centre–Right party emphasizing Montenegrin nationality

Political Overview

Yugoslavia was created at the end of World War I principally from the debris of two great multi-national empires — the Habsburg and the Ottoman. The "Piedmont" around which the new state was constructed was the former Serbian kingdom. Partly as a result of their numerical predominance, and partly because Serbia was the only element of the new entity to possess its own army, a constitution was imposed which strongly favoured the position of Serbs in the political process.

Governing typically with support from the Slovene clerical and Bosnian Muslim land-owning parties, Serbian politicians used official patronage and colonization associated with the land reform programme as their principal instruments in the attempt to Serbianize regions which they regarded as historically theirs — especially Macedonia, Kosovo and the Sandžak.

Frustrated by the way in which ethnic strife (especially between Serbs and Croats) stifled political and economic development, King Alexander inaugurated a royal dictatorship in 1929, which lasted until his assassination in 1934. Movement towards political normalization was in process when Yugoslavia was invaded in 1941.

The Axis invasion of April 1941 resulted in the division of the country between German and Italian zones of occupation. Some areas (especially Slovenia and parts of the Adriatic coast) were absorbed directly by Germany and Italy; the greater part of Macedonia went to Bulgaria, parts of the north to Hungary, and an array of puppet states was established in Serbia, Montenegro and Croatia. In the last of these, an indigenous fascist regime conducted a programme of racial extermination along Nazi lines, but directed against Serbs as much as Jews.

Two movements of resistance were set up early in the war: a royalist, Serb, army under Draža Mihailović (the "Chetniks"), and a communist movement, led by Josip Broz "Tito" (the "Partisans"). Having radically different political and economic aspirations, civil war soon developed between these two forces, which overlay (and often obscured) the struggle against the occupier.

Partly as a result of their greater success in securing Allied recognition and assistance, and partly because of the extreme narrowness of Chetnik aspirations, the communist forces ended the war victorious. The Yugoslavia re-established in 1945 was given a federal form, in the attempt to accommodate the regional and ethnic diversity on which the "first Yugoslavia" had foundered.

Unlike other areas of central and eastern Europe, therefore, the post-war communist regime was not founded principally upon occupation by the Soviet army. Tito's regime was, nevertheless, committed to the same communist model of politics. It moved rapidly to eliminate effective opposition, established a one-party regime, and embarked upon a programme of the nationalization of resources and centralized economic planning.

The Yugoslavs, however, retained a great sense of their independence, and were expelled from the Cominform in 1948, accused of ideological and political deviation and lack of party discipline. In the attempt to combat the effects of their isolation, the distinctive "Yugoslav road to socialism" which was expounded subsequently, stressed three lines. Close economic co-operation with the capitalist West made for economic development and the expansion of trade. The creation and evolution (after 1953) of "workers' self-management" enabled the Yugoslavs to affirm their continuing socialist credentials. Commitment to the Non-Aligned Movement distanced Yugoslavia from the Warsaw Pact (Warsaw Treaty Organization) countries, while denying that it had become militarily engaged with the West, and provided an influential international platform.

In spite of these apparent discontinuities in its development, the "new Yugoslavia" exhibited many continuities with its past. It emerged from the war with more than 75% of its population engaged in peasant agriculture. The post-war period has featured a constant effort to escape from economic backwardness, and to turn Yugoslavia into a modernized and industrialized state. This was undertaken initially through Soviet-style forced-march, centrally planned industrialization, but since the economic reforms of 1965 a much more diverse and flexible set of measures has been adopted. Although great progress has been made, the legacy of extreme differences of level of economic development between the country's regions has remained, providing occasion for a succession of political conflicts.

In spite of its elaborate play of distinctiveness, the Tito regime retained an emphatic commitment to the "leading role" of the Communist Party (known in Yugoslavia as the "League of Communists"). In this respect the process of destalinization has been vigorously and effectively resisted by Yugoslav communists. Above all, the Yugoslav economy remained heavily politicized, in spite of the elements of "market socialism" which nominally attended the development of self-management.

The political strains which have attended this process have been exacerbated, and given a particular form, in Yugoslavia by the continuing importance of the country's extreme ethnic diversity. A difficult balancing act has been attempted between the affirmation of the rights of ethnic groups and the insistence on the unity of the federation. This was managed, on the whole successfully, under the charismatic leadership of the late President Tito. After his death in May 1980, however, the achievement of unity became ever more precarious, and the wounds of pre-war and wartime hostility reopened.

A particular hazard which has been associated with the growing autonomy of the country's republics has been the loss of federal monetary control, which has been regarded as the principal cause both of the international debt crisis of the later 1970s and early 1980s, and of the period of hyper-inflation of the late 1980s.

This combination of sharpening inter-regional conflict and economic near-catastrophe initiated a process of radical change in Yugoslavia sooner than in most of the other communist-controlled states — a process which was already well advanced at the end of 1988.

Ethnicity and the conflict of nationalities

The most conspicuous feature of Yugoslav political life during the past decade has been the central part which ethnicity has played. Among the countries of central and eastern Europe Yugoslavia rivals the Soviet Union in terms of the complexity of its ethnic structure. In addition to the ethnic "charter groups" of South Slavs, from which the country takes its title (Croats, Macedonians, Montenegrins, Muslims, Serbs and Slovenes, to which should probably be added the 1.2 million who defined themselves as "Yugoslav"), the census of 1981 recorded 20 others as sufficiently numerous to merit separate mention. Most numerous among these are Albanians, Magyars, Gypsies and Turks. The numerical significance of such groups varies considerably between regions (see Table 7). This pattern is a direct result of the way in which the state of Yugoslavia was carved out of the two multi-ethnic empires which formerly dominated the Balkans — the Habsburg and Ottoman.

Yugoslavia's federal organization into six republics (and before their absorption into the

Table 7: Ethnicity in Yugoslavia by Republic; census of 1981
(Ethnic groups > 1%: percentages)

Territory	Ethnic group	%	Representation of principal ethnic group in territory
Yugoslavia	Serbs		36.3
	Croats		19.7
	Muslims		8.9
	Slovenes		7.8
	Albanians		7.7
	Macedonians		6.0
	Yugoslavs		5.4
	Mongenegrins		2.6
	Magyars		1.9
	Others		3.7
Bosnia & Hercegovina	Muslims	39.5	81.5
	Serbs	32.0	
	Croats	18.4	
	Yugoslavs	7.9	
	Others	2.2	
Croatia	Croats	75.1	78.0
	Serbs	11.6	
	Yugoslavs	8.2	
	Others	5.1	
Macedonia	Macedonians	67.0	95.5
	Albanians	19.8	
	Turks	4.5	
	Serbs	2.3	
	Romanians	2.3	
	Muslims	2.1	
	Others	2.0	
Montenegro	Montenegrins	68.5	69.2
	Muslims	13.4	
	Albanians	6.5	
	Yugoslavs	5.3	
	Serbs	3.3	
	Others	3.0	
"Inner Serbia"	Serbs	85.4	59.8
	Yugoslavs	4.8	
	Muslims	2.7	
	Montenegrins	1.4	
	Albanians	1.3	
	Gypsies	1.0	
	Others	3.4	
Kosovo	Albanians	77.4	70.9
	Serbs	13.2	
	Muslims	3.7	

Table 7: (*Continued*)

Territory	Ethnic group	%	Representation of principal ethnic group in territory
	Gypsies	2.2	
	Montenegrins	1.7	
	Others	1.8	
Vojvodina	Serbs	54.4	13.6
	Magyars	18.9	
	Yugoslavs	8.2	
	Croats	5.4	
	Slovaks	3.4	
	Romanians	2.3	
	Montenegrins	2.1	
	Gypsies	1.0	
	Others	4.3	
Serbia: Republic	Serbs	66.4	75.9
	Albanians	14.0	
	Yugoslavs	4.7	
	Magyars	4.2	
	Muslims	2.3	
	Croats	1.6	
	Montenegrins	1.6	
	Gypsies	1.2	
	Others	4.0	
Slovenia	Slovenes	90.5	91.7
	Croats	2.9	
	Serbs	2.2	
	Yugoslavs	1.4	
	Others	3.0	

Serbian republic in September 1990, two autonomous provinces) is a reflection of these facts. Ethnic complexity in itself might not have imposed insuperable political problems. The political salience of ethnicity in Yugoslavia stems principally from other specific features of the history and pattern of distribution of its constituent groups, which over the past two years have come to be specially relevant to the understanding of political developments in the country.

The majority of Yugoslavia's regions are ethnically mixed. Only the republic of Slovenia has more than 90% of its population drawn from its dominant ethnic group: in Macedonia, Montenegro and Serbia that proportion is closer to two-thirds.

The republic of Bosnia and Hercegovina is notable for its mixed population: roughly one third Serb, one fifth Croat and around 40% who consider themselves "Muslim" by nationality. These are not Turks left behind from the Ottoman empire, but indigenous, Serbo-Croat-speaking Slavs who are the descendants of those who embraced Islam in the 15th and 16th centuries. The extent to which a specifically religious commitment to Islam is a part of their cultural identity is debatable, and they do not identify themselves closely with other Islamic groups in Yugoslavia — such as the Albanians.

Also sensitive in this respect are parts of Croatia, which have substantial Serb settlements along the border with Bosnia; the former autonomous province of Vojvodina, which has a large Magyar population; and western Macedonia, which in recent years has become heavily settled by Albanians. The first of these experienced outbreaks of serious violence in July and August, and again in October 1990 when local Serbs attempted to set up an autonomous region on Croatian territory.

The region which has dominated Yugoslav politics more than any other in the period in question is the former autonomous province of Kosovo. Three-quarters of its inhabitants were Albanian at the census of 1981, and a combination of differential birthrates and emigration of Serbo-Croat speakers subsequently has increased that proportion dramatically. The struggle to introduce a revised constitution for the republic of Serbia focused in particular on the desire of Serbs to restore the authority of the republic over the two autonomous provinces which were nominally a part of Serbia, but which were seen to be slipping increasingly into the *de facto* control of other ethnic groups.

A second important indication of ethnic dispersion is found in the proportions of each group which reside in their "home" republic. Only in the case of Slovenes and Macedonians does this figure exceed 90%. A permanent issue in Yugoslav politics, therefore, has been the position and rights of ethnic minorities in each region, and since every group is a minority in the whole federation, the power balance between them at the federal level.

A key point of conflict in this regard has been the definition of certain "nationalities". This arises particularly because of the territorial claims which on historical grounds are advanced by the larger nations. Many Serbs do not, for this reason, recognize the existence of Macedonians, Montenegrins and Muslims as "nationalities", asserting that they are "really" Serbs. The same is true of Croats in relation to Muslims, whom they claim to be "Croats of the Islamic faith".

Historical traditions of the identity between ethnic groups and territory raise specially severe problems in relation to two areas: Kosovo and Macedonia. Serb claims to rule Kosovo as of right are premised upon the fact that the area was in the 13th and 14th centuries the heart of a Serbian empire. Strident advocacy of such claims has been the hallmark of the Movement for Serbian Renewal, led by Vuk Drašković. Albanians point to the antiquity of Albanian settlement in the region, and to the fact that it has long been a region of mixed ethnic composition. The conflict over Macedonian identity has a similar basis, and has provided an ideological focus for the new Macedonian nationalist parties.

Talk of the rights of minorities, or the appropriate powers of republics, hinges centrally on these issues. The whole constitutional process could be wrecked by them. At the same time, a simple division of Yugoslavia into an array of independent states would be compromised by the dispersion of nationalities, which must inevitably leave large minorities in all of the envisaged new states. An amicable division of Bosnia and Hercegovina is impossible along ethnic lines, as there is no clear geographical segregation of Serbs, Croats and Muslims — and the legitimacy of the last of these groups is contested by the other two. The sad fact of the matter is, that the breakup of Yugoslavia is not conceivable without a civil war, particularly over the future of Bosnia. Although public attention in Yugoslavia and abroad naturally has been focused on the dramatic conflict in Kosovo, where the majority Albanian population has sought republican status within the federation, in many respects the key to the future of Yugoslavia is Bosnia.

The politics of nationality are complicated further in Yugoslavia by three other facts. Lines of ethnic difference are emphasized by their coincidence with other significant differences, such as language and religion. Croats and Slovenes are typically Roman Catholic: others typically Orthodox, with the exception of the Islamic groups already mentioned. Albanians, Macedonians, and Slovenes are distinguished by their own languages. There are other differences of political tradition — particularly relating to the nature and role of the state — which date back to the earlier empires. Above all, the more recent history of inter-war and wartime conflict lends a degree of bitterness and hostility to any consideration of nationality in Yugoslavia.

The struggle for economic reform

The process of economic reconstruction is considered in detail below; but three points are appropriately made in this context. Yugoslavia shares with the other countries considered in this volume the problems of movement away from a politicized economy. This process presents difficulties of a particular form in Yugoslavia.

The need for economic change has been disguised in Yugoslavia both by the real moves away from overt central planning in the past, and by failure to appreciate the fact that the changes which were achieved following the post-1965 reforms were often more real than apparent. Indeed, there is good reason to believe that in the period after 1974 the Yugoslav economy underwent a kind of "restalinization" of some aspects of its economic organization, particularly through the effects of the *Zakon o udruženom radu* (the Law on Associated Labour — the basic statute which formerly defined and regulated the system of self-management in work organizations).

Furthermore, because of the greater success of Yugoslavia's political élite in defending their claims to legitimacy, it has been possible for economic "conservatives" to mount a relatively effective rearguard action in the face of demands for wholesale economic reconstruction.

The importance of these two points is reflected in the continuing political strength of former communists in several areas of the country, ranging from the election of Milan Kučan to the Slovene presidency to the outstanding success of Slobodan Milošević in Serbia.

Finally, a central feature of the Yugoslav economy has been the acute disparities of level of economic development which characterize its various regions and republics. Consequently a special twist is given to the rivalry between republics, and to the struggles relating to constitutional reform, in that these can be interpreted at one level as economic conflicts between developed and under-developed countries.

In all of these respects, although there is nothing resembling the problems of acute shortage and maldistribution which are encountered in the Soviet Union, the economic dimension of politics in Yugoslavia resembles that of the SU more closely than the other eastern and central European countries.

The development towards political pluralism

Although Yugoslavia has now gone through the process of replacing the former hegemony of the League of Communists with a form of "pluralism", in one important respect it is still not possible to say that there has developed a "democratic" politics. At the heart of this problem is the dominant part which ethnicity plays in the creation of political identity and political institutions. A plenitude of parties contested the cycle of elections, which began with the choice of presidential candidates offered to voters in Slovenia in April 1989 and ended with the free elections to the republican Assemblies, which were completed in December 1990: but an analysis of their character presents a discouraging picture. On the whole four types of parties can be identified.

Possibly the largest group have "constitutional" aims — they are based upon the demand for parliamentary democracy itself, and an attendant array of civil liberties. These are probably ephemeral, and if Yugoslavia survives into a further cycle of elections will be absorbed into parties of the fourth type.

There are several issue-oriented parties — especially the Greens. While such parties might become a long-standing feature of the political scene, experience elsewhere suggests that they will remain marginal.

By far the most significant, not only in their number but also their electoral success, are the ethnic parties, which everywhere since December 1990 hold power at the republican level, and consequently will call the shots at the federal level. An important feature of their platforms is that they are typically vague on issues of social and economic policy, and the greater part of their energies and self-definition are addressed to changes in the constitutional structure of the country. They challenge the legitimacy of the present state.

Finally, there are what could be called "general" parties, which seek to aggregate interests around a programme, the central concerns of which have to do with social and economic policy. Many of the reformed fragments of the LCY are of this type, as are the various Social-Democratic parties. While these too will be a persisting feature of any continuing Yugoslav politics they have performed poorly in the recent elections. It is also important to note that since the effective demise of the LCY at its XIVth Congress in January 1990, they have in most cases specifically republican aspirations. (Ante Marković's "Alliance of Reform Forces" did not contest the elections to all of the republican Assemblies.)

There is a sense in which what could be emerging in Yugoslavia is a mirror image of politics in the majority of Western European countries, in which the political contest takes place largely over issues of economic interest, within a generally uncontested constitutional framework. While tested at the periphery (for example, by the Scottish, Irish or Basque nationalists), by and large constitutional issues only become prominent in relation to the failures of the system to answer to economic interests. In Yugoslavia, on the other hand, it seems that questions of economic interest are almost a taken-for-granted background to the party struggle. With some latitude, there is general agreement that a movement towards a more open, market-oriented and depoliticized economy is desirable, even among those who retain a commitment in general terms to socialism. The energy of political contest is directed instead to constitutional issues, and especially to those which arise from Yugoslavia's multi-ethnic composition.

Because of the complexity of Yugoslavia's ethnic structure (and especially the geographical distribution of ethnic groups) the electoral contest has taken the form of an exercise in ethnic nose-counting. The political process revolves around the resolution of constitutional problems which will advantage or disadvantage (depending upon their outcome) one ethnic group or another. The day-to-day mechanisms of the economy which might have an impact impartially upon all sections of the community (inflation, stabilization, economic development, European integration etc.) might therefore be seen as reserved from the political contest. Ante Marković was wiser than he knew when he said that the government could continue without the League of Communists.

Whereas it is possible to envisage positive outcomes from this situation — a professionalized, effective government getting on with the job of governing, while the politicians slug it out — disastrous possibilities seem more likely. Unstable and shifting coalitions might regularly use their veto to interfere with the process of government, and indeed, take their bat home if their ethnic interests are not seen as adequately served within a constitutional framework whose legitimacy is challenged fundamentally. The latter pattern certainly came to typify politics in Yugoslavia between the wars, and the early signs are that this will continue. Indeed, the process may already have gone too far to prevent the complete disintegration of the country.

The problems of constitutional reform

The process of constitutional reform has been under way since 1987, resulting by the end of 1988 in the passage of a total of 37 amendments to the Constitution of 1974 through the Federal Assembly. So far-reaching were these changes that they would merit consideration as a new constitution — in effect the country's fifth post-war constitution.

Much of the work of constitutional revision has been subsequently consolidated in specific legislative acts as components of the Marković government's reform programme — especially the replacement of the former Law on Associated Labour.

The process of constitutional revision is complicated, however, by the fact that it necessarily encompasses the revision of the republican constitutions. Already it has become clear that developments at this level contradict either federal legislation proposed in the post-1987 round of reforms or the federal constitution itself. At the heart of the matter is an important question of principle, namely, the delineation of the respective rights of the republics and the federation.

Should the federal constitution emerge as a consequence of rights and duties devolved to it by the republics; or does the federation enact a framework which determines what is permitted as the sphere of influence of the republics? If the former is the case, then the subsequent series of republican constitutions has in effect sent the process at the federal level back to square one. If the latter holds, then the federation faces the probably insuperable task of enforcing conformity in those republics whose own constitution-making activity has disregarded federal constraint.

The most dramatic instance of conflict in this respect emerged in 1989 over the revisions proposed for the Slovene constitution, which envisaged that the republic would have the right to secede from the federation, and the power to limit the freedom of action of federal armed forces within its own territory.

Although this is the most controversial case, the problem is by no means confined to Slovenia. By the end of 1990, three republican assemblies had still not ratified the federal proposals for constitutional change. Since the several republican proposals which have been ratified by their own assemblies during 1990 actually embody diametrically opposed constitutional principles on some points, it is obvious that there are extreme difficulties here.

Even if the negotiation over constitutional change is allowed to go ahead reasonably expeditiously, without the intervention of political catastrophe, constitutional experts do not expect that it can be completed before the end of 1992 or even 1993.

The establishment of effective civil rights

The need for effective judicial protection of civil rights has emerged with particular urgency as a consequence of the situation in Kosovo, although it has been a problem throughout the post-war period. Indeed, the historical tradition in Yugoslav law of assuming that an action is forbidden unless it is specifically permitted by law (much older than the communist regime) makes for recurring difficulties in relation to human rights.

Amnesty International, reporting on Yugoslavia in 1982, expressed concern over the number and severity of cases of political imprisonment in Yugoslavia. The vast majority of these have related in one way or another to the country's ethnic conflicts, and by far the greatest number to successive states of emergency in Kosovo.

Several articles of the Federal Criminal Code have been repeatedly criticized both within Yugoslavia and abroad for their potential for abuse in relation to political activity; particularly Articles 114 (dealing with "counter-revolutionary endangering of the social order"), 118 (dealing with "hostile propaganda"), 133 (dealing with "verbal delicts"), and 136 (dealing with "association for purposes of hostile activity"). A further article (134) deals with "incitement to national, religious or racial hatred". Each of these is not only formulated rather loosely, but construed in practice with severe and arbitrary results. Especially contentious is the fact that it has been possible until recently in Yugoslavia, not only to be tried for "verbal delicts" (for expressing opinions) but for expressing these in private. Article 133 was abolished in December 1989.

Civilian alternatives to the regular compulsory military service for men were made possible for conscientious objectors only in March 1989. Previously all men over the age of 18 were obliged to spend 12 months in military training.

A delegation from the European Parliament, which visited Kosovo in June 1989 in order to examine adverse reports about the politico-legal position in the province, was forced to abandon its mission, claiming that its work was obstructed by the local authorities, and even that its members had been threatened with violence. There have also been a succession of draft resolutions placed before the US Congress, which have sought to make continuing American aid dependent upon an improvement in Yugoslavia's performance with respect to civil liberties, the most recent of these being the resolution introduced by Senator Alfonse D'Amato in October 1990. In July 1989, Yugoslavia's Ambassador to the USA was ordered to return as he was deemed insufficiently effective in countering such hostile criticism of his country.

Although the Marković government has been notably more sensitive than its predecessors to the need for adequate protection for civil liberties, the severity of civil disorder problems, especially in Kosovo, has not made effective progress easy, and there are still substantial numbers of "hard-liners" in key positions in Yugoslav politics, especially in Serbia, and in the military. The frequency with which civil liberties issues featured in the platforms of parties during the elections of 1990 is testimony to the widespread concern in the country about such matters.

Yugoslav indifference to international public standards in this area extends abroad. A long history of assassinations by Yugoslav government agents of politically active émigrés was drawn to public attention again in May 1989, when Vinko Sindičić was gaoled in Kirkaldy, Scotland for an attempt on the life of Nikola Štedul, the Croat leader of an extreme political faction.

The problem of debureaucratization

Among the most urgent, but least recognized of the outstanding issues which remain to be addressed in the Yugoslav political system is the problem of dismantling its huge bureaucratic apparatus. Attention has been given to the creation of new institutions — political parties, business organizations, and to a lesser extent independent trade unions. Yugoslavia is burdened to an incredible degree, however, with an apparatus of officialdom which has ostensibly to do with representation, delegation and self-management, but which in fact has had more to do with patronage and control.

The range of such organizations is immense, and encompasses not only the "socio-political organizations", such as a functionless "trade union" movement and the Socialist Alliance. The hierarchy of municipal, republican and federal institutions produces considerable duplication of functions. Among the most conspicuous generators of bureaucracy is the apparatus of *SIZovi* (*SIZ = Samoupravna Interesna Zejednica* — "Self-managing Community of Interest": the organizational device through which utilities and social services are managed). It has also long been recognized that one of the greatest disincentives to the generation of a network of small enterprises in Yugoslavia (a repeatedly expressed concern) has been the burden of administration which is routinely carried by any work organization within the system of self-management.

Although recent legislative changes are expected to provide opportunity for change here, any real results so far lie in the future. For as long as questions relating to the fundamental constitutional structure of the country — and indeed, the question of its very existence — dominate Yugoslav politics, problems of this more mundane character are unlikely to be addressed.

The role of the military in Yugoslav politics

The situation of the military in Yugoslav society, and especially the question of the political role of the armed forces, is particularly sensitive in contemporary Yugoslavia. Ever since the death of Tito there has been recurrent speculation about the possibility of direct military intervention fed by the example of the Jaruzelski coup in Poland. As the disintegration of the federation appears ever more likely, this eventuality can not be discounted. Throughout the period 1989–90, public statements by senior officers of the armed forces repeatedly warned that they would not stand by and watch the breakup of the country. The formation of a "party of the generals" in November 1990, with which two members of the Marković government are known to be associated, along with former Minister of Defence Admiral Mamula, has lent realism to this scenario. There are three aspects — interlinked, and all embedded in the country's recent past — to this problem.

The post-war regime emerged from a war (the "National Liberation Struggle") in which the party and military apparatuses were intimately intertwined. The Yugoslav National Army (YNA) was always heavily politicized in its professional core. It had its own party structure, and its own representation — the equivalent of republican status — in the Central Committee of the LCY. The "party of the generals" is, to a large extent, only a continuation of the former YNA party organization.

Military service was originally an important means of access to political position; it remained significant subsequently as a credential of political worthiness; and it has continued to ensure a privileged voice in the shaping of political affairs. Yugoslav politics has thus been relatively highly militarized throughout the post-war period, to an extent which has only recently been seriously challenged. (This has been a particular focus of contention in recent Slovene politics.)

Military values and experience have lain at the heart of the structure of legitimation of the Yugoslav regime. Although the regular class rhetoric of communism has been strongly in evidence in Yugoslavia, this has always been thickly overlaid by reference to the victory over the occupier in the war of liberation, as the justification for the rule of the League of Communists. The armed forces have been seen, and have seen themselves, as the custodians of the unity of the country and of its charter mythology. Compulsory military service has had important functions with respect to communicating central ideological traditions.

For a variety of reasons, Yugoslavia has failed to develop a range of federation-wide institutions of civil society which could provide a real basis for social cohesion (such as religious, educational or economic organizations). Nearly all organizations have a regional basis. Since 1974 even the League of Communists has been steadily regionalized, to the point of its disappearance during 1990. Only the armed forces have cut across these divisions, giving reality to its self-definition as the custodian of political unity.

The armed services have consequently felt themselves to be carrying a particular burden in relation to the political conflicts which have racked the country: and because of their history, might well find themselves in a position in which they feel they ought to intervene. The consequences of their doing so, however, would be grave. Because of its close association with the old regime, the YNA in some regions of the country finds its legitimacy faces particularly serious challenge. The forces have, as the home of some of the country's staunchest communists, come to been seen as particularly resistant to the whole process of democratization. Although the YNA itself has taken a back seat in Kosovo in relation to the militia, the experience of disturbances in the province has tended to identify the army with political oppression. Because (for a variety of historical reasons) the professional officer corps has come to be dominated heavily by Serbs and Montenegrins, the YNA is to some extent seen by other nationalities as the instrument of particular national aspirations, rather than as the genuine embodiment of the common interest. There is little doubt that if current political instability did result in some kind of military coup, the result would be far from the sullen resignation with which Poles greeted the accession to power of Jaruzelski.

For these reasons, the nature and political role of the armed forces in Yugoslavia are now items high up on the agenda of Yugoslav politics.

Economic Overview

Yugoslav governments have been approaching the need for economic reform in one way or another ever since the late 1970s. The country's problems were at first considered only in terms of the need for "stabilization". As difficulties mounted it became obvious that a more radical approach was required. The ill-fated Mikulić government (which resigned over the obstruction of its budget in December 1988) began to address this requirement seriously, but could not secure the necessary political support. Only with appointment of Ante Marković has Yugoslavia been offered a clearly defined, integrated package of reforms which grapple with the need for fundamental institutional reconstruction in the economic field.

The most enormous expectations, on the part of both Yugoslavs and others, have rested on the shoulders of Marković and his streamlined "cabinet of experts". They have produced a programme which in spite of opposition in some circles has earned respect; and it is possible to point to some important results. Their programme is far from complete, however, and the chances of its achieving completion are intricately tangled with the non-economic, constitutional and political questions already mentioned, which could wreck the entire enterprise.

Reform of the currency

A prime concern of the reform programme has been to ensure that Yugoslavia is not artificially sheltered from the world economy. Marković's first aim was the introduction of economic realism, very much in line with the expectations addressed to Yugoslavia by the IMF in 1983, and other international creditors who had funded the debt of US$20 billion which he inherited. Two related lines of approach provided the basis of this campaign: the convertibility of the dinar and the control of inflation. These are discussed in detail below: it is important to acknowledge here that these measures have undergirded the entire economic reform programme, and stand among its greatest successes to date.

Monetary reform was only a headline statement in relation to a more substantial programme of institutional restructuring, aimed at depoliticizing the economy, regulating it through market institutions, and creating a far more flexible organizational framework.

The Law on Enterprises (December 1988)

This replaced the Law on Associated Labour (*Zakon o udruženom radu* — *ZUR*) introduced in 1976. The principal provisions of the earlier law related to the structure of self-managing enterprises, which were divided into two types. The Basic Organization of Associated Labour (*Osnovna organizacija udruženog rada*) and the Complex Organization of Associated Labour (*Složna organizacija*). These replaced "enterprises" as the units of economic organization in the social sector, in that Basic Organizations were frequently sub-divisions of former enterprises, although the integrity of their operation could to some extent be restored by their recombination as Complex Organizations. The old *ZUR* remained controversial throughout its existence. Introduced under the banner of further consolidating workers' self-management, it has been since interpreted by both Yugoslav and external observers as a key aspect of the deepening politicization of the economy after 1974, and one of the principal contributing factors to Yugoslavia's intensifying economic problems after that date. Its abolition was therefore anticipated as an essential element of any movement towards a more market-based, less politicized economic order.

The new Law on Enterprises reconstituted the firm, or enterprise, in a more "natural" sense, and indeed established the legal right to set up almost any conceivable type of economic enterprise. It envisaged not only the continuation of "social ownership", but also the consolidation of the private sector within enlarged limits, and the setting up of joint-stock companies. Private interests were free in principal to acquire holdings in socially owned units. The provisions of this legislation remained extremely general and problematic, and were given essential increased specificity in several further statutes.

Foreign Investment Law (January 1989)

This extended the provision for the involvement of foreign capital in Yugoslav enterprises. Foreign participation in joint ventures with Yugoslav firms has been possible since 1967, although there have been limits on the proportion of the investment which could be in foreign hands, the types of enterprise which could enter into these kinds of arrangements, and the conditions under which profits would be taxed and repatriated. Such joint ventures have also remained firmly bound by the provision of the Law on Associated Labour. Consequently the growth of this type of activity has been relatively slow and has never met the expectations of the Yugoslavs.

The new Law allows a much freer range of possibilities for the development of co-operation between Yugoslav and foreign economic partners, and includes the possibility of privately owned Yugoslav ventures engaging in such agreements. Foreign investors are also permitted to own real estate in Yugoslavia directly for the first time since 1945.

Law on Social Capital (December 1989)

A key part of the process of reorganization is the creation of a framework within which it might be possible to restructure the ownership of formerly socially owned enterprises. This is seen as an essential precondition for the creation of a market economy. The problem has had two aspects: the first concerns the designation of new forms of ownership — the possibility of the privatization of socially owned assets — and the second concerns the creation of provisions whereby economic entities acting in the market could be declared insolvent. Both of these have turned out to be extraordinarily sticky problems, and at the time of writing no complete solution has been found to either of them. Failing in the attempt, however, the government can not so far be said to have really managed to grasp the nettle of economic restructuring, and created effective mechanisms for the *de facto* depoliticization of the Yugoslav economy.

An early beginning appeared to be made with respect to the first of these problems with the passing of a Law on Social Capital in December 1989, which aimed to facilitate the transformation of socially owned enterprises, either through the sale of a part of their capital to other socially owned enterprises, or to private interests, be they corporate or individual.

There has been the most enormous controversy surrounding this legislation, which at the time of writing is still not ratified by the republican Assemblies. Argument has raged over both the theoretical (juridical and moral) aspects of the problem as well as over the practicalities of the process. An important aspect of the emergence of a strong sense of republican economic autonomy has been the articulation of the demand that the republican governments ought to be able to retain an element of control over at least the "commanding heights" of "their" economies. Particularly sensitive is the position of very large firms whose activities are of potential importance to all parts of the Yugoslav economy, which are based in republican capitals, such as the oil and petrochemical conglomerate *INA* (based in Zagreb) and the Yugoslav National Airlines (*JAT* — based in Belgrade). Critics have seen untrammelled movement towards privatization — or the unregulated power to acquire resources within the republic even by socially owned interests based elsewhere — as posing a fundamental threat to the development of greater republican autarky. There does not appear to be a significant difference on this issue between representatives of the newly formed democratic movements (who otherwise have been vociferous advocates of the market principal) and those who continue to urge socialist solutions to Yugoslavia's problems.

The strength of these feelings and the power of the interests involved emerged during the course of an international conference held in Zagreb in October 1990, addressed to the general issues relating to the privatization process in eastern Europe. Yugoslav speakers were far from being the only ones to express concern about the problem. The range of disagreement among leading political figures in Yugoslavia is significant. The upshot of the debate so far has been that hardly any progress has been made towards the restructuring of ownership and control in the Yugoslav economy. What has been regarded as an urgent prerequisite for escape from the country's economic difficulties has turned into something of a political quagmire.

Financial Operations Act (February 1989)

Turning to the closely related problem of the creation of means of handling the liquidation of those enterprises which are economically non-viable, we find a similar lack of concrete achievement. An early start was made on this by the Marković government, with its Financial Operations Act, of February 1989. Previously the obstacles to winding up any enterprise which was chronically incapable of paying its own way has been regarded as one of the most obvious elements of the politicization of the Yugoslav economy. This has been closely linked in the past to the characteristics of the banking system (see below) which have also been subject to new legislation. A significant step towards resolving this problem was taken by provisions contained in the Financial Operations Act, which specified the conditions under which bankruptcy could be declared. A 60-day tolerance limit was specified for arrears, before proceedings could be initiated.

In practice, however, as with other major elements of the Marković reform programme, there have been significant departures from the new legal norms when it has come to the crunch. The most important role in shaking out unviable enterprises was supposed to be played by the banks, through their control of credit. There is ample evidence that, to date, they have been either reluctant or unable to play the part for which they were cast. The bankruptcy of the Slovene ski equipment company *Elan* in October 1990 (previously regarded as a model enterprise, and tipped for profitable privatization) may be a straw in the wind.

The reform of banking

Yugoslav and foreign experts have been broadly agreed ever since the IMF restructuring package was negotiated in 1983 that reform of the country's banking system is necessary. An important element in the generation of Yugoslavia's economic malaise (some would argue, its most important cause) has been the virtually complete lack of monetary discipline exercised by successive federal governments.

Reform of the banking system has been complex, and in common with other elements of the reform programme, can not be regarded as complete. The details of banking reform are considered under Key Economic Sectors below.

Some outstanding problem areas

In spite of the level of attention often given to the differences which separate Yugoslavia from the centrally planned economies of the CMEA, they continue to have one feature in common. One of the weakest elements of the Yugoslav economic system has always been, and still is, in the area of marketing and distribution. The importance of these weaknesses has been mitigated, in comparison with other countries, by the long-established system of peasant markets. These have made for continuous and relatively plentiful supplies of fruit and vegetables. Other commodities, such as meat and dairy products have remained erratic in their availability and quality, although shortages and queues on the scale typically found in some other parts of central and eastern Europe are unfamiliar in Yugoslavia.

There has been much talk, but as yet no specific proposal, for the long-awaited and much needed reform of the taxation system. (Although a proposal is currently under consideration to strengthen the direct economic leverage of the federal government by the levy of a 3% turnover tax.) These important developments can not be contemplated, and indeed none of the outstanding problems listed above can be addressed properly, pending the achievement of some kind of constitutional settlement.

These reforms add up to an ambitious and realistic attempt to come to grips with the country's economic problems and provide a framework for the creation of a more market-oriented and depoliticized economy. As such they have been widely acclaimed by outside observers. The chief difficulty, however, lies in the fact of their dependence upon the *constitutional* reforms which would render them effective. At the time of writing, however, the achievement of this is far from secure, so that economic reconstruction may be overtaken by political disintegration.

Some important economic indicators

The shortness of the time-fuse which is currently burning in Yugoslavia is suggested by the trajectory of some key economic indicators over the past two years. Following the announcement of the Marković programme in June 1989, and the gradual unfolding of the detail of this in legislative drafts, there was little immediate impact on economic performance. Conspicuously, inflation continued to soar, reaching a peak now acknowledged to have been around 2,700% p.a. by the end of 1989. Unemployment stood (officially) at 14%; Gross Social Product had declined by 3.7% on the year and industrial productivity was slumping.

The revaluation of the currency introduced in January 1990 (for detail see below), which pegged the dinar to the Deutschmark, yielded immediate results in the fight against inflation, and the general stabilization of the economy, with exports in particular surging ahead. The foreign external hard currency debt was reduced significantly, from more than $20 billion at the beginning of 1989 to an estimated $15.5 billion by the middle of 1990. Official reserves climbed from around $1.8 billion in April 1989, and are estimated at around $8.8 billion by the end of 1990.

On their own, financial measures could have no more than the effect of purchasing breathing space. Consequently, the failure of the federal government to secure the organizational changes it sought, have seen a return to the downward spiral. Inflation has re-emerged, and is expected to reach between 120–130% p.a. by the end of the year. Although the balance of trade has remained favourable, industrial production is expected to have declined by around 11%, GNP by around 10% and real wages by more than 2% during 1990.

Key Economic Sectors

Agriculture

Throughout the entire post-war period agriculture has been a poor relation of the urban and industrial economy in Yugoslavia. Early attempts to collectivize rural production were abandoned in 1953, and since then there has been a stable pattern of a dual structure. A social sector consisting of roughly 2,500 relatively large enterprises cultivates around a fifth of the agricultural area, with relatively capital-intensive methods. This is responsible for by far the greater proportion of grain production and industrial crops such as sugar beet and oil seeds. The overwhelming preponderance of agricultural land area (more than 80%) is in the hands of individual peasant cultivators, who until 1989 were limited to plots of no more than 10 hectares, but in practice were typically far smaller. On these are produced, very often by part-time farmers, the great proportion of fruit and vegetables, meat and dairy produce, which service the needs of both rural and urban populations. Taken together, agriculture employs about 2.4 million, or nearly a quarter of the labour force.

Having abandoned enforced collectivization, rural policy can be summed up as "benign neglect", allied to sustained pressure to ensure the sale of produce through the social sector "co-operatives". This situation has not been changed appreciably within the general reorientation of the economy.

No evidence is yet available as to the extent to which changes in the limits on landholding and employment in the private sector may offer effective incentives to retain labour on the land and reverse the steady process of post-war senilization of the farm population. Only in Slovenia has there been any clear sign of the re-emergence of the pre-war tradition of independent co-operative organization among farmers.

Inclement weather has meant that the years 1989–90 have not been good ones for agricultural productivity. Yugoslavia does have great agricultural potential, however, with a reserve of undercultivated land. Yugoslavs do not at present go hungry: but lacking substantial inputs of capital, training and above all organization, that potential remains dormant. Yugoslav agriculture makes an important contribution to the viability of the tourist industry. Agricultural produce, especially meat products and live animals, regularly contributes 7–8% of Yugoslavia's export trade.

Manufacturing industry

Some general issues affecting Yugoslav manufacturing industry, relating to the reorganization of the self-management system, have been mentioned above.

In common with much of eastern and central Europe, Yugoslavia shares general problems of industrial location, obsolescence of plant, and lack of adequate financial discipline. To the locational difficulties which attend "political factories" everywhere, Yugoslavia adds the special problems which result from the attempt to ensure republican industrial autarky.

The Yugoslavs have been far more successful than their eastern neighbours in the past in developing both production and marketing links with the West (see below). Whereas there is a general expectation that the economic reforms will result in the closure of many outdated or inefficient enterprises, and a radical shakeout of labour in many others, the overall prospects for manufacturing industry in Yugoslavia are fair. (The current decline in output is believed to be attributable to political factors as much as to the characteristics of industry itself.) The picture is highly uneven, however, and something of this variety can be conveyed by attention to particular areas of activity.

The *automobile industry* embodies both the greatest strengths and weaknesses of Yugoslav industry. The *Crvena Zastava* complex, based in Kragujevac, has had a very difficult time, indicated by collapse of the attempt to market the Yugo in the USA. There has been an attempt to put together new models more suited in design and standard of finish to the European market, but these have yet to prove themselves.

In contrast one can turn to the experience of the *IMV* plant at Novo Mesto in Slovenia. For several years this had been producing under licence versions of the Renault 5, largely for domestic markets. In 1988 it became evident that the enterprise was facing serious difficulties, and in any economic reorganization would probably end up as one of the casualties of the new Yugoslavia. A bold plan was conceived for its rescue, which involved the appointment of a "trouble shooter" to take charge of the scheme, and the temporary suspension of self-management law for the period of reconstruction. The group was divested of several of its subsidiaries whose work was not obviously related to the needs of vehicle production. The internal structure of the group was completely revamped. As a consequence of this, the plant has now been accepted as an integral member of the *Renault* "family", and a major producer of Renault 5s. There has been substantial capital injection. One of the "lame ducks" of Yugoslav industry has achieved the status of exemplar of what can be done with Yugoslav industry given the right leadership and the right opportunities.

Shipbuilding is one of the important strengths of Yugoslav manufacturing industry which have attracted insufficient attention in relation to their economic importance. In a period in which there has been markedly excess capacity in shipping construction in the world, Yugoslavia's yards, such as "3 Maj" in Rijeka and "Brodosplit" in Split, have defended their corner well.

The *textile industry* illustrates well one of the general problems of Yugoslav industry, in the constraints imposed by inadequate investment resulting in technical obsolescence. The industry has had a good record in relation to exports, contributing around 9% to the Yugoslav total volume. The workforce makes up around 17% of the Yugoslav total, and delivers 10% of the total social product.

The industry faces acute difficulties with regard to international competition, and is the subject of export restriction quotas from both the European Community and the USA. In spite of this, it has reduced over the last five years its dependence on the Comecon market by around a half. The Yugoslavs have started to take advantage of their spare capacity and relatively cheap labour to process semi-finished materials on behalf of foreign partners, with significant effect.

They face, however, the need to invest heavily in order to maintain their strength — investment recently has been in short supply — and the need to reorganize. It has been estimated that if the Marković plan for economic restructuring does go ahead, about 15%

of the country's 400 textile firms could be put out of business.

The major strengths of Yugoslav manufacturing industry are in food processing, metalworking, electrical machinery and equipment, electricity generation, and textiles, each of which accounts for 7–9% of total industrial output.

Transport

Transport is one of the areas of economic activity which has been most sensitive to its political context. A substantial programme of modernization has been under way since the mid-1970s, the achievements and limitations of which have reflected the overall process of political fragmentation. The electrification of the Rijeka-Zagreb rail link (Croatia) and the enhancement of port facilities at Koper (Slovenia), for example, serve distinctively republican rather than generally Yugoslav conceptions of need.

The international trunk road between Zagreb and Belgrade is still not completed, in spite of repeated credits from the World Bank ostensibly for this purpose. Consequently, although the important Karawanken tunnel is on the eve of opening (linking Austria and Slovenia), the Yugoslav section of this major trans-continental road link continues to be fractured by domestic political rivalries.

An early bloom among the crop of tentative results of economic liberalization has been the floating of a joint-stock company to finance the long overdue replacement for the Adriatic highway, from Rijeka to Dubrovnik. Italian and other foreign interests are believed to be involved, as well as domestic investors. Although the general concept has been mooted for at least 10 years, a start to construction is not yet in sight.

Regionalism is apparent in the recent steady expansion of the *Adria* airline (based in Zagreb) as a competitor, as much as a charter-complement, to the "national carrier", *JAT*.

Tourism

Discussion of Yugoslavia's economic performance would be incomplete without reference to tourism, which along with the earnings from Yugoslavia's shipping concerns, has been a principal source of invisible earnings, especially since 1965. These currently exceed $2 billion annually, from around 9,000,000 foreign visitors, who spend more than 50,000,000 bed-nights in the country. Recorded income in this sector is believed to be heavily under-estimated. Tourism has provided one of the principal stimulants to a growing private sector, which provides at least a third of registered tourist accommodation, together with an important segment of catering and other facilities. Foreign tourists are drawn principally from Germany, Italy and Austria, with important contingents also coming from the Netherlands and the UK.

Finance

Reorganization of the country's financial structure has been the centrepiece of the Marković reform programme. At the heart of this endeavour has been the creation of a fully convertible dinar. The new currency was launched at the beginning of January 1990. One new dinar was exchangeable for 10,000 of the old, and was pegged until June in the international market at 7:1 against the Deutschmark. This had several important effects immediately upon Yugoslav finances. The dual monetary structure of the country was eliminated overnight (previously the DM had operated almost as a second, unofficial currency), and the black market for foreign exchange almost eliminated. Enormous reserves of privately held currency (largely earnings of Yugoslav workers in foreign countries) were "liberated" — it no longer became necessary for private individuals to hold these as a security against an increasingly worthless domestic currency. It became easier to harmonize Yugoslav prices with world prices. The change had a spectacular impact upon the rate of inflation, which within four months dropped from an annual rate of around 2,700% to almost zero.

Several critics at the time argue that the new dinar was somewhat overvalued, and they have perhaps been partly vindicated by the subsequent devaluation of the dinar at the close of the year, to 11:1 DM.

Convertibility is an important indicator of the greater integration of the Yugoslav economy with that of western Europe, in comparison with other countries of eastern and central Europe. It is also a highly significant symbol of the broader aspirations of the Marković government in that direction.

The second major move made by the Marković administration in relation to financial restructuring has been the reform of the banking system. Although there has been a National Bank of Yugoslavia (*Narodna Banka Jugoslavije*) which has issued currency, and exercised some other functions in relation to the federal system of monetary institutions, it has not acted as a "National Bank" in the sense in which that phrase is more widely used in Europe and elsewhere.

Banks in general formerly have had the character of "Self-managing Communities of Interest" (*Samoupravne interesne zajednice — SIZovi*), which means that they have operated neither as direct instruments of central government policy nor as independent corporations. In common with other general services in Yugoslavia (such as those providing educational and health services) they have been run by committees which have included significant representation of their clients. In the case of the banks, this has meant that a powerful influence on their policy has been the voice of their creditors. Taken together with the legal obstacles to declaring workers redundant, or closing enterprises, this structure has virtually guaranteed that credit has been available on demand to pay wages bills or settle other accounts. The National Bank itself has thus had little or no leverage by which it could constrain the flow of credit to either persons or enterprises.

Another characteristic of the banking system which has exacerbated the country's financial problems is the fact that banks have shared since the mid-1960s in the general movement towards the republicanization of decision-making. Republican and even municipal banks were contracting foreign loans quite independently of any federal control or monitoring. The National Bank therefore had no effective control either over the accumulation of foreign, as well as internal, indebtedness.

An important feature of the Yugoslav financial scene which legislation also had to confront was the sea of inter-enterprise credit on which the economy floated, the dimensions of which even today remain unclear. The relatively uncontrolled issue of promissory notes surfaced spectacularly as a problem in 1987, when the Bosnian firm *Agrokomerc* was exposed as the source of a multi-million pound flow of entirely unsecured credit. The attempt to prosecute the firm's director, Fihret Abdić, for his part in this largely foundered upon the discovery that he was distinguished from many others only by the scale of an operation the illegality of which was in doubt.

Three of the legislative measures introduced by the Marković government are relevant to the attempt to rectify this situation, and introduce a degree of financial probity.

The *Financial Operations Act* (February 1989) was the earliest of these measures, which included in its provisions the transformation of the commercial banks into shareholding companies, and the substitution of shareholders in place of "founders" (principally large enterprises and local government representatives among their creditors). The commercialization process has only been partial, however, in that shareholders are still subject to important constraints, and there is nothing like free, inter-bank competition.

In June 1989 further legislation followed, increasing the autonomy of the National Bank of Yugoslavia, authorising majority voting in decision-making (in place of unanimity), and ensuring closer linkage between the granting of credit and credit-worthiness.

Finally, the *Law on the Rehabilitation of Banks* (December 1989) allowed the National Bank to impose uniform insolvency ratios (equity: assets, 1:15); ceilings on the foreign borrowing of domestic banks; and tighter provisions for the licensing of new banking enterprises.

Although it is clear that these measures have played a part in the reduction of the earlier levels of hyper-inflation, it is also the case that the power of republican governments has enabled the strict provisions of these laws in some measure to be evaded. Fearing the political consequences of the sudden imposition of rigorous credit control upon financially insecure enterprises, which were allowed to over-extend themselves in the past, banks have continued to cushion them against disaster. The need to tighten up control in this respect is suggested *inter alia* by the return of the inflationary spiral in the last quarter of 1990.

Energy

Yugoslavia is not an energy-rich country. It has supplies of lignite and poor-quality coal, and is quite well endowed with opportunities for hydro-electricity generation. Nevertheless, it is currently necessary to import about 40% of its energy requirements. There is a small proven capability for domestic oil/gas production, and the possibility in future of exploiting geothermal sources. Some progress has been made recently in the Dalmatian islands with the use of solar energy, where there are small, localized concentrations of population remote from larger sources of supply. The overall energy position presents Yugoslavia with several problems.

In an attempt to diversify its energy sources Yugoslavia built one nuclear reactor for power-generation purposes, in 1981, at Krško in Slovenia. This has always been subject to local criticism on safety grounds, and in the wake of the Chernobyl disaster a decision was taken not to build a second. A proposal to close Krško is being canvassed seriously.

The characteristics of its coal supply present Yugoslavia with the problems of environmental pollution in its use which are encountered in other countries of the region. In this respect, several Yugoslav cities and manufacturing areas are renowned for the severity of their dirty atmosphere. Zenica (Bosnia — known as the dirtiest town in Yugoslavia), and Jesenice (Slovenia) are examples.

Brown coal/lignite use is not the only source of problems in this respect. Automobile exhausts contribute heavily to the problem in Belgrade and Ljubljana. In Bor (Serbia) the river Mlada is dead as a consequence of mining and metal processing effluent, and a similar catastrophe was narrowly averted in Montenegro's Tara gorge in 1987.

The degree of concern extends well beyond these examples, however, and the first conference of Yugoslav ecologists met in June 1989, in Zenica. There are signs (including the emergence of Green parties) of rising public and political consciousness.

The Gulf crisis in 1990 presented Yugoslavia with some difficulties regarding its oil supply, as it had hitherto been a substantial customer of Iraq (largely in return for military hardware, of which Yugoslavia is a significant producer and exporter). On the whole, however, Yugoslavia has fared relatively well in the oil market, as the conditions under which it has contracted to purchase oil have benefited from recent movements of the value of the dollar. Oil accounts for around two-thirds of the country's imports of energy, not only for fuel but also as raw material for its large chemical industry.

New technology

Yugoslavia is not one of the most technologically innovative of states. In 1989 Yugoslav nationals filed internationally 1,699 patents for new inventions or products, amounting to 0.11% of total world registrations. Bearing in mind the scale of the very substantial "brain drain" from the country, however, and the resulting concentration of research and development activity in the major industrial powers, this level of performance is not low for a country of this size and level of economic development. Measured by other criteria, there are several areas in which Yugoslav technology is found, if not in the first rank of world developments, at least among the second rank.

In general, Yugoslavia's strengths in R&D reflect its major industrial interests, in electrical engineering and chemicals. In the spring of 1990 plans were announced to develop a large "science park" outside Belgrade, involving collaboration between the Pupin Institute and Stanford University. Pupin's principal concerns are in electronic process control and robotics — areas in which the Zagreb firm *Rade Končar* is also strong.

Yugoslavia has its own capability in computer manufacture, principally through the Slovene combine *Iskra*. A consortium of the country's largest electronics and engineering concerns work together on specifically military projects, and in military aviation and artillery construction Yugoslavia has a good reputation for the relatively sophisticated status of its products.

The relatively advanced nature of much R&D work in Yugoslavia (for example in its pharmaceutical firms, *Galenika*, in Belgrade, and *Pliva* in Zagreb) relates in part to the success of Yugoslav enterprises in establishing over the years effective links with foreign partners.

Foreign Economic Relations

Foreign trade

Yugoslavia has consistently shown a deficit over the post-war period in its trade in merchandise. In 1989 this amounted to a deficit of $521 million in the last quarter, and $782 million on the year. For the first half year of 1990, the deficit was $1.6 billion. Total volume of trade has risen steadily over the 1989–90 period, and expanded imports partially

Table 8:   Foreign trade, 1988–89 (%)

	Imports (cif)				Exports (fob)			
	1988		1989		1988		1989	
TOTAL		100.0		100.0		100.0		100.0
OECD		55.7		54.2		51.1		51.4
EC		38.8		38.9		36.8		36.9
Comecon		27.2		29.0		33.7		34.8
FRG	(1)	17.2	(1)	16.9	(3)	11.3	(3)	11.5
Italy	(3)	10.4	(3)	10.6	(2)	15.0	(2)	15.1
USSR	(2)	13.3	(2)	14.5	(1)	18.7	(1)	21.7
USA	(6)	5.5	(4)	4.8	(6)	5.6	(4)	4.7
UK	(12)	2.3	(15)	1.8	(11)	2.6	(10)	2.6

Note: Figures in brackets: rank-order of individual states.
Source: Yugoslav Statistical Office.

reflect the rising demand for industrial raw materials. This deficit is regularly balanced by invisibles, however, the most significant of which is foreign tourism. Trade performance is summarized in Table 8.

The pattern of foreign economic relations

The changing pattern of Yugoslavia's economic relations with foreign countries should be considered in association within the wider picture of its foreign relations.

Discussion within Yugoslavia throughout 1989–90 has centred in the main on the future of the country's links with the EC. Clearly, trade with the EC countries is becoming increasingly significant, and now covers approaching 40% of the total. The Marković government has indicated publicly and repeatedly that it would like to take Yugoslavia into the EC, and the currency reform already discussed should be seen as related to that ambition. This expectation is fundamentally placed in question, however, by the internal political state of affairs, as the EC has let it be known that "the European Community would like the Yugoslav ship to sale into European waters, but not that the several Yugoslav nations should arrive separately in the life-boats".

An initial agreement with the EC was signed in 1980, which was renewed on an interim basis in 1985; a further agreement was negotiated for the period 1987–91, which provides for controlled access to the European market for Yugoslav goods. Yugoslavia's prospects with the EC are not advanced by the continuing difficulties in its relations with Greece, over Macedonia, and in particular, by the bitter dispute over the use of water from Lake Dojran.

In advance of any possibility of joining the EC, developments within the *Alpe-Adria* group have turned out to be increasingly important in relation to Yugoslavia's economic relations. Italy in particular is becoming not only an important trading partner, but an active co-operator with Yugoslavia in the realms of transport planning and construction and environmental control. A vital stimulus in this respect has been tourism, on which an important conference of the members of the *A-A* group took place in Dubrovnik in March 1989. Italy and Yugoslavia share a particular interest in this respect, of course, in the use and condition of the northern Adriatic. There are regular and effective inter-governmental contacts between the two countries at all levels.

Although Yugoslavia has been a socialist country throughout the post-war years, it has not been a member of Comecon. (It has enjoyed "associate" status since 1964.) Trade with the CMEA countries makes up nearly a third of Yugoslavia's total. This has been the source of some embarrassment, in that massive trade surpluses have accumulated with the Soviet Union in recent years, and there have been repeated inter-governmental discussions in the attempt to rectify the balance. The deteriorating Soviet economy is a cause of some concern to the Yugoslavs. The situation is more balanced with other countries of the bloc. The link with Romania in connection with energy production (the Iron Gates) is especially important.

Foreign debt

Among the most serious of Yugoslavia's economic problems, and among those given most attention outside the country, have been the size of the country's foreign debt, and the costs of debt servicing. The level of indebtedness rose spectacularly through the late 1970s, to the point at which Yugoslavia was forced to approach the IMF for help in rescheduling, in 1983. There has been a succession of subsequent agreements, both with the IMF and commercial banks. The demands of servicing a debt of some $20 billion reached a peak debt service ratio of 45% in 1986, and have declined steadily since, to 36% in 1988, and an estimated 30% at the end of 1990. Debt service will consume around $4 billion per annum for the foreseeable future.

Joint ventures

The changing legal framework governing investment in Yugoslavia by foreign firms, and joint ventures between Yugoslav and foreign partners, has already been discussed above. Following the introduction of the new laws, Yugoslav government sources were expecting an additional inflow of investment amounting to around DM 40 billion in 1990. At the time of writing, no information is available regarding the degree of their success.

In the past, in spite of the willingness of the Yugoslavs to promote foreign investment, the restrictive conditions of ownership and control proved to be a substantial disincentive. It is too early to determine whether the new legal framework has removed those barriers.

Although only providing a minor contribution to Yugoslavia's economic stability, it is worth noting that Yugoslavia is unusual among the countries of central and eastern Europe in being the home base for several firms which have invested successfully abroad. The Slovene heating engineering firm *Gorenje* is one illustration of this.

Principal Personalities

Abdić, Fikret. Former general manager of the Bosnian enterprise *Agrokomerc*, who was at the centre of the collapse of the company in 1987, and stood trial in 1988 on fraud and other charges. Acquitted in 1989, he retained the loyalty of many of the company's workers, and returned to politics in the republic. The *Agrokomerc* affair was the first of a series of scandals to disturb Bosnian politics during the later 1980s.

Bučin, Nenad. A former teacher, born 1934, Montenegrin. Held posts in the Montenegrin LC and Socialist Alliance (SA) since 1969. Member of the presidency of the LCM 1980-82, and senior positions in the SA since then. Elected to the Federal State Presidency in 1989. An ardent and articulate supporter of an integrated Yugoslav market, and a depoliticized economy.

Drašković, Vukašin (Vuk). Serbian poet and novelist, born 1946, who emerged in 1989 as a significant challenger to Slobodan Milošević for leadership of Serbian nationalism. Founder of the Serbian Movement for Renewal.

Drnovšek, Janez. Slovene, born in 1950; gained a Ph.D in economics, having studied in Norway and the USA. Known also as an accomplished linguist. Worked as an economist in industry, and later as director of the Ljubljanska Banka. Brief experience in diplomatic service (Cairo). Elected to the Federal Assembly in 1984, and has held several other posts at republican level. Elected Slovene representative on the Federal State Presidency in 1989. Known for quiet diplomacy, and as a committed democrat and advocate of economic reform.

Gligorijević, Slobodan. Born in 1920, a Serb with partisan experience. Former academic economist from Belgrade University. Extensive political career, both within Serbia and the Federation, including General Director of the Bank of Yugoslavia, President of the Serbian Republic and member of the Federal Executive Council (FEC). Elected as President of the Federal Assembly in 1989.

Gračanin, Petar. A Serb, born in 1923; former partisan and professional soldier. Formerly active in LC organization within the armed forces. Now retired as a General in the Yugoslav National Army, to take a position as Minister of the Interior in the Marković government, where he is regarded as a political concession to Serb nationalism. Principal advocate within the Cabinet of the policy of repression in Kosovo. A leading figure in the "party of the generals", formed in November 1990.

Horvat, Branko. Yugoslav, born in 1928. Zagreb professor of economics, well known also outside Yugoslavia for translations of his works on the Yugoslav economy. Leader of the Association for a Yugoslav Democratic Initiative, one of the first independent groups to emerge in Yugoslavia, based in Zagreb, even before parties were officially permitted.

Izetbegović, Alija. Bosnian Muslim, imprisoned in 1946 for his political views, he emerged during the recent free elections in Bosnia as the leader of the newly founded Democratic Action Party. Believed to be a devout Muslim, who is concerned to revive the specifically religious dimension of Muslim nationality.

Janša, Janez. Slovene political activist and former editor of the journal *Mladina*, jailed in 1989 for his part in the Slovene "military secrets" trial. He took office as the republic's minister of defence after the elections of 1990, and played a key part in the developing controversy over the independence of Slovene defence policy.

Jović, Borisav. A Serb born in 1928, who gained experience as a planning official in local government, before joining the *Crvena Zastava* engineering firm. Subsequently acquired extensive experience as a civil servant at both republican and federal level, especially in the field of economic planning. Diplomatic service briefly with the CMEA and Italy. Member of the republican Assembly since 1980; CC of the Serbian LC, 1986–88; president of the Serbian Assembly 1988 and Serbian representative on Federal State Presidency 1989. Reputed to be closely allied to Milošević, and an advocate of continuing strong central control in the economy.

Kadijević, Veljko. Born in 1925, a Serb from Croatia. Former Partisan, and a career military officer, although always had a strong orientation towards ideological and organizational issues. General in the Yugoslav National Army, and Federal Minister of Defence in the Marković government. A staunch supporter of communist hegemony, and defender of the federation, although reputed to be liberal in economic affairs. One of the group of highly politicized senior military figures who founded the "party of the generals" in November 1990 (along with Admiral Stane Brodet, General Simeon Bunčić, General Stevan Mirković, Admiral Pater Simić and former Defence Minister Admiral Branko Mamula).

Kučan, Milan. A Slovene, born in 1941, who rose through the University LC organization and Youth Organization in Ljubljana, to the Slovene CC after the Sixth Congress. Known for his accessibility and openness to public opinion. Leader of the process of "humanizing the party" in Slovenia, and an advocate of contested elections. Although a communist, he himself was elected as republican president in a free election in May 1990.

Lončar, Budimir. Croat born in 1925, former Partisan, followed by a military career to 1950. Moved to diplomatic service, where in addition to various posts within the State Service for Foreign Affairs, he has held diplomatic office including Consul General in New York, Ambassador in Indonesia, Malaysia, West Germany and the USA. Deputy Foreign Minister 1984–87 and Foreign Minister from February 1988. Believed to be fairly strongly western-oriented, and the principal force making for the realignment of Yugoslav foreign policy.

Marković, Ante. A Croat from Hercegovina, born in 1924. President of the Federal Executive Council (FEC) of Yugoslavia ("Prime Minister") since January 1989. Partisan experience. Formerly director of the Zagreb-based engineering enterprise *Rade Končar*. President of the Republican Executive Council of Croatia, 1982–86. Principal architect of the current reform programme.

Marković-Milošević, Mirjana. Serbian professor of sociology in Belgrade born in 1942, member of the Belgrade LC Praesidium in 1989. Although married to Slobodan Milošević, she has made a career in her own right, and has a reputation as a "communist feminist". Said to be more radical than her husband, and certainly more articulate. Expected to be increasingly influential.

Mesić, Stipe. Croat, born in 1934, studied law. Active in the communist youth organization. Became mayor of his home town in Slavonia. Fell foul of the authorities for his involvement with Croatian national movement during the "Croatian Spring" of 1971–72, and subsequently imprisoned for a year. An early activist in the formation of Tudjman's "Croatian Democratic Union", of which he became secretary. Subsequently elected as the party's candidate for the Federal State Presidency in 1990. Known as a realist and pragmatist rather than an ideological visionary.

Milojević, Jelena. A Serb from Vojvodina, born in 1943. Elected as president of the Socialist Alliance in 1989. A sociology graduate. One of the few women to make a successful political career in Yugoslavia.

Milošević, Slobodan. Serbian, born 1941, former economist in industry, and between 1978–83 president of the Associated Bank of Belgrade. Member of the CC of the Serbian LC since 1983. Rose to prominence in 1987, when he took control as president of the Belgrade LCY. In succeeding years led a vigorous movement of Serbian nationalism, enforcing constitutional change in his own republic and through his command of nationalist mobs intimidating governments in other republics. Elected as president of the Serbian Republic in 1989. With the disintegration of the LCY, founded his own party, the Serbian Socialist Party, in 1990.

Pančevski, Milan. Macedonian, born in 1935 into a revolutionary working class family. Trained in technical school; but most of his career has been spent in political functions within the LC and the SA. Former member of the CC of the LC in Macedonia, its executive secretary, and president. President of the Praesidium of the LCY at its dissolution in 1990. Notable both as an old-style political career politician and a key figure in the former Macedonian political establishment.

Pregl, Živko. A Slovene born in 1947, who worked his way up through the party apparatus in Slovenia. Vice-Premier in charge of the economy in the Marković administration, and a key figure in the reform programme.

Rupel, Dmitrije. A Slovene born in 1947, professor of sociology at Ljubljana University. Leader of the DEMOS coalition which successfully challenged the LC in the Slovene elections of 1990.

Sapundžiu, Riza. Albanian, born in 1925. Former Partisan. Long experience in municipal government in his native Peć. Career in industry and banking, including as a Governor of the National Bank of Yugoslavia, and Yugoslav delegate to the World Bank from 1982. Executive Director of the World Bank. Member of Federal State Presidency elected 1989.

Simoneti, Marko. Slovene, former member of the Marković administration, and an expert on privatization. Resigned in December 1990 following the Slovene republican elections, in order to take a post in the newly formed Slovene government.

Slokar, Jože. A Slovene born in 1934. Holder of a succession of functions within the LC with a particular concern for the economy. Cabinet position with Marković.

Šuvar, Stipe. Born in 1937, a Croat. Former academic sociologist from Zagreb University. Long experience as a student activist, and publicist. Held a number of positions within the Croatian LC, principally concerned with ideological and cultural affairs. Emerged as a Tito loyalist after the "Croatian Spring" of 1971–72. Croatian CC member since 1982, and of its presidency since 1986. Elected to Federal State Presidency 1989. A staunch federalist, and a leading communist intellectual.

Todorovski, Gane. Macedonian poet, translator and professor of literature at the University of Skopje, born in 1929. He emerged as a political figure in the election campaign of 1990, as a leader of the "All-Macedonian Action Committee".

Tudjman, Franjo. A Croat, born in 1922. Joined the Partisans, and rose to the rank of General in the Yugoslav National Army. Later retired to practise as a historian. His commitment to communism was replaced by a vigorous nationalism, which got him into trouble in the "Croatian Spring" of 1971. In 1981 he was imprisoned under Article 133, after giving interviews to foreign journalists. Emerged during 1989 as founder and leader of the Croatian National Union which he led to victory in the 1989 elections. President of the Croatian Republic.

Tupurkovsi, Vasil. A Macedonian born in 1951, who began an early political career in the Macedonian Communist Youth Organization, and served a variety of political functions in the republic. Emerged as an important figure in the new generation of Macedonian politicians when he defeated senior figures to become Macedonian representative on the Federal State Presidency in 1989. The press gave headline notice to the first occasion on which he was seen wearing a tie.

Vllasi, Azem. Albanian, born in 1947, who worked his way up through LC youth organization and the provincial party apparatus after qualifying as a lawyer. Acquired a reputation as a pliant tool of Serbian interests in Kosovo, and a loyal communist, until 1988, when he was dismissed from his party and government positions for his alleged support for the striking Trepča miners, and charged with counter-revolutionary activity. Acquitted in 1990, and emerged from prison as a Social Democrat. As one of the younger and more vigorous Albanian politicians, it is likely that he will continue to play an active and influential role in the Albanian national movement.

Zelenović, Dragutin. A Yugoslav from Vojvodina, born in 1928. A mechanical engineer with extensive practical experience in industry, and latterly as an academic at the University of Novi Sad. Member of Federal State Presidency from 1989.

The Media

Yugoslavia has not had formal censorship in the post-war years, although a strong degree of *de facto* control over publication has been exercised. Under the threat of prosecution, and subject to the informal control of intervention by LC activists, there has been consequently a fairly high degree of self-censorship. Even so, publications such as the Slovene student publication *Mladina* have sustained a reputation for hard-hitting and entirely independent social and political comment. There has been a recent move to relax the statutory controls which are relevant here; nevertheless, in the changing political climate there is still evidence of direct political interference in the work of the media.

In May 1989 journalists from Bar were suspended for their sympathetic coverage of strike action. Following similar suspensions of TV journalists in Novi Sad (accused of giving greater coverage to the Tudjman election campaign than to a speech by Milošević) a new independent union of journalists was set up, which now has branches in all major cities.

In October 1990 a new all-Yugoslav TV network *YUTEL* began broadcasting, designed to escape from the particularism of the existing republican stations. Its transmissions have been boycotted in Serbia.

In general these restrictions on the action of journalists have reflected the strengthening of control by nationalist interests. The former TV Zagreb now proclaims itself "Croatian" TV. It is known that the prestigious *Politika* group has moved steadily under the control of the Milošević faction. In the process a number of the group's most eminent journalists have left, and many now write for *Borba*. Formerly regarded as a turgid party mouthpiece, this paper has emerged in the past two years as an increasingly respected source of relatively balanced and independent comment. The Yugoslav news agency *TANJUG* has also displayed a consistently pro-Serb slant, and some of its staff have been very active in the establishment of the new Union. Most seriously of all, the Albanian language media in Kosovo have been either suppressed or no longer have any meaningful degree of independence.

Because of the generally regional basis of the press and broadcasting media, it is still very hard to obtain accurate, balanced and full information on a federation-wide basis. (*Politika*, for example, is a Belgrade paper; *Delo* is Slovene and *Nova Makedonija*, Macedonian.) This parochialism contributes in no small measure to the tendency towards general paranoia which makes Yugoslav politics so unstable and volatile. This localization of the media is suggested in the fact that there are 28 registered daily papers in Yugoslavia, and more than 250 registered radio and TV stations or local relays. The most widely read daily paper is *Politika* (circulation about 240,000 in 1988).

Foreign Relations

The non-aligned summit

Continuing its tradition of involvement with the Non-Aligned Movement (NAM) Yugoslavia hosted the ninth Summit of Heads of Government of the Movement in Belgrade, in September 1989. Delegations from the 102 member-countries took part, together with representatives of 30 guest or observer states, including for the first time all of the Warsaw Pact (Warsaw Treaty Organization) countries, and representatives of nearly 40 international organizations. In spite of the public relations display which accompanied the event, there are reasons to question the extent to which participation in the NAM is still the centrepiece of Yugoslavia's foreign relations.

New diplomatic orientations?

In spite of the public display of "business as usual" at the summit of the NAM — and the emphatic repetition of old formulae by Yugoslav diplomats since then — it has become clear that within Yugoslavia a fairly comprehensive critique of the centrality of the movement to Yugoslavia's foreign relations has both been formulated, and has begun to gain a measure of significant support. The nature of the new thinking is suggested clearly by the title given to Foreign Minister Budimir Lončar's address to the meeting of ministers for foreign affairs of the Balkan states in Tiranë, in October 1990: "The Europeanization of the Balkans". Most importantly, the new orientation already seems to be reflected in the conduct of the country's diplomatic affairs.

The critique of former policy rests on three points: (i) too strong an identification with the non-aligned group of nations tends to separate Yugoslavia from Europe, whereas a closer integration with Europe is and ought to be the central goal of Yugoslav foreign policy; (ii) Yugoslavia's close involvement with the NAM has placed it in close association with some very undesirable figures in the international scene, which does no good at all when it comes to consolidating a new European orientation, and establishing its credentials as an open and democratic polity; (iii) the NAM is widely perceived as being a movement of Third World countries, which undermines Yugoslavia's aspiration to be seen as not only "European", but also as a reasonably sophisticated, primarily industrial economy, providing a respectable standard of living for its peoples.

Although there will continue to be good reasons why Yugoslavia's diplomatic service will wish to play down these shifts of position, there is little doubt that a new orientation is being formulated. In fact, all of the significant, specific developments with respect to Yugoslavia's foreign political relations in the period 1989–90 point clearly in that direction.

Meetings of the Foreign Ministers of the Balkan States

This interesting new forum for political and economic co-operation in Europe was launched in Belgrade in 1989, and followed in October 1990 by a second meeting in Tiranë. (The third meeting was scheduled to take place in Sofia in the autumn of 1991.) The communiqué issued at the end of the conference referred to a very wide range of common concerns around which it was anticipated that the parties to these talks could co-operate, including matters relating to transport and communications, health and environmental issues, as well as the more obvious economic questions, such as trade. Noteworthy among the issues raised, however, was the repeated emphasis on the need for the Balkan states to ensure a concerted and effective representation in other European intergovernmental organs.

The growth of Alpe-Adria links

This series of discussions, which dates back to a conference in Venice in 1978, involves representatives of relevant regions from within Austria, Germany, Hungary, Italy and Yugoslavia. Fifteen such regional governments are involved, with four others as observers.

Their work has focused upon several important issues of common practical concern, including transport, environmental protection and the strengthening of trade links. The real level of interest of these discussions within Yugoslavia is suggested by the fact that at first they were only thought to be of interest to the republics of Slovenia and Croatia. The group has recently been joined on an "observer" basis, however, by both Bosnia-Hercegovina and Montenegro.

The A-A group is expected to assume growing significance in the region as a whole, both as a mechanism for initiating action as well as a forum for discussion. Closely related to this development is the signing of the "Adriatic Initiative" by Italy and Yugoslavia in September 1990.

Yugoslav contacts with international bodies

The confirmation of Yugoslavia's new diplomatic orientation is found as clearly as anything else in the country's steady pursuit of firmer links with several very important international bodies. There has been a joint EFTA-Yugoslav Committee in existence since 1978, and Yugoslavia has indicated its intentions of applying to become a full member. Since 1961 Yugoslavia has had observer status with the OECD. An attempt is currently under way to upgrade this to full member status. Finally, the prospect is being taken very seriously of making a formal application for membership of the EC.

Some negative indications

Even the occurrence of rather negative events points in the same direction. In July 1989 Yugoslav-American relations were affected by the Kosovo problem, when the Yugoslavs recalled Ambassador Živorad Kovačević from Washington following his failure to head off criticism in Congress of Yugoslavia's human rights record. On this occasion Yugoslavia was revealed as very sensitive to criticism from the West, which in an earlier period might have been brushed aside.

One of the most interesting features of the Gulf crisis in 1990, and the international movement against Iraq following its invasion of Kuwait, has been the complete silence of the NAM. As a very substantial customer of Iraq's oil and food and a significant source of Iraq's military equipment, Yugoslavia might have been expected to be fairly vocal in the attempt to launch a concerted diplomatic initiative among the non-aligned nations to secure a resolution of the problem. (Iraq was the sixth in rank order of Yugoslavia's trade partners in 1989.) There has been no such initiative, and as far as it is possible to ascertain from publicly available sources, nor has one been contemplated.

Foreign relations and internal politics

The significance of Yugoslavia's foreign relations posture for its internal politics has often been underestimated. It is, however, doubtful whether after the mid-1960s non-alignment continued to yield much external benefit to the country. It remained significant, however, as an ideological flag to be waved internally, serving two purposes. It buttressed the claims of the Tito regime and its successors to play a major role in world affairs. Through the association of the NAM with decolonization and the defence of the rights of small nations, it provided a thinly disguised metaphor of the regime's advocacy of national self-determination on the domestic stage.

It might be argued that an important effect of this was to contribute to the insulation of Yugoslav politicians and public alike from the realities of their country's position in the world, and thus contribute to the manner in which domestic (especially ethnic) squabbles have been carried on in oblivious disregard of the need to address genuine and deep seated problems. The recent infusion of European realism into Yugoslav foreign affairs thinking has probably arrived far too late to make any significant difference to the course of events which is about to unfold.

EAST-WEST ECONOMIC RELATIONS
AND COMECON

Vladimir Sobell

One year after the fall of communist regimes in the countries of Eastern Europe the liquidation of the former Soviet bloc took another turn. On January 6, 1991, the member-countries of the socialist "common market" — the Council for Mutual Economic Assistance (CMEA, also known as Comecon) — decided to disband the CMEA. A new body was due to be set up on the CMEA's ruins, the Organization for International Economic Co-operation (OIEC). The successor is, however, destined to remain a mere shadow of the former CMEA. It is to have mainly a consultative and information function in addition to its "undertaker" role of winding down the CMEA. Yet this is not the end of the story since, like communism itself, Comecon has left a deep imprint on the member-countries' economies and its legacy will take many years to overcome.

The foundation of Comecon

Comecon was founded in January 1949 in the wake of Soviet rejection of the US-sponsored Marshall Plan for post-war reconstruction of Europe both as an alternative to the Marshall Plan and as a vehicle for the promotion of Soviet-type economic development in the new communist states. It could therefore be seen as economic pillar of the emerging Soviet bloc and as a tool by which Stalin sought to pre-empt the emergence of a central or Balkan regional integrative grouping which might have excluded the Soviet Union. Apart from the Soviet Union, the founding countries included Bulgaria, Czechoslovakia, Hungary, Poland and Romania (another key member — the former GDR — joined soon after its foundation). Comecon's membership gradually grew. Albania joined in 1949 but was inactive throughout the CMEA's existence. Other members included Cuba (joined in 1972), Vietnam (1978) and Mongolia (1962). Yugoslavia held associate membership. At the point of its dissolution there were also several countries with the co-operant status. These included developing countries with pro-Soviet orientation (Afghanistan, Angola, Ethiopia, Iraq, Mozambique, Nicaragua, and Democratic Yemen) but also Finland and Mexico.

Most Western analysts (and subsequently also East European economists) viewed the CMEA primarily as a political rather than purely economic organization, insofar as its main objective was not maximization of economic welfare but the promotion and maintenance of Soviet centrally-planned economic systems throughout the region. A leading American authority on the CMEA, Franklyn Holzman, for example, described the CMEA as a "trade destroying customs union" — a reflection of the fact that participation in the CMEA entailed net trade reduction. Such conclusions were justified in view of the excessive (and by any standards irrational) reorientation of the European member-countries' trade away from their traditional inter-war Western partners (mainly Germany) towards the

Soviet Union and isolation from the West. Typically, a European member of Comecon conducted at least 50% of its total trade with the Soviet Union, but in some especially faithful countries such as Bulgaria and Czechoslovakia nearly 80% of their trade in the late 1980s was taken by the USSR. The CMEA trade evolved along a "radial" pattern: a large portion of total trade with the Soviet Union along with relatively little trade with other CMEA members and an even smaller share with Western countries.

See Tables 1–5 below for an overview of internal and external CMEA trade.

Trade within Comecon

Intra-CMEA trade generally disregarded the conventional standards of comparative advantage — resources moved in accordance with political, ideological and technological rather than purely economic criteria. Thus all member-countries constructed heavy steel and iron industries and industries such as heavy engineering and petrochemicals regardless of their endowments with the needed energy and raw materials. Requisite energy and raw materials had to be supplied by the Soviet Union in ever increasing volumes; by the early 1960s all non-Soviet members of the CMEA became net importers of energy and raw materials. Since prices of these goods were determined artificially in intra-state agreements, Comecon in its last phase amounted to little more than a vehicle by which the Soviet Union subsidized the East European communist regimes (in addition to Cuba, Mongolia and Vietnam).

In fact it was not just a matter of subsidization. The East European countries' link with the CMEA was vital inasmuch as it provided them with the opportunity to purchase energy and raw materials (the so-called "hard" goods) from the Soviet Union, in return for their largely uncompetitive manufactures ("soft" goods) in sufficiently large volumes to keep their increasingly bankrupt economies going. As the technological level (and with it the competitiveness) of East European manufactures increasingly diverged from that of the Western countries, their ability to stand alone without Soviet support evaporated. In the end, this became the only glue that held the CMEA together (apart from the purely political commitment by the communist regimes).

After Comecon

The demise of communist rule and the dissolution of the CMEA thus marks a sea change in the economic environment of East European countries and is certain to mark one of the milestones in the region's economic history. The pattern established since 1949 will be reversed, but this time the shift should be understood as a return to normality after decades of Stalinist deformation. The member-countries will increasingly be reoriented towards the West, especially towards the EC (mainly Germany), and they will gradually revive their economies while abandoning all vestiges of Soviet-style communism by basing their economies and foreign trade on conventional market criteria. The early stages of this process are already well under way. The formal dissolution of the CMEA in January 1991 was preceded by several years of declining intra-CMEA trade; 1990 saw an especially dramatic fall as the Soviet Union substantially reduced exports of oil — perhaps the single most important hard commodity — by about 20% to Eastern Europe.

If earlier the East European countries had in common their participation in the CMEA "integration", then in post-communist development they share the problems of structural and systemic adjustment posed by their disengagement from the CMEA. What is the nature of these problems?

Problems of economic adjustment

As noted above, participation in the CMEA was synonymous with communism and with the maintenance of the Soviet-type centrally planned economy. Comecon was thus indirectly responsible for a series of distortions which are remarkably similar in each member country. Studies comparing the structural composition of East European economies have found that all of them display an excessive weight of industry in total economic activity in relation to their level of development (in comparison with market economies of similar size and development); moreover, within industry there has been a tendency to over-emphasize heavy industrial branches such as mining, metallurgy and heavy engineering. Similarly, all CMEA countries suffer from relatively under-developed light and services industries. Their agriculture is also larger (in relation to their level of development) than it would have been had they been conventional market-based economies. The CMEA countries' foreign trade is also substantially smaller (in relation to their GDP) than it should have been.

Another important feature, in many ways related to their "over-industrialization", has been their relatively high consumption of energy and raw materials both in absolute terms and in relation to their GDP. They consume about twice as much energy per unit of GDP as do the Western countries. This has had disastrous repercussions in the degradation of the environment. Comparisons of the levels of atmospheric pollution have shown that the East European countries generally emit several times the amount of pollution per unit of GDP as do the Western countries. One Western study concluded that all European members of the CMEA emit about two-and-a-half times as much sulphur dioxide per unit of GDP as do the Western countries, but the disparities are much more pronounced if individual countries are compared. If the amount of sulphur dioxide emitted per unit of GDP by former West Germany equals 100, then the comparable figure for what was the GDR is 490, for Czechoslovakia 485, for Hungary 386, for Poland 332, for Romania 279, for Bulgaria 229 and for the USSR 236. Another structural distortion worth noting is the CMEA countries' tendency to undertrade, that is have smaller than "normal" trade in relation to their level of development and size.

Structural distortions have been accompanied by chronic macro- and microeconomic imbalances. In fact it could be concluded that the communist economy meant an inherently imbalanced economy (communist economic theory in fact admitted this insofar as it asserted the primacy of "conscious" planning — that is intervention in the spontaneous working of the market). In practical terms this was responsible for the all-pervasive shortages of virtually anything. In his celebrated study (*Economics of Shortage*, 1980) the Hungarian economist Janos Kornai depicted shortages as the main distinguishing feature of Soviet-type centrally planned economies. If in a market economy firms are "demand constrained", that is they would produce more if there was more demand for their products, then socialist enterprises were "supply constrained" — they would produce more if they had more supplies. Given the chronic shortages, the authorities were under intense political pressure to continue to subsidize enterprises indefinitely. Over time, enterprises became habituated to what Kornai termed a "soft budget constraint", that is a situation when managers and workers knew they would be kept going regardless of their performance.

In fact it was not only the enterprises which operated on a "soft budget constraint".

The state, which managed its enterprises in this way, itself followed such principles. Chronic budget deficits, which grew larger and larger in the last years of communism, were "financed" by printing money. The East European currencies, apart from remaining inconvertible, came to be virtually worthless (in terms of Western hard currency) by the time communist rule collapsed. The imbalance was also responsible for severe inflationary pressures which, however, remained suppressed because prices in a traditional centrally planned system were strictly controlled. Inflation was manifested in the form of excess spending power in relation to the available goods (queueing), but countries such as Poland or Yugoslavia, which did attempt to introduce "market socialism" and partially or fully freed their prices, plunged into a hyper-inflationary spiral.

Most CMEA countries are heavily externally indebted and some have experienced severe difficulties with servicing their foreign debts. Poland has repeatedly rescheduled its debts and by the early 1990s it was clear that a decisive proportion of debts would have to be written off by Western government creditors. Hungary, which had the highest *per capita* debt, managed to avoid the same fate only with great difficulty. Bulgaria was forced to suspend repayments of its debt and interest in the course of 1990. Chronic balance-of-payments problems of the CMEA countries were ultimately rooted in the communist-type centrally planned system, because this system lay at the root of the uncompetitiveness of East European exports.

All of the former communist countries were likely to follow their specific roads on their return to capitalism, but since their structural and systemic distortions were essentially identical they were bound to pass through the same stages. They had all to stabilize their economies to overcome shortages and suppressed inflation. This, in practice, meant that prices of most goods had to be freed (increased) and all-pervasive subsidies removed; the way to this led through a political minefield as inflation must first be released into the open, or become "transparent". The same was true of unemployment, which under the communist system remained hidden. They must also begin gradually to restructure their economies (increase the share of services), and modernize their industries to make them more in line with the pattern observable in the market economies, and they must indeed place their economies on a market footing by creating the basic institutions of a market economy — the private ownership of the means of production and the capital market (including the stock exchange). Wholesale nationalization and growth of the state, it was clear, would be followed by similarly rapid denationalization. Typically a state holding agency was set up which prepares enterprises for privatization by converting them into joint stock companies. Various schemes for stock disposal of shares have been considered, including distribution to the population of vouchers exchangeable for shares at only nominal prices or free. Small businesses were being privatized by more conventional methods such as auctions. Privatization in Eastern Europe, however, is likely to be "active" or "creative" rather than passive; that is to say it will materialize mainly through closures of large state enterprises and the growth of new private ones rather than merely by privatization of existing firms.

The process of reform

Following the final demise of communism in late 1989 all CMEA member-countries initiated moves towards political pluralism — freely contested elections were held in each country — and preparation of economic reforms leading to a decisive break with the communist economic system. Poland led the way by implementing on January 1990 an IMF-backed stabilization programme. Prices of most goods were freed and subsidies removed. Effective brakes were imposed on increases of wages. The Zloty was drastically devalued and made "internally convertible" (enterprises and private individuals were able to exchange unlimited amounts of the Zloty for hard currency and vice versa). After initial acceleration of inflation, Polish hyper-inflation was spectacularly cured — the economy was largely stabilized. However, the price to pay for this success was a dramatic fall in output and a rapid growth of unemployment — unemployment increased from zero in early 1990 to about 7% of the total labour force by the end of that year. The former East Germany followed suit; it had virtually no other option if it was to reunite with West Germany. Following the currency union of June 1990, when the East German Ostmark was abolished and the Deutschmark became the legal tender in the former GDR, the East German economy dived into a deep recession as East German enterprises could not compete with their West German counterparts.

Developments in the other East European countries have been more gradual as political conditions precluded a decisive break with the past. Czechoslovakia slowly prepared legislation for reforms amidst political struggles over the direction of economic policy. The first real steps towards radical reform were made in January 1991 when a wide range of prices were freed and subsidies removed. Unemployment began to rise. Hungary never completely discontinued its modest market-oriented reforms under communism and had already been monitored by the IMF when Hungarian communism finally vacated the scene. The new democratically elected government headed by József Antall did not therefore need to execute a complete policy turnaround. Nevertheless, Hungary is facing a harsh adjustment as it continues to make its approach ever closer to a market system at a time of severe pressure on its balance of payments in view of its disastrous external situation.

The Balkan members of the CMEA have been undergoing a somewhat different development. The first free elections in Romania ushered in a victory of the National Salvation Front led by President Ion Iliescu which the opposition parties view as a neo-communist organization. Indeed Romania's new-born democracy is perhaps the most fragile of all the post-communist countries; the regime's image was seriously tarnished in June 1990 when pro-NSF demonstrators were brutally beaten by regime-mobilized thugs. Nevertheless, despite the neo-communist current in the NSF, the leadership has conceded the inevitability of radical economic reforms. A surprisingly youthful and competent government was assembled by Prime Minister Petre Roman and a radical reform programme was approved. The implementation of the programme has, however, run into serious problems already in the early stages — Romanian workers are refusing to accept the necessary sacrifice (inflation and unemployment) and the government has been forced to delay and water down its plans.

Bulgaria's path also differed from that of the northern tier of the CMEA. Its first free elections returned the communist party (renamed the Bulgarian Socialist Party) to power, but Prime Minister Andrei Lukanov was unable to form an effective government as the opposition refused to co-operate with the former communists in a government of national unity. Lukanov prepared a programme of radical reforms but was forced to resign in December 1990. The opposition Union of Democratic Forces (UDF) which engineered Lukanov's fall ostensibly advocated a more radical reform than that prepared by Lukanov, but at the point of writing (January 1991) Bulgaria's political scene was still unstable and details of its economic policy unclear. There could, however, be no doubt that any post-communist government would have to act resolutely along the lines pioneered by Poland. Bulgaria joined the IMF in September 1990 and given its balance of payments crisis it will have to follow the IMF's prescriptions if it is to restore its international solvency.

Despite these differences between the central European and Balkan members of the former CMEA (explicable in terms of different historical backgrounds and social conditions), the northern and southern tier of the CMEA can broadly be interpreted as moving in the same direction. If in the north the removal of the old system is apparently controlled and the break with communism relatively clean, then the process in the south has been more chaotic and less clear cut. The sharp contraction of output in Poland in 1990 may have been induced by the tough medicine administered by the government, but it is remarkable that output contracted nearly as sharply in Romania and Bulgaria in the wake of the spontaneous disintegration of the communist administration and the ensuing power vacuum.

Problems of internal and foreign trade

As noted above the collapse of communism in each CMEA member country has been matched by a parallel development on the intra-bloc level in the shape of the disintegration of the CMEA. Apart from the contraction of mutual trade, which accelerated in 1990 mainly because of Soviet failure to supply contracted deliveries of oil, the death of the CMEA has been manifested in the transition in January 1991 to hard currency accounting, at prevailing world market prices, in intra-Comecon trade. This heralds the end of Soviet subsidization of the CMEA member economies through the exchange of "hard" for "soft" goods. Theoretically at least, from this point trade between the Soviet Union and its former communist allies is to be conducted in the same way as trade among standard market economies.

This step has of course administered a sharp shock, made disastrously worse by the Gulf crisis, to East European economies, as suddenly they must pay world market prices for their oil and in hard currency or goods which the Soviet negotiators consider equivalent to hard (that is Western) manufactured goods. In effect this entails a massive shift in intra-CMEA terms of trade in favour of the Soviet Union: while Soviet energy and raw materials command firm, and easily definable, world market prices, the East European manufacturers (theoretically at least) obtain very low prices compared with their Western counterparts.

Precise estimates of this shift in the terms of trade cannot yet be made because it is uncertain how East European products will in the end be priced (indeed developments in late 1990 and early 1991 indicated some willingness on the part of the Soviet Union to refrain from excessive harshness in judging the value of imported East European products; it could be argued that Soviet enterprises will not be under pressure to penalize the East Europeans as long as the Soviet economy itself remains committed to the centrally-planned system). Nevertheless, it is certain that East European surpluses in ruble trade with the Soviet Union will be transformed into dollar deficits. Calculations carried out in Hungary, for example, suggested that a Soviet deficit with Hungary in 1989 of the tune of R 800 million would be transformed into a surplus of about $1.5 billion had trade been accounted in hard currency and at world market prices. Soviet calculations suggest that the Soviet Union could transform its deficit with Eastern Europe into an $11 billion surplus in 1991 after the new system is adopted; an IMF study of the Soviet economy concluded similarly that the Soviet surplus with Eastern Europe would be between $6.6 billion and $9.9 billion in 1991.

Fortunately for the East Europeans they may be able to soften the shock of the transition by converting their accumulated ruble surpluses with the Soviet Union, estimated at about 10 billion rubles by the end of 1990, into dollars at relatively favourable rates. Hungary negotiated the rate of 90 cents per Transferable Ruble (TR, a unit of account in intra-Comecon trade, similar but not identical to the Soviet Ruble) while Czechoslovakia managed a slightly better rate of TR 1 = $1; this could give Czechoslovakia a $3 billion cushion. Nevertheless, there can be no doubt that the collapse of Comecon will impose severe strain on the East European economies especially since it culminated at the time of the crisis in the Gulf. Some estimates have suggested that the loss of markets in the former GDR, higher prices of energy and losses of trade with Iraq (most East European countries counted on importing oil from Iraq to recover their credits there) will cost the East Europeans about $7 billion in 1991. Should the prices of oil rocket to $50 or more per barrel the East European economies would not be able to cope. They would require massive Western aid or loans to cover their balance-of-payments requirements and Hungary would most likely default on its debt payments. The alternative would be a dramatic collapse in East European output and trade in 1991 and beyond.

Alternative forms of association

The demise of Comecon automatically placed on the agenda the question of a successor organization. Although, as noted above, the member-countries agreed to maintain a CMEA replacement in the form of the OIEC, none of them are interested in restoring the old Soviet-centred CMEA; indeed the OIEC has been conceived (at least by some members such as Czechoslovakia) merely as a politically expedient substitute for the CMEA so as not to unnecessarily upset the Soviets. In fact no East European government is seriously interested even in creating a new regional organization excluding the Soviet Union. Proposals for a Central European Payments Union (CEPU) advanced by some Western specialists have so far received little attention in Eastern Europe, the main reason being the unwillingness to form another "poor men's club" in central and Eastern Europe. Instead all East European governments desire as speedy as possible an admission into the EC.

Although it is recognized both by the Community and East European governments that the East European economies are not in a position to enter the EC at this point, the East Europeans hope that they will be able to do so by the end of the 1990s. The former GDR, which automatically became a member at the point of its reunification with West Germany, is an exception. In this case a crash admission to the EC was possible because of massive West German economic aid, the adoption of West German currency, standards, legislation and rapid restructuring expected in the coming years.

Yet, if viewed in broader terms, it appears that the process of reintegration of former CMEA countries with Western Europe is already well under way. It is possible to point to several dimensions in which this process (of catching up with the former GDR) is taking place. First of all, the East European countries have initiated the creation of the political and economic preconditions — a pluralistic democracy and the creation of a market economy. Such a fundamental systemic (political and economic) convergence is a precondition for meaningful economic reintegration and eventual formal admission.

In the past, East-West was not a normal trade insofar as on the Eastern side it was managed exclusively by state authorities (it was also grossly suboptimal — trade with the CMEA, including the USSR accounted for a mere 7% of the total external trade of the EC, approximately the share taken by Sweden or Switzerland alone). The decentralization of decision-making authority to the level of individual enterprises, which is an intrinsic part of the reforms, will mean that trade between East and West will be managed on the level of individual firms and that East-West trade will increasingly be conducted in the same way as trade between any other countries. The creation of balanced market economies in Eastern Europe will mean that the region will increasingly begin to operate with real prices (instead of the former administratively determined "prices") which will also fully reflect world market prices. Simultaneously, policies will be applied leading to the convertibility of East European currencies. This usually entails a sharp devaluation, often to the level of the former black-market exchange rate, followed by additional domestic inflationary pressure. But despite such a shock, a meaningful albeit rudimentary link is created with the Western economies. In general terms it can be concluded that the painful progress towards balanced economies and market-driven domestic systems, with a large private sector and functioning capital markets, will also lay the foundations of their reintegration with the EC. It will also enable the East European economies to participate properly in the world economy at large.

Eastern Europe and the West

In the meantime, the European community can be expected to "deepen" as well as "widen" its integrative process — by progressing towards a monetary union and expanding its membership by admitting Austria and possibly other EFTA members. In this way, when the East European countries are ready to join formally by the end of the 1990s they will be joining a larger yet still more closely knit economic grouping. The opening up of Eastern Europe will have important repercussions in the West. A study by the Centre for Economic Policy Research (*Monitoring European Integration: The Impact of Eastern Europe*, October 1990) argued that the rebuilding of Eastern Europe with the aid of Western capital is likely to bring financial instability and force realignments in the European monetary system in the wake of a surge for German capital (the impulse for the realignment is a fundamental asymmetry in the EC, as Germany is better equipped to meet the demand for capital goods than any other Western country). The study also envisages a substantial fall in West European farm prices as Eastern Europe and the Soviet Union become in the medium term net exporters to the West of agricultural goods and energy.

One of the most important conclusions of this study is that Eastern Europe has a comparative advantage in research-skilled workers as a percentage of the total workforce (higher than the southern EC countries or middle-income countries such as Argentina, Hong Kong, Mexico and South Korea), many of whom have been working in the defence industries — one of the few areas where East Europe successfully competed with the West. The relative abundance of such personnel is combined with relative shortages of skilled production and commercial workers. Eastern Europe is, therefore, likely to specialize in the production of high-tech goods rather than labour-intensive goods. A corollary is that future East-West trade is likely to resemble present-day West-West trade: there will be flows in both directions of relatively sophisticated manufactures. Intra-industry trade, driven by economies of scale, is likely to predominate.

East European reconstruction will require massive flows of Western capital; the Centre for Economic Policy Research study estimates the amount of capital needed at $1,350 billion to $2,910 billion over the next 10 years, which on an annual basis represents about 15–30% of total investment of the EC and 5–10% of total OECD investment (the estimate includes the former GDR and excludes the USSR). Nothing near such massive Western investment in Eastern Europe has occurred so far, but these are still early days. Once the East European reforms are well under way, the economic and political scenes reasonably stable and the currencies progressing towards convertibility, the needed resources may be expected to be forthcoming. Western companies will be attracted by growing opportunities in the opening East European market and also the region's ability to serve as a bridgehead to the Soviet Union as well as a base from which to export to the EC. Already some large, psychologically important, deals have been concluded. In late 1990, for example, the German car maker *Volkswagen* won a 33% stake in Czechoslovakia's *Skoda*. *Volkswagen* plans to spend DM 9.5 billion over the next 10 years on expansion and modernization of *Skoda*'s car output as well as on a generous social programme of the company. *VW*'s share in *Skoda* could reach 70% by 1995.

Following the fall of communism, debate culminated in the West concerning the merits of a Marshall Plan-type programme of assistance to Eastern Europe. In the end the general conclusion was that loans and grants alone would be of little use — first it would be necessary to reform the East European economies to ensure that any finance that might be forthcoming was not wasted. The major difference between the European recipients of Marshall Plan aid and East European countries today is that the former already had reasonably functioning market economies — a factor completely lacking in today's Eastern Europe. Official aid should therefore concentrate on helping with the creation of the institutions of market economies (for example the stock market), management training, the promotion of small private enterprise and general economic advice.

The European Bank for Reconstruction and Development

In the summer of 1989, after the formation in Poland of East Europe's first government including non-communist ministers, a multilateral official aid to Poland and Hungary was launched by 24 Western governments and the EC. Later, this programme, co-ordinated by the EC, was extended to the other ex-communist countries (it was known as the PHARE programme, an abbreviation of its French title). A major milestone was reached in 1990 with the setting up of a new institution — the London-based European Bank for Reconstruction and Development (EBRD) — designed exclusively for the purpose of East European reconstruction. The EBRD is to channel funds to private sector projects, but aid to the East European public sector (especially the infrastructure) is not excluded in recognition of the surviving dominant role of the state in Eastern Europe. The EBRD is destined to become the pivot of Western financial backing of East European reconstruction in the years to come, but its activity will be supplemented by the World Bank, the European Investment Bank (EIB — the EC's own development bank), and bilateral aid from Western governments. Continued support for East European countries' balance of payments can be expected from the IMF (all European CMEA members — except the Soviet Union — are now IMF members).

Even before the fall of the communist regimes the EC either concluded or was negotiating extensive trade agreements with all CMEA countries, including the Soviet Union, but excluding Romania. These agreements envisaged a varying degree of the EC's openness to imports from Eastern Europe depending on an individual country's progress toward democracy and a market economy. Poland and Hungary obviously led the field as the EC lifted all quantitative restriction on their exports from January 1989. By September 1990 this concession was extended to all East European countries.

The former CMEA members continue to move rapidly up the ladder. In December 1990 the EC offered Czechoslovakia, Hungary and Poland the prospect of negotiating so-called "second generation" agreements, also referred to as "European agreements"; Romania and Bulgaria were expected to follow suit once their political scene had stabilized and economic reform had progressed. These could enter into force in January 1992. They aim for the establishment of special association with the EC, meaning a phased introduction of a free trade area for industrial products, free movement of capital and improved movement of persons (these provisions match, and in some respects surpass, the present status of the EFTA countries). The EC is to move more rapidly towards free trade than the associated countries thereby assisting their recovery. Association Councils are to be created at ministerial level with each associate member to supervise the agreement and to provide a forum for dialogue. These agreements are to last indefinitely and are to have a "value in themselves" insofar as they are "distinguished from the possibility of accession to the Community". On the other hand the "possibility of accession" would not "be affected by the the conclusion of association agreements" (Communication from the Commission to the Council and European Parliament, September 1990).

Table 1: OECD trade with CMEA countries (in $US millions)

EXPORTS

	Bulgaria	Czecho-slovakia	GDR*	Hungary	Poland	Romania	Eastern Europe	USSR	CMEA
1970	328	786	431	627	891	704	3,767	2,656	6,423
1975	1,098	1,879	1,129	1,835	5,487	2,004	13,432	12,527	25,960
1977	903	2,086	1,195	2,322	5,054	2,338	13,898	13,544	27,442
1978	1,109	2,338	1,490	2,995	5,615	3,028	16,574	15,601	32,175
1979	1,235	2,763	2,399	2,986	6,065	3,783	19,233	19,197	38,429
1980	1,605	2,964	2,482	3,292	6,490	3,904	20,737	21,545	42,282
1981	1,862	2,344	2,451	3,208	4,299	3,045	17,210	22,065	39,275
1982	1,547	2,145	1,714	2,876	3,227	1,686	13,195	22,752	35,946
1983	1,561	1,941	1,976	2,586	2,892	1,296	12,252	22,494	34,747
1984	1,451	1,892	1,801	2,509	2,947	1,398	11,998	21,889	33,887
1985	1,871	2,189	1,494	2,819	3,108	1,434	12,915	20,884	33,799
1986	2,202	2,744	1,917	3,468	3,376	1,643	15,351	20,574	35,925
1987	2,353	3,331	2,486	3,902	3,962	1,315	17,349	20,556	37,905
1988	2,429	3,576	2,951	4,000	4,965	1,257	19,177	24,909	44,086
1989	2,420	3,657	3,150	4,659	6,212	1,218	21,316	28,733	50,050

Note: * Without intra-German trade.
Source: OECD.

Table 2:   OECD trade with CMEA countries (in $US millions)

IMPORTS

	Bulgaria	Czecho-slovakia	GDR*	Hungary	Poland	Romania	Eastern Europe	USSR	CMEA
1970	241	726	410	535	1,064	552	3,528	2,846	6,374
1975	398	1,638	1,035	1,247	3,170	1,655	9,143	8,929	18,072
1977	516	1,878	1,133	1,675	3,908	1,905	11,015	12,211	23,226
1978	581	2,182	1,412	1,907	4,392	2,341	12,816	13,974	26,789
1979	919	2,758	1,638	2,543	5,118	3,253	16,229	20,042	36,270
1980	979	3,197	2,096	2,806	5,604	3,411	18,093	24,687	42,781
1981	837	2,725	2,184	2,493	3,610	3,545	15,394	24,235	39,629
1982	796	2,672	2,361	2,260	3,327	2,583	13,999	25,416	39,415
1983	731	2,619	2,415	2,319	3,290	2,757	14,132	24,625	38,757
1984	740	2,711	2,336	2,534	3,972	3,692	15,985	25,611	41,596
1985	714	2,636	2,314	2,608	3,933	3,464	15,669	23,303	38,972
1986	747	3,102	2,482	2,993	4,214	3,577	17,114	20,348	37,462
1987	760	3,493	2,596	3,697	4,913	4,066	19,524	22,856	42,380
1988	745	3,818	2,743	4,090	5,714	4,029	21,138	23,636	44,774
1989	794	4,134	2,895	4,495	6,159	3,876	22,354	25,668	48,022

Note: *Without intra-German trade.
Source: OECD.

Table 3: OECD trade with CMEA countries: Shares of individual countries in CMEA total in %

EXPORTS

	Bulgaria	Czecho-slovakia	GDR*	Hungary	Poland	Romania	Eastern Europe	USSR	CMEA
1970	5.1	12.2	6.7	9.8	13.9	11.0	58.6	41.4	100.0
1975	4.2	7.2	4.4	7.1	21.1	7.7	51.7	48.3	100.0
1977	3.3	7.6	4.4	8.5	18.4	8.5	50.6	49.4	100.0
1978	3.4	7.3	4.6	9.3	17.5	9.4	51.5	48.5	100.0
1979	3.2	7.2	6.2	7.8	15.8	9.8	50.0	50.0	100.0
1980	3.8	7.0	5.9	7.8	15.3	9.2	49.0	51.0	100.0
1981	4.7	6.0	6.2	8.2	10.9	7.8	43.8	56.2	100.0
1982	4.3	6.0	4.8	8.0	9.0	4.7	36.7	63.3	100.0
1983	4.5	5.6	5.7	7.4	8.3	3.7	35.3	64.7	100.0
1984	4.3	5.6	5.3	7.4	8.7	4.1	35.4	64.6	100.0
1985	5.5	6.5	4.4	8.3	9.2	4.2	38.2	61.8	100.0
1986	6.1	7.6	5.3	9.7	9.4	4.6	42.7	57.3	100.0
1987	6.2	8.8	6.6	10.3	10.5	3.5	45.8	54.2	100.0
1988	5.5	8.1	6.7	9.1	11.3	2.9	43.5	56.5	100.0
1989	4.8	7.3	6.3	9.3	12.4	2.4	42.6	57.4	100.0

Note: *Without intra-German trade.
Source: OECD.

Table 4: OECD trade with CMEA countries: shares of individual countries in CMEA total in %

IMPORTS

	Bulgaria	Czecho-slovakia	GDR*	Hungary	Poland	Romania	Eastern Europe	USSR	CMEA
1970	3.8	11.4	6.4	8.4	16.7	8.7	55.3	44.7	100.0
1975	2.2	9.1	5.7	6.9	17.5	9.2	50.6	49.4	100.0
1977	2.2	8.1	4.9	7.2	16.8	8.2	47.4	52.6	100.0
1978	2.2	8.1	5.3	7.1	16.4	8.7	47.8	52.2	100.0
1979	2.5	7.6	4.5	7.0	14.1	9.0	44.7	55.3	100.0
1980	2.3	7.5	4.9	6.6	13.1	8.0	42.3	57.7	100.0
1981	2.1	6.9	5.5	6.3	9.1	8.9	38.8	61.2	100.0
1982	2.0	6.8	6.0	5.7	8.4	6.6	35.5	64.5	100.0
1983	1.9	6.8	6.2	6.0	8.5	7.1	36.5	63.5	100.0
1984	1.8	6.5	5.6	6.1	9.6	8.9	38.4	61.6	100.0
1985	1.8	6.8	5.9	6.7	10.1	8.9	40.2	59.8	100.0
1986	2.0	8.3	6.6	8.0	11.2	9.5	45.7	54.3	100.0
1987	1.8	8.2	6.1	8.7	11.6	9.6	46.1	53.9	100.0
1988	1.7	8.5	6.1	9.1	12.8	9.0	47.2	52.8	100.0
1989	1.7	8.6	6.0	9.4	12.8	8.1	46.5	53.5	100.0

Note: *Without intra-German trade.
Source: OECD.

Table 5:   OECD Exports to CMEA by country (%)

Exporting country	1980	1984	1985	1986	1987	1988	1989
FRG	22.3	21.0	21.7	25.2	26.2	25.4	26.1
France	11.0	8.7	8.6	7.7	8.1	7.6	7.0
Italy	6.5	7.3	7.7	8.0	9.5	8.2	9.3
Great Britain	6.2	5.1	4.5	4.8	4.8	4.8	4.4
EC 12	56.3	51.1	52.9	55.3	58.4	55.3	56.7
Finland	6.6	8.2	9.4	10.0	8.7	8.4	7.5
Switzerland	2.5	2.2	2.5	3.1	3.9	3.8	3.3
Austria	5.0	5.6	5.6	6.0	6.5	6.4	5.9
Western Europe	75.1	70.9	74.3	78.1	81.5	78.3	78.3
USA	9.1	12.3	9.5	5.5	5.8	8.3	10.6
Japan	8.4	8.8	9.9	10.8	8.7	8.9	7.5
Australia	3.1	2.5	2.3	2.4	2.0	2.1	
Canada	4.2	5.5	4.0	3.2	2.0	2.5	1.5
Overseas	24.9	29.1	25.7	21.9	18.5	21.7	21.7
OECD TOTAL	100.0	100.0	100.0	100.0	100.0	100.0	100.0

Source: OECD

THE WARSAW TREATY ORGANIZATION

Stephen White

The Warsaw Treaty Organization (WTO) was established by the Treaty of Friendship, Co-operation and Mutual Assistance signed in the Polish capital on May 14, 1955. The signatory states were the Soviet Union, Bulgaria, Czechoslovakia, the German Democratic Republic (GDR), Hungary, Romania and Albania. The Treaty contained a collective defence obligation by which, according to Article 4, the parties would individually or collectively come to the assistance of a member-state subject to armed attack in Europe by any state or group of states. Article 5 provided for the establishment of a Joint Command of the members' armed forces. Article 6 established a Political Consultative Committee (PCC), which would meet twice a year, as the main formal organ for political consultations within the alliance. Article 3 provided for consultation on international questions affecting the member-states' common interests. It was also indicated in Article 5 that the alliance was seen as contributing to the maintenance of Marxist-Leninist political systems in Eastern Europe, referring to the protection of the "peaceful labour of their peoples" in addition to defence against aggression and a guarantee of the territorial status quo.

The WTO as a military alliance

The formal basis of Soviet-East European security relations had been established earlier through a network of bilateral mutual assistance treaties signed in 1948. The USSR's occupation and Sovietization of Eastern Europe had allowed the creation of a geographical buffer zone between the USSR and Western Europe. This forward defensive zone was covered by an integrated air defence network from 1948 and provided a staging area from which Soviet armed forces stationed in Eastern Europe might be able to launch an invasion of Western Europe. As East European armed forces began in 1949 to receive Soviet equipment and were enlarged and restructured on Soviet organizational lines they assumed a titular role in Soviet military strategy in Europe.

The military Joint Command was set up in Moscow in early 1956, while in the same year the PCC created a Secretariat and Permanent Commission which was intended to facilitate common stances on foreign policy issues. The new alliance appears to have played only a very minor military role in the first half-decade of its existence, despite the post-Stalin Soviet leadership's desire to place greater stress on formal institutional channels in Soviet-East European relations in the economic and military spheres.

The USSR's relative neglect of the WTO as a military organization in its first few years of existence suggested that operational military factors were not the primary Soviet motives in establishing it in 1955. The prospect of such an alliance had been raised by the USSR in the East-West diplomatic exchanges of 1954–55 over the Paris Agreements, which provided for the entry of a re-armed Federal German Republic into the Western European Union and the North Atlantic Treaty Organization (NATO). The Warsaw Treaty was described as a response to West Germany's entry into NATO. At the July 1955 Geneva Conference the East proposed a non-aggression treaty between the two blocs and the creation of a pan-European collective security system: the WTO would be dissolved in the event that NATO were also dismantled, a position that was to be publicly reiterated on many future occasions. The WTO may thus have been conceived initially as a bargaining counter in the mid-1950s' exchanges over European security and the role of Western Germany in the Western alliance system.

The only immediate military advantage accruing to Moscow from the Warsaw Treaty lay in the new basis provided for the continued presence of Soviet troops in Hungary and Romania after the Soviet military withdrawal from Austria pursuant to the Austrian State Treaty of May 15, 1955. In the aftermath of the Soviet military suppression of the October 1956 Hungarian uprising, the USSR signed new status-of-forces agreements governing the stationing of Soviet troops in Poland, Hungary, the GDR and Romania and in 1958 withdrew its forces — as a result of host government pressure — from Romania. The East European forces were relieved of their Soviet commanders as a concession to national feelings. Despite the existence of the Joint Command of the WTO, the USSR seemed to attach little importance to the contribution of its East European allies to Soviet military strategy, as the Non-Soviet Warsaw Pact (NSWP) forces had first to undergo reorganization and re-equipment in order to serve a useful military role in an East-West conflict.

Changes in Soviet military doctrine in the early 1960s, including large cuts in Soviet ground forces and preparation for rapid offensive nuclear operations in a European war, led the USSR to accord greater significance to the potential wartime roles of NSWP forces and to seek to integrate them more effectively into Soviet military planning. The WTO consequently acquired military functions of its own. In 1961, with the erection of the Berlin Wall and stabilization of the GDR, it became possible to institute large-scale multinational exercises involving most member-states and their number increased dramatically in the rest of the decade. These were part of a broader effort at military integration including modernization of the NSWP forces and weapons standardization.

In 1969 the military institutions of the WTO were reformed and expanded. The membership of the Joint Command was altered so as to remove the East European Ministers of Defence from a status of formal subordination within this organ to the WTO Commander-in-Chief, a position which has always been occupied by a Soviet officer and Deputy Defence Minister. The Joint Staff of the Joint Armed Forces was created with, again, a Soviet Chief-of-Staff, Soviet First Deputies and East European deputies. A Military Council was set up, together with a Technical Council. Finally, the irregular meetings of Defence Ministers occurring in the 1960s were institutionalized in the form of a Committee of Defence Ministers as the highest consultative body in the WTO for discussion of military matters.

The reconstitution of the Joint Command and establishment of a Joint Staff suggested that the alliance had become a distinct entity in its own right for the wartime command of the armed forces of its member-states. However, available evidence suggests that the WTO has not had a wartime operational command structure of its own nor its own mobilization and logistic support arrangements. It seems that in wartime NSWP forces would come under the command of the Soviet General Staff and would be organized in Soviet-designated fronts. The bulk of East European forces would have been delegated to rear security roles ensuring the passage of Soviet divisions from the USSR to the Central Front. To ensure the capacity for surprise attack through initially un-reinforced offensive operations employing forces already in place near the NATO-WTO line of contact, the USSR evidently planned to rely primarily on its own resources at the outset of an East-West War.

The 1969 reforms did, however, underline the value Moscow attached to select East European elements of the WTO Joint Armed Forces in its offensive military strategy, particularly from the armed forces of the Northern Tier states of Poland, the GDR and, to a lesser extent, Czechoslovakia. Available evidence suggests that all of the six East German divisions, three or four Polish divisions, two or three Czech divisions and a very small proportion of Hungarian and Bulgarian forces were assigned to the WTO Joint Command in the late 1970s/early 1980s. The majority of WTO joint exercises have involved the Northern Tier armies and modernization has been concentrated in the elements of Polish and East German forces apparently assigned for service in joint battle groups integrated with the Soviet formations that would form the bulk of the forces of the wartime joint fronts. The armed forces of Bulgaria and Hungary participated in multilateral exercises much less frequently and their modernization lagged behind that of the Northern Tier states.

Despite planning to rely largely on its own forces in the conduct of a major military offensive against Western Europe, the USSR has had to concern itself with the political *reliability* of East European armed forces. The "Prague Spring" of 1968 and the purging of, and mass resignations from, the Czech officer corps following the Soviet-led invasion of Czechoslovakia cast a long shadow over what had been one of the largest and best East European military establishments. Five Soviet divisions were stationed "temporarily" on Czech territory in the aftermath of the crisis to deter further political turmoil. Despite doubts as to Czech willingness to fight in any conflict with the West, the structure of the WTO was relied upon to ensure that some Czech formations would participate in joint force groupings closely integrated under Soviet command.

Poland has had the largest and one of the best equipped military establishments in Eastern Europe and the Polish authorities seemed to accept the assignment of some of their formations to integrated offensive roles. As with the GDR, the national interest lay in a rapid military thrust into West Germany that would bring victory before Polish territory became a target for NATO nuclear strikes. Thus, the USSR could count on the Polish military to fight for a reasonable period of time in an East-West war. However, the 1980–81 Polish crisis strengthened Soviet concern for the security of rail links through Poland to the Group of Soviet Forces in Germany. The imposition of martial law in December 1981 did little to enhance the reliability of Polish conscripts in the event of war with the West, and the continuing tensions in Poland probably caused Moscow to view its Polish ally as more of a liability than an asset.

Military integration was taken furthest in the GDR where, despite their small number, East German army divisions were well equipped to take part in a rapid offensive against West Germany. They came under the direct authority of the WTO Joint Command even in peacetime. The Romanian armed forces in effect were withdrawn from the WTO military structure in the late 1960s as Ceauşescu, concerned to assert his independence from Moscow, reoriented them exclusively towards the defence of Romanian national territory against external aggression from any quarter. Among the East European members of the WTO the forces of the three Northern Tier states were the most relevant to Soviet war planning and the WTO framework was designed to ensure that select elements of GDR, Polish and Czech forces would be available at the outset of a war in Europe to contribute to Soviet offensive operations. Yet the USSR's "coalition warfare" doctrine probably placed little faith in the reliability of its key allies in a protracted and increasingly destructive military conflict with NATO.

In the mid-to-late 1960s the Brezhnev leadership in the USSR sought to employ the WTO as an institution through which to strengthen the political cohesion of the socialist bloc and to enhance its role in foreign policy co-ordination. East European responses showed a desire for more genuine consultation within the alliance and an enhanced role for the non-Soviet allies in the making of WTO military policy. The 1969 reforms of the military institutions of the WTO appeared to accord a greater degree of formal equality to the East Europeans. Yet the Soviet effort to deepen integration in the WTO prompted a protracted debate in East European politico-military circles. Many of the issues raised by the East Europeans in the late 1960s' debate stemmed from the USSR's domination of policy-making in the alliance — a characteristic of the WTO that the 1969 reforms did little to alter — and some of the bones of contention subsequently resurfaced.

The lack of any effective East European voice in the higher military bodies of the WTO was criticized most vociferously by Romania. Bucharest argued that the post of WTO Commander-in-Chief should be rotated among the member-states rather than always being filled by a Soviet general. The USSR's allies should also be consulted through the WTO on Soviet planning and doctrine for the use of nuclear weapons. Most significantly, the allies should be allowed to develop their own national military doctrines. Similar military-political concerns were echoed by Polish and Czech military officers, the latter explicitly formulating and openly airing their professional and national grievances during the 1968 Prague Spring.

In the mid-1960s, issues of *burden-sharing* were first raised in the WTO. There were complaints about the unfair offset costs of Soviet forces in Eastern Europe and the constraints on modernization of the NSWP armed forces posed by the large size of their ground forces. Moscow's export of some of its most modern weapons systems to major Third World clients before their introduction into the allied armies caused resentment in the East European military establishments. However imperfect, the standardization of weapons and equipment in the WTO tended to benefit the USSR disproportionately as it dominated the development of all major weapons systems. Soviet predominance in collective decisions on weapons programmes ensured that military research and development benefited the Soviet defence industry.

On the other hand, the USSR has consistently shouldered the lion's share of the economic burden of the WTO's collective defence effort. This has been estimated in the West to be about 80% of defence spending in the alliance. Reflecting its wider superpower concerns, the USSR was estimated to spend 11–13% of GNP on defence in 1979, while the equivalent estimates for its WTO allies were: the GDR 6.3%, Czechoslovakia 2.8%, Poland 2.4%, Bulgaria and Hungary 2.1% and Romania 1.4%. At the November 1978 meeting of the PCC the USSR urged its allies to increase their defence spending by 5% p.a. as a response to NATO's recent adoption of its Long Term Defence Programme requiring 3% p.a. increases in defence budgets in real terms. East European responses varied considerably, but the inherent tensions over burden-sharing continued into the 1980s. Ceauşescu made the 1978 Soviet proposal public and denounced it, announcing a symbolic reduction in the Romanian defence budget. Though this move was coldly received in Eastern Europe, Hungary and Poland also signalled their own unease with Soviet demands for increased defence spending.

The WTO and the defence of socialism from within

The East European regional system has been the principal ideological extension of Soviet Marxism-Leninism, buttressing internal regime security in the USSR. The maintenance of this ideological as well as military buffer zone was the core objective of Soviet post-war policy in Europe. Party, state and military links with the East European regimes were designed to sustain the cohesion of the "socialist community". Stalin's death in 1953 led to the search for more refined channels of Soviet influence and control in the region and the establishment or revival of a network of multilateral organizations to replace some of the earlier levers of control and in order to defuse growing nationalist feeling in Eastern Europe.

Within 18 months of its inception the Warsaw Treaty was used by Moscow to justify, after the event, the Soviet military suppression in November 1956 of the Hungarian move toward a multi-party political system and a security policy of neutrality. Khrushchev thereby made explicit the WTO's role in the defence of socialism against internal threats and indicated that no ruling communist party could renounce its state's membership of the alliance without the concurrence of all its allies (especially the USSR). The USSR had not formally consulted the WTO in advance of the Soviet action, nor were the allies involved in the invasion itself. In the summer of 1968 the WTO provided the pretext for Soviet-East European manoeuvres in and around Czechoslovakia designed to increase the psychological pressure on the reformist Dubček leadership and to prepare the ground for implementation of the eventual Soviet decision — encouraged by East German and Polish calls for decisive action — to intervene in that country in August. The WTO exercises preceding the invasion were organized by the WTO Commander-in-Chief but command of the actual invasion was passed to the Commander-in-Chief of the Soviet Ground Forces.

Through symbolic participation by East German, Polish, Hungarian and Bulgarian military units, what was in effect a military intervention against an allied party leadership organized and led by the USSR gained the appearance of a collective act undertaken by the majority of the socialist community. During the 1968 Czech crisis and the crisis in Poland in late 1981 meetings of the WTO's PCC were employed in tandem with bilateral contacts to put pressure on the recalcitrant or ineffective national party leaderships. Multinational WTO manoeuvres were held around Poland in late 1981 on similar lines to the Czech-related actions in 1968.

The crushing of the Prague Spring was retrospectively rationalized in terms of the precepts of "socialist internationalism", given a sharper and more restricting interpretation under what became known in the West as the "Brezhnev Doctrine". This stressed the limited nature of the sovereignty of the states in the USSR's ideological sphere of domination. Each communist party had a responsibility to the other communist parties as well as to its own people. A threat to socialism in one socialist state was considered to be of common concern to all the members of the socialist community. Fraternal states were not obliged to respect the sovereignty of a state in which the socialist order was under serious threat from within, as state sovereignty could not be approached in an abstract, non-class manner. This doctrine afforded Moscow the right to intervene in allied countries in defence of or to restore the exercise of a "leading and guiding role" by the local communist party. After the invasion of Czechoslovakia five Soviet divisions were "temporarily" stationed in that country by an agreement in October 1968 and a May 1970 Soviet-Czech Treaty included the common internationalist duty to defend the gains of socialism and strictly to observe obligations under the Warsaw Treaty.

The military structures of the WTO seem to have been shaped by the USSR in such a way as to prevent the emergence in Eastern Europe of any national military establishment that would be capable of operating independently of, and therefore in opposition to, Soviet armed forces. Moscow's allies would thus be incapable of mounting effective resistance to a Soviet-led military intervention in their internal affairs. The system of joint WTO military exercises since 1961 facilitating the integration of allied forces into Soviet offensive nuclear doctrine minimized the ability of non-Soviet regular armies to conduct large-scale operations alone. Under the pretext of joint exercises Soviet troops were able to enter the territory of allied states in which no Soviet garrison existed and to increase their numbers in proximity to states in internal crisis.

The establishment of a unified alliance military doctrine of offensive coalition warfare deliberately precluded the adoption by the NSWP forces of the national defence of the homeland as their primary mission. Indeed, Soviet calls in the mid-1960s for greater military integration in the WTO prompted Polish, Czech and Romanian complaints about the absence of national military doctrines. Albania refused to participate in any WTO exercises, eventually leaving the alliance in 1968. After 1964, Romania refused to permit WTO exercises on its territory or to allow its troops to take part in exercises abroad. Romania did not take part in the intervention in Czechoslovakia and, alarmed by the possibility of Soviet pressure against itself, asserted the principle of exclusive national control of Romanian armed forces and moved to introduce an independent national doctrine of territorial defence.

In peacetime the East European forces assigned to the WTO Joint Armed Forces remain under national control, as confirmed by the 1969 reform of the alliance's military institutions which ignored earlier Soviet desires for supranational control of the WTO forced in peacetime. The 1969 changes improved the formal status of the non-Soviet military leaders. In addition to the reconstitution of the Joint Command, the new Committee of Defence Ministers would now meet annually. East European officers gained somewhat broader opportunities to contribute to military decision-making in the alliance through the new Military and Technical Councils and Joint Staff of the Joint Armed Forces.

Despite the concessions made to allied demands for increased alliance consultation, the reforms did not alter the practice whereby all top positions in the Joint Command and its Staff are held by Soviet officers. The Joint Command is directly subordinate to the WTO Commander-in-Chief and is composed of East European deputy commanders and Soviet officers charged with co-ordinating the interaction of allied service branches and special services. The Soviet WTO C.-in-C. also has liaison officers in the allied defence ministries. The Joint Staff operates to some degree outside the aegis of the CDM and PCC, under the direct control of the WTO C.-in-C. It plays the key role in integrating NSWP forces assigned to the Joint Command with the Groups of Soviet Forces in Eastern Europe and Soviet formations in the USSR's Western military districts and assigning joint missions. The C.-in-C. also appears to have other un-named agencies working under him to co-ordinate military doctrine, political work in the armed forces and officer education.

All these organs and agencies serve to weaken the NSWP states' control over their national armed forces. This pattern of activity, ultimately leading to the dispersal in wartime of selected NSWP units into larger Soviet-dominated formations, reflected the priority Moscow gave to common regime security in Eastern Europe as the main purpose of the WTO. With the exception of Romania, which successfully detached itself from these arrangements, the East European party leaderships largely supported this Soviet policy.

Soviet intervention capability, enhanced by WTO arrangements, helped to deter challenges to the existing monopoly of political power enjoyed by the ruling East European communist parties.

The WTO as an international diplomatic actor

One of the major reasons for the establishment of the WTO in May 1955 may have been to serve as a bargaining counter in the mid-1950s' East-West dialogue over European security arrangements. The likelihood of its dissolution declined, however, as the Warsaw Treaty acquired greater significance in legitimizing Soviet hegemony in Eastern Europe in the wake of the Soviet suppression of the Nagy regime in Hungary in November 1956. Despite the interlocking network of bilateral mutual assistance treaties that would continue to exist in its absence, the dissolution of the multilateral alliance would have been seen as evidence of a reduced Soviet commitment to enforce political orthodoxy and alignment with Moscow in the region.

In the mid-1960s Moscow attached greater importance to the WTO as a multilateral platform from which to launch Soviet proposals on East-West arms control and co-operation. The WTO's multilateral image was improved somewhat by the 1969 reform of its organs and the institutionalization of foreign policy consultations by the creation of a Committee of Foreign Ministers in 1976. This proved useful in the multilateral conference diplomacy that began in the 1970s on European arms control and in the Conference on Security and Co-operation in Europe (CSCE) in 1975. The USSR also tried to achieve common alliance declaratory stances on aspects of Soviet foreign policy outside Europe, with mixed results, reflecting the tension between the increasingly global involvements of Moscow and the more limited regional preoccupations of its allies. In 1969 and on several occasions in the 1970s, the USSR tried unsuccessfully to get a symbolic East European military presence on the Sino-Soviet border. The allies were highly reluctant to accept any formal extension of WTO obligations to extra-European areas.

Moscow's concern with foreign policy co-ordination provided its allies with the opportunity to press their own interests through WTO channels. In the late 1960s the East German leader Ulbricht sought alliance cohesion in the face of West German efforts to establish relations with East European states before intra-German relations had been normalized. In 1969–71 he used WTO meetings to urge Soviet caution in concessions to the West over Berlin and intra-German ties. His successor Honecker came to play the role of model ally in the 1970s, aware that the fullest possible integration in the socialist bloc offered the most reliable guarantee of the GDR's policy of demarcation toward West Germany.

The deterioration of superpower relations following the Soviet abandonment of the Geneva Nuclear and Space Talks in late 1983 was accompanied by Soviet attempts to rein back East-West dialogue in Europe. The GDR and Hungary were keen to limit the damage to European détente caused by the breakdown of the superpower arms control process, with Budapest stressing the important role of small states in preserving European détente. There followed a debate among WTO members on the role of alliance obligations and national initiatives in East-West relations in which the GDR — wary of Soviet willingness to manipulate improvements in intra-German relations as a way of punishing West Germany for its support of US/NATO positions — took the side of Hungary against the more orthodox Czech leadership. By the end of the Chernenko era, it had become clear that certain WTO allies, in addition to the longstanding maverick Ceauşescu, were increasingly reluctant to sacrifice their own national interests in East-West détente for the sake of foreign policy unity in the bloc.

In April 1985, with little fanfare, the Warsaw Treaty was renewed for 20 years, with provision for a further 10-year automatic extension. The Treaty's text went unaltered and there were no changes in the structure or processes of the organization. Less than five years later the continued existence of the WTO seemed in some doubt as the organization lost much of its original rationale with the end of the post-war division of Europe and of the Cold War in a broader sense.

The reduced utility of military power in Europe

At the end of 1988 the USSR had 29 divisions stationed on the territory of four of its WTO allies. In the Southern Tier, only Hungary hosted Soviet forces, of which there were 65,000, forming the Southern Group of Forces with their HQ in Budapest. In peacetime these forces are linked to the USSR's Southwestern Strategic Direction or Theatre of Military Operations. In the Northern Tier countries, Soviet forces are linked to the Western Strategic Direction. The Central Group of (Soviet) Forces "temporarily" stationed in Czechoslovakia since 1968 was comprised of 70,000 troops, headquartered in Milovice. The HQ for the Western Strategic Direction is at Legnica in Poland, which also hosts the HQ of the Northern Group of Forces, containing 40,000 Soviet troops. By far the largest Soviet military contingent abroad since World War II has been in East Germany. The Western Group of Forces (until recently known as the Group of Soviet Forces in Germany), with its HQ at Zossen-Wunsdorf, contained 380,000 troops in 1988. In 1989 the members of the WTO were estimated to have the following total armed forces personnel: USSR — 4,258,000; Poland — 412,000; Czechoslovakia — 199,700; GDR — 173,000; Romania — 171,000; Bulgaria — 117,500; Hungary — 91,000.

In February 1986 Gorbachev announced the concept of "reasonable sufficiency" as a central component of Soviet military doctrine. In May 1987 the concept was extended to the WTO in an alliance statement "On the Military Doctrine of the Warsaw Treaty Member States". The WTO declared its desire to reduce its military potential to a level sufficient for defence and repelling aggression. It sought to negotiate with the West the reduction of armed forces and conventional armaments to "a level at which neither side, while maintaining its defensive capacity, would have the means to stage a surprise attack against the other side or engage in offensive operations in general". The WTO claim to have shifted to a defensive doctrine cast doubt on its earlier assertions that its doctrine was defensive in nature. What the 1987 declaration did indicate, however, was that the technical or operational side of military doctrine would now be brought into greater conformity with its political side.

In the Conventional Forces in Europe (CFE) negotiations that began in March 1989 the USSR indicated its willingness to accept very large asymmetrical reductions in its forces in Eastern Europe and west of the Urals, making an offensive military strategy against the West impractical and severely constricting the political utility of Soviet military power in Eastern Europe. Such "new thinking" in Soviet conventional arms control policy supported the impression that the Gorbachev leadership had indeed fundamentally revised its definition of its security interests in Europe and the ways of achieving them. At the United Nations in December 1988 Gorbachev went further and announced that Soviet armed forces would be unilaterally reduced by 500,000 men by the end of 1990. This would include the withdrawal of 240,000 personnel from Eastern Europe and the USSR west of the Urals. Of these, 50,000 would come from six Soviet divisions to be withdrawn from the GDR, Czechoslovakia and Hungary and disbanded by 1991.

Gorbachev also announced the withdrawal of 10,000 Soviet tanks from Eastern Europe and the western USSR. Half of these would be taken from Soviet tank and motorized rifle divisions based in Eastern Europe, including six of the 14 Soviet armoured divisions then based in the GDR, Czechoslovakia and Hungary. Four tank divisions would be withdrawn from the GDR and one each from Czechoslovakia and Hungary. The removal of 5,000 Soviet tanks from Eastern Europe — about half of which would be the most modern types — would amount to a reduction of more than 50% in Soviet tank strength there. Soviet divisions remaining in the GDR, Poland, Czechoslovakia and Hungary were to be reorganized in such a way as to enhance their anti-tank and anti-air defensive capacity and reduce somewhat their ability to fight offensively. Soviet assault landing and assault river-crossing units and equipment — associated most clearly in NATO perceptions with offensive Soviet intentions — forward deployed in Eastern Europe were to be reduced. When completed, these reductions would almost completely remove any Soviet-WTO ability to launch a short-warning or surprise attack on the Central Front.

The end of the Brezhnev Doctrine

The new Soviet leadership under Gorbachev proved much more tolerant of domestic diversity in Eastern Europe, especially as the pace of economic and political reform in the USSR itself increased in 1987. The September 1986 Stockholm Agreement on confidence- and security-building measures in Europe repudiated the use or threat of force in relations between states, including those between states in the same alliance. In his November 1987 speech on the anniversary of the October Revolution, Gorbachev indicated that relations between Marxist-Leninist parties were to be subordinated to inter-state relations based upon peaceful coexistence. The joint Soviet-Yugoslav declaration of March 1988 declared that states were entitled to complete independence in internal affairs regardless of their socio-political system, "the forms and nature of their international alliances, or their geographic position".

In his address to the Council of Europe in Strasbourg in June 1989, Gorbachev reaffirmed that the Soviet concept of a "Common European Home" precluded the use or threat of force not only between but also within alliances. The subsequent WTO Summit meeting in Bucharest on July 7–8 collectively reiterated the Strasbourg line that the WTO members had the right to determine their domestic policies "without outside interference". Even before the East European upheavals of the autumn of 1989 it thus appeared that, in the words of the Hungarian delegation to the Bucharest PCC meeting, "the period of enforcing the so-called Brezhnev Doctrine is over once and for all".

The Soviet leadership refrained from an explicit condemnation of the 1968 suppression of the Prague Spring — the inevitable consequence of denouncing the Brezhnev Doctrine — until such an act would no longer, ironically, constitute interference in the internal affairs of the orthodox Czech party leadership. Although the Polish and Hungarian parliaments denounced the invasion of Czechoslovakia in August and September 1989 respectively, Moscow argued that an official re-evaluation of the events of 1968 had to await the Czech regime's own reassessment. With the resignation of those Czech party leaders associated with the post-1968 normalization, the new Czech leadership announced its own negative verdict on the invasion on December 2, while, the following day, the new coalition government called for talks on the complete withdrawal of Soviet troops from Czechoslovakia. On December 4 at the Moscow WTO Summit the alliance issued a collective denunciation of the violation of Czech sovereignty signed by the five states which had participated in the August 1968 invasion.

A new political environment

The official rejection of the Brezhnev Doctrine confirmed the earlier signs that Gorbachev had abandoned the USSR's ideologically oriented concept of its security interests in Eastern Europe: it no longer viewed the survival of Marxist-Leninist regimes in Eastern Europe as indispensable. The speed with which the Communist parties of Czechoslovakia, Bulgaria and East Germany moved to surrender their monopoly on political power in late 1989 took the USSR and the West equally by surprise. The bloody downfall of the Ceauşescu regime in Romania in the "Christmas Revolution" of 1989 was followed by the sudden imminence at the turn of the decade of German unification and the Soviet Communist Party Central Committee's decision in February 1990 to retreat from its political monopoly in the USSR itself. These events confirmed the change in status of Eastern Europe from that of a Soviet sphere of domination toward the role of an uncertain and potentially unstable sphere of security.

The inauguration of the Solidarity-led Polish government of Tadeusz Mazowiecki in September 1989 was accompanied by assurances that Poland would not withdraw from its alliance obligations to the WTO. Prior to a very successful visit to Warsaw by Shevardnadze in late October, the Polish government newspaper stated that Poland "respected the right of our Eastern neighbour to a security cordon and regarded it as the principal guarantee of our own security". In Moscow in November, Mazowiecki expressed his satisfaction that the WTO was ceasing to be an "instrument subordinate to ideology" and had begun to reflect the mutual interests of the member-states. He welcomed the emphatic recognition of complete national sovereignty contained in the October 27 Communiqué of the WTO Committee of Foreign Ministers. On February 11, 1990, Moscow signalled its acceptance of bilateral talks on withdrawal of the Soviet forces stationed in Poland.

With general elections due in March 1990, the Hungarian government continued to call for the WTO to adapt to changing East-West relations, while being careful to reaffirm Hungary's membership of the alliance and fulfilment of its obligations for as long as the WTO existed. Yet it was also made clear that Hungary aspired to eventual neutrality. Bowing to growing public pressure, Prime Minister Németh announced in January 1990 that the departure of all Soviet troops from Hungary as soon as possible was to be discussed with Moscow. By mid-February it was officially predicted that an accord would be reached within weeks.

On December 8, 1989, Moscow agreed to talks with the new Czech interim government on withdrawal of Soviet troops from that country. By the end of February the USSR had agreed to remove a substantial part of its forces before the Czech elections in June 1990, although an accord on their complete withdrawal by the end of the year, as demanded by Prague, had yet to be reached. The USSR began to reduce its forces in Eastern Europe as part of the unilateral Soviet armed forces cuts announced by Gorbachev in December 1988. The future levels of NATO and WTO forces and equipment from the Atlantic to the

Urals were under negotiation in the CFE. Moscow was therefore reluctant to reach bilateral accords with its allies on complete withdrawal of Soviet forces from their soil before a CFE agreement was reached with NATO.

The virtual collapse of the GDR in late 1989 brought the issue of German unification to the fore, raising sensitive questions about the future boundary between NATO and the WTO and German acceptance of the post-war western frontier of Poland along the Oder and Neisse rivers. While relieved at the fall of Honecker in October 1989, the USSR initially spoke strongly in favour of the continuing existence of a separate East German state as an inalienable part of the WTO and Soviet ally. However, by late January 1990, Moscow bowed to the strength of the unification tide and concentrated on managing its implications for the existing pattern of security arrangements in Europe. After the softening of the Soviet stance, the GDR interim Prime Minister Modrow on February 1 unveiled a four-stage plan for German unity. This envisaged military neutrality for the two Germanies on the way to federation. After also meeting Gorbachev, Gregor Gysi, the leader of its Communists (now organized in a renamed Party of Democratic Socialism), insisted that a unified Germany would have to be not only neutral but also demilitarized. This was reminiscent of the 1952 Soviet proposal for neutrality and demilitarization as the price for German unification.

Subsequent developments made it clear that the USSR would not ultimately insist on the withdrawal of West Germany from NATO as a condition of German unification. The Bonn government was resolutely opposed to this and Gorbachev did not demand German neutralization or demilitarization when Chancellor Kohl and Foreign Minister Genscher explained their plan to him on February 10, 1990. Bonn argued that a united Germany should remain in NATO. Measures would, however, be agreed to prevent a NATO Germany becoming a threat to Soviet security interests in Europe. East German territory would have "special military status"; no West German or NATO forces would be deployed on the territory of the East, and Soviet troops would be able to remain there for a transitional period. These principles in turn formed the basis for the discussions that took place between the Soviet and German leaders in Stavropol in the summer of 1990, following which the two Germanies established a unitary state on October 3 and retained membership of NATO although with a combined military force which did not exceed the size of the West German army before this date.

Towards a new type of alliance?

Even before the dramatic developments of the end of the 1980s Soviet leaders had begun to indicate that the nature of the WTO would soon have to be changed and its institutions reformed to reflect the shifts that had occurred in Soviet policy towards Eastern Europe and radical improvements in East-West relations. Gorbachev stated in Strasbourg that as the military confrontation in Europe was reduced so the WTO would be transformed from a "military-political" to a "politico-military" alliance. In Warsaw in late October 1989 Shevardnadze talked of a gradual shift to a more political defence arrangement in which problems of internal security within the alliance would be resolved by political means. He had recently stated that although all alliance obligations remained in force, co-operation in the WTO would have to be placed on a new basis. Gorbachev's military adviser Akhromeyev similarly raised the possibility of disbanding the military aspects of both Cold War alliances.

Exactly what form the revamped WTO would take remained a matter for speculation in early 1990. The outcome of general elections in East Germany and Hungary (March 1990), Bulgaria and Romania (May 1990) and Czechoslovakia (June 1990) and the attitudes towards Moscow of the new governments were bound to have a major influence on the alliance's future evolution. Moscow would certainly no longer be able to shape the reform debate to its own preferences. Military officials from several WTO states hinted in late 1989 that changes in both the political and military structures of the alliance were being discussed. Soviet General Chervov stated that the Political Consultative Committee would probably be replaced by a new supreme political organ that better reflected the political diversity of the member governments and the absence of ruling communist parties. The WTO command and control structure would also have to be modified to accommodate the more nationally-oriented military doctrines being developed by Czechoslovakia, Hungary and what was then still the GDR.

In October 1989, two leading Soviet commentators provided a further insight into possible Soviet thinking on how to adapt the WTO to the end of Soviet hegemony in Eastern Europe. A "mature political alliance" was needed to institutionalize "mature alliance relations" between politically diverse and genuinely sovereign member-states. The WTO would function purely as an inter-governmental organization. Political co-operation on internal alliance issues would have equal priority with East-West co-operation in building a "Common European Home". Its institutions would focus on co-ordination of the foreign policy aspects of East-West security issues (in relations with NATO and the EC) and on developing a mechanism for resolving conflicts between WTO member-states themselves that might arise due to territorial disputes and ideological differences. They proposed the setting up of a new international secretariat on NATO lines with a Secretary-General, to be sited in Eastern Europe. Each member-state would have a permanent diplomatic delegation to the WTO headquarters and permanent representatives to the alliance would meet regularly. Permanent and temporary committees would be established to examine a broad range of common military, technical, economic and social issues. There would also be a parliamentary body similar to NATO's North Atlantic Assembly.

By 1991, the future survival of even a radically reformed Warsaw Treaty Organization seemed far from assured. Changes in its methods of operation, institutions and military relationships would have to be considerable in order to transform the alliance into one which would be genuinely attractive to the populations of Eastern Europe and their freely elected, mostly non-communist governments. The image of the WTO as an arrangement that institutionalized Soviet political hegemony and the communist monopoly of power in Eastern Europe would be difficult to dispel, despite the popularity in the region of Gorbachev's *perestroika* and "new political thinking" in foreign and security policy. Growing popular pressure for the unilateral withdrawal of all Soviet forces from Eastern Europe, regardless of progress on multilaterally agreed conventional force cuts in Europe and the continued presence of some US forces in Western Europe, threatened to obscure the measure of common interest shared by Moscow and its allies. Tensions of this kind made it less easy, for instance, to conceive of the Warsaw Treaty in the 1990s as a partner in the negotiation of a new European security order within the framework of the Conference on Security and Co-operation in Europe.

Issues of this kind began to emerge in the 1990 summit, the first to take place since the collapse of communist government in Eastern Europe, and in the broader framework of East-West relations. The dominant issue, at the WTO summit in June, was the transformation of the organization from a "military-political" to a "political-military" one to take into account the new circumstances resulting from East-West détente, the election of democratic governments in Eastern Europe and the prospect of German unification. Prior to the meeting delegates spoke openly about their differences, and the summit itself was notable for its decision to open its proceedings to journalists. Hungary expressed its desire to leave the alliance, while Czechoslovakia favoured retaining the Pact until a pan-European security system had been established. A communiqué issued at the end of the meeting endorsed a consensus which committed member-states to retain the alliance for a transitional period while agreeing to appoint a committee to review the Pact on the basis that it represented "sovereign and equal states . . . built on democratic principles". The committee was expected to submit its report to a subsequent extraordinary meeting of Pact leaders.

Speaking to a conference in Copenhagen under the auspices of the Conference for Security and Co-operation in Europe in June 1990, the then Soviet Foreign Minister, Eduard Shevardnadze, announced further unilateral reductions in tactical nuclear forces in Europe, intimating that both NATO and the WTO could undergo "transformations" at their summits later the same year. He also underlined the need for new broader structures of security and co-operation based on the CSCE. Shevardnadze announced that in order to create favourable conditions for negotiations on the reduction of short-range nuclear weapons, the Soviet Union intended to withdraw 60 tactical missile launchers, over 250 nuclear artillery units, and 1,500 nuclear warheads from central Europe by the end of 1990. By the end of the year a total of 140 nuclear launchers and 3,200 nuclear guns would have been removed, leaving a "relatively very small amount" of Soviet battlefield nuclear weapons in Europe. The US Secretary of State James Baker met the Soviet Foreign Minister subsequently and welcomed the proposed cuts at a joint press conference.

Meeting in Prague in October 1990, WTO deputy foreign ministers and military commanders agreed to cut 490 tanks and 400 artillery pieces from their conventional arms holdings, clearing the way for the European arms treaty which was to be signed in Paris the following month. The agreement came in the wake of a fourth attempt, in as many weeks, to reach a consensus among members. The agreement, reached after a meeting on October 10–11, had ended in deadlock over the issue of Soviet tank quotas, and followed a decision by the Soviet Union to cut its allocation of tanks by 150 to 13,150 and its artillery by 500 to 13,200 pieces. The other Pact countries had originally demanded that the number of tanks allocated to the Soviet Union be reduced by 300.

The Paris conference, on November 19–21, 1990, brought together the 34 participants in the CSCE process. The meeting approved a "Charter for a New Europe" on November 21, which declared that the era of confrontation in Europe had ended and that the signatories would henceforth conduct their relations on the basis of "respect and co-operation". A far-reaching Treaty on Conventional Armed Forces in Europe, signed two days earlier, imposed equal ceilings on non-nuclear weapons located between the Atlantic Ocean and the Ural mountains, restricting each side to 20,000 tanks, 20,000 artillery pieces, 30,000 armed combat vehicles, 6,800 combat aircraft and 2,000 attack helicopters. Most of the cuts, which had been negotiated over a period of 20 months, were to be made by the Soviet Union and its WTO allies, which were expected to reduce their total arsenal by up to 40%. The treaty also provided for "declared site inspections" and some "challenge inspections", especially in the first 120 days. A joint declaration, finalized at Vienna on November 14, affirmed that its signatories were "no longer adversaries" and that "none of their weapons will ever be used except in self-defence".

The Treaty lost some of its force when it became clear that the United States would not be ratifying it until the Soviet Union had clarified its apparent relocation beyond the Urals of weaponry that should have been liquidated under the terms of the accord. This issue — the extent to which the Soviet military would be prepared to implement agreements concluded by their political superiors — was one of those relevant to the future of the WTO that still remained open in the early 1990s. Another was the institutional forms that the Pact would develop as it sought to acquire a more political character, a matter that became pressing after the announcement in February 1991 that the military command structure was to be dissolved. The largest questions of all, however, extended beyond the Warsaw Treaty Organization itself to wider issues of East-West relations in Europe. If the two pacts disappeared, what would take their place? Would the NATO member-countries be prepared to merge their alliance into a larger architecture of European security? And how would all the countries concerned deal with the conversion of their military industries and the redeployment of their armed forces? Developed as a response to the Cold War, both alliance systems were likely to find it difficult to adjust to the peaceful conditions they had helped to establish.

Note: This contribution draws upon the *Political and Economic Encyclopaedia of the Soviet Union and Eastern Europe* (Longman, 1990), and with respect to military data upon the International Institute of Strategic Studies' annual publication *The Military Balance* and the Stockholm International Peace Research Institute's yearbook *World Armaments and Disarmaments*.

DOCUMENTS

1. Treaty between the Federal Republic of Germany and the German Democratic Republic establishing a Monetary, Economic and Social Union (May 1990)

2. Treaty on Unification of the German Democratic Republic and the Federal Republic of Germany (August 1990)

3. Constitution of the Union of Soviet Socialist Republics

Treaty between the Federal Republic of Germany and the German Democratic Republic establishing a Monetary, Economic and Social Union

May 1990

The High Contracting Parties,

Owing to the fact that a peaceful and democratic revolution took place in the German Democratic Republic in the autumn of 1989,

Resolved to achieve in freedom as soon as possible the unity of Germany within a European peace order,

Intending to introduce the social market economy in the German Democratic Republic as the basis for further economic and social development, with social compensation and social safeguards and responsibility towards the environment, and thereby constantly to improve the living and working conditions of its population.

Proceeding from the mutual desire to take an initial significant step through the establishment of a Monetary, Economic and Social Union towards national unity in accordance with Article 23 of the Basic Law of the Federal Republic of Germany as a contribution to European unification, taking into account that the external aspects of establishing unity are the subject of negotiations with the Governments of the French Republic, the United Kingdom of Great Britain and Northern Ireland and the United States of America.

Recognizing that the establishment of national unity is accompanied by the development of federal structures in the German Democratic Republic.

Realizing that the provisions of this Treaty are intended to safeguard the application of European Community law following the establishment of national unity.

Have agreed to conclude a Treaty estab-

lishing a Monetary, Economic and Social Union, containing the following provisions.

Chapter 1
Basic principles

Article 1
Subject of the Treaty

(1) The Contracting Parties shall establish a Monetary, Economic and Social Union.

(2) Starting on 1 July 1990 the Contracting Parties shall constitute a monetary union comprising a unified currency area and with the Deutsche Mark as the common currency. The Deutsche Bundesbank shall be the central bank in this currency area. The liabilities and claims expressed in Mark of the German Democratic Republic shall be converted into Deutsche Mark in accordance with this Treaty.

(3) The basis of the economic union shall be the social market economy as the common economic system of the two Contracting Parties. It shall be determined particularly by ownership, competition, free pricing and, as a basic principle, complete freedom of movement of labour, capital goods and services; this shall not preclude the legal admission of special forms of ownership providing for the participation of public authorities or other legal entities in trade and commerce as long as private legal entities are not subject to discrimination. It shall take into account the requirements of environmental protection.

(4) The social union together with the monetary and economic union shall form one

entity. It shall be characterized in particular by system of labour law that corresponds to the social market economy and a comprehensive system of social security based on merit and social justice.

Article 2
Principles

(1) The Contracting Parties are committed to a free, democratic, federal and social basic order governed by the rule of law. To ensure the rights laid down in or following from this Treaty, they shall especially guarantee freedom of contract, freedom to exercise a trade, freedom of establishment and occupation, and freedom to form associations to safeguard and enhance working and economic conditions and in accordance with Annex IX, ownership of land and means of production by private investors.

(2) Contrary provisions of the Constitution of the German Democratic Republic relating to its former socialist social and political system shall no longer be applied.

Article 3
Legal Basis

The establishing of a monetary union and the currency conversion shall be governed by the agreed provisions listed in Annex I. Pending the establishment of monetary union, the legislation of the Federal Republic of Germany concerning currency, credit, money and coinage as well as economic and social union referred to in Annex II shall be implemented in the German Democratic Republic; thereafter, it shall apply, as amended, in the entire currency area according to Annex II, unless this Treaty provides otherwise. The Deutsche Bundesbank, the Federal Banking Supervisory Office and the Federal Insurance Supervisory Office shall exercise the authority accorded to them under this Treaty and said legislation in the entire area of application of this Treaty.

Article 4
Legal Adjustments

(1) Legal adjustments in the German Democratic Republic necessitated by the establishment of the monetary, economic and social union shall be governed by the principles laid down in article 2 (1) and the guidelines agreed in the Protocol; legislation remaining in force shall be interpreted and applied in accordance with said principles and guidelines. The German Democratic Republic shall repeal or amend the legislation referred to in Annex III and adopt the new legislation referred to in Annex IV prior to the establishment of monetary union, provided that no other time limit is fixed in the Treaty or in the Annexes.

(2) The proposed amendments to legislation in the Federal Republic of Germany are listed in Annex V. The proposed legislative adjustments in the German Democratic Republic are listed in Annex VI.

(3) In the transmission of personal information, the principles contained in Annex VII shall apply.

Article 5
Administrative Assistance

The authorities of the Contracting Parties shall, subject to the provisions of domestic law, assist each other in the implementation of this Treaty. Article 32 of the Treaty shall remain unaffected.

Article 6
Recourse to the Courts

(1) Should any person's rights guaranteed by or following from this Treaty be violated by public authority he shall have recourse to the courts. In so far as no other jurisdiction has been established, recourse shall be to the ordinary courts.

(2) The German Democratic Republic shall guarantee recourse to the courts, including recourse for provisional court protection. In the absence of special courts for public-law disputes, special arbitration courts shall be set up at ordinary courts. Jurisdiction for such disputes shall be concentrated at specific regional and district courts.

(3) Pending the establishment of a special labour jurisdiction, legal disputes between employers and employees shall be settled by neutral arbitration bodies to be composed of an equal number of employers

and employees and a neutral chairman. Their decisions shall be appealable in a court of law.

(4) The German Democratic Republic shall permit free arbitration in the field of private law.

Article 7
Arbitral Tribunal

(1) Disputes concerning the interpretation or application of this Treaty, including the Protocol and the Annexes, shall be settled by the Governments of the two Contracting Parties through negotiation.

(2) If a dispute cannot thus be settled, either Contracting Party may submit the dispute to an arbitral tribunal. Such submission shall be admissible irrespective of whether a court has jurisdiction in accordance with Article 6 of this Treaty.

(3) The arbitral tribunal shall be composed of a chairman and four members. Within a period of one month following the entry into force of this Treaty, the Government of each Contracting Party shall appoint two regular and two deputy members. Within the same period, the chairman and the deputy chairman shall be appointed in agreement between the Governments of the two Contracting Parties. If the periods specified in the second and third sentences have not been observed, the necessary appointments shall be made by the President of the Court of Justice of the European Communities.

(4) The period of office shall be two years.

(5) The chairman and members of the arbitral tribunal shall exercise their office independently and free from instructions. Before commencing their activities, the chairman and members of the arbitral tribunal shall undertake to carry out their duties independently and conscientiously and to observe confidentiality.

(6) The provisions governing the convening and the procedure of the arbitral tribunal are laid down in Annex VIII.

Article 8
Intergovernmental Committee

The Contracting Parties shall appoint an Intergovernmental Committee. The Commit-tee shall discuss — and where necessary reach agreement on — questions relating to the implementation of the Treaty. The tasks of the Committee shall include the settlement of disputes under Article 7 (1) of the Treaty.

Article 9
Amendments to the Treaty

Should amendments or additions to this Treaty appear necessary in order to achieve any of its aims, such amendments or additions shall be agreed between the Contracting Parties.

Chapter II
Provisions concerning Monetary Union

Article 10
Prerequisites and Principles

(1) Through the establishment of a Monetary Union between the Contracting Parties, the Deutsche Mark shall be the means of payment, unit of account and means of deposit in the entire currency area. To this end, the monetary responsibility of the Deutsche Bundesbank as the sole issuing bank for this currency shall be extended to the entire currency area. The issuance of coin shall be the exclusive right of the Federal Republic of Germany.

(2) Enjoyment of the advantages of monetary union presupposes a stable monetary value for the economy of the German Democratic Republic, while currency stability must be maintained in the Federal Republic of Germany. The Contracting Parties shall therefore choose conversion modalities which do not cause any inflationary tendencies in the entire area of the monetary union and which at the same time increase the competitiveness of enterprises in the German Democratic Republic.

(3) The Deutsche Bundesbank, by deploying its instruments on its own responsibility and, pursuant to Section 12 to the Bundesbank Law, independent of instructions from the Governments of the Contracting Parties, shall regulate the circulation of money and credit supply in the entire

currency area with the aim of safeguarding the currency.

(4) Monetary control presupposes that the German Democratic Republic establishes a free-market credit system. This shall include a system of commercial banks operating according to private-sector principles, with competing private, cooperative and public-law banks, as well as a free money and a free capital market and non-regulated interest-rate fixing on financial markets.

(5) To achieve the aims described in paragraphs 1 to 4 above, the Contracting Parties shall, in accordance with the provisions laid down in Annex I, agree on the following principles for monetary union:

— With effect from 1 July 1990 the Deutsche Mark shall be introduced as currency in the German Democratic Republic. The bank notes issued by the Deutsche Bundesbank and denominated in Deutsche Mark, and the federal coins issued by the Federal Republic of Germany and denominated in Deutsche Mark or Pfennig, shall be sole legal tender from 1 July 1990.

— Wages, salaries, grants, pensions, rents and leases as well as other recurring payments shall be converted at a rate of one to one.

— All other claims and liabilities denominated in Mark of the German Democratic Republic shall be converted to Deutsche Mark at the rate of two to one.

— The conversion of bank notes and coin denominated in Mark of the German Democratic Republic shall only be possible for persons or agencies domiciled in the German Democratic Republic via accounts with financial institutions in the German Democratic Republic into which the cash amounts to be converted may be paid.

— Deposits with financial institutions held by individuals domiciled in the German Democratic Republic shall be converted upon application at a rate of one to one up to certain limits, there being a differentiation according to the age of the beneficiaries.

— Special regulations shall apply to deposits of persons domiciled outside the German Democratic Republic.

— Action shall be taken against abuse.

(6) Following an inventory of publicly owned assets and their earning power and following their primary use for the structural adaptation of the economy and for the recapitalization of the budget, the German Democratic Republic shall ensure where possible that a vested right to a share in publicly owned assets can be granted to savers at a later date for the amount reduced following conversion at a rate of two to one.

(7) The Deutsche Bundesbank shall exercise the powers accorded it by this Treaty and by the Law concerning the Deutsche Bundesbank in the entire currency area. It shall establish for this purpose a provisional office in Berlin with up to fifteen branches in the German Democratic Republic, which shall be located in the premises of the State Bank of the German Democratic Republic.

Chapter III
Provisions concerning Economic Union

Article 11
Economic Policy Foundations

(1) The German Democratic Republic shall ensure that its economic and financial policy measures are in harmony with the social market system. Such measures shall be introduced in such a way that, within the framework of the market economy system, they are at the same time conducive to price stability, a high level of employment and foreign trade equilibrium, and thus steady and adequate economic growth.

(2) The German Democratic Republic shall create the basic conditions for the development of market forces and private initiative in order to promote structural change, the creation of modern jobs, a broad basis of small and medium-sized companies and liberal professions, as well as environmental protection. The corporate legal structure shall be based on the principles of the social market economy described in Article 1 of this Treaty, enterprises being free to decide on products, quantities, production processes, investment, employment, prices and utilization of profits.

(3) The German Democratic Republic, taking into consideration the foreign trade relations that have evolved with the member countries of the Council for Mutual Economic Assistance, shall progressively bring its policy into line with the law and the

economic policy goals of the European Communities.

(4) In decisions which affect the economic policy principles referred to in paragraphs 1 and 2 above, the Government of the German Democratic Republic shall reach agreement with the Government of the Federal Republic of the Germany within the framework of the Intergovernmental Committee appointed in accordance with Article 8 of this Treaty.

Article 12
Intra-German Trade

(1) The Berlin Agreement of 20 September 1951 concluded between the Contracting Parties shall be amended in view of monetary and economic union. The clearing system established by that Agreement shall be ended and the swing shall be finally balanced. Outstanding obligations shall be settled in Deutsche Mark.

(2) The Contracting Parties shall guarantee that goods which do not originate in the Federal Republic of Germany or the Democratic Republic are transported across the intra-German border in accordance with a customs monitoring procedure.

(3) The Contracting Parties shall endeavour to create as soon as possible the preconditions for complete abolition of controls at the intra-German border.

Article 13
Foreign Trade and Payments

(1) In its foreign trade, the German Democratic Republic shall take into account the principles of free world trade, as expressed in particular in the General Agreement on Tariffs and Trade. The Federal Republic of Germany shall make its experience fully available for the further integration of the economy of the German Democratic Republic into the world economy.

(2) The existing foreign trade relations of the German Democratic Republic, in particular its contractual obligation towards the countries of the Council for Mutual Economic Assistance, shall be respected. They shall be further developed and extended in accordance with free-market principles, taking account of the facts established by monetary and economic union and the interests of all involved. Where necessary, the German Democratic Republic shall adjust existing contractual obligations in the light of those facts, in agreement with its partners.

(3) The Contracting Parties shall cooperate closely in advancing their foreign trade interests, with due regard for the jurisdiction of the European Communities.

Article 14
Structural Adjustment of Enterprises

In order to promote the necessary adjustment of enterprises in the German Democratic Republic, the Government of the German Democratic Republic shall, for a transitional period and subject to its budgetary means, take measures to facilitate a swift structural adjustment of enterprises to the new market conditions. The Governments of the Contracting Parties shall agree on the specific nature of these measures. The objective shall be to strengthen the competitiveness of enterprises on the basis of the social market economy and to build up, through the development of private initiative, a diversified, modern economic structure in the German Democratic Republic, with as many small and medium-sized enterprises as possible, and thereby to create the basis for increased growth and secure jobs.

Article 15
Agriculture and Food Industry

(1) Because of the crucial importance of the European Community rules for the agriculture and food industries, the German Democratic Republic shall introduce a price support and external protection scheme in line with the EC market regime so that agricultural producer prices in the German Democratic Republic become adjusted to those in the Federal Republic of Germany. The German Democratic Republic shall not introduce levies or refunds vis-à-vis the European Community, subject to reciprocity.

(2) For categories of goods in respect of which it is not possible to introduce a full price support system immediately upon the entry into force of this Treaty, transitional arrangements may be applied. Pending the

legal integration of the agricultural and food industry of the German Democratic Republic into the EC agricultural market, specific quantitative restriction mechanisms shall be allowed for sensitive agricultural products in trade between the Contracting Parties.

(3) Without prejudice to the measures to be taken under Article 14 of this Treaty, the German Democratic Republic shall, within the limits of its budgetary means and for a transitional period, take suitable measures to promote the structural adaptation in the agricultural and food industries which is necessary to improve the competitiveness of enterprises, to achieve environmentally acceptable and quality-based production, and to avoid surpluses.

(4) The Governments of the Contracting Parties shall agree on the specific nature of the measures referred to in paragraphs 2 and 3 above.

Article 16
Protection of the Environment

(1) The protection of human beings, animals and plants, soil, water, air, the climate and landscape as well as cultural and other material property against harmful environmental influences is a major objective of both Contracting Parties. They shall pursue this objective on the basis of prevention, the polluter pays principle and cooperation. Their aim is the rapid establishment of a German environmental union.

(2) The German Democratic Republic shall introduce regulations to ensure that, on the entry into force of this Treaty, the safety and environmental requirements applicable in the Federal Republic of Germany are the precondition for the granting of authorization under environmental law for new plant and installations on its territory. For existing plant and installations the German Democratic Republic shall introduce regulations to bring them up to standard as quickly as possible.

(3) The German Democratic Republic shall, along with the development of the federal structure at Land level and with the establishment of an administrative jurisidiction, adopt the environmental law of the Federal Republic of Germany.

(4) In further shaping a common environmental law, the environmental requirements of the Federal Republic of Germany and the German Democratic Republic shall be harmonized and developed at a high level as quickly as possible.

(5) The German Democratic Republic shall harmonize the provisions governing promotion of environmental protection measures with those of the Federal Republic of Germany.

Chapter IV
Provisions concerning Social Union

Article 17
Principles of Labour Law

In the German Democratic Republic freedom of association, autonomy in collective bargaining, legislation relating to industrial action, corporate legal structure, codetermination at board level and protection against dismissal shall apply in line with the law of the Federal Republic of Germany; further details are contained in the Protocol on Guidelines and in Annexes II and III.

Article 18
Principles of Social Insurance

(1) The German Democratic Republic shall introduce a structured system of social insurance, to be governed by the following principles:

1. Pension, sickness, accident and unemployment insurance shall each be administered by self-governing bodies under public law subject to legal supervision by the state.

2. Pension, sickness, accident and unemployment insurance including employment promotion shall be financed primarily by contributions. Contributions to pension, sickness and unemployment insurance shall, as a rule, be paid half by the employee and half by the employer in line with the contribution rates applicable in the Federal Republic of Germany, and accident insurance contributions shall be borne by the employer.

3. Wage replacement benefits shall be based on the level of insured earnings.

(2) Initially, pension, sickness and accident insurance shall be administered by a single institution; income and expenditure shall be accounted for separately according to the type of insurance. Separate pension, sickness and accident insurance institutions shall be established, if possible by 1 January 1991. The aim shall be to create an organizational structure for social insurance which corresponds to that of the Federal Republic of Germany.

(3) For a transitional period the present comprehensive compulsory social insurance cover in the German Democratic Republic may be retained. Exemption from compulsory social insurance cover shall be granted to self-employed persons and professionals who can prove that they have adequate alternative insurance. In this connection, the creation of professional pension schemes outside the pension insurance system shall be made possible.

(4) Wage-earners whose earnings in the last wage accounting period before 1 July 1990 were subject to a special tax rate under Section 10 of the Ordinance of 11 December 1952 on the Taxation of Earned Income (Law Gazette No. 182, p. 1413) shall receive until 31 December 1990 a supplement to their pension insurance contribution amounting to
— DM 30,— for monthly wages up to DM 600,—,
— DM 20,— for monthly wages of more than DM 600,— up to DM 700,—, and
— DM 10,— for monthly wages of more than DM 700,— up to DM 800,—.
Earnings from several employments shall be counted together. The supplement shall be paid to the wage-earner by the employer. Upon application the employer shall be reimbursed for these payments from the budget.

(5) The ceilings for compulsory insurance cover and for contribution assessment shall be fixed according to the principles of social insurance law applying in the Federal Republic of Germany.

Article 19
Unemployment Insurance and Employment Promotion

The German Democratic Republic shall introduce a system of unemployment insurance including employment promotion which shall be in line with the provisions of the Employment Promotion Act of the Federal Republic of Germany. Special importance shall be attached to an active labour market policy, such as vocational training and retaining. Consideration shall be given to the interests of women and disabled persons. In the transitional phase, special conditions in the German Democratic Republic shall be taken into account. The Governments of both Contracting Parties shall cooperate closely in the development of unemployment insurance including employment promotion.

Article 20
Pension Insurance

(1) The German Democratic Republic shall introduce all necessary measures to adapt its pension law to the pension insurance law of the Federal Republic of Germany, which is based on the principle of wage and contribution-related benefits. Over a transitional period of five years account shall be taken of the principle of bona fide rights protection in respect of persons approaching pensionable age.

(2) The pension insurance fund shall use its resources exclusively to meet its obligations with regard to rehabilitation, invalidity, old age, and death. The existing supplementary and special pensions schemes shall be discontinued as of 1 July 1990. Accrued claims and entitlements shall be transferred to the pension insurance fund, and benefits on the basis of special arrangements shall be reviewed with a view to abolishing unjustified benefits and reducing excessive benefits. The additional expenditure incurred by the pension insurance fund because of such transfers shall be reimbursed from the budget.

(3) Upon conversion to Deutsche Mark current pension from the pension insurance fund shall be fixed at a net replacement rate which, for a pensioner who has completed 45 insurance/working years and whose earnings were at all times in line with average earning, shall be 70 per cent of average net earnings in the German Democratic Republic. For a greater or smaller number of insurance/working years, the percentage shall be

correspondingly higher or lower. The basis for calculating the upgrading rate for individual pensions shall be the pension of an average wage-earner in the German Democratic Republic, graduated to year of entry, who has paid full contributions to the voluntary supplementary insurance scheme of the German Democratic Republic, over and above his compulsory social insurance contributions. If there is no upgrading on this basis a pension shall be paid in Deutsche Mark which corresponds to the amount of the former pension in Mark of the German Democratic Republic. Survivors' pensions shall be calculated on the basis of the pension which the deceased would have received after conversion.

(4) Pensions from the pension insurance fund shall be adjusted in line with the development of net wages and salaries in the German Democratic Republic.

(5) The voluntary supplementary pension insurance scheme in the German Democratic Republic shall be discontinued.

(6) The German Democratic Republic shall make a government contribution to its pension insurance fund to offset its expenditure.

(7) Persons who have transferred their habitual residence from the territory of either Contracting Party to that of the other Party after 18 May 1990 shall receive from the pension insurance institution hitherto responsible a pension calculated to the regulations applicable to that institution for the period completed there.

Article 21
Health Insurance

(1) The German Democratic Republic shall introduce all necessary measures to adapt its health insurance law to that of the Federal Republic of Germany.

(2) Benefits which have hitherto been financed from the health insurance fund according to the legislation of the German Democratic Republic but which according to the legislation of the Federal Republic of Germany are not benefits covered by the health insurance fund shall, for the time being, be financed from the budget of the German Democratic Republic.

(3) The German Democratic Republic shall introduce continued payment of wages in the event of sickness which is in line with legislation governing continued payment of wages in the Federal Republic of Germany.

(4) Pensioners shall be covered by health insurance. The contribution rate of the relevant health insurance fund shall be applicable. The health insurance contributions of pensioners shall be paid in a lump sum by the pension insurance fund to the health insurance fund. The amount to be paid shall be determined according to overall pension payments before deduction of the proportion of the health insurance contribution payable by pensioners. This shall not affect the net replacement rate envisaged after conversion of pensions.

(5) Investment in in-patient and out-patient facilities of the health service of the German Democratic Republic shall be financed from budget funds and not from contribution revenue.

Article 22
Public Health

(1) Medical care and health protection are of particular concern to the Contracting Parties.

(2) While provisionally continuing the present system, which is necessary to maintain public medical services, the German Democratic Republic shall gradually move towards the range of services offered in the Federal Republic of Germany with private providers, particularly by admitting registered doctors, dentists and pharmacists as well as independent providers of medicaments and remedial aids, and by admitting private providers of independent, non-profit-making hospitals.

(3) The German Democratic Republic shall create the necessary legal framework for the development of the necessary contractual relations — particularly as regards remuneration — between health insurance institutions and providers of services.

Article 23
Accident Insurance Pensions

(1) The German Democratic Republic shall introduce all necessary measures to

adapt its accident insurance law to that of the Federal Republic of Germany.

(2) Upon conversion to Deutsche Mark, current accident insurance pensions shall be recalculated and paid on the basis of average gross earnings in the German Democratic republic.

(3) Accident pensions to be determined after the conversion to Deutsche Mark shall be based on the average gross monthly earnings in the twelve months prior to the accident.

(4) The provisions of Article 20 (4) and (7) shall apply mutatis mutandis.

Article 24
Social Assistance

The German Democratic Republic shall introduce a system of social assistance which shall correspond to the Social Assistance Act of the Federal Republic of Germany.

Article 25
Initial Financing

If, during a transitional period, contributions to the unemployment insurance fund of the German Democratic Republic and both the contributions and the government subsidy to the pension insurance fund of the German Democratic Republic do not fully cover expenditures on benefits, the Federal Republic of Germany shall provide temporary initial financing for the German Democratic Republic within the framework of the budgetary aid granted under Article 28 of this Treaty.

Chapter V
Provisions concerning the Budget and Finance

Section 1: The Budget

Article 26
Principles underlying the Fiscal Policy of the German Democratic Republic

(1) Public budgets in the German Democratic Republic shall be drawn up by the relevant national, regional or local author-

ities on their own responsibility, due to account being taken of the requirements of general economic equilibrium. The aim shall be to establish a system of budgeting adapted to the market economy. Budgets shall be balanced as regards revenue and expenditure. All revenue and expenditure shall be included in the appropriate budget.

(2) Budgets shall be adapted to the budget structures of the Federal Republic of Germany. The following in particular shall be removed from the budget, starting with the partial budget for 1990 as of the establishment of monetary union:

— the social sector, in so far as it is wholly or mainly financed from charges or contributions on the Federal Republic of Germany,

— state undertakings by conversion into legally and economically independent enterprises,

— transport undertakings by making them legally independent,

— the management of the Deutsche Reichsbahn and the Deutsche Post, which will be operated as special funds.

Government borrowing for housing shall be allocated to individual projects on the basis of their existing physical assets.

(3) National, regional and local authorities in the German Democratic Republic shall make every effort to limit deficits in drawing up and executing budgets. As regards expenditure this shall include:

— abolition of budget subsidies, particularly in the short term for industrial goods, agricultural products and food, autonomous price supports being permissible for the latter in line with the regulations of the European Communities, and progressively in the sectors of transport, energy for private households and housing, making allowances for the general development of income,

— sustained reduction of personnel expenditure in the public service,

— review of all items of expenditure, including the legal provisions on which they are based, to determine whether they are necessary and can be financed,

— structural improvements in the education system and preparatory division according to a federal structure (including the research sector).

As regards revenue, the limitation of deficits shall require, in addition to the measures under Section 2 of this Chapter, the harmonization or introduction of contributions and fees for public services corresponding to the system in the Federal Republic of Germany.

(4) An inventory shall be made of publicly owned assets. Publicly owned assets shall be used primarily for the structural adaption of the economy and for the recapitalization of the budget in the German Democratic Republic.

Article 27
Borrowing and Debts

(1) Borrowing authorizations in the budgets of the local, regional and national authorities of the German Democratic Republic shall be limited to 10 billion Deutsche Mark for 1990 and 14 billion Deutsche Mark for 1991 and allocated to the different levels of government in agreement with the Minister of Finance of the Federal Republic of Germany. A borrowing limit of 7 billion Deutsche Mark for 1990 and 10 billion Deutsche Mark for 1991 shall be established for the advance financing of proceeds expected to accrue from the realization of assets currently held in trust. In the event of fundamental change in conditions, the Minister of Finance of the Federal Republic of Germany may permit these credit ceilings to be exceeded.

(2) The raising of loans and the granting of equalization claims shall be conducted in agreement between the Minister of Finance of the German Democratic Republic and the Minister of Finance of the Federal Republic of Germany. The same shall apply to the assumption of sureties, warranties or other guarantees and for the total authorizations for future commitments to be appropriated in the budget.

(3) After accession, debt accrued in the budget of the German Democratic Republic shall be transferred to the assets held in trust in so far as it can be redeemed by proceeds expected to accrue from the realization of the assets held in trust. The remaining debt shall be assumed in equal parts by the Federal Government and the Länder newly constituted on the territory of the German Democratic Republic. Loans raised by Länder and

local authorities shall remain their responsibility.

Article 28
Financial Allocations granted by the Federal Republic of Germany

(1) The Federal Republic of Germany shall grant the German Democratic Republic financial allocations amounting to 22 billion Deutsche Mark for the second half of 1990 and 35 billion Deutsche Mark for 1991 for the specific purpose of balancing its budget. Furthermore, initial financing shall be made available from the federal budget, in accordance with Article 25, amounting to 750 million Deutsche Mark for the second half of 1990 for pension insurance as well as 2 billion Deutsche Mark for the second half of 1990 and 3 billion Deutsche Mark for 1991 for unemployment insurance. Payments shall be made as required.

(2) The Contracting Parties agree that the transit sum payable under Article 18 of the Agreement of 17 December 1971 on the Transit of Civilian Persons and Goods between the Federal Republic of Germany and Berlin (West) shall lapse upon the entry into force of this Treaty. The German Democratic Republic shall cancel with effect for the two Contracting Parties the regulations on fees laid down in that Agreement and in the Agreement of 31 October 1979 on the Exemption of Road Vehicles from Taxes and Fees. In amendment of the Agreement of 5 December 1989, the Contracting Parties agree that from 1 July 1990 no more payments shall be made into the hard-currency fund (for citizens of the German Democratic Republic travelling to the Federal Republic of Germany). A supplementary agreement shall be concluded between the Finance Ministers of the Contracting Parties on the use of any amounts remaining in the fund upon establishment of monetary union.

Article 29
Transitional Regulations in the Public Service

The Government of the German Democratic Republic shall guarantee, with due regard for the first sentence of Article 2(1), that in collective bargaining agreements or other settlements in the public administration sector the general economic and financial conditions in the German Democratic Republic and the exigencies of budget consolidation are taken into account, with any new service regulations being of transitional nature only. The Federal Representation of Staff Act shall be applied mutatis mutandis.

Section 2: Finance

Article 30
Customs and Special Excise Taxes

(1) In accordance with the principle set out in Article 11 (3) of this Treaty, the German Democratic Republic shall adopt step by step the customs law of the European Communities, including the Common Customs Tariff, and the special excise taxes stipulated in Annex IV to this Treaty.

(2) The Contracting Parties are agreed that their customs territory shall comprise the area of application of this Treaty.

(3) Equalization at the border between the fiscal territories for excise taxes of both Contracting Parties, except those of tobacco, shall be discontinued. Fiscal jurisidiction shall remain unaffected. Separate agreements shall be made to offset shifts in excise revenue.

(4) The movement of untaxed excisable goods between the fiscal territories shall be permitted as stipulated in the regulations on movements of untaxed goods within one fiscal territory.

(5) Tax relief for export goods shall be granted only upon proof of export to territories other than the two fiscal territories.

Article 31
Taxes on Income, Property, Net Worth and Transactions

(1) The German Democratic Republic shall regulate taxes on income, property, net worth and transactions in accordance with Annex IV to this Treaty.

(2) For the purposes of turnover tax there shall be no tax frontier between the Contracting Parties; in consequence, there shall

be no equalization of turnover tax burdens at the frontier. Fiscal jurisdiction shall remain unaffected. The right of input tax deduction shall extend to the tax on turnovers which are subject to the turnover tax of the other Contracting Party. Compensation for the reduced yield resulting from this shall be settled by special agreement.

(3) Where there is unlimited net worth tax liability in the territory of one Contracting Party, that Party shall have the exclusive right to tax; where there is unlimited net worth tax liability in the territories of both Contracting Parties, this shall apply to the Party with which the taxpayer has the closer personal and economic ties (centre of vital interests) or in whose territory he has effective management as a legal person. Property located in the territory of the other Contracting Party shall be assessed according to the regulations for domestic property applying in that territory.

(4) Where there is unlimited inheritance tax or gift tax liability in the territory of one Contracting Party, that Party shall have the exclusive right to tax transfers on which tax is payable after 31 December 1990. Where there is unlimited tax liability in the territory of both Contracting Parties, this shall apply to the Party with which the testator or donor had the closer personal and economic ties when the tax liability was incurred (centre of vital interests), or in whose territory he had effective management as a legal person. Paragraph 3, second sentence, shall apply mutatis mutandis to evaluation.

(5) Paragraph 4 shall apply accordingly to transfers of property by reason of death on which taxes are incurred after 30 June 1990 and before 1 January 1991. Transfers of property by reason of death from citizens of the Contracting Parties who had established residence in the territory of the other Party after 8 November 1990 or who for the first time had their customary abode there and who still had their residence or customary abode there at the time of death cannot be subjected to any higher inheritance tax than would be imposed where there is unlimited tax liability in the territory of the first-mentioned Contracting Party.

(6) Disclosure and notification obligations resulting from the inheritance tax and gift tax legislation of the Contracting Parties shall

in each case apply also with regards to the revenue authorities of the other Party.

Article 32
Exchange of Information

(1) The Contracting Parties shall exchange such information as is necessary for the execution of their taxation and monopoly legislation. The Ministers of Finance of the Contracting Parties, together with the authorities empowered by them, shall be responsible for the exchange of information. Any information received by a Contracting Party shall be treated as secret in the same manner as information obtained under the domestic laws of that party and shall be disclosed only to those persons or authorities (including courts and administrative bodies) involved in the assessment or collection of, the enforcement or prosecution in respect of, or the determination of appeals in relation to the taxes and monopolies falling within this Section. Such persons or authorities shall use the information for these purposes only. They may disclose the information in public court proceedings or in judicial decisions.

(2) The provisions of paragraph 1 shall not commit either Contracting Party

— to carry out administrative measures at variance with the laws and administrative practice of that or of the other Contracting Party;

— to supply information which is not obtainable under the laws or in the normal course of the administration of that or of the other Contracting Party;

— to supply information which would disclose any trade, business, industrial, commercial or professional secret or trade process, or information the disclosure of which would be contrary to public policy.

Article 33
Consulting Procedure

(1) The Contracting Parties shall endeavour to avoid double taxation in respect of taxes on income, property, net worth and transactions by reaching agreement on the appropriate delimitation of the tax base. They shall also strive to eliminate by mutual agreement any difficulties or doubts which result from the interpretation or application of their law on the taxes and monopolies that fall within this Section.

(2) To reach agreement as mentioned in paragraph 1 above, the Minister of Finance of the Federal Republic of Germany and the Minister of Finance of the German Democratic Republic may communicate directly with each other.

Article 34
Structure of the Revenue Administration

(1) The German Democratic Republic shall create the legal basis for a three-tier revenue administration in line with the Revenue Administration Act of the Federal Republic of Germany, incorporating the amendments arising from this Treaty, and shall establish the administration accordingly.

(2) Before the establishment of monetary, economic and social union, the first priority shall be to set up efficient tax and customs administration.

Chapter VI
Final provisions

Article 35
International Treaties

This Treaty shall not affect the international treaties which the Federal Republic of Germany and the German Democratic Republic have concluded with third countries.

Article 36
Review of the Treaty

The provisions of this Treaty shall be reviewed in the light of any fundamental changes in the situation.

Article 37
Berlin Clause

Consistent with the Quadripartite Agreement of 3 September 1971 this Treaty will, in accordance with established procedures, be extended to Berlin (West).

Article 38
Entry into Force

This Treaty, including the Protocol and Annexes I–IX, shall enter into force on the date on which the Governments of the Contracting Parties have informed each other that the necessary constitutional and other national requirements for such entry into force have been fulfilled.

Done at Bonn on 18 May 1990 in duplicate in the German language.

For the	For the
Federal Republic of Germany	German Democratic Republic
Dr Theo Waigel	Dr Walter Romberg

Protocol on Guidelines

To supplement the Treaty establishing a Monetary, Economic and Social Union, the High Contracting Parties have agreed on the following guidelines which shall be binding in accordance with the first sentence of Article 4 (1) of the Treaty.

A. General Guidelines

I. General Provisions

1. The law of the German Democratic Republic will be modelled on the principles of a free, democratic federal and social order governed by the rule of law and be guided by the legal regime of the European Communities.

2. Regulations which commit individuals or state institutions, including the legislature and the judiciary, to a socialist system of law, a socialist body politic, the aims and targets of centralized economic control and planning, a socialist sense of justice, socialist convictions, the convictions of individual groups or parties, socialist morality, or comparable notions, will no longer be applied. The rights and obligations of parties to legal relations shall be bounded by public morals, the principle of good faith, and the necessity of protecting the economically weaker party from undue disadvantage.

3. Authorizations should be required only for compelling reasons of the common weal. Their preconditions shall be clearly defined.

II. Economic Union

1. Economic activity should primarily occur in the private sector and on the basis of competition.

2. Freedom of contract will be guaranteed. Intervention in the freedom of economic activity must be kept to a minimum.

3. Business decisions shall be free from planning targets (e.g. regarding production, purchase, deliveries, investment, employment, prices and utilization of profits).

4. Private enterprises and liberal professions will not be subjected to worse treatment than state and cooperative enterprises.

5. Prices will be freely set, except where they are established by the government for compelling reasons in cases where the economy as a whole is affected.

6. For economic activity, the freedom to acquire, dispose of and use land and other factors of production will be guaranteed.

7. Enterprises under direct or indirect state ownership will be managed according to the principles of economic efficiency. They will be organized competitively as quickly as possible and transferred to private ownership as far as possible. The aim is to open up opportunities for small and medium-sized enterprises in particular.

8. In respect of posts and telecommunications, the regulatory and organizational principles contained in the Structure of Posts and Telecommunications Act of the Federal Republic of Germany will be adopted step by step.

III. Social Union

1. Everyone has the right to form or join organizations to safeguard and enhance working and economic conditions, to leave such organizations and to remain outside them. Furthermore, the right to be active within such organizations is guaranteed. All agreements which restrict these rights will be void. Trade unions and employers' associations will be protected as regards their establishment, existence, organizational autonomy and proper activity.

2. Trade unions and employers' associations able to conclude collective agreements must be freely formed, not include members

from the other side, be organized on a supra-company level and independent, and accept existing legislation on collective bargaining as binding; they must also be able to conclude collective agreements by exerting pressure on their bargaining partner.

3. Wages and other working conditions shall not be determined by the state but through free negotiation between trade unions, employers' associations and employers.

4. Legislation providing for special participation rights for the Free German Trade Unions' Federation, company-level union organizations and union management will no longer be applied.

B. Guidelines for Individual Fields of Law

I. Judicial System

1. Regulations providing for the participation of collectives, social organs, trade unions, works, social prosecutors and defenders in the judicial system and their right to be informed about proceedings will no longer be applied; the right of trade unions to advice and legal representation in labour disputes will remain unaffected by this provision.

2. Regulations on cooperation between the courts and local representations of the people and other organs, the duty of judges to inform the latter, as well as criticism of the courts will no longer be applied.

3. Regulations concerning the involvement of public prosecutors in the judicial system will only be applicable in criminal cases and in family law, parent and child and guardianship cases.

4. Principles contained in the Criminal Code of the German Democratic Republic which relate to the socialist system of law and the socialist body politic, as well as regulations which serve to maintain a centrally planned economy, conflict with a future unification of the two German states or are contrary to principles of a free democratic state, will not be applied to offences committed after the entry into force of this Treaty.

5. Provisions of the Criminal Code which relate to socialist property will not be applied to offences committed after the entry into force of this Treaty; regulations concerning personal or private property will also be applied to other property and assets after the entry into force of this Treaty.

6. To this extent that the legislation referred to in Annex II provides for fines or penalties and cannot be incorporated in the system of sanctions of the German Democratic Republic, the German Democratic Republic will adapt it to its own law as far as possible in line with the legislation of the Federal Republic of Germany.

II. Economic Law

1. For the purpose of establishing collateral for credits, rights equivalent to those in the Federal Republic of Germany, especially rights in rem. will be created in the German Democratic Republic.

2. Conditions for a free capital market will be created in the German Democratic Republic. They will include particularly the liberalizations of interest rates and the admission of tradeable securities (stocks and bonds).

3. Conditions will be created so that administrative decisions and other rulings made by authorities referred to the third sentence of Article 3 of the Treaty can be enforced against persons domiciled in the German Democratic Republic, if necessary by compulsion.

4. The existing insurance monopoly in the German Democratic Republic will be abolished, premium control removed from those insurance branches where tariffs are not part of the business statutes, and current legislation and rules on general conditions for insurance companies repealed.

5. Existing barriers in the payment transaction system of the German Democratic Republic will be removed and its structuring under law promoted.

6. Foreign trade and payment will be free. Restrictions shall be permissible only for compelling reasons in cases where the economy as a whole is affected, on the basis of intergovernmental agreements. The German Democratic Republic will abolish its external trade monopoly.

7. In order to achieve a comparable basis, the German Democratic Republic will adjust its statistics to those of the Federal Republic of Germany and, in cooperation with the Federal Statistical Office or the Deutsche Bundesbank, make information available in accordance with federal statistical standards for the following areas: labour market, prices, production, turnover, foreign trade and payments and retail trade.

III. Building Law

In order to establish a reliable basis for construction planning and investment, the German Democratic Republic will create as soon as possible a legal framework consistent with the Building Code and the Regional Planning Act of the Federal Republic of Germany.

IV. Labour and Social Law

1. Employers in the German Democratic Republic may agree with employees from the Federal Republic of Germany who are temporarily employed in the German Democratic Republic that the labour legislation of the Federal Republic of Germany be applied.

2. Persons in temporary employment may be exempt from compulsory social insurance if they have other cover.

3. The regulations of the German Democratic Republic governing occupational safety and health will be adapted within an appropriate transitional period to the industrial safety laws of the Federal Republic of Germany.

4. In changing its legal minimum period of notice for employment contracts, the German Democratic Republic will not exceed the statutory minimum periods of notice applicable in the Federal Republic of Germany in respect of wage-earners and salaried employees.

5. The German Democratic Republic will create a legal basis for summary dismissal for important reasons in conformity with Sections 626 and 628 of the Civil Code of the Federal Republic of Germany.

Statements for the record

At the signing of the Treaty between the Federal Republic of Germany and the German Democratic Republic establishing a Monetary, Economic and Social Union, the following statements were made with reference to the Treaty:

1. The two Contracting Parties state the following with regards to the second sentence of Article 2(1) of the Treaty: Freedom of movement within the meaning of this provision also includes the entry into the currency area of individuals, including members of ethnic minorities, who are in possession of an identity card, a passport or document in lieu of a passport of the Federal Republic of Germany or the German Democratic Republic.

2. The German Democratic Republic states that it will grant national and enterprises of all members states of the European Communities equal treatment with individuals and enterprises of the Federal Republic of Germany on a reciprocal basis in so far as the jurisdiction of the European Communities might be affected and in so far as nothing to the contrary is explicitly agreed in this Treaty; the protocol (to the EEC Treaty) on German internal trade remains unaffected by this provision.

3. The two Contracting Parties understand the three-month FIBOR within the meaning of the third sentence of Article 8 of Section 4 (1) of Annex I to be the respective interest rate which is determined in Frankfurt/Main every three months on the second business day prior to the beginning of an interest period, according to Section 2 (3) of the Conditions for the Bond of the Federal Republic of Germany of 1990 (Securities Code No. 113–478) without the discount envisaged in it.

4. In connection with Section 1 (3) of Annex IV the German Democratic Republic states: To ensure competition for public contracts appropriate directives will be established without delay and applied by public authorities with effect from 1 January 1991 at the latest.

Bonn. 18 May 1990

For the	For the
Federal Republic of Germany	German Democratic Republic
Dr Theo Waigel	Dr Walter Romberg

Treaty on Unification of the German Democratic Republic and the Federal Republic of Germany

August 1990

(abbreviated text)

Preamble

The Federal Republic of Germany and the German Democratic Republic resolved to complete the unification of Germany in peace and freedom as an equal member of the community of nations in free self-determination,

– starting from the desire of people in both parts of Germany to live together in peace and freedom in a democratic and federal social state based on a legal order,

– with grateful respect for those who helped freedom break through, who unerringly held on to the task of creating German unity and completing it,

– conscious of the continuity of the German history and mindful of the responsibility resulting from this for a democratic development in Germany which remains committed to respect for human rights and peace,

– in the endeavour to make a contribution to the unification of Europe and to the construction of a European peace-time order by German unity in which borders no longer separate and which guarantees all European nations that they can live together in confidence,

– conscious of the fact that the inviolability of frontiers and the territorial integrity and sovereignty of all states in Europe within their borders is a basic condition for peace, have agreed to conclude a treaty on creating German unity with the following regulations:

Chapter 1: The effect of accession

Article 1
Länder

(1) With the coming into effect of the accession of the German Democratic Republic to the Federal Republic of Germany in accordance with Article 23 of the Basic Law on 3rd October 1990 the Länder of Brandenburg, Mecklenburg-Western Pomerania, Saxony, Saxony-Anhalt and Thuringia will become Länder of the Federal Republic of Germany. The rules of the constitutional law on the formation of Länder in the German Democratic Republic of the 22nd July 1990. . . . The 23 boroughs of Berlin will form the Land of Berlin.

Article 2
Capital

The capital of Germany is Berlin. The question as to the seat of parliament and government will be resolved after the establishment of the unity of Germany.

Chapter II: Basic Law

Article 3
Coming into effect of the Basic Law

With the coming into effect of the accession the Basic Law for the Federal Republic of

Germany of 23rd May 1949 in the version of 21st December 1983 will come into force in the Länder of Brandenburg, Mecklenburg-Western Pomerania, Saxony, Saxony-Anhalt and Thuringia, as well as in the part of the Land of Berlin where it was hitherto not in effect, with the alterations resulting from Article 4, in as far as nothing different is specified in this Treaty.

Article 4
Changes to the Basic Law conditional on accession

The Basic Law ... will be changed as follows:

1. The preamble will be worded as follows: Mindful of its responsibility to God and mankind, filled with the desire to serve peace in the world as an equal member in an united Europe, the German People has made this Basic Law by virtue of its constitutional power. The Germans in the Länder of Baden-Württemberg, Bavaria, Berlin, Brandenburg, Bremen, Hamburg, Hesse, Mecklenburg-Western Pomerania, Lower Saxony, North Rhine-Westphalia, Rhineland-Palatinate, Saarland, Saxony, Saxony-Anhalt, Schleswig-Holstein and Thuringia have completed the unity and freedom of Germany in free self-determination. This Basic Law is valid for the whole of the German people.

2. Article 23 (area of applicability of the Basic Law) will be rescinded.

3. Article 51 Paragraph 2 of the Basic Law will be formulated as follows: "Each Land shall have at least three votes, Länder with more than two million inhabitants shall have four, Länder with more than three million inhabitants shall have five, Länder with more than five million inhabitants shall have six, Länder with more than seven million inhabitants [shall have seven], and Länder with more than twelve million inhabitants eight votes."

4. The previous text of Article 135a (Old liabilities) will become Paragraph 1. The following Paragraph will be added after Paragraph 1:

"Paragraph 1 shall have corresponding application to liabilities of the German Democratic Republic or its legal entities and to liabilities of the Federation or other corporate bodies and institutions under public law, which are connected with the transfer of properties of the German Democratic Republic to the Federation, Länder and communes, and to liabilities which are based on measures taken by the German Democratic Republic or its legal entitites."

5. The following new Article 143 will be added to the Basic Law:

"In the part of Germany which has acceded law can diverge from the stipulations of this Basic Law at the latest until 31st December 1995 in as far as and as long as complete adaption to the constitutional order cannot yet be reached because of the varying conditions. Divergences must not violate Article 19 (Restriction of basic rights), Paragraph 2 and they have to be compatible with the principles cited in Article 79 (Amendment of the Basic Law), Paragraph 3. Article 41 of the Unification Treaty and regulations for its implementation are valid in so far as they envisage that expropriations on the territory named in Article 3 of this Treaty will not be revoked."

6. Article 146 (Duration of validity of the Basic Law) will be formulated as follows:

"This Basic Law, which will be valid for the whole of the German people after the completion of the unity and freedom of Germany, will lose its validity on the day that a new Constitution comes into force, that has been resolved freely by the German people."

Article 5
Future changes to the Constitution

The governments of the two contracting parties recommend that the legislative bodies of the united Germany deal within a period of two years with the issues raised in connection with German unification concerning changes of or amendments to the Basic Law, in particular:

– as regards the relations between the Federation and the Länder in accordance with the Prime Ministerial Joint Resolution of 5th July 1990,

– as regards the possibility of a new structure for the Berlin/Brandenburg region diverging from the provisions of Article 29 of the Basic Law through the agreement of the Länder involved,

– as regards the considerations concerning incorporating provisions on state objectives into the Basic Law, as well as

– with regard to the question of the application of Article 146 of the Basic Law.

Article 6
Special Regulation

Article 131 of the Basic Law (Legal position of former members of the public service) will for the present not be put into force in the area named in Article 3:

– as regards the considerations concerning incorporating into the Basic Law state objective regulations, as well as

– concerning the question of applying Article 146 of the Basic Law.

Article 7
Financial Constitution

The Financial Constitution of the Federal Republic of Germany will be extended to the area named in Article 3, in so far as is not determined otherwise in this Treaty.

For the distribution of the tax revenue to the Federation and to the Länder and the communes in the area named in Article 3 the regulations of Article 106 of the Basic Law apply (distribution of tax revenue), with the proviso that:

1. Up to 31st December 1994 Paragraph 3, Clause 4, and Paragraph 4 are not applied;

2. Up to 31st December 1996 the share of the communes in income tax revenue is passed on under Article 106 Paragraph 5 of the Basic Law by the Länder to the communes not on the basis of the income tax payments of their inhabitants but according to the number of inhabitants of the local authorities;

3. Deviating from Article 106, Clause 7 of the Basic Law, an annual share of at least 205 of the Land share of the total revenue from joint taxes and of the total revenue of the Land taxes as well as an annual share of 40% of the Land share from the resources of the German Unity Fund under Paragraph 5 no. 1 shall accrue to the communes by the 31st December 1994.

Article 107 of the Basic Law (fiscal adjustment) applies in the area named in Article 3, with the proviso that up to 31st December 1994 between the present Länder of the Federal Republic of Germany and the Länder in the area named in Article 3 the ruling of Paragraph 1 Clause 4 is not applied and an all-German fiscal adjustment between the Länder does not take place.

The all-German Länder share of the turnover tax will be divided up into an eastern and a western share in such a way that the average turnover tax share per inhabitant in the Länder of Brandenburg, Mecklenburg-Western Pomerania, Saxony, Saxony-Anhalt and Thuringia amounts in the years

1991 to 55%
1992 to 60%
1993 to 65%
1994 to 70%

of the average turnover tax share per inhabitant in the Länder of Baden-Württemberg, Bavaria, Bremen, Hesse, Hamburg, Lower Saxony, North Rhine-Westphalia, Rhineland-Palatinate, Saarland and Schleswig-Holstein. The share of the Land of Berlin will be calculated in advance according to the number of inhabitants.

The area mentioned in Article 3 will be included in the arrangements of Articles 91a (participation of the Federation on the basis of federal legislation), 91b (co-operation of Federation and Länder on the basis of agreements) and 104a (apportionment of tasks to Federation and Länder) paragraph 3 and 4 of the Basic Law including the relevant implementing statutes under the terms of this Treaty with effect from 1st January 1991.

Upon the establishment of German unity the annual payments from the German Unity Fund will be as follows:

1. Eighty-five per cent in special support of the Länder of Brandenburg, Mecklenburg-Western Pomerania, Saxony, Saxony-Anhalt and Thuringia as well as the Land of Berlin to cover their general financial requirement, and distributed to these Länder in proportion to their number of inhabitants without taking into account the number of inhabitants of Berlin (West), as well as

2. Fifteen per cent to meet central public tasks in the area of the aforementioned Länder.

In case of fundamentally changed conditions scope for further assistance for the appropriate equalisation of the financial resources for the Länder in the area named in Article 3 will be examined jointly by the Federation and Länder.

Article 8
Transference of Federal Law

With the coming into effect of the accession, Federal Law will come into force in the area named in Article 3, in so far as it is not restricted in its area of validity to particular Länder or parts of the Federal Republic of Germany and in so far as no other provisions are made by this Treaty, particularly its Appendix I.

Article 9
Continued application of GDR law

The law of the German Democratic Republic which applies at the time of the signing of this Treaty, and which is Land Law according to the listing of competences in the Basic Law, remains in force in so far as it is compatible with the Basic Law, without taking into account Article 143, compatible with the Federal Law that comes into force and with the immediately valid law of the European Communities and in so far as no other provision is made in this Treaty. The law of the German Democratic Republic which is Federal Law under the listing of competences in the Basic Law and which does not affect matters governed in a federally uniform way, applies under the conditions of Clause 1 as Land Law until the federal legislative applies a ruling. . . . The church taxation law decreed by the German Democratic Republic applies . . . (with the exception of East Berlin) as Land Law.

Article 10
EC Law

With the coming into effect of the accession, the treaties on the European Com-munities, including changes and additions, and the international agreements, treaties and decisions which have come into force in connection with these treaties apply in the area named in Article 3. . . .

Chapter IV: Treaties and Agreements under international law

Article 11
Treaties of the Federal Republic of Germany

The Treaty parties start from the premise that treaties and agreements under international law to which the Federal Republic is a Treaty party, including those treaties that establish membership of international organizations or institutions, will retain their validity and that the rights and obligations resulting from this will also apply to the area cited in Article 3, with the exception of the treaties named in Appendix I. In as far as adjustments are necessary in individual cases the All-German government will contact the respective Treaty partners.

Article 12
Treaties of the German Democratic Republic

The Treaty parties are agreed that the German Democratic Republic's treaties under international law are to be discussed with the Treaty partners of the German Democratic Republic during the establishment of German unity from the standpoint of the protection of confidence, the interests of the states involved and the Treaty obligations of the Federal Republic of Germany, as well as according to the principles of a free, democratic state order under the rule of law in order to settle and/or establish whether they should have continued validity or require adjustment or abolition.

A united Germany will establish its position on the transition of the German Democratic Republic's treaties under international law after consultations with the respective Treaty partners and with the European Communities in so far as their competences are affected.

Should a united Germany intend to join international organizations or other multilateral treaties to which the German Democratic Republic but not the Federal Republic of Germany belongs then agreement will be made with the respective Treaty partners and the European Communities, in so far as their competences are affected.

Article 13
Transfer of Institutions

Administrative bodies and other institutions serving public administration or the administration of justice in the area named in Article 3 shall be subordinate to the government of the Land in which they are located. Institutions with a supra-regional sphere of activity will be transferred to the joint responsibility of the Länder concerned. . . . In so far as the institutions or parts of institutions have fulfilled tasks until the time of the accession coming into effect which under the listing of competences in the Basic Law fall to the Federation, they shall be subordinate to the responsible supreme Federal authorities. They shall settle the transfer or the liquidation.

The named institutions also include cultural, educational, scientific, and sporting institutions, and radio and television institutions, whose legal entity is the public administration.

Article 14

Joint institutions of the Länder . . . will until a final ruling continue to be run as joint institutions of the . . . (five GDR) Länder.

Article 15
Transitional regulations for the Land administration

The Land spokesmen in the Länder (without Berlin) named in Article 1 and the government commissioners in the Areas shall continue to fulfil their tasks from the coming into affect of the accession until the election of the Prime Ministers in the responsibility of the Federal government and shall be subject to its instructions. . . . The other Länder

and the Federation will provide administrative help in developing the Land administration . . . at the latest until 30th June 1991.

Article 16
Berlin

Until the creation of an All-Berlin Land government, the Senate of Berlin and the Magistrat [East Berlin Council] will exercise the tasks of the All-Berlin Land government.

Article 17
Rehabilitation

The parties in the Treaty affirm their intention that a legal basis be created without delay so that all persons can be rehabilitated who have been the victims of politically motivated criminal proceedings or other legal decision that was contrary to the rule of law or unconstitutional. The rehabilitation of these victims of the unjust SED regime shall be linked to an appropriate ruling on compensation.

Article 18
Continued validity of judicial decisions

Decisions taken by Courts of the German Democratic Republic before the coming into effect of the accession shall remain effective and can be executed according to the law either adopted according to Article 8 or as it continues to remain in force according to Article 9. This law will also be applied to the examination of the compatibility of decisions and their execution with constitutional principles. Article 17 remains unaffected. Those sentenced by a criminal court of the German Democratic Republic are granted by this Treaty . . . the individual right to bring about final decisions through judicial appeal.

Article 19
Continued application of public administrative decisions

Administrative acts by the German Democratic Republic passed before the coming into effect of the accession remain valid. They may be rescinded if they are incompatible with constitutional principles or with the provisions of this Treaty. As for the rest the regulations concerning the existing force of administrative acts remain unaffected.

Article 20
Legal position of the Civil Service

The legal position of members of the civil service at the time of the accession is as agreed in the transitional arrangements of Appendix I. Public tasks (sovereign authority within the meaning of Article 33 Paragraph 4 of the Basic Law) must be entrusted to public servants as soon as possible. Civil service legislation is to be introduced under the terms of the arrangements agreed in Appendix I. Article 92 of the Basic Law (organization of the courts) remains unaffected. Military law is to be introduced under the terms of the arrangements agreed in Appendix I.

Chapter VI: Public assets and debts

Article 21
Administrative assets

The assets of the German Democratic Republic which serve directly specified administrative tasks will become Federal assets. In so far as . . . they were not primarily intended for administrative tasks which according to the Basic Law are to be carried out by Länder, local authorities or other bodies of public administration. In far as administrative assets were primarily used for tasks of the former Ministry for State Security/Office for National Security, the Trust Agency is entitled to them unless . . . they have already been transferred to new social or public purposes. In as far as administrative assets do not become Federal assets . . . those bodies of public administration are entitled to them which are responsible for that administrative task in accordance with the Basic Law. . . .

Article 22
Financial assets

. . . Financial assets, excluding social insurance assets, will come under Federal trust administration, in as far as it has not been transferred to the Trust Agency. . . . Through Federal law the financial assets are to be shared out to the Federal government and the Länder named in Article 1 in such a way that the Federal government and the Länder each receive a half of the total value of the assets. Assets that the Federal government receives after this are to be used to carry out public tasks in the area cited in Article 3. . . . (That) is not valid for state assets used for the provision of housing which is owned by the state-owned housing enterprises. These assets will be transferred to the ownership of local authorities with the simultaneous taking on of the pro rata debts upon the coming into effect of accession. The local authorities will gradually transfer their housing stock to a market-economy housing sector, taking into account social concerns. During this process privatization is to be carried out at a quicker pace to promote the formation of individuals' ownership of housing. . . .

Article 23
Debt ruling

With the coming into effect of accession the total debts of the national budget of the GDR that have accumulated up to this time will be taken over by a special Federation fund without legal status which will fulfil the debt servicing commitments. The special fund will be empowered to take up credits for the repayment of debts of the special fund, to cover accruing costs of interest and of the procurement of credits and for the purpose of purchasing debt instrument of the special fund as part of market support.

The Federal Finance Minister shall administer the special fund. . . . The Federation is responsible for the liabilities of the special fund. From the day of the coming into effect of the accession until 31st December 1993 the Federation and the Trust Agency will each reimburse half of the interest payments made by the social fund. . . .

With effect from 1st January 1994 the Federation and the Länder named in Article 1 and the Trust Agency will take over the total debts accruing to the special fund on 31st December 1993 according to Article 27 Paragraph 3 of the Treaty of 18th May 1990 on Monetary, Economic and Social Union. . . . The special fund will be dissolved with the expiry of 1993.

With the coming into effect of the accession, the Federal Republic of Germany will enter into the guarantees, warranties and sureties taken on by the German Democratic Republic at the expense of the state budget up until unification. The (GDR) Länder and Berlin . . . shall jointly and severally take on a countersurety of 50% for the guarantees, warranties and sureties transferred to the Federal Republic. . . .

Article 24
Foreign debts

Settlement shall take place on the instructions and under the supervision of the Federal Finance Ministry.

Article 25
Trust Agency assets

The Trust agency law of 17th June 1990 will continue to be valid with the following proviso: In accordance with the Trust Agency law, the Trust Agency will continue to be entrusted with the task of making competitive and privatizing the former publicly-owned enterprises. It will be a direct federal institution under public law. The technical and legal supervision is the job of the Federal Minister of Finance. . . .

The number of the administrative council members of the Trust Agency will be increased from 16 to 20, for the first administrative council to 23. Instead of the two representatives elected from among the People's Chamber the Länder mentioned in Article 1 will be given one seat each on the Trust Agency's administrative council. Notwithstanding Paragraph 4 section 2 of the Trust Agency Law the chairman and the other members of the administrative council will be appointed by the Federal government.

The contracting parties affirm that the publicly-owned assets will be used exclusively and solely for the benefit of measures in the territory mentioned in Article 3, irrespective of the budgetary entity. . . . Within the framework of the structural harmonization of agriculture trust agency proceeds may in individual cases also be used to pay off debts of agricultural enterprises. . . .

The authority granted to the Trust Agency through Article 27 Paragraph 1 of the Treaty dated 18th May 1990 to take up credits is to be increased from a total of up to DM 17,000 million to DM 25,000 million. The aforementioned credits are to be repaid as a rule by 31st December 1995. . . .

According to the provisions of Article 10 Paragraph 6 of the Treaty dated 18th May 1990 opportunities are to be provided for savers to be allowed later on a guaranteed share in the publicly-owned assets at the reduced conversion rate of 2:1.

Interest and redemption payments for credits taken up before 30th June 1990 are to be suspended until the DM-opening balance sheet has been established. Interest payments due are to be paid to the Deutsche Kreditbank AG via the Trust Agency.

Article 26
Reichsbahn [East German Railways]

The ownership and all other real rights . . . become the Deutsche Reichsbahn assets special fund of the Federal Republic of Germany with the coming into effect of accession. . . . Together with the real rights the obligations and claims connected with them are transferred to the special fund. The Chairman of the Board of the Deutsche Bundesbahn [West German Railways] and the Chairman of the Board of the Deutsche Reichsbahn are responsible for co-ordinating both special funds. They are to work towards the goal of technically and organizationally merging the two railway companies.

Article 27
Post Office

The property and all real rights which are part of the Deutsche Post [East German Post

Office] special fund will become assets of the Federal Republic of Germany. They will be merged with the Deutsche Bundespost [West German Post Office] special fund. During this the obligations and claims connected with the real rights will at the same be transferred to the Deutsche Bundespost special fund. The assets which serve sovereign and political aims together with the relevant obligations and claims will not become part of the Deutsche Bundespost special fund. . . .

Article 28
Promotion of the Economy

Upon accession the area named in Article 3 will be included in the existing Federal rules on the promotion of the economy. In this the particular needs of structural adaptation will be into account during a transitional period. . . . Specific programmes of measures will extend to the following areas: regional promotion of the economy, improving economic framework conditions in local areas, the development of medium-sized firms, modernizing the economy and freeing enterprises from debt after examining individual cases.

Article 29
Foreign Trade Relations

The foreign trade relations of the German Democratic Republic which have grown up, in particular existing Treaty obligations to countries of the Council for Mutual Economic Assistance, enjoy protection of confidence. They will be . . . further developed and expanded.

Chapter VII: Employment, Social Affairs, Family, Health, Environmental Protection

Article 30
Employment and Social Affairs

It is the task of the All-German legislator,
– to codify as soon as possible a new and uniform law of contracts of employment, as well as the public law on working hours including the permissibility of working on Sundays and holidays and the particular protection of women at work,
– to reformulate and update public health and safety at work in agreement with European Community legislation and that part of the health and safety at work laws of the German Democratic Republic which conforms to it.

Employees may on completion of the 57th year, in the area mentioned in Article 3, receive a pre-retirement sum for a period of three years, but not longer than the earliest possible receipt of an old-age pension from the statutory retirement pension fund. The amount of the pre-retirement sum is 65% of the final average net emolument. . . . Until 31st December 1990 women, on completion of their 55th year, may receive pre-retirement payment for a maximum period of five years. . . .

Persons whose pension from the statutory pension fund commences in the period from 1st January 1992 to 30th June 1995, will
– receive a pension always at least of the same amount which would have resulted on 30th June 1990 according to the pension law valid until then in the territory mentioned in Article 3 without taking into consideration payments from additional or special pensions systems,
– be granted a pension even if on 30th June 1990 a pension claim had existed according to the pension law in force until then in the territory mentioned in Article 3.

As for the rest the transition is to be characterized by the objective of realizing, with the harmonization of wages and salaries in the territory mentioned in Article 3, also a harmonization of pensions for those in the remaining Länder. . . .

Article 31
Family and Women

It is the task of the all-German legislator to develop further legislation on equality between men and women . . . (and) to structure the legal position from the standpoint of the compatibility of family and profession in face of the different legal and institutional starting points in the employment of mothers and fathers. In order to guarantee the continuation of institutions looking after children during the day in the area named in Article 3 the Federal government will share the cost of these institutions for a transitional period until 30th June 1991.

Article 32
Independent Associations

. . . The building up and expansion of independent welfare institutions and an independent youth support sector in the area named in Article 3 will be promoted within the framework of responsibilities laid down in the Constitution.

Article 33
Health Service

It is the task of the legislator to create the prerequisites for swiftly and lastingly improving the level of in-patient provision of care for the population of the area named in Article 3 and adapting it to the situation in the rest of the territory of the Federation. In order to avoid deficits in expenditure by health insurance institutes on medicines in the area which has acceded the All-German legislator will make rules with a time limit by which the price paid to the manufacturer will be reduced in accordance with the rules on the price of pharmaceuticals by a proportion which corresponds to the difference between income from obligatory contributions in the area which has acceded and the Federal area of today.

Article 34
Environmental Protection

. . . It (is) the task of the legislator to protect man's natural basis for life, taking into account the principles of precautions, the pollutor [pays] and co-operation and to promote uniformity in ecological living conditions at a high level, or at least at that achieved in the Federal Republic of Germany. Ecological restructuring and development programmes are to be drawn up for the area named in Article 3 for the promotion of the cited goal within the framework of the rules on responsibility laid down in

the constitution. Planning measures to prevent dangers to the population's health is a priority.

Article 35
Culture

. . . The cultural substance in the area named in Article 3 must suffer no harm. The fulfilment of the cultural tasks including the financing of them is to be secured, whereby the protection and promotion of culture and art are the duty of the new Länder and communes in accordance with the allocation of responsibilities in the Basic Law. The hitherto centrally managed cultural establishments will be transferred to the ownership of the Länder or communes in which they are situated. Co-financing by the Federation will not be ruled out in exceptional cases, particularly in the Land Berlin. . . . The Cultural Fund (of the GDR) will be continued until 31st December 1994 in the area named in Article 3 as a transitional arrangement to promote culture, art and artists. Co-financing by the Federation in the framework of the allocation of responsibilities in the Basic Law is not ruled out. . .

Article 36
Broadcasting

The "GDR Radio" and the "German Television" will continue to be run until 31st December 1991 at the latest by the Länder named in Article 1 as a public institution, independent of the state and with legal status. . . . The bodies of the institution shall be the broadcasting commissioner [German: Rundfunkbeauftragte] and the broadcasting advisory council [German: Rundfunkbeirat].

The broadcasting commissioner will be elected by the People's Chamber on the suggestion of the Prime Minister of the German Democratic Republic. If no election by the People's Chamber comes about, the broadcasting commissioner will be elected by a majority by the Land spokesman of the Länder named in Article 1 and by the Mayor of Berlin. The broadcasting commissioner will manage the institution and represent it in law and extra-judicially. . . . The broadcasting advisory council will consist of 18 recognized personalities from public life as representatives of socially relevant groups. . .

The institution will be financed primarily from income from broadcasting licence receipts from listeners and viewers resident in the area named in Article 3. . . . The institution (is), in line with the federal structure of broadcasting, to be dissolved by a joint State Treaty of the Länder named in Article 1 or to be transferred into institutions of public law of individual or several Länder. Should a State Treaty not come about by 31st December 1991, the institution will then be dissolved with the expiry of that period. . .

Article 37
Education

School, vocational and academic qualifications or certificates of competence gained or recognized by the state in the German Democratic Republic will continue to be valid in the area named in Article 3. . . . Their equivalence will be ascertained on application by the authority responsible in each case. Federal and EC laws on the equivalence of examinations or certificates of competence as well as specific regulations in this Treaty have priority. The right to hold vocational descriptions recognised by the state or academic degrees and titles conferred remains unaffected in any case.

The usual procedure of the Conference of Ministers of Culture for recognizing teacher-training qualifications will be valid. The Conference of Ministers of Culture will make relevant transitional rules. Certificates in accordance with the system of trained vocations and the system of skilled work, final examinations and examinations for apprentices in recognized trained vocations are equal to one another. The regulations required for restructuring the school system in the area named in Article 3 will be made by the Länder named in Article 1. The necessary rules on recognizing certificates from schools will be agreed by the Conference of Ministers of Culture. . .

Students who change colleges before concluding their studies will have their studies and examinations hitherto recognized in accordance with the principles of Paragraph 7 of the General Rules for Degree Examination Regulations (ABD) or within the framework of the rules valid for the admissability to state examinations. The right to matriculation confirmed on final certificates from engineering and vocational colleges in the German Democratic Republic will be valid in accordance with the decision by the Conference of Ministers of Culture of 10th May 1990 and Appendix B to it. Further reaching principles and procedures for the recognition of vocational college and university-level education are to be developed within the framework of the Conference of Ministers of Culture.

Article 38
Science and Research

Science and research will continue to form an important basis for state and society in a united Germany. An assessment of publicly supported institutions by the Scientific Council, which will be concluded by 31st December 1991, will serve the necessary renewal of science and research while retaining high-performance institutions in the area named in Article 3, whereby individual results are to be put into effect step by step beforehand. . .

With the coming into effect of accession the Academy of Sciences as a society of academics will be separated from research institutes and other institutions. The decision on how the Academy's society of academics is to be continued will be taken in accordance with Land law. The research institutes and other institutions will continue to exist in the first instance until 31st December 1991 as Land institutions in the area named in Article 3, in as far as they have not been disbanded beforehand or transformed. . . . Contracts of employment . . . will continue to exist until 31st December 1991 as temporary contracts with the Länder. . .

The intent (of the same regulations) is valid for the Construction Academy and the Academy of Agricultural Sciences as well as institutions coming under the Ministry of Food, Agriculture and Forestry. The Research Council of the German Democratic Republic is disbanded with the coming into effect of the German Democratic Republic's accession.

Article 39
Sport

The sports structures being transformed in the region named in Article 3 will be switched to self-administration. The public authorities will promote sport in both a non-material and a material way.

Top level sport and its development will, insofar as it has proved its worth, continue to be promoted in the region named in Article 3. This promotion will be within the framework of the rules and principles valid in the Federal Republic of Germany. Within this framework the Research Institute for Physical Culture and Sport in Leipzig, the Research and Development Department for Sports Equipment in Berlin (East) and the IOC-recognized Doping Control Laboratory in Kreischa, near Dresden, will be continued or appended to existing institutions.

The Federal government will support disabled sport until 31st December 1992.

Chapter IX: Transitional and final regulations

Article 40
Treaties and Agreements

The obligations from the Treaty of 18th May 1990 on the creation of a Monetary, Economic and Social Union between the Federal Republic of Germany and the GDR continue to be valid, as long as nothing different is set in this Treaty or the agreements become irrelevant in the course of the establishing of German unity.

In as far as rights and obligations from other treaties and agreements between the Federal Republic of Germany or the Federal States and the German Democratic Republic have not become irrelevant in the course of creating German unity they will be taken over, adapted, or carried out by the internal legal entities responsible.

Article 41
Issues concerning assets

The Joint Statement by the government of the GDR and the government of the Federal Republic of Germany of 15th June 1990 on the settling of open questions of property is part of the Treaty. In accordance with specific legal rules there will be no return of property rights over plots of land or buildings if the relevant plot of land and building is required for urgent purposes of investment, which are to be more closely laid down, on a sure planning basis, serves the setting up of a location for a trading enterprise and is of particular value for promoting this investment decision in terms of the national economy, and above all creates or preserves jobs. Compensation for the former owner is also to be regulated in the law. Besides this the Federal Republic of Germany will not pass any laws which contradict the Joint Statement.

Article 42
Bundestag Deputies

Before the accession of the German Democratic Republic comes into effect the People's Chamber will elect 144 deputies as well as a sufficient number of substitutes on the basis of its composition on 1st September 1990 to be sent to the 11th Bundestag. The parliamentary groups represented in the People's Chamber will make relevant proposals. . .

Article 43
Bundesrat

From the formation of the (GDR) Länder until the election of the Prime Minister the Land plenipotentiary can take part in sessions of the Bundesrat with an advisory vote.

Article 44
Upholding of rights

Rights from this Treaty in favour of the German Democratic Republic or the Länder named in Article 1 can be claimed by each of these Länder after the accession comes into effect.

Article 45
The coming into effect of the Treaty

This Treaty, including the protocol enclosed and Appendices I to III, comes into force on the day when the governments of the GDR and the Federal Republic of Germany have informed one another that the required internal state conditions for the coming into force have been fulfilled. After the establishing of German unity the Treaty remains in force as Federal Law.

Protocol notes –

1. On Article 1: The boundaries of the Land of Berlin are stipulated by the law on the establishment of a new Berlin municipality of the 27th April 1920 [as received] with the proviso . . . that all areas in which elections to the House of Representatives or the Berlin City Council have taken place shall form a part of the districts of Berlin. The Länder of Berlin and Brandenburg shall examine and document the resulting boundaries within a year.

2. On Article 9: The two parties to the Treaty shall note the statement by the Land of Berlin that the church tax law applicable in Berlin (West) shall be extended to that part of Berlin in which it was not so far applicable from the 1st January 1991.

3./4. On Article 13: . . . in as far as institutions are wholly or partially transferred to the Federation, suitable staff are to be recruited on the appropriate scale in order to meet the requirements needed to fulfil tasks.

5. On Article 16: The two parties to the Treaty shall note the announcement by the Land of Berlin that the Mayor shall be appointed member of the Bundesrat on the 3rd October 1990 and that the members of the city government as well as other members of the Berlin Land government shall be involved in deputising for the appointed Bundesrat members.

6. On Article 20: The introduction of the civil servant law according to the provisions agreed in Appendix I shall take effect in line with the principles on functions of a permanent nature which are decisive for the staffing levels of the Federal Republic of Germany.

7. On Article 21: The Länder shall be informed about any further appropriation of property under military use. The affected Länder are to be consulted before property hitherto used by the military, which becomes a federal asset, are given over to a new use.

8. On Article 22: The publicly-owned property and land used by housing co-operatives for housing purposes . . . shall ultimately be transferred to ownership by the housing co-operatives while retaining their proper use.

9. On Article 35: The Federal Republic of Germany and the German Democratic Republic declare in connection with Article 35 of the Treaty: There is freedom to affirm Sorb nationality and exercise Sorb culture. The freedom to preserve and continue the development of Sorb culture and Sorb traditions shall be ensured. Members of the Sorb people and their organizations have the freedom to cultivate and to preserve the Sorb language in public life. The allocation of responsibilities in the Basic Law remains untouched.

10. On Article 38: Agreements made by the Academy of Sciences, the Building Academy and Academy of the Agricultural Sciences of the German Democratic Republic with organizations in other states or with international organizations will be examined according to the principles laid down in Article 12 of the Treaty.

11. On Article 40: Cases in which the Federal government has approved the taking over of the costs for the medical treatment of Germans from the area named in Article 3 will be settled by the Federal government.

12. To Appendix II, Chapter II, Section III, no. 2 (party assets) (not yet published): The parties have a claim to equal opportunities in preparation for and competing in elections. Money or assets having a monetary value which have come into the hands of the parties neither via membership subscriptions nor by donations nor by state contributions to election expenses, in particular the assets of former bloc parties and the PDS in the German Democratic Republic, may not be used either for preparation for the election

or for the election campaign. The parties are obliged to give affidavits by their treasurers on this and to have the renunciation of the use of such monies confirmed by accountants on 1st December 1990. In as far as parties in the Federal Republic of Germany merge with former bloc parties of the German Democratic Republic they have to provide a final balance and an opening balance at the moment of their merger by 1st November 1990 which correspond to the criteria of Paragraph 24 Section 4 of the law on parties.

Protocol statement to the Treaty: Both parties to the Treaty agree that the commitments in the Treaty are made without detriment to the rights and responsibilities of the Four Powers with reference to Berlin and Germany as a whole which still exist or to the results still to come from the talks on the external aspects of the creation of German unity.

3

Constitution (Fundamental Law) of the Union of Soviet Socialist Republics

Adopted at the Seventh (Special) Session of the USSR Supreme Soviet (Ninth Convocation) October 7, 1977

This edition includes amendments to the Constitution made in December 1988, December 1989, March 1990, and December 1990

The Great October Socialist Revolution, carried out by the workers and peasants of Russia under the leadership of the Communist Party headed by Lenin, overthrew capitalist and landowner rule, broke the fetters of oppression, established the dictatorship of the proletariat, and created the Soviet state, a new type of state, the basic instrument for defending the gains of the revolution and for building socialism and communism. Humanity thereby began the epoch-making turn from capitalism to socialism.

After achieving victory in the Civil War and repulsing imperialist intervention, the Soviet government carried through far-reaching social and economic transformations, and put an end once and for all to exploitation of man by man, antagonisms between classes, and strife between nationalities. The unification of the Soviet republics in the Union of Soviet Socialist Republics multiplied the forces and opportunities of the peoples of the country in the building of socialism. Social ownership of the means of production and genuine democracy for the working people was established. For the first time in the his-

tory of mankind a socialist society was created.

The strength of socialism was vividly demonstrated by the immortal feat of the Soviet people and their Armed Forces in achieving their historic victory in the Great Patriotic War. This victory consolidated the influence and international standing of the Soviet Union and created new opportunities for growth of the forces of socialism, national liberation, democracy, and peace throughout the world.

Continuing their creative endeavours, the working people of the Soviet Union have ensured rapid, all-round development of the country and steady improvement of the socialist system. They have consolidated the alliance of the working class, collective-farm peasantry, and people's intelligentsia, and friendship of the nations and nationalities of the USSR. Socio-political and ideological unity of Soviet society, in which the working class is the leading force, has been achieved. The aims of the dictatorship of the proletariat having been fulfilled, the Soviet state has become a state of the whole people.

In the USSR a developed socialist society has been built. At this stage, when socialism is developing on its own foundations, the creative forces of the new system and the advantages of the socialist way of life are becoming increasingly evident, and the working people are more and more widely enjoying the fruits of their great revolutionary gains.

It is a society in which powerful productive forces and progressive science and culture have been created, in which the well-being of the people is constantly rising, and more and more favourable conditions are being provided for the all-round development of the individual.

It is a society of mature socialist social relations, in which, on the basis of the drawing together of all classes and social strata and of the juridical and factual equality of all its nations and nationalities and their fraternal co-operation, a new historical community of people has been formed — the Soviet people.

It is a society of high organisational capacity, ideological commitment, and consciousness of the working people, who are patriots and internationalists.

It is a society in which the law of life is concern of all for the good of each and concern of each for the good of all.

It is a society of true democracy, the political system of which ensures effective management of all public affairs, ever more active participation of the working people in running the state, and the combining of citizens' real rights and freedoms with their obligations and responsibility to society.

Developed socialist society is a natural, logical stage on the road to communism.

The supreme goal of the Soviet state is the building of a classless communist society in which there will be public, communist self-government. The main aims of the people's socialist state are: to lay the material and technical foundation of communism, to perfect socialist social relations and transform them into communist rela-

tions, to mould the citizen of communist society, to raise the people's living and cultural standards, to safeguard the country's security, and to further the consolidation of peace and development of international co-operation.

The Soviet people,

— guided by the ideas of scientific communist and true to their revolutionary traditions,

— relying on the great social, economic, and political gains of socialism,

— striving for the further development of socialist democracy

— taking into account the international position of the USSR as part of a world system of socialism, and conscious of their internationalist responsibility,

— preserving continuity of the ideas and principles of the first Soviet Constitution of 1918, the 1924 Constitution of the USSR and the 1936 Constitution of the USSR,

hereby affirm the principles of the social structure and policy of the USSR, and define the rights, freedoms and obligations of citizens, and the principles of the organisation of the socialist state of the whole people, and its aims, and proclaim these in this Constitution.

I

Principles of the Social Structure and Policy of the USSR

Chapter 1
The Political System

Article 1

The Union of Soviet Socialist Republics is a socialist state of the whole people, expressing the will and interests of the workers, peasants and intelligentsia, the working people of all the nations and nationalities of the country.

Article 2

All power in the USSR belongs to the people.

The people exercise state power through Soviets of People's Deputies, which constitute the political foundation of the USSR.

All other state bodies are under the control of, and accountable to, the Soviets of People's Deputies.

Article 3

The Soviet state is organised and functions on the principle of democratic centralism, namely the electiveness of all bodies of state power from the lowest to the highest, their accountability to the people, and the obligation of lower bodies to observe the decisions of higher ones. Democratic centralism combines central leadership with local initiative and creative activity and with the responsibility of each state body and official for the work entrusted to them.

Article 4

The Soviet state and all its bodies functions on the basis of socialist law, ensure the maintenance of law and order, and safeguard the interests of society and the rights and freedoms of citizens.

State organisations, public organisations and officials shall observe the USSR Constitution and Soviet laws.

Article 5

Major matters of state shall be submitted to nationwide discussion and put to a popular vote (referendum).

Article 6

The Communist Party of the Soviet Union and other political parties, as well as trade union, youth and other public organisations and mass movements shall take part in the elaboration of the policy of the Soviet state and in the running of state and public affairs through their representatives elected to the Soviets of People's Deputies and in other ways.

Article 7

All political parties, public organisations and mass movements, in performing the functions envisaged by their programmes and statutes, shall act within the framework of the USSR Constitution and Soviet laws.

The formation and activities of parties, organisations and movements intent on changing by violence the Soviet constitutional system and the integral unity of the socialist state, undermining its security or inciting social, ethnic or religious strife shall be prohibited.

Article 8

Work collectives shall take part in discussing and deciding state and public affairs, in planning production and social development, in training and placing personnel, and in discussing and deciding matters pertaining to the management of enterprises and institutions, the improvement of working and living conditions, and the use of funds allocated both for developing production and for social and cultural purposes and financial incentives.

Work collectives shall promote socialist emulation, the spread of progressive methods of work and the strengthening of production discipline, educate their members in the spirit of communist morality, strive to enhance their political consciousness and raise their cultural level and skills and qualifications.

Article 9

The principal direction in the development of the political system of Soviet society is the extension of socialist democracy, namely, increasing participation of citizens in managing the affairs of society and the state, continual improvement of the machinery of state, growing activity of public organisations, strengthening of the system of people's control, consolidation of the legal foundations of the functioning of the state and of public life, greater openness and publicity, and constant responsiveness to public opinion.

Chapter 2
The Economic System

Article 10

The economic system of the USSR shall develop on the basis of the property of Soviet citizens and of collective and state property.

The state shall create the conditions needed for the development of different forms of ownership and shall guarantee equal protection thereof.

The land, the resources therein, the waters and plant and animal life in their natural state shall be the inalienable property of the peoples living on the given territory, shall be managed by local Soviets of People's Deputies and shall be granted for use by citizens, enterprises, institutions and organisations.

Article 11

The property of a citizen of the USSR shall be his personal assets and shall be used for the satisfaction of his material and intellectual needs and for economic and other activities not prohibited by law.

An individual may own any property designed for consumption and production which has been acquired with his earned incomes and in any other legal ways except for certain types of private property which are prohibited to individuals.

For the running of farms and subsidiary plots and for other purposes envisaged by law, individuals shall have the right to possess land for lifelong use, with right of bequeathal thereof.

The right to inherit property shall be recognised and protected by law.

Article 12

Collective property shall be that of leasehold or collectively-owned enterprises, co-operatives, joint-stock societies, economic organisations and other associations. Collective property shall be formed through the transformation by legal methods of state property and voluntary sharing of the property of individuals and organisations.

Article 13

State property shall be federal property, that of the Union and Autonomous Republics, of the Autonomous Regions, Autonomous Areas, Territories, Regions and other administrative territorial entities (communal property).

Article 14

The source of the growth of social wealth and of the well-being of the people, and of each individual, is the labour, free from exploitation, of Soviet people.

The state exercises control over the measure of labour and consumption in accordance with the principle of socialism: "From each according to his ability, to each according to his work". It fixes the rate of taxation on taxable income.

Socially useful work and its results determine a person's status in society. By combining material and moral incentives and encouraging innovation and a creative attitude to work, the state helps transform labour into the prime vital need of every Soviet citizen.

Article 15

The supreme goal of social production under socialism is the fullest possible satisfaction of the people's growing material, cultural and intellectual requirements.

Relying on the creative initiative of the working people, socialist emulation, and scientific and technological progress, and by improving the forms and methods of economic management, the state ensures growth of labour productivity, heightened production efficiency and quality of work, and dynamic, planned, proportionate development of the economy.

Article 16

The economy of the USSR is an integral economic complex comprising all the elements of social production, distribution and exchange on its territory.

The economy is managed on the basis of state plans for economic and social development, with due account of sectoral and territorial principles, and by combining centralised direction with the managerial independence and initiative of individual and amalgamated enterprises and other organisations, for which active use is made of management accounting, profit, cost, and other economic levers and incentives.

Article 17

In the USSR, the law permits individual labour in handicrafts, farming, the provision of services for the public, and other forms of activity based exclusively on the personal work of individual citizens and members of their families. The state makes regulations for such work to ensure that it serves the interests of society.

Article 18

In the interests of present and future generations, the necessary steps are taken in the USSR to protect and make scientific, rational use of the land and its mineral and water resources, together with the plant and animal kingdoms, to preserve the purity of air and water, ensure reproduction of natural wealth, and improve the human environment.

Chapter 3
Social Development and Culture

Article 19

The social basis of the USSR is the unbreakable alliance of the workers, peasants, and intelligentsia.

The state helps enhance the social homogeneity of society, namely the elimination of class differences and of the essential distinctions between town and country and between mental and physical labour, and the all-round development and drawing together of all the nations and nationalities of the USSR.

Article 20

In accordance with the communist ideal — "The free development of each is the condition of the free development of all" — the state aims to give citizens more and more real opportunities to apply their creative energies, abilities, talents, and to develop their personalities in every way.

Article 21

The state concerns itself with improving working conditions, safety and labour protection and the scientific organisation of work, and with reducing and ultimately eliminating all arduous physical labour by comprehensive mechanisation and automation of production processes in all branches of the economy.

Article 22

A programme is being consistently implemented in the USSR to convert agricultural work into a type of industrial work, to extend the network of educational, cultural and medical institutions, and of trade, public catering, service and public utility facilities in rural localities, and to transform hamlets and villages into well-planned and well-appointed settlements.

Article 23

The state pursues a steady policy of raising people's pay levels and real incomes through increased productivity.

In order to satisfy the needs of Soviet people to a greater extent, social consumption funds are created. The state, with the broad participation of public organisations and work collectives, ensures the growth and just distribution of these funds.

Article 24

In the USSR, state systems of health protection, social security, trade and public catering, communal services and amenities, and public utilities, operate and are being extended.

The state encourages co-operatives and other public organisations to provide all types of services for the population. It encourages the development of mass physical culture and sport.

Article 25

In the USSR there is a uniform system of public education, constantly undergoing improvement, which provides general education and vocational training for citizens, serves the communist education and intellectual and physical development of the youth, and trains them for work and social activity.

Article 26

In accordance with society's needs the state provides for planned development of science and the training of scientific personnel and organises the application of the results of research in the economy and other spheres of life.

Article 27

The state concerns itself with protecting, augmenting and making extensive use of society's cultural wealth for the moral and aesthetic education of the Soviet people, for raising their cultural level.

In the USSR development of professional, amateur and folk arts is encouraged in every way.

Chapter 4
Foreign Policy

Article 28

The USSR steadfastly pursues a Leninist policy of peace and stands for strengthening the security of nations and broad international co-operation.

The foreign policy of the USSR is aimed at ensuring international conditions favourable for building communism in the USSR, safeguarding the state interests of the Soviet Union, consolidating the positions of world socialism, supporting the struggle of peoples for national liberation and social progress, preventing wars of aggression, achieving universal and complete disarmament, and consistently implementing the principle of the peaceful coexistence of states with different social systems.

In the USSR war propaganda is banned.

Article 29

The USSR's relations with other states are based on observance of the following principles: sovereign equality; mutual renunciation of the use or threat of force; inviolability of frontiers; territorial integrity of states; peaceful settlement of disputes; non-intervention in internal affairs; respect for human rights and fundamental freedoms; the equal rights of peoples and their right to decide their own destiny; co-operation among states; and fulfilment in good faith of obligations arising from the generally recognised principles and rules of international law, and from the international treaties signed by the USSR.

Article 30

The USSR, as part of the world system of socialism and of the socialist community, promotes and strengthens friendship, co-operation and comradely mutual assistance with other socialist countries on the basis of the principle of socialist internationalism, and takes part in socialist economic integration and the socialist international division of labour.

Chapter 5
Defence of the Socialist Motherland

Article 31

Defence of the Socialist Motherland is one of the most important functions of the state, and is the concern of the whole people.

In order to defend the gains of socialism, the peaceful labour of the Soviet people, and the sovereignty and territorial integrity of the state, the USSR maintains armed forces and has instituted universal military service.

The duty of the USSR Armed Forces to the people is to provide reliable defence of the Socialist Motherland and to be in constant combat readiness, guaranteeing that any aggressor is instantly repulsed.

Article 32

The state ensures the security and defence capability of the country, and supplies the USSR Armed Forces with everything necessary for that purpose.

The duties of state bodies, public organisations, officials, and citizens in regard to safeguarding the country's security and strengthening its defence capacity are defined by the legislation of the USSR.

II
The State and the Individual

Chapter 6
Citizenship of the USSR.
Equality of Citizens' Rights

Article 33

Uniform federal citizenship is established for the USSR. Every citizen of a Union Republic is a citizen of the USSR.

The grounds and procedure for acquiring or forfeiting Soviet citizenship are defined by the Law of Citizenship of the USSR.

When abroad, citizens of the USSR enjoy the protection and assistance of the Soviet state.

Article 34

Citizens of the USSR are equal before the law, without distinction of origin, social or property status, race or nationality, sex, education, language, attitude to religion, type and nature of occupation, domicile, or other status.

Equal rights of citizens of the USSR are guaranteed in all fields of economic, political, social, and cultural life.

Privileges for individual categories of citizens shall be established only on the basis of the law. No one in the USSR may enjoy unlawful privileges.

Article 35

Women and men have equal rights in the USSR.

Exercise of these rights is ensured by according women equal access with men to education and vocational and professional training, equal opportunities with regard to employment, remuneration, and promotion, in social, political, and cultural activity, and by special labour and health protection measures for women; by providing conditions enabling mothers to work; by legal protection, and material and moral support for mothers and children, including paid leave and other benefits for expectant mothers and mothers, and gradual reductions in working time for mothers with growing children.

Article 36

Citizens of the USSR of different races and nationalities have equal rights.

Exercise of these rights is ensured by a policy of all-round development and drawing together of all the nations and nationalities of the USSR, by educating citizens in the spirit of Soviet patriotism and socialist internationalism, and by the possibility to use their native language and the languages of other peoples of the USSR.

Any direct or indirect limitation of the rights of citizens or establishment of direct or indirect privileges on grounds of race or nationality, and any advocacy of racial or national exclusiveness, hostility or contempt, are punishable by law.

Article 37

Citizens of other countries and stateless persons in the USSR are guaranteed the rights and freedoms provided by law, including the right to apply to a court and other state bodies for the protection of their personal property, family, and other rights.

Citizens of other countries and stateless persons, when in the USSR, are obliged to respect the USSR Constitution and observe Soviet laws.

Article 38

The USSR grants the right of asylum to foreigners persecuted for defending the interests of the working people and the cause of peace, or for participation in revolutionary and national-liberation movements, or for progressive social and political, scientific or other creative activity.

Chapter 7
The Basic Rights, Freedoms, and Duties of Citizens of the USSR

Article 39

Citizens of the USSR enjoy in full the social, economic, political and personal rights and freedoms proclaimed and guaranteed by the USSR Constitution and by Soviet laws. The socialist system ensures increased rights and freedoms of citizens and continuous improvement of their living standards as social, economic, and cultural development programmes are fulfilled.

Enjoyment by citizens of their rights and freedoms must not be to the detriment of the interests of society or the state, or infringe the rights of other citizens.

Article 40

Citizens of the USSR have the right to work (that is, guaranteed employment and pay in accordance with the quantity and quality of their work, and not below the state-established minimum), including the right to choose their trade and profession, type of job and work in accordance with their inclinations, abilities, training and education, with due account of the needs of society.

The right is ensured by the socialist economic system, steady growth of productive forces, free vocational and professional training, improvement of skills, training in new trades or professions, and development of the systems of vocational guidance and job placement.

Article 41

Citizens of the USSR have the right to rest and leisure.

This right is ensured by the establishment of a working week not exceeding 41 hours for workers and other employees, a shorter working day in a number of trades and industries, and shorter hours for night work; by the provision of paid annual holidays, weekly days of rest, extension of the network of cultural, educational and health-building institutions, and the development on a mass scale of sport, physical culture, camping and tourism; by the provision of neighbourhood recreational facilities, and of other opportunities for rational use of free time.

The length of collective farmers' working and leisure time is established by their collective farms.

Article 42

Citizens of the USSR have the right to health protection.

This right is ensured by free, qualified medical care provided by state health institutions; by the extension of the network of therapeutic and health-building institutions; by the development and improvement of safety and hygiene in industry; by carrying out broad prophylactic measures; by measures to improve the environment; by special care for the health of the rising generation, including prohibition of child labour, excluding the work done by the children as part of the school curriculum; and by developing research to prevent and reduce the incidence of disease and ensure citizens a long and active life.

Article 43

Citizens of the USSR have the right to maintenance in old age, in sickness, and in the event of complete or partial disability or loss of the breadwinner.

This right is guaranteed by social insurance of workers and other employees and collective farmers; by allowances for temporary disability; by provision by the state or by collective farms of retirement pensions, disability pensions, and pensions for loss of the breadwinner; by providing employment for the partially disabled; by care for the elderly and the disabled; and by other forms of social security.

Article 44

Citizens of the USSR have the right to housing.

This right is ensured by the development and upkeep of state and socially-owned housing; by assistance for co-operative and individual house building; by fair distribution, under public control, of the housing that becomes available through fulfilment of the programme of building well-appointed dwellings, and by low rents and low charges for utility services. Citizens of the USSR shall take care of the housing allocated to them.

Article 45

Citizens of the USSR have the right to education.

This right is ensured by free provision of all forms of education, by the institution of universal, compulsory secondary education, a broad development of vocational, specialised secondary, and higher education, in which instruction is oriented toward practical activity and production; by the development of extramural, correspondence and evening courses; by the provision of state scholarships and grants and privileges for students; by the free issue of school textbooks; by the opportunity to attend a school where teaching is in the native language; and by the provision of facilities for self-education.

Article 46

Citizens of the USSR have the right to enjoy cultural benefits.

This right is ensured by broad access to the cultural treasures of their own land and of the world that are preserved in state and other public collections; by the development and fair distribution of cultural and educational institutions throughout the country; by developing television and radio broadcasting and the publishing of books, newspapers and periodicals, and by extending the free library service; and by expanding cultural exchanges with other countries.

Article 47

Citizens of the USSR, in accordance with the aims of building communism, are guaranteed freedom of scientific, technical and artistic work. This freedom is ensured by broadening scientific research, encouraging invention and innovation, and developing literature and the arts. The state provides the necessary material conditions for this and support for voluntary societies and unions of workers in the arts, organises introduction of inventions and innovations in production and other spheres of activity.

The rights of authors, inventors and innovators are protected by the state.

Article 48

Citizens of the USSR have the right to take part in the management and administration of state and public affairs and in the discussion and adoption of laws and measures of All-Union and local significance.

This right is ensured by the opportunity to vote and to be elected to Soviets of People's Deputies and other elective state bodies, to take part in nationwide discussions and referendums in people's control, in the work of state bodies, public organisations, and local community groups, and in meetings at places of work or residence.

Article 49

Every citizen of the USSR has the right to submit proposals to state bodies and public organisations for improving their activity, and to criticise shortcomings in their work.

Officials are obliged, within established time-limits, to examine citizens' proposals and requests, to reply to them, and to take appropriate action.

Persecution for criticism is prohibited. Persons guilty of such persecution shall be called to account.

Article 50

In accordance with the interests of the people and in order to strengthen and develop the socialist system, citizens of the USSR are guaranteed freedom of speech, of the press, and of assembly, meetings, street processions and demonstrations.

Exercise of these political freedoms is

ensured by putting public buildings, streets and squares at the disposal of the working people and their organisations, by broad dissemination of information, and by opportunity to use the press, television, and radio.

Article 51

Citizens of the USSR shall have the right to unite in political parties and public organisations and participate in mass movements contributing to their greater political activity and to the satisfaction of their diverse interests.

Public organisations shall be guaranteed the necessary conditions for the successful accomplishment of their statutory tasks.

Article 52

Citizens of the USSR are guaranteed freedom of conscience, that is, the right to profess or not to profess any religion, and to conduct religious worship or atheist propaganda. Incitement of hostility or hatred on religious grounds is prohibited.

In the USSR, the church is separated from the state, and the school from the church.

Article 53

The family enjoys the protection of the state.

Marriage is based on the free consent of the woman and the man; the spouses are completely equal in their family relations.

The state helps the family by providing and developing a broad system of childcare institutions, by organising and improving communal services and public catering, by paying grants on the birth of a child, by providing children's allowances and benefits for large families, and other forms of family allowances and assistance.

Article 54

Citizens of the USSR are guaranteed inviolability of the person. No one may be detained except by a court decision or on the warrant of a procurator.

Article 55

Citizens of the USSR are guaranteed inviolability of the home. No one may, without lawful grounds, enter a home against the will of those residing in it.

Article 56

The privacy of citizens, and of their correspondence, telephone conversations, and telegraphic communications is protected by law.

Article 57

Respect for the individual and protection of the rights and freedoms of citizens are the duty of all state bodies, public organisations, and officials.

Citizens of the USSR have the right to protection by the courts against encroachment on their honour and reputation, life and health, and personal freedom and property.

Article 58

Citizens of the USSR have the right to lodge complaints against the actions of officials, state bodies and public bodies. Complaints shall be examined according to the procedure and within the time-limit established by law.

Actions by officials that contravene the law or exceed their powers, and infringe the rights of citizens, may be appealed against in a court in the manner prescribed by law.

Citizens of the USSR have the right to compensation for damage resulting from unlawful actions by state organisations and public organisations, or by officials in performance of their duties.

Article 59

Citizens' exercise of their rights and freedoms is inseparable from the performance of their duties and obligations.

Citizens of the USSR are obliged to observe the USSR Constitution and Soviet laws, comply with the standards of socialist conduct, and uphold the honour and dignity of Soviet citizenship.

Article 60

It is the duty of, and a matter of honour for, every able-bodied citizen of the USSR to work conscientiously in his chosen, socially-useful occupation, and strictly to observe labour discipline. Evasion of such work is incompatible with the principles of socialist society.

Article 61

Citizens of the USSR are obliged to preserve and protect socialist property. It is the duty of a citizen of the USSR to combat misappropriation and squandering of state and socially-owned property and to make thrifty use of the people's wealth.

Persons encroaching in any way on socialist property shall be punished in accordance with the law.

Article 62

Citizens of the USSR have a duty to safeguard the interests of the Soviet state, and to enhance its power and prestige.

Defence of the Socialist Motherland is the sacred duty of every citizen of the USSR.

Betrayal of the Motherland is the gravest of crimes against the people.

Article 63

Military service in the ranks of the USSR Armed Forces is an honourable duty of Soviet citizens.

Article 64

It is the duty of every citizen of the USSR to respect the dignity of other citizens, and to strengthen friendship of the nations and nationalities of the multinational Soviet state.

Article 65

A citizen of the USSR is obliged to respect the rights and lawful interests of other persons, to be uncompromising toward anti-social behaviour, and to help maintain public order.

Article 66

Citizens of the USSR are obliged to concern themselves with the upbringing of children, to prepare them for socially useful work, and to raise them as worthy members of socialist society. Children are obliged to care for their parents and help them.

Article 67

Citizens of the USSR are obliged to protect nature and conserve its riches.

Article 68

Concern for the preservation of historical monuments and other cultural values is a duty and obligation of citizens of the USSR.

Article 69

It is the internationalist duty of citizens of the USSR to promote friendship and co-operation with peoples of other lands and help maintain and strengthen world peace.

III
The National-State Structure of the USSR

Chapter 8
The USSR — a Federal State

Article 70

The Union of Soviet Socialist Republics is an integral, federal, multinational state formed on the principle of socialist federalism as a result of the free self-determination of nations and the voluntary association of equal Soviet Socialist Republics.

The USSR embodies the state unity of the Soviet people and draws all its nations and nationalities together for the purpose of jointly building communism.

Article 71

The Union of Soviet Socialist Republics unites:
the Russian Soviet Federative Socialist Republic,
the Ukrainian Soviet Socialist Republic,
the Byelorussian Soviet Socialist Republic,
the Uzbek Soviet Socialist Republic,
the Kazakh Soviet Socialist Republic,
the Georgian Soviet Socialist Republic,
the Azerbaijan Soviet Socialist Republic,
the Lithuanian Soviet Socialist Republic,
the Moldavian Soviet Socialist Republic,
the Latvian Soviet Socialist Republic,
the Kirghiz Soviet Socialist Republic,
the Tajik Soviet Socialist Republic,
the Armenian Soviet Socialist Republic,
the Turkmen Soviet Socialist Republic,
the Estonian Soviet Socialist Republic.

Article 72

Each Union Republic shall retain the right freely to secede from the USSR.

Article 73

The jurisdiction of the Union of Soviet Socialist Republics, as represented by its highest bodies of state power and administration, shall cover:

1) admission of new republics to the USSR; endorsement of the formation of new autonomous republics and autonomous regions within Union Republics;

2) determination of the state boundaries of the USSR and approval of changes in the boundaries between Union Republics;

3) establishment of the general principles for the organisation and functioning of republican and local bodies of state power and administration;

4) ensurance of uniformity of legislative norms throughout the USSR and establishment of the fundamentals of the legislation of the Union of Soviet Socialist Republics and Union Republics;

5) pursuance of a uniform social and economic policy; direction of the country's economy; determination of the main lines of scientific and technological progress and the general measures for rational exploitation and conservation of natural resources; the drafting and approval of state plans for the economic and social development of the USSR, and endorsement of reports on their fulfilment;

6) drafting and approval of the consolidated Budget of the USSR, and endorsement of the report on its execution; the management of a single monetary and credit system; determination of the taxes and revenues forming the Budget of the USSR; and the formulation of prices and wages policy;

7) direction of the sectors of the economy, and of enterprises and amalgamations under All-Union jurisdiction, and general direction of industries under Union-Republic jurisdiction;

8) issues of war and peace, defence of the sovereignty of the USSR and safeguarding

of its frontiers and territory, and organisation of defence; direction of the USSR Armed Forces;

9) state security;

10) representation of the USSR in international relations; the USSR's relations with other states and with international organisations; establishment of the general procedure for, and co-ordination of, the relations of Union Republics with other states and with international organisations; foreign trade and other forms of external economic activity on the basis of state monopoly;

11) control over observance of the USSR Constitution, and ensurance of conformity of the constitutions of Union Republics to the USSR Constitution;

12) settlement of other matters of All-Union importance.

Article 74

The laws of the USSR shall have the same force in all Union Republics. In the event of a discrepancy between a Union Republic law and an All-Union law, the law of the USSR shall prevail.

Article 75

The territory of the Union of Soviet Socialist Republics is a single entity and comprises the territories of the Union Republics.

Chapter 9
The Union Soviet Socialist Republic

Article 76

A Union Republic is a sovereign Soviet socialist state that has united with other Soviet Republics in the Union of Soviet Socialist Republics.

Outside the spheres listed in Article 73 of the USSR Constitution, a Union Republic exercises independent authority on its territory.

A Union Republic shall have its own Constitution conforming to the USSR Constitution with the specific features of the Republic being taken into account.

Article 77

Union Republics shall take part in the solution of problems within the jurisdiction of the USSR at Congresses of USSR People's Deputies, in the USSR Supreme Soviet, in the Presidium of the USSR Supreme Soviet, in the Federation Council, in the USSR Cabinet of Ministers and other bodies of the USSR.

A Union Republic shall ensure comprehensive economic and social development on its territory, facilitate the exercise of the powers of the USSR on its territory, and implement the decisions of the highest bodies of state power and administration of the USSR.

In matters that come within its jurisdiction, a Union Republic shall co-ordinate and control the activity of enterprises, institutions, and organisations subordinate to the Union.

Article 78

The territory of a Union Republic may not be altered without its consent. The boundaries between Union Republics may be altered by mutual agreement of the Republics concerned, subject to ratification by the Union of Soviet Socialist Republics.

Article 79

A Union Republic shall determine its division into territories, regions, areas, and districts, and decide other matters relating to its administrative and territorial structure.

Article 80

A Union Republic has the right to enter into relations with other states, conclude treaties with them, exchange diplomatic and consular representatives, and take part in the work of international organisations.

Article 81

The sovereign rights of Union Republics shall be safeguarded by the USSR.

Chapter 10
The Autonomous Soviet Socialist Republic

Article 82

An Autonomous Republic is a constituent part of a Union Republic.

In spheres not within the jurisdiction of the Union of Soviet Socialist Republics and the Union Republic, an Autonomous Republic shall deal independently with matters within its jurisdiction.

An Autonomous Republic shall have its own Constitution conforming to those of the USSR and the Union Republic, the specific features of the Autonomous Republic being taken into account.

Article 83

An Autonomous Republic takes part in decision-making through the highest bodies of state power and administration of the USSR and of the Union Republic respectively in matters that come within the jurisdiction of the USSR and the Union Republic.

An Autonomous Republic shall ensure comprehensive economic and social development on its territory, facilitate the exercise of the powers of the USSR and the Union Republic on its territory, and implement decisions of the highest bodies of state power

and administration of the USSR and the Union Republic.

In matters within its jurisdiction, an Autonomous Republic shall co-ordinate and control the activity of enterprises, institutions, and organisations subordinate to the Union or the Union Republic.

Article 84

The territory of an Autonomous Republic may not be altered without its consent.

Article 85

The Russian Soviet Federative Socialist Republic includes the Bashkir, Buryat, Daghestan, Kabardin-Balkar, Kalmyk, Karelian, Komi, Mari, Mordovian, North Ossetian, Tatar, Tuva, Udmurt, Chechen-Ingush, Chuvash, and Yakut Autonomous Soviet Socialist Republics.

The Uzbek Soviet Socialist Republic includes the Kara-Kalpak Autonomous Soviet Socialist Republic.

The Georgian Soviet Socialist Republic Republic includes the Abkhazian and Adzhar Autonomous Soviet Socialist Republics.

The Azerbaijan Soviet Socialist Republic includes the Nakhichevan Autonomous Soviet Socialist Republic.

Chapter 11
The Autonomous Region and Autonomous Area

Article 86

An Autonomous Region is a constituent part of a Union Republic or Territory. The Law on an Autonomous Region, upon submission by the Soviet of People's Deputies of the Autonomous Region concerned, shall be adopted by the Supreme Soviet of the Union Republic.

Article 87

The Russian Soviet Federative Socialist Republic includes the Adyghei, Gorno-Altai, Jewish, Karachai-Circassian, and Khakass Autonomous Regions.

The Georgian Soviet Socialist Republic includes the South Ossetian Autonomous Region.

The Azerbaijan Soviet Socialist Republic includes the Nagorno-Karabakh Autonomous Region.

The Tajik Soviet Socialist Republic includes the Gorno-Badakhshan Autonomous Region.

Article 88

An Autonomous Area is a constituent part of a Territory or Region. The Law on an Autonomous Area shall be adopted by the Supreme Soviet of the Union Republic concerned.

IV
Soviets of People's Deputies and Electoral Procedure

Chapter 12
The System of Soviets of People's Deputies and the Principles of Their Work

Article 89

The Soviets of People's Deputies, i.e. the Congress of USSR People's Deputies and the USSR Supreme Soviet, the Congresses of People's Deputies and the Supreme Soviets of Union and Autonomous Republics, the Soviets of People's Deputies of Autonomous Regions, Autonomous Areas, territories and other administrative-territorial entities, shall constitute a single system of bodies of state power.

Article 90

The term of the Soviets of People's Deputies shall be five years.

Elections of USSR People's Deputies shall be called not later than four months before the expiry of the term of powers of the Congress of USSR People's Deputies.

The term and the procedure for elections of People's Deputies of Union and Autonomous Republics, and of local Soviets of People's Deputies shall be determined by the laws of the Union and Autonomous Republics.

Article 91

The Congress of People's Deputies and sessions of the Supreme Soviets and local Soviets shall settle the most important matters of national, republican and local significance or call a referendum.

The Supreme Soviets of Union and Autonomous Republics shall be elected directly by the voters, or by Congresses of People's Deputies in those republics which provide for the creation of such congresses.

The Soviets of People's Deputies shall form committees and standing commissions, and executive, administrative and other bodies accountable to them.

Executives elected or appointed by Soviets of People's Deputies, with the exception of judges, may not hold their posts for more than two terms in succession.

Any official guilty of poor performance in his job may be released from his post before the expiry of his term.

Article 92

Soviets of People's Deputies shall form people's control bodies combining state control with public control by the working people at enterprises, institutions, and organisations.

People's control bodies shall check on

conformity with the law and on fulfilment of state programmes and assignments, combat breaches of state discipline, narrow localistic tendencies and departmental attitudes, mismanagement, wastefulness, red tape and bureaucracy; they shall co-ordinate the work of other control bodies and help improve the structure and functioning of the state apparatus.

Article 93

Soviets of People's Deputies shall administer all sectors of state, economic, social and cultural development, either directly or through bodies instituted by them, taking decisions, ensuring their execution, and verifying their implementation.

Article 94

Soviets of People's Deputies shall function on the basis of collective, free and constructive discussion and decision-making, of glasnost, of systematic reporting back to them and the people by their executive-administrative and other bodies set up by the Soviets, and of involving citizens on a broad scale in their work.

Soviets of People's Deputies and the bodies set up by them shall take into account public opinion, submit for public discussion major questions of national and local importance and systematically inform the citizens about their work and decisions taken by them.

Chapter 13
The Electoral System

Article 95

The elections of People's Deputies shall be held in single-candidacy or multi-candidacy districts on the basis of universal, equal and direct suffrage by secret ballot.

Some People's Deputies of Union and Autonomous Republics may be elected from public organisations if this is provided for in the constitutions of those republics.

Article 96

Elections of People's Deputies from electoral districts shall be universal: citizens of the USSR who have reached the age of 18 shall have the right to vote.

To be elected a People's Deputy, a citizen of the USSR must have reached the age of 21.

A citizen of the USSR cannot simultaneously be a People's Deputy to more than two Soviets of People's Deputies.

Members of the USSR Cabinet of Ministers, Councils of Ministers of the Union and Autonomous Republics and executive committees of the local Soviets of People's Deputies, with the exception of the chairman of these bodies, and also heads of departments, sectors and administrations of the executive committees of the local Soviets and judges cannot be elected deputies to the Soviet which appoints or elects them.

Mentally ill people who have been recognised incapable by the court and persons who have been sentenced to terms of imprisonment by the court shall not have the right to vote. Those who have been detained in accordance with the Code of Criminal Procedure shall not vote.

Any direct or indirect restriction of the electoral rights of citizens of the USSR is inadmissible and shall be punished by law.

Article 97

Elections of People's Deputies from electoral districts shall be equal: in every electoral district each voter shall have one vote; all voters shall exercise the franchise on an equal footing.

Article 98

Elections of People's Deputies from electoral districts shall be direct: People's Deputies shall be elected by citizens by direct vote.

Article 99

Voting at the elections of People's Deputies shall be secret: checking on the voters' exercise of the franchise is inadmissible.

Article 100

The following shall have the right to nominate candidates for election to People's Deputies from electoral districts: work collectives, the staff of specialised secondary and higher schools, as well as neighbourhood and army unit meetings. Bodies and organisations which have a right to nominate candidates for election to People's Deputies from public organisations shall be determined in accordance with the laws of the USSR and Union and Autonomous Republics.

The number of candidates to People's Deputies shall not be limited. Any participants in the election meetings may propose candidates, including himself.

There may be any number of candidates on one ballot paper.

Candidates for People's Deputies shall take part in the election campaign on an equal footing.

With a view to providing equal conditions for all candidates for election to People's Deputies, expenditure on the election campaign and elections of People's Deputies shall be the responsibility of the appropriate election commissions, which shall draw on a common fund created by the state, as well as by voluntary donations of enterprises, public organisations and individuals.

Article 101

Preparations for the election of People's Deputies shall be made openly and publicly.

Elections shall be supervised by electoral commissions of representatives elected by meetings (conferences) of work collectives, public organisations, the staff of specialised secondary and higher schools, and also neighbourhood and army unit meetings.

Citizens of the USSR, work collectives, public organisations, the staff of specialised and higher schools, and servicemen in their units shall be guaranteed the right to free and comprehensive discussion on the political, business and personal qualities of candidates for People's Deputies, as well as the right to campaign for and against them at meetings, in the press, and on television and radio.

The procedure for holding elections of People's Deputies is determined by the laws of the Union of Soviet Socialist Republics and Union and Autonomous Republics.

Article 102

Voters and public organisations shall give mandates to their deputies.

The appropriate Soviets of People's Deputies shall examine electors' mandates, take them into account in drafting economic and social development plans and, in drawing up the budget, organise the implementation of the mandates, and inform citizens of the results.

Chapter 14
People's Deputies

Article 103

Deputies are the plenipotentiary representatives of the people in the Soviets of People's Deputies.

In the Soviets, People's Deputies deal with matters relating to state, economic, and social and cultural development, carry out the decisions of the Soviets, and exercise control over the work of state bodies, enterprises, institutions and organisations.

People's Deputies shall be guided in their activity by the interests of the state as a whole, take the needs of their constituents and the interests of the public organisations that have elected them into account, and work to implement the mandates they have received from their voters and public organisations.

Article 104

People's Deputies shall exercise their powers, as a rule, without discontinuing their regular employment or duties.

During meetings of Congresses of People's Deputies, sessions of Supreme Soviets or local Soviets of People's Deputies, and in order to exercise their deputy's powers in other cases stipulated by law, deputies shall be released from their regular employment or duties and compensated from the appropriate state or local budget for the expenses connected with their work as deputies.

Article 105

Deputies have the right to address inquiries to the appropriate state bodies and officials, who are obliged to reply to them at a Congress of People's Deputies or a session of a Supreme Soviet or a local Soviet of People's Deputies.

Deputies have the right to approach any state or public body, enterprise, institution, or organisation on matters arising from their work as deputies and to take part in considering the questions raised by them. Heads of state or public bodies, enterprises, institutions or organisations concerned are obliged to receive Deputies without delay and to consider their

proposals within the time limit established by law.

Article 106

Deputies shall be provided with conditions for the unhampered and effective exercise of their rights and duties.

The immunity of Deputies, and other guarantees of their activity as Deputies, are defined in the Law on the Status of Deputies and other legislative acts of the USSR and of Union and Autonomous Republics.

Article 107

Deputies shall report on their work and on that of a Congress of People's Deputies, a Supreme Soviet or a local Soviet of People's Deputies to their constituents, and to the work collectives and public organisations that nominated them or to the public organisations that elected them.

Deputies who have not justified the confidence of their constituents or public organisations may be recalled at any time by a decision of a majority of voters or the public organisations that elected them, in accordance with the procedure established by law.

V

Higher Bodies of State Power and Administration of the USSR

Chapter 15
The Congress of USSR People's Deputies and the USSR Supreme Soviet

Article 108

The highest body of state power of the USSR shall be the Congress of USSR People's Deputies.

The Congress of USSR People's Deputies is empowered to consider and resolve any issue within the jurisdiction of the Union of Soviet Socialist Republics.

The exclusive prerogative of the Congress of USSR People's Deputies shall be:

1) adoption and amendment of the USSR Constitution;

2) decision-making on questions of the national and state structure of the USSR within the jurisdiction of the Union of Soviet Socialist Republics;

3) determination of the state borders of the USSR; endorsement of border changes between the Union Republics;

4) definition of guidelines for home and foreign policies of the USSR;

5) approval of long-term state plans and most important national programmes for the economic and social development of the USSR;

6) election of the USSR Supreme Soviet and of the Chairman of the USSR Supreme Soviet;

7) endorsement of the Chairman of the USSR Supreme Court, the USSR Procurator-General, and the Chairman of the USSR Supreme Arbitration Court;

8) election of the USSR Committee for Constitutional Supervision on the initiative of the Chairman of the USSR Supreme Soviet;

9) revocation of legislative acts passed by the USSR Supreme Soviet;

10) decision-making on holding a nation-wide vote (referendum).

The Congress of USSR People's Deputies shall adopt laws of the USSR and decrees by a majority vote of USSR People's Deputies.

Article 109

The Congress of USSR People's Deputies shall consist of 2,250 deputies, to be elected in the following order:

750 deputies from territorial electoral districts with equal numbers of voters;

750 deputies from national-territorial electoral districts on the basis of the following representation: 32 deputies from each Union Republic, 11 deputies from each Autonomous Republic, 5 deputies from each Autonomous Region and one deputy from each Autonomous Area;

750 deputies from All-Union public organisations on the basis of the representation established by the Law on the Election of USSR People's Deputies.

Article 110

The Congress of USSR People's Deputies shall meet in its first session not later than two months after the elections.

The Congress of USSR People's Deputies, on the recommendation of the Credentials Commission elected by it, shall decide on the eligibility of deputies, and, in cases when the election law has been violated, shall declare the election of the deputies concerned null and void.

The Congress of USSR People's Deputies is convened by the USSR Supreme Soviet.

The Congress of USSR People's Deputies shall meet in regular session at least once a year. Extraordinary sessions are convened on the initiative of the USSR Supreme Soviet or on the proposal of one of its Chambers, the USSR President, at least one-fifth of the USSR People's Deputies, or on the initiative of a Union Republic in the person of its supreme body of state power.

Following elections, the first sitting of the Congress of USSR People's Deputies shall be conducted by the Chairman of the Central Electoral Commission for Electing USSR People's Deputies and subsequently by the Chairman of the USSR Supreme Soviet.

Article 111

The USSR Supreme Soviet shall be the permanent legislative and control body of state power of the USSR.

The USSR Supreme Soviet shall be elected by secret ballot from among the USSR People's Deputies at the Congress of USSR People's Deputies and shall be accountable to it.

The USSR Supreme Soviet shall consist of two chambers: the Soviet of the Union and the Soviet of Nationalities, each having equal numbers of deputies. The Chambers of the USSR Supreme Soviet shall have equal rights.

The Chambers shall be elected at the Congress of USSR People's Deputies by general ballot. The Soviet of the Union shall be elected from among the USSR People's Deputies representing territorial electoral districts and the USSR People's Deputies representing public organisations, taking into account the size of the electorate in a Union Republic or region. The Soviet of Nationalities shall be elected from among USSR People's Deputies representing national-territorial electoral districts and the USSR People's Deputies representing public organisations on the basis of the following representation: 11 deputies from each Union Republic, 4 deputies from each Autonomous Republic, 2 deputies from each Autonomous Region and one deputy from each Autonomous Area.

The Congress of People's Deputies shall annually re-elect one-fifth of the deputies to the Soviet of the Union and the Soviet of Nationalities.

Each Chamber of the USSR Supreme Soviet shall elect a Chairman and two Deputy-Chairmen. The Chairmen of the Soviet of the Union and of the Soviet of Nationalities shall preside over the sittings of their respective Chambers and conduct their affairs.

Joint sittings of the Chambers shall be conducted by the Chairman of the USSR Supreme Soviet, or alternately by the Chairmen of the Soviet of the Union and of the Soviet of Nationalities.

Article 112

The USSR Supreme Soviet shall be annually convened by the Chairman of the USSR Supreme Soviet for regular sessions (autumn and spring), each lasting from three to four months.

Extraordinary sessions shall be convened by the Chairman of the USSR Supreme Soviet on his own initiative or on the proposal of the USSR President, a Union Republic in the person of its supreme body of state power, or at least one-third of the members of one of the Chambers of the USSR Supreme Soviet.

A session of the USSR Supreme Soviet shall consist of separate and joint sittings of the Chambers, and of meetings of the standing commissions of the Chambers and committees of the USSR Supreme Soviet held between the sittings of the Chambers. A session may be opened or closed at either separate or joint sittings of the Chambers.

Upon the expiry of the mandate of the Congress of USSR People's Deputies, the USSR Supreme Soviet shall retain its mandate until the formation by a newly-elected Congress of USSR People's Deputics of a new USSR Supreme Soviet.

Article 113

The USSR Supreme Soviet shall:
1) name the date of elections of USSR People's Deputies and approve the composition of the Central Electoral Commission for the Election of USSR People's Deputies;
2) when proposed by the USSR President, form and abolish ministries and other central organs of state administration of the USSR;
3) on the recommendation of the USSR President, approve the appointment of the Prime Minister. At a session, it shall approve and/or reject candidates for membership of the USSR Cabinet of Ministers and of the

USSR Security Council, and give its consent to their release from office;

4) elect the USSR Supreme Court and the USSR Supreme Arbitration Court, appoint the USSR Procurator-General, approve the collegium of the USSR Procurator-General's office and appoint the Chairman of the USSR Control Chamber;

5) regularly hear reports of the bodies which it forms or elects and of the officials whom it appoints or elects;

6) ensure uniformity of legislative regulation on the whole territory of the USSR and establish the fundamentals of legislation of the USSR and the Union Republics;

7) within the competence of the Union of Soviet Socialist Republics, juridicially regulate the procedure for the implementation of citizens' constitutional rights, freedoms and duties, relations of ownership, the organisation of economic management and social and cultural development, the budget and financial system, payments and pricing, taxation, environmental protection and the utilisation of natural resources, and other relations;

8) interpret laws of the USSR;

9) establish the general principles of the organisation and activity of republican and local bodies of state power and administration, and to determine the fundamentals of the legal status of public organisations;

10) submit the drafts of long-term state plans and the most important All-Union programmes of economic and social development of the USSR for endorsement by the Congress of USSR People's Deputies; approve state plans for economic and social development of the USSR and the State Budget of the USSR; exercise control over the course of the fulfilment of the plan and budget; approve the reports on their fulfilment; in case of necessity make changes in the plan and the budget;

11) ratify and renounce international treaties of the USSR;

12) exercise control over granting loans, rendering economic and other assistance to foreign states, and concluding agreements on state loans and credits received from sources abroad;

13) outline planning of defence and state security; introduce martial law or a state of emergency throughout the country; declare a state of war should it become necessary to fulfil international commitments on mutual defence against aggression;

14) take decisions on the utilisation of contingents of the USSR Armed Forces should it become necessary to fulfil international agreements on maintaining peace and security;

15) institute military and diplomatic ranks and other special titles;

16) introduce orders and medals of the USSR; institute honorary titles of the USSR;

17) issue All-Union acts of amnesty;

18) have the right to rescind decisions of the USSR Cabinet of Ministers in the event of their being inconsistent with the USSR Constitution and laws of the USSR;

19) rescind decisions and directives of the Councils of Ministers of the Union Republics should they fail to conform to the Constitution and laws of the USSR;

20) in the period between Congresses of USSR People's Deputies decide on the holding of a nationwide referendum (referendum of the USSR);

21) resolve other questions within the competence of the USSR except those which are within the exclusive competence of the Congress of USSR People's Deputies.

The USSR Supreme Soviet adopts laws of the USSR and resolutions.

The laws and resolutions adopted by the USSR Supreme Soviet may not contradict the laws and other acts adopted by the Congress of USSR People's Deputies.

Article 114

The right to initiate legislation at the Congress of USSR People's Deputies and at the USSR Supreme Soviet shall be vested in: USSR People's Deputies; the Soviet of the Union; the Soviet of Nationalities; the Chairman of the USSR Supreme Soviet; the standing commissions of the chambers and committees of the USSR Supreme Soviet; the USSR President; the Federation Council; the USSR Committee for Constitutional Supervision; the Union and Autonomous Republics through their supreme bodies of state power; Autonomous Regions; Autonomous Areas; the USSR Supreme Court; the USSR Procurator-General; and the USSR Supreme Arbitration Court.

The right to initiate legislation shall also be granted to public organisations in the person of their All-Union bodies, and to the USSR Academy of Sciences.

Article 115

Draft laws submitted for consideration by the USSR Supreme Soviet shall be debated by its Chambers at separate or joint sittings.

A law of the USSR shall be deemed adopted when a majority of the deputies have voted for it in each Chamber.

Draft laws and other major matters of state may be submitted for nationwide debate by a decision of the USSR Supreme Soviet taken on its own initiative or on the proposal of a Union Republic through its highest body of state power.

Article 116

Each Chamber of the USSR Supreme Soviet has the right to consider any question within the competence of the USSR Supreme Soviet.

Questions of social and economic development and of the development of the state, which are of common significance to the whole country, of the rights, freedoms and duties of citizens of the USSR, of foreign policy, and of defence and state security of the USSR are subject, above all, to consideration in the Soviet of the Union.

Questions of ensuring national equality and the interests of nationalities and ethnic groups in combination with the common interests and requirements of the Soviet multinational state, and perfection of the legislation regulating interethnic relations are subject, above all, to consideration in the Soviet of Nationalities.

Each Chamber adopts decisions within its competence.

A decision adopted by one of the Chambers shall, if necessary, be submitted to the other Chamber and in the event of approval by it shall acquire the force of a decision of the USSR Supreme Soviet.

Article 117

In the event of a disagreement between the Soviet of the Union and the Soviet of Nationalities, the matter at issue shall be referred for settlement to a conciliation commission, formed by the Chambers on a parity basis, after which it shall be considered for a second time by the Soviet of the Union and the Soviet of Nationalities.

Article 118

The work of the USSR Supreme Soviet shall be organised by the Presidium of the USSR Supreme Soviet, headed by the Chairman of the USSR Supreme Soviet. The Presidium of the USSR Supreme Soviet shall include the Chairman of the Soviet of the Union and the Chairman of the Soviet of Nationalities, their deputies, the chairmen of the standing commissions of the Chambers and committees of the USSR Supreme Soviet, other USSR People's Deputies — one from each of the Union Republics, as well as two representatives of the Autonomous Republics and one representative of the Autonomous Regions and Autonomous Areas.

The Presidium of the USSR Supreme Soviet shall prepare for sessions of the Congress and of the USSR Supreme Soviet, coordinate the work of the permanent commissions of the Chambers and committees of the USSR Supreme Soviet, and organise nationwide discussion of draft laws of the USSR and of other vital state issues.

The Presidium of the USSR Supreme Soviet shall ensure the publication of laws of the USSR and other acts passed by the Congress of USSR People's Deputies, by the USSR Supreme Soviet, by its Chambers, and by the USSR President in the languages of the Union Republics.

The decisions of the Presidium of the USSR Supreme Soviet shall be issued in the form of resolutions.

Article 119

The Chairman of the USSR Supreme Soviet shall be elected by the Congress of USSR People's Deputies from among USSR People's Deputies, by secret ballot, for a term of five years and for not more than two consecutive terms. At any time the Chairman may be recalled by the Congress of USSR People's Deputies by secret ballot.

The Chairman of the USSR Supreme Soviet shall report to the Congress of USSR People's Deputies and to the USSR Supreme Soviet.

The Chairman of the USSR Supreme Soviet shall issue resolutions on the convocation of the USSR Supreme Soviet, and decrees on other matters.

Article 120

The Soviet of the Union and the Soviet of Nationalities shall elect from among the members of the USSR Supreme Soviet and other USSR People's Deputies standing commissions of their Chambers to carry out legislative work and to make a preliminary review of matters coming within the jurisdiction of the USSR Supreme Soviet, to promote the implementation of laws of the USSR and other decisions adopted by the Congress of USSR People's Deputies and the USSR Supreme Soviet, and to supervise the performance of state bodies and organisations.

With the same aims the Chambers of the USSR Supreme Soviet may set up committees of the USSR Supreme Soviet on a parity basis.

The USSR Supreme Soviet, including both its Chambers, may set up, when they find it necessary, commissions of inquiry and audit, and commissions on any other matter.

The standing commissions of the Chambers and the committees of the USSR Supreme Soviet shall annually replace one-fifth of their members.

Article 121

The laws and other decisions of the Congress of USSR People's Deputies and the USSR Supreme Soviet, and resolutions of its Chambers, shall be adopted, as a rule, after a preliminary review of the drafts by the corresponding standing commissions of the Chambers or committees of the USSR Supreme Soviet.

Officials of the USSR Cabinet of Ministers, the USSR Supreme Court, the USSR Supreme Arbitration Court, and the collegium of the USSR Procurator-General's office, and the Chairman of the USSR Control Chamber shall be appointed and elected upon the conclusions of the appropriate permanent commissions of the Chambers or committees of the USSR Supreme Soviet.

All state and public bodies, organisations and officials must abide by the demands of the commissions of the Chambers and commissions and committees of the USSR Supreme Soviet and provide them with necessary materials and documents.

The recommendations of the commissions and committees must be considered by state and public bodies, institutions and organisations. The results of such examinations and the measures adopted shall be reported to the commissions and committees within the terms set by them.

Article 122

A USSR People's Deputy shall have the right during sessions of the Congress of USSR People's Deputies and of the USSR Supreme Soviet to address enquiries to the USSR Cabinet of Ministers and to the heads of other bodies formed or elected by the Congress of USSR People's Deputies, or by the USSR Supreme Soviet; and during sessions of the Congress of USSR People's Deputies to address enquiries to the USSR President. The body or official to whom the enquiry is addressed shall be obliged to give a verbal or written reply within three days during the current Congress or current session of the USSR Supreme Soviet.

Article 123

USSR People's Deputies shall be entitled to be freed from their duties at their place of employment for the term needed for the performance of their deputies' functions at the Congress of USSR People's Deputies, at the USSR Supreme Soviet, in its Chambers, commissions and committees, and among their electors.

A USSR People's Deputy may not be prosecuted or arrested, or receive a court-imposed administrative penalty without the sanction of the USSR Supreme Soviet, and between sessions, without the consent of the Presidium of the USSR Supreme Soviet.

Article 124

The USSR Committee for Constitutional Supervision shall be elected by the Congress of USSR People's Deputies from among people well-versed in politics and law and shall consist of a Chairman, a deputy chairman and 25 members, including one from each Union Republic.

The Committee for Constitutional Supervision shall be elected for a term of ten years.

The persons elected to sit on the Committee for Constitutional Supervision may not simultaneously be part of those bodies whose acts are supervised by the Committee.

The persons elected to sit on the Committee for Constitutional Supervision shall be independent in carrying out their duties, the USSR Constitution being their only authority.

The USSR Committee for Constitutional Supervision:

1) shall submit to the Congress of USSR People's Deputies at the latter's request reports on whether the USSR draft laws and other acts put before the Congress conform with the USSR Constitution;

2) at the request of no less than one-fifth of USSR People's Deputies, the USSR President, or the supreme bodies of state power of the Union Republics, shall present to the Congress of USSR People's Deputies its conclusions on the constitutionality of the USSR laws and other acts adopted by the Congress.

— on the instruction of the Congress of USSR People's Deputies and at the request of the USSR Supreme Soviet, shall present its conclusions on the conformity with the USSR Constitution and USSR laws of the decrees passed by the USSR President;

3) on the instruction of the Congress of USSR People's Deputies or at the request of the USSR Supreme Soviet, the USSR President, the Chairman of the USSR Supreme Soviet, or the supreme bodies of state power of the Union Republics, shall present to the Congress of USSR People's Deputies or to the USSR Supreme Soviet its conclusions

on the conformity of the constitutions of the Union Republics with the USSR Constitution and of the laws of the Union Republics with those of the USSR;

4) on the instruction of the Congress of USSR People's Deputies or on the initiative of at least one-fifth of the members of the USSR Supreme Soviet, the USSR President, or the supreme bodies of state power of the Union Republics, shall present to the USSR Supreme Soviet or to the USSR President its conclusions on the conformity of the acts adopted by the USSR Supreme Soviet and its Chambers and of draft acts submitted to these bodies for consideration, with the Constitution and laws of the USSR as adopted by the Congress of USSR People's Deputies, and also on the conformity of the resolutions and orders of the USSR Cabinet of Ministers with the laws of the USSR as adopted by the USSR Supreme Soviet. It shall in addition present its conclusions on the compatibility of international agreements and other commitments of the USSR and of the Union Republics with the Constitution and laws of the USSR.

5) on the instruction of the Congress of USSR People's Deputies or at the request of the USSR Supreme Soviet, its Chambers, the USSR President, the Chairman of the USSR Supreme Soviet, the permanent commissions of the Chambers and committees of the USSR Supreme Soviet, the USSR Cabinet of Ministers, the supreme bodies of state power of the Union Republics, the USSR Control Chamber, the USSR Supreme Court, the USSR Procurator-General, the USSR Supreme Arbitration Court, or the All-Union bodies of public organisations and the USSR Academy of Sciences, it shall present its conclusions on the conformity with the Constitution and laws of the USSR of the normative legal acts issued by other state bodies and public organisations which, in accordance with the USSR Constitution, are not under the procurator's supervision.

The Committee for Constitutional Supervision may, on its own initiative, submit reports on whether the acts of the highest bodies of state power and administration of the USSR and other bodies formed or elected by the Congress of USSR People's Deputies and the USSR Supreme Soviet conform with the Constitution and laws of the USSR.

Should any one act or any of its provisions fail to conform with the Constitution or laws of the USSR, the Committee for Constitutional Supervision shall make its report available to the body which introduced the act so that it may be modified to conform with the USSR Constitution. The Committee's report shall suspend enforcement of the act or any of its provisions found to be at variance with the USSR Constitution or USSR legislation, with the exception of USSR laws passed by the Congress of USSR People's Deputies, and the constitutions of Union Republics. An act or any of its provisions found by the Committee to violate the rights and freedoms of citizens shall cease to be valid once the relevant report is issued.

The body which introduced the act shall bring it in conformity with the USSR Constitution or with USSR legislation. Should the act fail to be modified accordingly, the Committee for Constitutional Supervision shall request, respectively, the Congress of USSR People's Deputies, the USSR Supreme Soviet, the USSR President and the USSR Cabinet of Ministers to abrogate acts which have been introduced by the bodies or officials accountable to them and which fail to conform with the Constitution or laws of the USSR.

The Committee's report may be rejected by the Congress of USSR People's Deputies, with two-thirds of the votes of the total number of USSR People's Deputies.

The work of the USSR Committee for

Constitutional Supervision shall be governed by the Law on Constitutional Supervision in the USSR.

Article 125

The Congress of USSR People's Deputies and the USSR Supreme Soviet shall supervise all government bodies accountable to them.

The USSR Supreme Soviet shall direct the activities of the USSR Control Chamber and hear on a regular basis its reports on the results of supervision of the supply and spending of money out of the federal budget and the management of federal property.

The organisation and procedure of the work of the USSR Control Chamber shall be regulated by laws of the USSR.

Article 126

The working procedure of the Congress of USSR People's Deputies, the USSR Supreme Soviet and their organs is determined by the regulations of the Congress of USSR People's Deputies and the USSR Supreme Soviet and by other laws of the USSR issued on the basis of the USSR Constitution.

Chapter 15 (1)
The USSR President

Article 127

The head of the Soviet state, the Union of Soviet Socialist Republics, shall be the USSR President.

Article 127 (1)

Any citizen of the USSR not younger than thirty-five and not older than sixty-five years old may be elected USSR President. No single person may remain USSR President for more than two terms.

The USSR President shall be elected by citizens of the USSR on the basis of universal, equal and direct electoral right by secret ballot for a term of five years. The number of candidates for the post of USSR President shall not be limited. The election of the USSR President shall be ruled valid if at least fifty per cent of the voters have taken part. A candidate who gains more than fifty per cent of the total number of votes cast in the election, in the USSR overall and in a majority of the Union Republics, shall be regarded elected as President.

The procedure for the election of the USSR President shall be determined by a law of the USSR.

The USSR President may not be a People's Deputy.

The USSR President may receive a salary for this post only.

Article 127 (2)

Upon assuming the post, the USSR President shall be sworn in at a session of the Congress of USSR People's Deputies.

Article 127 (3)

The USSR President shall:

1) act as a guarantor of the rights and liberties of Soviet citizens, and of the Constitution and laws of the USSR;

2) adopt the necessary measures to protect the sovereignty of the USSR and of the Union Republics, the security and territorial integrity of the country, and to implement the principles of the national-state structure of the USSR;

3) represent the Union of Soviet Socialist Republics inside the country and in international relations;

4) head the system of the organs of state administration and ensure their co-operation with the highest bodies of state power of the USSR;

5) present to the Congress of USSR

People's Deputies annual reports on the state of the nation and inform the USSR Supreme Soviet on key issues of domestic and foreign policy of the USSR;

6) form the USSR Cabinet of Ministers, taking into account the opinion of the Federation Council and after consultation with the USSR Supreme Soviet, make changes to it, present to the USSR Supreme Soviet a candidate for the post of Prime Minister; dismiss the Prime Minister and members of the USSR Cabinet of Ministers after consultation with the USSR Supreme Soviet;

7) present to the USSR Supreme Soviet candidates for the posts of Chairman of the USSR Supreme Court, the USSR Procurator-General and the Chairman of the USSR Supreme Arbitration Court and then present these officials to the Congress of USSR People's Deputies for approval; submit proposals to the USSR Supreme Soviet and the Congress of USSR People's Deputies on the dismissal of the said officials, with the exception of the Chairman of the USSR Supreme Court;

8) sign laws of the USSR; have the right within two weeks to return a law with his objections to the USSR Supreme Soviet for further discussion and voting. Should the USSR Supreme Soviet confirm its original decision by a two-thirds majority in both Chambers, the USSR President shall sign the law;

9) have the right to repeal resolutions and instructions of the USSR Cabinet of Ministers and decisions of ministries of the USSR and other bodies accountable to it; have the right to suspend resolutions and instructions of the Councils of Ministers of the republics on questions within the jurisdiction of the USSR should they violate the USSR Constitution and laws of the USSR;

9.1) head the USSR Security Council, which shall be given the task of elaborating recommendations for the implementation of a national policy on the defence of the country, maintaining its effective state, economic and ecological security, eliminating the aftermaths of natural disasters and other emergencies, and ensuring stability and the observance of law and order in society. Members of the USSR Security Council shall be appointed by the USSR President, taking into account the opinion of the Federation Council and upon consultation with the USSR Supreme Soviet;

10) co-ordinate the work of state bodies to ensure the country's security; be the Supreme Commander-in-Chief of the USSR Armed Forces; appoint and dismiss the supreme command of the USSR Armed Forces and award the highest military ranks; appoint judges to military tribunals;

11) conduct negotiations and sign international treaties of the USSR; accept the credentials and letters of recall of diplomatic representatives of foreign countries accredited to him; appoint and recall diplomatic representatives of the USSR in foreign countries and international organisations; award the highest diplomatic ranks and other special ranks;

12) award the orders and medals of the USSR and honorary titles of the USSR;

13) decide questions of granting citizenship of the USSR, relinquishing and depriving of Soviet citizenship and the granting of asylum; have the power of pardon;

14) declare general or partial mobilisation; declare a state of war in the event of an armed attack on the USSR and submit this question forthwith to the USSR Supreme Soviet; impose martial law in individual areas in the interests of the defence of the USSR and the security of its citizens. The procedure for imposing martial law and its regime shall be determined by law;

15) in the interests of ensuring the security of citizens of the USSR, warn of the imposition of a state of emergency in individual areas and, if need be, impose it at the request or with the consent of the Pre-

sidium of the Supreme Soviet or the highest body of state power of the Union Republic concerned. Should the USSR President fail to receive such consent, he shall impose a state of emergency and immediately submit his decision to the USSR Supreme Soviet for approval. A resolution of the USSR Supreme Soviet on this question shall be considered passed if it receives at least two-thirds of the votes of the total number of its members.

In the circumstances listed in the first part of this clause the USSR President may establish temporary presidential rule while observing the sovereignty and territorial integrity of the Union Republic concerned.

The regimes of a state of emergency and presidential rule shall be determined by law;

16) in the event of differences between the Soviet of the Union and the Soviet of Nationalities of the USSR Supreme Soviet which cannot be settled in accordance with Article 117 of the USSR Constitution, consider the dispute with the aim of achieving a mutually acceptable solution. Should no agreement be reached and the threat of disruption of the normal work of the highest bodies of state power and government of the USSR arise, the USSR President may propose that the Congress of USSR People's Deputies elect a new USSR Supreme Soviet.

Article 127 (4)

The USSR Vice-President shall be proposed by, and elected together with, the candidate for USSR President. The USSR Vice-President shall perform, upon the instructions of the USSR President, some of the latter's functions and act for him in his absence or should he be unable to perform his duties.

The USSR Vice-President may not be a People's Deputy.

Article 127 (5)

The USSR President, guided by and in fulfilment of the USSR Constitution and USSR laws, shall issue decrees binding throughout the territory of the country.

Article 127 (6)

The USSR President shall enjoy the right of immunity and may be recalled only by a Congress of USSR People's Deputies should he violate the Constitution and laws of the USSR. Recall shall be effected by a vote of at least two-thirds of the total number of deputies of the Congress of USSR People's Deputies on the initiative of the Congress or the USSR Supreme Soviet and taking into consideration the conclusions of the USSR Committee for Constitutional Supervision.

Article 127 (7)

Should the USSR President be unable to perform his duties for any reason, his powers shall be transferred to the USSR Vice-President until a new USSR President is elected, or, should this prove impossible, to the Chairman of the USSR Supreme Soviet. The election of a new USSR President shall be held within a period of three months.

Chapter 15 (2)
The Federation Council

Article 127 (8)

The USSR President shall head the Federation Council, which shall be composed of the USSR Vice-President and the Presidents (senior state officials) of the republics. Senior state officials of the autonomous territories and regions shall have the right to participate in the sessions of the Federation Council with the right to vote on questions of concern to them.

On the basis of the principles of home and foreign policy of the USSR, determined by the Congress of USSR People's Deputies, the Federation Council shall co-ordinate the activities of the highest bodies of state administration of the USSR and the republics, monitor compliance with the Union Treaty, elaborate measures to implement the nationalities policy of the Soviet state, ensure the participation of the republics in deciding questions of national importance and elaborate recommendations for settling ethnic disputes and conflicts.

Questions affecting the interests of peoples that do not have their own national-state structures shall be considered in the Federation Council with the participation of representatives of these peoples.

Article 127 (9)

The members of the Federation Council shall be the highest state officials of the republics and shall represent and defend the sovereignty and legitimate interests thereof and participate in deciding all questions considered by the Federation Council.

The members of the Federation Council shall ensure the implementation of the decisions of the Federation Council in their republics; supervise compliance with these decisions; receive from the federal bodies and officials all necessary information; have the right to appeal against decisions of federal bodies of state administration should they violate the legitimate rights of a republic; represent the USSR abroad on the instruction of the USSR President, and perform other duties.

Article 127 (10)

Decisions of the Federation Council shall be taken by a majority of not less than two-thirds of the votes and formalised in decrees of the USSR President.

The Chairman of the USSR Supreme Soviet may attend the sessions of the Federation Council.

Chapter 16
The USSR Cabinet of Ministers

Article 128

The USSR Cabinet of Ministers shall be an executive-administrative body of the USSR and shall be subordinate to the USSR President.

Article 129

The USSR Cabinet of Ministers shall be composed of the Prime Minister, his deputies and ministers of the USSR.

The structure of the Cabinet of Ministers shall be established by the USSR Supreme Soviet upon the proposal of the USSR President.

The heads of government of the republics may participate in the work of the USSR Cabinet of Ministers with the right to vote.

Article 130

The USSR Cabinet of Ministers shall be accountable to the USSR President and the USSR Supreme Soviet.

A newly-formed Cabinet of Ministers shall present to the USSR Supreme Soviet a programme of action for its term of office.

The USSR Cabinet of Ministers shall report on its work to the USSR Supreme Soviet at least once a year.

The USSR Supreme Soviet may pass a vote of no confidence in the USSR Cabinet of Ministers, in which case the latter shall resign. A resolution on this matter shall be passed by a majority of at least two-thirds of the total number of members of the USSR Supreme Soviet.

Article 131

The Cabinet of Ministers shall be authorised to decide questions of state administration within the jurisdiction of the USSR insofar as under the USSR Constitution, they are not within the terms of reference of the Congress of USSR People's Deputies, the USSR Supreme Soviet or the Federation Council.

Article 132

The USSR Cabinet of Ministers shall ensure the following:

1) The implementation jointly with the republics of a single financial, crediting and monetary policy, based on a common currency; the drafting and execution of the federal budget; the implementation of federal economic programmes; the establishment of inter-republic development and disaster relief funds;

2) the management jointly with the republics of single fuel, energy and transportation systems of the country; the management of the defence plants, space research projects and the federal communications and information, meteorology, geodesy, cartography, geology, metrology and standardisation systems; the implementation of a co-ordinated policy in the field of environmental control, ecological safety and nature conservation;

3) the implementation jointly with the republics of federal food, health, social security, employment, mother and child care, cultural and educational programmes, fundamental research and development projects designed to encourage scientific and technological progress;

4) the adoption of measures to ensure the country's defence and state security;

5) the implementation of Soviet foreign policy, regulation of the external economic activities of the USSR, co-ordination of the foreign policy and external economic activities of the republics, and customs services;

6) the implementation on consultation with the republics of measures to ensure respect for law and citizens' rights and freedoms, the protection of property and public order and to combat crime.

Article 133

The USSR Cabinet of Ministers shall issue resolutions and instructions on the basis and in pursuance of laws of the USSR and other decisions of the Congress of USSR People's Deputies, the USSR Supreme Soviet and decrees of the USSR President, and verify their implementation. The resolutions and instructions of the USSR Cabinet of Ministers shall be compulsory throughout the territory of the USSR.

Article 134 — This article was deleted in December 1990.

Article 135

The USSR Cabinet of Ministers shall co-ordinate and direct the work of the ministries of the USSR and other organs accountable to it.

To co-ordinate decisions pertaining to state administration, in the ministries and other central bodies of state administration of the USSR collegiums shall be formed from heads of the appropriate organs of the republics.

Article 136

The terms of reference of the USSR Cabinet of Ministers, the procedure of its work and relations with other state bodies and the list of ministries and other central bodies of state administration of the

USSR shall be determined by a law of the USSR.

VI
Basic Principles of the Structure of the Bodies of State Power and Administration in Union Republics

Chapter 17
Higher Bodies of State Power and Administration of a Union Republic

Article 137

The highest bodies of state power of Union Republics shall be the Supreme Soviets of Union Republics, or Congresses of People's Deputies in those republics which provide for the creation of such congresses.

Article 138

The powers, composition and procedure for the activity of the highest bodies of state power in Union Republics shall be determined by the constitutions and laws of Union Republics.

Article 139

The Supreme Soviet of a Union Republic shall form a Council of Ministers of the Union Republic, i.e. the Government of that Republic, which shall be the highest executive and administrative body of state power in the Republic.

Article 140

The Council of Ministers of a Union Republic issues resolutions and orders on the basis of, and in pursuance of, the legislative acts of the USSR and of the Union Republic, decrees of the USSR President and the USSR Cabinet of Ministers, and shall organise and verify their execution.

Article 141

The Council of Ministers of a Union Republic has the right to suspend the execution of resolutions and orders of the Councils of Ministers of Autonomous Republics, to rescind resolutions and orders of the Executive Committees of Soviets of People's Deputies of Territories, Regions, and cities (i.e. cities under the Republic's jurisdiction) and of Autonomous Regions, and in Union Republics not divided into regions, of the Executive Committees of district and corresponding city Soviets of People's Deputies.

Article 142

The Council of Ministers of a Union Republic shall co-ordinate and direct the work of the Union-Republican and Republican ministries and of state committees of the Union Republic, and other bodies under its jurisdiction.

The Union-Republican ministries and state committees of a Union Republic shall direct the branches of administration entrusted to them, or exercise inter-branch control, and shall be subordinate to both the Council of Ministers of the Union Republic and the corresponding Union-Republican ministry or state committee of the USSR.

Republican ministries and state committees shall direct the branches of administration entrusted to them, or exercise inter-branch control, and shall be subordinate to the Council of Ministers of the Union Republic.

Chapter 18
Higher Bodies of State Power and Administration of Autonomous Republics

Article 143

The highest bodies of state power of Autonomous Republics shall be the Supreme

Soviets of Autonomous Republics, or Congresses of People's Deputies in those republics which provide for the creation of such congresses.

Article 144

The Supreme Soviet of an Autonomous Republic shall form the Council of Ministers of the Autonomous Republic, i.e. the Government of that republic – the highest executive and administrative body of state power of that Autonomous Republic.

Chapter 19
Local Bodies of State Power and Administration

Article 145

The bodies of state power in Autonomous Regions, Autonomous Areas, Territories, Regions, districts, cities, city districts, settlements, rural communities and other territorial-administrative entities, formed in accordance with the laws of Union and Autonomous Republics, shall be the corresponding Soviets of People's Deputies.

Organs of territorial public self-government, citizens' meetings and other forms of direct democracy may function in accordance with republican legislation within the system of local self-government, alongside the local Soviets of People's Deputies.

Article 146

Local Soviets of People's Deputies shall deal with all matters of local significance in accordance with the interests of the whole state and of the citizens residing in the area under their jurisdiction, implement decisions of higher bodies of state power, guide the work of lower Soviets of People's Deputies, take part in the discussion of matters of Republican and All-Union sig-

nificance, and submit their proposals concerning them.

Local Soviets of People's Deputies shall direct state, economic, social and cultural development within their territory; endorse plans for economic and social development and the local budget; exercise general guidance over state bodies, enterprises, institutions and organisations subordinate to them; ensure observance of the law, maintenance of law and order, and protection of citizens' rights; and help strengthen the country's defence capacity.

Article 147

Within their powers, local Soviets of People's Deputies shall ensure the comprehensive, all-round economic and social development of their area; exercise control over the observance of legislation by enterprises, institutions and organisations subordinate to higher authorities and located in their area; and co-ordinate and supervise their activity as regards land use, nature conservation, building, employment of manpower, production of consumer goods, and social, cultural, communal and other services and amenities for the public.

Article 148

Local Soviets of People's Deputies shall decide matters within the powers accorded them by the legislation of the USSR and of the appropriate Union Republic or Autonomous Republic. Their decisions shall be binding on all enterprises, institutions, and organisations located in their area and on officials and other citizens.

Article 149

The executive and administrative organs of local Soviets of People's Deputies shall be the executive committees or other organs elected by them.

The executive and administrative organs of local Soviets of People's Deputies shall report at least once a year to the Soviets that have elected them and also at meetings at citizens' places of employment or residence.

Article 150

The executive and administrative organs of local Soviets of People's Deputies shall comply with laws, decrees of the USSR President and other decisions of the highest bodies of state power and administration of the USSR and the republics, taken within their terms of reference.

The executive and administrative organs of local Soviets of People's Deputies shall be directly accountable to the Soviet that has elected them and to the higher executive and administrative organ.

VII
Justice and Procurator's Supervision

Chapter 20
Courts of Law

Article 151

In the USSR justice is administered only by the courts.

In the USSR there are the following courts: the USSR Supreme Court, the Supreme Courts of Union Republics, the Supreme Courts of Autonomous Republics, Territorial, Regional, and city courts, courts of Autonomous Regions, courts of Autonomous Areas, district (city) people's courts, and military tribunals in the Armed Forces.

Article 152

All courts in the USSR, with the exception of military tribunals, shall be formed by the election of judges and people's assessors.

People's judges of people's district (city) courts and judges of territorial, regional and city courts shall be elected by the corresponding higher Soviets of People's Deputies.

The judges of the USSR Supreme Court, Supreme Courts of Union and Autonomous Republics, courts of Autonomous Regions and Areas shall be elected respectively by the USSR Supreme Soviet, Supreme Soviets of Union and Autonomous Republics, and Soviets of People's Deputies of Autonomous Regions and Areas.

People's assessors of people's district (city) courts shall be elected at meetings of citizens at their places of residence or work by a show of hands and people's assessors of higher courts by respective Soviets of People's Deputies.

Judges for military tribunals shall be appointed by the USSR President, and people's assessors shall be elected at meetings of servicemen by open voting.

The judges of all courts shall be elected for a term of ten years. The people's assessors of all courts shall be elected for a term of five years.

Judges and people's assessors may be recalled following the procedure established by law.

Article 153

The USSR Supreme Court is the highest judicial body in the USSR and supervises the administration of justice by the courts of the USSR and Union Republics within the limits established by law.

The USSR Supreme Court shall consist of a Chairman, Vice-Chairmen, members and people's assessors. The Chairmen of the Supreme Courts of Union Republics are *ex officio* members of the USSR Supreme Court.

The organisation and procedures of the USSR Supreme Court are defined in the Law on the USSR Supreme Court.

Article 154

The hearing of civil and criminal cases in all courts is collegial; in courts of the first instance cases are heard with the participation of people's assessors. In the administration of justice people's assessors have all the rights of a judge.

Article 155

Judges and people's assessors are independent and subject only to the law.

Judges and people's assessors shall be ensured conditions for the free and effective discharge of their rights and duties. Any interference in the administration of justice by judges and people's assessors is impermissible and punishable by law.

The inviolability of judges and people's assessors and other guarantees of their independence are established by the Law on the Status of Judges in the USSR and other legislative acts of the USSR and Union Republics.

Article 156

Justice is administered in the USSR on the principle of the equality of citizens before the law and the court.

Article 157

Proceedings in all courts shall be open to the public. Hearings *in camera* are only allowed in cases provided for by law, with observance of all the rules of judicial procedure.

Article 158

A defendant in a criminal action is guaranteed the right to legal assistance.

Article 159

Judicial proceedings shall be conducted in the language of the Union Republic, Autonomous Republic, Autonomous Region, or Autonomous Area, or in the language spoken by the majority of the people in the locality. Persons participating in court proceedings who do not know the language in which they are being conducted shall be ensured the right to become fully acquainted with the materials in the case, the services of an interpreter during the proceedings, and the right to address the court in their own language.

Article 160

No one may be judged guilty of a crime and subjected to punishment as a criminal except by the sentence of a court and in conformity with the law.

Article 161

Colleges of advocates are available to give legal assistance to citizens and organisations. In cases provided for by legislation citizens shall be given legal assistance free of charge.

The organisation and procedure of the bar are determined by legislation of the USSR and Union Republics.

Article 162

Representatives of public organisations and of work collectives may take part in civil and criminal proceedings.

Article 163

Economic disputes in the USSR shall be settled by the USSR Supreme Arbitration Court and the organs created in the republics in accordance with their laws for the settlement of economic disputes.

Interference by any organs, organisations or officials in the activities of judges in settling dispute shall be prohibited.

The organisation and procedure of the work of the USSR Supreme Arbitration Court shall be established by a law of the USSR.

Chapter 21
The Procurator's Office

Article 164

Supervision of the accurate and uniform observance of the laws of the USSR by all ministries and other organs of state administration, enterprises, institutions, organisations, local Soviets of People's Deputies and their executive and administrative bodies, political parties, public organisations and mass movements, officials and citizens shall be exercised by the USSR Procurator-General, the Procurators-General of the republics and the Procurators-General accountable to them.

Article 165

The USSR Procurator-General is responsible and accountable to the Congress of USSR People's Deputies and the USSR Supreme Soviet.

Article 166

The Procurators-General of the republics shall be appointed by the highest bodies of state power of the republics upon consultation with the USSR Procurator-General and shall be accountable to them. In supervising the observance of the laws of the USSR, the Procurator-General of the republics also shall be accountable to the USSR Procurator-General.

Article 167

The term of office of the USSR Procurator-General shall be five years.

Article 168

The procurator's bodies shall perform their duties independently of any local organs.

The organisation and procedure of the work of the procurator's bodies shall be established by legislation of the USSR and the constituent republics.

VIII
The Emblem, Flag, Anthem, and Capital of the USSR

Article 169

The State Emblem of the Union of Soviet Socialist Republics is a hammer and sickle on a globe depicted in the rays of the sun and framed by ears of wheat, with the inscription "Workers of All Lands, Unite!" in the languages of the Union Republics. At the top of the Emblem is a five-pointed star.

Article 170

The State Flag of the Union of Soviet Socialist Republics is a rectangle of red cloth with a hammer and sickle depicted in gold in the upper corner next to the staff and with a five-pointed red star edged in gold about them. The ratio of the width of the flag to its length is 1:2.

Article 171

The State Anthem of the Union of Soviet Socialist Republics shall be approved by the USSR Supreme Soviet.

Article 172

The Capital of the Union of Soviet Socialist Republics is the city of Moscow.

IX
The Legal Force of the USSR Constitution and Procedure for Amending the Constitution

Article 173

The USSR Constitution shall have supreme legal force. All laws and other acts of state bodies shall be promulgated on the basis of and in conformity with it.

Article 174

The USSR Constitution may be amended by a decision of the Congress of USSR People's Deputies, adopted by a majority of not less than two-thirds of the total number of USSR People's Deputies.

INDEX